THE YALE-HOOVER SERIES ON STALIN, STALINISM, AND THE COLD WAR

POLICING STALIN'S SOCIALISM

REPRESSION AND SOCIAL ORDER

IN THE SOVIET UNION, 1924–1953

DAVID R. SHEARER

Hoover Institution
Stanford University
Stanford, California

Yale University Press
New Haven and London

Published with assistance from the Mary Cady Tew Memorial Fund.

Set in Sabon and City types by The Composing Room of Michigan, Inc.
Printed in the United States of America.

Library of Congress Cataloging-in-Publication Data

Shearer, David R., 1952–
    Policing Stalin's socialism : repression and social order in the Soviet Union, 1924–1953 /
David R. Shearer.
        p. cm. — (The Yale-Hoover series on Stalin, Stalinism, and the Cold War)
    Includes bibliographical references and index.
    ISBN 978-0-300-14925-8 (pbk. : alk. paper)   1. Police—Soviet Union—History.
2. Political persecution—Soviet Union—History.   3. Social control—Soviet Union—
History.   4. Soviet Union—Social conditions.   5. Political purges—Soviet Union—
History.   6. Socialism—Soviet Union—History.   7. Stalin, Joseph, 1879–1953—
Influence.   8. Soviet Union—Politics and government—1917–1936.   9. Soviet
Union—Politics and government—1936–1953.   I. Title.
    HV8224.S3756   2009
    363.20947'09041—dc22   2009005138

A catalogue record for this book is available from the British Library.

This paper meets the requirements of ANSI/NISO Z39.48–1992 (Permanence of Paper).

10   9   8   7   6   5   4   3   2   1

Contents

Illustrations follow p. 218

Acknowledgments

This book has been a long time in the making, and I owe many debts of gratitude to people and institutions. I could not have completed the many research trips to archives and libraries without the generous support of the International Research and Exchanges Board, the National Endowment for the Humanities, and the National Council for Eurasian and East European Research. I am also indebted to the Dean's Office of Arts and Sciences, the International Studies Office, and the Department of History of the University of Delaware for key financial support and leave time. I owe a great deal to Alain Blum and Vladimir Berelowitch and the Institut national d'études démographiques and the Centre d'études du monde russe, soviétique et post-soviétique (Ecole des hautes études en sciences sociales). Several stays at these institutes provided a haven in a beautiful city, and the pleasant atmosphere in which I wrote much of this book. Similarly, I owe thanks to Paul Gregory and to the Hoover Institution and Archives. Research trips to the Hoover Archives were richly rewarding, and the series of summer workshops there provided a stimulating and productive atmosphere among congenial colleagues. The summer workshops led eventually to my decision to publish in the Yale-Hoover Series on Stalin, Stalinism, and the Cold War, and I am grateful to Jonathan Brent of Yale University Press for publishing this book. My thanks, too, to Vadim Staklo at Yale who has been always professional and cordial. I owe a great deal of gratitude to Gavin Lewis. His close and thoughtful editing has turned a manuscript into a book.

My participation in conferences proved important to the formulation of ideas in this book, and I am grateful to the organizers for including me. My thanks, especially, go to Norman Naimark, Ron Suny, and participants in the seminar "Revolution and State Terror," Center for Advanced Study in the Behavioral Sciences, Stanford University, 8–9 December 2006; Juliette Cadiot and members of the "Workshop on Categorization, Identification, and Recognition in the Imperial/Soviet Era: A Comparative Perspective," Watson Institute, Brown University, 7–8 February 2003; and Andrea Graziosi and Terry Martin and colleagues in the seminar "The Role of the NKVD in the Soviet Union under Stalin," Maison des Sciences de l'Homme, Paris, 25–27 May 2000.

In recent years, archivists in Russia have maintained both professional standards and hospitality while working in extremely difficult circumstances, and I am indebted to them most of all. I thank especially Galina Vladimirovna Gorskaia and Larisa Aleksandrovna Rogovaia (then) at the Russian State Archive for Socio-Political History, and Dina Nikolaevna Nokhotovich of the Russian Federation State Archive. I worked many long months in Soviet judiciary and procuracy collections of the Russian Federation State Archive, and I always found a professional and cordial reception there. I spent most of my time ensconced in the reading room of the Council of Ministers collection at the State Archive of the Russian Federation. Sofiia Viktorovna Somonova and Tatiana Zhukova made me feel at home in their reading room in a way that I will always treasure. This book would not have been possible without their advice, many cups of tea, and warm professional hospitality. Neither would it have been possible without the collegial help of Galya Kuznetsova. These archivists, as well as others, are part of this book. My special thanks also to Marina Doboronovskaia, Larisa Rogovaia (currently Assistant Director of the State Archive of the Russian Federation), and Nikolai Zelov for assistance in locating and reproducing photographs. Archivists at the State Archive of Novosibirsk Oblast provided a welcoming atmosphere during my several visits there. I am very grateful to Viktor Issaev of the Russian Academy of Sciences, Siberian Branch, a scholar and friend, who helped smooth my way in Novosibirsk. My thanks also to Sergei Krasil'nikov, Sergei Papkov, A. G. Tepliakov, and others at the Institute of History, Siberian Branch, Russian Academy of Sciences, for stimulating discussions and seminars.

Parts of chapter 6 first appeared in the articles "Social Disorder, Mass Repression, and the NKVD during the 1930s," *Cahiers du Monde russe* 42/2–4 (April–December 2001): 505–34, and "Crime and Social Disorder in Stalin's Russia: A Reassessment of the Great Retreat and the Origins of Mass Repression," ibid., 39/1–2 (1998): 119–48. Parts of chapter 8 first appeared as "Elements Near and Alien: Passportization, Policing, and Identity in the Stalinist State," *Journal of Modern History* 76 (December 2004): 835–81. I am grateful to both of these journals for their kind permission to reprint parts of these articles here.

Many individuals have read all or parts of this book as it evolved in manuscript form. I am grateful, especially, to the anonymous readers of Yale University Press for their constructive comments. Robert Gellately, Paul Gregory, Oleg Khlevniuk, and Lynne Viola were also gracious enough to read the manuscript, and I have benefited greatly from their suggestions and corrections. Similarly, I wish to thank other scholars for their comments: Jörg Baberowski, Alain Blum, Michael David-Fox, Sheila Fitzpatrick, Wendy Goldman, Andrea Graziosi, Marc Junge, Peter Kolchin, Eric Lohr, Terry Martin, Rudi Matthee, Nathalie Moine, Gabor Rittersporn, Peter Solomon, Ron Suny, and Amir Weiner. Much of my work overlaps with that of Paul Hagenloh, and I am grateful to Paul for many years of mutual work, shared observations, friendly arguments, and for his generosity of spirit. James Heinzen read large parts of the manuscript, and I am greatly indebted to him for his insights, encouragement, and guidance, for his sense of humor, and for our regular lunches at Penn. I am most grateful to Marina Dobronovskaia for her close reading of chapters, for her sharp eyes, and for her encouragement and companionship. The views expressed in this book are my own. Whatever faults that may remain are my own doing.

Newark, April 2009

Note on Transliteration

I have followed a standard transliteration system for Russian words, with the exception of well-known names beginning with E and Ia, such as Ezhov and Iagoda. I have written these as Yezhov and Yagoda in order to aid pronunciation. Similarly, I have transliterated the name Beriia as Beria.

Abbreviations and Glossary of Frequently Used Terms

Besprizornik(i)	Homeless child(ren)
Byvshie liudi	"Former people." Members of dispossessed middle and upper classes
Cheka	Acronym for the Extraordinary Commission to Combat Counterrevolution and Sabotage. The political police during the revolutionary war years 1917–22
Chekist	Political police official
d. (dd.)	File(s) (*delo[dela]*) (archive)
doc., docs.	Document(s). Bound set of pages, such as a booklet, often with no folio numbers (archive)
Edinolichnik	Private farmer, not belonging to a collective farm
EKO	Economic Crimes Department of the political police
Fond	Collection (archive)
GANO	State Archive of the Novosibirsk Oblast
GARF	State Archive of the Russian Federation
GIM	Chief Inspectorate of Police
GUGB	Chief Administration for State Security. Political police administration, 1934–41,

	under the Commissariat of Internal Affairs
GULAG	Chief Administration for Camps
GURKM	Chief Administration of Workers and Peasants Police (civil police) from late 1932
Kartoteki	Police card catalogs
kharbintsy	Workers on the Harbin branch of the Trans-Siberian railroad
Kolkhoz	Collective farm (formally, a cooperative of farmers)
Kolkhoznik(i)	Collective farm worker(s)
Komsomol	Young Communist Youth League
Krai	District. Usually larger than an oblast, and associated with frontier status
KSK	Soviet Control Commission (state inspectorate)
Kulak	"Rich" peasant
l. (ll.)	Folio(s) (*list[y]*) (archive document)
Lishenets (lishentsy)	Disenfranchised person (people)
MGB	Ministry of State Security. Political police, March 1946–March 1953
Militsiia	Shortened name for civil police
Militsioner	Civil police officer
MTS	Machine tractor station
MVD	Ministry for Internal Affairs, renamed successor to the NKVD from March 1946
Narkomiust' (NKIu)	People's Commissariat of Justice
Narkomfin	People's Commissariat of Finance
Narkompros	People's Commissariat of Education
Narkomzdrav	People's Commissariat of Health
NKGB	People's Commissariat of State Security, February 1941–March 1946
NKVD	People's Commissariat of Internal Affairs of the Russian Republic, 1918–30; All-Union Commissariat of Internal Affairs, 1934–46
OBKhSS	Department for Combating Theft of State Property

ob.	verso (*oboratnaia storona*) (document cites)
Oblast	Government administrative unit, larger than a region (*raion*), smaller than a district (*krai*)
OGPU	United (Combined) State Political Administration. Political police, 1922–34
OO OGPU	Operational departments (*operativnye otdely*) of the political police. Also the Special Department (*Osobyi Otdel*) of the political police whose members were assigned to military units
op.	Archive group
ORO	Operational-Investigative Department of the civil police
Osoboe soveshchanie	Highest sentencing board of the political police
Politotdel	Political Department. Used for political police administrations in machine tractor stations and on rail lines
Privod	Temporary police detention, short of formal arrest
Procuracy	State prosecutorial agency
Procurator	Prosecutor
Rabkrin (NK RKI)	State inspectorate agency
Raion	Region. Government administrative unit similar to a county
RGAE	Russian State Economic Archive
RGAKFD	Russian State Archive for Film and Photographic Documents
RGANI	Russian State Archive of Contemporary History
RGASPI	Russian State Archive for Socio-Political History
RKM	Acronym for civil police
RSFSR	Russian Soviet Federated Socialist Republic
Sotsvredelement	Socially harmful element
Soviet	A local governing council

Sovkhoz	State farm, in which farmers were paid salaries as workers
Sovmin	Council of Ministers. Replaced Council of People's Commissars from March 1946
Sovnarkom (SNK)	Council of People's Commissars. Highest government ruling body
Spetspereselentsy	Special settlers. Name for deported people
Spravka	Pass or affidavit
Svodki	Summary reports
Troika	Nonjudicial police sentencing board
TsIK	Central Executive Committee. Highest executive organ of the all-union or republic governments
Uchet	Surveillance registration
Ugolovnyi rozysk (UGRO)	Criminal Investigative Branch of the civil police
UNKVD	District- or oblast-level NKVD administration
URKM	District- or oblast-level civil police administration
Vedmilitsiia	Enterprise protection police
VTsIK	All-Russian Central Executive Committee. Highest government executive body of the Russian Soviet Federated Socialist Republic

Introduction

Policing, Social Order, and Repression under Stalin

Repression is an important weapon of a socialist state.
—*Andrei Vyshinskii, 1931*

IN NOVEMBER 1937, at the height of the great purges, a twenty-two-year-old Moscow resident, Kiril Korencv, was arrested and sentenced to eight years in a labor camp. With his arrest, Korenev became one of the millions of victims of Stalin's repressive police system—a typical story of false arrest and trumped-up charges. At the same time, Korenev's arrest was not typical, at least of the many such stories that have come down to us in memoirs and biographies. Korenev was not arrested, in the classic scenario, by jackbooted political police officers. There was no banging on the door in the early hours of the morning. No apartment search for supposedly incriminating evidence. Korenev was not whisked away in the "black raven" vans of the political police. Neither was Korenev charged with the usual litany of crimes of political opposition, spying, or anti-Soviet conspiracy. He did not endure endless days and weeks of interrogation, torture, and isolation in prison cells.[1] Korenev was arrested in daylight by civil police. He was charged with being unemployed, with having previous petty criminal convictions, and for associating with hooligans and criminal "elements." Korenev was jailed with a large group of people and he was sentenced quickly, without being isolated or interrogated.

While Korenev's story does not fit the well-known scenario of political repression, his experience was typical of that of many people who came into contact with the repressive apparatus of the Soviet state and police. And not just in 1937 and 1938. For much of the 1930s, public- or social-order repression was a main priority of the political as well as the civil police. Most histories overlook this kind of repression, and yet Stalin and other Soviet leaders regarded social order as one of highest priorities of state security. They considered social disorder, not political opposition, as the greatest threat to the regime and its policies. In the following chapters, I explore the reasons for this and the different phases, strategies, and campaigns of Stalinist social policing and surveillance. Repression under Stalin, I argue, was far more than politics by coercive means. Repression became a fundamental part of the way the Stalinist regime related to its citizens: the way the regime attempted to impose public order and reshape the Soviet social body.

Though extreme, Stalinist attempts to remake society through repressive means were not unique. It is a truism that states act on the populations they govern. Throughout history, rulers have attempted to create "pure" communities, or remake subjects or citizens according to some preconceived vision of a perfect, or at least a better, society. Some have argued that this is a peculiarly modern phenomenon, originating in the ideas of eighteenth-century European philosophers.[2] Whether this is true or not may be disputed. What is distinctive about nineteenth- and twentieth-century history is the array of social, political, statistical, and administrative technologies that governments have employed to try to remake their populations, and to do so in a "scientific" way.[3] Whether through policies that offer incentives or through methods of outright coercion, whether through welfare programs and rehabilitation or removal and physical extermination, modern states have accelerated the tempo and the scope of social intervention and reconstruction. The organizing effects of World War I gave impetus to these trends in all European and transatlantic countries, regardless of the ideological orientation of their governments. The power and ability of the state to intervene in and remake society grew enormously, especially, if not exclusively, in the twentieth century.[4]

Nowhere were these trends more pronounced than in the Russian Empire and its successor state, the Soviet Union. There, just at the end of World War I, a government took power whose leaders were inspired by a revolutionary and modernizing ideology of transformation, an antiliberal and collectivist ideology, which was put into practice in the reconstructed remains of an empire that already had a strong state tradition. From the beginning of the regime, Soviet officials used the full mobilizing power and repressive machinery of the state to try to engineer a perfect socialist society. As Marxist revolutionaries, the new Bolshevik government leaders used social class as the criterion of repression and privilege. In this new communist society, the working classes, and segments of the population close to the working classes, were good. Bourgeois and propertied classes were bad. Political leaders were obsessed with ways of identifying socially "near "and socially "alien" populations. They were determined to raise up the former and repress or exterminate the latter.[5]

Leaders of the Soviet state employed many means to repress what they regarded as alien or hostile segments of the Soviet population—from policies of social, economic, and political discrimination, to deportation or exile, to repression through incarceration and outright murder. During the 1930s, policies of repression, especially police repression, broadened and reached unprecedented levels under the dictatorial regime of Joseph Stalin, the general secretary of the ruling Communist Party. Police arrested, imprisoned, deported, killed, expelled, or in some manner coercively discriminated against millions of people in this period. This repression was perpetrated in the name of defending or perfecting socialism. It was carried out under the explicit orders of Stalin or with his tacit consent. The use of police violence and repression became a fundamental part of the Stalinist regime, a fundamental part of Stalin's method of rule. We cannot understand Stalinism or Soviet-style socialism without understanding the structure and policies of repression and policing during the years that Stalin ruled the Soviet Union. In the chapters that follow, I examine Stalinist policies of repression from the late 1920s through the death of the great dictator in 1953. And, as I noted above, much of the discussion that follows centers on social-order kinds of policing. Social-order repression was, I argue, far more pervasive than overtly political forms of repression, and targeted marginalized populations that leaders labeled "socially harmful elements" (*sotsial'no-vrednye elementy*). These *sotsvredelementy* included large numbers of rural inhabitants who had been dispossessed as class enemies, as well as other groups displaced by the revolutionary social and economic policies of the regime. The latter encompassed large numbers of indigents and itinerants, criminals, ex-convicts, members of religious sects, unemployed and orphaned youth, gypsies, the politically disenfranchised, and a range of other groups. These groups made up the social detritus of Stalin's industrial and agrarian revolutions from above.[6] Political leaders and police officials regarded these harmful or alien elements (*chuzhdye elementy*) as a serious threat to the state and its policies, so much so that the country's leaders turned to the police, political as well as civil, to bring order to the country. Under the command of Stalin's police head, Genrikh Yagoda, and with Stalin's backing, the political police, especially, expanded operational and administrative authority to take over institutions and problems of social governance, one after another—illegal migration and trade, indigence, the unemployed, civil and residence registration and census taking, orphan children and related problems of juvenile delinquency, and a massive wave of petty criminality.

Encroachment of political police into areas of civil governance was not entirely new in the 1930s. Political police involvement with certain types of criminality had roots in the 1920s, and even before the Revolution. During the tsarist era, political police—the gendarmerie—involved itself in policing banditry and contraband. The Bolshevik political police wielded broad jurisdiction during the revolutionary war years from 1918 through 1921, and was involved in policing banditry and certain types of criminality during the 1920s. The scale of police intervention during the 1930s, however, was unprecedented for a peacetime period. The conflation of public order with state security was unique to the Stalinist era and fundamentally reshaped the repressive policies of the Soviet regime.[7] More than that, the forced removal, redistribution, or elimination of suspect populations reached a level of mass social engineering that was also unique to the Stalinist era. Neither in the 1920s, nor after Stalin's death in 1953, did the Soviet regime employ methods of mass police repression to try to restructure the social, ethnic, and territorial boundaries of the country. This book examines how Soviet leaders came to equate social order with the political security of the state, and it places social-order policies of repression within the broader context of Stalin's repressive politics, Stalin's centralizing state revolution, and the history of police and policing under Stalin.[8]

MARTIAL LAW SOCIALISM

How was it that Soviet leaders came to regard petty criminals, itinerants, beggars, and other social marginals as such a threat? In the early chapters of this book, I explore this question by examining changes in the reality and representation of criminality and social order from the 1920s into the 1930s. Chapter 1 examines how criminality and social deviancy came to be politicized by Stalin and other leaders as a form of class war instead of "just" a social problem. The chapter explores particularly how criminals and others labeled as socially harmful became suddenly transformed into ubiquitous and dangerous enemies of the state and the Revolution. Part of this sudden change involved an ideological reinterpretation of deviancy and disorder. That ideological reinterpretation resulted, in turn, from the end of the mixed-market New Economic Policy of the 1920s, and Stalin's launching of a "socialist offensive" in the early 1930s. As the regime eliminated private trade and socialized land under state control, leaders drove the country aggressively toward a maximum effort to "build socialism." Building socialism involved a state-imposed program of crash industrialization, as well as a massive extension of state control over production, land, and trade. In the countryside, especially, social war broke out as the Communist Party and police confiscated property and forced peasants into state-controlled collective farms, *kolkhozy*. Those who resisted were branded as enemies, known as kulaks (*kulak* or *kulaky* in the plural). Supposed kulaks were shot by the thousands and rounded up and deported in the millions to special camps and penal settlements.

In early 1933, Stalin declared that the socialist offensive had succeeded, that the remnants of capitalism had been routed, and that the victory of socialism had been assured. With that pronouncement, definitions of deviancy, criminality, and other unacceptable forms of behavior changed. If crime and deviancy could be accepted and even tolerated as part of the compromise with capitalism of the 1920s, such tolerance was no longer possible after Stalin's announcement of socialist victory. Social disorder could be explained as nothing else but class hostility toward the new Soviet order, and as sabotage of Stalin's grand project to build socialism. As chapter 1 shows, the politicizing of criminality and antisocial behavior made (and makes) any discussion of crime and deviancy during the 1930s not only a discussion about social reality, but also a discussion about the ideology, perceptions, and priorities of Stalinist leaders.[9] At the same time, the threat that criminal and other marginal groups posed was more than a discursive turn, more than an ideological reinterpretation resulting from the end of capitalism.

The threat of social disorder in the late 1920s and early 1930s was real. Driven off the land, millions of impoverished peasants, as well as those in the former professional and intellectual classes, drained economic resources, endangered the state's already strained trade and distribution plans, and threatened to overwhelm the fragile infrastructure of the cities. Shunned as hostile, and with little chance to work or integrate, these marginalized populations did not fit into Stalin's socialism. These groups posed a danger to the social and economic stability of the country. So, too, did many more hundreds of thousands of other disaffected people whom the regime's officials deemed socially harmful. Massive disruption in the countryside caused by the state's collectivization and dekulakization policies, rapid and forced industrial development, and the widespread famine of 1932–1933 led to an administrative crisis in the country and widespread social instability. Weak and underdeveloped, welfare agencies and other organs of the civil government were unprepared to cope with the breakdown in social order caused by Stalin's agrarian and industrial revolutions. Viewing the rise in criminality and marginal populations as a political threat as well as a social and economic danger, the country's leaders turned increasingly to the political and civil police.

The problem with the police was that there were too few of them, at least in the early 1930s. Chapters 2 and 3 describe the woeful state of public order and policing in the late 1920s and early 1930s. These chapters chronicle the attempts by leaders, and especially Yagoda, to reorganize police and security organs and to create an effective national policing system. Much of that effort involved the administrative and operational integration of the civil and political police. This process remains a little-known but important aspect of Stalin's centralizing state revolution, and these chapters explore the origins, dynamics, and consequences of police integration.[10] As chapter 3 shows, the integration of civil and political police did more than professionalize and politicize the civil police. The process brought the political police into spheres of social governance and population control new to them. Increasingly, the political police, the OGPU in the early 1930s, took on tasks that had not been within their operational purview—administering local police forces and combating waves of petty criminality; cleansing cities, rail lines, and strategic areas of itinerants, beggars, orphaned and runaway children, hooligans, and other marginal populations; deporting socially undesirable and suspect ethnic populations from border areas; rounding up and dealing with the large numbers of orphans in the country; enforcing internal passport and residence laws; engaging in mass surveillance functions; even checking passenger tickets on trains.[11] Many OGPU officers found that these tasks were not what they had expected when they joined the state's security forces. Nonetheless, such tasks became a major part of the role of the political police during the 1930s, and drove many of the operational policies of the political police.[12]

Another important consequence of the political police's incursion into areas of social governance was to usurp from civil authorities enforcement of citizenship laws, and even the right to define citizenship. During the 1920s, as Golfo Alexopoulos has shown, the authority to repress someone as a social alien was accomplished primarily through the process of deprivation of civic rights, primarily voting rights, but also of other important social and economic privileges. That process, and decisions about disenfranchisement, lay within the jurisdiction of local government councils, the local soviets, and in community-based forms of repression.[13] In the early 1930s, however, the authority of local soviets over decisions on disenfranchisement was curtailed. Increasingly, as this book documents, identification and adjudication of social aliens and suspect populations came under the jurisdiction of police organs, exercised primarily though not exclusively through enforcement of internal passport and residence laws. This was a significant change, essentially taking the definition of citizenship—of social identity and social repression—out of the hands of the local institutions and placing it in the hands of the police organs. Social engineering that involved communities and was centered in civil government was replaced by a bureaucratized system of police repression administered under secret protocols and with little possibility of citizen redress.

While it is tempting to call what Yagoda created a police state, this is not an entirely accurate characterization. Certainly, Yagoda's police empire was at the heart of the Stalinist state. As powerful as police organs became, however, they never controlled the state apparatus, and policing organs and policies remained under the control of Stalin and the ruling elite of the Communist Party. Moreover, the phrase "police state" does not convey why, in fact, Stalin felt the need to create such an impressive state machinery of repression. He did not use a strong police apparatus to repress just for the sake of repression, or just to intimidate people into submission. Stalin needed a powerful police system in order, first, to subdue and remake the rural areas of the country, and second, to consolidate and defend the economic and social order that he created, especially in an increasingly hostile set of international conditions. What Stalin and Yagoda created might be more appropriately called martial law socialism, or, literally, militarized socialism. "Militarization" (*voennizatsiia*) was the term that Yagoda and others used to describe the integration of the police, and it is an appropriate description. The merging of political and civil police did, indeed, "militarize" the civil police, as well as bring the political police into the arena of social governance.[14] Specifically, this merging created a kind of militarized social gendarmerie, similar, in some ways, to the kinds of gendarme forces that existed in Russia prior to the Revolution, and which operated in European states during the nineteenth and twentieth centuries. Like its nineteenth-century counterparts, the task of Stalin's political and civil police was to maintain political and, more broadly, social order in the country.[15]

BOOKENDS

Stalin's declaration of socialist victory in 1933 transformed social marginals into class enemies, but to fight this new kind of enemy, Stalin made it clear that police organs had to change tactics. Campaigns of mass repression and administrative justice were to stop, and police were to find new ways to root out the enemies of the state. Chapters 4 and 5 examine Yagoda's attempts to transform political and social policing methods—to professionalize policing, end campaigns of mass repression, and focus policing on systematic methods of social surveillance and information gathering. These chapters describe efforts to establish informant networks, criminal and political catalog systems, and the simultaneous introduction of a countrywide system of internal passportization and residence registration. Literature is sparse on informant and mass social surveillance practices during the 1930s, and these chapters document what information is available.[16] Chapter 4 describes how informant networks were supposed to drive operational practice, and how this surveillance system worked, and did not work. Chapter 5 details the different types of registration systems, active and passive, and describes how information about individuals was written on cards, sorted, marked, and cross-filed into cataloging systems called *kartoteki*. Chapter 5 shows how increasingly diversified card cataloging systems became the primary basis for surveillance and policing work.

The catalog or registration systems, combined with informant and agent networks, were the key tools in a broad new technology of social surveillance. This new kind of policing was designed to prevent crime and sabotage before it happened. Policing was to be preventative, based on police ability to monitor suspicious elements, and to find criminals and saboteurs where they were hiding or masking themselves as loyal Soviet citizens. It was a system that was supposed to be secretive, automatic, and prophylactic, and it did not work. Chapters 6 and 7 show that, in fact, campaign and mass policing methods continued throughout the 1930s. For a number of reasons, old methods died hard. Authorities continued to use tried and true policing techniques as the most effective tools to maintain civil order, and to order society according to the leaders' hierarchy of hostile and loyal populations.

Little attention has been given to the campaigns of social repression of the 1930s.[17] In a traditional reading of Soviet history, there were two periods of mass violence perpetrated by the state during the 1930s. The decade began with a massive assault against peasant farmers, a social war in the countryside to eliminate smallhold farming, to bring land under the economic and political control of the state, and to deport or exterminate peasants who resisted what officially became known as collectivization. The regime branded those who were dispossessed or those who resisted collectivization as kulaks, and shipped them to labor camps or to agricultural penal colonies called "special settlements," *spetsposelki*. In the dekulakization campaigns of the first several years of the 1930s, the Stalinist regime dispossessed and executed or deported at least two million rural inhabitants of the country.[18] During these campaigns, political police, as well as local officials, were given broad, unchecked powers to try people before administrative sentencing boards made up of three officials, and hence called troikas, without recourse to judicial courts or due processes of legality.[19] Similarly, troikas were the main means that the regime used to condemn large numbers of people during the great purges at the end of the decade. If the 1930s began with the mass repressions of collectivization, the decade ended with the great purges of 1937 and 1938. The great purges were a paroxysm of state violence against society that was supposed to rid the country of dangerous enemies and potentially disloyal populations. The purges swept away hundreds of thousands of people in mass executions, and imprisoned hundreds of thousands of others.

The collectivization and the dekulakization campaigns are well known, as are the great purges. Much has been written about these events, but little about events in between. In most histories, the story goes that political leaders brought the most violent phase of rural repression to a close in 1932 and 1933. After that, the regime's leaders attempted to bring a measure of normalcy to Soviet society. Leaders banned the use of troikas, and prohibited the political police from using mass forms of nonjudicial repression. These changes were codified in the summer of 1934 in the subordination of the political police within a new all-union Commissariat of Internal Affairs, the NKVD.[20] Many authors describe formation of the NKVD as part of a strengthening of legal culture, a victory of judicial constraint on the power of the political police, and a development that was part of an overall policy to end, or at least limit, campaigns of mass repression and the nonjudicial sentencing authority of the political police. According to traditional periodization, the regime did not engage in campaigns of mass repression again until the sudden start of the great purges in 1937.[21]

This "bookends" interpretation of the 1930s needs qualification. In fact, the regime scaled down mass arrests in rural areas beginning in 1933, as most histories describe, but they reduced levels of mass repression in rural areas only to intensify operations of mass social repression in urban and other areas. Many hundreds of thousands of people were caught up in campaign-style sweeps of cities, industrial areas, rail lines, border zones, elite resorts, and other strategic regions. Those affected included criminals, ex-convicts, itinerants and beggars, orphan and unsupervised children, undocumented socially marginal populations, supposedly disloyal or potentially disloyal national minorities, and other undesirable or suspect categories of the population. Supposedly dangerous populations were identified and then isolated, mainly through deportation and exile, or by expelling them from cities, but at times through imprisonment and even execution.

Such policing efforts came to be known collectively as campaigns of "social defense" (sotsial'naia zashchita). To some extent, campaigns of social defense resembled "law and order" policing in other countries,

although there were some significant differences. Law and order policing was usually carried out on an ad hoc basis, and its different aspects
were often subdivided among civil police, courts, and social agencies. In
the Soviet Union of the 1930s, such policing was carried out on a systematic, mass scale, often using political as well as regular police, and
often using administrative or nonjudicial methods to deal with "offenders." In the Soviet Union, police became enforcers, judges, and jailers all in one. In chapters 6 and 7, I describe the social defense campaigns of the mid-1930s, which bridged and linked the two great
episodes of mass repression that began and ended the 1930s. These
chapters show that the use of troikas continued throughout the mid-
1930s. These chapters make the argument that formation of the NKVD
in 1934 did not so much constrain as consolidate and enhance police
power. Chapters 6 and 7 also differentiate types of repressive policies.
They show that attempts by some officials to reduce levels of repression
focused on specific kinds of political repression defined in the Soviet
legal code under statutes concerning anti-Soviet agitation. Few raised
objections about the nonjudicial campaigns of repression applied under
special police powers and extraordinary laws against socially undesirable or suspect ethnic populations. Heated debates during the mid-
1930s about levels of police repression overlooked the social defense
campaigns. The latter continued unabated throughout these years.

FROM CLASS WAR TO SOCIAL ENGINEERING

Much of the effort to cleanse Soviet society during the 1930s was
done through enforcement of, and mass policing campaigns associated
with, passport and residency laws. These laws were put into effect in
1933, and greatly broadened police powers. As chapter 8 shows, administration of the passport and residence registration system brought
police into the business of monitoring not just criminals and suspected
oppositionists but, potentially, the whole population. This was something new for police agencies, and their involvement in passport control
systems placed in police hands a powerful instrument of geographic as
well as social engineering. Control of passportization gave police the
authority to create officially sanctioned categories of identity—social,
ethnic, and occupational—and it involved police in the enforcement of
territorial zones of exile, exclusion, and internal colonization. Restric-

tions tied to passport identities amounted to a hierarchy of what officials described as "near" and "alien" elements and "distant" and "near" spaces. By the mid-1930s, policing agencies not only defined the status of citizenship, but the social and geographic construction of socialism in the Soviet Union.

THE CATEGORICAL IMPERATIVE

During the Stalin era, then, police repression encompassed more than the struggle against political opponents. Under Stalin, police repression and state violence became a form of social governance, a constitutive means of state. Mass forms of repression were an important instrument of that state, and Soviet officials in the 1930s understood mass repression in two ways. Mass repression (*massovye repressii*) could refer to quantity, the sheer numbers of people repressed at any one time or under any one operational order. After 1933, officials were charged, officially at least, not to engage in the repression of large numbers of people in this manner, regardless of whether repression was carried out by judicial or administrative means. Ignatii Barkov, for example, the chief procurator for Western Siberia, complained to the district Party head, Robert Eikhe, on several occasions, that punitive measures taken against citizens by local police or government officials reached a level that bordered on "mass" repression.[22] Similarly, I. A. Akulov, the prosecutor general of the country in 1935, reprimanded subordinates for allowing police to arrest large numbers of people in "campaign-style" methods of "mass" repression.[23]

If "mass repression" referred to quantity, the term also denoted repression by category or contingent. This kind of mass repression was carried out often, though not always, by administrative or nonjudicial means. The ways in which passport laws described the population reinforced this kind of mass policing, as did other factors such as the ingrained traditions of policing culture and the ineffective methods of traditional crime fighting. These various factors reinforced what can be called a "categorical imperative"—though not in a Kantian moral sense —in policies of social policing. Police directed repression not only against individuals, but, increasingly, against whole categories of the population that officials believed to be harmful, or alien. Although higher-ups officially discouraged categorical or campaign styles of policing, those same officials turned a blind eye to these kinds of practices. This was especially true as the focus of mass repression shifted in the early and mid-1930s from rural to primarily urban areas, and from "kulak" peasants to socially marginal groups. And, along with this shift, so too the character and the function of mass repression also changed. During the dekulakization campaigns of the early 1930s, the political police functioned as a political-revolutionary arm of the state. The purpose of repression was, literally, revolutionary—to extend state power, and to break and remake class (or more broadly, social) and economic relations. Repression was also decentralized and very public. The OGPU, and even certain bodies of local authority, were authorized to use nonjudicial, or administrative, forms of sentencing to enforce repressive measures, and the infamous troikas were set up to expedite political repression of large numbers of individuals. The regime made no attempt to hide its repressive purposes. The population was prepared and mobilized through mass propaganda campaigns for what the regime called class war. And, indeed, segments of the population were mobilized to participate in the state-sponsored violence of dekulakization. In this way, social repression was decentralized even to the point of giving local officials authority over arrest, property confiscation, incarceration, and even death.

It was, in large part, decentralization of violence that leaders sought to curtail by the 1933 orders to limit mass forms of repression in rural areas. During the mid-1930s, leaders did not so much end such repression as redirect its focus and, most important, remonopolize, professionalize, and secretize control over social violence. Campaigns of social defense, especially through enforcement of passport and residence laws, were conducted increasingly and, with only a few exceptions, by policing agencies. Such campaigns were conducted, by and large, outside the view of the public. Police were instructed specifically not to make a public display of sweep operations and group deportations. The way passport and residency laws were used by police to identify so-called dangerous elements was a secret one, involving an internal bureaucratic process of registering information in police surveillance catalogs. Repression, in other words, became a centralized, secret, professionalized, and bureaucratic process. The kind of mass repression that took place during the dekulakization campaigns of the first couple of years of the 1930s was the last within the pre-1939 borders that was based on popular mobilization toward revolutionary social goals; the last campaign based on a contract of violence between state and society for revolutionary purposes. After 1933, repression served more of a defensive than an outright revolutionary function. The regime employed repression to defend state interests and property and to protect state security defined as social order.[24]

THE GREAT PURGES

Mass social (and ethnic) purging by category drove the social defense campaigns of the mid-1930s, and that is the mechanism that was utilized in the great purges of the late 1930s. In chapters 9 and 10, I focus attention on the great purges of 1937 and 1938. Many histories of the "Great Terror" fixate on the political purges of the Party, military, and other institutions, portraying them as a sudden, pathological, and nearly inexplicable event. Other historians explain the purges as a desperate attempt by Stalin to secure control over a corrupt and anarchic political system.[25] I am one of a growing number of historians who distinguish institutional purges from mass social repression campaigns, the *massovye operatsii,* and who view the mass operations as a form of social prophylaxis.[26] Specifically, I argue that the mass purges of 1937 and 1938 cannot be separated from previous campaigns of both political and social repression. By placing them in context, I show that, in fact, the mass purges culminated at least a decade of policing policies, and were intended to rid the country "once and for all time" of socially "harmful" populations. I also agree with those scholars who argue that the prospect of imminent war and invasion, and the fear of "fifth-column" uprisings, motivated and determined the timing and level of violence of the purges. In chapter 9, I review arguments about the motivations for the purges. In chapter 10, I examine the combination of factors—central direction, bureaucratic momentum, and local peculiarities—that influenced the pace and dynamics of mass arrest operations. This chapter distinguishes rural from urban types of operations and shows that, in urban areas, at least, the mass purges were operationally similar to the campaigns of social defense of the mid-1930s. The purges also targeted the same populations. At the same time, the mass purges of the late 1930s differed from previous mass repression campaigns in at least two important respects. They killed many more people—nearly 400,000 in one and a half years

—and imprisoned hundreds of thousands more. The international context that motivated the purges was also different from the domestic context that motivated the social defense campaigns. The prospect of war and imminent invasion gave to the mass purges a scale and level of deadly intensity that were missing from the social defense campaigns of the mid-decade. Despite the increase in violence and scale, however, the mass purges did little to solve the underlying problems of social disorder or to secure the country against domestic threat. Drawing on police and government reports, I show that, in the few short years after the purges and before the German invasion, the country was plagued by many of the same problems as in the mid-1930s, and police were just as ineffective in solving those problems as in the earlier period.

Chapter 11 departs from previous chapters in that it examines the case of a single individual, Kiril Korenev. Korenev was arrested in 1937 as a socially dangerous element (he was purportedly unemployed and had a record as a petty thief), and was sentenced to a labor colony in Siberia. In 1938, due to the persistence of his mother, Korenev's conviction was overturned, and his case dismissed. Persistent searching by the NKVD, however, could not find Korenev. Korenev, it turned out, had escaped, fabricated new identities, and been rearrested no less than four times between 1937 and 1941, when he was finally identified. Based on procuracy and police documents, and from his own testimony and letters to his mother under assumed names, chapter 11 documents Korenev's escapes and how he lived outside the law. It also documents efforts by central authorities to track Korenev through his various identities. The story is significant for what it reveals about how people fell through the cracks in the policing system, and how they survived around the margins of official society; it also tells much, especially, about the dysfunctional aspects of a system designed to police society by population categories rather than by individuals.

Chapter 12 of the book surveys the shift in policies of policing and repression during and after World War II up through the mid-1950s. In this chapter, I describe the separation of civil and political policing, already begun in the very late 1930s, and the depoliticizing of "ordinary" criminality. I also describe the move away from administrative forms of mass repression toward an increasing reliance on traditional policing methods, public informant networks, and judicial forms of social disciplining. I argue that changes in policing practices reflected a demilitarization of the state after World II, as well as changes in notions of citizenship and the relation of citizens to the state, at least within the pre-1939 borders of the country. I contrast trends toward "normal" policing within the pre-1939 borders with policies in the country's newly acquired territories. In the occupied Baltic republics and in the western border regions of Ukraine and Belorussia, political and civil police carried out the same kinds of mass social and political repression that had been characteristic of the 1930s. These new territories were sealed off from the rest of the country for much of the 1950s and remained under special passport and policing regimes. They were only gradually integrated into the passport and policing system used in the rest of the country as they became "safe" for socialism.

IDEOLOGY, CULTURE, AND CONTINGENCY

In hindsight, it is tempting to impose an ideological or cultural rationality onto the mass police violence that characterized Stalinism of the 1930s. Such interpretations have taken several forms. In the classic formulations of Soviet totalitarianism, violence is seen as an inherent part of Bolshevik political culture and ideology. Vladimir Lenin and the Bolsheviks employed "red terror" unapologetically and ruthlessly against the new regime's enemies during the bloody struggle for Soviet power after 1917. Stalin's systematic use of state violence continued and extended this tendency to its logical and radical extreme.[27] Restated formulations of this argument portray Stalinist violence as an essential, "visceral" aspect of early Bolshevik mentality and culture. Bolshevik political culture was, at least in its ultimate Stalinist form, "utterly" destructive.[28] The use of violence against society was not unique to the Stalinist era or to Soviet history, of course, and many scholars have emphasized similarities between Soviet state violence and the exterminatory policies of Adolph Hitler's National Socialist Germany.[29] More recently, scholars have stressed continuities in the use of state forms of violence on a pan-European scale. These formulations are often couched within discussions of modernity and state intervention in society—the goal being to "sculpt an idealized image of the politico-social body."[30]

Such formulations are provocative, but too neat. Certainly, Stalin used state violence systematically and on a large scale. There was a rationality in Stalin's use of mass social violence. His goal, in some sense, was to reshape Soviet society. Yet in applying policies of mass police repression, Stalin and other Soviet leaders were not acting simply or only on ideological impulses to create an idealized body politic. Stalinist leaders used mass forms of violence and repression toward specific revolutionary ends, but also in response to a sequence of crises. The decade began with a state-sponsored revolutionary war in the countryside. In leaders' eyes, this revolutionary war mutated into a protracted social war on a broad scale. Toward the end of the decade, that social war played into yet another, broader, and even more dangerous threat. This last was the threat of invasion and military conflict with external powers. Each of these crises, in the collective view of Soviet leaders, either was unexpected or led to unexpected consequences, and each required emergency, martial law responses. Each crisis unfolded into the next in ways that the regime's officials may have caused, but did not anticipate. Ideology, culture, and personality shaped Stalin's perception of these crises, and predisposed the leader to apply policies of police repression in the manner he did. At the same time, arguments of ideology, culture, and personality do not go far enough. While offering a necessary understanding of mass police violence under Stalin, such arguments are insufficient to explain that violence. Reading the historical evidence forward reveals a more contingent and complicated set of scenarios— of a regime lurching from crisis to crisis during a period of interrelated and mounting dangers, culminating in the ultimate threat of annihilating international conflagration. It was the convergence of those circumstances, combined with Stalin's personality and background, which explains the peculiar virulence of Stalinism. This concatenation of circumstances and personalities was unique to the 1930s. Neither in the 1920s, nor after Stalin's death, did the Soviet regime engage in the kind of militarized and violent social repression that characterized Stalin's martial law socialism.[31]

Stalin's militarized kind of socialism dominated the Soviet state of the 1930s. As various scholars have noted, however, Stalin's socialism was not the only socialism, and Stalin's state was not the only state within the Soviet state.[32] The growing power and brutality of Stalin's militarized state eclipsed, but did not entirely destroy, the institutions of a weakened civil state. This book recounts, not only the repressive activities of police, but the efforts of those who sought to strengthen the institutions of the civil state, over against the growing power and influence of the political police and the Commissariat of Internal Affairs. Those who advocated a "new stage of socialism" based on constitutional and civil law were not, by and large, political intellectuals. They were neither political oppositionists nor those who suffered in the name of moral principle under Stalin's brutality. They did not regard themselves as anti-Soviet. They were often mid-level officials who worked in professional positions in bureaucracies, many in the judiciary and procuracy, or in the Soviet state's social agencies. Their actions or views did not make much difference in the great and immediate scheme of things, but they kept the civil and legal institutions of the state functioning, even as many fell, first into silence, and then into oblivion.[33]

Stalin's militarized police socialism was not the only kind of socialism, even for the Stalinists. For as much as police violence appears to have been an inherent characteristic of Stalinism, Stalinist leaders believed that mass social repression was a temporary, if necessary, aberration of socialist development. Such was Viacheslav Molotov's oft-quoted justification, made in the early 1970s, that the repressions of the 1930s were an emergency response in a life-and-death struggle, a continuation of the Revolution in the increasingly dangerous and threatening international conditions of war. This view was, I believe, sincere, if chilling; it was not simply an attempt to rationalize in hindsight.[34] The history of mass repression under Stalin was characterized by both its pervasiveness and its contingency. And, indeed, once the threat of war had passed, a number of Soviet officials, if not Stalin himself, began to rethink the idea of a militarized war state. Twenty years of Stalin's militarized socialism had resulted in social chaos, not in a carefully engineered society. The chapters that follow examine mass social repression in Stalin's state, and they recount the attempts to dismantle or mitigate Stalin's repressive machinery in the last years of the dictator's life.

1 A New Kind of Class War

In the current situation, a hooligan, a robber, a bandit—is he not the real counterrevolutionary?
—*Genrikh Yagoda, 1935*

IN JANUARY 1933, several hundred elite delegates of the Communist Party of the Soviet Union gathered in Moscow, as they did yearly, in the splendor of the Great Hall of the Central Trade Union Building. They were gathered for the yearly plenary session of the Party's Central Committee. They were there, specifically, to hear their leader, Joseph Stalin, discuss the state of the Party and the progress of the Party's revolutionary Five Year Plan to industrialize and collectivize the country. The white columns and high gilded ceilings of the Great Hall provided an appropriate setting for this gathering, for there, Stalin declared to a jubilant plenary session that the fundamental victory of socialism had been accomplished in the USSR. The Soviet leader reeled off the litany of "huge" successes of industrialization and collectivization during the previous several years. He looked ahead to the tasks that lay before the Party in the coming period of socialist construction. He cited Western "bourgeois" press accounts of stunning achievements. He declared that, despite hardships, despite hardened class resistance, and despite skepticism from many, the Party and the Soviet people had accomplished the "historic" tasks of the first Five Year Plan. Great factories had been erected and socialist farms had been organized. Soviet power ruled indisputably across the Soviet Union. Organized class resistance had been routed, Stalin declared, and in that lay a powerful victory. The remnants of the "dying" classes had been "knocked to their knees." They had been "driven from the factories and off the farms." They had been "scattered across the face of the USSR." The first Five Year Plan, Stalin pronounced, was a triumph for socialism and the Party.[1]

Not all was well, however. Even as Stalin hailed the victory of socialism, he sounded a warning that the country faced perhaps its most serious challenge yet. The Party, said Stalin in 1933, could not yet rest because the class war continued—not in the organized, open form of opposition, but in the form of "quiet sabotage" (*tikhoi sapoi*), specifically in the form of crime and lawlessness. Stalin's remarks about criminality have since been obscured by the more sensational interest in political forms of opposition and repression during the 1930s. Yet Stalin devoted a substantial part of his remarks to the 1933 plenary session to this new kind of class war. His descriptions of the dangers posed by crime and social disorder precipitated a major shift in both political and social kinds of policing, and in policies of social surveillance. In fact, Stalin and other Soviet leaders worried less about direct political opposition in 1933 than they did about lawlessness and social disorder. This chapter examines the realities and changing representations of crime and social order from the 1920s to the 1930s, and the ways in which deviancy and marginality came to be politicized by Soviet leaders.

CRIME AS CLASS WAR

In his remarks to the Central Committee's 1933 plenary session, Stalin laid out the dangers of criminality and social disorder. According to Stalin, remnants of hostile classes remained, even though organized class resistance had been broken. These hostile elements no longer had the force to engage in a direct attack against Soviet power, said Stalin, but they hated Soviet power and would attempt in any way possible to undermine the building of socialism. "They trick workers and *kolkhozniki*, they undermine Soviet power and the Party. They burn warehouses and break machines. They organize sabotage. They organize wrecking in *kolkhozy* and *sovkhozy*. . . ."[2] These kinds of direct wrecking activities amounted to anti-Soviet acts of sabotage, according to Stalin, but even these activities were not the main threat that the remnant capitalist classes posed to Soviet power. The most significant threat lay in the waves of pilfering and theft from factories, warehouses, freight trains, and farms, especially of such items as grain, coal, food, and other basic staple goods. Stalin made clear that he was talking about more than just a few desperate people. A single loaf of bread or some lumps of coal may not have amounted to much. Overall, however, this kind of theft occurred on a mass scale during the harsh years of the early 1930s. The cost to the Soviet economy ran into millions of rubles yearly.

Here was the greatest danger, according to Stalin, repeating the litany: ". . . theft and pilfering (*vorovstvo i khishchenie*) from factories and enterprises, theft and pilfering from railroad cars and trade enterprises, theft and pilfering from warehouses, and especially from collective and state farms." Stalin gave no credence to the obvious—that those caught stealing were, for the most part, poor workers and peasants who had no other recourse to try to stay alive. Stalin attributed mass theft to a campaign of deliberate sabotage. According to Stalin, anti-Soviet "former people" (*byvshie liudi*) acted according to the "deepest class instincts," knowing that the basis of the Soviet economy, and of Soviet power, lay in the socialization of property. Thus, a strike against socialist property meant a strike against Soviet power. As a result, the main activities of these "former people" was to organize mass stealing and theft of socialist, cooperative, and collective farm property.

Stalin chastised Party and local officials who turned a blind eye to pilfering, thinking that it amounted to petty crime and was unimportant in the overall scheme of priorities. On the contrary. Stalin emphasized that protecting socialist property in all its forms lay at the heart of socialist construction and Soviet power. He compared the sanctity and protection of socialist property under Soviet socialism to that of private property under capitalist law. He declared that, just as capitalist societies meted out harsh punishment for violating private property, so should socialist officials punish harshly even the slightest infraction against socialist property. Stalin defended the already infamous law of 7 August 1932, which made theft of socialist property, even petty pilfering, punishable by a long labor camp sentence and even by death. Socialist property theft, he repeated, was to be treated as seriously as any form of counterrevolutionary activity. To be indifferent to socialist property theft was tantamount to active cooperation in the destruction of Soviet power. He warned bluntly that it was the duty of "every communist, worker, and collective farmer" to enforce this law in its strictest application.[3]

Socialist property theft on the scale that Stalin described amounted to more than the sum of individual acts, according to the Soviet leader. What the Soviet Union faced was not just crime, but a whole new and unanticipated stage of class war, and this new stage of class war required, in turn, a new and forceful response. Here, not for the first time, Stalin put forward his famous argument about the strengthening of the socialist state as society approached the realization of full socialism. Stalin declared:

> Some comrades understood the thesis about class destruction, about creation of a classless society, and the withering (*otmiranie*) of the state as a justification for laziness and indifference, as a justification for the counterrevolutionary theory of the cessation (*potukhanie*) of class struggle and the weakening of state power. It can only be said that such people have nothing in common with our Party. . . . The destruction of classes will be achieved not by a cessation of class struggle, but by its intensification. Withering of the state will not be achieved by weakening of state power, but through its maximal strengthening, which is necessary to beat down the remnants of the dying classes and to organize defense against capitalist encirclement, which is far from destroyed and which will not end soon."[4]

As Stalin's comments show, his argument about strengthening the coercive power of the state did not result, initially, from fear of organized political opposition. Neither did it have much to do with the threat of capitalist encirclement. Stalin's reference to hostile external powers was a passing one. Stalin framed his comments about strengthening the state within his concern about the destabilizing consequences of social disorder.

Stalin focused his remarks specifically on the then widespread problem of theft and pilfering. Whether the Soviet leader had other types of criminal activity in mind is unclear, but his words carried exactly that import. Stalin's remarks placed the problem of criminality at the center of his address on reestablishing social order and building socialism in the country after the revolutionary upheaval of the previous three years. More than that, by linking class war and criminality, Stalin defined the latter not only as the central problem of social order, but social order as the central problem of state security. This new understanding deeply influenced police and OGPU policies in the mid-1930s, and turned the fight against crime and social deviancy—indeed, any kind of social disorder—from a matter of social control into a political priority in defense of the state. Thus, Stalin's remarks politicized, or more accurately statized, criminality and social deviancy in a way uncharacteristic of the 1920s and the period after his death. This speech also justified an increase in state power. This was to be tied to increased policing for the specific purpose of quelling social disorder. Stalin's January 1933 speech was one of the first to mention intensification of class war rather than its diminution, as the country moved closer to realizing socialism. That these pronouncements were occasioned by concern for domestic problems of criminality and social order highlighted all the more the link that leaders made between state security and social policing.

Other Soviet leaders repeated and expanded on Stalin's themes and on the threat that crime posed to the state and to the construction of socialism in the Soviet Union. These were no minor figures, but included the highest officials of the state and Party. An RSFSR Supreme Court review from 1935 reiterated Stalin's January 1933 speech. The review's author noted that Stalin's comments linking crime, social order, and class war provided the "starting point" for all criminal policy since. Stalin's defense of socialist property had "signaled the start of a sharp struggle against thieves and wreckers in the economy, against hooligans and embezzlers of socialist property."[5] Pavel Postyshev, a prominent Central Committee member, commented in a 1934 speech that "At present, the criminal element in our country is comprised of various dekulakized elements and elements made up of escapees from labor, concentration camps, etc. We need to understand that, because the base of activities of the routed class enemy . . . has been restricted, the class enemy all the more turns its attention to the criminal element, with which it is tied in its social origin."[6] A report of the USSR procuracy from the same year quoted Stalin's remarks about how professional and economic crimes were carried out by class enemies who had infiltrated into factories and enterprises, and who were hiding behind the mask of workers and collective farmers.[7]

In a 1935 speech to police officials, Genrikh Yagoda, then chief of the NKVD, made the specific link between class war, counterrevolution, and criminality. He reminded his audience that "For us, the highest honor is in the struggle against counterrevolution. But in the current situation—a hooligan, a robber, a bandit—is he not the real counterrevolutionary? . . . In our country . . . where the construction of socialism has been victorious . . . any criminal act, by its nature, is nothing other than an expression of class struggle."[8] We might reasonably assume that Yagoda was engaging in a bit of hyperbole in order to inflate the morale of his audience of policemen. Yet, according to his later critics, the NKVD chief emphasized similar priorities even in his communications with the GUGB, the successor agency to the OGPU, responsible not for social order but for the political security of the state and its leaders. According to Leonid Zakovskii, a senior OGPU/GUGB official under Yagoda, the latter stressed protection of state property as the foremost concern for OGPU operational and territorial organs in the struggle against counterrevolution. According to Zakovskii, Yagoda laid out this priority in one of his first directives as head of the NKVD in August of 1934. Zakovskii, as well as other critics such as Yakov Agranov, Yagoda's assistant chief, claimed that Yagoda maintained this emphasis in his operational administration of the GUGB throughout the 1930s.[9]

By and large, Yagoda's critics were correct. Throughout the 1930s, Yagoda, as well as other high officials, understood social and economic order as the primary task of the NKVD in defending the political interests of the Soviet state. At a 1931 conference of OGPU operational heads, one OGPU official confirmed that agents saw the hand of the counterrevolution behind all forms of organized criminal activity.[10] Writing in 1935, a leading specialist on crime and law, A. Shliapochnikov, echoed this assessment. Writing in a collection of articles on crime, Shliapochnikov provided one of the most articulate and detailed presentations of the argument that crime amounted to a new form of assault against the state. He offered a litany of stories and statistics on professional-economic crime, banditry, crimes of speculation, of stealing state property, and of hooliganism. Although much had been done to combat crime, in general, wrote Shliapochnikov, the state's response remained "weak" and "ad hoc" (samotek), especially against these "most dangerous" and "pervasive" kinds of crimes.[11] More to the point, according to Shliapochnikov, the problem of crime was no longer simply a matter of individual criminal activities. The rise in crime rates represented a dangerous alliance between traditional criminal elements and the state's enemies, the lower middle-class strata (melko-burzhuaznyi sloi). "An essential reason for the growth of a whole range of crimes," wrote Shliapochnikov, "is the alliance (smykanie) of the class enemy with the criminal element . . . which characterizes . . . the class

struggle at the present stage." Pilfering and theft had become transformed, in Shliapochnikov's words, from a petty criminal activity into
the "chief activity of class-dangerous elements . . . [as well as] backward
elements of the working class." In this new stage of class war, he continued, police repression needed to be strengthened; the purpose of law
and policing, and of repression in general, had to be redefined—to "repress disobedience (*stikhiia*)" in general, and not just to be tougher on
criminals.[12]

A NEW TAXONOMY OF CRIME

Organized political opposition to the Stalinist state was impossible,
of course, but in officials' perceptions, crime became its social equivalent. Soviet officials considered the waves of crime that swept the country in the early and mid-1930s as more than the sum of individual criminal acts. This is not to say that all criminals were motivated by
anti-Soviet sentiments or ideologies. The kinds of crime, and crime on
the kind of broad social scale that occurred in the 1930s, bear witness
more to mass social disobedience than to conscious resistance to the
state or the regime. Still, officials perceived crime, and more broadly, social disorder, as the social expression of a new kind of class war and as
a threat to the security of the state. The highest Party and state officials
believed crime and lawlessness posed a danger to the country's social
and economic order, and even to the stability of the regime. But, did
crime and, more broadly, social disorder, threaten the very foundations
of the state, as Stalin and other leaders claimed? How bad was criminality and social disorder during the early and mid-1930s? Was it as
bad as authorities claimed or feared? Who committed crimes, what motivated criminals in their activities, and what kinds of crimes were most
prevalent? What kinds of crimes most worried the regime's leaders, and
did those crimes reflect a real state of social breakdown or deep-seated
anti-Soviet opposition? These are pertinent questions, given the near
hysteria about crime and social disorder expressed by local and national
authorities, but they are also difficult to answer, since Stalin's speech in
January 1933 not only politicized crime but also the ways in which officials categorized and talked about crime. As a result, official discourse
from the 1930s tells us more about leaders' priorities and their understanding of state security than about the social dynamics of crime.

The way officials categorized crime changed from the 1920s to the 1930s, and the following two reports reflect that change. A 1930 report, for example, was one of the last to reflect a traditional reading of crime. The report, which ran to nearly two hundred pages, was prepared by the police for the head of the then Russian republic NKVD, A. A. Tolmachev. Based on incidents of police investigations, the report detailed crime trends during the last five years of the 1920s. The report contained no politicized language, no references to anti-Soviet elements, and the categories of crimes were laid out in a straightforward, literally descriptive manner. Crimes were grouped by the statutes covering them and organized as a compendium that would have been recognizable to professional policemen anywhere in Europe. No crime or set of crimes was given special attention for ideological or strategic reasons of state security. Each group was analyzed, first of all, according to incidence of occurrence—whether on the rise or declining—then by age group, region, season, and other such criteria. The "professions" of prostitution and panhandling were listed along with crimes of hooliganism, conditions of alcoholism, and child homelessness as "social anomalies" requiring the attention of social organizations as well as police. The report described banditry as a criminal problem, not as a form of political counterrevolution.[13]

The 1930 crime report represented a traditional nineteenth-century professionalized approach to policing as a nonpoliticized fight against statutory violations of law.[14] It reflected the separation, characteristic of the 1920s and again of the post–World War II era, between ordinary criminal and policing activities and opposition policing carried out by the political police. Tolmachev, of course, was soon removed from his position and the Russian NKVD was abolished as Stalin carried out his purge of the police and then merged it under centralized control of the political police.[15] For a time, after the merger, some police attempted to maintain professional independence and, by implication, a separation between "ordinary" and political kinds of crimes. A police official at a 1931 conference reiterated that, despite subordination to the OGPU, police operations should "under no circumstances" be politicized, nor should "objects" or "persons" of police attention be placed in a "political light" (*politosveshchenie*).[16] The subordination of police to the OGPU was already well underway, however, and Stalin's comments in early 1933 gave official sanction to the process of politicizing crime and other social "anomalies." Yagoda's comments from 1935, as well as others, cited above, show the extent to which policing and criminal activities became politicized.

The process of politicizing, or statizing, crime altered the way officials categorized threats to society and the state. Crime reports from the 1930s no longer organized crimes according to statute and frequency of occurrence. Officials ranked crimes according to their perceived danger to the state, or by the level of danger they posed to the fulfillment of state policy campaigns. State crimes (*gosudarstvennoe prestuplenie*) and crimes against administrative order became the most dangerous of crimes, in addition to outright political crimes adjudicated under the infamous statute 58 of the criminal code. Political crimes were included in the same discussions as other crimes, and the language of counter-revolution and anti-Soviet elements permeated all discussion of criminality and social order. Thus, a procuracy report on crime, written in 1935, started with a long section on the trend in political crimes, terror acts against state and Party officials, and crimes of wrecking. "Crimes of speculation" (*spekuliatsia*) came next. In contrast, the 1930 crime report, noted above, did not discuss political crimes, and it did not group crimes under vague headings such as speculation—a reference to profiteering—but listed crimes under their separate criminal statutes. In the 1935 procuracy report, the section on speculation was followed by categorical discussion of crimes against the governing order (*prestupleniia protiv poriadka upravleniia*). This category included, first and foremost, incidents of mass disorder, such as rioting or illegal strike activity (*massovye besporiadki*). Banditry and "resistance to and disrespect of [Soviet] power" also fell within this category. This last category also included short discussions of avoidance of military service, theft from and abuse of nationalized forest and land, violations of moonshine laws, and incidents of labor indiscipline. With the rapid extension of state monopoly, "occupational" crimes (*dolzhnostnoe prestuplenie* or white-collar crimes) became a major category of concern in the 1930s, especially as rapid and nearly unchecked bureaucratization followed inevitably from increasing state control over the economy. The procuracy's report devoted a lengthy section to these categories of crimes, which included bribery, embezzlement, illegal trade within state procurement and trade and banking organizations, and other kinds of graft and organizational corruption.[17] During the 1930s, officials extended the state's monopoly over crime and social disorder as they extended the state's monopoly over economic and social processes. Crime, in other words, became statized and was administered as a state monopoly, just as the economy was.

Crimes against persons and property together with hooliganism made up the last three categories discussed in the procuracy's 1935 crime report, but even here, the author's language politicized, or more to the point, statized, what had been previously regarded as nonpolitical, or nonstate, spheres of criminality. The author of this report discussed the dynamics of these types of crimes in terms of class enemy influence, but also as a direct and increasing threat to the state. Incidents of hooliganism, he noted, were decreasing from their highs during the late 1920s, but acts of hooliganism were beginning to take more dangerous forms than in previous years. No longer characterized by individual insults or rowdiness, hooliganism was characterized increasingly as a group form of disorder, which included physical beatings and other kinds of physical injury and, most disturbing, organized theft and other illegal activities that "cross over into outright banditry and counterrevolutionary crimes." The report accounted for this transformation by the supposed increase in numbers of recidivists and "declassed and class-harmful elements" that engaged in criminal activities.[18] In general, according to the procuracy report, courts needed to pay more attention to these types of crimes, not because they were on the increase, but because they were directed toward the disruption of production and cultural-educational work, and disorganization of the new Soviet way of life. These were dangerous crimes not because they occurred often, but because they threatened state interests. The report concluded this section with a reminder to the courts—not that they do more to fight statutory crime, but that they not underestimate the importance of their function to protect the state and to struggle against capitalist remnants.[19]

A draft report from May 1937 for a new criminal code also ranked crimes explicitly according to their perceived threat to the state. The report was written over the signature of I. A. Akulov, then head of the Central Executive Committee, TsIK, of the Soviet Union. In Akulov's summary, counterrevolutionary crimes came first, especially crimes of treason. Immediately behind in order of danger were crimes against socialist property, since, as Akulov wrote, the constitution and the law of

7 August 1932 viewed "pilferers" (*raskhititely*) of socialist property as enemies of the people. In third place were especially dangerous crimes against "state order," that is, *protiv gosudarstvennogo poriadka*. Interestingly, crimes in this category, such as hooliganism, illegal strikes, and other illegal gatherings, had traditionally been categorized under crimes against administrative order, or *poriadok upravleniia*. By 1937, "administrative order" had turned into "state order." All three categories of crimes were considered "state crimes," and were ranked as the most dangerous. A second section included crimes against defense of the Fatherland (*otechestvo*), such as avoidance of military duty. Only in a third section did Akulov include crimes against persons, or that threatened the life or health of Soviet citizens. In Akulov's reading, protection of the state came first, then defense of the Fatherland, then, and finally, the protection of citizens.[20]

THE PROBLEM WITH NUMBERS

Categorization according to the criterion of state security or policy fulfillment made clear what types of crimes leaders deemed most threatening to the regime, but such organization resulted in a good deal of confusion about actual crime trends. Traditional ordering of crimes, as in the 1930 NKVD report, ranked them according to their numerical incidence. With recategorization, this practice all but ceased, as reports and reviews grouped and analyzed criminality according to the categories described above. As a result, reports purportedly about crime trends were not really about crime, but about state priorities. To add to the confusion, different agencies kept their own statistics, which reflected the function of that bureaucracy within the state. The courts tracked convictions, the police counted arrests and numbers of cases initiated, and the procuracy reported numbers of cases processed and indictments issued. Agencies reported statistics in masses, yet there existed no central coordination or integration of materials. No attempt was made to standardize the kinds of statistics reported from different agencies, or to chart overall trends based on an analysis of all agencies' reporting. This lack of central coordination is surprising. The Soviet state was a highly bureaucratized and a highly centralized state. Its officials, arguably more than officials in any other country, kept meticulous records about everything. This tendency was exaggerated by the

Soviet commitment to planning—to economic and social engineering —and by Stalin's centralizing revolution of the late 1920s and early 1930s. Throughout the 1930s, however, no agency coordinated the collection and integration of statistical records to document crime. As one crime expert put it succinctly, "Criminal statistics still carry a purely departmental and compartmentalized character (*vedomstvennyi kharakter*)."[21]

Even more confusing, officials in each bureaucracy wrote and spoke about crime and criminals using statistics generated within that bureaucracy, but they wrote their reports as if their statistics reflected the overall state of crime and criminality. Rarely did one official reference differing statistics from another state agency, or acknowledge the peculiarities of his own figures. Thus, procuracy or judicial officials confidently described the "dynamics" of crime trends, but they used statistics that only counted the number of convictions for different kinds of crimes. Conviction rates, however, accounted for only a small percentage of the number of crimes reported, as some officials acknowledged. Assessments varied about the extent to which conviction statistics underrepresented real crime rates. A Russian republic Supreme Court review from 1936 estimated, overall, "about a 10 to 20 percent" difference, but this seems to overestimate, by far, the number of convictions in proportion to the numbers of crimes reported.[22] A 1935 report from the USSR procuracy's office provided what was probably a more realistic assessment, acknowledging that the number of actual crimes exceeded the number of judicial convictions "many times over."[23]

While statistics might be incomplete, it would be reasonable to conclude that the state's statistics provided at least an indication of social tendencies. Yet even this would be a dubious reading of official figures. Court and procuracy statistics did not describe trends in crime so much as they reflected the various and seasonal campaigns of the procuracy, the courts, and the political system that drove the state's criminal policies. The planting and harvest campaigns each spring and autumn were the two largest of these. During these times of the year, the state's prosecutorial and judicial apparatus was mobilized, as was the police. Other policing duties were undermanned and other types of crime went unreported or uninvestigated. Yet these were centrally initiated campaigns and affected all policing and judicial agencies more or less equally. At the same time, leaders in different bureaucracies pushed certain types of campaigns over others, according to the function of that agency or the policy dynamics within each bureaucracy. Thus, police might emphasize campaigns against hooliganism at the same time that procuracy officials were admonishing subordinates to be more diligent in pursuing cases that involved economic crimes.

The compartmentalized and campaign style of policing during the 1930s led to a bizarre situation in which different agencies issued contradictory reports on crime trends based on the different kinds of statistics each agency collected. A procuracy report published in 1934, which purportedly tracked crime trends, noted that, based on conviction rates, crimes of hooliganism and against private persons "rose sharply" during the last years of the 1920s. By 1929, such crimes comprised nearly one-third of all convictions in the Russian republic, up dramatically from approximately 3 to 4 percent of convictions before 1925.[24] In contrast, a Russian republic police report from 1930 described a significant decline in the number of cases of just such crimes investigated by police for exactly the same period. By 1929, according to police statistics, the number of cases of hooliganism and against individual persons dropped by more than half the number in 1925.[25] Similarly, while conviction rates dropped for nearly all crimes after 1933, government and police reports throughout the mid-1930s described the particular problems of theft of state property, speculation, banditry, hooliganism, and professional economic crime as growing worse, not better. These latter reports directly contradicted reports issued by the judiciary. While judicial officials described a decline of economic-professional crimes, based on rates of court convictions, the state inspectorate (*Kommissiia Sovetskogo kontrolia*, or KSK) reported an "outrageous" increase in the reporting of such crimes. In 1935, wrote a KSK report based on figures from the finance commissariat, the sum of money lost to embezzlement and outright theft of cash not only did not decline but, in fact, rose over 1934 figures. In 1934, this sum amounted to 120 million rubles, but in 1935 it rose again by several million rubles.[26] Another report, by the Institute of Criminal Law, noted not just an increase in the number of these types of crimes, but an increase in the proportion of these crimes to all crimes—from about 10 percent in the late 1920s to two-thirds of all crime reported in 1934. Interestingly, the latter report utilized police figures of cases reported rather than conviction rates. The same report declared that theft of state property, related professional-economic crimes, and crimes of speculation constituted the single most significant threat to the goals of socialist construction of the country.[27]

Occasionally, officials provided a rare and candid admission of the policy or campaign character of criminal statistics, their biased bureaucratic origins, and their lack of correspondence to social reality. A procuracy crime report from 1935, for example, noted with satisfaction a significant drop in crime rates from their highs in the late 1920s, the reconstruction period before the establishment of full socialism in the early 1930s. This was true, especially of crimes against persons and in rates of hooliganism—from a combined high of 40 percent of all court convictions in 1928 to only 10 percent in 1933. In one sentence, the report's anonymous author stated, confidently, that these figures represented a real and significant trend, a consequence of the establishment of full socialism in the country. In the next sentence, however, the author noted, apparently without contradiction, that the drop in numbers of such cases resulted "mainly" from a transfer of many cases from regular judicial courts to local comrades' courts. It went unstated but understood that, as a result, these cases would drop out of judicial statistics, as would the many cases listed under categories of hooliganism. In another part of the report, the author detailed several other reasons for the steep decline in conviction rates from the late 1920s to the early 1930s, all of which concerned judicial and repressive policies. The report noted that an increasing number of cases of hooliganism, as well as other kinds of cases, were handled "administratively," outside the court system, through police powers of exile and administrative fining of offenders. During the recent years, courts, too, ceased to hear many personal crimes cases, since "the attention of the [state's] investigative-judicial organs [had been turned] to the fight against other kinds of crimes." The latter, of course, was a reference to the nearly full attention given to the fight against crimes committed against the state during the collectivization and industrialization campaigns.[28] Such comments lay buried in the depths of a 266-page mass of statistical information and explanation, but they provided at least a small corrective to the report's stated claim to be a description of social reality.

The author of a 1936 review offered a more forthright caveat. The report in question was a Russian federation Supreme Court review that purportedly analyzed crime trends for the previous several years. The author of this report even registered a hint of professional protest and duress. The author cast doubt on the usability of the report in the very first pages by noting that, although the report supposedly described trends in criminality, it was based on court statistics that charted judicial conviction rates. The author acknowledged that "these two categories [actual crime rates and judicial conviction rates] are far from identical." Unfortunately, the author noted, the court was forced to use judicial statistics "because of the absence of specialized statistics on criminality." The text did not provide clues as to whether the writer believed such figures did not exist, or whether he was making a back-handed complaint about police secretiveness in withholding figures on reported crime investigations. In either case, this was a remarkable statement, and not the only such statement. Several paragraphs later, the author once again cast doubt on the veracity of the report as an accurate compendium of crime. Hinting at the campaign character of policing, the author wrote that, "In accordance with our charge to execute the specific directives of the Party and government, the material in this report is organized according to the most important of these directives. [Thus], we begin with fulfillment of the chief directives on protecting socialized (*obshchestvennoe*) property." This qualification made clear that, despite its title, the report was more about state security policies than about criminality.[29]

The changes in perceptions of social order described above are often difficult to see, or become obvious only in the comparative analysis of obscure documents and reports. Sometimes, however, new perceptions broke through the surface of older assumptions and were revealed in striking ways. One of the most telling illustrations of how economic crime became transformed into a category of political sabotage can be found in a document in the Novosibirsk archive, a memorandum prepared by the Western Siberian Procurator General, Ignatii Barkov, in March 1935. The document was a draft of instructions from Barkov to local prosecutors, edited by his deputy, a certain Pozdniakov. Barkov typed the draft instructions to warn subordinates against corruption and anti-Soviet tendencies in the work of judicial and prosecutorial cadres of the district. "It has come to our attention," he wrote, "that not a few justices and procuratorial officials have gone over to the side of our class enemies, have fallen under the influence of petty-bourgeois disobedience (*melko-burzhuaznaiia stikhiia*)." Having set the tone of the memorandum, Barkov then filled several pages with examples of such officials, their crimes, the consequences of those crimes in costs to the state, and the punishments given those officials. In one of the typed passages, Barkov discussed the negligence shown by a district prosecutor, Mikhail Zhdanov, in failing to prosecute to the fullest degree the case of a relative, a cousin named Khlebnikov, involved in an extensively organized smuggling and illegal trade ring. According to Barkov, Zhdanov tried to get a reduced charge or a light sentence for Khlebnikov, instead of doing his duty "to defend socialist property and to unmask this criminal." Worse, yet, charged Barkov, Zhdanov "benefited materially from Khlebnikov's criminal activities" by accepting money and gifts, "all the while declaring publicly the need to be vigilant against such crimes."[30]

Throughout the document, Barkov referred to corrupt officials such as Zhdanov's cousin as criminals (*prestupniki*) and to their activities literally as statutory crimes (*ugolovnye prestupleniia*). In editing the instructions, however, Pozdniakov, Barkov's assistant, made several substantive suggestions, one of which was to change the wording of "criminal" (*prestupnik*) to "enemy of the people" (*vrag naroda*). Pozdniakov made his suggestions by hand, using a black ink pen, and then signed his emendations using the same pen. Thus, in the references to Khlebnikov (the criminal), Pozdniakov's version read that Zhdanov (the judge and family relative) had failed to do his duty "to defend socialist property and to unmask *[not a criminal, as Barkov had written, but]* an enemy of the people," and that Zhdanov had "benefited materially [not from Khlebnikov's criminal activities, but] from the activities of an enemy of the people" (italics mine). Such a change of wording made a significant difference in how Khlebnikov and his activities should be viewed. An enemy of the people was no ordinary criminal, but a counterrevolutionary. Khlebnikov's activities were no longer "merely" statutory crimes, but constituted nothing less than an attempt to undermine Soviet power. In effect, Pozdniakov's alterations politicized Khlebnikov's criminal activities in a way Barkov's wording had not. Moreover, by calling Khlebnikov an enemy of the people, Pozdniakov made matters worse for Zhdanov. In Pozdniakov's version, Zhdanov attempted to aid, not just a criminal, which was bad enough, but a counterrevolutionary enemy of the state. No final version of the memorandum exists, and it is unclear how the finished set of instructions reads. In at least one way, however, the draft of this memorandum is of more historical interest than the finished version. The unfinished state of this document provides a glimpse into the process by which "ordinary" or statutory criminals became politicized as enemies of the regime, and the way statutory crimes became crimes against the state.

PROFESSIONAL-ECONOMIC CRIMES

Crime statistics may not tell us much about social reality, but they do tell us much about the priorities and perceptions of Soviet officials. They believed that certain types of criminality posed more of a danger to the state than other types. Certainly, officials believed that economic crimes posed one of the fastest-growing and most significant threats. It is difficult to confirm official assessments of economic, property, and occupational-professional crimes, since judiciary statistics were so skewed by anticrime campaigns and an emphasis on conviction rates. Still, officials reported a significant increase in these types of crime, and an increase in the proportion of these types of crimes to other crimes. That increase may have been due, at least in part, to the increased attention given to them by police and prosecutors. Yet the number and proportion of such crimes no doubt increased as the state expanded its monopoly into all aspects of the economic and commercial life of the country. The enormous amounts of money that the state poured into economic and industrial expansion created lucrative opportunities for graft, embezzlement, and other forms of white-collar crime. What is surprising, however, is that central authorities made little effort to gather overall statistics about the cost of these crimes. This is surprising, given the amount of concern expressed about administrative and financial corruption.

Some idea of the dimensions of economic crime can be gained from a comparison of police, Party, and other reviews for various years during the 1930s. The procuracy's review of crime for the first years of the 1930s, for example, showed a jump in the number of convictions for professional or occupational crimes, from 101,730 in the second half of 1932 to 189,159 at the end of 1933, to 179,891 for the first half of 1934. Similarly, the number of convictions for crimes against state property also jumped from 151,723 and 161,123 in the first and second half of 1932, respectively, to 241,914 in the second half of 1933, and then decreased to 166,548 in the first half of 1934.[31] A USSR Supreme Court review of all convictions for the interwar period showed a similar trend, if different numbers. According to Supreme Court numbers, convictions for professional-occupational crimes rose sharply from 67,517 in 1928 to a high of 308,322 in 1934.[32] As a proportion of all types of crime, including counterrevolutionary crimes, white-collar crime climbed steadily, according to the procuracy report, from 7.4 percent of convictions in 1928 to 33 percent in 1934. The proportion of crimes involving theft of state property rose from 20 percent in 1928 to 30.6 percent of all judicial convictions in 1934. The biggest jump in the latter category occurred, understandably, between 1928 and 1931, the period of intensive collectivization and dekulakization, when the proportion rose from 20 to 27 percent. These were the years of intense nationalization of the economy and the land and the creation of cooperative and state institutions to replace market mechanisms in supplying goods to the populace.[33]

In one of the few attempts to assess the cost of professional-occupational crime, a Supreme Court commission estimated that in Moscow and the Moscow oblast alone, over 25 million rubles in commodities had been lost in 1933 through theft or embezzlement. Yet this figure included only those commodities that passed through the *tsentrosoiuz* system, the system of cooperative retailers; it did not include any figures from the commissariats of light and heavy industries, from the commissariats of agriculture and collective farms, or from state bank and trading organizations.[34] The scattered statistics that existed from these latter commissariats suggested a situation no better than in the *tsentrosoiuz* network. Indeed, estimates of loss due to embezzlement and theft varied wildly, depending on the agency doing the review. In 1934, the state inspectorate agency reported an estimated loss of 120 million rubles for the Russian republic *tsentrosoiuz* system due to embezzlement and employee theft.[35] In another report, which covered the two-month period March–April 1932, police tabulated losses from just eleven district (*krai*) and oblast areas in the Russian republic. This report showed a loss of 4,673,030 rubles due, supposedly, to all types of occupational-economic crime during these two months. The police report cited above included no summary figures for the year, and the figures it provided were for fewer than half of the oblasts in the Russian republic, but the report stated that all types of economic and professional-occupational crimes were on the rise, and that officials expected a jump in such crimes during the spring planting season. Thus, a conservative extrapolation from the March–April 1932 figures gives an estimate of 28–30 million rubles for the year, perhaps even twice that amount, lost to the Russian republic due to professional-economic types of crime. Still, even an exaggerated extrapolation of a 55–60 million–ruble loss for 1932 comes nowhere close to the inspectorate report of a 120 million–ruble loss due to embezzlement and theft two years later in 1934, and that just within the consumer retailing system. No systematic attempts were made to reconcile such diverse figures or to establish some kind of trend pattern, but the loss to the state due to white-collar types of criminal activity was huge, certainly in the hundreds of millions of rubles yearly.

Examples of embezzlement and theft during this period are well known. In some light industry factories, the yearly cost of stolen goods amounted to well over 150 rubles for each worker in the factory.[36] At the Gorky automotive plant, finished cars disappeared right off the assembly line, and in Leningrad's Treugol'nik works thousands of pairs of galoshes were stolen during the course of the year 1932. Embezzlement of money or goods comprised the most common of these types of crimes. Most were committed by individuals in financial or administrative positions in state and cooperative organizations. The police report listed, especially, cashiers and financial workers in cooperative organizations, state trade organs, collective and state farms, banks and post offices, and agricultural machine tractor stations. Understandably, areas undergoing intensive industrial or economic development reported the highest number of cases. These included the Urals oblast, the central industrial region, the Western oblast, and the Ivanovo industrial region. All of these areas experienced new construction on a large scale and, as a result, money and goods flowed into the regions through cooperatives and construction offices, often with few or no safeguards.[37] Rural trade cooperatives and collective and state farm administrative organizations also became a focus for criminal activity, since they also functioned as funnels for money and goods coming into the countryside.[38]

Interestingly, professional-economic crime rates, while high in collective and state farm regions, were lower for the first time in late 1932 than the rates for similar crimes reported for urban and industrial areas. This would seem natural under the conditions of rapid industrial and urban growth during the early years of the 1930s. Yet for Bolsheviks, this was an especially disturbing trend since they equated urban space with socialist construction and therefore lower crime rates than in the supposedly backward, anticommunist rural districts.[39] In fact, economic crimes in general and professional crimes in particular were so rampant that police were overwhelmed. In March and April, 1932, alone, police registered over 27, 800 reported cases of economic crime in just the eleven oblasts and districts noted above.[40] This figure did not include Moscow and the Moscow oblast, nor did it include a number of other key areas, particularly the large territories of Eastern and Western Siberia. The latter comprised nearly half of the landmass of the Russian republic and one-third of its population. Moreover, according to the police report, nearly 80 percent of the cases it cited as solved—that is, with the guilty parties identified—were solved as a result of activities by social agencies and state inspectorates, not by police inspections or operational investigations.[41] As noted above, police expected an increase in such crimes, but not only because of seasonal agricultural campaigns. As the next chapter will show, police presence in outlying and new industrial and agricultural areas was minimal at best, and lower-level cooperative and state organs in these areas were often separated from oblast-level centers of inspection and control. Resources of the latter were also stretched thin and rarely reached outside of the major urban centers.[42] And even in major population centers, as well as in outlying areas, organized rings of criminals targeted financial departments for hiring themselves into positions of easy corruption. Insinuating themselves in this way was not difficult to do. Organizations were desperate for any kind of financially literate workers and rarely gave more than a cursory screening to new employees, if even that. Background checks were primitive even in those organizations that bothered with them. Employers had to rely, ultimately, on the word of the employee about his or her background. In the socially chaotic period of the early 1930s, it was relatively simple for a person to hide an unsavory past. As a result, police noted, "many" of those arrested and indicted for occupational and economic crimes were repeat offenders, some with numerous convictions already, and for serious crimes.[43]

The organized character of embezzlement schemes was a key to their success and to their scale. When one member of a gang found employment, he or she would find employment in the same office for his or her confederates. The size of some operations was truly audacious. B. D.

Miganov, who had been a Party member since 1918, headed the office that administered all railroad car and train station buffets for the Moscow railroad line. Following the pattern described above, Miganov staffed his office with confederates in crime from his previous positions in the Moscow-area restaurant administration and agricultural industry. He gathered around him a group that systematically embezzled over 280,000 rubles in a two-year period from 1932 to 1934. They hid their dealings mainly through the use of fictitious accounts, receipts, and purchase orders. "Hid" is not exactly the appropriate word, since their activities were well known to others in the administration. A police investigation uncovered that, in addition to Miganov's group, several other individuals were also siphoning off money, as well, as much as 17,000 rubles in one case, and 11,000 in another, all with Miganov's tacit knowledge. The administration's Party cell knew about these activities, but reported nothing. They, too, were being bought off by Miganov and his gang. The chief accountant of the buffet administration was in on the deal and regularly underreported the organization's balances to higher financial and administrative authorities. A police audit revealed a loss of about 500,000 rubles overall for the two-year period in which the group operated. The police report of this ring does not reveal how it was uncovered. When it was finally broken, thirty-one people in all were taken into custody.[44]

The Miganov ring was a large one, but not unusually so. Police files contain reports about many similar kinds of operations. Embezzlement and bribery were commonplace practices. In particular, the practice of bribery, *vziatochnichestvo*, was just as devastating economically as, and even more insidious than, crimes such as embezzlement and state property theft. Just as important to note, practices of bribery and embezzlement all too often shaded over into areas of accepted and even necessary administrative practice. It was the way things got done. The department head of a Moscow produce trust, a certain Ivanov, understood this. Ivanov was a "pusher" (*tolkach*), the person who was sent on business trips (*komandirovki*) to clear administrative log jams and get delayed goods moving, or secure smooth cooperation of other officials. Ivanov was good at his job. In his routine circuits of Moscow oblast vegetable markets and farms, Ivanov had established good working relationships that resulted in timely deliveries and even in overfulfillment of produce delivery plans and schedules. As it turned out, those working relations included a widespread system of bribery and kick-backs—to local farm officials, to train station depot managers and, of course, to local Party and state officials to sign needed release papers and to expedite bureaucratic matters. Bribes ranging from several hundred to several thousands of rubles per person also included prolonged drinking bouts, paid for by produce trust funds, whenever Ivanov was in a region. At least the assistant head of the trust, Gadshiev, knew about these arrangements and accounted for the bribery money as bonuses and prizes paid to local officials. Along the way, Ivanov and Gadshiev paid themselves hefty bonuses as well.[45]

Bribery and embezzlement were as corrosive as they were widespread, and police had little defense against these kinds of crime. Flurries of recommendations called for more officers to act as operative agents in financial and other organizations. Yet resources did not permit such widespread monitoring. In the whole of the Middle Volga territory, for example, only 386 operational officers worked in the criminal investigative branch of the civil police, the *ugolovnyi rozysk,* and only 18 of these operated in the *vedrozysk,* its enterprise section.[46] What the Soviets called economic and professional crime, or white-collar crime, continued to plague the state throughout the 1930s and well beyond.

CRIMES OF SPECULATION

Speculation—that is, trading on a person's own account to make a profit—also posed a major problem for the regime. By definition, such activities were regarded as exploitative and, more to the point, they threatened the state monopoly on profit and taxes. Thousands of people yearly were convicted under the 22 August 1932 law against speculation. In February 1934, Yagoda claimed that the police investigated about 10,000 cases of speculation each month, and these cases did not include large-scale crimes handled by the Economic Crimes Department of the OGPU.[47] An NKVD report to Sovnarkom declared that, in the country's "several" major cities, the police arrested 58,314 people for speculation during the first half of 1934. Police expelled from these cities another 53,000 people for speculation whose social profiles prevented their arrest under the 22 August law.[48] Even these numbers, however, give only a moderate impression of the scale of the problem that faced Soviet authorities. Despite harsh laws, yearly assessments concluded that "not enough was being done" against crimes of speculation, that the work of the campaign against speculation was "not being waged with sufficient strength," or, worse, that it was "not being waged at all."[49]

Most crimes of speculation were connected with buying and selling in commission stores, second-hand shops, and especially in public marketplaces and second-hand bazaars. According to an October 1935 report prepared for Sovnarkom, speculators "of all sorts" inundated market places. Yagoda, the police chief, hated markets as focal points for all sorts of activities by private traders, socially dangerous elements, and peasants. They were points of exchange that were almost impossible to control, but which were also vital to the country's economy. Banned entirely for a period at the beginning of the 1930s, private trade in public markets and bazaars had not only revived by 1934 and 1935; it flourished. So, grudgingly, conceded the October 1935 Sovnarkom report. In Rostov-on-the-Don, for example, ten thousand people thronged through the central marketplace on any given Sunday afternoon, although the city had licensed only one hundred selling booths there. In October 1935, Moscow's Iaroslavskii market regularly registered two thousand sellers to fill its one hundred sales stalls. On any given Sunday, over 300,000 people swarmed through the market buying and selling goods regardless of licensing procedures. The crowds of hawkers and buyers turned and twisted "without order" through the streets bordering the legal confines of the market.[50]

Illegal trade took many and often ingenious forms. The simplest involved the resale at high prices of scarce commodities purchased at state stores, or pilfered from factories, warehouses, trains, or other facilities that made up the state's production and distribution system. One of the most common practices involved sellers who met trains from the countryside as they arrived in the cities in the morning. There, on the platforms and out of the train windows, peasants did a brisk and furtive business selling farm products and commodities to urban middlemen. They, in turn, went straight to the cities' many markets and resold the goods at higher prices. In these cases, the traders were usually individuals working for themselves. But not always. Many entrepreneurs set up networks of middlemen and conducted illegal selling on a bulk scale. These "big speculators" (*krupnye spekulianty*) went so far as to establish direct contact with collective farm officials, with urban workshops and factories, or with bandit gangs seeking to sell stolen goods. Big speculators often gave themselves a thin legal cover by purchasing a license (*patent*) to set up as a private craft worker. A private craft worker (*kustar'*) could, legally, manufacture and sell items on a small scale, supposedly through the state's cooperative system. In fact, many *kustari* did not work, but acted as suppliers and purchasing agents for networks of small craft shops or domestic manufacturers, or as urban fences for rural bandit gangs. These networks dealt in scarce commodities, often in clothing or food items, and often operated in large volumes. The speculators Il'evskii, Shedrovskii, and Fel'tshtein, for example, were licensed legally to operate an artisan shop in Moscow. Instead, they put out materials to as many as twelve artisan manufacturers to make and sell women's berets and men's felt hats.[51]

Even a single individual could work up a relatively large-scale operation. Such was the case of citizeness Gur'eva, the wife of a worker at the Kuntsevo factory, No. 14. Gur'eva was at the center of a wholesale production and selling enterprise of women's blouses. She held an artisan's license, which allowed her to purchase materials legally from stores of the Moscow Cooperative Trade Association, Mostorg. At times, however, she purchased stolen bolts of cloth from contacts she had in public market administrations. Gur'eva made most of the blouses herself, but at times she engaged the help of two acquaintances, both legally employed seamstresses. Aside from the markup in prices, what made Gur'eva's activities illegal was that she sold and paid taxes on only a small percentage of her blouses through the state system. Most she sold privately in public markets or to other retailers. When police searched her flat, they found 200 partially sown blouses and 120 meters of cloth.[52]

Some speculators operated over long distances. A group of Kiev artisans, *Kievskie kustari,* contracted with a network of artisan workers in small villages to produce women's shoes. Using the name and legal transport license of a local Kiev city cooperative, the entrepreneurs shipped the finished products in batches of one to two hundred to Leningrad where they kept them "warehoused" in borrowed apartments. At certain intervals during the year, the entrepreneurs traveled to Leningrad. By prior arrangement, they paid the administrators of several markets to rent them sellers' stalls for two to three days. They would sell out their products and then "disappear" back to Kiev.[53]

Another common form of speculation exploited privileges in the Soviet tax code. The latter allowed workers holding trade union cards to receive significant income tax reductions, as much as 75 percent, according to one report.[54] At the same time, many workers applied for and received licenses to use their trade skills to produce and sell products on a small scale to state sponsored cooperatives. These *kustari* also benefited from similar tax privileges. While some reported their yearly incomes accurately, many such artisan workers failed to distinguish between wages, on which they paid reduced taxes, and profits from their private craft work activities, on which they should have paid significantly higher taxes. These artisan-entrepreneurs paid the reduced tax on the whole of their income. Thus, a certain machinist, Yanbaev, employed at the Liuberetsk factory, received three hundred rubles in wages per month. As a result of his side business activities, however, he received a yearly income of 25,000 rubles, but he reported this as wage income and paid the reduced tax of "only" 9,755 rubles. The report did not say what tax Yanbaev should have paid, but made it clear that he was cheating the government of tax revenues from his private income. Moreover, Yanbaev sold most of his wares for "exorbitant" profits in open markets rather than at set prices through the cooperative system.

One *kustar'*, a certain Kamenyi—a metalworker by trade—gave the tax break scam an ingenious twist by obtaining a psychiatric doctor's certification of his "nervous condition." This condition supposedly prevented Kamenyi from working in a collective setting, such as a factory or artisan workshop, since the pressure of such an environment led Kamenyi, an otherwise competent worker, to "break and ruin many parts." As a result, he was allowed to work individually, manufacturing small electrical heating products and, because of his nervous condition, not being assessed at the high tax rate on the sale of his products. In fact, Kamenyi struck a deal with a commission store in the Krasno-Presnensk area of Moscow. Under license as a buying agent for the store, he obtained metal parts, electrical cords, insulation, and other materials directly from state factories. He then set up a small workshop in the back courtyard of the store. There, Kamenyi manufactured heating devices—small water and room heaters—which the store then sold as private commission items, each supposedly purchased from different customers. Kamenyi and the store turned a profit of 150,000 rubles during the course of 1934, which they split in an unspecified proportion. The entire enterprise was illegal, of course, and Kamenyi hid most of his earnings. He reported only a fraction of this income, and on this he still paid only a licensed artisan's tax.[55]

Illegal and semilegal craft manufacture abounded and made many police officials wary of *kustari*. In the eyes of at least some officials, a craft or artisan's license was a legal license to speculate. A 1934 report surmised that only 4 to 5 percent of the eight thousand artisans registered with Moscow municipal authorities in fact sold their products to the state at legal prices. The rest, the report declared, took their goods to Moscow's private markets, where "they can sell them at speculative prices."[56] Yet to distinguish between profiteering and legal trade and manufacture often proved a difficult task, especially for items that were used. Who was to determine the fair price for an old pair of boots, or a used tool or piece of machinery, or for goods in general, when state prices varied from week to week and region to region? Procuracy officials often accused police officials of overzealousness, arresting innocent workers for trying to sell a pair of pants. Police, in turn, accused procuracy officials of laxness, turning a blind eye to all sorts of dubious practices.[57] Exploitation of the state system was relatively easy, and exploitation abounded in a system designed to eliminate exploitation.

Apart from marketplaces, commission stores provided another major channel for illegal buying and selling. Established in the late 1920s under license of the state's trade, cooperative, and even children's welfare organizations, these stores supposedly operated as a service to "honest" laborers. A commission store's task was to "realize" the private goods of workers "without resorting to middlemen or speculators." A worker might, for example, sell through a commission store a pair of boots or tools or single items of clothing or other private and used items. The store sold the goods at a price certainly no higher than state retail prices, took a commission of 20 to 25 percent, and gave the rest of the profit to the original owner. By the mid-1930s, some ninety-eight such stores operated in Moscow and Leningrad, with an officially reported turnover of 150 million rubles yearly. If we believe a 1935 survey of these stores, they engaged in a different and much more lucrative kind of business.[58]

In fact, concluded the 1935 inspectorate survey, lack of regulation of these stores had resulted in such widespread corruption that most commission stores no longer functioned as they were supposed to function. Instead, they focused their activities almost exclusively on speculative buying and selling, often acting as agents for the wholesaling of goods.[59] Most of this activity was illegal—selling stolen goods, for example, or reselling manufactured goods in short supply for higher than state prices —but because of the peculiarities of Soviet trade laws, some of these entrepreneurial practices fell within the law. In both cases, the quantities and sums of money were often large. A certain Krasnov, for example, purchased large quantities of boots in markets and state stores near where they were manufactured. In these locations, the boots were in plentiful supply, and Krasnov purchased them at state retail prices. Then, traveling to Moscow, where the boots were in short supply, Krasnov, with the connivance of store officials, resold the boots at a considerable markup through Moscow's commission stores. The turnover from this operation netted Krasnov alone over 100,000 rubles' profit. It is not clear how much the stores may have made off the transaction. Two other speculators profited similarly from the sale of boots to the sum of 400,000 rubles. In each of these cases, as in other cases of retailing of scarce goods, store managers hid the large single volume of sales under numerous fictional transactions with single individuals. According to one chart, markups ranged from 100 to 200 percent.[60]

The cases cited above were relatively small-scale operations, involving single individuals, but there were those who entertained grander visions. Several stores opened special departments in order to deal with larger operations, including the purchase and resale of large quantities of fabric, office equipment, valuable furs, and even heavy machine tools such as revolving turret lathes, drill presses, and welding stations. Some of this equipment was sold directly from the stores. In most cases, however, stores acted as middlemen, connecting buyers with sellers, either or both private parties and state manufacturers. Other stores sold sheet metal and other raw materials, technical instruments, and large quantities of newly manufactured furniture, as well as other items in short supply that either had been stolen or were newly manufactured. Stores actively solicited and competed for this kind of business by sending buying agents, ostensibly to investigate and deal with "complaints" from buyers. Leningrad stores, for example, regularly sent buying agents on *komandirovki* to such cities as Moscow, Kiev, Kharkov, and other major centers. These agents usually took their own commission of 3 percent of the turnover, or more, if they were particular good at what they did, or if they secured a particularly lucrative trade.[61]

Police campaigns of mass repression and deportation provided another source of big business for commission stores. Individuals and families selected for deportation to exile colonies as class-alien elements usually received only short notice of their impending exile. This gave them only a short time—a week to ten days—to settle their affairs and either sell or give away their possessions. Commission stores often provided the only outlet for such people to liquidate their holdings. In rural areas, the sale of these possessions did not usually amount to much, although rural buying agents and local council chairmen often benefited financially from the exile of class-alien elements from their regions. In urban areas such as Moscow and Leningrad, by contrast, the list of socially alien people often included individuals and families that had been prosperous and even wealthy before the Revolution. This was especially true of contingents of exiles deported from Leningrad during the infamous 1935 campaigns against "former people" and socially alien elements.[62] The forced and sudden liquidation of possessions by thousands of people created a buyer's market and a windfall for the city's commission stores. A number of stores benefited handsomely from the purchase of family heirlooms, jewelry, stylishly fashionable and high-quality antique furniture, furs, silver and gold service ware, and other possessions of those under deportation orders. These goods did not come cheap. Store buyers paid high prices for some of the goods they bought—11,000 rubles for two small antique "cabinets," for example—but purchase agents from commission stores found a ready market for these goods—for prerevolutionary furniture, in particular—in the country's new high-flying class of Soviet top managers. Stores did a "light restoration" and resold the antiques, sometimes in whole suites, to the Soviet elite.[63]

Antique furniture—especially of the Renaissance Revival, Empire, and Belle Epoque eras—was the rage in the 1930s for those who could afford it. According to the inspectorate report cited above, sales of antique furniture fetched "fabulously" (basnoslovno) high prices for the commission stores. The sums of money involved were, indeed, dazzling, although the percent of profit for the stores was not excessive compared to sales of other more mundane goods. The two cabinets mentioned above, for example, sold to the manager of the Karelian animal husbandry trust for 19,500 rubles. The manager used them to decorate his office. This sale represented a 44 percent profit for the store, a lucrative deal, to be sure, but not the 100 to 200 percent the stores made on other sales. Truly remarkable, however, was the amount of money available even to small-scale Soviet bureaucrats for this kind of indulgence. One administrator dropped 300,000 rubles during a two-month Leningrad buying spree. The administrator, a certain Nikonov, was chair of a local rural soviet, not a particular high position, yet he had both the time and the huge amount of money to buy "several" antique wardrobe cabinets, three armchairs, and four antique beds.[64]

This was wheeling and dealing on a high level, but it is not clear exactly what was illegal about these transactions on the part of the commission stores. The buyers no doubt misused funds in order to make their purchases, but what about the stores? The latter did not steal or resell deficit state goods at higher than official retail prices. There were no state price norms for such items. Neither could stores be accused of disrupting the state's economic and distribution plans. The morality of these transactions was certainly repugnant, but it cannot be said, at least on the basis of the examples given above, that stores left the original owners destitute. They could have done so, since sellers—usually people under deportation orders—were in a desperate situation. Store agents could easily have driven the price into the ground and left the sellers no choice. The inspectorate report that uncovered these practices noted that store agents paid high market value for the items they purchased. The report made no mention of improper accounting methods. In principle, the stores performed the function for which they were established, unless the turning of a profit, or the amounts of money or profit involved, made these transactions illegal. Still, the inspectorate report condemned these sales as speculative.

Reselling purchased property was a valuable business, but commission stores also turned a handsome profit from the sale of confiscated property, often undervaluing goods purchased from police, courts, and other state agencies, then reselling the same goods at high retail value. This was truly profiteering. On the other hand, this practice was, in essence, often a matter of one set of thieves besting another set of thieves. As numerous reports complained, money confiscated by court, government, or police officials, as well as the proceeds of confiscated goods, often went into the pockets of those doing the confiscating rather than into state coffers. If police or court officials turned to commission stores to sell confiscated goods, very likely this was an effort to realize profit from goods otherwise difficult to liquidate as cash.

The fight against speculation fell to several agencies. These included the civil police, the OGPU/NKVD, and Narkomfin, the Commissariat of Finance. The police criminal investigative branch, *ugolovnyi rozysk,* or the OGPU were supposed to handle large-scale crimes of speculation and the regular police the majority of small-scale violations. Narkomfin became involved because speculation resulted in violations of tax laws. All three agencies blamed the others for the state's ineffective war against profiteering. Sovnarkom's report claimed that organs of the NKVD (including both the regular police and undercover investigators) consistently failed to conduct any serious campaign against speculation. The Moscow police, the report said, issued fines to speculators—over five thousand in 1934 in the Yaroslav market alone—but did so only as a result of spot checks of sellers. Supposedly, the worst offenders escaped the attention of the police. In Kharkov, behavior of the police "effectively legalized speculation" by fining speculators five rubles apiece, no more than the registration price for sellers, and then allowing them to continue selling their wares at whatever price they could get.

Police received bribes to allow sellers to operate, but also received large sums of money from market administrators not to disrupt sales activities. These arrangements were even written into contracts. In 1935, in exchange for "keeping order" at Moscow's Yaroslav market, the market officials agreed to pay the Moscow police administration a sum of 156,978 rubles. In Kharkov, police officials demanded 30 percent of all rents paid for licenses at the city's markets. Market administrators in Leningrad agreed with police commandants to pay individual policemen a sum of 240 rubles per shift for their presence in the market. According to these agreements, police authorities had the right to suspend police activities at the marketplaces if market administrators failed to pay the amounts specified in their contracts. As a Sovnarkom report noted, such financial arrangements made it in police interests not to cause trouble at the markets by cracking down on speculators. This was especially true in those cases where *militsiia* received a share of the market's profitability. Sovnarkom's report emphasized that these types of kickbacks were most likely illegal and certainly unconscionable on the part of the RKM. "Without a separate contract," the report concluded, "the police, who are paid out of the state's budget, do not feel obligated to carry out their duty in fighting crime and keeping order in the markets."[65]

Narkomfin officials also made charges against the police, chastising them, especially, for failing to collect the huge sums of contraband money and taxes owed by speculators.[66] Sovnarkom criticized police laxity as well, but it reserved its harshest criticisms for local finance officials. The latter were so obsessed with fulfilling their financial goals that they failed in some localities to report sellers and artisans from whom they received large sums of "tax" money. While such practices brought revenue to local governments, they amounted to officially sanctioned forms of bribery. In Kharkov, local tax officials attempted to obstruct the police in arresting speculators at the city's markets, arguing that if they swept all the speculators from the streets, tax authorities would have no way to collect money from them. Similarly, municipal authorities turned a blind eye to speculation since cities received a substantial income from the profitability of their public markets. Revenue from Moscow's markets increased the city's budget by 3 million rubles in 1934. Stalingrad earned 556,000 rubles from sales in its public markets.[67]

The inability of police and municipal authorities to regulate trade in public markets transformed the markets from places of second-hand exchange into focal points of crime. Further, the ability of "speculators" to use public markets as a major outlet for their activities exacerbated related types of crime such as theft of state property, banditry, and professional-economic crimes. Despite harsh punishments associated with all of these kinds of crimes, they continued unabated, causing "serious harm" to the development of legal trade in the country.[68]

BANDITRY

No type of crime alarmed Soviet authorities more than banditry. Although authorities had made a concerted effort in the late 1920s to rid the country of the last of its bandit gangs, the upheavals of the early 1930s, especially in the countryside, brought about a resurgence of such activities. Some bandit gangs ranged across relatively large areas, but most operated in specific territories. Some bands comprised as many as fifty to sixty individuals, but most numbered no more than ten to twelve members. It is difficult to determine how widespread bandit activity was, but it existed in nearly every oblast. Most bandit activities occurred in parts of Ukraine, the Western oblast, much of the Urals and Western Siberian regions, and in the Northern Caucasus and Central Asian regions. In 1932, thirty-five bandit gangs operated in the Urals oblast alone.[69] Mounted, armed, and mobile, the most dangerous bandit gangs lived in sparsely populated and relatively inaccessible areas, such as forests or rugged hills. Bandit gangs were usually well armed, at times with weapons that allowed them to outgun local police authorities. The Fedoseev gang, for example, which numbered about fifty members, carried, in addition to individual revolvers and hunting rifles, three American Winchester repeating rifles, two bombs, and twenty grenades. Some local policemen refused to participate in the campaign to capture this band, since its members were so well armed.[70] Bandit gangs usually refrained from attacking individuals, except for sporadic robberies of travelers whom they happened to encounter on the road. At times, bands raided noncollectivized farms, but most targeted collective farm villages and Soviet institutions and facilities: trains, warehouses, especially grain warehouses during the planting and harvesting seasons, postal depots, police armories, MTS's, and other such facilities.

Gang members in the 1930s generally came from one of several backgrounds. Many, of course, were petty criminals by choice or "profession," but many, especially gang leaders, were dekulakized peasants who had escaped deportation and had stayed in their home regions. Or they were dekulakized peasants who had been dispossessed but not exiled, or peasants who had escaped from or had left labor colonies to which they had been deported as kulaks and "socially dangerous elements." Because of the social backgrounds of bandits, instructions to local police authorities warned that bandit gangs were to be regarded not just as criminal elements, but as counterrevolutionary insurgents against Soviet power. This was certainly the OGPU assessment of banditry, but it was also the assessment offered by the justice commissariat, usually more sober in its judgments than the OGPU. A procuracy report on crime for 1931 went so far as to claim that rural bandit raids aimed specifically to destroy *kolkhoz* property and that bandit gangs singled out rural Party, state, and police officials against whom they committed "acts of terror."[71] There was some truth to this assessment, if only because state institutions—collective farms, mail cars, storage facilities, etc.—provided the most lucrative targets for bandit activities. The procuracy report insisted that, because of the especially dangerous counterrevolutionary character of banditry, organizers and gang leaders should be subjected to the most extreme measures of social defense— shooting. Because of the political status accorded bandit gangs, campaigns against them often involved OGPU officers and troops, in addition to local police authorities. The other reason for OGPU involvement was that local authorities usually did not have the resources to pursue and eliminate bandit gangs in their territories.

Bandit gangs also drew heavily from non-Russian ethnic populations. According to one police report from the Urals in 1932, non-Russian gangs were especially difficult to trace and eliminate. Their members often had family ties and resided in the areas where they operated. As a result, local non-Russian populations not only protected the identities of bandit gangs from officials, they provided bandits with information about police movements. Information was also difficult to obtain because of ethnic and language barriers. Police authorities found it difficult to establish informant networks in non-Russian areas and required translators to interrogate local inhabitants about bandit activities.[72]

In areas where Bolshevik power was not firmly established, especially in non-Russian border areas, traditional bandit activities could become the center of popular uprisings. In the Southern Caucasus region, the mix of religion, anti-Russian sentiment, and local culture proved volatile. During the beginnings of collectivization in early 1930, several areas erupted in open revolt against the thinly spread police and military authority. According to an official report, the core of rebel forces formed around the organization and activities of the numerous bandit gangs that had traditionally operated in the area. In the Nagorno area, near the Turkish border, rebel forces numbered about one thousand armed and mounted men, operating in groups of fifty to sixty.[73] Centered in the Nagorno region, the rebellion spread until anti-Soviet forces held one-half of the Nakhichevansk republic, a region bordering Turkey to its west and Persia to its southeast, with a population of about 100,000 mostly rural and poor inhabitants. The capital city, Nakhichevan' (present day Nakhchivan) remained under Bolshevik control, but Soviet forces proved powerless to stop frequent raids on it and surrounding villages. Similar uprisings occurred simultaneously in neighboring Armenia, and Soviet officials greatly feared that the traditionally hostile ethnic groups would unite forces.

In this uprising, as in others, traditional banditry mixed with anti-Soviet, anticolonial, and Islamic religious sentiments. Rebels held the area for several months, even moving freely across the Turkish and Persian borders. They erected banners and carried placards with slogans that read "For the single gospel, the Koran! Down with Soviet power! For honor! For religion! For Freedom!" The arrival of regular Red Army troops, reinforced by OGPU forces and border police units, finally brought order to the area. Soviet forces lost about eighty troops, but few bandits were apprehended in the operation to subdue the region. Most escaped into the mountainous regions of the border areas. Because of the pressing need for troops elsewhere, Soviet authorities halted the campaign to pursue the bandits and withdrew forces to hold the valley areas against further outbreaks. After the rising, rebels drifted back to their previous lives, and regional police reports show that levels of traditional banditry continued in the area just as strongly as before the uprising.

Uprisings on the scale of the one that occurred in Nakhichevansk were unusual. Yet Soviet authorities feared their recurrence, which is why they saw banditry as a politically dangerous phenomenon and not just as a manifestation of rural crime. In Nakhichevansk, according to the official report, it was the "kulak-bandit elements" that were the key to the rising. Their activities and "agitation" decisively influenced large segments of the region's "middle" and even "poor" peasants to join the anti-Soviet movement.[74] So too, in the case of Nakhichevansk, the rising evoked earlier risings of the radical Islamic bands, the *basmachi,* which so threatened Soviet power in the early years of the revolution. While many groups engaged in banditry simply for reasons of petty theft, it is clear that many organized specifically for the reasons official reports stated: to fight against Bolshevik power. Dispossessed of their land and property, exiled and imprisoned, many of those "kulaks" who resorted to banditry felt they had no choice but to be outlaws, or at least little left to lose thereby. Thus, the activities of at least some bandit groups in the USSR during the 1930s fit Eric Hobsbawm's classic model of "primitive rebels."[75] These Soviet peasant rebels clearly fought a losing battle against the brutal encroachment of urban and, in some cases, colonial forces attempting to modernize the countryside through economic and military subjugation. In a larger context, the bandits of the 1930s can be seen as the last sporadic instances of armed resistance in the Eurasian peasant war that began in 1919, a war that was interrupted during the 1920s and which was renewed in the early 1930s. The geographic pattern of bandit resistance coincided with the pockets of greatest peasant resistance to Bolshevik power in 1919–21, to which the Bolsheviks returned with a vengeance during dekulakization in 1929–32.[76]

Despite repeated campaigns to wipe out banditry, bandit gangs continued sporadic activities. A 1934 procuracy report noted the menacing prevalence of gangs in rural areas, and cited a disturbing increase in banditry in the Western oblast and the Central Black Earth region. A year later the NKVD launched another major but unsuccessful drive to eradicate banditry.[77] In March 1935, the plenum of the Soviet Supreme Court noted the continued growth of bandit gangs and activity in Western Siberia, Central Asia, and Ukraine. The court referred to banditry, still, as one of the "most acute" forms of class war, "directed against socialist property and administrative order."[78] As in previous years, most gangs drew members from the ranks of escaped or deported kulaks and from local non-Russian populations. The court commission noted with alarm, however, a disturbing increase in the percent of bandits who were or who had been "working youth." And this despite successes in creating what the report called "a growing political consciousness" among kolkhozniki and the working young.[79] Throughout the mid-1930s, regional police reports describe operations intended to rid their areas of bandit gangs. Each anticipated that their region would soon be cleared of bandits. Yet, numbers of bandit gangs remained at about the same levels throughout the early and mid-1930s. As some were eliminated others arose in their place.[80]

HOOLIGANISM AND THE CRIMINALIZATION OF HOMELESS AND UNSUPERVISED CHILDREN

One of most disturbing signs of social disorder was the problem of homeless children (besprizorniki) and unsupervised children (beznadzorniki). The sheer numbers of this population created problems of social stability, as did the threat to order that resulted from the connections between homelessness and crime. The homeless and unsupervised population of children acted as a major source for recruitment into the Soviet Union's criminal class. Because of the social upheavals of the early 1930s, the population of such children in the RSFSR alone jumped dramatically from a low of 129,000 in 1929 to a peak of 400,000 in the late months of 1933, and these were only the children who were counted as they passed through children's homes or temporary gathering centers (*priemnye punkty,* or *priemniki*). These centers experienced a "massive" influx of children during 1933. The infamous Danilov Monastery in Moscow was one of the largest of these points.[81] These figures excluded Kazakhstan, for example, which had a population of around 43,000 homeless children in 1933 and 68,000 in 1934.[82] They also failed to include Ukraine, where, according to a Sovnarkom report, children's homes counted about 228,000 children in 1933.[83] In the whole of the USSR there existed well over half a million homeless children during the middle years of the 1930s.

Many of these children were orphaned, abandoned, or separated from home during the collectivization campaigns and famine of 1932 and 1933. In 1932, for example, a survey of children in state custody at the Danilov Monastery showed that only 15 percent of homeless children were homeless due to the death of both parents. More common reasons included poverty (18 percent), children fleeing home because of the "influence of the street and friends" (18 percent), and abandonment or "an unpleasant home situation" (29 percent). The next year, however, the death of parents accounted for nearly one-half (42 percent) of all children who were homeless. Moreover, almost half the children interviewed listed their parents' occupation as individual farmers (*edinolichniki*). The proportion of other reasons for homelessness remained about the same or declined. The draw of life on the street, especially, declined to account for only about 10 percent of homeless children in 1933.[84] As with the figures above, these figures described conditions only in the RSFSR. They did not include Ukraine, for example, where famine and collectivization took the heaviest toll on the population. In the Northern Caucasus region, also the scene of much of the collectivization struggle and famine, the number of homeless children soared to over 120,000 in just the last half of 1933.

The police, the courts, and the social welfare organs that ran children's homes were overwhelmed by the epidemic of homeless children. Police made monthly sweeps of urban areas to round up homeless children and place them in state institutions for adoption. In Moscow, police sweeps netted about 28,000 children in all of 1933, yet conditions in homes were so abysmal that "well over 50 percent" of children ran away. As of May 1934, officials estimated that about 45,000 boys and 15,000 girls between the ages of twelve and seventeen still lived on the streets throughout urban areas of Russia. This included about 2,000 to 3,000 in Moscow alone at any given time.[85] Children were highly mobile—a 1933 sweep of ten railroad lines in Western Russia brought in 4,000 unsupervised children riding illegally on trains. Moscow was, by far, the preferred destination for homeless and unsupervised children. In 1933 and 1934, well over half of all children who passed through the Danilov Monastery sorting point had come from outside the Moscow oblast. In 1933, 27 percent arrived from Ukraine.[86]

Having no home and no work, socially alienated because of their background and the violence that had made them homeless, many children turned to crime. Despite the "huge" effort and "enormous" expenditures committed by the government, Sovnarkom reported in May 1934 that homelessness among children continued to be a severe problem, and had led inevitably to a soaring child crime rate. Sovnarkom's report described the problem of unsupervised children and youth crime as "exceptionally dangerous." In 1933, the state spent over 261 million rubles, 35 million in Moscow alone, on the campaign to clear the streets of unsupervised and delinquent children.[87] In 1932, police in the capital detained or arrested 15,648 underage criminals between the ages of twelve and seventeen. Most of the criminal youths were apprehended for theft (87 percent in 1931, 27 percent in 1932, and 41 percent in 1933), and most came from what officials described as socially dangerous classes, that is families of noncollective farmers, or families of urban nonworker or nonprofessional backgrounds.[88] According to Sovnarkom's report, criminal youth gangs "terrorized" patrons and sellers at public markets and bazaars. Recidivist youth criminals cycled and recycled through children's homes. They influenced other children into a life of crime, which escalated from simple grab-and-run theft to assaults with knives (hooliganism), organized urban banditry, and murder.[89] The legal strictures against prosecuting youths as adults or putting them in adult prisons complicated police efforts to isolate child offenders and combat youth crime. Until 1935, when special labor colonies and work camps were established for delinquent children, police were forced simply to deposit underage criminals at children's registration and distribution centers. In Moscow in 1933, one-third of all those brought to children's distribution centers had been apprehended by police for criminal activities. Sovnarkom's report noted that these centers, and children's homes generally, were rapidly becoming no more than way stations for underage criminals.[90]

In the spring of 1935, the Soviet regime passed a series of draconian laws against hooliganism, which also dealt with the related problem of homeless and unsupervised children. These laws gave police wide powers to pick up street children, and to convict underage criminals under both judicial and administrative powers.[91] Despite such measures, underage crime and hooliganism continued to be a serious problem, or at least leaders perceived this to be the case. Moreover, surveys of underage convicts showed a disturbing trend. A survey in June 1936 revealed that, when apprehended for their crimes, 45 percent were homeless or had lived in children's homes. In contrast, 55 percent had lived with their parents, both of whom worked. By the mid-1930s, then, in contrast to even several years earlier, the crimes of most underage convicts did not result from social rootlessness, but from lack of parental supervision. Moreover, of those underage criminals who were homeless at the time of their arrest, the great majority (71 percent) had been on the streets, eluding police, for one to two years or more.[92] Even more disturbing, the "mass" of those who had been arrested was between the ages of twelve and fifteen, the youngest of two age categories, and had been caught in crimes in urban and industrial areas. Those between sixteen and seventeen numbered far fewer and their crimes tended to be in rural areas.[93]

Many interpretations could be placed on such statistics, but the interpretation that the authors of the survey imposed reflected the narrative that the problem of underage crime was still a serious one; it had not been solved at all, even by the draconian laws of 1935. Even more ominous, the laws that criminalized homeless and unsupervised children also linked youth crimes increasingly to anti-Soviet intent. Both procuracy and Supreme Court reviews in 1935 and again in 1936 warned local authorities to take this connection seriously. Hooliganism especially, noted a 1935 report by V. A. Antonov-Ovseenko, the Russian federation chief procurator, no longer involved just insults and "rambunctious" behavior (beschinstva); acts of hooliganism increasingly involved organized social violence by youth and assaults with weapons resulting in murder. In some localities, cautioned the report, youthful hooliganism crossed the boundary into forms of banditry and other counterrevolutionary crimes. Worst of all, even women were participating in hooligan gangs in increasing numbers. Antonov-Ovseenko offered no explanation for his observation, but he saw it as a worrisome trend, and as a direct threat to social and socialist order.[94] Regardless of the explanation, Antonov-Ovseenko's refrain was typical of most observers. On the one hand, the police often acted too harshly against minor violators. On the other hand, commentators criticized the special police courts for underage criminals for being, on the whole, too lenient with serious offenders.[95] In general, critics blamed all agencies—the police, the courts, the Commissariat of Education—for allowing high rates of recidivism among child-criminals, and for allowing continued "energetic adult influence" on children of class-alien and criminal elements.[96]

THE SOCIALLY HARMFUL ELEMENT

One of the most serious crimes in the view of Soviet leaders and police officials was that of being socially harmful. Social harmfulness was different from other types of criminality, since the designation "socially harmful element" (sotsial'no-vrednyi element) or "socially dangerous element" (sotsial'no-opasnyi element) constituted a social identity as well as a criminal category. Until 1935, there was no specific criminal statute that covered this category, but throughout much of the 1930s, leaders enacted decrees and engaged in numerous policing campaigns against social harmfuls, as being among the most threatening to the regime and the construction of socialist order. At the same time, this category is one of the most difficult to define, both as a social stratum and as a type of criminality.

The category of "socially harmful element" had existed since at least the 1920s, but during the 1920s, police and other officials attached this label to a specific population of people. People who fell into this category included those with at least two previous court convictions or four police detentions (privody).[97] During the 1930s, police began to apply this category more broadly to a range of socially marginal or deviant groups of people. These socially harmful or "alien" elements (chuzhdie elementy) included itinerants, the unemployed, actual or suspected petty criminals, and those found in violation of residence registration laws. A joint police and procuracy order from 1935 included in this category not only those in the "criminal world," but anyone who maintained ties with known criminals, or who was not gainfully employed. The category also listed "professional" beggars, violators of passport and residence laws, and unsupervised or orphan children picked up for crimes. In fact, those included in this category need not have committed a crime.[98] The category of socially harmful became a catch-all category for many kinds of persons. Included in this category were religious sectarians, those who had been dispossessed of property, and "former people." If caught in the wrong place at the wrong time—in a police raid to check identity papers, for example—such people became subject to summary arrest and sentencing by extrajudicial police sentencing boards for up to five years in corrective labor camps or deportation colonies.[99]

Redefining marginal, deviant, or otherwise undesirable populations as socially harmful carried a number of advantages. Police and state officials regarded socially harmful elements as a serious danger to Soviet order and to the state, more so than "mere" statutory lawbreakers, such as prostitutes or petty thieves. Thus, the redefinition of criminals and social deviants into a single category of socially harmful became a way for police officials to heighten the importance of their role in defense of the state. More practically, recategorization made policing easier, since it obscured social complexities and reduced all undesirables to a single neat category, instead of making up a hodgepodge of individual cases. Social marginals or deviants could be marked and repressed more easily under one nonjudicial law covering "dangerous elements" than under numerous criminal statutes. The latter process required the tedious completion of evidence and indictment forms and other laborious prosecutorial procedures. Arresting people under criminal code statutes also led to different kinds of sanctions, depending on the kind of crime. Conviction was not certain, and maximum sentences for most petty crimes were less than the five years that police boards could mete out to those identified as social harmfuls. Moreover, many statutory cases submitted by police were often returned by the procurator's office for violation of procedures or for insufficient evidence. Most advantageous of all, of course, was that police could arrest and extrajudicially exile or imprison an individual as socially harmful who had not committed a statutory crime, but who was in some way deemed a social danger.

Yagoda tried to take full advantage of this possibility. He had little patience for legal procedures, and he encouraged his subordinates to arrest lawbreakers and deviants as social harmfuls rather than indict them under various statutes of the criminal code.[100]

Criminalizing social marginals proved an ingenious device for police officials. A police report on people picked up in Leningrad in a 1934 roundup is revealing in this regard. The report included a list of names and short descriptions of sixteen people who had violated newly enacted internal passport and registration laws. Police routinely categorized these types of social ordinance violators as belonging to the socially harmful element. Five of the sixteen social harmfuls listed were women with no permanent residence or steady employment. All but one were in their twenties or early thirties, and all had been picked up by police on the streets several times previously. All were listed as having no defined home or employment. We cannot assume that any of these women engaged in prostitution, based only on the brief police descriptions, but police may very likely have made this connection. In any case, it did not matter whether these women were beggars and homeless, which was not a statutory crime in 1934, or whether they engaged also in prostitution, which was a crime. Laws about social harmfuls allowed police to categorize and arrest these women simply and neatly as violators of passport laws, and hence as socially harmful.[101]

As social harmfuls, the women identified in the Leningrad police report were quickly processed by police administrative boards. The violators were deported or exiled, according to the number of times they had been picked up. Unnecessary was the task of proving that they had committed a statutory crime. Irrelevant was the question whether they posed any real danger to the state. Also irrelevant and unnecessary were questions about why these women were homeless and without work, and whether, in fact, they worked as prostitutes or whether they were begging. For police, a simplified system of social categorization, combined with administrative adjudication, proved an especially effective way to deal with the human detritus of Stalin's socialism.

Soviet officials almost always used the phrase *sotsial'no-vrednyi element* in the singular, whether referring to an individual or to a group. The use of the singular amalgamated a complex mass of people into the same undifferentiated category of social danger. The category of socially harmful element—*sotsvredelement,* in the parlance of the day—

lumped together prostitutes and petty criminals, religious sectarians and itinerant beggars, hooligans as well as the déclassé, the dispossessed and the disenfranchised, and the unemployed and violators of residence and passport laws. These were the disobedient, or anarchic (*stikhiinye*) and "unorganized" (*neorganizovannye*) segments of the population— criminals and ex-criminals and social marginals. These unorganized segments of the population did not fit into one of the neatly defined social ranks—workers (*rabochie*), collective farmers (*kolkhozniki*), or white-collar employees (*sluzhashchie*)—created by the regime. Like dirt or trash, unorganized populations were "matter out of place." They were unproductive, in the perception of officials, "filth on the face of the cities"; they siphoned off state resources, and overwhelmed the fragile infrastructure of both urban and rural networks. Unorganized segments of the population were carriers of pollution and social contamination, both political and physical. They not only carried the "virus" of anti-Soviet attitudes; they were the primary cause, or so officials claimed, of the spread of epidemic diseases, especially typhus and tuberculosis, the great killers of the 1930s. Authorities contrasted "mobile and unorganized" groups within the population— "nomads, wanderers (*otkochevniki*), orphans"—to "local core populations (*mestnoe korennoe naselenie*)."[102] The latter were good, the former, bad.

The category of social harmful overlapped but was separate from the category of kulak. By 1933, as Stalin declared, the regime had supposedly defeated kulaks as an enemy class. They were contained in camps and, mainly, in the special settlements (*spetsposelki*) to which over one million dispossessed peasants had been deported. Officials, therefore, did not regard kulaks as part of the *sotsvredelement,* unless they had escaped and been caught for passport violations or petty criminality. Individuals who had served their time in exile and had fallen afoul of the law or residence laws would often be identified as former kulaks and *sotsvredelement.* Kulaks working and living in special settlements, however, were a different matter. Although regarded as anti-Soviet, kulaks after 1933 were supposedly harnessed to productive labor for the state. Confined within their settlements or labor colonies, kulaks were no longer a social or political danger. Not so social harmfuls, whom police regarded as a greater threat precisely because they were not contained, so that they represented a ubiquitous menace. There were, of course, many hundreds of thousands of peasants who had been dispossessed but not deported, or who had escaped deportation. These people, without permanent residence or work, were pushed to the social and economic margins of Soviet society, and they too often fell into the expanding ranks of social harmfuls.

The *sotsvredelement* became the main enemy in Stalin's new class war. During much of the 1930s, both civil and political police focused their attention on this vaguely defined category of the population. The political police—the OGPU/GUGB—were particularly involved in the campaigns against harmful elements, and had been for some time. The OGPU had won the right to arrest and exile social harmfuls as early as the 1920s, and the organs of state security never lost that right.[103] And as police broadened the definition of socially harmful elements, civil and political policing merged in the 1930s as both types of police engaged in large-scale campaigns to identify and monitor these populations. The political police also retained the right to remove and isolate these populations in camps, special settlements, or particular areas of the country. These campaigns against social harmfuls—the new class enemy—extended the campaigns of the 1920s to disenfranchise class enemies of the state and the Revolution, but did so in a different and more deadly way. In the 1920s, disenfranchisement was conducted by local civil authorities in campaigns that ascribed loyal or alien status to individuals in their communities. This often served as a way for communities to rid themselves of troublemakers, the weak or poor, or other unwanted populations. Local committees often solicited citizen participation in these campaigns through letters, denunciations, newspaper articles, meetings, and interviews. Police may have enforced bans on ostracized citizens, but disenfranchisement comprised a process of social cleansing controlled by local Soviet authorities.[104]

By 1930 and 1931, police became increasingly involved in dealing with the growing numbers of disenfranchised, dispossessed, and itinerant people. In December 1931, D. V. Usov, the assistant head of the OGPU inspectorate overseeing the police, tried to lay out an appropriate police response to what was clearly a growing threat to public order. On one hand, Usov took a hard line. He stated bluntly that the indigent and homeless were social parasites. He noted that, as class war intensified, class harmful "elements" would try to use certain "elements" of the poor and homeless against Soviet authority. He declared that it was the task of the police to fight resolutely against such social parasitism. On the other hand, Usov still acknowledged that the problems of indigence and homelessness were rooted in past cultural practices, the inability of "unstable and backward elements" to adjust to new Soviet conditions. Given this backwardness, the police's role in dealing with this segment of the population should be secondary and supportive, rendering assistance to the social agencies whose primary task it was to deal with these problems. Police were to take direct repressive action against indigents and homeless only if efforts by trade unions, social aid groups, and health agencies failed to have an effect. Usov cautioned local police, however, to be careful how they applied force. He reminded subordinates that, among "certain" segments of the population, the belief still held sway that homelessness and indigence were a form of pious asceticism. Such beliefs made dealing with wanderers and homeless people in many provincial areas a special problem. In these areas, he wrote, "cultural backwardness of the mass is encouraged by the fanatical moods of priests, who use the poor as a channel for anti-Soviet agitation and all manner of harmful rumors." In the end, Usov directed that police arrest only those "poor" who refused to work, but he recommended that these be isolated and exiled in order to "protect revolutionary order and public safety."[105]

As Usov's carefully worded directive shows, OGPU instructions in 1931 and 1932 still advised local officers that socially marginal populations came primarily under the jurisdiction of social agencies, and that police should intervene only when such groups posed a criminal or political threat. In early 1933, orders continued to distinguish, if only implicitly and for operational reasons, between socially marginal populations to be expelled from cities, and the overtly political categories of counterrevolutionaries, kulaks, and other dangerous anti-Soviet elements. Already, however, officials were beginning to blur the distinction among these categories. By 1934 and 1935, Yagoda, as well as others, conflated the categories entirely. He referred to socially marginal populations as socially dangerous (sotsial'no-opasnye), anti-Soviet, and even more dangerous than those supposed class enemies deported during dekulakization. What had happened to precipitate such a dramatic change in tone and definition was Stalin's speech to the Central Committee plenum in January 1933, in which he identified crime as a new form of class war, and criminals as the new class enemy. This speech politicized the campaigns against socially marginal groups, turning "unorganized" populations into "socially dangerous elements," and then into anti-Soviet counterrevolutionaries. Stalin's speech crystallized the growing concern among leaders about the threat of public disorder to the regime's policies and its very stability. Stalin's pronouncements allowed Yagoda to declare, without irony, that beggars and poor people were counterrevolutionaries and a danger to the regime. Stalin's speech made public order equivalent to state security—which it was, given the circumstances—and turned the campaign for public order into a new phase of class war.

CONCLUSIONS

In the 1930s, the regime ended the disenfranchisement campaigns. Officials' attitudes hardened toward deviant and marginal populations, now deemed not only alien, but dangerous. As the following chapters show, policies to deal with these groups came increasingly under the purview of the police, both political and civil. As a result, policies of social repression and definitions of citizenship that involved local communities and were centered in civil government became militarized within a system of centrally controlled policing. In the 1930s, it fell increasingly to the police rather than to civil authorities to define who was "near" (*blizko*) and who was "alien" (*chuzhdoi*), who was a loyal citizen and who a socially dangerous element. The curtailment of civil jurisdiction in favor of central police authority was characteristic of the Stalinist "revolution from above."

Apart from changing notions about class war, there were a variety of reasons why police and political leaders focused so intently on socially marginal populations during the 1930s. One of the reasons for this emphasis, as later chapters detail, lay in ideas about prophylactic policing. Other reasons lay in the social and economic dislocation of the early 1930s, and the underdeveloped nature of the country's policing forces. Stalinist leaders had cause to be concerned about a crisis of social order and a breakdown in civic governance. The following chapter describes the problems of police and policing during the late 1920s and early 1930s.

2 Police and Social Disorder

At present strength, the RKM cannot carry out its duties in any oblast or district.
—Genrikh Yagoda, 1932

THE PROBLEM OF CRIME and social disorder during the early 1930s was twofold. Stalin's industrial revolution and class war in the countryside created social dislocation on a near-biblical scale. Widespread dispossession of property, wholesale deportations, and forced population migration characterized the early years of the 1930s. Dispossessed and often starving, hundreds of thousands of peasants and other rural inhabitants, as well as those formerly belonging to the professional classes, took to the rail lines and roads and streamed into and through the cities and industrial sites. This massive unorganized movement of people drained economic resources and threatened to overwhelm the underdeveloped infrastructure of the cities and the social stability of the country. Large numbers of indigents and itinerants, criminals, unemployed youth, gypsies, the disenfranchised, and a range of other groups added to these mass migrations. Social displacement on such a scale heightened criminality and social disorder, and formed the background of Stalin's remarks in 1933 about the rising threat of criminality. Stalin, of course, cast the problem of social breakdown in the language of class war, and no official acknowledged publicly that widespread social dislocation was more the result of the regime's policies than of conscious class opposition. Regardless of the causes, leaders believed that rising crime rates and other social problems posed an imminent danger to the state and the goals of socialist construction.

This was one side of the problem of social order. On the other side, the Soviet state possessed inadequate resources to deal with widespread social disorganization. Social agencies were weak and quickly over-whelmed, and the state's policing agencies also experienced difficulty coping with the problems that suddenly confronted them. Stalin's so-cialist offensive extended the power of the state into new areas of the economy and society, and the Party's leaders had marshaled extraordi-nary resources, both financial and human, to achieve this victory—to subdue the peasantry, to defeat opposition to collectivization, and to press large-scale industrialization. The battle for Soviet power had been won in the countryside and in the cities. Maintaining Soviet order was another matter. The Party's central institutions of power were secure, but asserting civil and political authority in rural and even in many urban areas was difficult in the early 1930s. Apart from local Party au-thorities, the task of imposing some kind of civil order in the wake of Stalin's socialist offensive fell largely to a police force that was woefully inadequate to the task put upon it. This chapter explores the problems of policing and police during the first years of the decade, and the con-sequent problems of maintaining social order in the midst of chaotic social upheaval.

THE *MILITSIIA*

The civil police supposedly constituted the first line of defense of the state and society against its enemies. The problem with the police, how-ever, was that were very few of them. A report of the then Russian fed-eration NKVD from April 1930 addressed this problem bluntly. The report stated that police numbers were "entirely inadequate" even for the normal tasks of maintaining public order, let alone for the addi-tional tasks forced upon police by the state's socialist offensive. The So-viet regime could count on only 90,000 regular police officers in the whole of the RSFSR in 1930. This included 33,563 regular uniformed state police, nearly 53,000 police hired specifically to protect enterprises (*vedmilitsiia*), and 4,441 special investigative detectives (*ugolovnyi rozysk*). The number of regular state police, reduced by 1,000 from the previous year, constituted a force some four times smaller than that which had maintained order in 1913, the last peacetime year of the old regime.[1] Moreover, most of these police forces were concentrated in major cities and industrial centers. This left only 12,887 policemen to protect state interests and to keep public order in rural areas of the RSFSR. This was a pitifully small number. Officials established an average norm of one policeman for every 3,000 inhabitants. In major urban centers, the ratio was supposed to hover around 1:750–800 inhabitants, but overall in the Russian republic, the average ratio was 1:5,371. Outside of major cities, the proportion of police to population varied considerably, but was mostly on the thin side. In 1932, Yagoda could report that police presence in Ukraine, Belorussia, and the North Caucasus had reached satisfactory levels. In other areas, however, the situation was "catastrophic." In the middle and lower Volga areas of the country, for example, the ratio of police to citizenry dropped to one policeman for every 9–10,000 inhabitants. In the Urals, an especially lawless area because of the number of camps and deportation colonies, there was only one police inspector for every 15,400 people.[2] Each police inspector had to try to cover an average of 3,535 square kilometers of territory in his jurisdiction.[3] Western Siberia suffered a similar deficit, with a ratio of one inspector for every 14,000 rural inhabitants, and a jurisdiction that covered 5,513 square kilometers per inspector.[4] Fewer than 900 state police served in the whole of the Far Eastern territory, an area about one-fourth the size of the United States that stretched from the Arctic Ocean to the Chinese border. Fewer than 1,400 *vedmilitsiia* provided feeble protection for factories, mines, and other industrial sites and enterprises in the territory. In all, 137 criminal investigators worked in the whole of the Soviet Far East.[5]

A report from the Russian federation Executive Soviet (VTsIK) put the number of police somewhat higher than the NKVD, but also warned of a crisis in policing and public order.[6] In fact, the crisis of policing was worse than the average statistics described. If most areas had few police, many had none at all. The latter included 152 *raiony,* about 9 percent of the 1,675 *raiony* in the Russian republic in 1932. Another third made do with three or fewer police inspectors. *Raiony* with five or more included major towns where scarce police were concentrated, leaving outlying areas bereft of regular law enforcement.[7] Instead of the required minimum of two criminal investigators per village, most rural regional police organizations had none. Some regions were lucky enough to make do with one investigator to cover several *raiony*.

If policing in rural areas was inadequate, the situation in urban areas was not much better. The latter usually concentrated scarce police resources, but before 1932, most urban areas, with a few notable exceptions, had no separate police administration. In many towns, oddly, the police were administered from oblast- or even republic-level offices.[8] Moreover, numbers of urban police were also low. A police proposal for reorganization in 1932 declared that, despite some increases in personnel, levels and training were still not enough "to secure revolutionary order and public security in a number of cities, workers' towns, and industrial regions." The growth in police numbers "clearly lags behind the tempo of development of new cities and the expansion of existing cities."[9] Police administrations even in the areas around Moscow suffered a dearth of leadership cadres. In 1932, as much as one-quarter to one-third of "command staff" positions remained vacant in the Moscow oblast.[10] A police circular lamented the near complete lack of attention to formation of police units in outlying areas in general, and in "national" areas in particular, that is, areas where the majority of inhabitants were non-Russian. The latter fact was "especially" troubling at a time when the class war was intensifying in these areas, and local authorities needed to be able to rely on a loyal police force.[11]

If the numbers of police were low, so were the qualifications of police personnel. In the early 1930s, the police were an ill-trained, ill-equipped, and low-paid lot. The average monthly pay even for an investigative inspector was only 110 to 130 rubles in 1932, although this was supposed to be raised to 120 to 130 rubles in 1933. This was lower than the average monthly salary of an unskilled worker in the nonpriority consumer sectors of the economy. The chief of a precinct police station, the *uchastkovyi inspektor,* earned sixty to seventy rubles monthly, about as much as a sales clerk, and a rank-and-file policeman drew only fifty to sixty rubles monthly. In rural areas of Western Siberia, a local policeman could count on only thirty to forty rubles a month.[12] By mid-decade and the latter 1930s, the *militsiia* received pay and ration cards and some training that approximated levels in the military and political police. In 1932, however, most police officers were still on the second-tier ration list with access to fewer and lower quality goods than groups on the state's first-tier ration list.

Police were remarkably underqualified for their job. The Russian government's report from 1930 bemoaned this state of affairs, noting that two-thirds of all district and oblast police chiefs had no special training. This figure reached 80 percent among rural chief inspectors, even though, as the report pointed out, "on these shoulders rests the most serious task of defense of the Revolution."[13] This situation was made worse by the constant purging of supposedly untrustworthy elements within the police. Purging rid the police of many unsavory types, to be sure, but it also depleted the ranks of the *militsiia,* and especially the investigative branch, of experienced, well-trained officers. Many of the latter, usually not communists, had worked as professional policemen since before the Revolution. Thinning their ranks reduced the qualifications of the police overall. In a single year, 1929–30, the proportion of criminal investigative police with special training dropped from 18 to 16 percent.[14] Most police had had some form of military service to fall back on, but before 1931, they received no weapons training at all. Many local police had no weapons, and those who possessed them often did not know how to use them, or kept them in poor condition.[15] The eight policemen who served in the Trotsk region, outside of Leningrad, were relatively well armed. They shared two revolvers among them, plus a Browning. The *uchastkovyi inspektor* had in his arsenal several "Austrian" rifles for prisoner transport.[16] In most regions, however, police had few weapons. Numerous police circulars chastised local offices that did have weapons for the poor state in which they were maintained, and for a lack of security about how they were used and by whom. A 1931 circular described the weapons preparedness of the police, in general, as "catastrophic," and noted that local police were often outgunned by better-organized bandit gangs that operated in nearly every oblast in the country.[17]

Police work, even at the investigative and operational level, attracted few young and vigorous recruits. In 1932, in Western Siberia, only 20 to 25 percent of police officers were physically fit enough to carry out their full range of duties. This was especially true of the higher ranks, above the level of a patrol officer. Due to low pay and poor housing priorities, noted the report, the police profession seemed to attract "right and left (*splosh' i riadom*) . . . physical invalids or people in very weak health."[18] To make matters worse, even those policemen were ill-equipped for their tasks. Just a little over one-third of them possessed weapons in working order, few patrol officers had proper uniforms, and local governments denied the RKM adequate office space in scarce city buildings. Most outlying police stations had no telephone contact with their central police headquarters (this was true even in large cities), and very few police possessed adequate mechanized transportation, whether for prisoner exchange, operational activities, or even to drive to meetings.[19]

One report detailed the mundane problems of public-order officers in a typical rural area, again in Leningrad oblast. This particular region, unnamed in the report, was fortunate enough to have a policeman— one policeman, with the rank of inspector. As a result, the jurisdiction of the police inspector encompassed a number of villages and the inspector fell under the jurisdiction of, and supposedly reported to, a group of several rural government councils, or *sel'sovety*. "He does not have a permanent office," lamented the report, "and he travels around from village to village and *kolkhoz* to *kolkhoz*, often filling out forms and formulating documents in his own apartment. . . . [The inspector] also holds consulting hours for and carries out questioning of citizens in his apartment." The report noted dryly that, because of the inspector's lone status, lack of offices, and necessary peripatetic duties, no one could ever find him when he was needed. Moreover, local Soviet officials had no idea what the inspector did or how he spent his time. There was no paper and no station or office for logging duties, complaints, fines, or other such desiderata of a policeman's service. "The *sel'sovet* has no way to supervise [the inspector's] activities," noted the report. Such a situation was not only bad for maintaining public order, it opened up the possibility of abuse of office. Indeed, petty extortion, blackmail, and the levying of excessive fines remained a serious problem of abuse among police throughout the 1930s, in no small part exacerbated by low pay and lack of professional standards of conduct and support.[20]

The situation described above was typical, but it is interesting to note that the police inspector in that particular region was lucky enough to have an apartment and some means of transportation. Housing and transportation shortages for police were chronic. As a supposedly militarized force, equivalent to OGPU and military troops, police were supposed to live in state-allocated housing, or at the very least in barracks. Fewer than 5 percent did so, a function no doubt of a lack of housing, but also of the singular conditions of employment of most police inspectors. In Western Siberia, again reflecting trends in the rest of the country, only 5 percent of police lived in state-allocated housing. Most paid rent out of already meager salaries for rooms or small apartments. The situation in Novosibirsk was "especially extreme." Half the police force in that city was forced to rent private dwellings while, remarkably, 6 percent were registered as homeless.[21] Local governments were supposed to supply police with apartments allocated out of their living funds, but the 1932 police report from Western Siberia condemned the "total indifference" of local soviets to the housing and wage needs of the police.[22] Despite their obligations, district- and region-level soviets constantly paid wages late, mostly because the money was siphoned off to other priorities, including the lining of officials' own pockets. And the lack of training, weaponry, pay, and housing extended to transportation as well as other means of communication. Police cars and vans were scarce even in large cities and towns; they were nonexistent in rural areas. Many rural inspectors did not even have horses that they could count as their own. Police could not make rounds, get to crime scenes, respond when summoned, or even travel to meetings.[23] Many regional policemen were lucky if they had one horse for the whole region. In the early 1930s, less than one-half of all rural police had access to a horse.[24] In the Trotsk region of Leningrad oblast, the police apparatus could rely on two horses, but only if they were not in use. The horses were stabled and owned by a local medical clinic and a village soviet.[25]

Given such working conditions, it is no wonder that police either quit or turned to petty crime to get by. In both 1929 and 1930, turnover within the *militsiia* reached an average of 64 percent, nearly two-thirds of the force. The Far Eastern region saw a complete turnover of police two years running, and in the Urals, all but 7 percent quit and were replaced in 1930.[26] Corruption was endemic, leading to convictions for some form of criminality of 20 percent of rank-and-file police in 1929. In the same year, about 5 percent of higher-ups were convicted of statutory crimes. The 1930 internal report that provided these figures warned that criminal convictions were rising sharply from year to year within police ranks. The same report noted that convictions among *ugolovnyi rozysk* officers had reached 7.6 percent in 1929.[27] An investigation by the RSFSR procuracy went further still, and excoriated the investigative branch as a veritable den of thieves, con-artists, and extortionists.

The report, no doubt exaggerated for the procuracy's own institutional reasons, nonetheless pointed to serious problems. The report acknowledged the temptation toward criminality, given the low state of pay and work conditions, and called for improvements. "Low pay and poor work conditions lead many in the investigative apparatus to complete rottenness," reported the state's inspectorate organization, Rabkrin, in 1931. "[Officers] slide into outrageous forms of criminality." A procuracy investigation of police in Central Asia detailed a truly gruesome situation in which police, and especially criminal investigative branches, demanded "huge" bribes "for every privilege." This included bribes required from people to retrieve the bodies of relatives. Conditions in jails were "horrific" and, if relatives were unable to pay, police left prisoners locked up and bodies to lie for days in communal cells.[28]

According to Rabkrin's investigators, the problem of corruption and police criminality was only partly the result of low wages and poor work conditions. Criminality was endemic to the way that the *ugolovnyi rozysk* officers worked. The very nature of their undercover investigative work placed them in constant and intimate contact with the underworld of criminals and socially dangerous types. By insinuating themselves into the criminal world, by being such a part of it, investigative agents too easily succumbed to the influence of that world. Agents often worked with little supervision. They recruited hardened criminals as informants, since the latter knew the underworld, but then these groups of informants themselves became nuclei of gang activity. They fed selective information to their resident controllers who, in return for turning a blind eye, used their positions of privilege and protection to develop their own criminal contacts and activities. During police roundups, informants were often quietly released, or were warned in advance and easily avoided arrest. In a number of cases, agents became the leaders of gangs based around their groups of informants. Their criminal activities ranged from extortion to sexual blackmail to the operation of prostitution rings, smuggling activities, and other types of crimes far more serious than the usual excessive fining and petty abuse of office common among police. According to the procuracy, "this type of system not only harms the fight against the criminal element, but also puts the criminal investigative apparatus at risk of corruption, since in using these kinds of methods, officers often visit more than is necessary the dens (*pritony*) of criminals, get drunk with them, and collude with the criminal world." By relying on criminal elements for their information, the police had become dependent on that element. In the process, the police had become a part of the very criminal world they were dedicated to fight.[29]

Procuracy and state inspectorate officials were not the only ones to make the connection between corruption and poor wages and work conditions; police officials themselves understood this well. The Western Siberian police chief, M. Domarev, pointed explicitly to the connection between police conditions and police crime. In 1933, he warned Fedor Griadinskii, the chief of the district soviet, that low wages and failure of the district- and region-level soviets to provide adequate food supplies for local police were the cause of widespread corruption. This kind of corruption included outright theft and speculation in food and meat supplies, extortion of produce and meat from collective and state farms, and other activities by official agencies that tied them to local criminal elements. Domarev highlighted the obvious by pointing out that these kinds of activities compromised the police in their fight against those very criminal elements. Domarev urged the Western Siberian soviet to enact financial and administrative measures to improve the lot of police.[30]

Ironically, Domarev was removed from office and remanded to court custody just a year later for abetting exactly the kind of official criminality he deplored. The internal police review that led to his arrest provided a detailed accounting of official corruption. The review charged him with allowing a culture of laxness and corruption to pervade the Western Siberian police system. The review found that the police administration, "both the district central apparatus and in outlying areas," was "saturated" with criminal elements. One of the district's chief criminal investigators, a certain Ivanov, secretly operated a theft ring. In Tomsk, a police operative group systematically engaged in apartment robberies.[31]

The introduction of an internal passport system in 1933 provided yet another lucrative opportunity for graft, allowing regional police chiefs to do a brisk business in selling passport blanks. In Western Siberia, in 1933, "at least" 83,633 numbered blanks could not be accounted for. Presumably, officials sold these illegally to criminals and others instead of distributing them to legitimate citizens. OGPU investigators sent to Western Siberia uncovered yet another major embezzlement ring in the district's central supply department, which had systematically siphoned off several hundred thousand rubles' worth of supplies, confiscated property, cash, and other valuables. Regional police chiefs ran kickback schemes, overcharged fees, stole and sold horses from farms, and were found guilty of gross criminal negligence in the performance of their duties. Finally, there were the usual charges of bribery, excessive fining, and drunkenness.[32]

The Western Siberian report amounted to a scathing indictment of the police system, but it differed from inspections of other police organizations only in the excessive nature of the activities described. Central OGPU authorities conducted many such internal reviews, which became the stuff of weekly circulars, official reprimands, and orders that imposed sometimes harsher and sometimes milder punishments than that meted out to Domarev. These actions served both a moral and a practical purpose—to provide local authorities with a guide to proper police procedures and to warn of the consequences of too flagrant violations of central rules. The latter was an especially valuable function of published reprimands. Local police read about their hapless colleagues who came under the scrutiny of an internal review, and they learned which offenses carried harsh punishments and which carried lesser strictures. One enterprising police chief was found to have embezzled tens of thousands of rubles of confiscated property and fines over the course of 1933. Police were supposed to turn over this kind of money to other state authorities, but this particular police chief used it to send himself and his officers on resort vacations. Although embezzling was a serious crime, he was not relieved of his command. Yagoda ordered him suspended and jailed for only ten days, no doubt because he had used the embezzled funds for a good police cause.[33]

Police corruption was certainly not peculiar to the early 1930s. Criminality permeated and plagued the Soviet state throughout its existence, and this was no more or less true of the police than of any other bureaucracy. Yet such corruption was especially endemic to this period of the early 1930s because of the transitional character of those years. Many regional and local police bureaucracies were just coming under central state budgets, and were experiencing the first inflow of serious amounts of money from Moscow. At the same time, central authorities had not yet established full administrative control over local police agencies in order to control funds and personnel. This situation created conditions particularly conducive to the flourishing of official abuse and corruption. The living conditions and corruption described above for police in Western Siberia reflected a national pattern, or at least a national perception. An internal police report from 1931 went so far as to declare that most police forces in the country were "unreliable." A "significant" number of police personnel came from kulak or other anti-Soviet "alien" backgrounds and easily fell prey to the lure of the criminal milieu.[34] By 1934, the situation was little improved, at least according to Yagoda. In that year, 29,000 police officials were charged with some kind of criminality, nearly one-quarter of the total number of state police in the country. Most of these indictments carried fines or nonjudicial punishments such as temporary suspensions or demotion, but 9,000 of these indictments proved serious enough to be heard by military tribunals, and 5,000 of those cases ended in guilty verdicts and prison sentences.[35]

MOSCOW: POLICE AND PUBLIC ORDER

Cities such as Moscow and Leningrad fared better, not surprisingly, than rural or provincial areas in terms of police protection. In 1931, the Moscow oblast boasted a police force of 7,733 officers and 873 officers of the *ugolovnyi rozysk*. This number, 8,606, served an oblast population of about 9 million people, about 1 policeman for every 1,000 citizens. Figures for the number of police in the city itself are unavailable, but the population of Moscow in 1933 hovered at about 3.6 million. Since most of the oblast police were concentrated in Moscow proper, the ratio of police to population probably approached that of the norm of 1:750 or 1:800.[36] As expected, this was well above the norm for other areas of the country, and it approximated the numbers of police serving other major European cities, such as Berlin and London.[37] Still, the Moscow police force was much smaller than the force that patrolled the city before the Revolution, even though the population in the early 1930s was substantially larger than in the first decade of the twentieth century.

Moscow police received high marks for their appearance on the street and for operational discipline and professionalism. An internal police review from 1935 commended the force's efficient command structure, and its significant success in fighting major crimes such as murder and armed assault.[38] Still, the Moscow police force was plagued by many of the same problems that crippled policing in other areas of the country.

Turnover of officers continued to be a problem, many precincts seeing four to five new commanders in the course of a single year. Officers received little weapons training, and investigative techniques and informant and agent networks worked at an "extremely low level of operational success." More disturbing was an astute insight that policing work was not driven by priorities set forth for the police by higher authorities, but by the inertia of existing police methods and by the "specificity" of police contacts in the criminal world. In other words, police work continued to be dominated by a culture of tacit complicity, in which police "reeled in" petty criminals supplied to them by their agent contacts, while they left untouched the large speculators and organized criminal operations. It was the latter, especially, that cost the state "huge" amounts of money.[39]

The infrastructure and reach of the police system also suffered. The state's rapid colonization of the economy caught police short, unable to protect state assets from, among other threats, the mass pilferage that characterized the early 1930s. Similarly, the rapid rise in Moscow's population also stretched police resources thin. In 1932 alone, the city's population climbed by over half a million, from 3,135,000 to 3,663,000. Despite the goal to organize policing in all neighborhoods, police rarely ventured into the shantytown and flophouse districts of the city, and then only in force during organized raids.[40] Night patrols were still rare, even in Moscow, and even the center of the capital was not immune to the problems of social disorder. Hooligan gangs, usually of orphaned and migrant children, preyed on the city streets and used them as their playground. Large groups of ragged-looking children were a common, Dickensian sight in markets and poorer sections of the city. According to one report, in the two years 1931 and 1932, police apprehended 20,500 children on some kind of criminal charge, mostly for theft and hooliganism. Another internal police review claimed that, just in 1932, police apprehended 15,648 child criminals. Yet a third report noted that 13,500 underage criminals were arrested in the last half of 1931.[41] Whatever the numbers, they were large, and these were only underage criminals.

Citizens and sellers in the markets and bazaars of Moscow, as well as other cities, suffered pickpocketing and petty theft as a daily routine. Gang theft on the city's streetcars, for example, was not uncommon; gang members would swarm onto a car, front and rear, holding passengers and conductor at knifepoint, then jumping off and scattering before the next stop, or before police could be summoned. Thieves perfected the art of purse snatching as open streetcars rolled by on the streets. Some children took daring delight in roller-skating behind streetcars, holding on to the back rails for a thrilling ride. (This was indeed, dangerous, given the cobblestone paving of streets and streetcar lines). Even high government officials complained of being harassed by criminal youth gangs. The problem of unsupervised children running loose on the streets of Moscow so incensed Yagoda that he demanded that all such children be rounded up and sent to child detention centers.[42]

In Moscow, as in other cities, the main problems confronting police were not high murder rates or other sensational crime problems, but the daily plague of "petty criminality, theft of socialist property, and hooliganism." The streets were embarrassingly full of beggars, homeless children, prostitutes, and undocumented individuals—the flotsam and jetsam of déclassé "elements" left in the wake of the great Stalinist project to build socialism in one country. And that was Moscow, the major city, the seat of government and center of Soviet power. The situation was worse by far in other areas. In a 1932 report to Sovnarkom, Yagoda again lamented that, at its current strength, the police could not, "even in a single republic, krai, or oblast," fulfill the tasks of maintaining revolutionary order and public safety. Yagoda described as "especially strained" regions of new industrial and transportation construction "where populations grow at a rapid tempo and draw an influx of criminal elements."[43] The largest accumulations of criminal, kulak, and anti-Soviet elements were also to be found, logically, in areas of the country designated for exile and special settlements. With its penal settlements in the north and new industrial centers in the southwest, the Western Siberian district fit Yagoda's description of an "especially strained" area. He singled out the district as one of several areas severely understaffed by police and "not well protected."[44]

WESTERN SIBERIA: POLICE AND PUBLIC ORDER

Reports from Western Siberian police, OGPU officials, and local authorities confirmed Yagoda's laconic assessment. As one official wrote, criminals and socially dangerous elements "pour into the district from both east and west."[45] Escapes from colonies, prisons, and penal camps added to this flood. In any year, tens of thousands of escaped prisoners and deportees made their way to cities and industrial sites, crowding the roads and the rivers, and looking for work on collective and state farms or in local towns and villages.[46] These populations were nearly indistinguishable from the tens of thousands of ragged-looking in-migrants looking for work or fleeing from unsettled conditions in the western and Central Asian areas of the country. In the second half of 1933 alone, over 50,000 Kazakhs crossed the border into the Western Siberian district to escape the famine and hardships of collectivization in their native land. These were impoverished, starved people, who had been stripped of their livelihoods and who, in the panicked assessment of one official, threatened the order and economic balance of the areas where they settled.[47]

As the numbers and proportion of "socially dangerous" populations rose rapidly in Western Siberia during the early years of the 1930s, the number of police in fact dropped. Reorganization and purging of police ranks in 1930 and 1931 resulted in a reduction of civil police in the district from 2,736 to 2,327. In Novosibirsk, the number of police dropped from 276 to 197 even as the population grew from 146,000 to 180,000. In the provincial center of Bisk in the industrial and agricultural lands west of Novosibirsk, only 69 police officers served a city of 53,000 in 1932. In Novo-Kuznetsk, the number of police officials increased in 1930 and 1931 from 24 to 38, but the population during the same year soared from 28,000 to over 100,000.[48] In Novosibirsk, police ranks were stretched so thin and jails were so overcrowded that prison officials allowed prisoners to "guard" themselves. Prisoners came and went "as they please, individually and in groups."[49] In rural areas, the lack of police and OGPU units required one chief inspector, along with two to three officers, to cover over 5,000 square kilometers and 10,000 to 15,000 or more inhabitants. In non-Russian areas of the *krai*, Soviet police authority hardly existed.[50]

Officials in the cities of Omsk, Tomsk, Barnaul, and Novosibirsk vied for the dubious distinction of having the highest crime rates. Officials' reports implied a perverse pride in how bad crime could be in their respective cites. In 1934, a special envoy from the district's Party committee wrote that in Omsk, crime was so rampant that "literally, every inhabitant is terrorized. . . . Every citizen fears going out, even to work, fears for his life, even at home, sleeping in his own bed." According to the envoy, incidents of theft, aggravated assault, physical intimidation (*izdevatel'stvo*), hooliganism, and murder—even of whole families—occurred not only at night, but in broad daylight, on public streets. Citizens of Omsk could not be certain of a safe journey home after work, he wrote. They could not take for granted that their homes would be safe while they were out, or that their "wives, parents, and children" would not be "raped, beaten, killed or robbed at any moment in their beds."[51]

If Omsk was a "lawless" city, so was Tomsk, the largest major city in the northern part of the *krai*. Tomsk lay at the edge of the Narym, one of the largest and most infamous territories of exile settlement in the country. The city and its environs were the debarkation point for almost all shipments of exiles and criminals before their final transport to camps and colonies. One of the largest labor colonies for underage criminals and homeless children in the USSR operated not far from the city limits, within the Tomsk *raion*, with an average population of three thousand inmates. Several thousand prisoners also crowded the city's prisons and jails. As a result of its location, criminal and exile elements "pour[ed]" into the city, especially in the spring and summer months when roads and rivers became passable once again. According to a 1933 police report, criminal and escaped exile populations "saturate" Tomsk to its "absolute maximum limit." "Clearly," boasted the police review, Tomsk occupied "a unique position" because of crime.[52]

Novosibirsk, the administrative capital of Western Siberia, was not to be outdone by its provincial satellites, and a 1933 police report detailed the rise in criminality and social disorder in that city. Crime rates indeed rose dramatically in Novosibirsk during the early 1930s. Based only on the number of officially reported cases, police calculated that, during 1933, incidents of banditry (organized gang theft) and aggravated robbery jumped 312 percent. Many of these involved systematic looting by organized groups of apartments and stores, "even down to the window frames." Simple robbery (without use of weapons) increased 129 percent; incidents of hooliganism rose 214 percent; and cases of speculation, or selling of state goods for private profit, climbed 155 percent. Incidents of theft of state property reached 424 percent over the number of such cases reported in 1932: 955 versus 182 incidents, respectively. Interestingly, the number of known murders dropped during 1933 from 152 to 97. Cattle rustling in Novosibirsk oblast fell by 20 percent in 1933, and in the last two months of 1933, incidents of theft of socialist property also fell by 66 percent.[53]

The Novosibirsk report gave several reasons why that city found itself in a "uniquely unfavorable situation . . . in comparison to most large cities in the Union."[54] The main reason, as the police report acknowledged bluntly, was that Western Siberia served as a social dumping ground for the rest of the country. The police report minced no words, declaring that "The OGPU and the courts exile and deport socially harmful and socially dangerous elements through Novosibirsk from the central regions of the Union." This created severe strain on the already strained policing forces in the territory, but worse was the fact that, due to understaffing of regular and political police, a "significant" proportion of those "contingents" was able to flee from their places of confinement. Police estimated that, in a period of nine months during 1933, 12,362 inmates escaped from camps of the Siberian Gulag system. In addition, over 2,000 deportees were missing and presumed escaped from exile settlements in the Narym region, 48,000 kulaks went missing from labor colonies in the territory, and the number of children missing from children's homes and labor colonies also reached into the thousands.[55] According to the Novosibirsk police chief, all of these people were heading first and foremost for the city as their first destination after escape.

There was truth in these assessments, even if exaggerated. Novosibirsk was a fast-developing industrial and administrative center and a major rail junction and, very important, it was not a so-called "regime" city— it did not have special residence laws that allowed police administratively to deport undesirable people.[56] As a result of these conditions, Novosibirsk quickly became a magnet for "the wandering criminal element" (*gastroliruiushchii ugolovnyi element*) and for "professional cadres of orphans." The latter was an especially large problem, since, as the report claimed, the "central areas of the Union . . . saturate our territory with a significant number of orphans who then flee their settlements and head for Novosibirsk." Finally, there were the ubiquitous runaway kulaks. The latter, because of lax enforcement of passport and residency laws, obtained work easily enough in a labor-starved economy, especially in the burgeoning industrial centers of Siberia. Work gave them the coveted right to residency and an internal passport. This was the primary way that runaway kulaks "legalized" themselves and melted back into the general population.[57]

Novosibirsk was not unique, despite the lament of its police chief. As local reports show, similar patterns of criminality and social disorder prevailed in Omsk, Tomsk, and in many other "frontier" areas of the

Soviet state. The Novosibirsk report is interesting, nonetheless, for another reason. In a few short paragraphs, police officials offered a fairly accurate appraisal of several serious social problems associated with the state's modernizing and punitive social policies, and did so without ideological adornment. At the same time, the report utilized what were fast becoming reified social categories used by police and policy makers to organize and sort marginal populations. "Wandering" criminals (like wandering minstrels) and "professional contingents" of orphans were already beyond social redemption. Soon, police began to refer to these and other socially marginal groups not only as antisocial, but as anti-Soviet, and then as recidivists, and this, by the middle and late 1930s, opened the door for more drastic measures than exile. These groups already carried the epithet of "element," a term reserved for antistate, antisocial categories to be dealt with by special methods of social "engineering," primarily by "extraction" (iz"iatie) and deportation. Leaders already regarded kulaks as an anti-Soviet grouping, of course, but it is interesting to note that, unlike the peripatetic criminal elements, runaway kulaks, according to the police report, were seeking to work and settle. For a time, anyway, this positive social attribute worked in favor of those exiled under that rubric. Stalin even referred to kulaks as having the rights of "voluntary" labor. He explicitly rejected the label of "convict," and did not regard kulaks as part of the "dangerous" or "harmful" element—so long as they remained in their settlements, of course.[58] During the mid-1930s, the civil rights of many hundreds of thousands of kulaks were restored as a result of their having "proved" themselves worthy through work in the labor and farm colonies to which they had been exiled in the early part of the decade. That reprieve did not last long, since those once designated as kulaks were targeted again in the mass repressions of 1937 and 1938. Still, during most of the 1930s, officials made the distinction between kulaks, willing to settle and work, and "professional" criminals and orphans whom they regarded as dangerous and harmful.

YOUTH CRIME, PUBLIC ORDER, AND ANTI-SOVIET CONSPIRACIES

Western Siberian police officials, like those in other areas of the country, reserved special concern for the increasingly menacing problem of youth crime, which was associated with the problem of homeless children and escaped inmates from youth-criminal labor camps. Tens of thousands of homeless or unsupervised children ran loose in Siberia throughout the early and mid-1930s. Police ascribed much of the surge in crime to them, especially petty theft in marketplaces and other public areas. State-operated youth homes were so overcrowded that, beginning in 1933, local officials solved their problems of vagabond youth in a simpler way than constant repatriation to orphanages. Police engaged in periodic sweeps of their streets or roads, gathering up homeless children. After each sweep, police drove these children over the border to a neighboring region or to larger cities and dropped them there. This was done not only with children but with adult criminals as well when local jails overflowed. As a result, reported the chairman of the Tomsk city soviet in 1934, "the streets, markets, bus and streetcar stops, train station, stores, and other enterprises of [the city] are flooded by groups of adult and homeless underage recidivist criminals who create all manner of disorder and who terrorize the population."[59] Tomsk police could not confine underage criminals to state homes in the city since they, too, were overfilled. In April 1934 1,475 children were housed in the city's homes for underage children, which had a total capacity of fewer than 1,000.

In Novosibirsk, police officially attributed over one hundred crimes in April 1934 to children between the ages of ten and sixteen.[60] These ranged from individual acts of pickpocketing and grab-and-run crimes all the way to organized gang thefts of stores and apartments, and even murder. In April 1934, a police report noted that one of the newest techniques of grab-and-run theft involved youth criminals who stole women's gold earrings, ripping them off the hapless victims' ears as they raced past on the sidewalks.[61] Many youth crimes involved knives, but occasionally also guns. While many such crimes were perpetrated by individuals, the increasingly frequent appearance of organized youth gangs worried police. For several months in 1934, a gang of "up to thirty" members operated in Novosibirsk under the leadership of two adult repeat offenders, Shorkin and Prud. Most members of this gang were between sixteen and eighteen, but at least ten were under sixteen years of age. They engaged in armed robbery, murder, and over fifty apartment thefts. The gang was armed with hunting rifles, two Smith and Wesson revolvers, a Browning revolver, and several other handguns. A similar gang of twenty members also worked the streets of Novosibirsk during 1934. Several of the members of this gang had belonged to the Shorkin-Prud gang and had escaped from jails or youth homes after its breakup.[62]

At times, officials saw political motivation in gang activities, even counterrevolutionary activities disguised as hooliganism. The inspector of the district's Party central committee, M. Floren, drew such a conclusion after his tour of Tomsk in 1934. After meeting with workers of the Rudzutak railroad repair works, Floren reported: "I gained the strong impression that workers [living in the city's factory district] were literally terrorized by hooligan elements, and that these elements were not just plain hooligans, but political organizers of terrorist acts against the state and workers." According to Floren's report, the workers with whom he met saw similar dark maneuverings behind what was probably systematic gang activity. One worker, he wrote, "expressed his apprehension that, if war should break out, these elements will certainly be even more active, and that government organs should take decisive measures now, or, in the event of war, it will become even worse."[63] While the worker may or may not have read political motivation into such a statement, the inspector chose to do so, and his assessment reiterated the line Stalin had taken in 1933. For Floren, systematic gang activity had to be connected to broadly organized anti-Soviet political movements, with plans to disrupt Soviet order on the home front in the event of war. Authorities often ascribed political motivations to crime, depending on what they determined the criminal's social background to be. In general, however, police in the early 1930s still regarded the category of hooliganism as "ordinary" crime, not motivated by anti-Soviet attitudes. This distinction began to break down as ordinary crime became increasingly politicized, and as youth crime became increasingly pervasive. The blurring of lines between political and ordinary crime, as expressed in Floren's report, began to occur regularly after 1934.

PUBLIC ATTITUDES TOWARD THE POLICE

People's attitudes to the police were complicated. People looked to the police to protect them from what many believed was an epidemic of crime and lawlessness. At the same time, at least according to internal police reports, many people blamed the police, at least in part, for widespread social disorder. Public opprobrium of the police appears to have had little to do with general feelings of opposition to the Soviet state's policies of collectivization and dekulakization; nor did censure of the police derive from simple disgust with apparent police ineffectiveness in combating crime. Public attitudes toward the police were specific: the police force was corrupt and in league with criminals.

The reputation of police as corrupt and ineffective was widespread during the early 1930s among the public and among high police officials themselves. A police report from 1932 listed "improving relations with the public (*so storony obshchestvennosti*)" as one of seven priorities for the coming period, along with other "fundamental" changes in organization and operational work.[64] In his report on crime in Omsk, Floren emphasized that the negative public image of the police proved a deterrent to the latter's effectiveness. He illustrated public attitudes by recounting what he claimed to be typical conversations overheard in public places by police eavesdroppers. One such exchange occurred at an outlying bus depot among four women conductors on break. One described a night robbery of her neighbor's apartment—apparently a systematic gang robbery, in which the thieves took everything: "even the shutters and windows—they robbed the apartment clean!" According to Floren's informant, the women became "agitated" upon hearing this story and repeatedly asked each other why such robberies had "blossomed" in recent times. "Why can't they get them?" asked one woman. "Before, the police would have arrested someone; they would have found the culprits," she said, "but now, nothing." A third conductor declared that the matter was "all clear. These [robberies] don't happen without the participation of the police." As proof of police collusion with criminal elements, all the women agreed that they had witnessed numerous occasions when police tried to "run away" when they saw someone being beaten and robbed on the street, or when police officials denied such an incident occurred if it was reported by a citizen.[65]

It is telling that the women who described these incidents should attribute motives of collusion to police rather than fear. In his autobiography, Nicholas Voinov, an orphan during the 1930s, corroborated the women conductors' impressions, but he added the element of intimidation. Voinov described in the towns where he lived a widespread system of orphan, or *besprizornik,* criminal organizations. In addition to thievery, which was their primary means of livelihood, the activities of *be-*

sprizornik gangs included protection racketeering, police bribery, and revenge murders of public (even NKVD) officials. According to Voinov, many police routinely avoided confrontations with gangs and stayed out of gang affairs in the urban areas where gangs operated. Police did so because they were bribed to look the other way, but also out of fear of retaliation should they intervene. According to Voinov, whole sections of cities, at least in provincial towns, were run by gangs, largely teenage orphan gangs, who extorted protection money from police and local administrative officials.[66] M. Floren, the Party's inspector sent to Omsk, believed the problem of corruption and official criminal activity was so bad in that city that he recommended to the district's Party committee a sweeping purge not only of the Omsk police, but also of the city's NKVD organization, the local Party committee, and the city soviet. Such drastic steps were necessary, he wrote, to restore "public trust" (*obshchestvennoe doverie*) in the organs of Soviet authority and to allow "the workers and civil servants of Omsk to live without fear and to participate peacefully and securely in the construction of socialism."[67]

OGPU

If police networks were stretched thin across the Soviet territories in the early 1930s, so were networks of the OGPU, at least according to assessments by that agency. Before the formation of OGPU units in the system of machine tractor stations in 1932, Yagoda reported a total of 17,298 OGPU staff in the country. This figure rose to 20,898 by the beginning of 1933.[68] This included the central administrative apparatus, and the "special organs," *osobye organy*. The special organs included the special departments (*osobye otdely,* or OO) stationed in military units, the secret political departments (*sekretnye politicheskie otdely,* or SPO) in oblast and district offices, and the economic crimes and transportation departments (EKO, and TO or DTO, respectively). Yagoda's figure of 20,898 excluded OGPU officers staffing places of confinement and working in nonoperative positions such as police academies. This figure also excluded border forces, the *pogranichniki,* and about 50,000 internal militarized forces of the OGPU.[69] This figure corresponds roughly to the 19,400 staff reported by Petrov and Skorkin, using archive sources from the NKVD. In all, according to the latter scholars, OGPU forces in the country varied from about 25,000 to

28,000 officers in the early 1930s.[70] This number included about 2,000 officials in the central apparatus and another 3,000 in OGPU school administrations and prison administrative positions. Slightly fewer than 6,000 officers staffed regional bureaus of the OGPU or worked as special plenipotentiaries in regions. Another 600 to 800 officers worked in OGPU bureaus in "population centers" outside of the major capital cities of the country. At the beginning of 1933, a little over 5,000 officers staffed transport departments, up from 4,598 listed at the beginning of 1931.[71] The latter operated in groups out of offices in train stations in major towns or cities, or at "operational points" (*operativnye punkty*) at key junctions. In the Moscow oblast, there were as many as 61 such departments, each of which controlled one or two operational points. In Western Siberia, there existed only 20 operational points, established at major rail centers in towns such as Novosibirsk, Tomsk, Barnaul, Omsk, Barabinsk, Biisk, and other smaller towns with rail junctions. In Kazakhstan, the OGPU staffed 27 points, 38 points in the Far Eastern district, and 13 in Sverdlovsk oblast.[72] Another 3,283 officers made up special operational "sectors." These operational "sectors" were formed in oblast and *krai* centers (75 in all) and each was staffed by 20 to 30 officers. These were to be used for special operations and to supplement the staff of regional offices. Regional bureaus were supposed to be staffed with up to three officers, yet in the early 1930s, only 20 percent of the country's rural regions were fully staffed. Most regions had at least two officers, but nearly one-third of all regions had only one OGPU officer. According to one OGPU official in 1931, political police informant networks were spread so thin across the countryside that the civil police had a more thoroughly developed system of information and policing than did the OGPU.[73]

During the dekulakization and collectivization campaigns, of course, OGPU numbers in the countryside increased and were supplemented by special OGPU forces, Party plenipotentiaries, and even by the infamous urban factory gangs, sent to the countryside to help with collectivization. This level of occupation of rural areas did not last. As the Party and police scaled back dekulakization and collectivization campaigns, OGPU special units and other groups withdrew from the countryside, leaving the state's new salient vulnerable to sabotage and criminal activity. By 1932, OGPU troops had withdrawn their protection from most agricultural warehouses, farms, and other rural areas, as well as from many state industrial sites. The transfer of thousands of OGPU officers to work in the understaffed judicial and procuracy systems, the police, and other state organs also depleted OGPU numbers. OGPU troops continued to keep guard on railroad lines, key junctions, some major roads, and industrial enterprises of significance. Yet, even these forces were overburdened. In late 1931, A. A. Andreev, the transportation commissar, warned Stalin in a letter that the numbers of OGPU troops within the railroad system were "obviously insufficient" to keep the roads cleared of kulak elements and to pressure rail administrators to fulfill their tasks.[74] A June 1932 memorandum to Sovnarkom reported that just under 46,000 armed guards served to protect railroads under the Commissariat of Transportation, but the OGPU memorandum projected a need for a total force of over 60,000 guards. Yagoda regarded even this increase as minimally acceptable and, to his chagrin, Sovnarkom initially refused even that increase. The request was vetoed by the powerful hand of the state's finance commissariat. Commissar Grin'ko's terse memo on the matter noted simply that there were inadequate funds for such an increase.[75]

In the face of central budgetary strains, a November 1933 report from the Western Siberian Soviet to the Russian federation Sovnarkom registered a common complaint. OGPU cutbacks in the wind-down from collectivization had left storage warehouses, timbering sites, and machine and tractor stations in the territory's major collective farms without proper protection. After 1932, these sites were no longer guarded by troops of the state's political police, nor even by regular police. Hired security guards—usually pensioners or demobilized and often invalided Red Army soldiers—patrolled these and the territory's other major industrial facilities. The Siberian officials requested immediate and extraordinary funding of three hundred new police officer positions. Central authorities denied the request, again citing budget constraints, this time to the chagrin of local authorities.[76]

POLITOTDELY

The vacuum of authority in outlaying and rural areas was partially filled by Political Departments, *politotdely*, of Machine Tractor Stations, the MTS. The MTS controlled heavy machinery for a number of collective or state farms, and were manned by Party and OGPU political officers, along with contingents of mechanics and other service personnel. The assistant chief of each MTS was the chief political officer and an OGPU operative. It was the responsibility of the political officer to keep track of political problems in villages and farms, but the MTS political officers played a much broader role. Despite the existence of village soviets and local Party organizations, the MTS political officers represented political, and sometimes civil, authority in rural areas outside the towns. Local *militsiia* constables, usually based in the largest of several villages, deferred to resident political officers, and the latter nearly always became involved in the investigation of, and reported on, any serious crimes that occurred in their areas. Collective and state farm chairmen also took orders from the MTS chief political officer, especially if the farm chairmen were not Party members. In addition to all their other duties, MTS political officers were charged with strengthening Communist activities in their regions. Thus, they reported regularly on their efforts to establish or expand local Party cells, to set up reading and study circles, foster Young Communist Youth League organizations, and where possible, start local newspaper publishing. The MTS political officers were powerful in their bailiwicks. Their regular reports to the Party central committees in their districts provide detailed information about daily life in rural areas of the country.

Formation of the political departments caused friction at times with territorial Party organizations, but the *politotdely* carried "much power" in their local areas, according to Lazar Kaganovich in 1934. Peasants looked to the political officer not only as the main political representative, but as the main representative of Soviet power in general in the regions. Political officers often found themselves adjudicating civil as well as political affairs, and engaged in agricultural and even educational matters, in addition to writing reports to Party authorities on political attitudes among local inhabitants. This is not surprising, given the paucity of both civil and political authority in outlying areas.[77]

Creation of the *politotdely* was a stroke of genius. Established in 1933, these organizations effectively extended Soviet power into the countryside. By the end of the year, close to 3,400 political departments operated in machine tractor stations in either collective or state farms. These departments were staffed by 25,000 Party workers, of whom about 3,000 were OGPU operatives working as assistant chiefs.[78] This amounted to a considerable political and policing force in areas that lacked both. In

1934, leaders considered subdividing and multiplying the number of machine tractor stations and political departments. They worked so well in the countryside that Kaganovich, commissar of transport, attempted to re-create them on railroad lines. *Politotdely* did not work well there, however, and were suspended by the end of 1934, as they were in rural areas. Despite their success as levers of political and social control, *politotdely* created jurisdictional conflicts. Leaders decided in both cases to strengthen the power and reach of local Party organizations, rather than confuse lines of authority with political departments in machine tractor stations or in railroad line administrations.[79]

VEDMILITSIIA

Apart from the OGPU and the *militsiia*, three other types of policing forces operated in urban and rural areas. Officers of *vedmilitsiia*, or enterprise police, were considered an extension of the regular police force —some of these units were armed and had the right to make arrests— but their salaries were paid by the enterprises they patrolled. At times, the *vedmilitsiia* also patrolled the neighborhoods bordering on an enterprise if, as was often the case, there was no regular police presence in the area. As the numbers of state police declined from the mid-1920s, the numbers of the *vedmilitsiia* grew rapidly. By 1930, the *vedmilitsiia* numbered nearly 59,000 in the Russian republic, as opposed to only 37,600 regular police. One report claimed a 314 percent increase in the numbers of *vedmilitsiia* from 1926 to 1930.[80] By 1932, the *vedmilitsiia* numbered 82,000 overall in the Russian republic, nearly twice the number of regular state police. In Western Siberia, the number of *vedmilitsiia* reached 8,586, nearly four times the number of regular police.[81]

Such large numbers of *vedmilitsiia* resulted from one or a combination of several reasons. One report made virtue out of necessity by claiming that such increases represented the fulfillment of the Soviet ideal of citizen participation in governmental administration. More realistically, the same report cited a second reason, which had to do with the rapid expansion of industry and the simultaneous decline in police numbers due to local budget constraints.[82] In fact, regular state police were stretched so thin that enterprises were forced to hire *vedmilitsiia*, regardless of ideological considerations. In these cases, *vedmilitsiia* filled the policing gap created by the state's sudden economic and industrial expansion. In at least some instances, however, state enterprises preferred not to rely on the regular police for protection of their property, even if such was available, and hired their own *vedmilitsiia*. If managers had the money, many preferred to hire a security force on which they knew they could rely. A 1932 report revealed still another motive tied to the lucrative character of contracts associated with the *vedmilitsiia* system. The report in fact claimed that the number of *vedmilitsiia* was "bloated" far beyond necessity, and beyond the qualifications of those employed as enterprise police. As it turned out, enterprises paid for the services of enterprise police, and these contracts brought in good money for local police officials. "A number of *krai* and oblast [officials]," admonished the report, "have not yet gotten beyond the idea that the *vedmilitsiia* is a cash cow (*doinaia korova*)." Accordingly, local police pressured or persuaded enterprises to accept large police forces, and they hustled contracts with "small and unimportant" enterprises simply to bring in more money. As a result, the numbers of *vedmilitsiia* mushroomed in a "spontaneous" way that alarmed central police authorities. The latter worried that the *vedmilitsiia* were turning into what amounted to legally licensed gangs, armed, with little supervision, and a source of potential conflict with regular police authorities. In the meantime, the defense of important state land and buildings suffered from a lack of qualified security personnel.[83]

SEL'ISPOLNITELI

The system of village bailiffs, *sel'ispolniteli*, existed from the tsarist period. It is not clear how, exactly, these officials functioned, either under the tsars, or in the 1920s and early 1930s, or how many there were still officially registered by the early 1930s.[84] The institution was apparently abolished or simply lapsed, but in the early 1930s, official reports still referred to them. In the absence of effective police presence in rural areas, both civil police and the OGPU insisted that village bailiffs be more fully utilized. One of the last references to them appeared in a set of recommendations by the OGPU in late 1932 for strengthening policing authority outside of cities. The recommendations criticized local civil police officials for not integrating bailiffs into operational plans. The recommendations urged a "maximal" coordination of bailiffs' activities and a systematic program of policing instruction for bailiffs. The OGPU insisted on an increase in both numbers and qualifications for *sel'ispol-niteli*. Except for this, however, no mention of bailiffs was made again. Apparently, such recommendations belonged to the period of hectic planning during the early 1930s, when police and OGPU officials sought almost desperately to use any means available to extend policing authority in the countryside.[85]

OSODMILTSY

A large number of vigilante police organizations filled the void created by the lack of state or enterprise police forces. These groups supplemented regular policing functions, and police classified them under the rubric of voluntary associations for cooperation with the police, or *obshchestva sodeistviia militsii (osodmil)*. *Osodmiltsy* were organized in small units, or cells, and their numbers grew dramatically during the early 1930s. In 1930, police counted 2,500 cells with 26,177 individuals, but by spring 1932, about two thousand cells operated in the Western Siberian territory alone. Membership in the Western Siberian groups numbered close to fifteen thousand individuals.[86] As the number of vigilante policing organizations mushroomed, the state attempted to bring them under some kind of control. A Sovnarkom decree from spring 1932 organized the "societies" into "brigades," and subjected them to direct regulation by the *militsiia*. Henceforward, the *osodmiltsy* became known officially as *brigadmiltsy*. The new regulations limited numbers and restricted membership to "leading workers." Brigade members were supposed to undergo police instruction. The new regulation allowed brigade members to be armed, but only with registered police weapons. By spring 1934, police officially praised the "revolutionary" work of over 325,000 organizations, some 80,000 in cities and 245,000 in rural areas.[87]

The large number of *osodmiltsy* in rural areas is not surprising, given the lack of police presence outside the cities. In the first years of the 1930s, citizens organized voluntary policing units especially on the new collective and state farms and in areas of intense state industrial activity, such as the shantytown outskirts of larger towns and cities. The Urals and Western Siberian areas boasted the largest number of such groups, no doubt due to the significant influx of new migrants, both forced and voluntary, and the dramatic population shifts associated with industrialization, collectivization, and the arrival of large numbers of deportees and social marginals being settled or settling in these regions of the country. These were areas where regular police were spread thin, but which experienced significant in-migration and population movement.[88]

Voluntary police units took on some of the most common policing functions, such as patrolling residence, work, and recreation areas to protect against theft and hooliganism. *Osodmil* units did not have the right to arrest but could only hold individuals until regular police units arrived to make an arrest, and in the early 1930s, they also did not have the right to carry firearms. The most significant change involved abolishing what was deemed the "territorial" organizations of *osodmilty* and reorganizing units along "institutional" or enterprise lines. Police hailed this reform as a voluntary and spontaneous movement. In fact, this voluntary reorganization meant that many villages were forced to disband their only community policing forces and organize guard patrols attached to specific points of state importance. The circular outlining the change recommended that the new brigades be organized in groups of twenty in such places as machine tractor stations, grain collection points, factory shops, and other enterprises. On the other hand, voluntary brigades were also encouraged to patrol places where large numbers of people gathered, such as markets and bazaars. Police were instructed to provide minimal training for brigade members and to work closely with the brigades. And in keeping with their new status, brigade members were allowed to carry firearms issued from police armories, though these had to be turned in at the end of each shift.[89] In 1937, police recognized 350,000 members of the *brigadmiltsy* across the country.

Officially, the police welcomed the *osodmiltsy* and *brigadmiltsy* as a complementary force. Officials estimated that if such organizations were fully utilized, they would do the work of an additional 22,000 to 25,000 police officers. In a period when the RKM was stretched thin, these organizations could free the regular police from "the most routine" patrol functions to concentrate on "operational" or investigative matters. The *osodmiltsy* also provided a source of recruits and an inexpensive training school for regular officers. In Western Siberia, for example, police in 1932 hired 262 *osodmiltsy* into the district's operational units, thirty-two of them into unit leadership positions.[90] At the same time, RKM of-

ficials worried about the unsupervised vigilante activities of citizen police forces. "Despite their successful development," wrote a police officer in 1930, "many of these groups still operate without statutes (*za-
konodatel'nykh aktov*) that regulate their activities."[91] In addition,
police worried that large numbers of *osodmiltsy* did not indicate direct
popular support or enthusiasm for Soviet authority. "Many" trade
unions, for example, refused to recognize or work with these groups, especially the newly formed *brigadmiltsy,* when they organized in a factory. Unions feared that these voluntary police organizations amounted
to little more than legally sanctioned hooligan and criminal gangs. There
was probably some basis to this fear, since most *brigadmiltsy* in factories tended to be young men between the ages of eighteen and thirty.[92]
In fact, the formation of local vigilantes highlighted the weakness of the
state's civil authority. Many of the societies for cooperation with the
police organized out of necessity, because police could not protect outlying neighborhoods and farms. Even more telling, at least some farm
and factory communities refused establishment of regular *militsiia* stations, preferring to organize their own vigilante patrols. In doing so,
they saved the expenses that accompanied allocation of offices and living space for salaried police officers. Very likely, they also saved themselves the added cost of police protection in the form of bribes and kick-
backs.[93] This was cause for concern to police. As a 1932 police report
noted, local administrations often hired semi-invalids or retirees with little training as guards for warehouses and other storage and production
areas. This practice allowed farm and factory managers to use the more
physically capable in their work force for other tasks. Police officials
understood the economic motives behind these decisions, but warned
that such practices placed much of the state's property in danger of theft
or arson. To the police, such practices were an indication of the still
low priority given to the task of protecting and respecting socialist property.[94] From the point of view of the RKM, the large number of voluntary policing organizations were both a help and a hindrance in their attempt to establish Soviet authority and social order.

CONCLUSIONS

During the late 1920s and early 1930s, the Stalinist regime drove the
Soviet Union into a major economic and social revolution. Collec-

tivization and dekulakization campaigns extended Soviet power deep into a hostile countryside. Forced industrialization and destruction of market mechanisms, likewise, extended state power into the economy, transforming urban areas and creating new industrial cities. Stalin's revolution required a massive mobilization of state resources, and created social dislocation on an equally massive scale. The regime was not prepared for the social chaos that resulted from its policies. Social agencies were underdeveloped and weak. Both political and civil police were stretched thin across a large territory. The civil police, in particular, operated amid a chaotic state of affairs. Underfunded, understaffed, and underqualified, the civil police was a disorganized and corrupt institution. As it was constituted, the *militsiia* was inadequate to the task of maintaining social order and protecting state property and interests.

Political police could not fill the vacuum left by the absence of civil authority. Establishing Soviet political power throughout the country was difficult enough; maintaining Soviet order was another and ultimately more difficult task. Stalin understood that his plans for the country would require a strong policing presence, as well as harsh policies of social repression. In the late 1920s and early 1930s, he turned to Genrikh Yagoda, assistant chief of the political police, to create a centralized and unified policing system. The following chapter describes Yagoda's efforts to create such an institution.

3 A Soviet Gendarmerie

*I believed and still believe it inexpedient to transfer the police . . . to the
OGPU. . . . The merger of these organs . . . would not be consistent
with the essence of one or the other.*
—*I. Bespalov, Russian federation judicial official, November 1930*

GENRIKH YAGODA BUILT Stalin's policing system. A diminutive
and decadent man, Yagoda was, according to most characterizations,
Stalin's faithful executor.[1] He did what the great leader bid. Yet Yagoda
was intelligent and resourceful, and had a tremendous capacity for
work. As assistant head of the political police, and then as head of the
OGPU and NKVD, he built up the structures of policing and repression
that characterized the Stalinist regime. He took disparate bureaucratic
organs and forged a police empire at the center of the Stalinist state. By
the time Yagoda was removed in late 1936, he had unified under one
commissariat all civil and political policing functions and all punitive
and correctional organs. Further, he enlarged police jurisdiction to encompass major areas of social policy. Under Yagoda, the police filled the
partial vacuum created by a weak civil state. Stalin's patronage facili-
tated police expansion, of course, but heightened police power was in
no small measure also the doing of Yagoda. This chapter examines
Yagoda's takeover of the civil police, his creation of a unique kind of Soviet policing system, and his maneuverings to form a unified policing
administration under a single commissariat.

Yagoda accomplished his goal in 1934 with the creation of the all-
union Commissariat of Internal Affairs, the NKVD (*Narodnyi komissariat vnutrennikh del*). The NKVD combined the civil and political po-

lice administrations, the country's border forces, fire fighting administration, and all carceral institutions for both political and civil detainees.
Reforms transferred the OGPU wholesale into the new commissariat,
and the political police became known as the Chief Administration
for State Security (*Glavnoe upravlenie gosudarstvennoi bezopasnosti,*
GUGB). The leaders of the old OGPU became the department heads of
the new NKVD, and the GUGB dominated the commissariat.[2] The
NKVD was one of the cornerstones of Stalin's centralizing state revolution, but its existence and power were not a foregone conclusion. In
order to realize his centralizing plans, Stalin, through Yagoda, had to
break and re-create bureaucracies. This process plunged Yagoda into a
fight against powerful rival agencies, and it was also unconstitutional, as
critics noted. Centralization of police administration also ran counter to
numerous Party resolutions to decentralize administration, and it abrogated the authority of republic and local governments to control their
own internal affairs. Still, Yagoda created the Stalinist policing system in
a few short years, but he did so against resistance from powerful figures
and institutional forces.[3]

Yagoda's maneuverings not only centralized policing power. Reforms
merged the civil and political police in a way that resembled the police
gendarme system of the late tsarist era. In the Soviet context, this meant
the merging of the civil police, the *militsiia,* and the political police, the
OGPU. One of Yagoda's most impressive achievements was to transform the *militsiia* from a local and disorganized constable force into a
militarized policing system under control of the OGPU. At the same
time, changing perceptions of class war gave new direction to the political police as an organ of social control and public order. The conflation of social order and political policing, and the organizational
merger of the *militsiia* and OGPU, shaped the dynamics of repression
under Stalin. For the task of creating a unified social and political policing system, Yagoda was Stalin's man.

BACKGROUND

Throughout the 1920s, the different parts of what came to be the all-
union NKVD fell under control of several commissariats, and not even
central state administrations. The civil police, for example, was administered and largely funded by local soviets under nominal direction of

the republic-level commissariats of internal affairs. Throughout the 1920s, there was no union-level internal affairs commissariat. Prisons and other places of incarceration came under control primarily of the re-public-level commissariats of justice, although the OGPU administered a number of labor rehabilitation camps. The OGPU operated as an al-most independent agency, with authority similar to that of a commis-sariat-level administration, although it fell under direct political and ad-ministrative control of Sovnarkom, and of the Party's highest governing body, the Political Bureau (Politburo) of the Central Committee. This had not always been the case. In the early 1920s, the agency barely sur-vived an attack on its existence. After the end of the revolutionary and civil wars, in 1921 and 1922, powerful officials, led by Nikolai Bu-kharin and the finance commissar, Georgii Sokol'nikov, argued that an extraordinary secret police agency was no longer needed and could no longer be justified in the new socialist republic. During the revolution-ary and civil war period, 1917–22, the political police was known as the Cheka, an acronym for the Extraordinary Commission to Combat Counterrevolution and Sabotage. The defeat of the revolution's enemies gave the agency no further function, according to its critics. In 1922 and again in 1924, Sokol'nikov and Bukharin proposed cutting the agency's funding and personnel.[4]

In response to critics, Cheka leaders redefined the agency's name, image, and *raison d'être*. Re-creating the agency in a new guise was the doing primarily of Feliks Dzerzhinskii, first head of the Cheka and OGPU, and his deputy Iosif Unshlikht. Unshlikht, especially, played a key role in refashioning and strengthening the Cheka into what became known in 1922 as the State Political Administration, the GPU, and after 1923 as the Unified or Combined State Political Administration, the OGPU.[5] Unshlikht understood that the OGPU was no longer needed as a semimilitary organ of counterinsurgency, and he defended the role of the new OGPU as a political police protecting leaders and state se-curity. As a political police, the OGPU was to continue to fight the regime's political enemies, but it was also to operate as a social surveil-lance agency, gathering information about attitudes of different seg-ments of the general population, the intelligentsia, and the state bu-reaucracies.[6] At the same time, and in a significant development, OGPU leaders were also able to extend the role of the agency in defending the new Soviet social order. Against opposition from critics such as commissar of justice Dmitrii Kurskii, the OGPU gained jurisdiction over the fight against criminal banditry. OGPU officials argued that banditry shaded easily over into political opposition and outright insurgency. Banditry, therefore, presented a political as well as a social threat to Soviet order and should be dealt with by the political police. On a more practical level, officials noted that, having experience as a counterinsurgency organization, the OGPU was better prepared to confront bandit gangs that were heavily armed and contained, sometimes, dozens of members.[7]

Dzerzhinskii and Unshlikht successfully asserted the agency's jurisdiction over other categories of nonpolitical criminals. These included recidivists, "dangerous" speculators, and smugglers. As in the 1930s, so in the early 1920s, OGPU leaders argued successfully that recidivist criminals were socially dangerous and should fall under authority of the political police. This latter was an important point. During the 1920s, the OGPU fought for and gained control over what were described as socially dangerous individuals. The definition of a dangerous individual could be interpreted broadly, but in practice, it often meant unemployed and criminal segments of the population, especially individuals with more than two judicial convictions.[8]

Bringing civil criminals under jurisdiction of the political police required a change in the penal code, which involved a protracted fight with the Commissariat of Justice and the Russian republic's Commissariat of Internal Affairs, the NKVD RSFSR.[9] The OGPU won that fight and, in doing so, gained more than just the power to arrest. In addition, the OGPU regained the right, once belonging only to the Cheka, to sentence those under its jurisdiction by administrative sentencing boards that operated outside the judicial system, the troikas, which were not subject to the same evidentiary rules and rights of trial and defense as in a judicial hearing. The Cheka had used troikas ruthlessly and extensively during the revolutionary war years, and the image of the troika as a summary form of justice carried over into the 1920s. The sentencing authority of OGPU troikas was less during the 1920s than that wielded by those of the Cheka. During the 1920s, for example, OGPU troikas did not hear political cases, which were adjudicated by the OGPU's highest sentencing board, the *Osoboe soveshchanie*. Moreover, troikas did not have the right to pass death sentences, except in cases of banditry and certain types of armed robbery. Still, troikas possessed

considerable clout, including the right of administrative exile of criminals. The OGPU troikas of the 1920s passed sentences on several thousand people yearly during the middle and late years of the decade.[10]

Transformation of the Cheka into the OGPU secured its continued
existence, and not only as an agency to fight political opposition. By the
mid-1920s, OGPU leaders had managed to transform the agency from
a supposedly temporary organ of revolutionary justice into a permanent state institution with authority to defend public order as well as the
political security of the state. The ability of OGPU leaders to extend the
agency's jurisdiction into areas of civil order marked a turning point in
the history of the political police. This development opened the door to
the eventual abolition of the RSFSR NKVD in 1930 and the transfer of
its responsibilities to the OGPU.[11] These events also foreshadowed and
justified the much broader extension of OGPU authority in the 1930s.

The new policing functions of the OGPU created overlap with the republic-level NKVD organs, and with judicial administrations in the various republics. Predictably, overlapping functions gave rise to constant
tension and jurisdictional disputes. Conflicts arose particularly over social policing and punitive functions under authority of the NKVD. In
the Russian federation, the largest republic, these conflicts pitted Yagoda, as assistant head of the OGPU after 1926, against Vladimir Tolmachev, the head of the Russian NKVD. Throughout the 1920s, Yagoda and Tolmachev sparred with each other in a kind of bureaucratic
guerilla warfare, in which Yagoda sought to chip away at the jurisdictional authority of the NKVD, and to extend the operational purview
of the OGPU.

As Yagoda and Tolmachev fought over jurisdictional authority, Tolmachev wrestled with the unique problems of administering the NKVD.
The commissariat was miserably underfunded, and this affected its ability to administer the diverse areas over which it had nominal authority.
The condition of the *militsiia* was particularly bad. Due to a lack of
money, there was almost no central coordination of policies, operational standards, or training. Money for uniforms or offices was almost
out of the question, let alone funding for weapons or professional police training. Numbers were abysmally low, as noted in the previous
chapter.[12] Yet such disorganization was not just the result of under-
funding, neglect, or poor management; it also resulted from the revolutionary restructuring of the police after the civil war, and in reaction

to the organization of policing during the tsarist period. The tsarist political police, the *Otdel'nyi korpus zhandarmov,* operated as a classic nineteenth-century European gendarmerie, a policing force organized around military rank and discipline. Prior to reforms in the 1880s, the *Korpus zhandarmov* operated as an administration separate from the civil police. Reforms in the 1880s folded the *Korpus zhandarmov* into a general Department of Police, *Departament politsii,* which also incorporated the civil police. Both the civil and political police came under the jurisdiction of the newly created interior ministry, the head of which was also the head of the *Korpus zhandarmov.* In effect, the civil police became subordinate to the political police administratively and operationally. In the first decade of the twentieth century, the *Korpus zhandarmov* was transformed into what became known as the *Osobyi otdel* (Special Department) of the interior ministry. The name not only foreshadowed the name used for parts of the later Soviet apparatus, but the tsarist political police also gained the right to exile criminal and political suspects through an administrative court, operated by the *Korpus zhandarmov* and then the *Osobyi otdel,* called the *Osoboe soveshchanie.* This arrangement carried over into the Soviet period. The Soviet version of the *Osoboe soveshchanie* became, in the 1930s, especially, the primary means by which the OGPU exercised its judicial authority.[13]

After 1917, Feliks Dzerzhinskii preserved the tsarist organization of policing during the revolutionary war period, and this included control over civil policing and administrative arrest and sentencing of criminals as well as political oppositionists. With the advent of the New Economic Policy, however, some Soviet officials argued that the coercive organ of the political police should not be included within the system of socialist state building, and should under no circumstances have any ties to forces of public order such as the civil police. In 1922, VTsIK forced a separation of the civil police administration from the OGPU, placing it under the nominal administration of the Russian NKVD. At the same time, the government won a fight with the OGPU to transfer budgetary and operational control of the *militsiia* to local Soviet organs of power. The government stripped the OGPU of jurisdiction over statutory crimes and limited its administrative authority only to clearly defined cases of political opposition.[14]

By design, then, revolutionary reforms established the civil police, the *militsiia,* as a kind of local constable force rather than as a national policing system. The *militsiia* in the new Soviet republic worked in some ways like the British policing system that had developed in the late nineteenth and twentieth centuries. Local constables, *militsionery* in Russian, kept the civil peace. They adjudicated disputes and had only limited authority in criminal matters. The latter involved mainly an initial incident report of a crime. During the 1920s, *militsiia* officials were to have no part in political policing. Criminal investigations were conducted by the *ugolovnyi rozysk,* the state's criminal investigation organ, akin to the famed CID, the Criminal Investigation Division, of Britain. Like the CID, the *ugolovnyi rozysk* was an independent organ, not connected to the *militsiia,* but was also administered under the internal affairs commissariats of the different republics.

Decentralization of control and separation of political and civil policing, government officials claimed, was a democratic revolutionary response to the centralized and militarized policing system of the tsarist and early revolutionary eras. It also represented, no doubt, the high point of Soviet civil power. From 1922 forward, the reencroachment of the OGPU on Soviet authority continued apace, sometimes slowly, sometimes rapidly. The political police, still under Dzerzhinzkii's leadership, reasserted its authority already in 1923 and 1924 and, by the mid-1920s, had recast itself as an important bulwark of both state security and social order. OGPU leaders further asserted the agency's authority during the mid- and late 1920s, after Dzerzhinskii's death, when the OGPU came under leadership of V. R. Menzhinskii and his deputy, Yagoda. Yagoda was as aggressive as Unshlikht in his advocacy of OGPU authority. By 1928 and 1929, Yagoda, as well as others, called openly for subordinating the civil police and the *ugolovnyi rozysk* to OGPU control, as well as all prison and camp inmates in the country.[15]

Yagoda's proposals were, of course, motivated by political and bureaucratic ambition, but they carried all the more weight since they pointed up major problems. Reviews by several agencies, and even by the Russian NKVD itself, recognized that, by the late 1920s, civil policing in the country was in disarray. Decentralizing reforms may have been motivated by principles of democratic socialism, but they brought chaotic consequences. The Soviet government was never wealthy, but local soviets, in particular, operated in constant and dire financial straights. As a result, financial decentralization followed administrative decentralization and made for an impoverished policing system throughout the country. Moreover, apart from the low wages, lower public esteem, and inadequate training of the civil police, the NKVD either failed or refused to coordinate the welter of local practices. By the late 1920s, ranks, duties, and compensation varied considerably from locality to locality.[16] Worse yet, under control of local soviets, police inspectors found themselves burdened with a number of tasks not directly related to fighting crime or defending public order. Police duties included chasing errant cows, chickens, and other livestock. Police were mobilized to check tickets on local trains and settle disputes between neighbors. Constantly short of political propaganda instructors, local soviets often pressed police into the business of touring village meetings and explaining Party-government policies. Tolmachev complained that, in 1928, the NKVD received over 30,000 requests for non–police-related investigations, the largest single number of these, nearly 17,400, from the justice commissariat. In the half-year period from July through December of the same year, Tolmachev claimed that rural police, the most thinly stretched line of social defense, received 171,422 nonpolice calls from local soviets, and this was just in the central Black Earth region of Russia.[17]

Despite these kinds of complaints, Tolmachev continued to defend the local organization of policing. If Yagoda called for centralization of police administration, Tolmachev called for more decentralization. In 1927, Tolmachev proposed a complete separation of the NKVD from local policing, putting the latter under administrative and financial control of local soviets. As part of a citizen's police force, Tolmachev recommended a kind of police draft, in which professional police would be replaced by ordinary citizens selected, or drafted, for a two-year period to act as bailiffs (*ispolniteli*) in the areas where they worked and lived.[18] Such a proposal may have been motivated by practical realization of the NKVD's dismal lack of funding, but it was consistent with the original intent of government decrees about socialist construction and withering of the state. Tolmachev's proposal also followed specifically from Party decisions, taken at the Fifteenth Congress, to centralize planning within the state, but to decentralize administration. Tolmachev duly responded with his plans for police administration to fit this model.

Tolmachev's proposals opened the door for others to push through. A 1928 review by the Russian federation's inspectorate agency, Rabkrin, went still further. That report called for the near complete abolition of the NKVD, folding the NKVD's police and investigative administration into a single agency under jurisdiction of the justice commissariat.[19] Rabkrin's recommendations did not cede police or prisoner control to the OGPU, but the agency's criticism of the NKVD was an ominous sign. Such criticism became increasingly public and increasingly political in 1929 and 1930, and included open calls, from the Russian republic Rabkrin among others, for liquidation of the NKVD. In January 1930, however, in a turnabout from 1928, another Rabkrin report recommended that the OGPU take over all policing and criminal investigative functions from the NKVD.[20] This contradiction in proposals was not surprising. Until 1929, revolutionary socialists, such as Aron Sol'ts, still worked in the Russian Rabkrin, and still conducted their reviews with an eye toward Rabkrin's original charge—to reduce bureaucratism, corruption, and overcentralization within the government system. Increasingly, however, the Rabkrin system became politicized as Stalin's primary institutional weapon to undermine and take over control of key state sectors. Since 1926, the all-union Rabkrin was headed by Stalin's close ally, Sergo Ordzhonikidze, who replaced department heads and heads of important republic-level bureaus, and who initiated a series of major investigations of state agencies in 1929 and 1930. Rabkrin targeted major administrative levels of the state, found them woefully wanting and, using its authority, pushed through what usually amounted to centralizing reorganizations. Administrative restructuring often combined agencies and brought them under control of Stalinist appointees. Beginning already in 1928, and certainly by 1930, Rabkrin's investigations had become a highly politicized instrument by which Stalin secured control over the state apparatus. The 1930 report fit this pattern, focusing on political problems as well as issues of bureaucratic division of labor. Rabkrin's criticism of the NKVD's "soft" line toward criminals, prisoners, and anti-Soviet elements provided ammunition to Stalinists in the increasingly charged political atmosphere of the late 1920s.[21]

Rabkrin's recommendations echoed other criticisms. In another blow to the NKVD, an interagency commission recommended in June 1929 to transfer all convicts serving long-term sentences (over three years) from NKVD to OGPU jurisdiction.[22] Stalin endorsed this resolution, since he needed labor for construction projects, and specifically, for plans to build the Baltic–White Sea canal. At first, the Politburo accepted this proposal, but Tolmachev, acting in concert with Sovnarkom, was able to have the decision reversed. In doing so, the NKVD leader worked closely with A. I. Rykov, then still head of Sovnarkom, and one of the most outspoken critics of Stalin's industrialization plans. In late August, Sovnarkom, acting for the government, rejected the transfer of prisoners, as did the RSFSR Sovnarkom, then under the chairmanship of S. I. Syrtsov who also opposed Stalin on a number of Party and economic issues.[23] Stalin saw political conspiracy in this opposition to his economic plans. In a September letter to Molotov, Stalin described efforts to thwart his plans as "criminal." Stalin made clear his belief that the NKVD stood in the way of his goals, especially for OGPU control over forced labor prisoners. He expressed his view that Tolmachev and his commissariat were tainted by association with the Party faction that had resisted class war in the countryside and rapid industrialization. Stalin recommended to Molotov that it was time, finally, to dismantle the NKVD.[24]

TAKEOVER OF THE POLICE

The NKVD was rapidly losing its battle with the political police now, and the reasons for this were clear. The NKVD and the OGPU engaged in bureaucratic fights throughout the 1920s, with the justice commissariat often joining the fray over issues of incarceration and control of the country's custodial populations. While Yagoda often won battles against the NKVD, neither he personally nor the OGPU as an institution was sufficiently strong enough to achieve the ultimate goal of eliminating its bureaucratic rival. This gradual war of attrition entered a decisive phase when Stalin took a direct interest in policing matters. In 1929 and 1930, Stalin turned his attention to the task of constructing the kind of police system that he believed would be necessary to achieve his goals. Given his decision to push the country into rapid industrialization and forced collectivization, and to eliminate private market forces, the Soviet dictator anticipated a significant expansion in the country's forced labor population, and wanted to ensure that this population came under OGPU administration. Stalin also understood that he needed a reliable and effective police system to suppress anticipated resistance to his plans for radical restructuring of the economy. The NKVD's inefficiency, its limited jurisdiction, and its resistance to mass-based forms of repression all put the commissariat at odds with the leader's aims.[25]

Events moved rapidly after Stalin's letter to Molotov. In October 1930, Stalin and Molotov pressured the Politburo to endorse, again, the June resolution to transfer convicts to the OGPU. Then, in November, the Politburo took a secret decision to liquidate the Russian NKVD by the end of 1931. In the liquidation process, the various parts of the NKVD's empire were carved up and meted out to its two rival agencies. Administration of prisons fell to the justice commissariat, Narkomiust', while the newly established labor camp and settlements system went to the OGPU. At the same session, and also as part of the secret protocol, Politburo members appointed a commission to detail arrangements for transfer of leadership (*rukovodstvo*) of the *militsiia* and the *ugolovnyi rozysk* to the OGPU.[26] A Sovnarkom resolution of 15 December publicly established the civil police, the RKM, as an independent organization, but another secret protocol of the same date laid out the particulars of transfer to control by the political police.

The transfer was an odd and confusing arrangement, and typical of the welter of overlapping and conflicting administrative arrangements under Stalin's rule. According to the Party's secret protocol, police administrations were to remain formally under administration of the republic-level Sovnarkoms. Thus, police administration remained, nominally anyway, decentralized and part of the Soviet government. Local *militsiia* and *ugolovnyi rozysk* organs were officially subordinated to corresponding executive committees of the soviets. Operationally, however, they were "to conduct work under the direction of local OGPU organs."[27] In order to coordinate OGPU operational control, a Chief Inspectorate of Police (*Glavnaia inspektsiia militsii* or GIM) was to be established by the OGPU, and the work of local police administrations was to be directed by special OGPU plenipotentiaries, who answered to this new inspectorate. Plenipotentiary and inspectorate officials were to be regular OGPU officers assigned to oblast and *krai* level police organs. They were charged to bring police practice into line with and up to the standards of the OGPU. They were to oversee purging of undesirable elements in the police, raise professional levels of work, and instill a "Chekist" attitude in police toward their work and in their service to protect the state—that is, one of vigilance and just ruthlessness as supposedly possessed by the revolutionary-era Cheka. Most important, OGPU officers controlled key personnel decisions. Hiring and firing of staff was still to be carried out by local soviets, but in accordance with OGPU recommendations. As George Lin, the chronicler of the Russian NKVD, has written, "the government's liquidation resolution . . . was merely an official cover-up for an OGPU seizure of the police."[28] Nominally, then, civil police still operated under direction of the Soviet government and its local councils. Secretly, the *militsiia* was incorporated into Yagoda's growing police empire.

Why did the government set up such a strange set of conflicting competencies? Lin has argued that the secret nature of the OGPU's control over civil police reflected leaders' perception of public sensitivity to such an arrangement.[29] This is no doubt true, since political police control over civil police recapitulated to an uncanny degree the subordination of the imperial Russian civil police to the gendarmerie. In fact, the similarities became even more striking in the coming years, so much so that it is difficult to escape the conclusion that Yagoda & Co. looked back consciously to the imperial policing system for a model on which to build the Soviet police apparatus. The dual relationship that Stalin hit upon preserved the pretense of control by local soviets, while placing the political police in ultimate authority over the *militsiia*.[30] Yet the argument of public sensitivity, even of the leadership's embarrassment, only goes so far as an explanation. OGPU control over the police may have been written into secret regulations, but the administrative apparatus of control soon became apparent to all. It was an arrangement that could not be kept secret. The arrangement may have resulted, in part, simply from Stalinist leaders' penchant for conspiracy and secretiveness in any matters relating to the OGPU. But a major reason may also have been money. At a time when central state budgets were already under severe strain due to industrial expenditures, Stalin may not have wanted the added burden of central financing of police. The December 1930 arrangement called for raising police wages and rationing levels to those of the OGPU and the military, but this stipulation amounted to nothing more than wishful thinking. Civil police financing remained under local budgets, impoverished as they were, at least for the period of the state's budgetary crisis in 1930 and 1931.

CHEKIST IN SPIRIT AND METHOD

OGPU officials lost no time in trying to consolidate their hold over the *militsiia*, despite the formal and nominal administrative subordina-

tion of civil police to the local soviets. In pursuit of their goal, high police officials promoted a very different idea of policing from that which
had previously governed the work of civil constables. Already in 1931,
D. V. Usov, the newly appointed assistant head of GIM, put forward an
aggressive program for the new police. The goal of OGPU control, according to Usov, was to effect a complete transformation of the *militsiia*
from its "condition of apolitical inertness" into a "fighting organization" for the "construction of socialism and defense of revolutionary
order." In Usov's conception, the *militsiia* should be a main "pillar of
support" of Soviet power, sharing on every level in the "fighting spirit,
professionalism, and operational tempo" of the OGPU.[31] The function
of the policeman, according to Usov, was not just "to wave a baton
around," but actively to root out crime, impose public order, and protect state interests and property.

Hyperbole aside, questions arose about what exactly these words
meant and where, in particular, the line between civil and political policing was to be drawn. In remarks to OGPU police inspectors in May
1931, Usov was careful to distinguish the functions of the civil from
those of the political police. The *militsiia* was to remain primarily a
crime-fighting organization and not a political police, but in addition to
gaining new arrest and investigative powers, the *militsiia* needed to "operationalize" its work in the same manner as the Cheka. Toward this
end, Usov made an unequivocal argument for merging the criminal investigative apparatus into the civil police administration. This new combined agency was to have close working ties to the OGPU, in terms of
both passing on information and employing professionalized methods
of work. But herein lay a gray area. As Usov acknowledged, criminal activity often merged into political and anti-Soviet opposition. This was
especially true in the current stage of Soviet development, according to
Usov, and he cited the well-known litany of banditry, economic crimes,
and industrial wrecking as examples of overlap. It was inevitable, then,
that this overlap of crime and political opposition entailed an overlap
of civil and political policing.

The fight against certain types of criminality was not the only area of
overlap that Usov had in mind. Usov also discussed the problem of social monitoring, and the role that civil police were to play in that sphere.
This kind of overlap was not so much a problem in urban areas, according to Usov, where the OGPU had a well-established presence, but

rural areas presented a different problem. There, on the "periphery," as he described it, the OGPU was not strong. Potentially, local police had a much more widespread organization, despite the current deficits in personnel. It was precisely in rural and peripheral areas that the lack of OGPU presence necessitated local police networks to operate as an extension of the OGPU, fulfilling the functions of social surveillance and fighting political as well as statutory crime.[32]

Here, then, was an important aspect of what Usov meant by his call to "operationalize" police work along OGPU lines. For Usov, the operational basis of all Cheka work was, as he repeated often, the gathering of information, *osvedomlenie,* or surveillance.[33] Police were to gain enhanced authority to investigate crimes, and even act against criminals, but one of the main tasks of the new *militsiia* was also to act as an organ of social surveillance. Through daily contact with the population, police officials acted as a filter for information to use in their own investigative work, but to pass on to the OGPU. How, exactly, this was supposed to work is discussed in the next chapters, but it is important to note here that Usov laid out this social function of the police already in 1931.

In its current form, Usov lamented, the structure and culture of the *militsiia* were simply not up to this task, especially in peripheral areas, where the OGPU most needed the *militsiia.* The local ties of the police —to family, friends, and even the criminal world—were a particular problem, given the new role that Usov envisioned for the *militsiia.* In a remarkably candid aside, Usov regretted that Soviet police could not replicate tsarist practice, namely to resettle soldiers and gendarmes to areas far removed from their home villages. Due to labor shortages in industry, the police could not even draw recruits from urban workers to work in rural areas.[34] Usov approved the widespread purge carried out in 1930 and 1931 of supposedly alien, criminal, and other anti-Soviet elements in the police, thereby implying that one of the functions of the purge was to "sever" the community ties of local police.[35] Yet Usov pointed out that local police were still too much intertwined with the "alien" social milieu. Here was the logic of euphemism, in which "alien" meant "local." However, the task of separating the *militsioner* from such "alien" ties could not really be solved "mechanically" or "surgically" by police resettlement; it required a change in mentality and police culture. Therein lay the main problem. Usov depicted the ordinary *militsioner* stereotypically as still a peasant "just arrived from the village, the countryside." That kind of policeman, Usov declared, "has no political understanding, no sense of what is going on around him. They give him a baton, fifteen minutes of instruction, and say 'go to work.'" Usov contrasted this lack of professional instruction with the supposed years of specialized training that police received in capitalist countries.[36]

Usov's comments highlight the kind of Soviet gendarmerie that he and Yagoda envisioned. It was a vision of policing and state structure very much in contrast to the 1920s democratic ideal of organic ties to the community and the working population. On the contrary, both Usov and Yagoda demanded further professionalization, separation from social milieu, and operational secretiveness. And what of the function of police to protect civic rights and individual property, asked one of Usov's listeners at the 1931 OGPU conference? Usov's answer was circuitous but his meaning was clear. He declared that "in a whole series of localities, during dekulakization, some police officials, adhering to the idea that they should protect citizens' rights, failed to understand [dekulakization] policy." Local police had too often sided or at least sympathized with their neighbors against the harsh policies of collectivization. In the immediate future, Usov stated, the protection of state interests was to take precedence over the private rights of citizens.[37]

This single comment showed that the OGPU takeover of the police was more than just a matter of Yagoda's personal ambition, bureaucratic colonization, or bureaucratic efficiency. Usov could not have been more blunt in identifying the new role that leaders envisioned for the police as a state gendarmerie rather than as a community-based constable force. And despite his pessimism about the current state of police, Usov looked forward to this new gendarmerie as a highly trained, professionalized force. This was to be a policing force created through military-style training and discipline, and fully utilizing the latest operational methods of the OGPU. All this would require long-term training, but Usov noted that the most immediate plan to raise the professional level of police would involve a projected transfer of large numbers of OGPU personnel to work in command positions in the *militsiia*. In a further move to professionalize and integrate police, a 1931 directive ordered that all police cadre departments were to be transferred to administrative supervision by the OGPU. It took only a few months, then, after the secret incorporation of the civil police for the OGPU to abandon completely the pretense of local soviet control. Henceforward, civil police appointments were controlled by the political police.[38]

OPPOSITION

Such blatant Chekaization of the police provoked concern among a number of officials, and brought the police into direct conflict with procuracy and judicial agencies at all levels of the state system. Usov acknowledged the "sharp and open antagonism" that his proposals provoked, especially among officials in the justice commissariat. While he did not mention names, Usov very likely referred to the outspoken criticisms raised by N. Krylenko, the then Russian federation justice minister.[39] Responding to Usov's proposed guidelines, Krylenko expressed alarm that these proposed reforms threatened to turn the police into an independent investigative body, unaccountable either to local governments or to the state's procuracy system. Referring to the police's new investigative role, Krylenko wrote to Sovnarkom in September 1931, "Not one policeman works this way." Krylenko objected strenuously to appointment of police officials by the OGPU from above, rather than through election by local soviets. He reiterated the point that civil police officials, like all Soviet officials, were to be elected and were to be responsible to local authorities. He complained that police reforms, in general, violated a number of Russian republic laws and, most serious of all, that the OGPU had not consulted the Commissariat of Justice when establishing new administrative and operational guidelines for the police.[40]

Krylenko understood that the OGPU grab for the police involved more than a bureaucratic power game. As Krylenko pointed out, civil police subordination to the OGPU involved a fundamental threat to the Soviet constitutional state, and he was not alone in this view. An unsolicited letter from a Russian republic procuracy official, a certain I. Bespalov, articulated the same concern. Writing to one of Rabkrin's central officials, V. Ia. Grossman, in 1930, Bespalov added the following comment to a memorandum on an unrelated matter:

> I consider it necessary to underscore in written form that I regarded, and still regard it, inexpedient to transfer the police, places of confinement, and the apparatus for organizing forced labor to the OGPU. . . .

> [T]he OGPU is an organ for fighting especially dangerous social ele-
> ments, using specific methods, while the police and the administration
> of places of confinement are organs of broad mass influence (*shirokogo
> massovogo deistviia*), which use completely different methods of work,
> the main element of which involves broad social participation. The
> merger of these organs may result in changes to the character of the
> OGPU, or lead to the transfer of methods of the OGPU to the above-
> named organs, and this would not be consistent with the essence of one
> or the other organization.[41]

This was an extraordinary statement for several reasons. Bespalov made
this statement unsolicited, therefore giving it all the more the force of
conviction. Bespalov's comment also reflects his belief that Rabkrin was
one of the agencies behind the merger of the police and the OGPU, since
he clearly was addressing his comments, or so he thought, to someone
who he believed carried some authority in the matter. Bespalov still ad-
hered to the 1920s idea that the political police did not belong within
the civil state. The *militsiia* and rehabilitative institutions, by contrast,
were somehow still supposed to be part of a state engaged in socialist
construction, with broad public participation and accountability, and
this distinguished them from the secretive and punitive tasks of political policing. What Bespalov feared, as he wrote, was that the methods
of secretiveness and administrative political repression employed by the
political police would infect a public constable force under control of
that same political police. Bespalov worried that the *militsiia* would be
transformed into an organ of social repression instead of a local organization to protect revolutionary legality.[42]

Such criticism, while astute, carried no weight. Yagoda and the
OGPU lost no time in trying to subordinate the civil police. Yagoda,
Usov, and other OGPU leaders ignored the administrative fig leaf of Soviet authority, and insisted on strict hierarchical and professional subordination of police only to higher police authority and, ultimately, to
the OGPU. Occasionally, regional police reports included sections on
"community participation," but Yagoda never felt compelled to maintain the pretense of either Soviet or social accountability.[43] After the
OGPU takeover of the *militsiia,* Yagoda's yearly reports about police activities dropped any reference to community—*obshchestvennost'*—except in discussing the police-organized activities of the civilian vigilante
groups—the *osodmiltsy.*

Yagoda concurred in Usov's sense of urgency about transforming the *militsiia* into a militarized force, and he agreed that the *militsiia* should work in the "very spirit" and using the investigative methods of Chekists. At the same time, the secret policeman also cautioned against full Chekaization, as the process of militarization came to be called. Yagoda recognized the continuing constable function of the *militsiia* to uphold civil laws, distinct from the tasks of the political police, to uproot political enemies, protect state interests, and to wage class war. While Yagoda desired complete administrative subordination of the civil police, he still believed in maintaining functional and operational differences between the RKM and the OGPU. The police, in his conception, was to work as an auxiliary force to the OGPU in the establishment of social discipline and the protection of state interests and property. His conception of the *militsiia,* as he noted in late 1930, was of an organ of Soviet power somewhere "in the middle between the Chekist and the civil population (*grazhdanskoe naselenie*)."[44]

IN THE MIDDLE

In the middle was where police officials found themselves. Whatever the reasons for the new police arrangements—political, financial, bureaucratic—those arrangements left the *militsiia* sitting between two stools, precisely in-between and in limbo, neither one thing nor the other. One of the goals of the OGPU takeover, for example, was to militarize the police in order to raise operational, living, and disciplinary standards. Yet the conflicting administrative jurisdictions of 1931 and 1932 left police subject only to partial military jurisdiction. Police officials fell under military courts only for certain criminal offenses associated with operational and financial matters relating to professional duties. Other criminal actions were subject to civil courts.[45] At the same time, even though police supposedly came under military regulations, they were nonetheless allowed membership in the professional unions (whose protection was admittedly nominal). Worst of all for police, militarization did not affect budgetary allocations or salaries. Funding for most police remained under the constantly bankrupt budgets of district- and local-level soviets. Neither wages nor numbers rose significantly for at least a couple of years. As a disgruntled Yagoda noted, after transfer of police to OGPU control, his request for an immediate increase in *mi-*

litsiia numbers was refused on financial grounds.[46] Indeed, the situation was so confusing that in one draft of the police guidelines from 1931, Sovnarkom officials first included then struck the word "militarized" (*voennizirovannyi*) in describing the police as "an [a militarized] administrative organ of state power."[47]

Reforms of the RKM made clear Yagoda's intention to turn the police into an organ of social control, subordinate to the organs of state security, but if initial administrative confusion made this goal difficult to achieve, so did resistance from both political and civilian police organizations. OGPU officials were not pleased to find themselves assigned to work with *militsiia* organs. Likewise, officials in the RKM were ill disposed toward the kinds of tasks assigned them, especially during the policing campaigns in the countryside in the early 1930s. On top of this, local soviets continued, despite Yagoda's repeated protestations, to press civil police into traditional kinds of public and local government service.

Many OGPU officers looked on work with the RKM as either plenipotentiaries or as precinct inspectors as unworthy of a real Chekist and as a career dead end. Leaders attempted to counter this impression, insisting that assignment to the *militsiia* was an especially important operational task, and that control over the *militsiia* was one of the most important charges given to the OGPU by the government. At the same time, they acknowledged that OGPU commanders in fact used RKM assignments as an opportunity to rid themselves of incompetent and trouble-making subordinates, as well as ones with health problems and physical handicaps.[48]

OGPU overseers had good reason to worry about the reliability of the civil police as both a crime-fighting organization and as an organization "for the protection of state interests." OGPU officials distrusted the police because of the low level of police training and the large numbers of socially alien personnel within police ranks. Most important, OGPU officials were wary of working with police, partly because of the latter's traditionally strong local ties, personally and administratively, and, relatedly, because of extensive involvement of police with local criminal groups. For these reasons, and despite widespread purges, OGPU leaders were cautious about relying on local police during the massive dekulakization and collectivization drives of the early 1930s.[49] In fact, reports by Rabkrin noted that, in a number of regions, local authorities (including police and Party officials) resisted OGPU dekulakization operations.[50] Hence, OGPU leaders were particularly sensitive to the issue of police attitudes toward their new role, and they solicited frequent assessments from local inspectors on a range of issues dealing with police reorganization and operation.

A lengthy report from Western Siberia confirmed Usov's less than optimistic conclusion about police preparedness for new tasks. "The intensification of class war," wrote the head of the Western Siberian RKM in late 1931, "associated with the decisive attack against capitalist elements . . . has placed before the *militsiia* a heightened responsibility to defend and strengthen revolutionary order and public safety . . . and [to act as] an armed organ of the proletarian dictatorship." Unfortunately, concluded, the report, the police was not yet a capable force. This was due in large part to the continued lack of clarity about what the police was supposed to do. Lines of authority remained unclear and OGPU officials could not exercise full authority over police. Police received conflicting orders from above and from organs of local government. In addition, the poor work and material condition of police made it nearly impossible to maintain a stable force. Most telling, local police did not yet "feel" the Chekist spirit and discipline. The latter was expressed particularly in the continued "saturation" of police by supposedly "criminal and corrupt elements," and by local officials who were "too close to the alien element." All of this made for conditions of massive turnover and a serious breakdown in discipline. While police forces were certainly rife with criminality, the phrasing "too close to alien elements" was also bureaucratic code acknowledging what Usov also acknowledged—that local police officials were not prepared to carry out state policies of repression against local populations; they were not yet ready for their new role as part of a state gendarmerie.[51]

Numerous reports confirmed local police reluctance to participate in mass dekulakization campaigns. The same Western Siberian report cited above noted what it described as a "lack of initiative" by regional police to register and officially file criminal charges against peasants who had resisted collectivization, or who had failed to render sufficient grain amounts to fulfill state quotas. When they did bring charges, local police officials "did not always take the necessary class approach," meaning that they filed statutory criminal charges, but without the accompanying political charges. In numerous regions, local soviets and Party organizations had to take the initiative to arrest supposed kulaks for class sabotage of agricultural campaigns or of collectivization. Most disturbing of all, in "several" regions, police with family or personal ties to "counterrevolutionary elements" could not be trusted. As often as not, they sided openly with "anti-Soviet elements," in some regions arresting local officials rather than kulaks for criminal violations.[52]

Collectivization and dekulakization involved civil police in a number of new activities. One of the most draining and time-consuming tasks for the OGPU was the massive amount of manpower required to carry out deportations of tens and hundreds of thousands of peasants—to round them up, collect livestock and private possessions, get them loaded on trains and other transport, and then accompany deportees to the points of exile. As a result, OGPU officials hoped that many of these tasks could be turned over to local police. Police had experience in such matters going back to the 1920s, but only with court-convicted criminals, not administrative exiles. Thus, they had no experience in mass deportations, nor did they have experience in the direct political repression of the population. OGPU officials watched closely to see how police handled these new responsibilities.

In Western Siberia, the first two mass deportation operations carried out by civil police took place in autumn, 1931. The operations involved some 285,600 deportees, nearly 5,000 head of cattle, 11,000 horses, 1,800 cows, 2,200 sheep, 7,000 plows, and 15,000 carts. Slightly more than 1,000 police were mobilized for gathering, guarding, and transport duties.[53] They conducted the operations under OGPU supervision and, according to the Western Siberian OGPU police plenipotentiary, the operations went fairly well, all things considered. In general, police officials carried out the operations "without violating the . . . basic class political line, and without violating their basic punitive functions." This was an odd phrasing, written in the negative, as if the assumption was just the opposite. Indeed, the assumption was that policemen would not fulfill their duty with the requisite "Chekist spirit," and the inspector duly cataloged instances that revealed his lack of trust in the class vigilance of police. There was, for example, the police inspector who, because of "close ties to several of the local kulak deportees," allowed an entire contingent to escape its transport. Another local inspector violated basic political vigilance by transporting letters back to family members from exiled kulaks whom he accompanied to their colonies in the north. This was bad enough, but later operations revealed that these letters contained "inflammatory invective" against Soviet power, inciting others to engage in direct "counterrevolutionary resistance" to collectivization.[54]

It is difficult to know how widespread police resistance was, whether disturbing incidents cited by the OGPU resulted from conscious opposition or simple ignorance. Indeed, such information may well have been motivated by an unconscious desire to supply what plenipotentiaries believed their superiors expected to hear. Later reports seem to confirm this. In late 1931, OGPU officials again found disturbing signs of police reluctance, yet one year later, after the regime's crackdown on excesses by local officials, they found evidence of police overzealousness. In late 1932, an OGPU review of police found it "unacceptable" that local police administrations participated in outright coercive measures against peasants—forcing them to work in the fields, and searching peasants' huts for hidden grain.[55] Whatever the case, there appears to be sufficient evidence to believe that many police officials, for various reasons, were reluctant to take on their new roles. By the mid-1930s and later, police attitudes changed, and police officials fully participated in campaigns of social repression. In the first years of the decade, however, given the halfway conditions of takeover, the OGPU experienced difficulty in exerting control over police administrations.

Full subordination of police occurred only, and finally, in late December 1932, with formation of an all-union chief administration, the *Glavnoe Upravlenie Raboche-kres'tianskoi Militsii or* GURKM. Interestingly, the GURKM came into being as the all-union police administration responsible for introducing and enforcing the new system of nationwide internal passports and residence registration. Creation of the passport system and formation of the GURKM went hand in hand and marked a major step in the Stalinist regime's movement toward centralized policing and governance. The subordination of the civil police to the GURKM was also the final bureaucratic piece that allowed Yagoda to centralize administrative and funding control over the police, as well as operational authority. In addition, and significantly, the new GURKM came under the direct administration of the OGPU. No longer was the *militsiia* administered under republic-level Sovnarkoms, even as a formality; the GURKM was headed by a ranking officer of the

OGPU, G. E. Prokof'ev, assistant head of the OGPU, who worked directly under Yagoda's supervision. In the parlance of Soviet acronyms, the *militsiia* was now known officially as *GURKM pri OGPU* (that is, under OGPU control)—and with that reorganization, Yagoda finally wrested all police power away from the organs of the Soviet government.[56]

MORE REFORMS

As Yagoda attempted to reform and professionalize the police and OGPU, Party and state leaders implemented a range of other reforms that affected OGPU authority and jurisdiction. Many of these reforms resulted from mass repression campaigns associated with collectivization and dekulakization, and from policing campaigns to clean cities of undesirable populations. In leaders' eyes, these campaigns may have secured Soviet order, but they solved one problem by creating another. By early 1933, hundreds of thousands of detainees crowded the country's jails and lockups, quite apart from its camps, colonies, and prisoner settlements. Such large numbers overwhelmed local officials, who were uncertain how to process those that were being detained as socially harmful. The procurator general's office began to flood with complaints by local prosecutors about prison overcrowding and violations of legal procedures. By April 1933, police surveys showed a prison population of over 800,000, twice the legal capacity of these institutions.[57] In some areas, there were so many prisoners that police gave up trying to control them. In Novosibirsk, for example, police ranks were stretched so thin and jails were so overcrowded that prison officials allowed inmates to guard themselves. A number of inmates even found day work, leaving the prison in the morning to return at night. The jail, it seemed, was the cheapest place to live.[58]

The country's leaders responded in several ways to the dramatic rise in custodial populations. Yagoda's solution was to set up more police boards, and to expedite conviction and sentencing of social marginals outside the judicial system. Apart from speeding up the sentencing process by bypassing courts, Yagoda recommended expansion of penal settlements to hold the numbers he anticipated in the purge of cities. Already in February 1933, he submitted a detailed plan to Stalin, which he worked out with his deputy in charge of the GULAG, M. D. Berman.

The new settlements were designated for resettlement of what Yagoda described categorically as "anti-Soviet elements." Yagoda estimated that it would be necessary to set up a series of new labor settlements during 1933 and 1934 in Kazakhstan and Western Siberia to hold as many as two million individuals. This number included several categories. Among them were kulaks not yet deported from collective farm areas, individuals convicted of sabotage of agricultural and other campaigns, and labor-capable convicts with sentences up to five years to be transferred from prisons previously controlled by the justice commissariat. The main bulk of settlers in these colonies, however, were to be the large numbers who, in conjunction with new passport and residence laws, would be swept up in cities and factories and in cleansing operations of the country's western borders. These contingents, he cautioned, represented particularly dangerous elements—far more socially dangerous than the contingents of kulaks deported during the height of collectivization in 1930 and 1931. Yagoda and Berman laid out the number of settlements they believed would be needed, where exactly they were to be located, and the types of economic activity that each would conduct. The recommendation even detailed the numbers of houses needed, as well as livestock, administrative and service personnel, guards, machinery and equipment, seed grain, and costs of transport.[59]

Yagoda proposed a classic policing solution to the rapid growth in the country's custodial population—to expedite sentencing through administrative forms of repression and to build more places of penal servitude. Stalin and other leaders took a different and broader approach, which was to bring order to the country's penal system and to enact a number of measures designed to moderate the state's approach to police repression. Taken together, this set of interrelated reforms over 1933 and 1934 seemed to place institutional and legal constraints on the growing power of the OGPU, of Yagoda in particular. The Politburo dampened Yagoda's ambitions already in March 1933 by approving but scaling back his plans for new penal settlements. It agreed to the formation of colonies in Kazakhstan and Western Siberia, as Yagoda had proposed, but only for one million instead of two million settlers—500,000 in each region.[60] Further, Stalin tied the realization of this plan primarily to the redistribution of prisoners that overwhelmed the country's jails and labor camps, not to an influx of significant numbers of new arrestees or exiles.[61] Then, in late April, Stalin held a meeting with top OGPU officials in which he made clear, again, that the politics of repression were to change: that police were to adhere to legal procedures and the levels of repression overall were to be reduced.[62] Finally, in early May, the Politburo placed a further curb on the arbitrary authority of police and local authorities by forbidding the OGPU troikas to administer the death penalty without review by higher judicial authorities.[63]

These policy changes were formalized in a secret set of instructions that Stalin and Molotov sent to all punitive agencies and court officials on 8 May 1933. Quoted often as the 8 May instructions, this set of rules was recorded in the Politburo minutes from 10 May under the heading of reducing the prison population in the country.[64] The 8 May instructions carried the force of both the Politburo and the government, being signed by Stalin as general secretary of the Party and Molotov as head of Sovnarkom. The instructions covered a number of points, some already covered a year earlier in a June 1932 Politburo instruction. Indeed, the 8 May instructions rehearsed the same phrases word for word about the victory of collectivization in the countryside, and about the need to stop indiscriminate arrests in rural areas. It reinforced the requirement that only the police, the OGPU, and the procuracy had the right to arrest, and that all arrests needed the sanction of corresponding procuracy officials. The instructions called for an intensification of struggle against class enemies, but not by the now outdated methods of mass repression. The state's "blows" now were to be more "precise," more targeted in order to be most effective. The instructions detailed specific numbers of kulak deportations that were to continue from specified areas, but these were understood to be the last such mass deportations. Finally, the instructions confirmed the transfer of prisoners from jails and camps to colonies and settlements, and it specified 400,000 as the limit for prisoners to be held in the country's jails at any one time.[65] The instructions were comprehensive and specific and represented an attempt by the regime both to reduce, and to regain control over, the use of violence in Soviet society.

The 8 May instructions were followed by significant institutional reform in the summer. The most important of these reforms created a new and powerful all-union procuracy administration. This centralized bureaucracy replaced the procuracy offices that had been under jurisdiction of the republic-level justice commissariats. The new all-union procuracy oversaw activities of both courts and the punitive organs of police and the OGPU. As a central state regulatory organ, the new procuracy held the potential to act as a significant curb on the ambitions of Yagoda and his growing police empire. Yagoda, however, did not oppose the formation of the procuracy as much as did N. V. Krylenko, the head of the RSFSR justice commissariat. The new agency directly undercut his power as head of the largest single procuracy in the country, and he fought a losing battle in Sovnarkom to retain control over his procuracy.[66] The new USSR procuracy was placed under Ivan Akulov, a former OGPU administrator, but one who fulfilled his new role with some authority and independence. The real power behind the new procuracy was Andrei Vyshinskii, the former Russian federation prosecutor under Krylenko, who now took over a more powerful position than his former boss and rival. Vyshinskii used his position, first as deputy head, and after 1935, as head of the procuracy, to promote a greater adherence to legality and a more professionalized legal system within the country. He became quickly an advocate of judicial and legal reform and a significant thorn in the side of the political police under Yagoda.

The 8 May instructions and the formation of an all-union procuracy strengthened the institutions of legal procedure in the Soviet state and placed significant limits on police power. The 8 May instructions served as intended, to curtail the arbitrary mass repression of the peasantry, but these reforms did not end the legal use of administrative mechanisms of repression, nor the use of mass forms of repression. No sooner had the instructions been issued than the Politburo began to make exceptions to the policy of moderate repression. The original decree of 8 May that banned troika death penalties exempted the whole of the Far Eastern region, a huge swath of territory. Then, in July, the Politburo sanctioned sentences of death by firing squad against bandit "elements" by troikas in Western Siberia. In addition, the same resolution permitted the OGPU to mount operational sweeps to rid the district of bandit organizations and "déclassé elements." Following close on the heels of this exception came another ruling, in August, that allowed troikas to issue death sentences in a range of other territories, including the whole of Ukraine, the North Caucasus, Belorussia, Kazakhstan, and the Urals oblast. These measures were also limited to cases of banditry and other armed offenses, but such formal constraints seemed to have had little effect on the activities of troikas. In July, Krylenko complained to Stalin about the "tens of thousands" of cases still being adjudicated by troikas, many of which involved criminals and others outside the jurisdiction of the political police.[67] In the absence of effective civil policing, in other words, the political police were taking on the task of controlling criminality and maintaining social order, and doing so through the use of campaign policing methods and administrative forms of repression. That so many exceptions were made to the 8 May guidelines, and that so little was done to stop the continued use of troikas for repression of civil disorder, was an indication of how much the regime's leaders still believed that criminality presented a major threat to public order and state authority.[68] Thus, within months of the 8 May instructions, the regime had issued exceptions that effectively covered most of the country. By autumn 1933, the OGPU troikas were back in business everywhere except in the central areas of European Russia.

And even in urban areas of the Russian federation, Sovnarkom and the Politburo extended police powers, even as they scaled back police operations in rural parts. Extension of police and OGPU powers resulted from a perception among leaders that urban criminality, instead of decreasing, was becoming more of a problem. By late 1933, police and OGPU were already engaged in campaign operations associated with urban passportization, but whatever policing benefits had resulted from passportization seem to have been short-lived or insufficient. Something of a panic mood gripped Party and government leaders. In December 1933 and January 1934, the Politburo adopted a number of dramatic measures, first in Moscow and then in other cities, aimed at subduing urban criminals and other marginal populations. In late December, and under the heading "Struggle against criminals and déclassé elements," the Politburo suddenly mandated the death penalty for any participants in crimes of armed robbery. Further, the Politburo instructed the Moscow OGPU specifically to exile "by administrative sentence and to a distant place, out of [Moscow] oblast" anyone who had been convicted twice or more of robbery in the previous year. This injunction applied also to anyone who had been apprehended twice or more for hooliganism. The rule applied, in other words, to any individual who had even been temporarily detained in a police station for hooliganism under the *privod* procedure, without being actually arrested and convicted under a hooligan statute. The indigent poor and any déclassé elements picked up by police or OGPU were also to be deported, back to their previous residence out of Moscow, to OGPU penal settlements, or even to labor camps. In January, 1934, the Politburo extended similar procedures to Kharkov and instructed police there to deport up to two thousand déclassé elements. In a bow to the new injunctions against mass repression, and so as not to attract public notice, the police were told to be discreet, not to round up all two thousand at once, but to do so in groups of eighty to a hundred over the course of two to three months.[69]

More dramatic measures came in January with the dismissal of Georgii Prokof'ev as head of the GURKM and his replacement by L. N. Bel'skii, a longtime mid-level OGPU officer.[70] Not satisfied with Prokof'ev's efforts, the Politburo and Sovnarkom demanded of Yagoda and Bel'skii a new plan for 1934 that detailed "concrete measures" in the police fight against criminals and socially harmful elements, as well as for passportization. In the same first weeks of January, the Politburo demanded that Usov, still assistant head of the OGPU police inspectorate, take direct responsibility for the OGPU "to bring order to Moscow's streets and to cleanse (ochistit') them of filth."[71] What exactly the Politburo meant by this wording is unclear—whether leaders referred to social "filth" or to literal trash on the streets. There is no other context in which to interpret the instruction, and the wording was often used to refer to both aspects of what leaders regarded as trash. In either case, the instruction fit the adamant stance by Party and state leaders on cleaning up urban areas and making this task a priority of the political as well as the civil police.

Such measures fit into the regime's fixation on criminality and marginal populations as the most serious threat to its own survival. They reflected the typical overreaction to a perception of heightened social disorder, as well as the particularly Stalinist practice of acting against the regime's own laws.[72] Having enjoined police and OGPU officials to cease mass forms of repression in rural areas, the Party and government now demanded that police engage in what amounted to mass forms of urban repression. Still, the timing of these recommendations may have had a basis in social reality, reflecting the consequences of the prison reforms enacted in the spring and summer of 1933. Those reforms were supposed to reduce the country's prison population by transferring large numbers of prisoners to camps and penal settlements. In fact, of the nearly 468,000 prisoners affected by this order, only 68,378 were transferred. Police released nearly 400,000 people from prisons in the course of May and June, 1933. This included more than half of all prisoners held in jails in the Moscow oblast. In the capital, police freed as many as 18, 650 prisoners who had either been convicted or were under indictment.[73] Many of these individuals probably posed no real social threat, but were victims of passport sweeps—indigents, beggars, prostitutes, the unemployed. Many, however, could have been petty criminals —pickpockets, small-time thieves, burglars. Released from prison, a good proportion very likely remained in the city and the surrounding oblast. Released in the summer of 1933, they would have been unaffected by the initial passportization of the city, which ended in April. And given the lax enforcement of the passport regime, those released from jails could have found relatively easy ways to return to old habits and haunts. The draconian measures enacted by the Politburo in December reflected leaders' response to an ongoing crisis of social disorder, and a reaction to a real spike in criminality on the capital's streets.

Yagoda's policing plan for 1934 fit the get-tough mood of the country's political leaders. Submitted in January and co-signed by the new head of the police administration, Bel'skii, the report covered activities of the police for the whole country. Significantly, the report began with passportization, a sign of the importance Yagoda attached to this as a policing tool. The language of the plan was typical of Yagoda's categorical and histrionic style. "The OGPU considers it the first and foremost task of the *militsiia* to introduce the kind of [passport] regime in which not one citizen can reside [anywhere] beyond the limits specified in his passport and residence registration, creating that regime first in Moscow and Leningrad and then in the remaining . . . cities."[74] Anyone picked up without a passport or proper residence permit was to be sentenced by a police troika to a "concentration camp" or penal settlement, or deported to his home residence, depending on the social background and criminal record of the individual. The police chief ordered his subordinates to increase neighborhood patrols and police posts and to ensure that, using passport laws, streets of major cities were cleared daily of the indigent, hooligans, and unsupervised children. Police were to "root out" (*iskorenit'*) criminals from flophouses and send them to camps for ten years. The same applied to those arrested for hooliganism and knife fighting. Police were to send reinforced units regularly to sweep markets, bazaars, and other public places such as theaters and train stations of criminals and déclassé elements. Interestingly, Yagoda included this last injunction under the section of instructions for maintaining sanitary conditions and conditions of "good order" (*blagoustroistvo*) in cities.

Yagoda saved some of his most vituperative language for street children. Police were to pick up any unsupervised children disturbing public order, including and especially those caught roller-skating behind cars and trams, those trading in contraband cigarettes and other items, and any groups or gangs engaged in rowdy behavior (*beschinstvuiu-shchye*). Unsupervised orphan children were to be sent to children's homes or deported to their hometowns. Repeat child offenders were to be sent to special camps which Yagoda proposed to establish for underage criminals, with a minimum capacity of 10,000. Detained children who lived with parents, relatives, or guardians were to be held in separate detention centers and the adults responsible for the children were to be fined up to one hundred rubles.

Yagoda took advantage of the moment to propose an increase in police ranks, to be made up of demobilized soldiers and OGPU units. In addition, he proposed an increase in pay and ration levels, especially of meat, and an increase in training, most particularly weapons training. He recommended arming police in Moscow and Leningrad with rubber truncheons "in order to subdue hooligans, and for self-defense." Yagoda also took the opportunity to rehearse long-standing complaints against rival agencies. He requested Sovnarkom to upbraid the education commissariat, which was responsible for children's homes, and he demanded that they increase the number of homes and provide better security in them. He requested the justice commissariat to consider new law codes to sanction his recommendations for punitive measures, and he admonished the procuracy not to send cases to the police that did not involve specific operational measures such as search and seizure or arrest. Yagoda wanted an operational civil police force that matched his idea of the OGPU, and he demanded the "most stringent" discipline from his own ranks. The police chief promised punishment "to the maximum" for any police officials failing to fulfill the tasks he outlined.[75]

Reactions to Yagoda's proposals among high political leaders varied. No record exists of Molotov's reply, which would have been crucial coming from the head of Sovnarkom. But while Molotov may have agreed with the substance, it is difficult to imagine that he was positively disposed to the tone of Yagoda's report. Molotov's deadly prim style did not match the spluttering rhetoric of his police chief. Queried for his response, the then chief procurator, I. A. Akulov, replied rather laconically that some of the punishment measures proposed by Yagoda were "inexpedient." Some, he noted, went beyond the prerogatives allowed police in the 1930 regulations that subordinated that force to the OGPU. In the case of hooligans, Akulov argued that current incarceration for two years was too little, but he proposed five instead of the automatic ten suggested by Yagoda. Still, Yagoda got much of what he wanted, at least in terms of police force reform. Sovnarkom approved a rise in wages and numbers, and approved recommendations for uniforming police officers after the style of OGPU officers. More substantively, police rationing status and medical and other social welfare conditions of work were raised to the same levels as those of the OGPU and military. Apart from the specific punitive measures adopted already in December 1933, Sovnarkom and the Politburo withheld approval of Yagoda's recommendations for sentencing criminals and social marginals. As before, these bodies took a broader and more systematic view by recommending establishment of a commission to look into the state's overall policies of punishment, its legal institutions, and its legal procedures. In general, however, Sovnarkom and the Politburo endorsed the policing priorities set out in Yagoda's February 1934 plan.

YAGODA'S VISION

Yagoda laid out more than just a yearly plan. His report provided a vision of how policing should work. On paper, at least, that plan conformed both to the tough mood of the country's leaders and to the supposed turn away from methods of mass operations. In early March 1934, following up the plan approved by the government and Party, Yagoda sent out a rash of circulars articulating his vision for a number of specific tasks. Enforcement of passport and residency laws constituted the centerpiece of his social policing strategy. The daily maintenance of the passport and registration system was "the most important lever" that police and OGPU possessed to fight criminals and déclassé elements and, in doing so, to protect the vital interests of the state. And for Yagoda, in 1934, those vital interests were clear—protection of state property and public order.[76] Strict and daily enforcement of passport and residency laws would, according to Yagoda, free specially designated "regime" cities "completely" of the "criminal-hooligan element." In turn, such measures would clear urban areas of the anti-Soviet "element" since, in Yagoda's view, these two were actually one and the same "element." In cities without special passport and residence statutes, police could not simply expel unwanted populations, but passportization would at least allow police to identify and track the "criminal and suspicious element." This capability, in turn, would "significantly ease the task of the police to maintain order and reduce crime." Police were to increase and maintain the number of police posts in their areas. They were to make rounds of their precincts at least twice daily. They were to be in constant contact with a range of key people who would act as their eyes and ears. Shopkeepers, doormen, even shoeshine boys and others, especially building superintendents, could inform police about new or suspicious people in their areas, and police could check registration books of apartment houses on a regular basis, matching these with their own passport books at least once a month. In this way, Yagoda noted, police could maintain public order and secure control over the cities on a daily basis, not through fits and starts and in the old campaign manner of mass operations. Such measures would, according to Yagoda, allow police to achieve the ultimate goal of prophylactic policing, namely to prevent crime before it happened rather than to react to crime only after it occurred.[77]

To achieve this policing ideal required the proper kind of people, and Yagoda spilled a great amount of ink describing how police were to conduct themselves, and what relations the RKM was to have with the OGPU. It was the task, first and foremost, of the OGPU not only to act as a model, but to train and in practice lead the police. Yagoda requested large transfers of OGPU officers to staff police ranks. He demanded continuation of the review and purging of undesirable "elements" from the police that had begun in 1930. Police heads were to conduct thorough checks on acting policemen as well as on new recruits. In Yagoda's plan, each precinct head was to hold an officer's rank in the OGPU as well as in the RKM. Investigative units of the *ugolovnyi rozysk* were to coordinate any operations with the local precinct head, who would also be in the know about ongoing and potentially overlapping OGPU operations in his area. Yagoda lectured his subordinates on numerous occasions to treat citizens with courtesy, to listen to their complaints, and actually to respond to them. On the other hand, police were to show "a hard face to the hooligan, to the criminal, to the undocumented resident." At all times, police were to maintain a professional, uniformed, and imposing presence on the streets. This would reassure citizens and intimidate criminals and other suspicious individuals.[78]

FORMATION OF THE NKVD SSSR

The expansion of police tasks and jurisdictions led to still more centralizing reforms. By summer 1934, a Politburo commission, which included Yagoda and officials of the justice commissariat and the procuracy, made recommendations for re-formation of a commissariat of internal affairs, a new NKVD. This new NKVD was, in some ways, a re-creation of the old NKVD of the 1920s, but it was far more powerful. The new NKVD was a federal organ rather than a republic-level administration, and its jurisdiction was much broader than that of the old RSFSR NKVD, which controlled only the *militsiia*. Under the new NKVD SSSR, Yagoda realized what his predecessors could only dream of—control over all places of incarceration and over camps, colonies, and penal settlements. Even more significant, Yagoda now headed a combined police organization, controlling both the civil and the political police under one administration. The *militsiia* remained a chief administration—the GURKM —but was subsumed under the new NKVD. Organizationally, the OGPU remained relatively intact, but under the new NKVD it became also a chief administration, the GUGB, the Chief Administration for State Security. On paper, the GUGB was only one of several chief administrations within the new formation, including the police. In fact, all the leadership positions in the NKVD were held by the leading commanders of the GUGB, who simply transferred from the OGPU to the new commissariat.[79] The new NKVD became synonymous with the political police, which now directly subordinated the civil police.

The new NKVD fit neatly into Stalin's hypercentralized reorganization of power. However, the formation of this powerful new agency did not go unchallenged. In the early months of 1934, both Akulov and Krylenko wrote to Stalin expressing their opposition to the creation of an all-union commissariat dominated by the political police. Both officials criticized the broad powers of administrative repression given to political police troikas, and each warned that troikas were abusing their authority and processing "tens of thousands" (as Krylenko wrote) of nonpolitical offenders. Both men warned that the regime was placing too much reliance on extrajudicial forms of review and repression. Krylenko, in particular, recommended that the size and power of the political police be scaled back dramatically, and that troikas be restricted to the limited authority granted to them in the early 1920s. At that time, troikas had power only over cases of military insurgency and politically motivated banditry. Since the political police was an executive organ, rather than a governing organ, Krylenko recommended that it be re-formed at the republic level. In any case, he wrote, the political police should not be included in an all-union and independent commissariat.[80]

Stalin and other leaders pushed forward with reforms for an all-union commissariat, despite Krylenko's and Akulov's recommendations. At the same time, and for his own reasons, Stalin agreed, at least on paper, with the need to restrict the use of administrative methods of repression. Formation of the NKVD was accompanied by judicial reforms that gave primary punitive authority to courts and took that authority away from the political police. These reforms, supported by both Vyshinskii and Akulov, as well as by Krylenko, envisioned an end to the administrative powers of the police troikas. Civil and political police retained investigative and arrest powers, as did the procuracy, but state-administered repression would now pass into the realm of several different levels of courts. Regular and appeals courts remained the bulwark of the system of judicial punishment. Military tribunals continued to hear cases arising within the militarized sectors of the state, such as the military, police, border, and fire forces. In the late autumn, however, a new layer of courts was approved, "special collegium" courts, *spetskollegii,* established to handle the bulk of especially dangerous crimes against the state. These were the courts that were to take over most of the OGPU cases, which had been handled through the extrajudiciary administrative powers of the OGPU troikas. The *spetskollegii* were administered under the USSR justice commissariat and supervised by a special branch of the procuracy. They were established in accordance with all the rules of evidence that existed in regular courts, with the exception that they could meet in closed session, if a presiding judge chose. The *Osoboe soveshchanie* of the NKVD remained the only administrative court under authority of the political police, and this body was to hear only special cases of political crimes deemed too sensitive to try in regular courts.[81]

This turn of events was significant and, as Peter Solomon has written, amounted to a reiteration of the principles of a traditional legal order. Court reforms, especially, reinforced the foundation of a judicial state within which police actions could be defined as excessive or even illegal.[82] In June 1935, the Party's Central Committee reinforced legal constraints on police by reiterating procuracy supervisory authority over the NKVD, including the necessity for procuracy sanction of arrests.[83] However, these reforms did not represent exactly a return to a traditional legal order, although many in the Soviet legal system saw them in this way. The judicial state and the police state continued to coexist and Stalin, as in other aspects of governance, allowed these overlapping and conflicting authorities to operate in constant tension. Such a situation served Stalin's purposes of flexibility and a consciously balanced confusion of authority among subordinate power centers within the state.[84]

CONCLUSIONS

Subordination of the civil to the political police in 1930, then formation of the GURKM in late 1932 and, finally, formation of the NKVD in 1934 were the major turning points in the centralization of police administration. Centralization went hand in hand with subordination of civil to political police control, and subordination of the civil police hastened the merging of the functions of civil and political policing. Under this new administration, the civil police became gradually and then fully militarized; that is, police came under the same pay, training, and disciplinary regime as the political police and the military. With formation of the all-union GURKM, police became subject to disciplinary sanctions by military courts for any crime, not just for crimes committed in the line of duty, and officers were no longer subject to (or protected by) labor union regulations. This latter protocol, especially, reintroduced military-type ranks, uniforms, and organizational structure into the civil police. Formally, at least, these reflected the same ranks and professional standards as in the political police and regular army. Yagoda did not take militarization quite as far as in the OGPU. Civil police officers did not live in barracks, as did military and many political police units, but continued to live in their communities and act as a civilian police force. Indeed, Yagoda chided some local police administrations for overzealousness by forcing their police officers to live in barracks.[85] Still, full militarization of police was one more step in the militarization of civil government in general, and also in the reintroduction of the tsarist model of militarized policing.

Most important, financing of the RKM was transferred from impoverished local Soviet budgets to the all-union budget of the Chief Political Administration. As a result, work and living conditions of the police improved from their low point at the beginning of the decade. By the middle years of the 1930s, civil police had been integrated into the same rationing and rank system as the political police. RKM budgets rose year to year, though never enough for Yagoda, and much of the money went to hire more police and to train and equip them to a level comparable to that of the OGPU. Soviet authorities also spent considerable amounts of money on political training courses to raise the level of political reliability and professionalism of *militsiia* functionaries.

Increases in budgets worked, at least to increase numbers. By mid-decade, police numbers had expanded, and many of the new police officers were either demobilized army veterans or had been transferred from work in the OGPU. If in 1930, total police forces in the country numbered about 87,000, by late 1932, Yagoda reported a total force of 98,000 officers.[86] Figures for mid-decade are scarce, but by late 1934, Yagoda counted 124,000 police in a report to Sovnarkom.[87] By 1937, RKM forces had grown to a strength of 138,000. With the formation of the railroad police in 1937 and the expansion of special economic crime units, overall police numbers jumped, reaching 182,000 in 1938 and 213,439 officers by 1940.[88]

The civil police apparatus never quite lived up to the professional standards and tasks set for it, whether as a crime-fighting organization or as a force for social control. Nonetheless, the process of centralization and subordination, begun in 1930, established in the Soviet Union under Stalin the structure of a militarized policing system that was subordinate to its political branch. The policing system that Yagoda created —a Soviet gendarmerie—functioned well enough. The following chapters explore the role of the civil and political police during the 1930s as organs of social order, surveillance, and repression.

4 Informants, Surveillance, and Prophylactic Policing

In order to uncover and strike our enemy decisively, we need precise, accurate, and deep agent work, otherwise we run the risk of overlooking the enemy.
—Genrikh Yagoda, 1934

THE FIRST TWO YEARS of the 1930s were hectic years for Yagoda and the political police. During that time, the OGPU apparatus was fully engaged with dekulakization campaigns and the class war in the countryside. The OGPU played a leading role in dekulakization, and these campaigns of mass repression gave new life and direction to the political police. The agency found its justification, once again, as a revolutionary and counterinsurgency arm of the Party and state, just as in the period 1918–1921. Still, the OGPU strained to keep up with the pace of mass roundups, military campaigns against resistant peasants, transport of deportees, and policing the countryside. At the same time, OGPU officials found themselves suddenly hard pressed to manage the new penal settlements that had been established for kulaks and other anti-Soviet elements. As if all this was not enough, Yagoda was simultaneously pushing through a major overhaul of the policing system, attempting to incorporate, professionalize, and bolster the civil police as an auxiliary arm of the OGPU. Then, in summer 1932, Yagoda and the OGPU faced yet another new situation, even a potential crisis, as Stalin and the Politburo began to send signals to end the dekulakization campaigns.

The tapering off of dekulakization in 1932 and 1933 forced the OGPU, as in the early 1920s, to find a new role in Soviet society. In contrast to the early 1920s, however, *Chekists* in the early 1930s did not have to wait long for something to keep them busy. OGPU officers soon found themselves embroiled in Stalin's new kind of class war—against criminals, social marginals, and other undesirable populations. This, so declared Stalin in January 1933, required new methods of policing. For the political and civil police these new methods supposedly involved nothing less than a transformation of past practices and institutional culture. For the political police, as Yagoda never tired of saying, the new circumstances required a change from mass operations and methods of military-like counterinsurgency to targeted policing, undercover operational work, use of systematically gathered information, and sharp "incisive" blows against a ubiquitous enemy. From the civil police, Yagoda demanded professionalization and transformation from a hodge-podge of local constable forces into a disciplined national policing agency. The combined forces of the political and civil police were to root out enemies and criminals before they did their damage, not after the fact. In Yagoda's view, policing was to be prophylactic, not reactive.[1] Policing was supposed to protect state property and interests from potential sabotage by the regime's enemies, and from their alliance with the criminal underworld and socially disaffected segments of the population.

This and the next chapter examine Yagoda's attempt to create a prophylactic policing system, one that incorporated the latest scientific methods of social surveillance, social monitoring, and agent and undercover work. These were to be the primary tools appropriate to new circumstances, and information was to be the basis of this new policing. In principle, and for a time, anyway, Yagoda set great store in the processing of information gathered by a highly professionalized, secret, and widespread system of informants, agents, and undercover police. Indeed, even though police resorted often to campaign or mass methods of policing, Yagoda insisted that the most effective means of policing was through this kind of secret systematic information gathering. The point of policing, he stressed, was not to react in campaign style to events or problems that had already become a public danger or a political threat, but to use systematic methods of monitoring to prevent criminality and opposition from taking hold in society. Information was the key to prophylactic policing, the way to check wreckers, saboteurs, and diversionaries of all sorts, and to stop political opposition from organizing on any significant scale.

Yagoda failed to achieve the kind of prophylactic policing system he described. For various reasons, as this chapter shows, agent-operational work and informant types of surveillance never became truly effective during the 1930s. Certainly, police officials conducted operational surveillance of individuals and domestic spying on a large scale, and they gathered information from citizen denunciations and informant networks.[2] Despite Yagoda's urgings, however, operational methods of surveillance could not become the basis for prophylactic policing and widespread social monitoring, since they required too many people and too many resources, even for the police. Likewise, informant networks held great potential for gathering information about the population and were certainly widespread, but they remained underutilized. There were several reasons for this, but one of the most important was Stalin's warning, in 1933, about the new kind of class war that the regime faced. Fear of sabotage by class-harmful elements masking as loyal citizens permeated leaders' attitudes toward the population during the 1930s, especially after the supposedly successful collectivization and dekulakization campaigns had driven open class resistance underground. That fear affected police culture and practice.[3] As a result, following collectivization and the dekulakization campaigns, officials did not trust public participation in matters of policing and surveillance, although they certainly utilized denunciations in certain operations.[4] This distrust reinforced what was already a professional culture of secretiveness inside the police. In addition, and in the context of Yagoda's efforts at professionalization, working with informant networks ran counter to the image many police officials had of themselves as *Chekists*. Thus, for a number of reasons, the use of informant systems remained underdeveloped in both the political and the civil police during the 1930s.

The most successful instrument of social surveillance developed out of a bureaucratized process of information gathering, the system of *uchet,* or registration, which involved the gathering and categorical sorting in card catalogs of statistical and observed information about individuals and populations. Systems of registration had been the basis of political police surveillance during the 1920s, as limited as that was, and they became the basis of a massive system of public surveillance and policing during the 1930s.[5]

There were two different types of *uchet.* One type was active and directly related to direct physical surveillance of criminals or suspected oppositionists. This type characterized police activities during the 1920s and continued to play an important role during the 1930s. A second type of *uchet* was passive, the simple bureaucratic accumulation of statistical information about individuals belonging to various segments of the population. This information could then be used for various purposes of social policing or policymaking. This latter type of *uchet* became increasingly diversified during the 1930s, in part for reasons of bureaucratic logic, but also, and importantly, as police became increasingly involved in the administration of the internal passport and residence registration system. This brought police into the business of monitoring not just criminals and suspected oppositionists but large segments of the population. These card cataloging systems, or registries— *kartoteki*—contained information garnered from work records, police files, passports, residence cards, and other bureaucratized forms of social registration. Police officials, both political and civil, were obsessed with registries and the process of analyzing information. This was a scientific method of surveillance, in keeping with the scientific approach of socialism to social engineering. The *kartoteki* became the primary basis of both social surveillance and policing practices, more so than information gathered from informant networks or agent and undercover operations.

INFORMANT NETWORKS

Informant networks and agent-operational practices nonetheless constituted a significant though under-developed and controversial aspect of policing. As officials professionalized and extended police authority, they also extended the police's information gathering and surveillance systems. Both the civil and the political police engaged in social surveillance during the 1920s, but not on the scale of the 1930s, and not in ways that overlapped. During the 1920s, the OGPU stressed the importance of surveillance and information gathering about the population. As a number of scholars have shown, however, the "overwhelming majority" of its limited resources went toward outright counterinsurgency efforts to combat banditry and uprisings, to fight against recidivist criminals and other "anti-Soviet elements," and to establish the administrative exile and camp systems. The departments that gathered and processed surveillance information were relatively small, and the gathering of information about the population played a secondary role to the more direct struggle against the regime's real and perceived enemies.[6] During the 1930s, and after collectivization, the balance of resources expended changed considerably to give more priority to surveillance, but without diminishing the regime's capabilities to fight dangerous classes and harmful elements. The two functions in fact merged. Gathering information about the population served the goal of fighting enemies. Yagoda always understood that the two functions were intimately related, and incorporating the civil police into the OGPU broadened the scope of both the state's policing and its surveillance capabilities.

The political police gathered information about the population through a widespread system of informant and agent networks. The informant network consisted of two layers. The most basic layer was made up of general informants (*obshchie osvedomiteli*). These were ordinary people from different walks of life in factories, farms, state enterprises, offices, stores, and other places of employment. General informants were not paid and were not listed as OGPU or GUGB staff. They were recruited by and gave information to so-called resident agents. Resident agents were made up of the "more active" general informants, and each resident agent gathered information from at least ten and usually "several tens" of general informants. OGPU or GUGB officers had no contact with general informants, but did meet with and recruit residents. Residents were also not paid, nor were they on the political police staff. Most of the general informant networks were administered through the Secret Political Administration of the OGPU/GUGB and controlled by low-level functionaries at the oblast and *krai* level.[7]

The second informant level comprised the network of special informants (*spetsial'nye osvedomiteli*). These informants were recruited by and reported directly to political police officers. This system of informants was administered by officers in each of the operational departments of the OGPU/GUGB. Special informants reported on specific groups or individuals, on specific places or institutions, and usually gathered specialized information about activities, contacts, and work. Thus, the Economic Crimes Department (EKO), which dealt with wrecking activities, economic sabotage and diversion, and other economic and white collar crimes, operated a network of special informants within the Soviet trade and distribution system, in markets, and in any enterprise that dealt with economic activities. Analogously, the Special

Department (*osobyi otdel*, or OO), controlled informants in military institutions and ranks, and gathered information about spying, terrorism, and counterrevolution within the military and within any militarized institutions, including the civil police, fire brigades, and border forces. The Secret Political Department, SPO, in addition to running the general system of informants, operated special informants to infiltrate suspected counterrevolutionary groups. Finally, the Transport Department (TO), and the Operational Department (*Operotdel*), also ran their own special informant networks. In addition to these networks, a separate network of special informants worked under the GULAG administration in labor camps, colonies, and special settlements. Special informants were supposed to be "better qualified" than general informants, usually because they came from a particular milieu, such as the intelligentsia, the clergy, or were specialists in institutions. Most of these informants were also not paid, or they were not supposed to be paid, nor were they on GUGB staff rolls, although in some cases they might receive remuneration.[8]

In contrast to the system of informant networks, agent networks were made up of either career Chekist officers, specially trained for undercover work, or civilian operatives who were recruited and paid for their specialized knowledge or position. These agents were assigned to specific intelligence-gathering tasks, often in preparation for or in conjunction with an ongoing investigation or operation. Agents could be drawn from any rank of officers, or from any milieu, but were supposed to have some qualification for the task of their undercover work. As it turned out, many agents were individuals caught in compromised situations and turned by police to act as informants. Undercover officers operated by order of oblast and *krai* operational departments for special investigations, approved by the operational heads. Operations might last weeks or months. The number of operational agents in any oblast or *krai* depended on the initiative of the OGPU/NKVD in the locality concerned, and on the number of investigations in progress.

As the political police geared up for its expanded role in the realm of policing public order, the system of informants expanded accordingly. In a report to Stalin in early 1935, Nikolai Yezhov, acting in his capacity as a Central Committee secretary with control over security organs, counted 27,650 residents who received information from some

500,000 informants within the various levels of the GUGB. This number represented a doubling or more from the low point of 1924, when the then OGPU counted 10,000 to 12,000 residents. The number of informants in 1924 is difficult to establish, although Nicolas Werth has written that the two key departments then involved in informant work —the information and transport departments—numbered 26,520 and 12,580 informants respectively. These figures were nowhere near the size of the network a decade later, the number of informants having ballooned to nearly half a million.[9] Indeed, even this number may have been low. As Yezhov noted in his report, it did not include many informants who were not officially counted. In 1937, in an offhand comment to political police recruits, Yezhov noted that the number of political police informants reached into the "millions."[10]

Change in the overall size and structure of the political police also reflected its changing role in Soviet society from an instrument of class war to one concerned with public order and social monitoring. In 1922, the OGPU counted 90,000 officers working in nonmilitary parts of the agency, while 119,400 agents were assigned to military units or institutions. After severe cutbacks in 1923 and 1924, the OGPU counted 21,000 civilian and 76,000 military staff.[11] By 1930, that number had fallen to a low of 17,476 officers working as operational staff, with only 1,352 of those officers working in military units or institutions.[12] Numbers rose again rapidly to 25,573 by January 1935, but that included only 3,769 officers in the OO assigned to militarized sectors of the state.[13] If nearly 78 percent of the OGPU staff in 1924 was assigned to gather information about the military (76,000 of 97,000), by 1935 the GUGB assigned slightly less than 15 percent of its total staff to that task.

According to a 1935 report by Yagoda, most of the increase in OGPU/GUGB officers between 1930 and 1935 occurred through a strengthening of numbers in regional departments and machine tractor stations. These offices were the lowest in the bureaucratic hierarchy of the OGPU/GUGB and the ones most directly in contact with the public. In fact, the assistant political officer in machine tractor stations was, by designation, an OGPU officer. MTS officers, drawn mainly from staff of the Secret Political Department, numbered about five thousand by late 1934, when the political departments in the MTS system were closed.[14] These and regional officers provided the most immediate and direct source of information available to the political police about rural activities and moods, but it is not clear how and when, if at all, regional officers and MTS agents fit into the information gathering system. No formal structure existed to link management of informant networks from the oblast level with officers working in regional departments or in machine tractor stations. The latter certainly wrote regular reports to superiors, based on their investigative activities, but it is not clear if they knew of informants in their own areas of jurisdiction who were under the control of the oblast-level secret political or operational departments. It is reasonable to assume that they may have known the identity of residents, and perhaps acted as contact officers, but it is just as likely that they were not included in this information loop. Lack of coordination between various operational levels was a common scenario within the political police system.[15]

Other growth areas in the political police system were found in border regions, especially in Belorussia, Western Siberia, Kazakhstan, and the Far East.[16] Less expansion occurred in the operational departments, except for those related to organized crime, the EKO, and the *Osobyi otdel,* responsible for the system of informants in the military. In keeping with increased political priority assigned to economic crimes, the OGPU bolstered its economic department, increasing agent staff by 72 percent from 1930 to 1935, from 1,387 to 2,388 officers. This department experienced the largest increase in numbers of any of the operational departments during the 1930s. The *osobyi otdel* grew from 2,680 to 3,769. The least amount of expansion took place in the SPO, responsible for managing informant networks and gathering information on political opposition. In fact, Yagoda reported that in 1933 and 1934, 2,900 officers were drawn off SPO departments and reassigned to posts in machine tractor stations. As a result, that department underwent only a 13 percent increase in staff, from 4,252 to 4,831.[17] The Transport Department, the largest of the operational departments, and one of the most active in social-order policing, also underwent growth, from 4,598 to 5,383 officers.[18] By the mid-1930s, the two largest operational departments were the Economic and Transport departments. As noted above, significant expansion also took place in border offices, local offices, and machine tractor stations. These were impressive increases, especially in numbers of officers in direct contact with the public and informers, or in departments concerned with issues of public order. These changes reflected a significant shift in resources to the priorities of the 1930s.

CIVIL POLICE NETWORKS

The value of surveillance and secret information gathering was unquestioned inside the political police. Information was, to use Peter Holquist's memorable quotation, the "alpha and omega" of OGPU work.[19] This was not so in the case of the civil police. During the 1920s, surveillance practices and organs of the police had atrophied, even lapsed, due in large part to lack of budgets, personnel, and the general disarray of the Soviet state system. This was especially true in rural areas, where the NKVD operational and investigative apparatus, the *ugolovnyi rozysk*, was spread thin, and where almost no informant networks operated.[20] At the same time, many NKVD officials expressed an ideological hostility to secret forms of policing, and at least some police officials dismantled secret informant systems. These actions, although probably not widespread, represented a revolutionary reaction to the hated system of secret police informants of the prerevolutionary era. In the Urals, for example, police during the 1920s disbanded much of the informant system and used the money for buildings and other facilities. That experiment was based on the assumption that "society had reached such a level that it could itself, without any agent-informant apparatus, wage the fight against criminality and public disorder."[21] In the context of this democratic revolutionary idealism, the people themselves were to act as guardians of revolutionary order. Such had been the culture of the NKVD.

This same democratic revolutionary idealism had been behind the criticisms leveled in the late 1920s by the state's inspectorate agency, Rabkrin, about informant, agent, and secret investigative practices of the police. As numerous reviews showed, the *ugolovnyi rozysk* had earned itself a notorious reputation for corruption and criminal activity in its agent and surveillance work. In 1928, Rabkrin officials strongly condemned the *ugolovnyi rozysk* for having been taken over by the culture of criminality the agency was supposed to fight. At the time, Rabkrin officials blamed this corruption not so much on the lack of higher administrative control over agent and surveillance work as on the agency's "separation from the working masses." The remedy, according to the review, lay not in stricter professional enforcement but in the cultivation of "comradely" public cooperation and "revolutionary vigilance." In keeping with the revolutionary tone of the 1920s, Rabkrin officials recommended establishment of workers' control commissions to oversee activities of the *ugolovnyi rozysk,* to ensure that operational officers cease contact with criminals and other undesirable types, and to work more closely with trade union and other civic organizations to prevent crime.[22]

OGPU officials who took over the *ugolovnyi rozysk* and civil police scorned the "naïve" idealism of populist policing practices. "Cultivating the masses" to fight the regime's enemies was, at least in the context of policing practice, backward, ineffective, and even counterrevolutionary. At a May 1931 operational conference of civil police and OGPU officers, one OGPU officer scoffed at the Urals experiment in populist policing.[23] As they integrated civil police into the OGPU, political police officials moved quickly to reestablish informant and agent work as "the fundamental building bloc" of all policing activities. Purges of the *ugolovnyi rozysk* and then incorporation into the RKM brought a reorganization of the agency's informant, agent, and undercover operations. The *ugolovnyi rozysk* was integrated wholly as a section into the newly created Operational-Investigative Department of the civil police, the ORO, and its operational and surveillance operations were expanded and professionalized within the newly integrated system of civil and political policing.

Reorganization and expansion fit the new priorities of the new criminal investigative department. As a whole, police organs now took on a more active role in the fight against crime, social disorder, and anti-Soviet activities. The new police guidelines of 1932 granted police, in general, greatly expanded policing, investigative, and arrest powers, and this in turn led to a need for information about and surveillance of criminal activity on a much larger and more organized scale than had been the case under the old *ugolovnyi rozysk.* The new secret activities of undercover, agent, and informational work were supposed to replace old policing methods of simply reacting to crime. Surveillance work was now, in conjunction with operational activities, to anticipate and prevent crime through secret, professionalized methods of criminal and public surveillance.[24] In addition, police were also supposed to become an active part of the state's system of political-social surveillance, which required information-gathering about the general public, and not just about criminal activity. In effect, the *ugolovnyi rozysk,* like the RKM as a whole, now became an auxiliary arm of the political police, augmenting the latter's social surveillance and information-gathering capabilities.[25]

THE 1931 CONFERENCE

The task of creating a new, professionalized police operational and surveillance organization fell largely to D. V. Usov, the assistant head of the GIM, and to his deputy, an officer whose last name was Maurer, head of the inspectorate overseeing the ORO. Usov and Maurer devoted considerable time and energy to the establishment of a functioning and uniform operational system throughout the country. These police leaders organized special conferences and symposiums of operational directors, and both reviewed, amended, and approved instructions for informant and agent networks in different parts of the country.

Central OGPU and police authorities provided guidelines and instructions for development of informant and agent networks, especially at the May 1931 conference of OGPU and police operational chiefs, held in Moscow. Much of that conference focused specifically on the reconstruction and professionalization of information-gathering and undercover practices, and on the integration of those practices into informant and agent practices of the OGPU. OGPU and high police officials attending the conference discussed how networks were supposed to operate. Discussions were detailed, and included a number of working sessions in addition to general talks. Not surprisingly, the organizational structure adopted at that conference closely resembled the informant and agent system within the OGPU. As in the OGPU system, so in the civil police, informant networks were organized around two basic principles, or "categories" of networks. Secret Informational Departments (SIO) at the oblast, *krai,* city, and regional levels administered general informant networks (category I), while the OO of each oblast, *krai,* city, and region managed special informants and agents (category II).

Category I networks gathered information from the general populace and were organized around residents. As in the OGPU, residents were to be unpaid, ordinary but trustworthy citizens—preferably, and in some instructions, exclusively, drawn from Party members and members of the Communist Youth League, or Komsomol. In police parlance, residents were not referred to under that moniker, but were called "group leaders," or *gruppovody*. Each *gruppovod* was to manage information from an ideal number of ten informants. Also, as in the OGPU, civil police officers were not to meet directly with general informants, but only with group leaders, or residents.[26]

Networks of special informants and agents were organized according to the working subgroups of the Operational-Investigative Department. At this level of informant and operational work, ORO officers were to have direct contact with special informants and agents, but, of course, under the same "conspiratorial" conditions as in the OGPU system. Officers had more discretion about whom to use as special informants and agents, including even former convicts or criminals caught and turned into double agents. Again, as in the OGPU system, so in the RKM, any agent was to be thoroughly vetted for trustworthiness by case officers and by operational heads. Some special informants and agents were paid, although it is unclear on what basis and how regularly. They were to be used for specialized forms of information gathering, about individual people or groups of people, or for information about activities in specific places in preparation for, or in conjunction with, an ongoing operation. In the early 1930s, informant and agent activities centered, as did all operational work, on three groups: banditry and other crimes against persons; economic crimes; and property theft and fraud.[27]

It was no coincidence that police informant structures mirrored those of the OGPU. This was not just a matter of habit or bureaucratic cultural importation. OGPU officials wanted a police structure of information that would fit seamlessly into their own organization of information. Thus, police surveillance and agent work was structured in parallel to that of the OGPU, and even subordinated operationally to the political police, just as were police operational departments. At the same time, certain distinctions were to be maintained. Police operational officers were to bring a heightened political awareness to the management of informant and agent work, just as they were to operational activity, but "under no circumstances," declared the head of the ORO, Maurer, were police to allow "politicization" of their informant apparatus (whatever that meant) or to assign "on a systematic basis" political targets to their agents for observation. Police agents might be drawn into such tasks, but only under unique circumstances, and only under direct OGPU management.[28] Similarly, operational officers were to relay immediately to their

OGPU counterparts any information gathered by police agents or informants that "touched on political issues" or that was related to crimes that were "clearly anti-Soviet or of a class character." The latter included "counterrevolutionary agitation, distribution of counterrevolutionary publications, involvement in organizing anti-Soviet demonstrations or mass refusal to pay taxes, disruption of agricultural or timber quota payments, terror acts, diversionary activities, etc."[29]

Such neat distinctions proved difficult to apply in the daily practice of sorting information and conducting agent work. The more so since, as Maurer also declared, all forms of banditry and all information relating to socially dangerous elements belonged within the sphere of OGPU competence as politicized criminal activities. In agent and informant work, as in operational activities, overlap between civil and political police activities was considerable. Lines of separation easily blurred between social order and state security.

The police precinct system provided police with yet a third level or category of information gathering, and one potentially far more widespread than within the OGPU. In general, a precinct chief—*uchastkovyi inspektor*—was not supposed to be involved in running informant networks or agents. Inspectors were not to be used as either case officers or substitutes for residents, although exceptions could be made in rural areas, where regional offices were often located far from some of their outlying precincts. On occasion, noted one OGPU officer, if an inspector, especially in a rural area, was competent, and the regional center far away, that inspector could be trusted to manage a general informant network, but that network should be set up by an operational officer from the regional office.[30] Still, in laying out the framework of the police informant system, OGPU heads envisioned a third "category," a so-called auxiliary informant network, in addition to the general and special categories of networks. The auxiliary networks were to be made up of daily contacts that a precinct inspector cultivated with resident citizens and service personnel in his jurisdiction. This informant system was not to be formalized, but OGPU officials regarded it as the duty of every *uchastkovyi inspektor* to establish such an informal system. Inspectors were to transmit to regional police chiefs relevant information gathered through these contacts, either in regular semimonthly reports, or by extraordinary (*vneocherednye*) reports. Although not formally constituted in 1931, this layer of police surveillance became the basis for the formally constituted system of information gathering associated with the passport and residence system, inaugurated in early 1933. This system, especially as it evolved quickly into the passport registration system, provided a level of detailed information about citizens that had no equivalent in the OGPU. As OGPU officials understood, the auxiliary informant system, and its reincarnation under the passport system, held the potential for development of a surveillance system far more widespread and detailed than was possible within the political police.

SETTING UP THE NETWORKS

Based on the proposals worked up at the May 1931 conference, OGPU officials promised to send to oblast and *krai* heads working instructions on setting up networks and agent operations. By mid 1932, however, a number of oblast and *krai* police administrations still had no written instructions. In at least several instances, oblast-level OGPU police heads took the initiative to formulate their own temporary set of instructions. As these instructions show, local practices differed, sometimes considerably, but, in general, local instructions followed the recommendations set out in the May 1931 conference.

Instructions from oblast and *krai* operational chiefs provided a guide to the type of informants to recruit. In urban areas, people to be tapped as general informants included building superintendents and domestic service people, an excellent source of information—those who "know who lives in their building, their lifestyles, and habits."[31] Officials encouraged recruitment of prostitutes as special informants, for similar reasons, and especially because of their connections to the underworld of their clients. At a 1934 conference in Western Siberia, operational officers noted that in department stores, women made the best informants and the best temporary agents. They were more honest and more reliable in their work habits than men and generally provided more accurate and detailed information.[32] Chauffeurs, taxi drivers, trash men, and others who moved around the city or area because of their work made good sources, as did night guards, shoe shiners, artisan workers, store clerks, and street and market traders. Similarly, cafeteria workers and servers in bars, clubs, restaurants, and beerhouses were to be recruited. Instructions warned against recruitment of ex-convicts or former criminals, unless well vetted by higher police officials.

In rural areas, lists were similar to those in urban areas, but also included MTS workers, rural "activists," members of cooperatives, postal workers, and delivery people who routinely traveled about a region as part of their work. Instructions allowed for recruitment of private farmers, if well vetted as trustworthy, but expressly forbade use of Party or Komsomol members in either urban or rural areas as special informants or agents. In contrast, police were told to recruit primarily Party and Komsomol members as residents, and non-Party people only if thoroughly vetted. Moreover, residents, especially in rural areas, were supposed to be people who moved about as part of their daily work, such as circuit postal riders, insurance agents, and civil inspectors. Informants were not to be tied officially in any way to the police, and were to meet only with their resident or, when necessary, with the qualified police officers who ran the network. This latter seemed to differ somewhat from OGPU practice, in which informants were never to meet with OGPU officers, but only with residents.[33] Informants were never to be given weapons or any kind of document attesting to their connection with the police. Neither were informants or residents to meet with police in station houses or police buildings. Safe houses, or "conspiratorial apartments," were to be arranged for such meetings and passing of information. In the Urals, for example, police maintained secret apartments in at least twenty-three cities and towns for meetings with residents, informants, and agents. According to instructions, these were to be established only in urban or large industrial areas, such as Sverdlovsk, Cheliabinsk, and Slatoust. Presumably, the conspiratorial purpose of such places would have been difficult to carry out if set up in rural villages, although a list of these apartments included regional administrative centers as well as larger urban areas. The Urals instructions did not specify how contact was to be maintained with rural informants, but if these were to be recruited from people whose occupations made them mobile, then meeting in regional centers would have been a reasonable alternative to debriefing in smaller villages.[34]

Instructions also laid out the kind of information that was to be garnered from informants. Logically, police wanted information about favorite meeting and hiding places used by criminals. Thus, they wanted information about who came and went in "thieves' dens" (*pritony*) of all types: beer halls, apartments, especially in poorer and outlying districts of cities, workers' barracks, cheap hotels and hostels, markets, bazaars, railroad stations, dock areas, race tracks, cafés and other "dives" (*khazy i maliny*), and certainly in public parks and gardens. Police were particularly interested in information about individuals who seemed to have money but no visible means of work or steady employment. Police were told to gather information also and especially about "suspicious" people who frequented trade and supply enterprises and points of exchange. Also important was information about public contact within the Soviet economic system, such as information about people who worked in municipal departments, service areas of hospitals, warehouses, financial departments, and savings banks. In rural areas, networks needed to be "extensive" and gather information about people who worked in or frequented markets, agricultural and artisan cooperatives, communal distribution centers, feed and grain distribution and storage points, and collective and state farm livestock barns. Particular attention was to be paid to those in rural areas who worked in coops, and to those who seemed to be the most prosperous. In the early 1930s, a prosperous lifestyle was, in itself, a sign of illegal gain and corruption.[35]

As in the OGPU, police special informants were supposed to provide information about specific people or places, and often in preparation for special operations. One of the primary goals of the special informant network and of agents was to infiltrate directly into the criminal world. In contrast to instructions not to recruit criminals as general informants, police were encouraged to recruit former criminals and prostitutes as special informers. Special informants were also not to be regularly paid, although they could be remunerated from time to time. Unlike informants, even special informants, agents were to be salaried police officers or highly qualified civilians and specially trained for their work. Their primary use was for infiltrating professionally organized crime rings in order to gather information for major sting operations. All agents came under direct control of the police Operational Department and its crime subgroups. These agents were to have a wide intraregional jurisdiction.[36]

HOW THEY WORKED

Information about the workings of police networks comes from either the early 1930s, the period of reorganization and first expansion, or from the postwar period which will be covered in a later chapter. The material from the early 1930s is sketchy, at best, but material exists for some cities and oblasts, especially from the Moscow and Urals areas. Formally, police maintained a large informant network in Moscow. The size of civil police networks in Moscow was large, but was still smaller than that of the political police. The operational departments and *ugolovnyi rozysk* of the oblast police listed 11,171 informants as of June 1932, both general and special. A survey of eighty regions, however, revealed a more modest number of 6,805 working informants. This number did not include the network of auxiliary informants, supposedly working under each precinct inspector. Including the latter would have pushed numbers much higher, potentially far higher and with potentially more systematic coverage of the population than possible for the political police. By December 1932, the number of informants working for police operational departments in 131 of the 146 *raiony* of the Moscow oblast numbered 10,455.[37] This amounted to a significant expansion in just a few months, but the head of the oblast police informational-statistical sector, one Boikov, regarded this number still as low. Even so, police could not muster enough qualified residents or officers to manage even this number of informants. Boikov noted that informants were run directly by officers in operational departments. No resident system had yet been established, even though the number of informants had expanded. This caused a severe work strain on police, since most regional police departments, even in the Moscow oblast, had no more than two qualified operational officers. Burdened by their investigative responsibilities, operational officers had little time—and little inclination, admitted Boikov—to devote to setting up and running informant networks. As a result, productivity suffered. In the last three months of the year, the Moscow oblast's network of some 10,455 informants had generated only 6,120 reports, a disappointingly low number, according to a review by a ranking OGPU inspector, one Rozanov. This number of reports had produced, in turn, "only" 2,474 solid leads in solving crimes or uncovering criminal activities.[38] According to Rozanov, such a low level of productivity required a personal explanation from Boikov, the more so since operational officers violated the most basic rule of conspiracy by meeting with informants themselves, rather than gathering information through residents. The practice of meeting directly with informants not only detracted from the other investigative duties of operational officers, but exposed their identities as police officers.[39]

Police in the Urals experienced problems in setting up informant networks similar to those of their Moscow colleagues. In late 1932 and early 1933, police relied on a network of informants and agents that numbered only 8,553 operatives for the entire Urals oblast. Most of these informants worked for the three major operational departments (antibanditry, antitheft, and economic), and most were located in Sverdlovsk, the oblast capital. Officials claimed that they could not adequately cover outlying and rural areas of the oblast, and that their information from these areas was sparse.[40] Police complained of insufficient informants and agents even in urban areas. In the Yegoroshinsk region of Sverdlovsk, local police officials could count on only 48 informants, but they figured that they needed at least 148 for all the enterprises and parts of the region that needed to be covered.[41] In the whole of the oblast, only five agents worked out of the police antibanditry unit, and this in one of the most bandit-ridden territories of the country. The anti–theft and fraud department could count on only two agents.[42]

In the Urals, as in Moscow, operational officers did not take well to working with informant networks. The head of the Urals oblast police Operational Department, Griazanov, remarked on this, and it seems to have been a general reaction. Running informant networks out of operational departments may have had a certain bureaucratic logic, but doing so ran counter to the image that operational officers cultivated of themselves as professional and elite undercover investigators, and interfered with their primary duties as undercover investigative officers and agents. The head of the Western Siberia Operational Department, Sharov, underscored the problem in a report from 1934. Choosing his words carefully, he wrote that operational officers "undervalued" the effectiveness of general informant work. Operational officers, he remarked, felt that informant networks were little more than venues for gossip-mongers, who otherwise encroached on the time and sphere of authority of operational departments. Thus, operational officers were reluctant to be assigned to informant work, and expressed "bad feeling" toward officers who worked with general informants. Many officers tended to dismiss or not trust the information gathered through general informant networks.[43]

Still, and despite this reluctance, pressure continued from the center to set up large-scale informant networks. Caught between these two

pressures, and squeezed as well by personnel shortages, Ural police officials hit on a solution which seems to have become widespread practice. In Sverdlovsk, Griazanov conceived the idea to involve precinct
officers more actively in the informant system. At first, instructions recommended that precinct inspectors not be used as contact officers for
residents, or be involved in running informant networks. These officers
were not experienced enough for the kind of management needed of the
information gathered through networks. By late 1932, however, at least
in Sverdlovsk and in the Urals, police officials understood that, lacking
manpower in the operational and information departments, it made
sense to draw in the local precinct inspectors. As Griazanov noted in a
special conference, operational officers, especially in outlying areas and
in heavy-crime urban areas, were often overwhelmed simply by their
investigative work. They had little time to do the routine work of meeting with and digesting information from residents and informants.
Precinct inspectors, on the other hand, were already well situated to operate informant networks. The latter were, supposedly, in daily contact
with the kind of people to be utilized as informants.[44]

By October 1932, Griazanov reported on the successful completion of
a trial period involving twenty-two inspectors, among the most experienced in Sverdlovsk, who had recruited and were receiving information
from forty-six informants. The information was valuable, he claimed, including the whereabouts of wanted criminals, locations of weapons
stashes, and leads on several major cases of theft of state property. Based
on this initial success, Griazanov went further to claim that integrating
precinct inspectors into the informant system would be a "breakthrough"
organizational innovation, especially in the fight against speculation and
theft of socialist property. As proof of this claim, Griazanov noted with
satisfaction a jump in the number of informant reports from 6,997 in
summer to 8,593 in the autumn of 1932, which had led to an increase
in the number of agent operations from 532 to 660 during the same
period.[45] Griazanov noted that in Sverdlovsk, there were some one
hundred precinct officers. He speculated that if each of these developed
a network of ten informants, it would yield an immediate result of a
thousand-person informant system, just in that city alone. Shifting the informant system to the precinct level would satisfy the central authorities'
craving for numbers and, in turn, would free up special departments to
concentrate on their agents and investigations.[46]

Integrating precinct inspectors into the informant management system may have made sense administratively. Precinct inspectors were the police officers most directly in contact with the public, and on a widespread scale. Moreover, beginning in 1933, precinct officers were already charged to administer informant networks as part of passport work. At the same time, such a solution violated the original intent of the informant system, which was to establish a consistently high-grade level of information from the public, sifted and analyzed by professional operational officers. Decentralizing the administration of general informant networks to the precinct level cheapened the value of the information, at least in the eyes of higher officials. This practice led to a bloated informant system, with little control by qualified personnel over who was giving information. Initial results from the Sverdlovsk experiment may have been weighted by the use of especially competent inspectors, or by Griazanov's particular skewing of results in order to make his scheme look a success. More than likely, the success of the Sverdlovsk experiment resulted from the typical method of campaign work, in which an intense effort for a short period of time produced the desired outcome.

By December, a conference on informant work revealed a more sobering and typical picture. In general, operational and investigative officers gave little credence to the information coming from precinct level networks. Operational officers tended to rely on their own sources of information. Central authorities often chided operational departments for ignoring precinct informant networks, even when the former set up operations in a locale. Elite operational units often did not bother to inform local precinct officers of their presence during agent operations, which led to overlapping and even harmful disruption of police informant and undercover activities.[47] For their part, precinct officers were as reluctant as operational officers to take on informant management duties. Already overburdened by too many demands, they had little patience or training for the time-consuming tasks of gathering, sifting, and registering all the information that came their way. In Sverdlovsk, as elsewhere, turnover among informants remained high and productivity low—the latter measured by numbers of reports generated by informants—and these were signs of a casual attitude toward recruitment and exploitation of sources.[48] Judging by reports and circular letters, precinct officers paid little enough attention to passport and registration tasks, let alone to the systematic management of informant networks.[49]

Throughout the 1930s, use of informant and agent information remained a "weak spot," a "bottleneck" at the operational as well as at the precinct level.[50] This was true not just in provincial areas, but even in the police force of a major urban center such as Moscow. In July 1932, an internal police review complained that, for the most part, the operational parts of the Moscow oblast police worked very poorly. Operational and investigative departments shunned agent and informant work and concerned themselves mainly with petty cases not requiring investigative or agent-operational activity. In a number of regions of the oblast, agent and informant activity was nonexistent. Heads of departments generally took no active part in informant and agent work, and neither for that matter did operational officers. In a particularly biting comment, the reviewer, the assistant head of the oblast police, Odintsov, noted that leadership and oversight over the small amount of agent and informant activity that existed was conducted more actively by the oblast procuracy office than by heads of the police operational departments.[51] This latter remark was certainly meant to sting, given the jurisdictional rivalry and often the bad feeling that existed between police and procuracy officials.

The criticisms above were written in 1932, but three years later, the situation showed little improvement. Based on an inspectorate report from July 1935, Yagoda criticized the Moscow ugolovnyi rozysk and operational departments for continued lack of serious attention to both agent and informant work. Investigators and operational officers foisted management of networks onto lower staff and residents. As in 1932, so in 1935, heads of departments took little or no part in network management, and only about 15 percent of staff officers worked actively with informant networks. The review showed that only 30 percent of the formally constituted networks were active in producing information, and many city branch departments had no active networks at all. Yagoda noted that only 7 percent of all cases brought to charge by the Moscow ugolovnyi rozysk resulted from leads provided by informants or agents. The situation was far worse in the city and oblast operational departments, where fewer than 1 percent of cases were generated by informant or agent leads. In general, criminal investigations were not linked to agent work, especially in areas of large-scale crime and state property theft. As a result, operational departments and the *ugolovnyi rozysk* networks "reeled in" petty crooks and thieves, but had little success breaking open large-scale organized crime gangs whose activities cost the state "huge" losses.[52]

What was true for Moscow was true elsewhere, and even more so. Sporadic use of networks went hand in hand with lax management, and resulted in outright corruption. As a rule, department heads took little or no part in oversight of informant work. Information gathered by general informants often "went nowhere," but sat unprocessed in secretarial files. More seriously, department heads did not bother themselves with agent review or vetting. This task they left to lower-level officers who actually ran agent networks. In turn, operational officers were not careful about who they used as informants and agents. They took "whomever was there." In many cases, police operational-statistical bureaus had no record of agents who worked for operational departments, which meant that officers did not inform superiors of agent recruitment; nor, therefore, were agents properly vetted for reliability. As a 1934 circular noted, "In many police departments, the agent apparatus takes in people who are not vetted and not experienced, and in equal measure, drops agents without good reason or warning, and without informing higher officials."[53] The consequence of such mismanagement, claimed Yagoda, was predictable. Many agents were unreliable criminal types, "double-dealers" (*dvurushniki*) who manipulated information, investigations, and police activities for their own protection or criminal advantage.[54] According to internal police investigations, in fact, the agent and informant system was riddled with criminals. Rather than acting as a means to infiltrate the criminal world and to seek out undesirables, the network had turned into a conduit for criminal infiltration of the police, as well as "saturation" by socially dangerous types.

Despite general improvements in regular street policing, informant and agent work remained ineffective and corrupt. The problem proved so intractable that, instead of trying to reform the system from within, Yagoda initiated a wholesale sweep of the agent system. In late 1934 and early 1935, GUGB officers and units were assigned to purge and reconstruct, almost in its entirety, the police informant and agent network system within the state sectors of the economy. Yet, as sweeping as this reform was, it addressed only one aspect of this type of policing. As Yagoda noted, serious deficiencies still plagued informant and agent op-

erations in rural, cooperative, and other nonstate sectors.[55] Mismanagement, underutilization, and corruption remained an endemic problem in the police informant and agent system.

Internal police reviews portrayed a nearly moribund system of agent
and information work, and yet the system could not have been as dysfunctional as these reports suggested. Other reports show a system that
functioned on at least some basic level. During the course of 1934, for
example, Moscow city and oblast police operations uncovered at least
six major fraud and embezzlement rings. These rings usually included
up to ten to twelve people, working in different sectors of the Soviet
trade and distribution apparatus. In one sting operation, *ugolovnyi
rozysk* agents rolled up a ten-member gang working within the Moscow
oblast cooperative union. The gang members engaged in "mass" theft
of goods and embezzlement through fraudulent bookkeeping, selling at
inflated prices, and passing off low-quality products to retailers. Over
the course of a year, the gang embezzled close to 60,000 rubles. Another operation resulted in the arrest of thirty-one individuals working
in the Moscow Railroad buffet administration. All were allegedly involved in a single embezzlement ring in which each took a cut from falsified deliveries and bills. Losses over the course of a year amounted to
500,000 rubles.[56] In the same year, in the Gor'kii district, *ugolovnyi
rozysk* working out of the city of Dzerzhinsk uncovered a sixteen-mem-
ber gang of escaped kulaks who were living under assumed names and
falsified documents. The group, six of whom were related, claimed to be
a cooperative of poor peasants, all living in a local village, who had obtained a license to dig and sell peat fuel. Apparently, the group came to
the attention of police through sales of manufactured goods in local
markets, which were in short supply. These goods were very likely
stolen or illegally purchased, and their sale "gained a highly profitable
income" for what was otherwise a modest cooperative venture. The
members of the so-called cooperative were so well off, according to the
undercover report, that each owned at least one horse, several cows,
and other livestock, as well as domesticated birds.[57]

These operations had a certain success, including against some major
crime rings, but they still amounted to very little within a system of corruption that cost the state hundreds of millions of rubles a year. The
very size and relative openness of some of these fraud and embezzlement activities suggests that they were widespread, that they operated
often with impunity—especially when they bribed police to turn a blind

eye—and that the NKVD was still relatively ineffective in policing major crime. As Yagoda noted on numerous occasions, informant networks worked best at uncovering petty crimes and criminals. The most effective policing of crime was through mass policing of public order— the campaign-style sweeps of markets, transportation networks, and city streets. This was the kind of policing that officials disliked, but tolerated, since it was effective.[58]

Interesting, too, is how Yagoda's reaction to police corruption differed from that of the authors of earlier inspection reports. In the late 1920s, still in keeping with revolutionary ideals, Rabkrin had recommended a thorough "proletarianization" of the informant and agent system, indeed of the entire *ugolovnyi rozysk*. Infusion of workers, and oversight by workers' soviets, was supposed to bring social accountability, and this view reflected a deeply ingrained revolutionary mistrust of secret state policing methods. Yagoda's response to corruption, in keeping with his predilection to mistrust public accountability, was just the opposite. Yagoda preferred in-house methods of purging, further professionalization, and further subordination of the civil police to political police supervision.

POLITICAL POLICE NETWORKS

When Yagoda criticized civil police, he often referred to the OGPU and GUGB as models of how police should work, yet an analogous process of expansion and devaluation seems to have taken place in the management of informant networks within the political police. This was the conclusion reached by Yezhov in a series of 1935 reports. Then still a Central Committee secretary with oversight over the security organs, Yezhov put the overall number of general informants in the country at about 500,000. He admitted, however, that this number was a guess. In a series of reports to Stalin in the first months of 1935, Yezhov could state only that the GUGB operated 27,650 residents and slightly fewer than 271,000 general informants. These acted within the "organized" or socialist state sector of the economy and society. Yezhov could not say for certain how many residents and informants operated within the "unorganized" sectors of the population. In fact, there existed no central control over or registry of informants within the general populace —of those known as "house informants" (*dvorovoe osvedomlenie*). Surprisingly, there also existed no registry of informant networks in the

military and in transport. Nor, for that matter, was there any centralized registry or review of special informants or even of agents working
out of territorial (oblast and *krai*) departments of the NKVD.[59]

As proof of chaotic management, Yezhov reported that numbers of
informants listed officially within the GUGB varied widely from area
to area, but with little relation to population density or strategic considerations. In 1935, only 1,200 OGPU informants operated in the
whole of the Saratov *oblast,* a huge swath of territory along the Volga,
while the OGPU office in the Severnyi *krai* reported 11,942 informants
in that sparsely populated territory. As expected, the NKVD saturated
the Moscow oblast, where it had 3,625 residents and nearly 22,000
general informants. This was more informants even than the civil police
maintained, and the number did not include military or "house" informants. During the mid-1930s, the GUGB maintained constant agent
observation of nearly seventy streets and public squares in the capital
and at least two hundred enterprises, schools, barracks, scientific institutions, villages, farms, industrial sites, and warehouses in the oblast. In
contrast, the Western Siberian UNKVD fielded 2,900 residents and
18,452 general informants to cover one of the largest territories in the
country and one of the most industrially important, with some of the
largest labor camps and special settlements.[60]

Yezhov sharply criticized the way the informant system was organized. Officers never met with informants, he noted, which was as it
should be, and residents chose their own informants, but this meant
that operational officers had no direct control over their sources of information. At the same time, at least according to Yezhov's findings,
residents exercised little discretion over their choices of informants and,
in any case, met infrequently with them. Since they were not paid and
were overburdened with their own working lives, residents devoted little time to managing their networks.[61]

Agent work was the foundation of Cheka activities, wrote Yezhov,
but operational heads, let alone rank-and-file officers, paid little attention
to proper oversight of networks. Agents, as well as residents and their informants, were too often managed by low-level, unqualified officers.[62]
Operational heads exercised little control over agent selection or vetting
and, as in the civil police, agent and informant recruitment by officers
was haphazard, or often done in campaign style in response to pressure
from higher authorities. The head of the Leningrad Special Operations

Department, for example, in response to a critical inspector's report, issued a general memo to the entire staff instructing that each member recruit at least ten informants or agents. As a result, according to Yezhov, within a month the department was "choked" with agent and informant information, most of it useless and much of it misleading.[63] Leningrad was not an isolated example. Recruitment methods were so chaotic and lax as to create an open door for criminals and oppositionists to infiltrate the "Cheka," and then turn it to their own nefarious purposes. Yezhov wrote of the same kind of "double agents" (*dvoiniki* was his word) in the GUGB as Yagoda had described in the civil police.[64] Yezhov claimed that background checks of political police informants revealed many to be hardened criminals or long-time oppositionists, chosen from among those already under arrest, or from those active in politically suspicious circles.[65] This was true not just of informants, but disturbingly, also of agents. Many came from among ranks of recidivist offenders, clerics, even opposition party members. In more than a few cases, according to Yezhov, informants and agents were drawn from among refugees or political exiles. With little or no control over agent selection, concluded Yezhov, it would be no wonder if many NKVD operatives were in fact active agents of hostile foreign governments.[66]

In the first two months of 1935, Yezhov wrote several reports, at Stalin's behest, vetting the GUGB in general, and the Leningrad branch in particular. The timing and focus of the reviews were no accident. Yezhov conducted his reviews and submitted his reports in the wake of the murder in December 1934 of Sergei Kirov, the Leningrad Party chief and Stalin's close confidant. Yezhov's assignment was to uncover the reasons why the GUGB had been compromised in such a way as to allow a murderer to gain access to a high Party leader. It is clear from the reports that Yezhov was not just looking for a lapse in security. Operating on the assumption that Kirov's murder was a political assassination, Yezhov was looking for evidence of conspiracy and a fundamental flaw in the structure of the political police, a flaw that would open the NKVD to mass infiltration by the regime's enemies. Yezhov certainly understood the implications of his charge, either implicitly or explicitly. Thus, his ingenious conclusion that the GUGB had been massively compromised by infiltration through its informant and agent structure is not surprising, and its authenticity is all the more suspect.

Still, for all the political motivation surrounding his reports, and despite their highly politicized conclusions, Yezhov's criticisms of how the informant and agent system actually worked ring true—the bloated size, high rates of turnover, poor screening, low productivity, and casual use of informants. Throughout the 1930s, information from these networks was generally of poor quality, even as the numbers of informants soared, with little oversight. Officers tended to mistrust information gathered from network sources, and even Yezhov wrote of many overblown (*dutye*) cases arising out of informant and agent work.[67] Both Yezhov and Yagoda recommended a "sharp" cut in numbers of informants and agents, closer operational management and integration, and more intensive exploitation of networks.[68] In 1937, Yezhov claimed that, in accordance with this recommendation, informant and agent numbers had been cut in half in 1935, and then cut in half again in the spring of 1936.[69] If such a cut occurred, it seems to have had little effect. To the contrary, as will be seen in later chapters, the size of informant networks continued to grow rather than diminish. The GUGB as well as the civil police stressed numbers, not quality. Both the civil and the political police tended to work through the establishment of extensive informant networks casually used and frequently idle, rather than through the cultivation of closely monitored and intensively exploited sources. Other descriptions of the informant system support this description. In Western Siberia, for example, a Chinese immigrant, living in exile in the Prokop'evsk region, was the resident agent for a network of informants among Chinese inhabitants of the area. The resident, Soikin, worked for the GUGB and controlled a network of informants which, officially, numbered in the thousands.[70] Likewise, Yezhov wrote in his report that in some oblasts the numbers of even specialized informants ranged in the hundreds and sometimes thousands. In many cases, special informants and agents were far less qualified than those about whom they were charged to provide information.[71]

CONCLUSIONS

The informant system never developed into the basis of prophylactic policing that Yagoda had envisioned in 1931 and 1932. Overblown, mistrusted, and given low priority, material from informants was never reported, or it piled up in reports or documents that went unread or unused. Police turned to other methods to collect information about the population, such as cataloging information in cross-referenced file systems, that appealed more to the "scientific" turn of mind of high police officials. Cataloging systems also suited the bureaucratic and secretive methods of the police, more so than the imprecise information gathered from unreliable human sources. During the 1930s, as the following chapter shows, the catalog and registration system became the primary basis of both policing and surveillance.

5 Cataloging the Population

Police ... do not appreciate the broad application of statistical work.
—*Genrikh Yagoda, 1935*

AT THEIR OPERATIONAL CONFERENCE in May 1931, OGPU and civil police officials commented frequently and critically on the haphazard methods of reporting and processing of information of former times, and regaled each other with stories of the "old ways." They feigned incredulity at the lack of professionalism, even quaintness, which had supposedly characterized the Russian NKVD of the 1920s. Informant reports seemed to have had more to do with the belletristic aspirations of local operational heads than with professional police practice. One officer claimed, to the supposed surprise of his listeners, that many local police heads had simply sent postcards to higher authorities through the mail describing trends in their regions. In general, police reporting was not standardized. There was no way to coordinate analysis of trends across republics, even within republics. Reporting was chaotic and directly contradictory. Different sectors from the same oblast reported completely different statistics. Statistics that were collected were used for purposes of reporting to higher government bodies, but not for operational purposes to target particular crimes, criminal populations, or localities.[1]

Just as they attempted to professionalize operational and informant work, police officials in the early 1930s attempted to systematize and professionalize the processing of information. Desiring to bring a higher level of accuracy and effectiveness to police work, officials spent a great deal of effort, both in conferences and in circular memorandums, detailing forms and methods of reporting. OGPU inspectors modeled the structure and management of operational work in the civil police on practice within the OGPU, and they followed OGPU practice in setting up the processing of information within the police. And, as in operational matters, so too in reporting, officials sought to integrate civil police reporting activities into the overall OGPU system of surveillance. At the May 1931 conference, in particular, OGPU officials outlined for civil police operational heads the details of what to include in monthly and quarterly reports, how these were to differ from extraordinary reports, and how information was to be turned into operational activity. At first, police reporting combined statistical information with narrative description. The narrative aspects of surveillance soon atrophied, however, as officials turned increasingly to statistical and biographical information gathering on card catalog systems. During the 1930s, this system of *kartoteki* became the primary basis for both policing and surveillance activities.

CATEGORIZING AND PROCESSING INFORMATION

At the 1931 conference, high OGPU and civil police officials laid out a naively complicated system of police reporting. The most basic kind of reporting was done through the writing of regular monthly and quarterly reports, and also by the frequent reports, usually every ten days, requested during specific policing campaigns. Monthly and quarterly reports (*otchety*) provided a statistical overview according to a standard form, providing figures for arrests, incidents, crimes, and social profiles of criminals; another standard form provided staffing statistics and information on operational activity. These reports contained a narrative section as well, explaining statistics or summarizing trends. Operational officers often included short summaries of particular cases as examples, which they culled from daily logs.[2]

Reports were to be processed through the Statistical Information Department at the oblast level, whose operational subgroup would then feed material back to Operational Department heads for action. In addition to monthly reports, regional and oblast operational heads could send up extraordinary reports (*vneocherednyie doneseniia*). These were reports on unusual events or trends, and were sent directly to the operational heads at the next highest level for immediate action. These reports could often be more narrative in nature than statistical, especially when describing occurrences such as a train wreck or unusual bandit activity. Such reports included descriptions of measures taken and, often, requests for further instructions.[3]

Compilation of informant material was a separate process from that of operational reporting, but it followed a similar pattern of regular and extraordinary reporting. Information gathered by regional officers was to be filtered to higher police and OGPU authorities at the oblast, krai, and then republic levels. Thus, regional RKM and OGPU heads summarized informant information and passed it on to the Statistical Information Department at the oblast level. This information, in turn, was to be processed and passed back down to relevant operational heads for action. Agent information gathered during an ongoing investigation was sent directly to the operational heads in charge of the investigation. Although informant information was to be summarized and passed on in monthly and quarterly reports, operational officers in charge of networks and agents were required, at least according to the 1931 instructions, to gather and summarize informant information at least every three days. These "working summaries" (*rabochie svodki*) were to be shared with operational subgroups on banditry, economic crime, and theft, and were to serve as the basis for initiating operational activities.[4]

OGPU officers explained the new reporting system in detail. Still, some police officials failed to grasp the rationale behind it, and the relation between systematic statistical reporting and the new roles of the police. One question, in particular, was revealing, from an oblast police official who asked why local officials needed to compile such detailed monthly and quarterly statistical reports if they also filed extraordinary reports. The exchange that followed this question highlighted the operational and surveillance purposes of policing. The two types of reporting were necessary, explained an OGPU official patiently. These reports functioned together not just to report crime, criminals, and police informant activities, but to build a "normal" profile of a region, and then to identify crimes that "fall outside the ordinary pattern." By building a social-statistical picture of a region, police officials could identify and isolate, immediately and easily, any out of the ordinary activities, and the social types associated with those activities. Moreover, regular reporting created a history, an institutional memory that could be read easily by successive officials. Standardized statistical reporting and record keeping were a crucial part of prophylactic policing. It served operational and surveillance purposes to protect Soviet society and the state against its enemies. The 1931 policing conference was a key part of a new process in which police reporting became part of the state's growing statistical surveillance system of the population.[5]

KARTOTEKI

Regular and extraordinary reporting kept information flowing, and was supposed to be the lifeblood of operational and surveillance activities. If information was the lifeblood, then the heart of the system was *uchet,* the registration of information. Throughout the 1920s and into the 1930s, the political as well as civil police developed formalized systems for cataloging and cross-referencing information about activities—types of crimes or oppositional activities—and about individuals—biographical information about criminals, convicts, oppositionists, and others under suspicion or observation, as well as informants. Information in these registration systems was written on file cards and kept in card catalogs. Both civil and political police maintained an extensive and increasingly complicated system of *kartoteki.* The number of people registered (*na uchet*) in police surveillance and operational *kartoteki* at any one time is unclear, although by the late 1930s, the political police kept surveillance information on some 1.2 million people.[6] This provided a huge system of both archival and operational material to feed the social surveillance system of the Soviet state.

As in operational and informant areas of work, the RKM and OGPU/GUGB tried to maintain a functional differentiation in their registration systems. Thus, the civil police and the OGPU kept separate *kartoteki* for different categories of activities and people. Police were supposed to register information about civil crimes and criminals, while OGPU bureaus kept cards on political activities and those under political suspicion and active observation. In fact, and by design, police and OGPU catalogs often overlapped and duplicated each other. The information was cross-referenced across a wide range of activities and individuals, but was duplicated especially for certain types of individuals—escapees from prisons, camps, colonies, and special settlements; criminals convicted of or under suspicion for banditry, hooliganism, major economic and antistate crimes; and individuals classified as socially dangerous.[7] The OGPU/GUGB maintained separate registration systems, of course, for individuals who were under political suspicion or active surveillance, and those who were imprisoned in the Gulag. Special lists also existed for foreigners living in the Soviet Union, which included political refugees, and which also included markers for individuals who were not allowed to live in special regime areas.[8] Analogously, however, civil police maintained a *kartoteka* system listing former political as well as statutory criminal convicts residing in their areas of jurisdiction. In addition, information about criminals and criminal activities could be, and in many cases was, coordinated with information about political activities and the activities of subversive elements. Information about socially dangerous persons and about escapees, in particular, was shared by both the *ugolovnyi rozysk* and the corresponding level of the OGPU/GUGB.

The largest and most widespread *kartoteka* system was that of the passport and residence registration system. The *militsiia* was charged to administer the passport system and to maintain passport and residence catalogs. This *kartoteka* system differed from other systems in that it registered and categorized not just dangerous types, but everyone who carried a passport. Passport and residence registration thus provided police with a surveillance tool, potentially, of the entire population. *Kartoteki* of those denied residence in key cities, for example, were kept and duplicated by the police and the OGPU. Cards of people registered in these *kartoteki* also specified the reasons why a passport was denied. If a person who was refused a passport moved to a nonregime area, cards were to follow him or her to the new place of residence, and to both the local police and the OGPU. If a person issued a passport had a criminal record, reference to that record was registered in the passport *kartoteka* of his or her place of residence, as was information about people from supposedly alien or dangerous classes. A duplicate card was filed in police criminal registration catalogs and in the OGPU/GUGB catalogs of former convicts and suspicious or socially dangerous persons. As with operational and informant areas of activity, OGPU officials made certain that the police registration system could be easily coordinated with and integrated into the overall surveillance apparatus of the political police.[9]

The registration system used by the OGPU/GUGB evolved out of that agency's counterinsurgency and political policing functions of the 1920s. There was a continuity of OGPU registration practices, although greatly expanded, from the 1920s to the 1930s. In contrast, the civil police systems described above grew out of major reforms in the early 1930s, in keeping with operational subordination of the civil to the political police, and with the expanded emphasis on agent and surveillance functions. Police in the old Russian NKVD maintained information catalogs, but not on the scale and not in the standardized detail envisioned in the reforms of the early 1930s. Consistent with the familiar script of criticizing previous police administrations, police and OGPU officials in 1931 described the old registration system as "outdated . . . cumbersome, and irrational." Previous NKVD officials had "undervalued" the importance of information registration and the "specialist-statisticians" who were trained to maintain such a system.[10] In the old system, information was contained in separate catalogs according to different criteria: individuals with court convictions, those wanted by police or under investigation, those simply detained by police as suspicious persons, etc. Thus, information about any particular individual was scattered across several different types of registries. In the new system, all information about an individual was to be integrated and placed on a single card or set of cards. Each card was filed alphabetically by name, and included information about a person's physical characteristics, including gender, height, weight, hair and eye color, and distinguishing marks. Cards also recorded biographical information, especially about an individual's social background, social status, work record, political party affiliations, places of residence, as well as police or OGPU detentions and judicial convictions, and terms in prison, camp, or administrative exile, if any.[11]

In addition to written notations, cards were to be cut and punched in particular places, such as corners. These marks were to be standardized according to different indicators—at least by type of crime, type of conviction, and form of punishment. Cards could then be quickly and easily grouped by different categories and provide a fast way to cross-reference the study of crimes and criminals in a region or area. Chief criminal investigator Vladimirov, from the Moscow police, touted the technical and scientific advances of such a system. He boasted that chronometric studies had shown an efficiency improvement of 40 to 50 percent in the categorization of criminal statistics using punch cards over older methods of categorization by handwritten notation. In order to investigate certain trends and to make operational decisions, he explained, "You don't need to read anything, or make any decisions; all you need to do is to gather together all the cards with the same cuts or holes in them, and then to count the marks and other indicators." Cards could be shuffled or "cross-cut" in any way and the information used for any operational purpose.[12]

In addition to concentrating information about a person on a single card, police were instructed to broaden the scope of surveillance information kept about that person. Cards were to register information not only about a single individual; they were to include the names of that individual's immediate family members, close relatives, and regular contacts, especially those in the criminal world or from suspicious or socially alien backgrounds. In addition, cards were supposed to contain reference to any operational action taken against the named individual, and the names of any others who were the target of the same actions. All aliases were to be registered and cross-referenced to a separate auxiliary catalog of names, monikers, and street or underground nicknames. Fingerprints, when available, were also to be kept in an auxiliary registry under the person's name. Identifying information about fingerprints was to be cross-referenced to both the registry of aliases and the main biographical *kartoteka*. Photographs, when available, were to be included with card information, both in the main biographical registry, and in the auxiliary registries of aliases and fingerprints. Photographs and fingerprints of individuals who had not been arrested or convicted were usually not available, but the *privod* system of temporary police detention proved highly useful in this regard. In the course of *privod*, police could take photographs, prints, and biographical information. The individual would be freed, having been duly shaken up, and police would be able to list the person's name in a surveillance catalog, in other words to "fix" the individual "on *uchet*" (*vziat' na uchet*). Police often used this technique against known petty criminals, hooligans, and marginal people from suspect social backgrounds.

WHOM TO REGISTER

Questions arose at the OGPU-police conference in May 1931 about whom to place on *uchet* and what kinds of information to register. The discussions surrounding these questions, which were detailed and sometimes heated, along with OGPU, police, and NKVD memorandums during the 1930s, reveal a truly utopian vision of social surveillance. The scope of the surveillance and registration system was revealed, however, not just in grandiose statements, but in consideration of detailed and even mundane questions, for example, whether to put prostitutes on *uchet*. Resistance by some officials to this measure implied a perception, at least among some, either that prostitution was not a crime, or that prostitutes did not belong in the category of politically dangerous elements. The Moscow chief criminal inspector, Vladimirov, concluded that prostitutes probably should be put *na uchet* (though not as criminals or suspicious persons) for two reasons. The first reason, he stated flatly, was that there were simply so many of them. The second reason was that so many prostitutes were "associated with the criminal element." This interesting turn of phrase implied that, in Vladimirov's view, most prostitutes worked a living as best they could from the trade that they were forced into, and that prostitution, although an unfortunate social deviation, was not in itself politically or socially dangerous. Vladimirov went so far as to say that Moscow police operated a special network of informants among prostitutes to distinguish which "categories" of prostitutes were associated with the criminal element and which were not. Besides, prostitutes were subject to administrative exile and judicial punishment, and prostitution was a factor that, on the whole, influenced and was associated with the growth of crime.[13]

Vladimirov was a longtime police investigator, a street cop familiar with the reality of the criminal world. His curious musings about prostitution were based on practical police experience, and showed at least some feeling toward prostitutes as individuals not entirely responsible for the trade that economic or social circumstances forced them to ply. The moderator of the session in which Vladimirov spoke, however, was Maurer, a ranking OGPU officer and member of the OGPU police oversight inspectorate. Maurer had the final word on the matter of prostitutes, and he added a political to the criminal criterion for placing them on *uchet*. Echoing Yagoda's categorical statements about marginal social groups, Maurer stated that there could be no discussion about whether to include prostitutes on *uchet*. Prostitutes, he stated curtly, were part of the déclassé element and, because of that status, were clearly suspect. On both political and criminal grounds, prostitutes would be included in the *uchet* system.[14]

Apparently, nationality was not included in the working draft of information to be placed on registration cards. This in itself was interesting, and showed that, still, in 1931, issues of national identity did not play the kind of central role in repressive policies that they would come to play only one or two years later. Still, this was a contested issue at the May conference. Proposals from the floor suggested that nationality was a necessary piece of information to include on registration cards. The same Vladimirov countered that this was not a factor that influenced the character of a criminal. The nationality of a thief, he argued, had no significance; only the social factors that determined the crime and makeup of the criminal were important. Criminals who came from national minorities, for example, were criminals not because of their nationality, but because of the social milieu in which they lived. "Not true!" replied someone from the audience, as the discussion wound further into intricacies of nationality vs. social background. Interestingly, Maurer did not have as resolute a position on the issue of nationality as on the question of prostitution. He recommended only mildly that the issue be pursued in more detailed discussions in the working sessions of the conference. In fact, the issue did not remain long unresolved.[15] Police and OGPU registration forms carried a line for nationality as early as 1932. By that year, the question of nationality was already becoming a central issue in the state's politics of repression.[16]

Other questions arose, for example, whether everyone run in by the police on *privod* should be documented on surveillance cards. This would include ordinary drunks, as well as suspected criminals and socially dangerous individuals. Maurer replied that, at present, police were registering many of the wrong types of people; about one-third (35 percent) of those on police *uchet* were harmless. The main point of registration, he reminded officials, was to keep track of recidivists, as the most dangerous part of the criminal element. Others, who had no criminal record and who were detained for minor infractions, need not be registered, except for those with demonstrated ties to the criminal world, or those—and especially those—who were socially alien elements. The latter should be documented, regardless of how slight the infraction, because of the risk that they posed as potential criminals or as a source of social disruption.[17]

Former convicts were another category to be registered and kept under active observation. The head of the RSFSR RKM Secret Information Department, Larisov, stressed this point in a discussion that revealed the wide scope of the *uchet* system, and its tie to a vigorous system of operational surveillance. The purpose of registration, declared Larisov, was not just to create a passive statistical record, but to maintain constant observation of all suspicious people, including and especially former convicts. "Keep in mind," emphasized Larisov, "that that object [i.e. former convicts], especially that object, should remain constantly in our field of vision as a special category of registration and surveillance" (*kak osobouchetniki*).[18] On a different occasion, Yagoda also emphasized that operational work was not completed with the arrest of an individual under surveillance. That was the just the beginning. Police and OGPU should maintain constant agent observation of criminal and suspect apartments, of all connections, associates, etc., certainly after an individual's arrest, but even, in fact especially, after a convict was released from prison or camp.[19] Indeed, according to Larisov, a convict's *uchet* card was to be kept on permanent file. When a convict was released, his or her card was to be transferred to the active agent-operational file in the region where the former convict settled and registered his residency. There, operational officers were to maintain surveillance of the individual as an *osobouchetnik*.[20]

This was an extraordinary statement for two reasons. The system of surveillance as outlined by Larisov made a mockery of the official ideology and the policy of social rehabilitation through labor. Citizens who served out their sentences of confinement or exile were supposedly released with full rehabilitated rights. Through political reeducation and labor, they would supposedly reenter society as fully productive citizens. In the eyes of the security organs, however, and as Larisov's comments made clear, such individuals were still suspect as dangerous to the state. They, as well as their families and associates, were to be kept within the field of vision of the security organs.

Larisov understood the ideological implications of this order, and he at least tried to cover it with a fig leaf of justification. He argued that placing a person not under active suspicion of criminal or illegal political activity *na uchet* and under observation was, "after all, not a form of punishment but . . . a prophylactic measure." Criminality, Larisov reminded his audience, was on the rise, and the increasing threat to public order was most closely associated with socially alien and anti-Soviet elements. In the context of class war and the need for protection of socialist construction, constant observation of these groups only made sense.[21]

Apart from the breach of official ideology and policy, the surveillance tasks outlined by Larisov were practically impossible to implement. The logistics of such a surveillance system were enormous, given the increasingly large numbers of people placed in some sort of detention at one time or another. According to Larisov's formulation, all these millions of people would be under permanent police suspicion, and therefore under supposed police and OGPU observation after their release. Moreover, the millions of people on active registration would be compounded by the numbers of their family members, associates, and contacts, all of whom police were also to register and keep under some kind of surveillance. Yet despite overwhelming logistical difficulties, Larisov expressed no doubts about the feasibility of implementing such a surveillance system. Just the opposite. Larisov, like Yagoda and other high police officials, expressed every confidence in the effectiveness of the *uchet* system. Updated with a constant flow of residence and passport information, and of informant and agent information, *kartoteki* would provide the basis for a truly comprehensive system of population surveillance and policing. Residence, political, and criminal registration systems were supposed to work together in a seamless manner to allow police to catch undocumented persons, illegal residents, and escapees. Such a system would allow police to know the exact location at any time of any person deemed socially harmful or dangerous to the interests of the state, even if that person had not committed a criminal or political act. Yagoda reminded subordinates on numerous occasions that proper maintenance of residency registers, along with a steady flow of information from local informants and agents, offered political as well as civil police the most important means to identify and track criminals and dangerous elements in Soviet society.[22]

One of the most heated discussions among police and OGPU officials throughout the 1930s was generated by the issue of where to locate registration catalogs. This may have seemed a trivial matter at first glance, but it was important. Disputes about what information to keep at what level went to the core issue of the surveillance system—how to coordinate local and central information and operational activity. OGPU catalogs were kept on at least three levels—a central catalog in Moscow, at the oblast level, and at the regional (*raion*) level. Presumably, republic-level OGPU/GUGB administrations also maintained catalogs, but it is not entirely clear to what extent these catalogs duplicated the information at higher or lower levels. At the May 1931 police conference, some officials advocated a principle of strict centralization. Comprehensive union-wide catalogs should be maintained no lower than at the republic level, and some argued even only at the central RKM level, based on information passed up from regions and oblast officials. Others argued that such centralization was too cumbersome and denied to local and field officers the necessary flexibility and speed they needed in their work. Suspect individuals could easily slip out of a region while officers waited for information about their identity from Moscow or republic administrations. Trying to maintain comprehensive central catalogs also threatened to overwhelm central offices with too much information, creating backlogs and inefficiency as well. For these reasons, OGPU and police leaders decided that centralized catalogs would contain information only about especially dangerous individuals, or about individuals or groups whose activities encompassed cross-republic or international contraband and spying activities. Similarly, even oblast catalogs were to be limited to individuals engaged in large-scale criminal activities or whose activities included large numbers of regions. The most comprehensive catalogs were to be maintained by the secret information departments at the regional level. These catalogs would then provide the most direct access to information by regional operational officers, and could be easily updated by information flowing through the regional level offices. Regional-level *kartoteki* were also located most accessibly to the passport and residence catalogs to be kept at the precinct level in each region. In this manner, regional police and OGPU offices were to be the nerve centers, as it were, of operational and social surveillance activity.[23]

Here, in the registration and surveillance system, was the essence of Yagoda's vision of prophylactic policing, as well as proof, at least in police minds, that marginality, crime, and counterrevolutionary leanings all slid together. The system of *uchet* was one that, in its internal logic, reflected the policeman's positivist vision of universal social surveillance. OGPU and police officials congratulated themselves on the advanced technical and scientific aspects of the registration system. In theory, the system was detailed, completely integrated, and automatically cross-referenced. High police officials cited references to chronometric studies of efficiency. They described in rational tones the seamless flow of information in and through different departments. They explained the managerial intricacies of running a complex network of agents and informants. They lectured on the secret machinations of conducting operations and investigative activity. OGPU and police leaders laid out the plan of a smoothly integrated system of prophylactic surveillance and policing. All of this gave the impression of a highly tuned and humming bureaucratic machine, of many busy people in a complex process of calculated interaction.

REGISTRATION AND POLICING

The reality of policing was far more messy than the picture painted by officials. In practice, the registration system never really worked, at least not in the prophylactic way that Yagoda envisioned. The sources of information needed to feed the *kartoteka* system did not function well during the 1930s. As noted above, informant networks were notoriously inconsistent and the information they provided was of dubious value. Moreover, Yagoda criticized subordinates repeatedly for the episodic or campaign nature of operational surveillance, used only during specific cases and operations, and then curtailed once an arrest was made, or when other objectives became more important. In order for registration and prophylactic policing to be effective, scolded Yagoda, surveillance had to be constant, even of released convicts and of family and associates of arrested individuals. "Operational officers regard their work as complete when they arrest a criminal," Yagoda noted, "when, in fact, arrest is just the beginning of [operational and registration] work."[24]

The absence of updated operational and informant information was only one gap in the registration system. Officials rarely updated registration information through systematic checks of work and residence rolls, let alone through compilation of informant and agent information.[25] Many police officials in general paid little attention to *kartoteka* work, and inspections often revealed local registry offices in disarray. Lack of attention to registry work went hand in hand with lax enforcement of residence and passport laws. Police consistently allowed undocumented populations to settle in passportized areas, or allowed those to register who should not be allowed to live in a specially privileged area. "Police administrators in localities . . . don't do anything to stop the inflow of unwanted categories [of the population]," complained F. Fokin, assistant head of the OGPU in 1934.[26] Likewise, many police failed to enforce "deregistration" (un-registering one's current address and listing an intended new residence address) when a citizen moved from one place of residence to another. Police often failed, as well, to insist on identification of previous residences by people registering in a new town. In this way, officials had no way to track the previous places of residence of an individual.[27] Thus, lax enforcement of passport and residency laws provided yet another way for dangerous and suspicious individuals to slip through the cracks in the registration system.

As a result of these breaches, information in police registries became quickly outdated and ineffective as both a surveillance and an operational tool. This seems to have been a problem that afflicted both the political and the civil police. A Soviet Control Commission survey of political police catalogs in Voronezh oblast in November 1934 found "alarming" discrepancies in this regard. A spot check of registration information on seventy-five "socially alien and anti-Soviet elements" revealed that twenty-three did not work or reside at the places then currently listed on the NKVD cards. Further investigation showed that "most" of the twenty-three had not lived or worked at their current address for over one and a half years. They had, in other words, disappeared from the surveillance system; they were no longer within the field of vision of the NKVD.[28] When queried in a memorandum by Molotov, Yagoda claimed that the Voronezh case was an exception, and that in general, the NKVD had made great strides in documenting and isolating or removing the country's dangerous populations. In a note to Ian Rudzutak, vice chair of Sovnarkom, however, Molotov expressed his doubts, writing laconically that Yagoda's claim was "not especially convincing."[29]

Molotov had good reason to doubt Yagoda's claim. Yagoda's constant criticism of subordinates belied his reassurances to Molotov that the disarray in the Voronezh oblast NKVD administration was exceptional. Catalog information was often not coordinated with operational work to find missing persons, wanted individuals, or runaways. This lack of coordination created not just cracks in the penal system, but gaping holes through which poured hundreds of thousands of escapees. Officials in camps, colonies, prisons, and special penal settlements were slow, if they did not simply omit, to inform local NKVD offices (both the civil and the political police) of escaped prisoners or settlers.[30] Indeed, the camp and settlement prisoner registration systems were so inefficient that officials there often did not have accurate work and residence rolls. In many cases, it appears that they did not inform local police and GUGB officials of escapees because they did not know inmates had escaped. They did not or could not keep daily track of who was present and who not. Settlements, especially, required only a weekly, and sometimes only a monthly check-in at local police precincts. As a result, colony and settlement officers were especially liable not to know if individuals went missing.[31]

Compounding this problem, oblast-level GUGB offices did not, as a rule, coordinate search and other operational activities of regional branches of civil and political police. Lack of coordination led to lax enforcement and a chaotic situation. Lists distributed by oblast or central authorities of wanted criminals, escapees, and suspicious persons to be kept under observation were not cross-checked with local catalogs or passport registers. Often, as one NKVD survey reported, "nothing is done with [these lists]. They are shuffled into a pile and lie about the shelves of regional NKVD and police offices like waste paper."[32] According to Yagoda, civil and political police heads had little control over, or even knowledge about, what was happening in peripheral areas of their jurisdictions, especially in rural areas. In an August 1934 talk, Yagoda upbraided territorial operational heads, saying that the great majority of them did a "very poor" job leading their oblast and *krai* departments, and especially peripheral areas of their territories. "You are busy with all sorts of things, only not with operational work." Operational officers had "no clear picture of who lived and what was happening on the periphery." Consequently, peripheral areas of the country, and of each oblast and *krai,* became something of a haven for marginal populations to hide from authorities, at least for a time.[33]

Statistics on escapees reinforce this anecdotal evidence. OGPU settlements and colonies were only lightly guarded. It was relatively easy to run away from these penal settlements, although once away, life on the run in wilderness areas was itself a daunting prospect. In addition, many deportees had families with them, which also acted as a deterrent. Still, many hundreds of thousands fled deportation settlements, especially during the chaotic early years of the 1930s. OGPU and civil police succeeded in capturing only a small percentage of these escapees.

From 1932 through 1940 nearly 630,000 special settlers fled their exile, of which 235,000 were returned. This amounted to a return rate of only 37 percent. As Yagoda noted, most of these were discovered through passport sweeps, which meant that the passport system worked well enough in conjunction with mass sweep operations, but this was far from the ideal that Yagoda envisioned of an ironclad system of registration, surveillance, and operational work.[34] Many in that 37 percent were no doubt swept up in the specially ordered mass operations of 1937 and 1938, rather than caught in the steady working of the surveillance and operational system of the NKVD. Numbers from the early and mid-1930s bear this out. During the first half of the decade—from 1932 through 1935, when reforms were instituted—some 554,000 deportees fled settlements, while only about 178,000 were returned. This was a return rate of less than one-third (32 percent), significantly lower than the overall rate of return for the whole decade.[35] Many of these escapees changed their names, falsified documents, and otherwise melted into the peripheral landscape, into new industrial sites hungry for labor, and into the nonpassportized areas of the country, to try to eke out a life without being noticed. Their numbers testified to the chasm between theory and practice in the policing-surveillance system.

There were many reasons why the system did not work as Yagoda envisioned. One reason was that the system that the OGPU instituted in the early 1930s was a root-and-branch reorganization, not an adjustment to an already functioning system. The *kartoteka* system was created ex nihilo, at least within the civil police, as was the new police operational and surveillance system. The OGPU certainly had long experience with such work, but that organization also underwent rapid expansion, reorganization, and integration with the civil police. And all of this took place during massive campaigns of social repression on a coordinated union-wide scale. It is no wonder that the system did not work, given its newness and the large number of underqualified people who worked in the police and OGPU.

The problem lay not just in issues of scale, scope, and qualification, but also in numbers—specifically, in the lack of them. In practice, the burden of operational and surveillance work fell on the shoulders of officials at the regional level of the civil and political police. Despite significant expansion during the 1930s, this remained the least qualified and most understaffed level of both organizations. RKM organs could count on only three or four, maybe four or five, but often only two or three operational officers in most regions outside major cities. OGPU offices counted about the same number of operational officers, plus a driver, and one to two secretarial staff. According to the logic of the system, these individuals had to staff and run the three main operational departments (antibanditry, economic crimes, and antitheft). This handful of people was supposed to organize and manage informant networks, run agents, maintain surveillance operations, compile statistics and reports, keep criminal and passport registration catalogs, and conduct active investigations.

It was impossible for just a handful of people, let alone unqualified people, to fulfill all the tasks assigned to the different parts of the policing system. It is no wonder that registration work lapsed, that informant networks were not maintained, that reporting was slow and often incomplete, that operational work was sporadic. Local officials, pressed with too many demands and too few people, coped as best they could. Many engaged in the time-honored practice of fulfilling orders "on paper," as higher officials so often remarked. Many simply ignored orders and instructions from above. "It was not required," answered one local inspector, when asked why he had not fulfilled instructions to implement a fingerprinting system as part of the registration of criminals.[36]

All these problems encouraged noncompliance and simultaneously reinforced the campaign style of policing in fits and starts. Pressed for results, local officials mobilized officers and even non–police officials, or they launched operational campaigns on specific orders from above. Introducing the passport system, policing petty crimes such as speculation, searching for criminals, and sweeping areas for socially dangerous elements were all policies and tasks that the police and OGPU carried out in this way. These campaigns consumed time and energy and disrupted normal policing duties and routines. The crisis nature of these methods also worked against the smooth functioning of the policing and surveillance system.

REFORM AND FURTHER INTEGRATION

Police authorities implemented a number of reforms in order to normalize the policing and surveillance system. The problem of escapees, especially, drove many of these reforms.[37] Some reforms focused on the gathering and processing of information, while others centered on operational methods. All were designed to further integrate civil and political police, and many reforms brought the political police even deeper into the sphere of civil policing. Beginning in 1935, for example, efforts to find escaped prisoners, whether criminal or political, were coordinated under control of local political police offices.[38] Other reforms included expansion of and tighter control over prison and camp informant networks, and better integration of camp informant information with operational activities to find escaped prisoners. The creation of interregional operational sections was an especially important reform. Both the civil and the political police established these middle-layer administrations in the early 1930s. Such sections, staffing up to ten officers with support staff, were located in major towns, usually regional administrative centers, and worked to supplement personnel and to coordinate operational and surveillance activities. Many of these centers were dismantled after the dekulakization campaigns, but others remained as important organizations in outlying or geographically large regions. These operational centers proved particularly effective during mass operation campaigns. They directed and reinforced regional officers in rounding up targeted categories of the local population, in conducting mass sweeps of socially dangerous elements, in campaigns to check passports and residency papers, and in surveillance and other operational work.

Some of the most important reforms involved the flow and handling of information. In early summer 1935, Yagoda ordered that local informant catalogs be replicated at the central political police levels in republics and in Moscow, and in July 1935 he began the process of systematizing the fingerprinting and photographing of all custodial populations. Instruction teams were to be sent to all oblast-level NKVD administrations, as well as to oblast-level GULAG administrations, equipment was to be mobilized, and instructional material distributed. Parallel registration bureaus were to be established by the central GULAG and GURKM (passportization) administrations. Copies of fingerprints and photographs, even if already on file, were to be duplicated and included in corresponding oblast- and regional-level catalogs. A separate catalog system was to be set up at each administrative level and cross-referenced by name to an individual's main registration card.[39]

The instructions on fingerprinting and photographing supplemented a major reorganization of the criminal registration system in June 1935. Central authorities streamlined the paper reporting requirements from local police, for example, as they placed increasing emphasis on the collection and integration of card catalog information.[40] Most important, the catalog system was brought completely under GUGB management. According to Yagoda's instructions, *kartoteki* of criminals and suspicious persons were to be located not just in regional police offices, but were to be duplicated in their entirety at every level of the NKVD—at the oblast (or *krai*) and republic administrations, and in the central commissariat in Moscow. This instruction meant, in effect, that card catalogs came under control of political police officials, since they headed NKVD administrations at all levels higher than the region. Biographical cards were to be filed by name and were to include photographs, aliases, biographical histories, and references to fingerprints on file. Printed registration forms also included lines for information on social status; nationality; passport number; identifying physical characteristics; and record of convictions, deportations, and operational actions taken against the individual concerned. Fingerprint and street alias catalogs were to be organized parallel to and cross-referenced with biographical catalogs.

This reorganization affected the registration system of the civil police and was curiously selective. Civil police registration catalogs included certain kinds of information about criminals, socially dangerous individuals, and even politicals. In contrast, GUGB *kartoteki* at all levels except the *raion* level were to be comprehensive. Card catalogs of the political police were to include all information about individuals on *uchet* by both the GUGB and the *militsiia*. Moreover, all registration information, as well as the organization of all the different kinds of catalogs, was placed under the control of officers assigned by the statistical administrations of the GUGB. This latter administrative reorganization stood in contrast to previous practice, in which *militsiia* officials maintained responsibility over their own catalogs.[41]

In September 1936, Yagoda launched a major reorganization of the internal passport and residence registration system involving a process of duplication analogous to that of the criminal and political registration system. Like the reforms described above, reorganization of passport registration catalogs subordinated the civil police more closely to the GUGB. Beginning in late 1936, NKVD administrations in all cities with populations over 20,000 (some 360 cities by then) were to establish "branch" (*kustovye*) address bureaus. The catalogs in these bureaus were to consolidate and duplicate passport and residence information for surrounding regions. These bureaus, like all passport and residence bureaus, were used for many purposes—to establish demographic patterns for social and economic purposes, to check unwanted migration, to plan development, to find missing persons or relatives—but the bureaus were set up originally and specifically to act as "reference" *kartoteki* for police and GUGB searches and operational groups. They were to be established "alongside" (*pomimo*) catalogs of criminal, counterrevolutionary, and other suspicious persons, and they were to be used in conjunction with operational activities by both agencies. Civil police still managed passport and registration catalogs in localities, but the branch catalogs were located in NKVD offices in larger towns and cities. This meant that passport catalogs, like other registration catalogs, came under direct control of political police officers.

Like the other reforms, reorganization of the passport catalog system was intended to improve the effectiveness of both political and civil police operations against criminals, escapees, and "elements" dangerous to the state. The circular that ordered organization of branch bureaus was entitled "On searches for criminals," and in that same circular, Yagoda ordered the creation of yet another catalog system, this time of escaped prisoners and special settlers. Information in this *kartoteka* system was supposed to be coordinated between the GULAG administration and the various levels of the NKVD. This catalog system was to be updated monthly and cross-checked with information in the branch residence registration and passport catalogs.[42]

In his circular, Yagoda once again chided subordinates for failing fully to appreciate the importance of "statistical" policing work, first and foremost the collection of passport and residence information, but also other kinds of registration information, including fingerprint and photograph information. Yagoda reiterated instructions for effective distribution of wanted lists. He rehearsed procedural protocols for operational activities and coordination of information between GULAG and territorial police organs. Yagoda once again laid out jurisdictional distinctions between civil and political police operations but, as with criminal registration, he also placed all police search operations, civil as well as political, under GUGB operational control. The latter instruction, especially, contrasted with previous practice, in which civil police had independent jurisdictional responsibility to find and capture escaped exiles in their areas.[43] Oblast NKVD administrations were to report monthly to the GUGB in Moscow on the results of searches in their oblasts. In turn, oblast-level GUGB offices were to coordinate distribution of wanted lists and search activities.[44]

The proliferation of registration systems continued as authorities added more categories of the population to the list of those who supposedly threatened the regime, or who worked under police control. Those on registration included political oppositionists, social harmfuls, "common" criminals, recidivists, informants, agents and on and on. In April 1935, Yagoda renewed instructions for all precinct inspectors to create separate catalogs of known hooligans in their jurisdictions, as well as of individuals "without definite employment."[45] The expansion of surveillance lists and duplication of registration catalogs made sense operationally, but it also enhanced political police involvement in civil policing and population monitoring. The catalog system became the active operational archive of information that police, both civil and political, used to identify and remove criminals, marginal populations, and suspect individuals. Registration instructions maintained an operational distinction between civil and political police spheres of authority, but all registration systems were set up to integrate easily into the GUGB information and operational system. Regional and precinct police offices continued to maintain passport catalogs and address bureaus, but these also became a major source of social surveillance, and were placed ultimately under control of the political police.

CONCLUSIONS: CATALOGS AND MASS POLICING

Throughout the 1930s, Yagoda attempted to improve policing methods by pushing through a number of reforms. Several of these reforms involved increasing control by the GUGB over registration systems and operational activities of the civil police. Yagoda intended these changes to improve overall operational and managerial effectiveness, but not to blur lines of operational jurisdiction between civil and political policing. Yet these lines were already quite blurred by 1935, and Yagoda's reforms reinforced an already strong trend to subordinate the civil to the political police. Conversely, Yagoda's reforms entangled the political police further in matters of broad social surveillance and the policing of ordinary criminality and public order. Yagoda's very success in integrating political and civil policing would be used against him in early 1937, but not yet in 1935 and 1936. At the time, Yagoda was working with official sanction and in accordance with an official view, espoused by Stalin, that public order was a key priority of state security and therefore the legitimate, even urgent, business of the political police.

Changes to the policing system in the mid-1930s reinforced other changes, as well as the tendency to merge public order and state security. As other scholars have noted, during the 1920s, political police tended to rely heavily on narrative types of social surveillance, based on the regular production of reports (*svodki*) about popular moods.[46] In keeping with the positivist, scientific outlook of police officials, however, police began to move away from this narrative type of social monitoring. In the 1930s, police developed and relied increasingly on statistical methods of surveillance through the compilation of card catalog registries—the system of *uchet* and *kartoteki*. As this chapter has shown, the use of *kartoteki* proliferated, including separate registries for criminals, informants and agents, social marginals, even rowdy troublemakers and suspicious persons. These registries not only replaced *svodki*, they also took precedence over narrative forms of reporting through informant and agent networks.

The number and kinds of card catalog systems grew rapidly in the early and mid-1930s, including the passport and residence registration system. These systems grew to be one of the most effective social policing tools available to the regime, certainly more so than informant networks. By late 1936, Yagoda could write that operational activities and the use of registration information had improved over the chaotic practices of the early 1930s. Still, both of these aspects of policing were far from satisfactory. Despite some improvement, despite prodding from the center, and despite increasing control by the GUGB, informant, passport, criminal, and other registration systems continued to work far less effectively than central authorities wished.[47] Policing continued to be reactive rather than prophylactic. Informant networks remained underutilized. Informant information rarely drove operational activities. Agent surveillance continued to be episodic, in reaction to crimes already committed, rather than constant and pervasive. Police reporting described trends based on cases of arrests already made and profiles of crimes already committed and criminals already apprehended, not on analysis of information from surveillance networks. In a system that was understaffed with underqualified people, policing was not driven by the integral functioning of informant information, registration, and operational activities, but by political decisions of leaders implemented through campaign-style operations of repression.

To the extent that passport and other registration systems worked effectively, they did so in conjunction with these campaign-style operations, usually ordered from the center, and only when problems of criminality or public order became an urgent state priority. Thus, information about suspicious types picked up in mass police raids could be checked in various registries, particularly in passport and residence catalogs. At the operational conference in 1931, OGPU officials lauded the use of registration systems in conjunction with mass policing operations. They saw this combination as an effective tool to isolate criminals and socially dangerous populations.[48] In 1931, however, the use of mass forms of repression was still regime policy against peasants and socially marginal elements. By 1935, the situation had changed, and leaders saw the use of mass operations as a failure of prophylactic policing. Still, as the following chapter shows, campaign methods of social policing were effective. Officials resorted to their use, especially in conjunction with the rapidly developing systems of card catalog registration. During the mid-1930s, these campaigns reinforced a mobilizational style of policing, as much as did local inertia and problems of staffing and qualification. Mass repression did not end in 1933, it changed form.

6 The Campaigns against Marginals

What will we do now that we've liquidated the capitalist elements?
—OGPU official, 1934

IN FIGHTING STALIN's new kind of class war, the OGPU shifted its orientation from a revolutionary and counterinsurgency force to a social policing force, an organ increasingly involved in social control, surveillance, and the maintenance of public order. This was a new role for the political police, but one that Yagoda, with Stalin's backing, pushed aggressively. As the decade wore on, the OGPU and then the NKVD encroached on and colonized social policies that had previously come under the purview of other state organs, particularly the courts and social agencies. The political police's move into problems of social order militarized civil governance in a way unknown during the 1920s, and placed the political police at the center of the social and geographical construction of Soviet socialism.

This chapter examines the class war against social marginals during the mid-1930s, and the effect of that war on political police and policing, as well as the transformation of the civil police. Reforms of the civil police made clear Yagoda's intention to turn the *militsiia* into an organ of social control subordinate and equal in preparedness to the organs of state security. By placing it under the administrative control of the OGPU, Yagoda intended to "militarize" the police, but he did not intend completely to Chekaize it—for administrative merger to lead to operational merger. The police were to work as an auxiliary force to the OGPU in the establishment of public order and the protection of state interests and property. The fight against counterrevolutionary activities was to remain a prerogative of the OGPU, the organ of state security.

The neat distinction between civil and political police functions proved difficult to maintain. The distinction between social order and state security quickly blurred as the regime attempted to deal with the wide-scale social dislocation caused by its policies. In word and practice, leaders easily conflated public order with state security. As a result, enforcement of public norms and the protection of social space became the business of the political as well as the civil police. Likewise, and despite Yagoda's intentions, considerable overlap occurred, both administratively and operationally, between the *militsiia* and the OGPU. As the *militsiia* took on new functions as a social gendarmerie, the OGPU turned its attention from class war in the countryside to campaigns against socially marginal, suspect, and criminal populations in cities, arteries of communication, and other strategically important areas such as borders. These campaigns of social defense, as they were called, commenced in the summer and autumn of 1932, even as the regime began to scale back the mass repressions that had been unleashed in the Soviet countryside during collectivization and dekulakization. The campaigns against social marginals occupied much of the attention and operational energy of the political and civil police throughout the middle years of the decade.

The overlap of civil and political policing produced another consequence, also in contrast to official injunctions, in the continued use of campaign and nonjudicial methods of mass repression. There were several reasons for this. Administrative processing of large numbers of people had become ingrained in OGPU practice during the dekulakization and border cleansing campaigns of the early 1930s. That kind of counterinsurgency policing proved resistant to change, and carried over from OGPU practice to influence the operational culture of civil police and then the NKVD. As a result, police continued to use campaign and administrative methods of repression during the social defense campaigns of the mid-1930s. As it turned out, such methods were also the most effective way that authorities could utilize scarce resources. Throughout the 1930s, despite increases in budgets and personnel, civil police officials found themselves hard pressed. Lack of staff, lack of training, and lack of discipline, among other problems, continued to hamper policing efforts to react to and prevent crime and to maintain social order. Campaign-style cleansing operations in cities, regions, rail depots, marketplaces, and other areas compensated for the ineffectiveness of routinized policing methods. In many localities, sporadic and intensive policing campaigns became a norm rather than an exception. Finally, the very language of description of the population, with its broad categories of socially near, socially alien, and socially dangerous elements lent itself to mass types of policing methods. Description influenced practice as police turned increasingly to repression of categories—of whole groups of people—rather than of individual offenders. This categorical imperative came to characterize Stalinist policing culture during the 1930s.[1]

THE RAILROAD AND ANTIHOOLIGAN CAMPAIGNS

Involvement of the political police in problems of social order began in late 1932, not surprisingly in a series of campaign-like operations to bring order to the chaos on the country's rail lines. Ostensibly, the OGPU's transport forces were charged to defend the railroads against counterrevolutionary sabotage, that is, against the enemies of the state. OGPU officers regularly rode trains in order to provide security for military and special assignments as well as mail cars, or against heavy bandit attacks. They also provided protection of crucial railheads, yards, bridges, and junctions. Judging from correspondence, however, political police officials did not see it as their task to ensure civil order on trains or on the lines. That, according to the division of responsibility, was the task of the transport commissariat's guard force.[2]

Stalin had his own ideas about the role of the political police. Writing to Kaganovich from his vacation in Sochi in early August 1932, Stalin communicated his displeasure about the "outrageous" situation on the country's rail lines, in which "hooligans and orphans" disrupted trains and stations and brazenly robbed, "terrorized," and "physically intimidated" government officials. Stalin, interestingly, wrote nothing about passengers, only about government workers, *sluzhashchie,* who were the targets of harassment. Such a situation was intolerable, wrote Stalin. The OGPU was "asleep." "Where are they? What are they doing?" Stalin demanded that Kaganovich call the agency to account, and he singled out Deputy Commissar Georgii Blagonravov, by name.

Blagonravov was both deputy commissar of transport and head of the Transport Department of the OGPU. Clearly incensed, Stalin instructed the OGPU, through Kaganovich, to bring order to the railroads, even by placing armed troops on trains with authorization to "shoot hooligans on the spot."[3]

Stalin did not refer to mass operations in his note to Kaganovich, but he left no doubt that he expected immediate results. V. R. Menzhinskii, as head of the OGPU, and Blagonravov responded accordingly and as a result, police launched one of the first civil-order mass operations over a four-month period from April through August 1932. In a Politburo-sanctioned operation, OGPU units joined with railroad guard brigades, and even deputized activists of the Komsomol, in order to clean stations and trains and river traffic of "hooligans, orphans, and petty thieves." By checking tickets and identity documents, police hauled in just over 49,000 individuals of the "hooligan element" and detained 13,122 orphans. In all, 3,558 arrests were made from within these two categories, while an additional 8,288 arrests resulted from those caught with stolen goods. An additional 118,085 individuals were fined for minor disorder violations or for riding without tickets.[4]

Menzhinskii reported on this operation at the end of August. Since cases were still pending in court, his report did not include information about how the cases of those arrested were adjudicated. Menzhinskii warned Stalin, however, that despite the success of the operation in reducing hooliganism and theft, this reduction would be only temporary unless the transport commissariat took significant prophylactic measures to protect lines through systematic patrolling. Unfortunately, as Menzhinskii noted, the railroads were in no position to provide such protection, and the railwaymen's trade union refused to become involved in policing work. The union insisted that this was the job of the line brigades and the police.[5] Consequently, the government responded by transferring a large contingent of OGPU forces to permanent railroad duty. Already in June, Sovnarkom had moved to integrate troops of the OGPU internal forces into the regular guard force of the transport commissariat, especially to secure the railroads. By the beginning of 1933, the OGPU was to transfer as many as 20,000 troops, and this was to bring OGPU forces on the railroads to a total level of 54,120. Sovnarkom recommended an additional 3,251 troops for guard duty on water transport, and 820 for protection of various oil and refinery facilities. These troops were to retain their OGPU status, and the OGPU was to pay for their outfitting and housing, but they operated under the authority and at the command of the line directors to which they were assigned.[6] Such a situation must have caused a certain amount of resentment among OGPU personnel, but it was a clear indication of the mixing of political and civil policing that came to characterize the 1930s.

In order to utilize this new force to the maximum, Menzhinskii requested and the Politburo sanctioned at least two more mass operations, one of them immediately following the first operation. This second operation took place from September through November 1932, also against hooliganism and theft in the railroad system. The operation yielded 8,439 arrests for hooliganism and 3,224 arrests for theft. In the process, security units swept up an unspecified but large number of individuals categorized as part of the "socially dangerous and orphan element." Interestingly, 1,826 of those arrested for hooliganism found themselves in local comrades' courts, while 2,092 received regular court sentences of three years' imprisonment or more, including 361 individuals sentenced to death by shooting. Although 3,224 individuals were arrested for theft, 3,460 received sentences of incarceration, the latter number including previous detainees.[7] The most ominous aspect of the operation involved the unspecified but large number of people who were swept up as socially dangerous or as orphans. The number must have been significantly large, since 36,887 individuals listed in that category were sentenced to some form of forced labor, including 6,000 sent to labor camps. The rest were likely deported to labor colonies or possibly to special settlements, although the latter is less likely, since settlements until 1933 housed mainly agricultural laborers deported as a result of dekulakization. It is possible that many may have been sentenced to some form of labor in local jails. Finally, noted Menzhinskii's report, state security officers—charged with the defense of the state against its mortal enemies—issued fines to nearly 594,000 individuals for traveling without proper tickets or for other minor infractions.[8]

Operations on such a scale jammed the courts and created a serious backlog of cases. In response, the OGPU fell back on tried and true practices. As in the dekulakization campaigns, the mass campaigns on railroads and river transport prompted requests by the OGPU to process large numbers of people, especially those categorized as socially dangerous or harmful, through administrative arrest and extrajudicial troikas under OGPU control. Yagoda submitted his request in December 1932 to TsIK, the Central Executive Committee of the Soviets. He asked that troikas have authority over cases involving hooliganism, rowdyism (*debosh*), and, oddly, cases involving "people who ignor[ed] the authority of security personnel on highways and railroads, and in specially guarded places." The latter reflected, no doubt, a fact of Soviet life—that masses of people simply ignored regulations and the local officials who attempted to enforce them. Yagoda requested that the troikas be given the authority to pass sentence even up to shooting. Avel' Yenukidze, as secretary of TsIK, noted his approval for troikas as such, but struck out permission to shoot.[9] The latter was consistent with the effort to recentralize control over state-administered violence, and especially over the right to administer the death penalty. It is significant, however, that these sweeps helped establish the precedent for how the regime would deal with the vague category of "antisocial" and "socially harmful" groups, the largest single category of those detained and arrested in the railroad operations. It is not clear from the brief reports who exactly fell into this category, but police would continue to use and broaden it as the decade wore on.

The OGPU counted the antihooligan operation a tremendous success—so much so, that Menzhinskii requested an extension of special OGPU powers at least through February of 1933. In making such a request, Menzhinskii made clear that the OGPU had found a particularly effective "extrajudicial method by which to settle up [or get even—*rasprave*] with declassed hooligan-bandit elements." Indeed, the OGPU continued its operations, and not just through February. In March 1933, the Politburo again recommended a sweeping railroad operation using powers of administrative arrest and sentencing, this time focusing primarily on lines in Ukraine, the North Caucasus, the "Southeast," and Kazakhstan. As in earlier operations, the sweep was designed to clean lines and protect them from "infiltration" (*proniknovenie*) by "class-harmful, counterrevolutionary, and corrupt anti-Soviet elements."[10] The operation coincided with the formation of political departments (*politotdely*) along railroad lines, modeled after the *politotdely* in agricultural machine tractor stations. OGPU and police units continued to use undercover and investigative methods to fight against the organized transportation of stolen and contraband goods and against the organizations that used the railroads and postal systems for criminal purposes. Still, the most effective, or at least publicly visible, results came from operational sweeps. In the absence of regular and effective policing, OGPU operational groups routinely cleared yards, depots, stations, trains, and other facilities of gangs and drifters. At times, OGPU officers found themselves in the business of checking passenger tickets and freight manifests.

The antihooligan operations on the railroads were some of the first of the 1930s that became known as campaigns of social defense, *sotsial'naia* or *obshchestvennaia zashchita*. These operations were also some of the first to utilize political police and internal troops in campaigns to secure public order, as opposed to campaigns against political opponents or supposedly hostile classes. The railroad operations differed from the dekulakization campaigns in that the former were discrete operations conducted under specific orders under control of professional police officials. They did not involve any significant propaganda campaigns or attempts at broad social participation. They were not initiated to alter or remake social or economic relations, but to maintain social order and to protect state property and interests. The railroad campaigns did not involve mass repression on the scale of dekulakization, but they did involve the arrest and administrative adjudication of large numbers of people. Those caught up in the operations were detained or arrested not just for violating specific laws, but for fitting into the category of socially harmful or orphan. These campaigns were not the only or the last such meddling of the political police in matters of public and civil order, but they were typical, perhaps even the very model, of the kind of social policing that came to characterize the mid-1930s. The railroad operations were the beginning. Larger operations were to follow, and resulted from the chaos created by the regime's policies.

THE THREAT TO THE CITIES

By late 1932, forced collectivization and dekulakization had resulted in a critical, even dangerous, situation for the regime. These ruthless campaigns, as well as the resulting food shortages in the countryside, drove a large segment of the rural population off the land.[11] Hundreds of thousands of people who were not deported fled the villages and the countryside, if they could get past police patrols and checks. Many of these people headed for the cities and industrial sites, where distribution and rationing networks were already under serious strain. In 1931, alone, some 10.8 million people officially registered as new arrivals in towns and cities, while another 10.6 million arrived in 1932. Registered departures from urban areas for these years amounted to 6.7 million and 7.8 million respectively. New urban in-migration, then, reached some 4 million people in 1931 and close to 3 million people in 1932.[12] Many but not all of these immigrants arrived from rural areas. The overall drop in rural households from 1929 to 1932 amounted to about 1 million, which meant that many people were moving from cites to cities, most likely in search of food and work.[13] Still, whether from rural areas or other urban areas, new arrivals in cities put pressure on food and housing resources. The consequences were predictable. Serious disturbances broke out in a number of cities and towns, precipitated by food shortages. In the Belorussian town of Borisovo, several hundred people attacked grain warehouses, and demonstrations by women and children were not infrequent. Police reported strikes and demonstrations in other towns, while some of the most serious strikes occurred in the textile manufacturing centers of Ivanovo, north and east of Moscow. In some of these cases, crowds attacked police and OGPU offices and, even more disturbing for regime leaders, police in some instances sympathized with the demonstrators.[14] Then, in the midst of these troubles, severe grain shortages in late summer led to the collapse of the state's grain procurement plan. These events exacerbated flight from the countryside and food shortages in the cities. Thus, just as urban populations swelled in late summer and autumn 1932, regime officials were forced to cut grain allocations to the cities by as much as 16 percent from the already low levels in late summer 1931.[15] In the late autumn, the country lurched into the beginnings of a famine that lasted from November 1932 to June 1933 and took the lives of some 5 million people. By late 1932 already, masses of people began streaming out of the countryside toward the cities.

Soviet leaders became alarmed by the inundation of cities. Newcomers not only threatened social disruption but placed a strain on the state-controlled distribution and rationing system, as well as on the already severe shortage of housing, and this at a time when goods, services, and basic staples were already in scarce supply. The rise in urban unrest exacerbated fears of a major threat to the regime. In late summer, regime leaders decided to take action to protect the urban and industrial centers of the country. In early autumn, a series of measures tightened labor discipline and control over rationing cards in an effort to stem corruption in the distribution system. In October, for example, TsIK sent a decree to local soviets to ensure that access to rationed foodstuffs was tied strictly to productive employment and proof of urban residence.[16] In turn, concern over enforcement of this decree triggered a related concern over the ability of localities to control in-migration. A survey conducted in the summer by the Russian republic's statistical agency revealed what was already obvious. Major deficiencies in the system of residence registration allowed large numbers of people to settle in urban areas without proper permits.[17] Faced with such a situation, the Politburo prepared decrees and policies to act along two related lines: to clear cities of marginal populations and to interdict the mass flight of peasants from rural areas of the country.

The decrees that set in motion these policies deserve a close reading, since they formalized the use of large-scale repression as a means to secure public order. The first decree, from November 15, called for the cleaning out (literally, the unloading, or *razgruzka*) of major urban centers—Moscow and Leningrad foremost—of "superfluous people not engaged in production or work in enterprises." This measure was to be implemented as part of a new system of residence identification—internal passports—and a related strengthening of residence registration systems based on passport documentation. Significantly, the decree aimed at ridding cities not just or even primarily of class enemies, such as kulaks, but of a laundry list of socially "unproductive" populations: "criminals and other antisocial elements (*anti-obshestvennyi element*)." Interestingly, the decree referred to antisocial rather than socially dangerous elements, as in the harsher language of later formulations.[18] These populations were to be swept out of cities and then kept out through enforcement of a new system of passport and residence registration. Just as significantly, the decree and the operational orders that followed called for close cooperation between civil and political police in mounting sweep operations against the population categories listed. Similarly, a series of directives from late January 1933 called for the cooperation of civil and political police in operations to close off routes of out-migration from famine-plagued regions. Measures included roundups of people on roads, and especially along rail lines. In other measures, police as well as local authorities were instructed not to grant travel permits to peasants or to sell train tickets without proper authorization from workplaces or government authorities.[19] The regime, in other words, using outright police repression, was attempting to stem uncontrolled population movement from both ends—from the major source of that movement in rural areas to the primary destination of most migrants in the cities.

The language in the directives on out-migration from rural areas, and the operational reports associated with them, highlighted the focus of leaders on public order and not just on class war. The directives called for police to pick up, not kulaks, but "peasants" who were trying to leave certain Ukrainian and Northern Caucasus areas for cities and grain areas in the Central Black Earth and western regions of the country. A summary report from late January claimed that peasant flight was, of course, provoked by organized counterrevolutionary agitators and Polish agents. Much of the operational activity was directed against these supposed class and anti-Soviet enemies. Yet the same report showed that only a small percentage of those caught up in sweeps were "filtered" as kulaks or "White Guardists"—659, for example, out of 11,774 taken on the North Caucasus rail line during January. In all, 1,216 of the 5,000 people swept up in the Black Sea OGPU operational sector were identified as counter-revolutionaries.[20] Police took no legal punitive action against the great majority of detainees, who were returned to their home villages. In other words, repatriation meant that authorities did not regard returned peasants as class enemies, even though, in many cases, repatriation was as good as a death sentence, given the widespread famine conditions in the areas of flight. Still, these were some of the first operations, along with the antihooligan operations on railroads, which targeted populations for mass repression for the specific purpose of restoring social and economic order. One of the largest single operations took place on the Belorussian and Ukrainian lines in late January 1933. Police rounded up nearly 25,000 people in the week-long operation: 16,000 were returned to their villages; 1,016 were arrested; the rest remained under investigation as of the writing of the report.[21]

These antimigration operations turned the political police toward issues of public order and brought the civil and political police into close cooperation. In Ukraine, as elsewhere, the antiflight operations were carried out by a number of groups, but these were led by the special operational groups of the OGPU, the *operativnye otdely,* or OO OGPU. These interregional operational units were staffed by twenty to twenty-five officers, who worked with regional and MTS officers to mount sweeps of roads for fleeing peasants. They also, importantly, ran village agents who identified "organizers and agitators" who "provoked" peasants to flee. These units, in other words, used both informant investigations to target individuals and mass roundups of people on roads without proper documents. The units supplemented their numbers with local police and even local Soviet authorities and Komsomol members. The goal was "to create a cordon" along the main exit routes of peasants trying to make their way from eastern Ukraine to the Northern Caucasus and Black Sea areas, as well as to Dagestan. In similar types of operations, railroad units from the OGPU Transport Department worked the rail lines, trains, and train stations in mobile operational groups. These operations units concentrated their limited numbers on raids of key junctions and stations that served as "gathering points" for fleeing peasants. Civil police and OGPU units also conducted joint sweep operations in cities in order to find peasants residing in towns without proper residence permits.[22] Foreign consular officials reported, as early as August 1932, large police operations in Moscow and Kharkov to expel homeless beggars, prostitutes, and hungry peasants from the cities.[23]

As in other operations, the numbers of people involved proved too much for courts to handle, and the OGPU received permission to process detainees through administrative troikas. By early 1933, however, OGPU troikas were also overburdened with cases. As a result, the civil police took up the slack and set up some of the first *militseiiskie troiki.* These troikas, established at the city or oblast level, soon became widespread in the adjudication of passport violators. They were made up of the appropriate OGPU representative, the head of the police Operational Department, and the head of the oblast police organization. This last official was soon replaced by the head of the newly established Passport Department. As with dekulakization troikas, work of the police troikas was supposed to be reviewed by the appropriate procuracy official. The troikas first began work in the antimigration campaigns, and then continued as regular passport sentencing boards. A summary report from February 1933 showed that 145,190 "runaways" had been detained. Of this number, 108,478 were returned to their places of residence; 18,448 were held for some kind of judicial or nonjudicial indictment (*privlechenie k otvetstvennosti*); slightly more than 3,000 were sentenced immediately to exile in Western Siberia or Kazakhstan; and 11,659 were held for "filtration" to determine if they were kulaks or other anti-Soviet "elements."[24] One of the final reports concerning these operations, from mid-March, showed 219,460 detainees, of which 185,588 had been returned to their places of residence.[25]

THE PASSPORT CAMPAIGNS

The antihooligan and antimigration campaigns resulted in the arrest or detention of many tens of thousands of people, but it was the passport and resident registration system that proved the most important instrument for the regime in its campaigns against unproductive, criminal, and socially marginal populations. After mid-1932, these were the populations that officials believed most threatened the regime because of their inundation of cities and the disruption they caused in housing, food supply, and the distribution system of commodities. By issuing passports to citizens and reforming the domicile registration system, Soviet leaders hoped simultaneously to protect their major bases of support—urban working populations—and their ability to plan and control trade and distribution systems. The 15 November 1932 decree stated these goals in general. A second decree, of 15 December from Sovnarkom, identified the goals specifically: "to better count . . . and to cleanse the population of the USSR."[26]

The 15 November Politburo resolution served primarily to establish a commission that was charged to work out the details of a new passport law. No surprise that the commission was initially headed by V. A. Balitskii, a leading officer in the OGPU who was soon to be sent to Ukraine as a special plenipotentiary. In Ukraine, Balitskii oversaw the OGPU during the brutally harsh years of the famine and then until 1937. He departed Moscow just days after chairing the first commission report in late November, and the chair's position passed to Avel' Yenukidze. High-ranking OGPU officers continued to dominate the commission, including Yagoda, D. V. Usov, the assistant head of the OGPU police inspectorate, and G. E. Prokof'ev, an assistant OGPU commissar and soon to be first head of the all-union police administration.[27]

The commission worked quickly, examining passport systems under the tsarist regime and in other countries, and it submitted its final draft of a new law on 27 December. The law required all citizens over the age of sixteen who lived permanently in towns, workers' settlements, and state farms to possess a passport and to register that passport with local police in order to obtain a residence permit, a *propiska,* for the address listed in the passport. Passports were also to be issued to employees of rural machine tractor stations and to those working in transport. Those living in passportized areas without registered passports were subject to fines or expulsion. Repeat offenders were subject to prosecution and even prison and exile. Employees were required to register passports at places of work located in passportized areas and could not be hired without a passport. Any employee hired legally but who did not possess a passport could obtain a temporary passport that would then become permanent. Military and OGPU troops and officers fell into a special "militarized" category, to be issued passports which were then confiscated by their commands and replaced with special passes, or *spravki,* which served in place of passports while they were on active duty. In time, other categories, especially railroad workers, were also militarized in this fashion, which essentially tied these groups to their places of work, so long as their passports were held by the authorities.

In accordance with Politburo guidelines, passportization was to be carried out first in three major cities—Moscow, Leningrad, and Kharkov—which were heavily inundated with in-migrants, and in a hundred-kilometer radius around the first two and a fifty-kilometer radius around the last. Early in 1933, the commission extended this first wave of passportization to other "first-priority" cities—Kiev, Minsk, Rostov, and Vladivostok, then to industrial centers such as Kuznetsk, Stalingrad, and Baku—in all, thirteen cities and border areas. The passport commission anticipated passportization during 1933 and 1934 of other urban, border, strategic, and industrial areas.[28] A major section of the new law created the Chief Administration of Workers and Peasants Police, the GURKM, under control of the OGPU, to administer countrywide passportization, and a system of passport desks, *stoly,* to be established in each police precinct for distribution and control of passport and registration permits.[29]

On 14 January 1933, the passport commission and the new police administration issued detailed instructions for passportization. In addition to the published law described above, the GURKM issued a set of secret instructions to local police and OGPU offices. These instructions described in detail who was and who was not to be given a passport and allowed a *propiska,* under what conditions, and what actions police were to take against those denied passports or residence permits. These instructions also detailed for the first time a distinction between passportized areas of a first or "regime" category and all other passportized areas. In the first set of instructions, Moscow, Leningrad, and Kharkov received the designation of regime areas, but this list was soon expanded to include a number of cities, towns, and border areas. In nonregime areas, all citizens were to be issued passports who were not under criminal indictment or runaway kulaks. In regime areas, however, passportization was far more restrictive, and police were to deny passports and residence permits to a range of socially marginal groups. These included "persons not engaged in production or the work of institutions or schools, or who [are] not engaged in any other form of socially useful work." The list included several other categories: all persons who arrived in a regime area after 1 January 1931 and who did not have a formal letter of invitation for employment, anyone unemployed at the time of passportization, and persons, in the open-ended wording of the instruction, who were "obvious flitters" or who had been previously fired from a work place. All persons who had been disenfranchised (i.e. *lishentsy*) or who had a criminal record were not to receive passports or registration permits in regime areas, unless they were dependents of actively serving military personnel. Finally, those denied passports in regime areas included all refugees, except formal political immigrants, and all family members of any person listed under exclusion.[30]

Seasonal workers from *kolkhozy* fell under special instructions. This category of people became the subject of contentious debates, as Yagoda attempted to tighten restrictions on migration of "unorganized" or marginal and harmful populations. In the original instruction, however, seasonal workers, *otkhodniki,* were to be issued a temporary three-month passport if they possessed a formal letter of hire from an enterprise, and a pass, or *spravka,* issued by the collective farm or village soviet of their permanent residence. This temporary passport allowed these types of workers to obtain housing. After three months, their temporary passports could be exchanged for one-year passports, and then renewed for three to five years. At first, *otkhodniki* were issued passports by police offices in the cities of the enterprises that hired them. In February 1934, however, in the first of many moves to control such migration, police were instructed to cease this practice. After that date, passports were to be issued by the local soviets where peasants resided, before they traveled to passportized areas.[31]

Police planned passportization in major cities in two phases. The first phase was to take place in large factories and other workplaces that employed over two thousand workers. A second phase then passportized all those who could not be issued passports at a place of work. The latter included residents employed at smaller enterprises or offices, dependents, pensioners, the elderly, and the disabled. Police instructed enterprises to compile current lists of employees, which were to include information on biographical and work background, and to submit these lists prior to the passport distribution. Temporary passport desks were established in enterprises for the purpose of issuing passports, while permanent passport desks were to be organized at every precinct station, which would become the primary location for control over passport and residence registration in a neighborhood. Passports were to be issued on the basis of any one of several documents that could prove a person's employment history or residence qualifications. This, as well as any suspect or "compromising" information, was to be recorded in a card index system, to be filed at the precinct passport desk, and eventually duplicated and integrated into larger catalogs at higher levels of police administration. Citizens were to register and unregister their place of residence at the local precinct passport desk.

Social policing through passportization was supposed to work in both a passive and an active way. As a passive policing method, passportization worked by denying passports to socially undesirable populations. Anyone who was denied a passport in a regime locality was given ten days to leave and to inform police in writing where they intended to settle. Presumably, anyone not eligible for a passport in a regime locality, and who was not a criminal, would resettle and receive a passport in a nonregime locality. If, after the ten-day grace period, those denied a passport had not left, they were subject to a fine and police deportation. Review of documents for passportization was also supposed to identify any criminals or runaway kulaks who were so brazen as to try to apply for a passport and residence permit. Otherwise, police anticipated that illegals would leave rather than take the risk of being caught in a passport check. In either case, the objective of cleansing the area would be accomplished, and police anticipated that, eventually, illegals would be caught in the ensuing squeeze as the system of passportization was extended across the entire country.

This was all well and good, but police did not want simply to let the passport system act passively on the population. In early 1933, in preparation for the distribution of internal passports, civil and political police also geared up for a major offensive to identify and detain, or actively drive, unwanted populations out of cities. In Moscow, for example, Secret Order 009 of 5 January 1933, "On Chekist measures to introduce the passport system," set this process in motion. Yagoda issued the order even before the government's commission finalized details of the new passport law. "Chekist measures" meant active operations to identify and round up large numbers of people and then do something with them. Toward this end, the decree required local OGPU and police units in the city and oblast to compile two types of lists. The first type comprised all those who should be deported from Moscow as antisocial. It is not clear by what criteria police would judge someone as antisocial. Nor was it clear how the people who ended up on these lists differed from those who, when applying for passports, were denied them because of some compromising information or ineligibility due to residence or work criteria. Presumably, however, those on the antisocial lists would be more dangerous than those denied passports and subject to expulsion. The second type of list was to consist of individuals who fell into more dangerous categories of "counterrevolutionary, kulak, criminal and other anti-Soviet elements." These lists were to be compiled on the basis of different sources of information—police records and existing watch lists, work rolls, informant networks, and local responsible citizens. Lists were to be sent to the main administration of the Moscow oblast OGPU Operational Department, which would coordinate sweeps by local OGPU and *militsiia* units.[32] The order required the lists within one week. It also warned local OGPU offices to be certain to transfer files of individuals on watch lists to new residence locations after deportation of those individuals. Interestingly, it also allowed local operational departments temporarily to leave in place individuals who, otherwise slated for deportation, were important to ongoing agent investigations. Presumably, these individuals were either under surveillance or were acting as police or OGPU informants.

Initial passportization of the first-priority regime areas took place between January and the end of April 1933. During that period, police issued 6,596,514 passports in thirteen regime cities, and in the Leningrad and Moscow oblasts. Nearly 266,000 passport requests were denied, amounting to 4 percent of the total population that requested passports.

The largest contingent of those refused passports consisted of 76,670 individuals who had migrated to cities in 1931 and 1932, but who had no "socially productive" means of support. Other categories of socially undesirable populations included escaped kulaks (60,508), former convicts (34,338), *lishentsy* (21,926), those not engaged in socially useful work (34,851), and dependents of all these (28,379). An additional 7,310 individuals were taken into custody as a result of police sweep operations.[33] Those denied passports were either detained and deported or forced to make their own arrangements to leave the city.

As passportization got under way, and as operations began to sweep up people, a mass exodus from cities began. Reports estimated that Moscow emptied at a rate of about 1,000 individuals a day. By the last days of April 1933, Moscow had about 98,000 people fewer than in January. Most important, as an OGPU report noted, as a consequence of passport denials, sweep operations, and "voluntary" out-migration, at least 1,673 rooms became available in Moscow for new occupation. In Leningrad, passportization "freed" 3,380 rooms.[34]

Follow-up sweeps in regime areas after initial passportization also yielded significant results. Between summer 1933 and summer 1934, police detained 630,613 violators of passport laws living illegally in regime areas. These were in addition to the numbers swept up in the initial passport phase during the winter and spring of 1933. Most of these—slightly more than 360,000—were fined and expelled from cities. Another 3,400 were indicted and remanded to courts for hearings, while OGPU boards sentenced 65,661 to some measure of "social defense," meaning that they were sent to camps or to penal work settlements. The latter consisted mainly of individuals described as part of the "déclassé and criminal element."[35]

Initial successes in Moscow, Leningrad, and other regime cities encouraged police and Party officials to start the second and third phases of passportization. In April, Sovnarkom gave the go-ahead. Police ordered millions of passport blanks, registered their numbers, shipped the blanks to local authorities, and sent special plenipotentiaries and units to oversee local preparations for distribution. Officials began public enlightenment campaigns to prepare the affected populations. Likewise, G. E. Prokof'ev sent secret orders to organize police and local OGPU units for sweep operations.[36] In this way the police geared up for a major campaign of social engineering.

As part of that campaign, Yagoda issued a circular designed to regularize repressive measures associated with passportization. Police had conducted the initial passport operations with only vague instructions from central officials about punishments. As a result, the first passport campaigns had produced numerous complaints, from both citizens and local prosecutors, about the arbitrary and often harsh punishments meted out to passport violators, or to those denied passports. In order to avoid this, Yagoda issued Order 0096 on 13 August 1933, detailing the rules for the "nonjudicial repression of citizens violating laws relating to the passportization of the population." The order established special passport troikas at the republic, *krai,* and oblast levels to review and sentence violators of passport laws. The troikas were to be chaired by the OGPU plenipotentiary who exercised control over the police. Troika members were to include the head of the police Passport Department and the OGPU Operational Department, with participation of the local procurator. These troikas reviewed the cases of passport violators according to the lists sent to them from localities in their jurisdictions, and they were empowered to pass sentence on violators, subject to review by the OGPU central sentencing board, the *Osoboe soveshchanie,* in Moscow.

In his circular, Yagoda specified the kinds of sentences to be given for four categories of individuals. These included (1) those with no useful employment and disorganizers of industry; (2) *lishentsy* and kulaks; (3) people who had been released from prison or sentences of exile (but who did not have the right to live in the city from which they had been exiled); and (4) "criminals and other antisocial elements." Those in the last category were to be sent to labor camps for up to three years, while those in the other categories were to be sent to penal resettlement colonies (*spetsposelki*), or expelled to live outside a thirty-kilometer radius from a passportized city. The order was especially hard on repeat violators in any category, who were to be sent to labor camps for up to three years.[37] Interestingly, no clarification was given about how to identify someone as antisocial, or what was meant by employment that was not useful. This was left to local officials, specifically to those handing out passports. Thus, someone denied a passport and exiled to a settlement need not have committed a statutory crime. Similar rules applied to *lishentsy,* who need not have broken any law, but who were subject to repression. Repression under passportization thus extended and expanded the OGPU's right to apply administrative exile, and it confirmed a long-standing law, from at least 1924, which subjected social undesirables to criminal forms of repression even if they had not broken a law. The application of this practice would become increasingly widespread during the social defense policing campaigns of the mid-1930s.[38]

The second and third phases of passportization began in the spring and summer of 1933. Operational orders set in motion OGPU and police sweeps throughout the Soviet Union, and by the end of August 1934, police completed initial passportization of all designated areas in the Russian republic. This campaign resulted in the issuing of 27,009,559 passports, about 12 million to citizens living in regime cities, and nearly 15 million to citizens living in nonregime cities, towns, and rural areas.[39] As with the initial process of passportization, the issuing of passports, registration of residence, and special sweep operations set the country's marginal populations in motion. Hundreds of thousands of people fled the regime cities and industrial areas either as a consequence of being denied a passport or in advance of the passport campaign. In an August 1934 report to the Russian Soviet, Fokin, the head of the police Passport Department, counted 384,922 individuals who had been refused passports in the RSFSR. This figure amounted to slightly more than 3 percent of the overall number of citizens who received passports. In the border regions of Eastern Siberia, nearly 11 percent of the population had been denied passports and were either detained or forced to leave their places of residence.[40] One report claimed that nearly 35,000 people fled the metallurgical city of Magnitogorsk prior to passportization, while another noted that police detained and then expelled another 1,500 "parasitic elements" as a result of operations during the passport campaign in that city.[41]

By late summer 1934, police were able to assess longer-term trends in population movement as a result of passportization. Again, officials paid special attention to Moscow and Leningrad. They estimated that in 1932, the year before passportization, Moscow experienced a total in-migration of 40,000 to 45,000 people each month and had grown by over half a million from a population of 3,135,000 to 3,663,300. By the beginning of 1934, as a result of passportization and stricter residence laws, the city experienced an overall population decrease to a level of 3,613,000. This net population decline for the year of only 50,000 people nevertheless represented a huge shift in contrast to the estimated population growth had passportization not occurred. Based on

projected population growth from before passportization, police estimated that, as of 1 January 1934, the capital city had 578,000 fewer
people than it would have had if the city continued to experience the
same kind of growth that had characterized 1932, the year before passports were introduced. Leningrad's population was about 300,000 less
than projected, had passportization not occurred, and in fact underwent a total decline of 176,000 from 1 January 1933 to 1 January
1934.[42] Overall, during the first half of 1933, Soviet cities experienced
a total out-migration of nearly 400,000 people. This was the only period since the civil war years in which the population of cities actually
declined, and it was exceptional for the period of rapid industrialization
and urbanization during the 1930s.[43]

As a method of social control and as a policing tactic, passportization, and police operations associated with it, proved highly successful
—at least initially. Police campaigns achieved the immediate goals of
driving socially marginal populations out of cities and of relieving pressure on urban food and housing resources. The campaign also produced the added benefit of allowing police to quantify exactly, or so
they thought, the new enemies of the regime and to identify where they
were "hiding." A police report from August 1934, for example, presented a chart supposedly quantifying how many socially undesirable
types were living and working in nonregime cities that had been passportized. Unless they were under active indictment or were runaway
kulaks, these populations were supposed to receive passports in nonregime areas. This was in contrast to regime areas, where such people
were denied passports and forced to leave or suffer deportation or
worse. Indeed, passportization allowed police to track these socially
marginal populations. Thus, Fokin, the head of the passport police, reported that passportization had identified 158,000 former convicts living in nonregime towns that had been passportized as of August 1934.
Another 196,000 "social aliens" lived in the same areas, while passports had been issued to an additional 71,000 people without definite
means of support.[44]

OTHER SOCIAL DEFENSE CAMPAIGNS

Anticipating a large population movement resulting from passportization, police and OGPU officials set in motion their own populations,

not only to count but to round up the country's marginal and dangerous populations. Throughout 1933 and 1934, the OGPU mounted a number of operations in various cities and border and industrial areas. Some of these operations, while they coincided with passportization, seemed not to be connected directly with it, and required Politburo approval.[45] Many operations, however, were related to the passportization campaign and did not require specific approval. Passportization, in other words, gave political and civil police nearly unchecked authority to engage in mass policing operations. Many of these latter operations involved blanket sweeps of such locations as marketplaces, train stations, shantytowns, and workers' camps on the outskirts of cities. A large operation in August 1933, for example, focused on criminals, "social aliens," and contraband activities in the border regions around Leningrad. Some operations targeted specific groups rather than places. In June and July 1933, police mounted operations, based on passport and residence permit checks, to round up and deport gypsies and déclassé elements in Moscow. These campaigns resulted in the expulsion of several thousands of people. Déclassé elements were described mostly as recidivist criminals or people with a petty criminal record. They, along with 5,470 gypsies (1,008 families, including 1,440 men, 1,506 women, and 2,524 children) were exiled to labor colonies near Tomsk in Western Siberia. From Tomsk, gypsy families were dispersed further to various colonies "according to their ethnic distinction."[46]

One of most frequently targeted groups was, of course, the vague category of speculators. Given the severe shortages during the early 1930s in both food and commodities, it was not surprising that illegal selling skyrocketed. Local police were unable to contain the problem and, as a result, a Politburo decree from August 1932 involved the OGPU in the fight against speculators.[47] The decree covered only the selling and reselling of grain and bread, but police practice gradually widened to include all forms of profiteering, so that the decree became the basis for renewed policing campaigns throughout the early and mid-1930s, which involved both the *militsiia* and the political police. By April 1933, Yagoda reported a little over 54,000 people detained for speculation, of whom 32,340 had been convicted either in courts or by OGPU and police troikas. In the first half of 1934, the police and the OGPU had indicted 58,314 individuals, with an unspecified and higher number of people detained. Yagoda claimed, in fact, that police initiated about

10,000 cases each month.[48] Police and OGPU agents arrested a number of these people on an individual basis, but Yagoda was pleased to confirm that many had been discovered by mass sweeps of marketplaces and train stations. He noted that, in addition to the 58,314 indicted during the first half of 1934, 53,000 people had been expelled from the country's largest cities, presumably Moscow, Leningrad, Kiev, and other major centers. These sweeps were part of campaigns to clear cities of "the parasitic and alien element," and were tied to passportization of the populations in those cities.[49]

Passport laws gave police a powerful tool to rid cities of socially marginal populations. At the same time, these laws reinforced categorical and campaign policing methods, and brought the political police into the business of public-order policing. This latter followed from Stalin's redefinition of class war, and resulted in the blurring of categories of those to be repressed. Social marginals and ordinary criminals could now be reclassified as anti-Soviet and even as counterrevolutionaries. Such a situation perhaps made policing easier in cities, but caused confusion in other ways. During dekulakization, officials in special settlements often complained that OGPU roundups of kulaks included common criminals and other groups not supposedly targeted in these operations. Although this confusion occurred, it was not supposed to happen. Beginning in 1933, the targets of policing operations became even more confused. Orders for a cleansing operation often included a mixture of target groups—kulaks, as well as déclassé and generally "anti-Soviet elements." Operations in border areas swept in smugglers, as well as suspect national minorities and supposed spies, diversionaries, and criminals, in addition to "other anti-Soviet elements." Similarly, in Party and government resort areas in the Caucasus, police sweep orders amounted to a laundry list of undesirable populations. These operations involved OGPU as well as civil police units. The conscious meshing of categories reflected the general line toward conflation of social order and state security, especially in the orders for protecting state elites in resorts, and securing the country's borders.[50]

In June 1934, police issued orders for yet another sweep operation of rail lines, this one to last up to two months, against "professional hooligans, criminals, and unsupervised children." The first two categories were to be sentenced to six months to three years in a "concentration camp," while unsupervised children caught "hooliganizing" were to be sent to "special" camps of an unspecified nature. Interestingly, this operation was directed against more than just hooligan elements. In contrast to the earlier antihooligan campaigns, this new operation was folded into a campaign to reduce the large number of train collisions, the link being that criminal and hooliganizing "diversionaries" were causing havoc and contributing to massive rail disruptions. The campaign was to be coordinated and conducted mainly by units of the Transport Department of the OGPU, in conjunction with guard forces of the transport commissariat. As part of the operation, police officials were to check passport documents, and to renew passes only for those allowed access to railroad buildings, yards, and tracks. Officers were instructed to clear trains regularly of those riding on buffers, fronts, and roofs of locomotives and cars. This campaign was given Central Committee sanction in the form of a Party decree, since it involved such an important economic sector.[51]

It is difficult to assess overall numbers, but the mass repression associated with passportization and other campaigns of social defense in 1933 and 1934 certainly involved hundreds of thousands, perhaps close to a million people. The great majority of these people suffered either administrative expulsion from cities or forced migration to nonregime areas, or they were forced to return to starving villages from which they had fled. These hundreds of thousands of people, many of whom certainly died as the result of summary police actions, do not show up in statistics about repression, based as these are on numbers of custodial populations. These people were not arrested or convicted to any term of penal or colony servitude. Yet they were also victims of mass repression, or "social defense," as the regime's officials called it. Additionally, some tens of thousands were sentenced to one or another form of imprisonment, exile to labor colonies, or to what officials still called concentration camps, *kontslager,* of the newly formed Gulag system.

RENEWAL AND INTENSIFICATION

Police conducted social defense operations even as leaders were drafting plans to curtail administrative forms of mass repression. The Politburo instructions of 8 May 1933 and reforms during that and the following year seemed to signal a turn in policy toward a more balanced division of judicial and policing power. Constraint on police power seems also to be reflected in the following year's statistics. The year 1934 was a slow year for police and the OGPU, at least on paper. The number of arrests and convictions dropped off sharply from the previous years, from a high of over 500,000 arrests in 1933 to 205,173 in 1934. Convictions dropped correspondingly from nearly 240,000 to 79,000. This was the lowest number of arrests and convictions since mid-1929, when collectivization and dekulakization began in earnest.[52] Furthermore, for the first time in several years, an increasing number of cases were heard in regular courts rather than in administrative courts of the police. Indeed, the special powers of the OGPU troikas ended in the summer of 1934 with the reorganization of the OGPU and the police into the NKVD USSR. With this reorganization, all cases that had been adjudicated in nonjudicial or administrative fashion were transferred for review within the country's restructured court system. This included many cases heard in the police passport troikas, as well as the troikas of the OGPU. The yearly report on crime and repression by the chief procurator's office noted these trends. The report extolled the strengthening of legality in the country, and supported "this huge shift . . . in judicial policies," which "could not but result in the reduction of convictions and levels of state repression." As 1934 came to a close, officials in the procuracy believed that they had finally won a major victory over the political police.[53]

Statistically, then, 1934 saw a reduction in the levels of repression in the Soviet Union, but the drop in numbers of those arrested and convicted of crimes was deceptive. The statistics did not count the large numbers of people who were not arrested, but who, nonetheless, suffered deportation or other administrative forms of repression at the hands of the police. Moreover, the drop in numbers of those arrested may have had as much to do with the working out of administrative reforms as with a conscious change in policies. Several months passed after promulgation of reforms in July before the Party and government approved governing regulations for the new courts and policing systems. In the meantime, Yagoda and the police did not sit idly by. Police and OGPU kept busy, so much so that in August, Yagoda pressed Stalin to hurry up and approve regulations governing the operation of the new NKVD's *Osoboe soveshchanie*. Rather large numbers of arrestees were "piling up" (*skopilos'*), wrote Yagoda, as a result of operations associated with purging cities and transport of socially dangerous elements. The cases of these individuals were waiting to be heard in the OGPU's administrative court. Yagoda argued that the need to clear this backlog was great enough to justify permission for the *Osoboe soveshchanie* to start work even before the government approved formation of the new NKVD.[54] Thus, what may have seemed like a victory of moderating reforms did not overly upset the police chief. Yagoda used the reform process to consolidate his own policing empire. By late 1934, Yagoda had complete control over all policing organs within a powerful all-union commissariat. He also controlled all the country's custodial populations, providing a rich source of revenue for the NKVD and turning it into a powerful economic branch of the state. And Yagoda did not anticipate any slackening of police activities. Indeed, the next two years, 1935 and 1936, brought new campaigns of social repression. As in 1933 and 1934, many of these campaigns were associated with passportization and public order, especially with the renewal and exchange of passports originally issued in 1933. During the two middle years of the decade, police campaigns against social marginals intensified as the newly formed NKVD widened and systematized campaigns of social defense against indigents, displaced peasants, and illegal urban residents. The country's political leaders also carried out campaigns of mass police repression against suspect ethnic populations, even as they renewed and intensified repressive measures against social marginals, petty criminals, and illegal traders. Policing agencies were not weakened by reforms and reorganization in 1934. To the contrary, through colonization of social policies, the combined police organs in the NKVD continued to grow in power and jurisdictional authority.

OPERATIONAL ORDER 00192

The ban against use of troikas, instituted in late summer 1934, lasted only a few months. In early January 1935, Yagoda and Andrei Vyshinskii, by now the procurator general of the Soviet Union, gave instructions to reestablish special troikas to handle cases of passport violations by "criminal and déclassé elements." In 1935, as in 1933, during initial passport campaigns and operations against social harmfuls, the country's underdeveloped court system could not handle the crush of cases that passed through it. The attempt to pass from administrative to judicial repression broke down. Troikas were once again necessary to handle the overwhelming number of passport violations associated with passport exchange and the continuing purge of urban areas. The January special order from Yagoda and Vyshinskii sanctioned special "police boards" (*militseiskie troiki*) similar in makeup and function to the recently disbanded OGPU passport troikas. They were to operate at the republic, *krai,* and oblast levels, and included the appropriate head of the UNKVD (a political police official), the head of the corresponding level civil police (the URKM), and the corresponding procurator. In a letter to Stalin from 20 April, Vyshinskii explained that the formation of these troikas had been necessary due to the significantly large number of passport cases of socially harmful elements. These cases had clogged the judicial system and the *Osoboe soveshchanie.* They had led to overcrowding of preliminary holding cells and the consequent violation of Soviet law for holding individuals without indictment. Vyshinskii was writing to Stalin for approval of a draft Central Committee directive that would give approval to the continuation of these troikas, as well as permission for operations that would "achieve the quickest clearing (*bystreishaia ochistka*) of cities of criminal and déclassé elements."[55]

Vyshinskii's draft was short but revealing. His letter showed that the first, massive cleansing operations of cities in 1933 and 1934 had failed to solve the problem of unwanted populations in urban areas. By 1935, the pressure on resources was not as acute as in 1933 but, as Yagoda declared in a circular memorandum, failure to maintain passport laws had allowed unproductive and criminal elements to return in large numbers to the streets of the cities. The initial benefits of passportization had been short lived, and cities were filling up again at an unacceptable rate, and with the wrong people—the unproductive and unwanted—who would strain municipal resources and foster crime. A separate memorandum, from February 1935 by E. M. Iaroslavskii, a Central Committee member, noted that Moscow's streets were filled with beggars and itinerants.[56] Yagoda blamed local police for laxness in the enforcement of passport and residence laws. For local police, however, the problem must have been akin to scooping sand out of a hole. Each handful removed was replaced by almost the same amount trickling in from the sides. No matter how many social harmfuls police removed from the streets, they always returned, sometimes with the same face, sometimes with different faces.[57]

The courts could not prosecute offenders fast enough, and the problem lay not just in numbers. In his letter to Stalin, Vyshinskii stated that one of the primary functions of the troikas was to hear cases of criminal and déclassé elements "for which there is no foundation for transfer to a court." In other words, the troikas were designed to simplify and expedite the process of repression of undesirable populations by bypassing the judicial system's normal requirements for submission of evidence. Thus, the troikas could convict and pass sentence on an individual whose case might be quashed (*prekrashcheno*) by a regular court for lack of evidence. In order to preserve legal sanction, according to Vyshinskii, sentences for these types of cases were to be confirmed by the *Osoboe soveshchanie* on condition that there was no objection from the procuracy at any level.[58]

This was a duplicitous position for Vyshinskii to take, but not atypical. As Stalin's eager creature, Vyshinskii on several occasions sanctioned the use of extrajudicial methods of repression, even as he advocated the strengthening of legal procedures.[59] Thus, in this instance, Vyshinskii, supposedly a proponent of judicial reforms, also advocated the use of troikas to avoid judicial evidentiary standards and specifically to deal with socially dangerous populations. For a time—for most of 1935, in fact—the procuracy and the country's Supreme Court officially sanctioned the practice of passing to the *Osoboe soveshchanie* cases "of those from the socially dangerous element who have been accused of a crime, but for whose cases there is not enough evidence to secure a judicial conviction." The court and procuracy office issued this injunction even as Vyshinskii circulated a major directive to local prosecutors on strengthening revolutionary legality and improved procedures to supervise NKVD activities.[60] Whatever Vyshinskii's motives, court officials likely agreed to the directive about socially dangerous elements reluctantly, under pressure of leaders' fixation on this category of the population. Judicial officials soon rethought their position. A court directive from January 1936 amended this practice and required that cases lacking proper evidence should be directed to the appropriate procuracy official for review and not sent automatically to the NKVD's administrative court.[61]

Stalin responded to Vyshinskii's April 1935 letter and draft directive not by quibbling about legal procedures, but by cautioning, again, against the use of mass policing measures. In a note at the top of Vyshinskii's letter, Stalin replied that a "quick clearing is dangerous." Stalin recommended that clearing the cities should be accomplished "gradually, without jolts and shocks (*bez tolchkov*)," and "without excessive administrative enthusiasm (*bez . . . izlishnego administrativnogo vostorga*)," that is, without administrative excesses. Most likely, Stalin misread Vyshinskii's letter on purpose. By arguing that the use of troikas would lead to the quickest clearing of cities, the chief procurator was not suggesting a return to mass police operations, which he had staunchly opposed. Vyshinskii was referring to the expediting effects of troikas to supplement judicial mechanisms of repression. Still, Stalin decided to use Vyshinskii's language to deliver a warning. He recommended that operations based on the directive last one year, and with the rest of the draft, he agreed.[62]

The actual Central Committee directive is not yet available in declassified archive materials, but the joint procuracy-NKVD operational instructions are located in procuracy files. On 9 May 1935, Yagoda and Vyshinskii sent these instructions, Operational Order 00192, detailing the work of the new troikas, to all republic-, oblast- and *krai*-level NKVD administrations. The substance of the instructions is worth noting since they show the extent to which the definition of socially harmful elements had broadened. In the 1920s, police defined these elements narrowly as people with a criminal record. While they were suspect, they were generally not subject to summary arrest simply because of their socially deviant or marginal background. According to the new 1935 directive, however, socially harmful elements fell into one of several categories: persons with previous criminal convictions *and* "continuing uncorrected ties" to the criminal world; and persons with no criminal convictions, but with no definite place of work and ties with the criminal world. Other categories also included "professional" beggars, persons caught repeatedly in urban areas without proper residence permits, persons who returned to places where they were forbidden to live, and children over the age of twelve caught in a criminal act. All of these types of people were to be regarded as socially harmful. They were now subject to summary sentencing by the extrajudicial troikas of the NKVD for up to five years in corrective labor camps.[63]

Order 00192 was not meant to justify or set in motion mass police operations as such, but it became the basis for some of the largest NKVD campaigns of mass repression during the mid-1930s. Operations based on the order continued through the rest of 1935 and at least through the early months of 1936. Like earlier sweeps by civil and political police, these ones targeted particular city areas, especially flophouse districts where large numbers of itinerant workers and vagabonds slept; they focused on shantytowns in industrial districts, marketplaces, train stations and other urban public places, and particular farms and villages. By the end of the year, operations by the *militsiia* alone netted close to 266,000 people classified under the rubric "socially harmful element." This number was given in a report compiled by the criminal investigation section of the police, the *ugolovnyi rozysk*. According to this report, approximately 85,000 of these individuals came under the jurisdiction of NKVD troikas, while the cases of another 98,000 were sent for hearing within the regular court system. "Other measures of social defense" were applied to 64,448 individuals, which probably ranged from fines to deportation back to home regions or outside city limits. In October alone, police in Moscow and the Moscow oblast detained nearly 6,300 people for not having proper residence and work documents, or for other reasons that defined them as socially harmful types. From the start of the campaign to November, police brought in 26,530 people in Leningrad, and 38,356 in Moscow.[64]

The figures above covered only civil police activities. In a separate memorandum, Yagoda reported to Stalin that in 1935, the GUGB brought in (*privlecheno*) a total of 293,681 individuals. Some 193,083 of these were arrested. The case files of as many as 228,352 of those brought in were sent to courts or procuracy officials for further judicial action.[65] Yagoda listed 33,823 people whose cases were heard administratively through the *Osoboe soveshchanie*. In addition, he cited a total of 122,796 individuals whose cases were heard "by NKVD and police troikas" in 1935.[66] Presumably, the cases of most, though not all, of those heard in the *Osoboe soveshchanie* were of a political nature involving accusations of counterrevolution, and were not associated with mass operations against socially dangerous people. However, those listed as under adjudication by troikas would have been associated primarily, if not exclusively, with passport sweeps since, in 1935, with but a few exceptions, passport troikas were the only troikas in operation.

How do we account for the differences in numbers? Yagoda's figure of nearly 123,000 adjudicated through "NKVD and police troikas" is higher than the *ugolovnyi rozysk* figure of 85,000 for the first ten months, January through October. Certainly, *militsiia* operations against social marginals would have continued through November and December, but they would have had to account for as many as 38,000 individuals, or about 19,000 a month, to come into line with the figures cited by Yagoda. Operations on that scale would have been larger than the usual 9,000 to 10,000 a month in September and October, but they might have been possible if police were making an all-out effort at the end of the calendar year. Both of these figures disagree with the figure of 119,159 compiled by the interior ministry in 1953 for the number of people convicted by NKVD troikas in 1935.[67] Still, and despite the discrepancies, all three figures are close enough to provide a coherent picture. The scale of civil and political police operations against social marginals in the mid-1930s was significant, far more widespread than can be discerned by counting only the numbers of people who were sentenced to camps. GULAG records show only 19,642 people sentenced to terms in camps or colonies for passport violations in 1935.[68] This figure is far lower than the various numbers reported by policing officials of those who were swept up in passport operations, or who were processed through passport troikas for other reasons. In fact, tens of thousands of people found themselves subject to some form of administrative or judicial repression for being social undesirables, and for being in the wrong place at the wrong time. GULAG figures also do not account for the many hundreds of thousands more who were caught up in police sweeps or checks, held for a time, and then released, or whose cases were quashed for lack of evidence. In Western Siberia alone, this number reached into the tens of thousands per year during the mid-1930s. The district's chief procurator, Ignatii Barkov, complained that these numbers were of such a magnitude to constitute, in and of themselves, a form of mass repression.[69]

These kinds of numbers, along with fragmented reports from localities, suggest that local police ignored central instructions against mass sweeps. The very nature of the order against social harmfuls lent itself to campaign operations rather than daily enforcement of passport and residence laws.

If Yagoda was bothered by this, he gave little hint of it. He offered only mild reprimands and reminders to subordinates about the need for steady enforcement of passport laws. The reaction of local procurators to the order was exemplified by that of Barkov in Western Siberia. He followed the general line laid down by Vyshinskii and Yagoda, that the decree on socially dangerous elements provided the NKVD with a powerful weapon in the fight against criminals and other enemies of Soviet order. He declared that the new authority given officials under this decree allowed "a maximization of effort to sweep away criminal-déclassé and itinerant (*brodiachii*) elements, to reduce crime significantly, and to liquidate, especially, aggravated assault and armed robbery."[70] Regardless of what he may have thought privately, Barkov publicly saw no contradiction between the principles of socialist legality and the use of extrajudicial police methods against harmful populations. When it came to cases processed through the judicial system under statutes of the criminal code, Barkov hounded *militsiia* and GUGB officials constantly for their investigative sloppiness, violations of procedure, and abuse of rights. Yet he only rarely criticized police activities related to these administrative forms of repression.[71] In keeping with the language of the 8 May 1933 Politburo instructions, Barkov only recommended that police avoid "campaign-like mass operations." In the same sentence, however, he urged an increase in "daily sweeps of criminal-déclassé elements."[72]

As 1935 turned into 1936, both Yagoda and his police chief, Bel'skii, took stock of the campaign against socially dangerous elements. Whatever the two policemen may have thought about police methods, they counted the social defense campaigns based on Order 00192 a major success. Both emphasized how well the campaigns had worked by noting in reports to Sovnarkom that crime rates in regime cities had declined significantly, due specifically to the purging of those areas under special passport laws. Conversely, crime in rural areas was not declining nearly as rapidly as in urban areas. One of the main reasons, apart from fewer numbers of police, Yagoda emphasized, was that the government and Party directives to clear cities of "parasitic and itinerant elements" had not been extended to rural parts of the country.[73] In fact, because of the success of sweep operations, Yagoda recommended in his March report that Sovnarkom grant a continuation of the work of the NKVD troikas to sweep déclassé elements from cities and workers' settlements. When queried for his reaction to this request, Vyshinskii replied that he had no objections in principle. He noted only that the matter needed to be discussed in a special commission, since there existed "special directives" governing the work of these troikas.[74]

INTENSIFICATION OF ANTICRIME CAMPAIGNS

Sovnarkom approved Yagoda's request, and police troikas continued their work through 1936. Likewise, campaign-style operations continued, and not only in the form of passport sweeps to catch undocumented residents and social aliens. The mass campaigns of 1935 and 1936 also coincided with a harsh turn in policies toward criminals and other social marginals. In March 1935, for example, the Politburo renewed, for the third time since 1931, a directive to shoot individuals convicted of aggravated theft. At first, this directive applied only to several large urban areas, but an increasing number of local officials elsewhere appealed for permission to follow it in order to thwart continuing high crime rates.[75] In April came a new law intensifying measures against juvenile crime, which was followed closely by a new law politicizing and increasing police latitude in dealing with hooliganism and dangerous criminals. April and May brought Party and government directives on child homelessness, as well as a renewed campaign against banditry and speculation. At first, and in accordance with reforms from late 1934, the state's punitive organs applied these new laws and directives through judicial means of repression, but the NKVD order against social marginals, issued in May 1935, gave police the means to broaden the jurisdiction of troikas, and to process criminals and other social undesirables through administrative police boards.

Using passport and residence laws to catch criminals and prevent criminality was a logical step, at least for police. Early on, Yagoda and other leaders understood the close connection between undocumented people and crime. Time and again, Yagoda lectured subordinates on the use of passport laws above all as a way to catch criminals, escapees, and other dangerous types. He encouraged subordinates to send wanted criminals and recidivists caught in passport sweeps to passport boards and, ultimately, to the *Osoboe soveshchanie*. Conversely, he advised local police not to waste time indicting recidivist thieves arrested for statutory crimes through regular courts; better to try them before passport troikas. Administrative repression of criminals and other undesirables under passport laws was quicker and more certain to result in an appropriately punitive sentence, according to Yagoda, than sending the cases through the court system. Yagoda did not trust the judicial system and was suspicious of court officials. According to the police chief, indictment through courts was laborious and often led to a dilution of charges or a softening of sentences.[76]

NKVD officials openly encouraged police to bypass courts and judicial standards and to utilize administrative forms of repression against an increasingly wide variety of criminal and socially marginal populations. Police understood that sweep operations, combined with the use of passport and residency laws, worked especially well to catch certain categories of criminals, especially petty speculators and thieves operating in cities.[77] And in the mid-1930s, despite constant directives to fight speculation, both organized and petty speculation continued to grow. By 1936, petty trading had become an increasingly serious problem in the eyes of regime leaders, especially after the reestablishment of private trade in 1935 and the weaning of the country off rationing and back onto a market and money economy. Legalization of private trade opened up new possibilities for the criminal "element" to engage in anti-state activities. As a result, petty forms of speculation reached "unacceptable" proportions, creating, or so officials believed, serious disruption of the state's planning and distribution system and corresponding deficits of and long lines for scarce goods.[78] As NKVD circulars made clear, agent networks and undercover investigations by the Economic Crimes Department of the OGPU could not cope with the scale of this activity. Whatever headway civil and political police made against organized networks of traders was nullified by the massive selling "from hand to hand" (*iz ruk v ruki*) that took place daily across the country.[79] Given this situation, regime leaders and police turned to campaign-style operations as the most effective way to compensate for the inability of normal policing methods to reduce this type of criminal activity. In October 1935, and again in July 1936, the Central Committee and Sovnarkom authorized civil and political police to organize campaigns against small-time "speculators." The joint government-Party orders took the form of directives signed by Molotov and Stalin. The 19 July 1936 directive ordered the police to submit a plan for a one-time sweep operation, "using administrative procedures," in Moscow, Leningrad, Kiev, and Minsk. The directive provided a guide figure of five thousand speculators to be arrested and subjected to show trials or to be expelled from these cities.[80]

Police operations to carry out the government directives exemplified the continued use of campaign-style policing methods, but those operations also highlighted the process of bureaucratic inflation. Sovnarkom's directive of July 1936 called for special operations in four major cities. In turn, the NKVD operational order called for campaigns in all major cities. Sovnarkom's directive recommended that police expel (vysylat') speculators and place a residence ban of four years on those expelled from the four cities to be cleansed. In turn, the police order called for full exile (ssylka) of speculators to Kazakhstan, and a residence ban of five years. The police order geared up the whole police machinery for a special effort. Police heads were directed "immediately" to pull officers off regular duty and other cases—especially those working in any economic crime units, in the criminal investigation departments, those engaged in agent work, and regular beat officers—to create special operational units for the "active struggle" of the campaign. The police order detailed which statutes to apply to which types of cases, and ordered that illegal traders caught in Moscow, Leningrad, Kiev, and Minsk be sent through police troikas, as a way to expedite "the quickest emptying" (razgruski) of those cities of speculators.[81]

Yagoda's order for the antispeculation campaign typified the way in which officials perpetuated mass forms of repression, despite the supposed ban against such methods. The language of the order smacks of Yagoda's penchant for military jargon and military-like mobilization. A policing operation against petty profiteers reads like a grand battle plan. It is replete with urgent movements and sweeping priorities. Resources were to be organized and focused for an all-out effort that supposedly would roll back an enemy with decisive blows. It must all have sounded boringly familiar to local police officials: one more campaign in a string of campaigns that would have little effect, but that had to be carried out.

The use of police troikas was a new twist, however. These troikas had been set up specifically to prosecute passport violators, not to adjudicate regular criminal cases. Sovnarkom's original directive for the antispeculation campaign allowed for "administrative" processing of speculators, but this phrase referred to police authority to expel individuals from cities; it did not refer to the use of police administrative hearing boards to send people to prison or exile. The latter was a detail added by Yagoda. The operational order further specified that police heads report on the progress of the campaign once every ten days, and once every three days in the four cities marked for special operations. By the end of August—that is, within one month of the police order— troikas had convicted 4,000 individuals in these four cities, while regular courts had convicted 1,635 individuals as part of the antispeculator campaign. This number stood in contrast to the 5,000 that had been convicted by courts for the whole period, January through May 1936. Moreover, the August figures did not yet include the results of the campaign in all other cities and oblasts besides Moscow, Leningrad, Kiev, and Minsk.[82] As this and other campaigns showed, police used administrative sentencing boards for more than prosecuting passport violators; once passport troikas were in place, police used them increasingly to deal with continuing problems of illegal trade, commodity shortages, and criminality in general.

NATIONALITIES AND FORMER PEOPLE

Civil and political police groups mounted other operations against populations that the regime's leaders perceived as harmful or politically dangerous. As early as 1933 and 1934, police began to target specific nationalities in some of the last operations against kulaks. The year 1933 saw the great mass exodus of Kazakhs during collectivization in Soviet Central Asia. In the western borderlands of Ukraine and Belorussia, kulak, social defense, and nationality campaigns overlapped. Operational orders to target suspect national groups highlighted the way leaders confused and conflated categories of social deviancy, state security, and the suspect "enemy nations" against whom their paranoia was growing.[83] Border-cleansing operations in 1933 and 1934 were directed against the usual categories of kulaks, spies, diversionary, and anti-Soviet elements. In the western borderlands, however, police units were directed to pay special attention to families of Polish and German backgrounds who likely had cross-border ties in Poland.[84] In August 1934, Central Committee directives alerted local Party committees to take special note of foreign nationals or anyone of non-Soviet national origins working in their enterprises.[85] Nationality operations intensified in 1934 in Karelia, Ukraine, and Belorussia. Already, the regime's leaders were beginning to turn their attention from class enemies and so-cial marginals to ethnic minorities.

Nationality campaigns began in earnest and on a large scale in 1935. Political police units, using police and local party activists, engaged in large-scale deportations of suspect national minorities to Siberia and Central Asia, especially from the western and Far Eastern border zones. In the two years 1935 and 1936 GUGB operations targeted hundreds of thousands of Finns, Poles, Germans, Koreans, and Ukrainians living in border areas, whom the regime suspected of cross-border loyalties.[86] The largest of these operations occurred in the winter and spring of 1935 and displaced some 412,000 Germans and Poles from Ukrainian and border areas to the eastern parts of Ukraine. Then, again, in spring and summer 1936, somewhere between 45,000 and 60,000 were shipped from border areas to Kazakhstan.[87] In 1935, Yagoda also rec-ommended the removal of several thousand Soviet citizens of Greek ori-gin living in the Black Sea border regions. The latter campaigns, espe-cially, mixed nationality with earlier kulak operations, Yagoda noting in his recommendations that the "Greek populations" had been espe-cially resistant to collectivization in 1930 and 1931.[88]

The regime regarded these populations with suspicion, especially within the context of rising international tensions during the mid-1930s. Party and state leaders regarded it as entirely within the authority of the state to remove these populations as a precautionary measure. Yet officials did not regard them as ipso facto anti-Soviet. Even the popu-lations that were to be resettled were not supposed to be deprived of their rights as Soviet citizens. Vyshinskii insisted, for example, that the "Greeks" to be moved from the Black Sea areas were to be compen-sated for their displacement, except for those arrested under specific charges. Party and police officials were supposed to distinguish care-fully between those who were to retain their rights as fully enfranchised citizens and those who should be categorized as socially dangerous or anti-Soviet. The latter were to be arrested, or if not arrested, "filtered" and sentenced through special troikas to camps or labor colonies. In some instances, high GUGB officials provided operational officers with approximate figures of how many individuals to arrest or detain as dan-gerous. In writing to a local prosecutor about border-cleansing opera-tions in July 1935, Vyshinskii noted that two thousand households had been selected for removal after NKVD initial investigation of over six thousand households. On what basis these investigations were carried out is not clear, but they could very well have been based at least in part on review of passport catalogs, since the operation involved a border area and would have been passportized. Also, and most likely, NKVD plenipotentiaries relied on reports from and interviews with local Soviet authorities and Party secretaries.[89]

One other peculiarity of these deportations was that tens of thousands of people displaced from their homes and livelihoods were never counted among the "repressed." As with tens of thousands of socially marginal people, nationality deportees who were not arrested would not have showed up in figures for camps, colonies, or penal settlements. Thus, they would be missed in any survey using these sources to document repression during the 1930s. It is only with a wave of research in nationality studies that we know about such forms of mass repression, even though they occurred on a large scale.[90]

One of the best-known of the mass social operations of mid-decade was the Leningrad purge of "former people" in the winter and early spring of 1935. That campaign was aimed at ridding the city of supposedly anti-Soviet and potentially disloyal populations from the former bourgeois, professional, and intellectual classes. The purge was closely tied, as well, to increased housing demand in the city. Purge results were always accompanied by figures on how many apartments had been freed up for new occupancy.[91] The Leningrad campaign coincided with related campaigns to clear ethnically Finnish populations from border areas in Leningrad oblast and the Karelian border areas close to the city, and from the Kalinin oblast. Some 11,700 "former people" were exiled from Leningrad as a result of the city's purge. Another 23,217 "kulak and anti-Soviet elements" were deported from nearby border areas to special labor colonies in Western Siberia, Kazakhstan, and Tadzhikistan. An additional 23,565 people were exiled from the Kalinin oblast and Belorussian border areas. The Leningrad operations were carried out under the leadership of L. M. Zakovskii, the newly appointed NKVD and GUGB head of Leningrad and the Leningrad oblast. Zakovskii made the original recommendation for the city's purge, basing his request on housing space and the threat to the city from socially dangerous populations. Zakovskii reported directly to Yagoda, who in turn recommended that Stalin and the Politburo approve it. These related purges were some of the largest single purge operations of the middle years of the 1930s.[92]

CONCLUSIONS

Social defense and nationality operations of the mid-1930s such as those described here differed from the earlier operations of dekulakization and collectivization. They were not intended to extend state power or to revolutionize economic and social relations. They were designed, specifically and consciously, to defend the Soviet state's new salients: to secure state property, territorial borders, and the socialist economic organization of the country. At the same time, such operations did, in fact, continue the revolutionary restructuring of the Soviet polity. By 1935 and 1936, both civil and political police were deeply involved in the cleansing and shaping of Soviet society. Despite the ban on nonjudicial and mass forms of repression, these methods, and the police who administered them, had become a constitutive part of the state's programs for social and ethnic reformation. Indeed, the mass operations against *sotsvredelementy* and national minorities worked so well that the country's leaders applied the same methods to resolve other social problems. Sweeps of orphan children became the primary method, in particular, to resolve the growing and related problems of juvenile homelessness and youth crime. As both of these problems worsened in the early 1930s, leaders turned increasingly to the police to intervene in the state's policies regarding juveniles. In so doing, the Stalinist regime both criminalized and politicized juvenile homelessness and delinquency in a way not characteristic of the 1920s. The following chapter examines police colonization and militarization of a problem that had long been the purview of civil governance.

Figure 1. 1913 internal passport for S. G. Bagdatev. Page 1. GARF, f. 8005, op. 1, d. 2.

Figure 2. 1913 internal passport for S. G. Bagdatev. Pages 2–3. Note line 2, listing social status as urban dweller (*meshchanin*) of the town of Shusha. Note also no line for nationality. GARF, f. 8005, op. 1, d. 2.

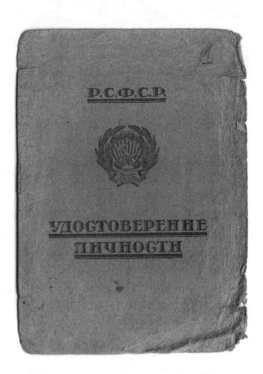

Figure 3. 1925
identification
booklet for
N. M. Zhdanov.
Front cover.
GARF, f. 4789,
op. 1, d 10.

Figure 4. 1925 identification booklet for N. M. Zhdanov. Reverse of front cover and p. 1. The middle stamp at left notes the issue of a foreign travel passport. The stamp across the middle of the page at right notes the issue of an internal passport to replace this document. GARF, f. 4789, op. 1, d. 10.

Figure 5. 1925 identification booklet for N. M. Zhdanov. Pages 2–3. Note that in Figures 3–5 there is no line for social status, in contrast to both prerevolutionary and 1930s internal passports. Note, however, line 4 on p. 1 (Figure 4) listing occupation (*rod zaniatia*) as white-collar employee (*sluzhashchii*). In Zhdanov's 1933 passport (Figure 6) this line became the line for social status (*sotsial'noe polozhenie*), also listed as white-collar employee. Note no line for nationality. GARF, f. 4789, op. 1, d. 10.

Figure 6. 1933 internal passport for N. M. Zhdanov. Page 1. At left, handwritten notation of Zhdanov's death, 31 December 1934, registered with the Civil Registration Bureau (ZAGS). Note line 3 for nationality (Russian) and line 4 for social status, listed as white-collar employee (*sluzhashchii*). GARF, f. 4789, op. 1, d. 10.

Figure 7. 1933 internal passport for N. M. Zhdanov. Pages 2–3. GARF, f. 4789, op. 1, d. 10.

Figure 8. Civil police personnel preparing internal passports for issue, 1935. Photo courtesy of RGAKFD.

Figure 9. Issuing internal passport, 1933. Note the image of a young, stylish, civil service worker issuing a passport to an older woman in traditional garb. Photo courtesy of RGAKFD.

Составной шкаф для хранения дубликатов
кеннкарт

Figure 10. German identification card catalog. Photo taken as part of a Soviet civil police commission trip to Berlin to study National Socialist population registration systems, summer 1945. GARF, f. 9415, op. 5, d. 463.

Figure 11. Citizen registration cards from a German catalog. Summer 1945. GARF f. 9415, op. 5, d. 463.

Figure 12. Meeting of mid-level operational commanders of civil police, city of Kimry, 1932. Print from a cracked glass negative. Photo courtesy of RGAFKD.

Figure 13. Meeting of operational officers of civil police, Ukraine, 1931. Photo courtesy of RGAFKD.

Figure 14. Aron Sol'ts speaking at a conference of judicial and procuratorial heads, 1934. Seated, among others, are Ivan Akulov, far left, and Nikolai Krylenko, far right. Photo courtesy of RGAFKD.

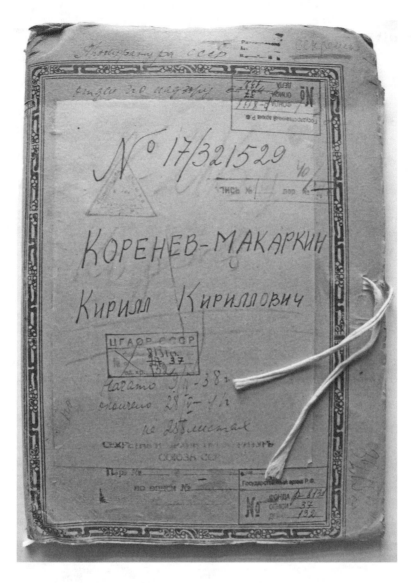

Figure 15. Procuratorial file for Kiril Korenev, containing 255 pages. GARF, f. 8131, op. 37, d. 132.

Figure 16. Employee pass for Kiril Korenev at *Komsomol'skaia Pravda*, 1937. GARF, f. 8131, op. 37, d. 132.

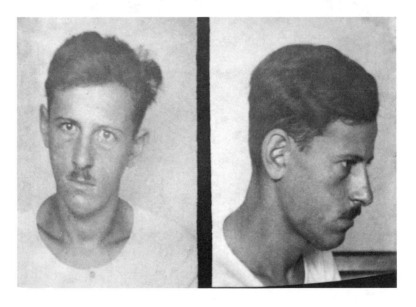

Figure 17. NKVD arrest photographs of Kiril Korenev, alias Emel'ian Makarkin, April 1938. GARF, f. 8131, op. 37, d. 132.

7 Policing Juveniles, Policing Debates

What we need is more legality and less expediency.
—*Andrei Vyshinskii, 1936*

THROUGHOUT THE 1920S and into the first years of the 1930s, many officials regarded hooliganism and child homelessness as related problems, but as ones that fell within the purview of the state's social agencies. Police readily agreed with this assessment. As late as 1930, a Russian NKVD report on hooliganism took a "soft" line, referring to hooliganism as a social "anomaly," describing it primarily as an educational and cultural matter, not one for the police. The largest contingent of hooligans, noted the report's anonymous author, consisted of workers and peasants. This fact alone, according to the report, refuted the opinion, then gaining ground, that hooliganism was some form of political protest, fomented by déclassé and harmful elements against Soviet power. Instead of taking a hard line of police repression, the report called for social agencies and trade unions to do a better job of cultural education among youth. The latter conclusion was born out by data taken from arrested hooligans, which proved their isolation from social agencies and youth groups. In any case, noted the report, police repression would prove wholly inadequate, since data already showed a public reluctance to identify youth offenders to police. This latter fact confirmed, as well, the widespread perception that the problem of juvenile delinquency was one dealt with more effectively through community rather than police action.[1]

After police were subordinated to the OGPU in 1930, this soft approach began to change, especially as juvenile crime rates and the numbers of street children began to rise dramatically and visibly during the early 1930s. This chapter describes police colonization and militarization of policies toward juveniles. It follows the hardening attitude of police and leaders toward homelessness and hooliganism, the politicizing of what had been considered a social anomaly, and the effective methods used by Yagoda to usurp jurisdiction over a growing problem of social disorder.

FIRST STEPS

As early as 1931, and as part of his aggressive plan for police expansion, D. V. Usov, the first OGPU head of the police, began pushing for greater police involvement in juvenile policy. In August, Usov issued a circular alerting local police to the growing menace of both child homelessness and delinquency. In order better to understand the dimension of these problems, he required that local officials prepare reports, to be submitted no later than December, on the local situation of homeless children. Interestingly, in a draft of the circular, Usov struck out a last phrase "and on its causes" from the final version. Usov did not wish to open the door to local officials to speculate on the social or political nature of child homelessness and crime; he did not want local officials to make clear the connection between child homelessness and its origins in the state's brutal policies of collectivization and dekulakization.[2]

Usov finessed these connections in a separate circular issued in December 1931, and he tried to lay out an appropriate police response to what was clearly a growing threat to public order. On one hand, Usov took a hard line. Consistent with his general attitudes toward the indigent and homeless, he called for resolute police action against juvenile homelessness and criminality. On the other hand, Usov still acknowledged that the police's role in dealing with this segment of the population should be secondary and supportive, rendering assistance to the social agencies whose primary jurisdiction it was to deal with wayward and orphan children.[3] Still, Usov did not trust social agencies and, in his August circular, he prepared the way for police to challenge the effectiveness of the state's social policies. Usov asked that local police not only provide statistics on homelessness and child crime; he wanted to know, as well, what measures were being taken by organs such as educational organizations, the Association of Friends of Children, local health commmisariats, and the children's commissions under local soviets. In other words, Usov wanted to build up evidence against local relief organizations. He wanted specific data on the numbers of the "juvenile criminal element" apprehended and given over to the various social organs, and he wanted information on the extent to which juvenile delinquents were sent to closed "reformatories" and to open labor colonies.[4]

By mid-1933, Usov had the information he wanted, and the criminal investigation section of the RKM submitted a critical report on youth crime for 1931 and 1932. This was an odd report. It documented the rise in juvenile crime rates and the inadequacy of social agencies to respond to youth problems, but its own statistics seemed to contradict its conclusions about the social origins and political significance of delinquency. Moreover, the conclusions of regional officials did not fit the overall line that Usov wished to develop. Moscow police officials raised a warning about rising youth crime rates, but the Far Eastern section of the report noted that, while child homelessness was on the rise, it was a problem that was still easily dealt with by the region's social organs.[5] The report's authors included a warning that the population of youth offenders was heavily infiltrated by alien elements, and that underage criminals were being manipulated by class enemies to commit crimes, such as arson, against Soviet order. Yet a chart on social background, included in the report, showed that roughly 40 percent of child offenders convicted during the period of late 1931 and early 1932 were children of working-class families. The second-largest category consisted of children of state white-collar workers (13 and 10 percent respectively for the last half of 1931 and the first half of 1932) and of poor *kolkhozniki* (6 and 4 percent). In another curious twist, the report placed the category of "socially dangerous element" under the list of crimes for which children were convicted rather than as a type of social status. The report discovered that fully 39 and then 48 percent of convicted youth offenders were guilty of being socially dangerous. These percentages made this "crime" as prominent among youth as the traditional crime of petty thievery, for which 46 percent of youth criminals were convicted during each period of the study. Here, in the manipulation of categories and in the statistical sleight of hand that made "socially dangerous" a crime, police found the "proof" that juvenile delinquency was becoming part of the class war against the Soviet state. All other statistics revealed a rather typical picture of youth criminality. Most juvenile delinquents engaged in traditional activities of pickpocketing and simple theft. Only about 5 percent of juvenile felons were convicted under hooligan laws, and none under laws against Soviet order. The report did note a disturbing trend of recidivism, that is, offenders having previous convictions or *privody* with police.[6]

The police report linked the rise in youth crime rates to the worsening problem of child homelessness, and it sharply criticized the uncoordinated approach to the latter. The anonymous authors noted that, due to lack of communication, there did not even exist clear statistics about the problem (apart, of course, from those collected by police). The work of both social agencies and special juvenile courts, the Komones, was entirely unsatisfactory, which brought police efforts to nothing. Worse still, the lack of effective social agencies forced the police into ineffective methods of mass sweeps of children off streets and transport routes. Once apprehended, police had no control over placement or holding of children, who were turned over to social agencies or juvenile courts. Children's homes and vocational institutions were so poorly run that they acted as revolving doors and as mills for the production of juvenile delinquents. Juvenile courts often gave light sentences even to serious child offenders. As a result, chided the report, homeless children and delinquents ended up right back on the streets. The problem was especially pronounced for children under sixteen years of age. This group made up half of all those picked up by police, either for criminal offenses or as homeless, but these children fell through the cracks in the system. Juvenile courts refused to try children under sixteen years of age, and children's homes offered conditions little better and sometimes worse than those on the streets. Homes were either lax in supervision or cruel and exploitative. Either way, current practices failed to address this growing segment of disaffected youth.[7]

The report's recommendations were predictable. Noting the rise in numbers of street children and the increasing influence of déclassé elements among that population, the report called for more active police involvement. Police should continue aggressive sweeps of urban areas, but then have control over centers for placement of those brought in. The report recommended that the Komones courts be abolished and their functions be given to the police. The report also called for police to establish labor regime colonies for youth offenders in order to reeducate and reintegrate wayward juveniles as productive members of Soviet society.[8]

The call to establish special colonies for homeless children may have seemed harsh, but it was not only a police recommendation. One year earlier, Krylenko and A. S. Bubnov, the head of the Russian federation education commissariat, Narkompros, noted an alarming rise in numbers of homeless children entering children's homes. Like the police report in 1934, Krylenko and Bubnov noted the revolving-door character of these homes, which acted only as way-stations and breeding grounds for juvenile delinquents. Part of the problem, argued the two officials, was that children's homes were located close to major urban centers. It was easy for children to walk out and make their way to nearby cities. Thus, Krylenko and Bubnov recommended that, in order "to radically resolve" this situation, Narkomiust' and Narkompros be allowed to establish several large colonies for homeless children, with varying levels of security, in "faraway regions" (*otdalennye raiony*) of the Northern Krai. Such a solution, they believed, would discourage children from running away, given the isolation and difficult conditions that runaways would face. It is not clear what action the Central Committee or the government took on this proposal, but it was quickly superseded by similar demands from the NKVD.[9]

THE POLITBURO COMMISSIONS

Police officials pressed their recommendations as part of a Politburo-established commission on child homelessness and juvenile crime. The commission was formed in late winter or early spring 1934 under leadership of V. Ia. Chubar', a presidium member of Sovnarkom. It included representatives from all relevant social agencies, as well as high police officials including Ia. S. Agranov, Yagoda's deputy, and prominent individuals such as M. I. Kalinin and N. A. Semashko, head of the Children's Committee of the Russian federation Central Executive Committee, VtsIK. Semashko was a major advocate of child policy reform and deeply involved in running the system of children's homes. Deliberations of the commission from summer 1934 through December of that year and then to a final draft decree in April 1935 give a rare glimpse of how the NKVD took over a major sector of the state's social policies. The succession of draft decrees and commission materials shows how the condition of child homelessness became criminalized in essence, and how juvenile delinquency became politicized as a threat to Soviet order and security.

The first drafts of the commission's work reflected a traditional emphasis on social agencies. Although highly critical of the education and health commissariats (Narkompros and Narkomzdrav) and other welfare organizations, the commission did not call for any fundamental shift in policy. Members demanded an increase in budgets, expansion of the network of children's homes, and increased funding for vocational institutions. The draft decrees in July and again in September 1934 demanded serious and specific measures to improve conditions in homes, professionalization of staff, and increased discipline and security. Both drafts called for greater diversification of labor and vocational colonies and institutions within the system run by Narkompros.[10]

New and controversial measures included formation of special courts for youth offenders between the ages of twelve and sixteen years. The draft decrees did not say whether these should be placed under jurisdiction of the ineffective Komones system or under Narkomiust'. The commission recommended that children under the age of fourteen should be forbidden to travel on any kind of long-distance transport, such as railroads and riverboats, unless accompanied by a parent or legal guardian. Laws were to be changed to increase legal penalties for adults who drew children into criminal activity and for parents and guardians whose children or charges became involved in crime for lack of supervision. The commission proposed an increase in budgets for aid to indigent parents and for adults in rural areas willing to adopt homeless children. Most controversial of all was a proposal, recommended by a subcommittee on juvenile crime, for a one-time ten-day sweep operation to be mounted by police in urban areas.[11] This sweep would gather up all street children, who would be deposited temporarily in an expanded system of placement centers run by Narkompros until commissioners in each center would decide where to send them. Commission members were to consist of representatives of the local police, educational, health, and court systems. Children not apprehended in a crime might be sent back to parents or relatives, placed for adoption, or placed in vocational institutions. Those with a criminal background could be sent to vocational colonies. Children convicted of a serious crime or with a recidivist background could be sent to a new system of closed incarceration centers to be set up by Narkomiust'.[12]

Prominent commission members such as Kalinin and Semashko fought against inclusion of repressive measures, and they did so successfully at first. Kalinin made clear his objection to establishment of a system of special courts and closed carceral institutions. He objected in principle to a systematic campaign of repression against juvenile offenders.[13] Semashko, while very critical of Narkompros, called for a significant expansion of social welfare programs to aid homeless children. Such arguments apparently had an effect since, on the specific recommendation of Kalinin, the commission's December 1934 draft struck out the entire section that recommended police action against street children.[14] At the same time, the December draft retained the recommendation that special courts and carceral institutions be set up for juvenile offenders. A most ominous change also stipulated that carceral institutions be placed under NKVD jurisdiction rather than under Narkomiust'. This latter change in administrative jurisdiction resulted from general reforms that placed all places of incarceration under the NKVD, but the change, nonetheless, foreshadowed harsher measures to come.[15]

The December draft decree, however, was not the last word on the issue of juvenile policy. For reasons unclear, but probably related to hardline dissatisfaction, the Politburo reconstituted an expanded children's commission under Kalinin's chairmanship. The new commission included Yagoda instead of Agranov, thus giving the police more weight on the commission. The commission also included, among others, K. Voroshilov, a loyal Stalinist and head of the armed services. At first glance, Kalinin's chairmanship heralded continuation of the "soft line" on juvenile issues, but draft recommendations put forward by the commission in February 1935 swung dramatically in favor of greater police involvement. The February draft cut back budgets for Narkompros for expansion of children's homes, a measure strongly opposed by Nadezhda Krupskaia, an education specialist and a member of the commission. Instead, the February proposal recommended that the NKVD establish its own system of vocational centers and colonies for wayward children. This draft also called for more extensive policing measures. A recommendation for police sweeps of streets was put back in the list of recommendations, but not just as a one-time operation.

The draft decree enjoined police to engage in "systematic" sweeps of streets, markets, and railroad stations in all urban areas. The children rounded up were to be either placed in children's homes or sent to NKVD colonies.[16]

In yet another draft in March and a final one in April, the NKVD extended its jurisdiction even further, while the role of social agencies was cut even more drastically. Indeed, Narkompros, which had been the primary government organization to deal with homeless children and juvenile delinquents, was cut almost entirely out of the picture. Narkompros would retain a "formal" system of homes for wayward children, but with no budget. These homes were to be supported entirely by the garnished wages of parents and guardians of the children in them.[17] Instead, the NKVD was given the task to set up the main system of institutions for homeless and juvenile delinquents. On paper, this was to be an extensive empire. The NKVD was to take over vocational institutions and colonies, as well as special "isolators" for serious child offenders. Moreover, the NKVD was now to take over the reception and placement "points" (*priemniki-raspredeliteli*) where street children were placed temporarily before further placement or adjudication. Police were not supposed to hold children in these reception points for more than one year before they were released to relatives, sent on to NKVD-run schools or colonies, or remanded to courts, but the reception points were to be administered under a "strict regime." This was to prevent the problem of runaway children ending up back on the streets, a problem that had plagued the previous system run by Narkompros.[18] As a result of these changes, then, children picked up on streets, regardless of whether they had committed a crime, would now find themselves entirely in the hands of the police—picked up by police and placed, as virtual prisoners, in what amounted to police-run strict-regime internment centers. This would be a homeless child's first and primary contact with state authority.

Prominent specialists objected to these recommendations. Semashko certainly did, as did Nadezhda Krupskaia, when solicited for her opinion. Krupskaia was a strong advocate of socially ameliorative solutions to the problems of homeless children and juvenile crime. She opposed harsh police measures, at least by implication. The root of the problem of homeless children, unsupervised children, and delinquency, she argued, lay in social changes and changes in family situations, primarily in the expansion of women in the work force, the consequent absence of working parents at home, and the severe strain on housing in recent years. These problems would be solved not by criminalizing children, but by increasing social assistance to families and community welfare and educational organizations.[19] Still, and regardless of objections, the NKVD's policing solutions won out over more moderate proposals. The police recommendations were adopted into law by a joint Sovnarkom and Central Committee decree from 31 May 1935 "On the struggle against homeless and unsupervised children."[20]

The ability of NKVD officials to impose their will on the state's social policies reflected the growing authority of that commissariat, and specifically of Yagoda's ability to manipulate policy. The sudden swing in recommendations after December 1934 most certainly was connected to his participation in Kalinin's commission, but it also coincided with deliberations of another Sovnarkom commission on fighting crime and improving the work of the police. The latter commission came under the chairmanship of Ian Rudzutak, deputy chair of Sovnarkom, and met at the same time as the children's commission under Chubar'. Yagoda sat on the crime commission and wrote the main draft decrees for consideration by it, as well as sitting on Kalinin's children's commission. He attributed such importance to the issue of juvenile crime that he convinced the crime commission to devote three of its five major reform recommendations to it.[21] His recommendations anticipated almost point for point the measures finally adopted by the Kalinin's commission on homeless children. Yagoda urged the crime commission to lower the age of criminal responsibility to thirteen; he asked that the NKVD be allowed to establish carceral institutions and special corrective labor colonies for juvenile offenders; and he encouraged tougher penalties for adults who drew children into crime or who allowed children to drift into crime through negligence.[22]

Despite procuracy attempts to mitigate some of the harsher measures, Yagoda's draft resolution on child crime made its way almost completely intact into the final TsIK and Sovnarkom law on 7 April 1935. That law, "On measures to fight juvenile crime," allowed full application of adult laws against children down to the age of twelve who were apprehended for murder, attempted murder, aggravated assault, and armed robbery.[23] A secret addendum from 20 April informed courts and procuracy officials that measures applied to juvenile offenders should also include the death penalty.[24] The April 7 law on juvenile crime came out of the recommendations made by Rudzutak's policing commission, but the deliberations of that commission certainly influenced the workings of the commission on children. The Central Committee approved the hardline resolution on homeless and unsupervised children on 31 May. This latter decree incorporated both substantive policy recommendations and language that characterized the 7 April law against juvenile offenders.

Yagoda was not the only official working behind the scenes. Other political leaders influenced the turn toward hardline juvenile policies. Both Molotov and Stalin, though not members of either the children's or the crime commission, took a direct hand in writing the final draft for the children's commission report. Molotov edited a preliminary draft and, in a handwritten insertion, Stalin recommended that the age of criminal responsibility be dropped from sixteen to twelve years of age. Yagoda recommended age thirteen, but the final draft reflected Stalin's preference. Also preferring hard measures, Stalin expressed dissatisfaction with a section, written by Vyshinskii, that called for "educational-medical" measures as well as punishment to deal with juvenile delinquency. In the margin of Vyshinskii's draft, Stalin underscored this recommendation and noted that it was "incomprehensible" (*neponiatno*). The final draft made no mention of educational–medical measures.[25]

Other powerful figures weighed in. In late March, Voroshilov, a member of Kalinin's children's commission, wrote a strong letter addressed simultaneously to Stalin (as the Party's general secretary), Molotov (as head of Sovnarkom), and to Kalinin (as chair of the children's commission). Reacting to newspaper accounts of what he described as "monstrous" forms of juvenile hooliganism, Voroshilov vented his outrage at the "laxness" of courts in dealing with underage criminals.[26] He repeated information, which he garnered from L. D. Vul', head of the Moscow police, about the thousands of "registered" juvenile hooligans loose on the streets of Moscow. By registered, Vul' meant juvenile delinquents known to police and listed in police surveillance catalogs. These were not just the ordinary run-of-the-mill hooligans, but "especially malicious juvenile hooligans." Roaming those same byways were, "without dispute," at least eight hundred juvenile bandits "capable of anything." In his letter, Voroshilov noted that Kalinin's commission would be making its final recommendations soon, but he lamented that those recommendations would still be ineffective. "The purging (*ochistka*) of Moscow of the population of homeless and criminal youth will not be resolved," wrote Voroshilov, "since not only Vul', but Khrushchev, Bulganin, and Yagoda as well, declare that they have no possibility to place the homeless due to the absence of children's homes. As a result, they cannot fight [effectively] against this open sore [*sic*]." As late as March, apparently, as Voroshilov's mixed metaphor suggested, the takeover and expansion of children's institutions within the NKVD was still not a done deal, and Voroshilov's letter may have given impetus in that direction. He argued that police should have authority not only over homeless but also over unsupervised children in order to secure the capital from the growing problem of "'children's'" hooliganism. Coincidently, or not, the final draft decree of Kalinin's commission gave nearly full jurisdiction over youth institutions to the NKVD, and it gave police authority, for the first time, to repatriate homeless children to their original home regions rather than to place them in Moscow's children's homes.[27]

HOOLIGANISM

Decrees by both the commissions under Rudzutak and Kalinin, as well as Voroshilov's letter, reflected a growing fear of hooliganism and its association with socially dangerous types. One of the five major recommendations by Rudzutak's crime commission covered hooliganism, and the final April 1935 draft by the Kalinin commission included a section "On the fight against juvenile hooliganism on the streets." Such a section, referring specifically to hooliganism, had not appeared in earlier drafts. In previous drafts, juvenile delinquency had been covered under the rubric of "juvenile law violations" or "juvenile crime." The last-minute inclusion of language about hooliganism—it first appeared in March, just weeks before submission of a final draft—escalated juvenile delinquency into a major social danger. The discursive switch from "juvenile crime" to "hooliganism" allowed police greater leeway to criminalize and deal harshly with what had earlier been seen as a social anomaly. Suddenly, according to Kalinin's commission on children, it was "absolutely intolerable" that "on streets of the capitals and major cities there exist outrageous hooligan outbursts (*vykhodki*) by children and juveniles." Examples of such outrages included fights, insults hurled at adults, and riding on streetcar bumpers. Consequently, police were enjoined "to take personal responsibility . . . to ensure a normal and cultured order on city streets, and to secure appropriate behavior of children in public places." And, of course, the latter translated into the habitual call for "systematic clearing of streets of homeless and hooliganizing children." This language, along with the expanded jurisdiction already granted police over juvenile policies, effectively criminalized child homelessness and equated it with the growing threat of hooliganism. Such language clearly and automatically linked homelessness with criminal and socially dangerous behavior.[28]

Apparently, the head of the VTsIK children's commission, N. A. Semashko, wrote the section on hooliganism and police responsibility. Yagoda objected to the language in that section, with its implied criticism of police, as well as its additional stipulation that local city councils establish special commissions to monitor police compliance with the order to clear streets of homeless and hooligan children. Civil authorities were to have the power "to bring to strict responsibility" both rank-and-file police and commanders who took a lax attitude toward these duties. The language of this stipulation sounded tough, and Yagoda did not like the implied criticism that the police had not done or could not do its job.[29] He did not protest too much, however, and the stipulation remained in the commission's final draft. Yagoda could afford to tolerate this aspersion on the work of the NKVD. He had gotten everything he wanted from the new laws on child homelessness and crime. The power granted to city councils to reprimand police was a fig leaf, masking the fact that the NKVD had colonized a major sphere of social policy and usurped prerogatives and money that had belonged to local governments. The NKVD had brought yet another aspect of public order under its jurisdiction.

The association of child delinquency with hooliganism was all the more ominous since, by 1935, officials saw political as well as social danger in the growing problem of youth crime. As noted above, Rudzutak's crime commission devoted a significant section to hooliganism, and both procuracy and Supreme Court reviews in 1935 and again in 1936 warned local authorities to take seriously the connection between youth crime and anti-Soviet intent. Hooliganism, noted a 1935 Russian procuracy report, no longer involved just insults and "rambunctious" or "disorderly" (*beschinstva*) behavior; acts of hooliganism increasingly involved organized social violence by youth and assaults with weapons resulting in murder. In some localities, cautioned the report, youthful hooliganism crossed the boundary into forms of banditry and other counterrevolutionary crimes.[30] A USSR Supreme Court document from 1935 described hooliganism as all the more dangerous since it involved acts that "disrupt . . . public order (*poriadok upravleniia*), and the organs of Soviet power that maintain public order." More to the point, hooliganism was one of the most dangerous crimes, since the victims of hooligan acts could be anyone. Thus, in the odd logic of the court, hooligan acts that disrupted public order—fights in a café, a movie house, or on the street—were more serious than acts directed against individual persons. The former involved the disruption of public space and order, and therefore were a direct attack against the Soviet state. Citing Stalin's by now famous January 1933 formulation of crime as class war, the court document declared that, as the economic and political power of the Soviet state increased, so the necessity increased to fight decisively against hooliganism.[31]

OPERATIONS AGAINST CHILDREN AND HOOLIGANS

Police lost little time in acting on the newly promulgated homeless children, antihooligan, and juvenile crime laws. By spring 1935, police were engaged in mass roundups of homeless and unsupervised street children, many of whom were sent to NKVD labor colonies. According to Yagoda, territorial and railroad police detained (*zaderzhano*) nearly 160,000 homeless or unsupervised children in the second half of 1935 as a result of sweeps. Of these, 62,000 were sent to NKVD colonies, while another 74,000 were returned to parents or relatives. Narkompros or Narkomzdrav homes received 13,700 children and, according to Yagoda, the rest—about 10,000–were arrested, charged with crimes, and given over to courts for trial.[32] As with passport and other campaign operations, NKVD assessments of results varied considerably from figures given by other agencies. According to a 1938 VTsIK report, territorial and railroad police rounded up many fewer children— about 62,000 children in the last half of 1935—than the 160,000 that Yagoda claimed, and slightly over 92,000 children during 1936. According to VtsIK figures, Narkompros and other nonpolice agencies

brought about 16,560 children to placement centers in the second half
of 1935. This brought the total number of children entering placement
centers to 78,560 in that period. In the VtsIK version, close to 14,000
of these children were deported to NKVD youth labor colonies in 1935,
and about 17,000 in 1936. Police returned another 18,000 children to
parents in the last six months of 1935. According to VtsIK, nearly half
of the children entering placement centers in the second half of 1935—
35,000 out of 78,560—went to children's homes run by Narkompros
or Narkomzdrav.[33]

As the figures above show, VTsIK's numbers from its 1938 report
were less than half those given by Yagoda in his 1936 report. Moreover, the two reports disagreed in assessment of the role of the NKVD
in dealing with children once they were detained. According to Yagoda's
report, nearly 40 percent of the children taken off streets in the last half
of 1935 were sent to NKVD colonies, while VTsIK recorded less than
25 percent sent to such colonies. According to VTsIK, the great majority—nearly half—ended up in non–police-run children's homes. Despite these discrepancies, both reports emphasized the dramatically increased role played by the NKVD in dealing with the problem of street
children. Both reports noted the large shift in administration of placement centers from Narkompros to the NKVD. Yagoda reported that, by
June 1935, 260 centers had changed hands, meaning that 23,000 children living in these centers suddenly found themselves under police jurisdiction instead of under the administration of social welfare agencies.[34] This was in addition to 22,000 children in centers or colonies
already run by the NKVD. In all, according to the VTsIK report, some
325,000 children were taken off the streets between spring 1935 and
August 1937. Urban and railroad police roundups accounted for slightly
more than 259,000 of these children. Most of them were not homeless
but "unsupervised," and were returned to parents—about 147,335, according to VtsIK. Nearly 100,000 homeless children were sent to homes
run by social agencies such as Narkompros or Narkomzdrav, while
40,000 were placed in NKVD colonies or were sentenced to prison
terms. Yagoda's report for 1935 may have disagreed considerably with
the VTsIK figures for that year. Overall, however, the proportions of figures from VTsIK for the two years covered by its report corresponded
to the proportions offered by the NKVD. Yagoda claimed that about 40
percent of homeless children fell under NKVD administration in the

second half of 1935, while the VtsIK figures showed about the same proportion for the two years covered by its report.[35]

DEBATES ABOUT REPRESSION

The continued use of administrative forms of repression led, in 1935, to a series of heated discussions among high officials and bureaucracies over the levels, kinds, and functions of repression. Some of these disagreements are well known. In early 1936, a series of letters from Vyshinskii and Krylenko to Party and state heads articulated a concern about the growing numbers of people arrested under laws against counterrevolution. Both men complained that levels of political repression, as defined by rising conviction rates under statute 58, had reached unjustifiable levels. Vyshinskii's first letter was dated February 1936, and sent to both Molotov, as head of Sovnarkom, and Stalin, as head of the Central Committee.[36] The letter precipitated a heated exchange with Yagoda, since Vyshinskii blamed Yagoda's police for significant increases in the state's custodial populations. Yagoda, in turn, blamed the courts and procuracy for the great majority of increases in the country's prison and camp populations.[37] These exchanges illustrated the highly compartmentalized character of the state's policing and procuracy agencies, and the difficulties of accounting for repression during the 1930s. Vyshinskii and Yagoda could not even agree on the numbers of people in the state's penal system arrested for political crimes, or on how they got there. Yagoda put forward an overall figure of 293,681 "brought to criminal responsibility" in 1935, of which 193,083 were arrested. He gave a moderately low figure of 33,823 people convicted by the NKVD's *Osoboe soveshchanie* in 1935. The great majority of those repressed, he argued—some 228,352—were dealt with by the procuracy and courts. Vyshinskii put the number of NKVD convictions at over 150,000 at least, including those processed through passport police boards, as well as through the *Osoboe soveshchanie*. He also pointed out that 90–95 percent of individuals convicted by courts had been arrested by the organs of the NKVD. According to Vyshinskii, procuracy organs had initiated only 5 to 10 percent of these cases. Thus, he wrote, nearly all of the figures for those convicted by courts should be tallied under the NKVD, not the courts. Vyshinskii noted further that the number of political convictions would be much higher if family members were counted

who were exiled with those actually convicted. Consequently, concluded
Vyshinskii, the number of those exiled from Leningrad during the 1935
purge of the city amounted to two to three times more than the 5,130
people officially counted by police. According to procuracy numbers,
over 11,000 people suffered exile—4,833 heads of families and 6,239
family members.

Vyshinskii put forward two other criticism of the NKVD that bear on
the question of how repression was defined in the 1930s. The chief
procurator sharply condemned not only the number of arrests and convictions by the NKVD, but the number of arrests of citizens whose cases
had been dismissed or quashed by prosecutors; these were cases that
never went to a judicial court or to an administrative sentencing board,
but ones that involved unjustified detention of citizens. Vyshinskii put
the number of citizens who suffered this kind of abuse at well over
800,000 for 1935 alone. And these were cases initiated only by the civil
police, not by the GUGB. Thus, according to Vyshinskii, between half
a million and a million citizens had been unjustifiably detained or arrested by police. This was a staggering number of people, Vyshinskii
wrote; their detention amounted to a form of repression that Yagoda refused to acknowledge.[38]

Vyshinskii's other criticism—his main criticism—was that too many
people were passing through the administrative sentencing apparatus
of the NKVD, whether the *Osoboe soveshchanie* or the police troikas.
To be sure, Vyshinskii expressed concern about the numbers of people
being repressed, but the main issue that exercised him was the use of
nonjudicial forms of repression. With the formation of the NKVD in
1934, the state was supposed to curtail sharply the use of administrative methods of repression. Cases of state crimes were supposed to be
processed by the procuracy and courts. Only the most dangerous political crimes were to come under the administrative sentencing jurisdiction of the NKVD. In one respect, then, Vyshinskii's criticisms were jurisdictional, a matter of bureaucratic turf; he was asserting the authority
of the procuracy and the courts against that of the NKVD in the state's
policies of repression.

Issues of legality also came into play. Vyshinskii noted that procedures of evidence were not as stringent in proceedings of the *Osoboe
soveshchanie* as in courts. Nonjudicial sentencing boards required neither corroboration by witnesses, nor even the presence of the accused.

As a result, wrote the chief procurator, proceedings of the *Osoboe soveshchanie* and police troikas lent themselves too easily to mistakes and abuse. In order to resolve these problems, Vyshinskii's primary recommendations to Stalin and Molotov were to increase the participation of courts in cases of political repression, to reduce the number of cases moving through the *Osoboe soveshchanie,* and to restrict still further the jurisdictional competence of the latter body.[39]

Apart from jurisdictional and legal issues, however, the disputes between Vyshinskii and Yagoda turned on a more fundamental difference of opinion about the function of repression. Here was the essential issue that separated the two men. For Yagoda, the purpose of repression was to defend the security of the state against its enemies. The practice of repression was to be carried out ruthlessly and efficiently, even secretly, out of the eye of the public and public institutions. Despite his protestations to the contrary, Yagoda cared little for legal procedures and courts, which he believed mostly hindered the task of defending the state from its enemies in the most effective way. For example, he reminded operational heads of the NKVD that their central task was the protection of state security, but only by working "on the basis of revolutionary legality." On the face of it, this was an admonition that officers should work according to the law and legal procedures. In the same breath, however, he quoted Stalin to make clear what he meant by that phrase. Keep in mind, he reminded his audience, that according to Stalin's instructions, "'the chief task of revolutionary legality in our time is the defense of socialized (*obshchestvennaia*) property.'"[40] Such a comment amounted to a backhanded swipe at procuracy and judicial complaints that police often ignored revolutionary legality, understood as adherence to laws and legal procedures. Yagoda's twist to the oft-used phrase would not have been lost on his audience as a tacit endorsement, backed by Stalin's authority, of aggressive policing policies. Such comments, and Yagoda's attitudes in general, fostered an open antilegal culture within the OGPU, to such an extent that many OGPU officers allegedly boasted that they had read neither the state's criminal codes nor the criminal procedural codes. According to Yagoda, even many operational heads of the political police did not know that the procuracy possessed supervisory authority over NKVD investigations.[41] Complaints by procuracy and court officials were legion about the lack of procedural accuracy and blatant illegality in the NKVD.[42]

For Vyshinskii, as for Yagoda, the purpose of repression was to defend the state. In contrast to Yagoda, however, Vyshinskii argued that the purpose of repression was also educational, serving the goal of social disciplining. According to Vyshinskii, the practice of repression was not to be kept secret, but made very public. Vyshinskii believed that public courts were a proper forum for the civic and political education of the citizenry, and hence that they were the most appropriate place to try political cases. This difference of views between Yagoda and Vyshinskii over the function of repression was at the heart of many disputes between the procuracy and the NKVD. One of the most absurd examples of this difference arose in 1936 over the issue whether to allow repetition in open court of anecdotes, comic verses, and slanderous epithets about Soviet power or the country's leaders. Yagoda wished these to be suppressed for reasons of security, and so as not to make the courts into a forum for the spread of anti-Soviet slander. Vyshinskii argued that they should be allowed under rules for presenting evidence, but also, and mainly, in order to educate listeners in the ways that the state deals with those who slander it. In the end, Sovnarkom resolved the matter by ordering that the content of slanderous remarks be entered into the court record, but recited only in closed sessions of courts. Such a Solomon-like resolution was an attempt to address the concerns of both Yagoda and Vyshinskii.[43]

Vyshinskii expressed his views about repression and law most articulately in the course of a series of debates held in the state's Institute of Criminal Policy, administered under the justice commissariat. Many of the state's most important legal specialists worked in this institute, including high-level functionaries in the justice and procuracy agencies. The institute published the proceedings of these debates in 1935 in a multivolume collection titled *Problems of Criminal Policy*. In his contribution, Vyshinskii laid out his vision of repression under Soviet law, and especially the relation between judicial and nonjudicial forms of repression.[44] Vyshinskii argued, as might be expected, for a reduction in the use of the police system of extrajudicial punishment. While he conceded that the latter was necessary in a rare number of cases, he argued that punishment and law, indeed "the further advancement of proletarian democracy," should be based "firmly and consistently" on "the single universal process of law."[45] At first glance, these phrases may seem like a call for moderation, legal process, and a return to principles of individual protection within a socialist democracy. Yet the insistence on due process, Vyshinskii wrote, was not to protect the rights of the accused; the central question was how useful this or any form of repression was in protecting and furthering the interests of the state (*gosu-darstvo*). According to Vyshinskii, the advantage of due process within the judicial system was that it was open to public *view*, not to public *scrutiny*. Vyshinskii was not calling for a moderation of administrative repression in favor of citizens' rights—in fact, he often criticized the courts for their "weak" sentencing practices.[46] According to Vyshinskii, the court system, including the use of due process, was one of the most effective tools "for organizing public opinion," and for "educating the masses to discipline in the interests of strengthening the authority of the state."[47] Extrajudicial forms of repression were not open to public view, but were hidden and therefore not as effective as a means of disciplining the masses.[48]

THE CIVIL VS. THE MILITARY STATE

Other procuratorial and judicial officials criticized the NKVD, and increasingly so, in the middle years of the 1930s. Krylenko and Vyshinskii were not alone in the call to reduce levels of political repression. Antonov-Ovseenko, the Russian federation chief procurator, also called for a decrease in repression, and not just in political forms of repression. Speaking to a joint procurator-judicial conference in July 1936, Antonov-Ovseenko called for an end to all administrative forms of repression, not just against political criminals, but also, and especially, against socially harmful groups. He was harshly critical of the NKVD and the "tendencies" toward arbitrary repression within the police. Such tendencies, he declared, were "still very much alive." Antonov-Ovseenko condemned the self-reinforcing idiocy of such policies, which criminalized social marginals and then made them into enemies by the very fact of their marginality. "We scatter the declassed element about, which, in itself, acts to bring forth a criminal class." Branded as "harmful," socially marginal people could not find work, and turned to criminality as the only and last resort. Antonov-Ovseenko read several letters from people who had suffered this kind of experience to illustrate the point that police policies of repression proved a major source of crime and criminality. After reading one letter, Antonov-Ovseenko noted that, though short, it said much.[49]

In his remarks, Antonov-Ovseenko focused specifically on the repression of social marginals, and this set him at odds not only with police, but with his superior, Vyshinskii. It did so, because, when Vyshinskii criticized levels of repression, he was careful to make distinctions. In his February letter to Stalin, Vyshinskii cited three sources of increase in administrative forms of repression: arrests for counterrevolutionary agitation, arrests for planning or attempting terror acts against Party and state officials, and arrests of those identified as socially dangerous or socially harmful. Vyshinskii wrote that his objections to administrative methods of repression specifically concerned arrests in the first two categories, and specifically excluded social cleansing operations.[50] Vyshinskii gave no explanation for not including arrests of social marginals in his complaint. Possibly, he believed that miscarriage of justice or procedure was less of a danger in the troikas that adjudicated socially dangerous elements, since these troikas supposedly included prosecutorial personnel. But decisions by the *Osoboe soveshchanie* were also subject to procuratorial review. Another possible explanation may have followed from Vyshinskii's didactic view of repression. He may have believed that little didactic purpose was to be served by a public display of repression of marginal populations. More important were the political and social lessons to be taught by open judicial repression of political crimes. Whatever the reason, Vyshinskii's remarks made clear that he did not oppose the use of repression so much as the way the police conducted it. Nor did he oppose the use of administrative forms of repression when it concerned the category of socially harmful elements.

Vyshinskii's apparent lack of concern for repression of socially marginal populations set him apart from Antonov-Ovseenko, and it is likely that the latter's comments in July were aimed at his boss as much as at the police. Vyshinskii's letter was written and his exchange with Yagoda took place in February; Antonov-Ovseenko addressed his remarks about social marginals to his colleagues in July. It is not certain whether the Russian chief procurator was privy to the Vyshinskii-Yagoda exchange, but it is reasonable to assume that Antonov-Ovseenko was informed about it. If so, it is also likely that he chose his topic deliberately for the July meeting of procuracy heads—the more so since Vyshinskii sat on the podium of the conference as Antonov-Ovseenko made his remarks. Indeed, Vyshinskii had given the lead address, in which he again stressed the need to strengthen legality. For those in the know, Antonov-Ovseenko's remarks appeared as a clear but implicit rebuke of Vyshinskii.

Nor was the Russian procurator alone in his criticisms, which were echoed by other procuracy officials at the July 1936 conference. A number of officials reiterated the need to end all forms of administrative repression. Several called for significant restrictions to be placed on the NKVD. One procurator, a longtime official working in the "special" department that oversaw policing in border regions and transport zones, noted that the NKVD in these areas were nearly a law unto themselves, since all citizens there came under their special jurisdiction. Even the local procurators in border regions and along transport routes were materially dependent on the NKVD for transportation and even food and housing. As a result, procuratorial oversight, especially in border regions, was weak, and many procurators were living "in the pocket" of the NKVD. Several officials vigorously challenged this assertion, but others reiterated the charge and included this kind of corruption in the list of practices and policies that needed to be changed.[51]

The longtime inspector and procuracy official A. Sol'ts also addressed the issues of repression, police high-handedness, and the need for legality. And he, too, took a swipe at Vyshinskii. Echoing Antonov-Ovseenko, Sol'ts stressed, especially, the dysfunctional effects of campaign-style policies of repression. He noted that such campaigns always ended with the need for procuracy and judicial officials to review the cases of thousands and tens of thousands of innocent citizens who had been arrested. This was an enormous waste of resources and time, noted Sol'ts, not to mention the worse consequence that thousands of lives were disrupted and often ruined by such policing measures. Like other officials at the conference, Sol'ts called for greater legality and increased restrictions to be placed on the arrest authority of the NKVD. Yet Sol'ts distinguished his remarks from those of his superior, Vyshinskii. Sol'ts challenged Vyshinskii openly but subtly by diplomatically pointing up the hypocrisy of the chief procurator's call for greater legality. Referring directly to Vyshinskii, Sol'ts made the comment that greater legality should not be read simply as a call for transferring harsh administrative forms of repression to the courts. Greater legality did not mean imposing the harshest judicial sentence possible in every case, but in applying the law fairly in defense of citizens' rights, and in consideration of mitigating circumstances, as well as in defense of the socialist state.[52]

Officials at the July conference were emboldened by the promulgation of the new constitution of 1936. Many made their remarks about legality with references to statutes and protections guaranteed in that document. Ignatii Barkov, the Western Siberian procurator, commented that the constitution provided the foundation for a new era of protecting citizens' rights.[53] The procurator Radchenko remarked that, with publication of the new constitution, procuracy and judicial officials should turn greater attention to the construction of a strong civil state. Radchenko cited the rising number of civil cases pending in courts, nearly 2 million in 1935 in the RSFSR, and declared that more resources should be devoted to overseeing property and other civil rights of citizens. Cases involving housing, alimony, land, and other forms of property, and a host of other questions, needed to be reconciled with the civil codes adopted in the new constitution, and with the general concept of socialist legal order (*sotsialisticheskii pravoporiadok*).[54] Radchenko's colleagues sympathized—some more, some less—with his call to reorder priorities. Several pointed out that such a shift in focus was still premature. Yet despite such disagreements, the tenor of the conference reflected a sense among procuracy and judicial officials that the time was finally at hand to settle up, to exert their authority over the police, and to move the state away from policies of repression toward a greater reliance on law, judicial process, and a strong legal culture.

A MIXED ASSESSMENT

The musings of legal experts and judicial officials had little effect on NKVD policies, despite procuracy efforts to enforce legal and procedural sanctions. Stalin chose, for his own reasons, not to adjudicate the debates about repression that divided the procuracy, the judiciary, and the police. The Stalinist regime continued to use both judicial and administrative forms of repression during the 1930s. Although debates arose over the extent and forms of political repression, only a few officials raised objections to the continued use of administrative and campaign policing methods against marginal and national minority populations. These methods worked well enough that the country's leaders applied them to resolve a number of social problems. Indeed, by the early months of 1936, Yagoda was able to paint a generally favorable picture of the NKVD's efforts to fight crime and establish public order. His March 1936 report to Sovnarkom stood in sharp contrast to the dire picture he had presented just two years earlier.[55] As a result of reforms, reorganizations, significant increases in personnel, and increased professionalism, Yagoda declared in his 1936 report, police had made significant advances toward the goal of securing social order and curbing criminality. Most violent crimes had been reduced to insignificant levels. He boasted that there were fewer murders in the whole of the Soviet Union in 1935 than in the city of Chicago.

Yagoda noted that certain types of crimes continued to be a problem, including simple robbery, organized forms of hooliganism, speculation, and theft of socialist property. While not as widespread as in the early 1930s, these types of crimes persisted, according to Yagoda, despite efforts by police to eradicate them. Lack of supervision of homeless children also continued to be a problem, and in 1934 and 1935 incidents of armed banditry also rose. According to Yagoda, however, professional qualifications and educational levels of the police had risen, as well as police discipline. Cases of corruption and crimes committed by police officers had fallen off considerably in the previous years, but Yagoda noted that much still had to be accomplished to raise the professional and "cultural" levels of the country's police force.[56]

Yagoda's internal NKVD report in early 1936 echoed the positive tone of his report to Sovnarkom, but with similar cautions. Overall, according to Yagoda, the police had secured order in the country and had achieved "notable successes" in the struggle to reduce crime and establish social order.[57] Yet whatever success the NKVD achieved in fighting crime and establishing social order was not due to the establishment of regularized policing methods. Even by the middle 1930s, the country still had no effective police system for the daily maintenance of order. Despite expansion of the *militsiia,* the number of police in the country in 1935 was still half what it had been before the 1914–18 war.[58] Police in most cities, even major urban centers, had yet to establish a police post system for daily patrols in neighborhoods. In provincial cities such as Novosibirsk, the large working-class neighborhoods had no regular police patrol system. In Barnaul, an industrial center five hours south of Novosibirsk by train, few police ventured out into the outlying shantytown districts of the city.[59] Attempts to establish night patrols, even in large cities, had largely failed and had been abandoned, and citizen vigilante groups continued to grow in areas that lacked effective police forces. Many rural areas, according to Yagoda, remained outside the effective range of policing abilities.[60]

CONCLUSIONS

Most important, and despite his optimistic reports, Yagoda had failed to change policing culture. Local police enforced passport and residence laws only sporadically. By Yagoda's own reckoning, the most effective policing mechanisms were the mass campaigns against socially harmful elements. In the absence of a regular policing system, the clearing or *iz"iatie* campaigns became the primary method for the regime to fight criminality and other forms of public disorder, to rid the cities of unwanted or marginal populations, and to protect cities and other vital spaces such as border regions and elite resorts. Throughout the middle 1930s, and despite government and Party policy to end mass forms of repression, many hundreds of thousands of people were swept up in large-scale arrests, deportations, and punitive expulsions. Mass or categorical forms of repression did not end with dekulakization in the early 1930s. While mass arrests and deportations in rural areas tapered off after 1933, they increased in intensity and scope in urban areas and border zones as police attempted to purge these areas of criminals, marginal elements, and potentially disloyal national minorities. Operational groups of both the political and civil police continued to investigate large-scale organized crimes, but small-scale crimes, such as speculation and petty theft, burgeoned out of control and were most effectively handled by mass police sweeps of markets, train stations, flophouse districts, and other areas where such people operated. The NKVD handled the single most troubling problem of social disorder during the middle 1930s—homeless youth and juvenile crime—in the same way. The other major problem that threatened social order during the 1930s stemmed from the various categories of "socially dangerous elements," and the regime handled this problem in the same manner. The use of administrative forms of justice and mass policing remained an integral part of police culture and practice throughout the 1930s.

8 Passports, Identity, and Mass Policing

The passport system is the first, most important line of defense of the revolution.
—Genrikh Yagoda, 1935

The OGPU categorically opposes . . .
—Genrikh Yagoda, 1934

THE SOVIET REGIME employed many means to categorize, monitor, and act upon its citizens, but the most detailed and comprehensive was the internal passport and domicile registration system. Introduced in the early 1930s as a mechanism to protect urban areas from mass migration, the passport system quickly evolved into a complex set of policing tools. As previous chapters have shown, campaign methods of social policing using passport and residency laws supplanted an inadequate and still underdeveloped police system. Authorities applied passport and residency laws to combat waves of criminality and social disorder, and to police deviance and marginality. At the same time, police used the passport system to impose officially sanctioned identities on the population. These identities were predefined in sets of instructions and were written into corresponding passport lines, based on police scrutiny of documents provided by the passport holder. The passport system ascribed social, occupational, and ethnic-national identities directly to all who received an internal passport, and indirectly to those who were not issued passports. In this way, the passport system extended the categorizing tendencies of the Soviet regime and formalized a uniquely Soviet system of social taxonomy.

The passport system functioned not only to categorize or "photograph" the country's population, but also to bind it to particular places.

Issuance of a passport was tied directly to the registration of the passport number to a specific residence and place of work. In turn, passport laws permitted some populations to live and work in privileged cities and areas, and barred other populations from those areas. Here was a powerful policing tool, as well as a tool of identification. Categorization of the population through passport identities allowed officials (or so they believed) to quantify, monitor, and restrict the movement of undesirable populations, and to cleanse strategic areas, such as borders and elite resorts. Residency restrictions placed on different populations created a complex mosaic of what officials described as near and alien elements and distant and near spaces. Passportization, in other words, was tied to a particular vision of internal colonization as well as to a corporate ordering of the state. That ordering was a geographic as well as a social, ethnic, and occupational construct.

This chapter examines the social-geographic aspects of the passport system, and the role of the police in administering that system.[1] The latter is an especially important part of the following discussion. Through administration of the passport system, and especially through repressive measures associated with it, OGPU and then NKVD leaders found themselves involved in realms of social policy and policing new to them. Registration of criminals and dangerous populations had long been part of policing, but administration of the passport system, in all its complexities, engaged police in processes of social engineering and surveillance on a broad scale. Social engineering on the scale of the passport system was new for both the political and the civil police and required new skills. By necessity, police had to become masters of statistical descriptions of the population, a sphere of expertise long dominated by demographers. As police officials moved into the realm of population statistics, they inevitably came into conflict with professionals in the State Statistical Administration, who were in charge of census and other civil registration systems in the country. Conflicts between the NKVD and officials of the statistical administration in the middle 1930s have been well documented.[2] Here, that takeover is emphasized as yet another aspect of police militarization of the sphere of social politics.

Administration of the passport system also involved police officials in the colossal new task of administration of labor camps and penal colonies and settlements. This theme has also been well documented. Less well known is how authorities identified whom to deport, where dangerous populations should be sent, and under what conditions, if at all, "alien elements" could be reintegrated back into society. Certainly, Stalin and other political leaders had the final say in these matters, but as this chapter shows, police officials also played a key role. Through the daily administration of passport laws, police officials decided who fit into which categories of the population. More to the point, it was police officials who decided how to fill out passport lines identifying social status, and what to write in passport card catalogs about undesirables. The country's passportization and residency registration system provided the regime one of its major instruments for naming and rearranging the population of the country. Through administration of the passport system, police played an active role in that process.

The task of identifying citizens and social aliens was also new to the police. Identification of social aliens fell under the jurisdiction of local soviet officials during the 1920s and the early years of the 1930s. This authority derived from the control local officials exercised over election and disenfranchisement laws.[3] During the 1920s, civil and political police enforced laws of inclusion and exclusion, but police did not decide who was a privileged citizen and who a social alien. Those decisions were made by local communities and their elected representatives. In Stalin's militarized state, identification and adjudication of social aliens and suspect populations was transferred from the jurisdiction of local civic government to the purview of police. This was accomplished through the authority given police to engage in administrative forms of repression associated with social defense campaigns and passport laws. Social engineering that had involved whole communities and was centered in civil government was replaced by a bureaucratized system of police repression, administered largely under secret orders, and with little possibility of citizen interaction and redress.

Officials believed that passport categories of identity represented social reality and they enacted policies of privilege and punishment, of inclusion and repression, based on those categories. Despite the existence of other means of documenting identity, the passport system became a primary means by which Soviet officials defined the social and ethnic composition of Soviet society, the degree of loyalty of different populations, and the geographic distribution of those populations. Through administration of the passport system, the civil police was transformed from an agency fighting crime and defending public order to one of mass social engineering and surveillance. Likewise, the function of the political police broadened from counterinsurgency and fighting political opposition to social engineering on a mass scale.

THE CATEGORICAL IMPERATIVE: SOCIAL POLICING AND THE BUREAUCRATIZATION OF IDENTITY

The Soviet passport system was created for the purpose of identifying and isolating marginal and supposedly dangerous populations. The all-union civil police administration, the GURKM, was created formally and specifically to administer the union-wide passport system.[4] As a result, the creation of social identities through passport categories became intertwined with bureaucratic processes of population surveillance and repression. Indeed, the passport system functioned to bureaucratize and make automatic both the formative process of social identity and the business of surveillance. The one process entailed the other. A passport fixed an individual occupationally, ethnically, and socially through categories written into the passport document. Residence registration of a passport at the local or regional police office placed a person geographically. If a person left a locale, he or she was required to "unregister" the current residence and to indicate the new address. Upon arrival at the new address, the passport holder was, in turn, required to reregister his or her passport and new residence at the new location. If the system worked correctly a citizen could not have a social identity that was not open to police scrutiny.

Identity and surveillance worked through the ascribed categories in the actual passport document, but also through more detailed information that police kept in passport *kartoteki*. These catalogs were supposed to be located in each passport office, or "table" (*stol*), in local police offices, regional passport centers, and a central catalog system at the Commissariat of Internal Affairs in Moscow. Cards for each passport number documented information contained in the passport, but also the background, previous residences, previous convictions, or other possibly "compromising" information for each passport holder. Information in passport catalogs was based on documents or affidavits provided by the passport holder when the passport was issued, and then was supposedly updated by local officials and police whenever new information was registered. The system was supposed to work automatically, so that any new information filed at a local passport office was sent on in duplicate to the regional and central catalogs.

The passport system was notoriously inefficient. Many police gave low priority to the daily tasks of maintaining passport files, or of following the strict procedures for issuing or checking passports and residence registrations. Police inspectorate surveys showed that, even in large cities with professionalized police forces, residence rolls registered tens and hundreds of citizens who did not actually live in a precinct, or who had moved and had not "unregistered," or who lived in a region but who had no residence registration. In a major city, such discrepancies could add up to tens of thousands of people who were not properly documented. Yet for all its faults, the passport system worked well enough to give the regime a powerful social instrument. Passportization and enforcement of residency registration laws were designed to make Soviet society visible, transparent to the eyes of the police, even as citizens went about their daily lives. And as Alain Blum and Nathalie Moine have noted, the passport system was more precise and detailed in its creation and collection of information about citizens than other statistical apparatus—more so even than the census and the civil registration system for gathering information on births, deaths, marriages, and other family changes.[5] As a result, the passport and domicile registration system soon replaced other means of social monitoring. Police continued to keep files on individuals under direct agent observation, but direct observation of individuals was selective and required intensive use of manpower. Likewise, relying on reports from the vast and cumbersome network of resident police agents and "poorly qualified" informants was costly and of dubious value.[6] In contrast, passportization provided a truly mass means of social identification and monitoring. The first passport distribution campaigns began in 1933 and, by the end of 1934, slightly more than 27 million people over the age of sixteen had been issued passports. This number represented about 20 percent of the adult population, and only covered the Russian republic, the largest of the Soviet republics. How many citizens were passportized in the whole of the Soviet Union by 1934 is not known, but the 27 million figure included about 12.7 million people in so-called regime areas—major urban areas such as Moscow and Leningrad, strategically important sites, industrial regions, military land and buildings, and border regions—and another 15 million people in nonregime areas. Towns with under 10,000 population were not passportized; neither were most rural areas, especially collective farms, although state farms were passportized.[7] By the end of the 1930s, passportization extended to approximately 50 million citizens in a total population of 162 million.[8] A simple comparison between the approximately 1.2 million people who were listed in surveillance registers (*na uchete*) in the late 1930s and the 50 million people with registered passport information shows that the difference in scale of surveillance was dramatic.[9] The passport system, if maintained correctly, held the potential to monitor all citizens automatically, universally, and secretly, providing police and other authorities an instrument to find and identify any individual at any time. If informant networks and direct surveillance were the "eyes that must see but not be seen," then passportization was even more so.[10]

This bureaucratization of identity and surveillance had several important consequences. As passportization began to take effect throughout the country, passport and residency laws became one of the major weapons police used in the fight against crime. This was probably not one of the originally intended functions of passportization, but resulted mainly from the weakness of regular policing methods in the country. Once police grasped the implications of passportization, however, they were quick to employ it to the full extent. By the mid-1930s, operative groups of both the civil and political police were using mass passport sweeps in cities as a primary way to bring in tens of thousands of people who fit the profile of socially harmful—criminals and associates of criminals, the unemployed, beggars, prostitutes, itinerants, and other socially marginal populations. Yagoda, as well as the head of the police, L. N. Bel'skii, emphasized on numerous occasions the importance of passport laws and police passport troikas as primary crime-fighting tools and as instruments for the maintenance of public order. Yagoda urged his police officials to bypass cumbersome judicial procedures and to use passport sweeps, especially, as a way to identify, capture, and convict recidivist criminals and other socially dangerous types.[11]

If the use of passport laws shaped public policing practice, it also contributed to changes in the methods and function of repression. Beginning in 1933, with the curtailment of forced collectivization and dekulakization, the regime's leaders relied less on campaigns of social mobilization, and more on the techniques of policing agencies to carry out policies of social repression. Police not only enforced exclusionary laws, but defined who was a loyal citizen and who an "alien." Police carried out repressive policies under secret orders based on a police-controlled, bureaucratized system of social identity. In turn, police-controlled passport sweeps—so-called "social defense" campaigns—became a primary tool of repression. The use of the passport system did not precipitate this shift in methods, but the categorizing mechanism of passports allowed police officials to distance themselves from public participation. Passportization allowed the police to professionalize, bureaucratize, and make secret the business of repression. Accordingly, professionalization, bureaucratization, and secrecy fit the function of repression after 1933, which served more to protect institutions of state power and state property than to break and remake social power relations. Defense of the state was the clear goal of the campaigns of social defense and the campaigns against suspect ethnic populations during the mid-1930s. The passport system brought to these campaigns of repression a technology of secrecy and a level of social engineering impossible before its implementation.

Passportization bureaucratized aspects of social surveillance as well as repression. For example, along with other forms of registration, it made sense out of the decision in 1932 to cease the regular summary reports, *svodki,* which had been used since tsarist times by police to take the barometer of popular attitudes toward the regime and its policies. *Svodki* were prepared on a regular basis by local police authorities and then filtered at higher administrative levels for consumption by political and governmental bodies. The *militsiia* also compiled monthly and quarterly *svodki* on crime in their areas. In 1933, the OGPU ceased the regular collection of these reports and continued them only on an ad hoc basis, upon request, and on specific topics.[12] With passportization, *svodki* became redundant as a mechanism of social monitoring. Police no longer needed to try to gauge psychological attitudes or public moods. Through passport and residency laws, officials could (or so they thought) systematically categorize, quantify, and locate or relocate, with reliable exactness, loyal and potentially dangerous populations. Here was social engineering on a large scale, and the beauty of the system, for the police, was that it was automatic, professionalized, and secret from the public.[13]

One of the most important consequences of passportization was to encourage officials and citizens to think in the same collective and categorical terms. In officials' eyes, moreover, passportization reduced the population from a mass of individuals to a range of simplified types. This was done simply by a line on the passport giving a person's social status, or *sotsial'noe polozhenie*. Circulars from the early and mid-1930s instructed local police how to define individuals under the three basic categories of worker, peasant, and white-collar employee. Peasants could be subdivided further into poor, middle, or kulak peasants. Apart from these basic designations, other complications arose, and a person could be identified more specifically by occupation as an artisan (*kustar'*), student, pensioner, domestic worker, and even pejoratively as someone "from the capitalist . . . or déclassé . . . remnants—a trader, a religious sectarian, or without defined employment." Reformed social types might be listed as artisans, for example, with a notation of former status as kulaks. Instructions often mixed occupation with social background as a way to define social status, but it was police who defined these categories. And it was police, particularly local police officials, who decided which individuals fit into which categories of social status. In this way, police officials took on a significant role in defining social identities through their administration of the passport system.[14]

The use of these kinds of identify categories permitted officials to speak of and write about the country's populations as "organized" and "unorganized." Organized populations—those which had been categorized by passportization and residency laws—were good. Unorganized populations—people who had no passports or who did not fit into one of the neatly defined social ranks created by the regime— were bad. Like dirt or trash, unorganized populations were "matter out of place." They were the carriers of pollution and social contamination, both political and physical. In a January 1933 circular, for example, police and health officials ascribed the spread of epidemic diseases, especially typhus, to "mobile and unorganized groups within the population—nomads, wanderers (*otkochevniki*), orphans—who are the main transmitters of . . . infectious illnesses among local core populations (*mestnoe korennoe naselenie*)."[15] Similarly, in a 1932 report, police officials described the presence of socially marginal people as filth or dirt (*zagriaznenie*) "on the face of our cities." In the same report—in fact, on the very next page—authorities also charged local police to lead the fight for public hygiene. Thus, in making cities models of socialism, the report admonished local officials first to cleanse the social trash from the streets, referring to "dangerous" and "unorganized" elements, and then to clear the literal trash, as well.[16] Similarly, Yagoda warned throughout the mid-1930s of the social dangers created by hiring labor migrants outside of organized state contracts. Laborers, especially from rural areas, who sought employment outside of organized contracts between farms and factories were certain to be from the "socially dangerous element"—criminals, fortune seekers, runaway kulaks—who would disrupt production and "contaminate" regime areas.

Passportization of the population not only encouraged people to think in categorical terms, but in categories created by the regime. As noted in chapter 1, suspected prostitutes, for example, need no longer be caught in the specific act of solicitation to be arrested. These women, many of whom had no "defined place of employment or residence," could now be picked up and sentenced to harsh punishment as violators of passport and residency laws, or simply as socially harmful. Similarly, it was in connection with the passport system that the category of "socially harmful element" (sotsvredelement), which had existed for a long time, became formally codified as a legally punishable social identity. As described in chapter 6, Operational Order 00192, from May 1935, defined who fit the profile of a socially harmful "element." This category included persons with previous criminal convictions and "continuing uncorrected ties" to the criminal world, and persons with no criminal convictions, but with no definite place of work and ties with the criminal world. The category also included "professional" beggars, persons caught repeatedly in urban areas without proper residence permits, persons who returned to places where they were forbidden to live, and children over the age of twelve caught in a criminal act. All of these types of people were to be regarded as socially harmful. They were now subject to summary arrest and sentencing by troikas for up to five years in corrective labor camps.[17]

Procuracy officials often objected to the police tendency to abuse the "socially harmful" designation, but their harsh criticisms of police practice revealed a common acceptance of the social reality of this category. In 1936, for example, a procuracy official, Khaevskii, noted with outrage that police officials issuing passports to released convicts would, at times, list the individual's occupation as *sotsvredelement*. This practice was, of course, a bit of mean humor and against regulations, and Khaevskii correctly underscored the damaging implications of carrying such a passport. In his complaint, however, Khaevskii did not challenge the validity of this category to describe identity, only its inappropriate application to particular individuals. Even in criticizing the police, Khaevskii revealed the extent to which officials and citizens internalized social categories created by police.[18]

Despite the success of passportization in standardizing social identities, some misunderstood the purpose of passportization and the social categories it created. Many local officials, at least in Western Siberia, were enthusiastic about passportization, since they believed that it would allow them to rid their jurisdictions of former kulaks, marginal types, and other groups belonging to the "socially alien element." They failed to understand that, in nonregime areas, those were exactly the people whom higher officials wanted passportized, in order to monitor them. What local officials did not understand, and what higher officials had to explain, tactfully, was that passportization was not designed to bring local regions into socialism by cleansing them of alien populations, but to use local areas as social dumping grounds for those same populations expelled from regime areas.[19]

There were those who understood this and other functions of passportization, and theirs was an understanding not to the liking of police. Police kept close track of what the populace was saying about passportization, especially of those who criticized it. One of the most common complaints was that it was just "one more way" for the regime to make money off the backs of the people. One disgruntled person described passportization as "nothing more than a way to tie people to specific places, just one more plot by the Communists, from whom one can't ever expect anything good, anyway." Some equated Soviet passportization to its tsarist equivalent, both of which defined people's identities and restricted their freedom "as the regime sees fit." Others complained that passportization, which created social differences, was incompatible with the goal of creating a classless society. Another critic hit close to the mark when he described passportization as a second wave of social purging and colonization, akin to dekulakization. During the first Five Year Plan, "Soviet rulers threw out the kulaks and exiled them. During the second Five Year Plan, they thought up passportization, and they'll use it to find more 'kulaks' to settle in various places. And in doing so, they'll turn over a huge profit."[20]

PASSPORTIZATION AND PENAL COLONIZATION

Throughout the 1930s and beyond, the Soviet regime engaged in the systematic and large-scale displacement of purportedly anti-Soviet and suspect populations. In addition to massive dekulakization campaigns, police deportation and passport operations during the mid-1930s purged cities of socially marginal populations. The regime emptied large areas of the Ukrainian and Belorussian borderlands of Polish, German, and other "anti-Soviet" populations. Similar campaigns removed Finnish populations from Karelia and social marginals and "former" and "declassed" people from major cities such as Moscow, Leningrad, Kiev, and industrial centers such as Magnitogorsk, Dneprostroi, Kharkov, and other sites. In 1935, Yagoda proposed to ship "Greeks" and "other anti Soviet contingents" from the Black Sea border regions. Two years later, Koreans were deported en masse from the border areas of Siberia. The great purges of 1937 and 1938 again targeted peasants and social marginals, as well as certain national minorities. Deportation of ethnic communities accelerated during and after World War II, when Chechens and other minorities suffered the cataclysm of forced relocations.[21]

All of these operations involved both political and civil police in the movement and custodial administration of large numbers of people, many millions of whom ended up not in the labor camps of the GULAG, but in the system of penal settlements run by the NKVD. These special settlements (*spetsposelki*), as they were called, occupied large tracts of land in specially designated areas of the country. Many other deportees were simply exiled from their original homes and restricted to particular regions. The latter exiles were not placed under armed guard, but were forbidden to move or travel out of the regions to which they were relocated.[22] A 1935 directive from the NKVD summarized which areas of the country had been designated as dumping grounds for socially harmful or dangerous populations. These areas included Western Siberia, especially the wild and hostile northern Narym regions; large portions of Central Asia, especially the northern arc of Kazakhstan, as well as the northern regions of Uzbekistan; parts of Eastern Siberia—interestingly called the "Far" East—and sections of northern-central Russia, called the Northern District, or *krai*. The word *krai* in Russian literally means "edge." As the names imply, these areas were located at the edges or margins of the Soviet state, though not always at its geographic extremities. Generally, authorities regarded these areas as "distant" (*udalennyi*)—either geographically or in terms of economic development—from the central and major "socialist" core of the country. Thus, contingents of people whom the police deported were, literally, extracted or "distanced" (*udalit'*) from socialist society.[23]

Such "distant" areas became the equivalent of the Soviet frontier. Officials thought about these areas as frontier lands. Throughout the 1920s, for example, OGPU officials regarded Western Siberia as an area whose indigenous population was "hostile" to Soviet power, and even by 1936, the district was listed in NKVD pay and supply registers under areas designated as "extreme" and "distant" (*otdalennye*) duty areas.[24] Similarly, Party officials assigned to Western Siberia thought of themselves as the bringers of modern socialist civilization to the district. One Party official described the Western Siberian *krai* as an "outpost of socialism in the east."[25] Thus, these areas were more than just social dumping grounds for unwanted populations. In fact, they took on the dual characteristics of many frontier lands. They were places to be assimilated, but also places of exile, places of both freedom and bondage.[26] The resources of these underdeveloped lands were crucial to the Soviet state, and the regime spent much effort to develop and integrate frontier lands into the core of the state. At the same time, officials found these areas convenient places to isolate dangerous populations and to use those populations as a source of cheap labor. The use of forced labor to exploit resource-rich but underdeveloped lands became a vital part of Soviet state policy under Stalin.[27]

Police and other officials regarded the hundreds of thousands of exiled people who worked and lived in these "distant" areas as penal or forced labor. The regime sent these populations far away from the core areas of the Soviet state in order to protect socialist spaces and populations. But there was another reason, as well, why these populations ended up in such "distant" locations. Police and government officials also regarded these exiles as settlers, literally as "special settlers" (*spetspereselentsy*), who played a key part in taming, or "mastering" (*osvoenie*) what officials believed were the frontiers of the Soviet state.[28] As such, the experience of these special settlers mirrored that of penal colonists in other times and places. In fact, the Soviet state shipped these *spetspereselentsy* to live and work in labor "settlements" or colonies (*trudposelenie*) in much the same way that the British crown exiled penal and political prisoners to settle the Australian territories in the eighteenth and nineteenth centuries. Like the French in South America and the British in Australia and New Zealand, Soviet leaders utilized penal colonists to exploit and develop not only agricultural lands, but also timber and fishing resources, trapping and animal husbandry, and metallurgical and mining industries.[29]

The forced colonization program epitomized the militarization of state social policies. Penal colonists were forced into settlements, as prisoners, which were grouped into military-like reservations. Each reservation was referred to as a *komendatura*, and was administered by uniformed political police troops of the OGPU/NKVD. Yet, these populations were held in their regions of exile not so much by armed guard as by enforcement of passport restrictions that limited movement out of the regions of their exile. As kulaks or social harmfuls, *spetspereselentsy* had no passports. They were not allowed to leave the regions where they were settled, even after the reservations were "demilitarized;" that is, after colonists were restored their voting and other civil rights, and the settlements were integrated into local civil administrative government. After restoration of their rights, the former kulaks were issued passports. They were restored "all their citizen's rights, including the right to vote," but with restrictive stamps in their passports forbidding travel and settlement outside their regions. In absurd bureaucratic police logic, a circular from March 1935 explained to local authorities that they were to tell former kulaks that they had full rights, "except the right to leave the area of their settlement." And it was local police, of course, not the OGPU officers, who were responsible for enforcing these passport and residence restrictions. Information on settlers was kept in police registry catalogs, and settlers were required to report once a month to the local police station to register their presence in the address book.[30] Thus, the *militsiia*, through administration of passport laws, played an important role in the repressive policies of the regime toward its custodial populations, and in the regime's plans for forced exploitation of colonial areas.

THE GEOGRAPHY OF FORCED MIGRATION

Passportization functioned as an instrument for social cleansing of cities and border areas, and as a means to maintain control over large numbers of the state's penal and exile populations. It also produced a related effect, that in addition to the many people arrested as dangerous elements, many more people simply left cities or areas where they believed that, for one reason or another, they would be denied passports, or worse, would be arrested as socially harmful elements. Thus, in addition to its association with forced deportation, passportization produced a large and involuntary out-migration of undesirable populations from regime to nonregime areas. In the first half of 1933, as a result of the first wave of passportization in the largest cities, urban areas of the country experienced a net loss of nearly 400,000 people. As noted in chapter 5, this was the only period since the civil war years in which the population of cities actually declined, and it was exceptional for the period of rapid industrialization and urbanization during the 1930s.[31]

The combination of deportation and forced migration of undesirable populations created a geographic mosaic of socialist and nonsocialist parts of the country. Officials could look at maps and cite statistics, as did Yagoda, to see the progress of constructing socialism in the country. This was not a progress measured along a single front. Generally, however, the social-geographic construction of Soviet state socialism in the mid-1930s corresponded to an east-west and an urban-rural divide. By the mid-1930s, the number of cities or industrial sites in the country which carried the designation of a regime area had grown from the original three (Moscow, Leningrad, and Kharkov) to thirty-seven.[32] Regime status not only brought certain privileges of supply and police protection—the right to limit settlement of unwanted populations—but also lifted a place into the ranks of full socialism. In his report on crime for 1935, for example, Yagoda, as well as other police officials, boasted about the positive effects of passportization in cleaning up the cities and making them "models" of socialism.[33] In fact, Yagoda recommended that the powers granted the police in regime cities be extended to rural and other nonregime areas.[34] Regime status, however, did not always connote safe, even if it denoted socialist. In 1934, for example, Sovnarkom granted regime status to the whole of the Eastern Siberian *krai*, precisely because it was a dangerous place. Eastern Siberia was "overrun" with escapees and criminals, but it was also strategically vital because of its resources, and it had a long and contested border with Japanese-occupied Manchuria.[35]

As more and more areas were designated regime areas, unwanted populations were pushed out and then into nonregime cities and areas. Officials in the latter areas attempted, desperately at times, to cope with the massive influx of purportedly anti-Soviet and other undesirable populations. This was especially true of the Urals and Western Siberian areas. Soviet authorities used these districts as favored dumping grounds for populations deported by police, but these parts of the country also became major destination points for populations driven out of regime areas by passportization. Cartographically, these areas were still part of the European core of the Soviet Union, from which most migrants came. They were not as extreme in distance or climate as the more eastern and Asian regions. In addition, much new industry was being constructed in these parts of the country and, throughout the 1930s, many of these sites were nonregime areas. Thus, citizens who were denied passports in regime areas could receive passports and find work in the industrial and mining centers of Western Siberia and the Urals. For the same reasons, these areas also became magnets for illegal immigrants. The demand for labor in these areas was so great that local officials tended to enforce residency laws loosely. As a result, these areas drew many tens of thousands of escaped kulak and other deportees, as well as ex-convicts and released former kulaks. By law, the latter could not settle in regime areas, nor could they return to their original homes. Thus, they, like other second-class citizens, tended to congregate in economically developing but socially marginal areas of the country.

During the early 1930s, especially, Western Siberia was flooded with the social detritus of the new Stalinist civilization. Problems associated with the deluge of both free and forced in-migration during the first half of the decade overwhelmed local authorities. As one frustrated official wrote, criminals and socially dangerous elements "pour into the district from both east and west."[36] In the second half of 1933 alone, over

50,000 homeless Kazakh children crossed the border into the Western Siberian district to escape the famine and hardships of collectivization in their native land. In the course of just a couple of years, hundreds of thousands of Kazakhs had fled north and east to Siberia.[37] And, according to a 1937 report by the head of the Western Siberian NKVD, Sergei Mironov, as many as nine thousand "socially dangerous" individuals lived in the Kemerovo mining regions in the southwestern areas of the district. As a result of in-migration of undesirable populations, Mironov reported, the areas of the Donbass and the Narym, particularly, had become infested with anti-Soviet and other marginal populations. According to Mironov, 208,400 exiled kulaks lived in the Narym and Kuzbass areas, not to mention former kulaks; another 5,350 individuals lived under administrative exile and included White officers, active bandits, and former (tsarist) police officials. The district was overrun, Mironov continued, with large populations of itinerants, gypsies, beggars, orphans, and criminals.[38]

A similar situation obtained in Kazakhstan as in the Urals and Western Siberia. When Mikhail Shreider arrived in the republic's capital, Alma-Ata, in 1938 as assistant head of the NKVD and head of the republic's police force, he was struck by the "huge" number of criminals there, and in Kazakhstan in general. Shreider described the state of crime in Alma-Ata as "catastrophic." Shreider quickly understood the dual reasons for this. As a penal dumping ground, Kazakhstan was home to a number of large labor camps, colonies, and special settlements, particularly the large Karagandinsk camp, sprawled out along the border separating Kazakhstan, the Altai, and Western Siberia. Lack of a passport regime in Alma-Ata compounded the problem, making the city a haven for large numbers of escapees and socially marginal populations that had fled passportization and regime areas in the European parts of the country. The situation in Kazakhstan, Shreider mused, resembled closely a similar situation he had faced as head of the police in Western Siberia, where he served prior to his appointment in Alma-Ata.[39]

Some local officials tolerated the influx of illegals and populations the regime regarded as socially harmful or marginal, in the belief that the labor benefits to local industry outweighed the social costs. Others adopted a different strategy. Throughout the 1930s, many local officials petitioned Sovnarkom to grant their areas regime status so that they could mount sweeps to clean out unwanted in-migrants. These areas were often located adjacent to regime cities, border regions, or key industrial areas. As many noted in their requests, passportization of nearby regime areas precipitated an outflow of criminals, anti-Soviet elements, and social marginals into their areas. As a result, these areas became staging grounds or bases for groups conducting criminal activities in adjacent regime areas, such as smugglers or gangs of thieves and pickpockets. Those engaged in more organized types of crime—illegal manufacture or trade—might also base themselves close in these non-regime areas, which also drew those who hoped to establish residency close to a regime city, and then use that as a base in order to find employment and a coveted apartment there. Yagoda was especially sensitive to this kind of "back-door" infiltration of regime cities.[40] As often as not, however, areas adjacent to regime cities or regions provided the only refuge for those kicked out of their homes, but who had neither the means nor the desire to move farther afield. Whatever the reasons, these areas filled up with people who had nowhere else to go or who hoped to gain residency or regain it in a neighboring regime area. Occasionally, Sovnarkom would grant requests for regime status, based on recommendations by the NKVD. In most cases, however, central authorities refused these requests and left local officials to fend for themselves.[41]

Mikhail Shreider fell into the category of those regional officials who attempted to purge their areas of marginal populations. As an assistant NKVD commissar and head of the Kazakhstan police, Shreider lobbied successfully in 1938 to have Alma-Ata included in the list of regime cities. When the city was granted that status, Shreider responded immediately with a campaign of passportization that included mass expulsions. As he noted in his memoirs, however, social cleansing of the city carried a heavy cost in the forced expulsion of large numbers of professionals—doctors, engineers, educators—who had been exiled to Kazakhstan as "former" people. Many of these had been first exiled in the mid-1920s, as part of the disenfranchisement campaigns of that decade. As former *lishentsy*, these individuals were, potentially, "socially harmful elements." They were, therefore, subject to further deportation from regime cities, according to the decree on social harmfuls of May 1935. Shreider estimated that as many as half of the many thousands exiled in 1938 from Alma-Ata belonged to what he described as the city's best citizens. A number of these included specialists work-

ing in the republic-level administrative apparatus. Even the Party secretary of the republic, Mirzoian, tried to intercede on their behalf. Shreider claimed to have made hundreds of exceptions, striking names off deportation lists of those with irreplaceable expertise. In retrospect, he
criticized the "lack of foresight" that went into the 1935 law defining
socially harmful elements. Still, he remarked, "there was nothing to be
done. We were required to fulfill the decrees of the Central Committee
and Sovnarkom." In the course of several weeks, Shreider signed the
exile orders of a "huge list" of citizens, a list that filled a whole bound
volume.[42] According to the logic of passport and residence laws, these
people were forced to move to still more provincial regions, either un-
passportized or passportized as nonregime areas. The numbers of such
people driven from their homes, not just once, but twice or more, mul-
tiplied across the whole of the Soviet Union in the 1930s. Such people
must be counted in the hundreds of thousands, if not millions. Socially
repressive measures associated with passportization created a forced exodus of populations on a massive scale.

ESSENTIALIZED IDENTITIES AND
DEGREES OF SEPARATION

Once a person was categorized into a particular identity, it was nearly
impossible to expunge it. One's social identity, especially a suspect identity, became formalized through special notations stamped in one's passport, and then recorded in NKVD *kartoteki*. These notations referred to
particular paragraphs in the passport regulations, which denoted past
criminal convictions or other stigmatizing characteristics such as prior
deportations. These notations affected where a person could live, work,
and travel, and the privileges and rights to which a person had access.
Yet passport and residence laws in the USSR did not simply include or
exclude on an either-or basis. A person's civic status was marked by degrees of restrictions that affected, to varying degrees, the right to vote,
the right of movement, and access to goods and residence privileges.
These varying degrees of restrictions might be called degrees of social inclusion or separation. These civic restrictions were also tied to geographic location, so that alienness became a matter of degree or grada-
tion, depending on the kind of travel and residence restrictions, and
restrictions on civic rights, assigned to any particular population. More-

over, residence restrictions, as listed in passport notations, remained permanently in force for certain categories of the population. The regime rarely allowed the complete reintegration of those consigned to a socially marginal or harmful category, even when deportees or prisoners were officially released and supposedly granted full citizen's rights. The massive review of dekulakization cases in 1934, for example, freed tens of thousands of peasants whose cases procuracy officials judged to have been wrongly adjudicated. At first, these freed peasants were allowed to return to their original homes, supposedly with full citizens' rights, and with the hope and expectation that they would integrate back into Soviet society by joining a *kolkhoz*. Members of this category of citizens, however, were forbidden to seek restitution of confiscated property. If someone insisted on establishing a separate household as a *edinolichnik*, that person was forced to rent back the original or other land from the state.

Also in spring 1934, TsIK began a process to restore civil rights to peasants who had been exiled as kulaks in the early years of the decade. Over the course of the next years, special settlements were demilitarized, and the settlers in them were granted full citizenship rights once again. These former kulaks—and they were referred to as former kulaks —had supposedly earned their full citizenship, replete with passport and voting privileges, through honest labor working on the penal farms. These individuals, however, were not allowed to return to their original homes, or seek residency in any regime areas. Yagoda even pressed for a directive that, while granting "full" rights, nonetheless restricted former kulaks to live and work within the region where they had been exiled. TsIK issued that decree in January 1935.[43]

Former criminal convicts fell into yet another category of restrictions. Those released from jail or camps were allowed to return to their original homes, a condition of reintegration that placed former criminals in a higher social status than former kulaks. Depending on the type of crime, however, individuals in this category were also forbidden to seek residency in regime cities, unless they fulfilled certain supposedly well-defined and stringent conditions.[44] In fact, before reforms in August of 1936, almost no ex-convict was allowed to travel to or reside in a regime area. After heated debate, Vyshinskii convinced Sovnarkom to reduce the list of crimes considered especially dangerous that carried this restriction. With the adoption of new regulations, Sovnarkom reduced the list of "most serious crimes" (*samye derzkie prestupleniia*) to four—theft (*grabezh*), armed assault (*razboi*), murder, and aggravated assault—in addition to the host of specifically political crimes against the state.[45] Vyshinskii was unable, however, to convince Sovnarkom to place a time limit on residence restrictions.

INCORRIGIBLES AND SOCIAL ATAVISM

Within the caste system described above, some social elements could be redeemed and partially reintegrated, depending on the circumstances, but there were some categories of people who could never be redeemed.[46] During the Stalinist regime, those who fell into the category of former kulak or recidivist, as well as members of certain ethnic groups—Germans, Poles, Finns—were never rehabilitated or allowed to repatriate. The police attempted to keep these groups separate from the healthy segments of socialist society by placing them in camps and guarded colonies, and restricting them to certain geographic areas of the country. As noted above, even kulaks who had been granted civil rights were restricted to the regions of their exile. In 1937, Vyshinskii, for example, made a special point to remind subordinates of the distinction between former kulaks and criminals. Certain categories of criminals, he clarified, could return to their original homes after release, while former kulaks and recidivists could not do so.[47]

Permanent restrictions placed on certain categories of the population reflected a shift in official attitudes during the mid-1930s toward an atavistic or essentialized view of social identity.[48] The events that led to permanent residence restrictions on former kulaks exemplified this shift, which began with the 27 May 1934 TsIK decree that allowed for restoration of full rights to exiled peasants. With the promulgation of that decree, a mass exodus began from special settlements. This mass flight triggered, in turn, something of a panic among high police and political officials. As of December 1934, about 32,000 labor colonists had been restored their rights, according to a report from M. D. Berman, head of the Gulag system. In a memorandum to Yagoda, Berman explained that, of those 32,000, about 8,000 elected to remain in their labor settlements, only about 25 percent. Berman recommended that mass restoration of rights be rescinded and that former kulaks not be allowed to return to their original homes.[49] Yagoda immediately ordered his deputy not to allow former deportees the right to travel away from their place of exile until the issue could be clarified at higher levels. Yagoda then wrote to Stalin to request that this "gap" in the TsIK decree be plugged. In that letter, Yagoda clarified his reasons to restrict movement, which were twofold: (1) because mass exodus of former kulaks would disrupt the state's plans "to master inhospitable places," as he phrased it, and (2) because the return of *spetspereselentsy* to their former homes would be, again in his phrase, "politically undesirable." Yagoda's second reason, of course, nullified any pretense to the ideology of rehabilitative labor, declaring, in essence, that once a kulak, always a kulak. In any case, Yagoda declared, the NKVD had to take action to stop the "massive" outflow of former kulaks back to the western parts of the Soviet Union.[50]

On 25 January 1935, TsIK issued an amended decree denying former kulaks the right to leave their regions of settlement. Still, Yagoda was not satisfied with these measures. In his view, restrictions should be applied to all other exiles that applied to former kulaks. His deputy Berman not only agreed with this, but in a report from late February 1935 urged him to seek a TsIK resolution to the same effect. The report dealt with completion of the urban social cleansing campaigns against déclassé elements initiated in association with the original passportization drives of 1933 and 1934, and also with the transfer to settlements of all those in camps with five or fewer years left in their terms of confinement. Berman noted that a number of those convicted already in 1930 and 1931 were reaching the end of their terms and were being released. They, in turn, were returning to their original homes. This, he warned, should be stopped, and he recommended that Yagoda seek to include these "contingents" under the 25 January kulak decree. The powerful assistant NKVD commissar, G. A. Molchanov (head of the Secret Political Department) agreed with this, and Berman even included a draft decree to be signed by M. I. Kalinin and A. S. Yenukidze, the heads of TsIK. Yagoda submitted the draft and, even before the issue was decided, distributed orders in March to settlement commandants and police heads to prevent the movement of ex-convicts and other freed deportees. To Yagoda's undoubted chagrin, Akulov, the then procurator general, blocked the resolution and it did not pass.[51] Yagoda could have taken some heart in knowing that the list of crimes for which conviction carried permanent residence bans in regime areas was still a long one. Still, barring ex-convicts from regime areas was not the same as isolating them permanently in "distant" areas.

Yagoda's attitudes may have been extreme among Soviet leaders, but they pervaded police culture and informed policing practice. Judging from procuracy complaints, police routinely denied unrestricted passports to ex-convicts, regardless of passport laws. In a 29 June 1935 order, Yagoda issued instructions not to give passports to any released prisoners that would allow them to live in regime areas. This order stood in direct violation of the passport statutes that covered which violators could and could not return to or live in regime areas of the country.[52] In a similar instance in 1935, Yagoda received reports that some local NKVD officials were releasing "large numbers" of recently arrived deportees. Under orders from the RSFSR procurator general, local administrators were ordered to free detainees if, on their arrival at labor colonies, there were no arrest or transport papers for them, or if such papers were not in proper order. Noting that deportees, once exposed to the underside of Soviet life, could not return to normal society, Yagoda instructed local officials to ignore the procurator's orders and to hold detainees, even if proper arrest and processing documents were missing.[53] Procuracy officials complained repeatedly about violations of this kind, apparently to little effect, but also, and importantly, even after Yagoda's removal in late 1936, which indicates that this kind of practice pervaded police culture and was not peculiar to Yagoda. In July 1937, the procuracy official and Sovnarkom member Leplevskii reported to Molotov that the commission reviewing the criminal codes was stalled over the issue of allowing ex-convicts back into major cities and industrial cities. He pointed to the leading NKVD member on the commission, Berman, who insisted that they should be kept out. Leplevskii criticized this position, noting the large number of laws allowing many ex-criminals access to regime areas.[54]

Recidivism, in fact, presented an interesting category. Soviet criminologists rejected many of the prevailing European explanations of recidivist criminal activity as biologically rooted or as the result of general sociological deformations. M. N. Gernet, the great Russian and then Soviet criminologist, wrote vehemently against the biological cum racial theories of Cesare Lombroso, the Italian phrenologist who so influenced thinking on recidivism and deviance in the late nineteenth century. Gernet proposed a "sociological" explanation of crime, as a function not of biology, but of social conditions, a theory compatible with but not dependent on a Marxist class analysis.[55] G. I. Volkov, a Soviet procuracy official and specialist on criminality, agreed, and went further, arguing that even general improvement of social conditions would not, alone, solve problems of crime. In Marxist fashion, Volkov wrote that the elimination of crime from society required a change in social relations of whole classes to political power and production.[56] Thus, only Soviet socialism provided the conditions for the complete eradication of crime and recidivism. As a result of these kinds of ideas, many social theorists as well as government figures encouraged the promotion of skilled training and job placement for criminal convicts as a way to integrate them into a healthy socialist society. The corrective labor camp system, as well as the labor colony system, was supposedly based on this principle of social redemption through work under conditions of Soviet socialism.

Yagoda paid lip service to this social-determinist view and often made reference to the rehabilitating function of labor camps and colonies. At the same time, Yagoda pointed to statistics showing that many crimes were committed by individuals with former convictions. How, then, was recidivism to be explained under Soviet conditions of socialism? Yagoda minced no words. He reviled recidivists. He believed, as did many other European criminologists and policemen, that recidivism was an atavistic trait and that repeat offenders constituted a class of unredeemable people. He believed, however, that recidivism was socially not biologically rooted. The majority of severe crimes in the country, he argued in a 1936 report, were committed by a hard core of criminals, but these criminals also fit the category of socially harmful elements, specifically the déclassé element.[57] Yagoda explained criminal recidivism, in other words, as the expression of an anti-Soviet social orientation. As such, according to Yagoda, recidivist criminals were incorrigible because they were inherently hostile to Soviet power, and they could never be rehabilitated.[58]

Here, in criminological form, was Stalin's idea of criminals and marginal populations as the new class enemy. The danger that these groups posed was not associated with class, as defined by property—these populations possessed no property, except through theft—but with class as defined by productive contribution or service to the state. Consequently, and as attitudes hardened toward deviant or marginal groups, Yagoda urged local police and GUGB officials to intensify their sweeps of socially harmful elements, based on Order 00192, and to enforce pass-port laws all the more stringently. Indeed, this hardening of attitudes found expression in the increasingly categorical application of passport and residence restrictions. In the early years of the 1930s, for example, police in regime cities applied exile orders flexibly to residents who had at one time been deprived of voting rights, or who were not engaged in "socially useful production." According to operational instructions that accompanied passportization, such people were to be either deported out of cities or exiled to special settlements. However, police had the dis-cretion to apply this measure selectively. If a person in this category was not engaged in anti-Soviet or otherwise suspicious activities at the time of passportization, and if that person had relatives in the city or was a longtime resident, then police were instructed not to apply deportation or exile measures against him or her. In a March 1935 directive, how-ever, the head of the police Passport Department, Fokin, and the assis-tant police commissar, Markar'ian, issued an order countermanding the previous instructions. Police now were to apply exile orders categori-cally. All former *lishentsy,* as well as socially marginal people, were to be deported from regime cities, regardless of their current circum-stances.[59] Stricter enforcement of passport laws and laws against "so-cially dangerous elements" would, in Yagoda's reckoning, rid the coun-try simultaneously of anti-Soviet and hard-core criminal elements, since they were one and the same. Such social incorrigibles, according to Yagoda, had to be removed from socialist society permanently and not allowed the possibility of reintegration.[60]

Vyshinskii, among others, opposed such categorical policies, and soon after Yagoda's removal in late 1936, the chief procurator tried to revive policies of social reintegration for recidivist criminals. In the early months of 1937, Vyshinskii established a program, in cooperation with the NKVD, to amnesty recidivists and to place them in socially useful work if they would give themselves up to police. In a report to Sov-narkom and to Stalin, Vyshinskii claimed that his commission, working in conjunction with the police, had found work for over six hundred recidivists. As proof of the effectiveness of his program, the chief procu-rator produced letters from several municipal government heads sup-porting his initiative. In addition, he proffered testimonials from self-de-scribed "recidivist-thieves." Each spoke well of his former "profession" and its supposed code of honor, but each expressed gratitude for the chance to "work honestly." One repeated his pleasure at having been issued a legal passport, along with receiving regular pay and a place to live.[61]

N. I. Yezhov, Yagoda's successor, proved somewhat more flexible in his policies toward recidivists. Yezhov supported Vyshinskii's project and cooperated in the amnesty and placement program. Yezhov went so far as to make recommendations to Sovnarkom in April 1937 for establishment of a commission, run by trade union councils, to take over the placement program. In a memorandum to Sovnarkom and to Stalin, however, Yezhov could not help but underscore what he believed to be the social danger posed by repeat offenders. Using arrest and conviction statistics from 1936, Yezhov emphasized that a significant proportion of serious crimes were committed by what he described as the "contingent" of recidivist criminals. According to Yezhov, criminals with prior convictions often made up the core leadership "cadre" of criminal gangs. Each month, he wrote, over 60,000 criminal offenders were released from confinement at the end of their sentences, but the NKVD could place only six to seven thousand of these in jobs immediately after release. The rest, warned Yezhov, "disperse across the country and, without work, begin to commit crimes again, even on the very road out of the camp."[62] Yezhov acknowledged that many former convicts could not find work because of prejudice against them, but many, he argued, simply did not want to work honestly, even if offered jobs. Yezhov quoted one thief, still serving time in a labor camp, who arrogantly proclaimed (apparently to a prisoner informant) "I don't want to work when I get out of here. I like to travel around to different cities and rob. I love the sun, the open air, and the campfire. I will sit here only until summer, then, absolutely, I will take off."[63]

Yezhov warned that, given such attitudes, it was necessary to keep recidivists under strict control, even as he supported Vyshinskii's placement program. Yezhov proposed that Sovnarkom allow camp sentencing boards to extend sentences of recidivists automatically for up to three years should they engage in the slightest tendency toward disobedience or "hooliganism." Vyshinskii opposed this recommendation, as did his deputy, G. Leplevskii (also a Sovnarkom member), and the head of the justice commissariat, N. Krylenko. All three argued that any individual had to be sentenced for a specific crime, not for something so vague as "disobedience," and in any case, such sentencing power should belong to special judicial boards, not to the NKVD troikas. Leplevskii, in addition, noted in a letter to Molotov (as head of Sovnarkom) that NKVD officials continued to insist that all ex-convicts, regardless of crime and number of convictions, be barred from residency in regime cities and industrial areas. Referring to the August 1936 reforms of passport laws, Leplevskii complained that such a demand was unconstitutional, since only those convicted of the most serious crimes were now forbidden from regime zones. Leplevskii's letter revealed the extent to which essentialism pervaded police and other NKVD practices toward former criminals and other social marginals.[64]

DEPORTATION BY CONTINGENTS

Collective deportations by category often distinguished administrative policies of repression from regular political and criminal sentencing. Unlike victims of judicial repression, whose cases were handled individually, victims of collective, or categorical, deportations were generally kept together, or sent to several different places in discrete "contingents" (*kontingenty*). The largest and most widely scattered diaspora, of course, developed in the early 1930s with dekulakization. In the early 1930s, the regime exiled these so-called kulaks to areas mostly in the eastern reaches of the Ural oblast, large sections of Western Siberia, especially its northern regions, areas in the Northern *krai,* and parts of Kazakhstan. Most of these contingents came from the western agricultural parts of the country. Since "kulak" was a class category, the contingents included different ethnic groups, but primarily Ukrainians, Belorussians, and Russians. Kulaks resettled from the Primorsk areas of the Pacific in the early 1930s were sent mainly to the northern Caucasus, while some contingents were settled in the lower Volga basin.[65]

Police tried not to mix different types of contingents. Thus, national minorities deported from border regions in the mid- and late 1930s were not integrated into existing colonies. Police forced these groups to establish new colonies primarily in the sparsely populated areas of Central Asia: most often in Kazakhstan, northern Uzbekistan, and parts of Tadzhikistan. Officials settled contingents of the Finnish-Karelian deportation of 1935 in the Vologda and Western Siberian areas, but police placed these contingents in their own colonies. The Finnish-Karelians were kept separate from existing kulak colonies.

To some extent, keeping categories of displaced populations separate was a consequence of discrete operational initiatives, but there was another intent behind these policies. Officials made it clear that class enemies were not to be mixed with criminals who might be from socially "near" elements. One group might contaminate the other or disrupt policies directed at a particular category. Officials perceived this to be a particularly widespread problem during dekulakization. In their haste to banish class-hostile peasants from their regions, many local authorities took the opportunity to get rid of other unwelcome social types, such as criminals, itinerants, and beggars. These they rounded up and dispatched in the same "echelons" as kulak class enemies. On the receiving end, commandants of colonies often complained that large numbers of people in these criminal categories were mixed in with the kulak contingents under their charge. The criminals created no end of headaches. Recidivists, in particular, brought crime and, as social "disorganizers," adversely affected the general morale of their colonies. Criminals were also the ones most likely to try to escape settlements and colonies. OGPU officials repeatedly warned local officials not to mix criminals in with kulaks, but to sentence hard-core criminals to well-guarded, strict regime labor camps.[66]

Other distinctions held, as well, and created anxieties when violated. The déclassé "former people" who were exiled from Leningrad in 1935, for example, were sent to colonies in Western Siberia and the Northern *krai*. Judging by complaints, however, groups in this contingent were, for some reason, apparently mixed in with other colonies or dispersed into the general population outside of regime areas. More than a few commandants, often from lumbering and agricultural colonies, complained that members of the "Leningrad contingent" did not fit into their colonies, or were not suitable for the work in which these colonies were engaged. The "Leningraders" aroused enough concern that special directives reminded colony administrators not to allow these déclassé intellectuals and "former" people to work as teachers, no matter what their formal qualifications or experience.[67]

STATE SECURITY VS. ECONOMIC MODERNIZATION

Rationalization of social repression through passport and residency laws allowed Soviet leaders to bureaucratize and quantify problems of population control and state security. Authorities believed in the social reality of the categories they created. They also believed that, through manipulation of geographic and social categories, they could secure the safety of the state. In the eyes of Soviet leaders, the passport system fixed populations socially and put them in their place geographically. This was all to the good. Yet in nearly every case of change in passport regulations or procedures, Yagoda's arguments for social control and state security came into conflict with other priorities. Local authorities and economic leaders, in particular, complained that increasingly restrictive stamps placed in passports hindered labor movement and contributed to the growing problem of shortages in critical professions. Passport and residency laws, in other words, strangled rather than controlled labor migration and threatened fulfillment of economic plans even as they enhanced population control. In May 1934, P. Lobochenko, the head of the Ukrainian republic Sovnarkom, pleaded with Molotov to relax current passport and registration laws for *otkhodniki*—rural inhabitants who left farms in order to find work in urban factories. Under existing law, *otkhodniki* could not gain passport and residency permits in urban factory areas unless they were hired through collective agreement contracts with state or collective farms. Lobochenko requested that Sovnarkom permit registration of *otkhodniki* who were hired by factories or other enterprises on an individual basis, outside of the formal collective agreement contracts.[68]

Lobochenko's request was not radical. He agreed that any individual hired in this manner should hold a valid passport or an affidavit (*spravka*) from a collective farm head or a village soviet allowing that individual to seek employment outside the farm. Still, Lobochenko warned that, should police enforce current laws, some of the largest factories in Ukraine would lose a "significant number" of their workers. Factory managers would have to fire many of their individually hired employees, since these would be in violation of hiring and residence laws, and police would deport them out of the cities in which factories were located.[69]

Yagoda attempted to block Lobochenko's request for change in residency laws, and his letter to Sovnarkom reveals his near hysterical fear at the prospect of unorganized population movement. Yagoda's letter also provides a good example of the kind of static and simplified categories in which the police thought. "The OGPU," wrote Yagoda, "categorically opposes the registration of individuals arriving spontaneously and individually (*samotekom, v individual'nom poriadke*), in regime cities to look for work." Equating individual initiative with social danger, Yagoda asserted that "only an insignificant number of real collective farm workers come to cities on their own." According to Yagoda, the "basic mass" of individuals arriving in cities as collective farm workers" came, in fact, from the "class-alien and criminal element." People in this "element" had been forced out of regime cities by passportization, had secured passports in nonregime areas using false *spravki,* and were attempting to "infiltrate" back into cities and large enterprises. Yagoda admitted how easy it was to obtain false *spravki.* He wrote that *spravki* from *kolkhoz* heads or even from village soviets were useless. Such documents were no guarantee of a person's acceptable social status, since "the majority of kulaks, thieves and other such types already have these '*spravki.*'" Consequently, reasoned Yagoda, "spontaneity" in hiring practices could lead only and inevitably to "saturation (*zasorennost'*) of cities and enterprises by the socially alien element." Unable to restrain himself, Yagoda added a further jibe by noting "as is already the case in cities of the Ukrainian SSR." To clinch his argument and, content not just to insult Ukrainian practice, Yagoda added that allowing *kolkhozniki* to seek work outside organized hiring agreements would lead to another obviously undesirable situation: individuals would leave farms and search for other work simply to improve their situation. The danger in this, he concluded, was that it would contribute to high turnover rates and would foster the creation of a "cadre" of "rolling stones" (*letuny*) and "production dis-organizers."[70]

Yagoda's language is revealing of the insidious way that the passport system created a categorical social reality of identity. In Yagoda's mind, anyone not fitting into an organized passport category of the population was, by definition, suspect of being a social harmful. Just as bad was anyone who took individual initiative to better his lot in life by trying to move to a new place of employment. Yet despite Yagoda's forceful opposition, Sovnarkom acceded to Lobochenko's request, and residency laws were relaxed to allow for the kinds of situations described by the Ukrainian leader. A reluctant police head, L. N. Bel'skii, issued the order, but only, he noted, "at [Sovnarkom's] suggestion."[71] Interestingly, the police or Sovnarkom or both had rejected a similar request in April 1934 from the heads of the Donetsk oblast Party and government organizations. Perhaps, as head of a major republic Sovnarkom, Lobochenko's arguments carried more weight, but a year later, in August 1935, Sovnarkom rejected a request by Leningrad government and Party officials to extend the April 1934 decision to cover the hiring of *edinolichniki,* peasant farmers who had not incorporated into the collectives. Writing for the OGPU, G. E. Prokof'ev, Yagoda's assistant, made arguments similar to those made by Yagoda the previous year about the social contamination of unorganized populations, especially *edinolichniki,* an already suspect category. According to Prokof'ev, the large unorganized masses of labor migrants arriving daily in cities were certain to be "saturated with runaway kulaks, criminals, rolling stones and," referring specifically to *edinolichniki,* "individuals trying to avoid payment of taxes after having sold off their households."[72] These groups should not be allowed to contaminate factories and settle in regime cities. The NKVD, wrote Prokof'ev, stood resolutely against the proposal to grant residence permits to *edinolichniki* seeking factory work. Moreover, he noted, the timing of the Lenigraders' request was unfortunate. Granting that request, he wrote, would nullify the effectiveness of ongoing operations in the city to expel the "socially alien and criminal element."[73] The prospect of mass spontaneous labor migration by rural inhabitants evoked fears of social contamination, and all the more so if those migrants were or had been independent farmers.

OTMETKI

The NKVD won its argument with the Leningrad authorities, but Yagoda remained worried about the contamination of socialist spaces. By late 1935, and despite certain successes, Yagoda concluded that passport and residency laws were not working as they should. Current measures had proven insufficient to "solve the problem of cleansing regime localities of the socially alien and criminal element." Undesirables continued to flow into urban areas, often as part of the daily throngs of people arriving on trains to buy and sell goods at public markets. In addition, Yagoda complained, those who should not be allowed to live in regime areas were getting around existing passport and residency laws. Individuals expelled ("distanced") from one regime "point," explained Yagoda, simply received legal passports in nonregime cities, then, finding work in a different regime city, resettled there. Since such passports carried no notations about having been expelled from one regime locality, police officials in another regime locality had no way to know that the individual seeking residence in their city was an undesirable *sotsvredelement.* Yagoda claimed that former exiles and ex-convicts with passports were infiltrating back into regime areas in this manner. As a result, according to Yagoda, what was occurring was not a cleansing of regime areas, but merely the exchange among regime cities of socially alien and criminal populations.[74]

In December 1934, Yagoda had tried and failed to have a special stamp placed in passports of criminals and others forbidden to live in regime areas.[75] In late 1935 and early 1936, he pressed the issue of travel and residency restrictions yet again in Sovnarkom. It is worth dwelling on this series of exchanges, since they reveal the thinking of high state officials and the differences of opinions among them. Thus, in December 1935, still concerned about social contamination by marginal and other anti-Soviet populations, Yagoda recommended that a special stamp or notation (*otmetka,* plural *otmetki*) be placed in the passports of "all those . . . forbidden to live in regime points." The notation was to read simply "For nonregime localities." Such a stamp was necessary, Yagoda argued, to seal the breach in the defenses of socialist cities, which he described in his accompanying letter to Sovnarkom officials.[76]

There are two points that need to be made about Yagoda's proposal. First, Yagoda overstated his case. As Sovnarkom members well knew, numerous restrictions were in place, including passport stamps and special passes, supposedly to prevent the illegal movement of former convicts and exiles. Moreover, police in any city, especially regime cities, were charged to check the background of any citizen applying for residency, and that check was specifically to include contact with police in former places of residence. On the other hand, as officials also knew, police were lax in maintaining passport and residency records and in conducting such background checks. Moreover, individuals who wanted to hide part of their past could do so with relative ease. As Yagoda noted, a citizen could move several times, legally, in nonregime areas, and thereby obscure traces of having lived in and been expelled from a regime city. To Yagoda's constant irritation, local police often did not check the first previous residence situation of in-migrants, let alone the third or fourth. (In this case, geographic "distancing" worked to the advantage of marginal people rather than to their disadvantage.)

Second, Yagoda's proposal was ambiguous, and the ambiguity hinged on how broadly or narrowly to interpret his language. In his letter to Molotov, the police chief recommended placing permanent notations in the passports of all those "forbidden [by current passport laws] to reside in regime localities." Yagoda made the proposal ostensibly in order to keep criminals, kulaks, former exiles, and other marginal and anti-Soviet elements out of regime cites. Archive documents suggest that at least some officials, including Vyshinskii, initially understood the proposals to be directed specifically against those populations. Thus, when Sovnarkom's secretary, Miroshnikov, submitted the proposal to Vyshinskii for the procuracy's response, Vyshinskii replied only that he had no objections "in principle" to the kind of notation Yagoda proposed. Such a notation, after all, would only formalize procedures and regulations already in place.[77]

It soon became apparent, however, that Yagoda had a much more sweeping proposal in mind. At least a few officials became convinced that Yagoda's intention was to place the notation "For nonregime localities" in passports of all citizens—not just undesirables—who were not specifically allowed to live and work in regime areas. The implications of such a proposal were staggering. In a letter to Molotov, Leplevskii, the Sovnarkom member and procuracy official, pointed out that, apart from the clearly unconstitutional nature of the proposal, police and other NKVD organs would be incapable of enforcing such a proposal; they could not even enforce existing passport regulations.[78] But setting aside constitutional issues and problems of enforcement, such a proposal would have made it difficult for all citizens to gain access to the major capital cities of the country. Leplevskii reminded Molotov that the original passport commission approached the issue of restrictive stamps in passports "with great caution." He warned that even a narrow interpretation of Yagoda's proposals presented serious problems of both enforcement and potential abuse.[79] Moreover, Leplevskii reminded Molotov that Sovnarkom's original passport instructions already included a detailed list of crimes for which a person would forfeit the right to live in a regime city. Leplevskii urged Molotov and Sovnarkom to reject Yagoda's recommendations. What was needed was not more regulations, but stricter enforcement of current regulations.[80]

When Vyshinskii finally understood the import of Yagoda's proposal, he too joined in a protracted fight to quash it. Vyshinskii not only objected to the specific proposal, he went further to urge a reduction in the number of crimes entailing exclusion from a regime area. Vyshinskii also argued that a statute of limitations be placed on residence bans— from three to five years, depending on the severity and type of crime committed. It was unfair, he argued, to deny an individual full civil rights who had paid his debt and had rehabilitated himself. Sovnarkom's legal advisor endorsed Vyshinskii's proposals and recommended that Yagoda and Vyshinskii draw up a joint resolution based on them.[81] Molotov apparently also leaned toward Vyshinskii's recommendations, since he criticized Yagoda's draft at a Sovnarkom steering commission meeting. Yagoda, however, found Vyshinskii's draft reforms "unacceptable," and after two months of negotiation, the two still could find no common ground.

In late April 1936, Yagoda summarized his objections to the procuracy's reforms. He was typically adamant and categorical in his comments. According to Yagoda, placing a statute of limitations on residency restrictions would lead to the "immediate return to regime localities of all those who we expelled [literally, distanced—*udalili*] in 1933: that is, it will bring to nothing the results of [our] purge of regime areas." Yagoda argued, somewhat lamely, that there was little danger of a lifelong residency ban under current laws. Through the various amnesties that the state offered, ex-convicts had the right to petition for removal of criminal convictions from their records. If approved, this process would also and automatically remove any residency limitations. Yagoda noted that he had no objections to Vyshinskii's shortened list of crimes entailing a residency ban, but then he suggested an additional fourteen criminal statutes, with various subsections, violation of which he felt should be reinstated in the "shortened" list. Yagoda objected to the provision allowing full freedom of movement and residence to released exiles and former convicts not covered under the new list of grievous crimes. He objected to provisions giving procuracy officials closer supervision over police passport enforcement, and he objected in principle to Vyshinskii's insistence on a narrow application of the *otmetki* issue. Placing a notation in passports of only those convicted under specific criminal statutes would allow "refugees and all sorts of other types" to settle freely in regime areas: that is, people who, under current law, were forbidden to do so. As if his point was not already clear, Yagoda emphasized it by reiterating that "such a provision will give the right to refugees to live in regime cities." Yagoda could not even bring himself to articulate the reasons why such a scenario was undesirable. He declared, simply, that "The incorrectness of such a recommendation needs no proof."[82]

After three more months and much wrangling, the NKVD and the procuracy finally agreed to a compromise set of reforms. The 8 August 1936 revised passport instructions represented a partial victory for each side. Sovnarkom adopted Vyshinskii's shortened list of crimes that carried a residency ban in regime areas, but this list included Yagoda's fourteen additions. Sovnarkom also endorsed Vyshinskii's demand that ex-convicts and freed exiles, not convicted under the specific list of crimes, be granted full rights to live where they chose. (This provision did not apply to former kulaks.) Sovnarkom refused to take a stand on Vyshinskii's recommendation that a statute of limitation be placed on any residency ban. Instead, members tabled that issue for consideration within the context of an ongoing review of Soviet criminal codes. That review, begun as early as 1934, was still far from completion in 1936, so this postponement represented at least a partial victory for Yagoda. Sovnarkom endorsed Yagoda's recommendation for a notation placed in passports of those forbidden to live in regime areas, but the NKVD lost its fight over the major issue of how broadly to apply that notation. Sentiment within Sovnarkom favored the procuracy's recommendation that a more specific notation be placed in passports of only those citizens convicted of any of the specific list of crimes included in the instructions. Sovnarkom endorsed Vyshinskii's narrow wording of the notation to read: "Issued on the basis of point 11 of SNK resolution of 28 April, 1933." The reference was to point 11 in the original passport instruction listing the crimes for which conviction carried residence restrictions. This wording replaced Yagoda's vaguer and more ambiguous wording: "For nonregime localities." In deference to Yagoda, Sovnarkom included a specific reference to refugees, who were also to be banned from living in regime cities.[83]

Police continued to improve the effectiveness of the passport system, adding fingerprinting and photographing by the end of the decade. They continued also to work on the problem of keeping track of individuals as they moved from residence to residence. Failure to register a point of destination when permanently leaving a residence and failing to register a previous residence upon arrival in a town or passport region were the single biggest problems of the passport system in the 1930s. So was the related problem of automatically coordinating information about changes in residence. If citizens registered their passports when settling in a new residence, they often did not bother to register their departure or their destination when leaving a former residence. A little over 5 percent of the population failed to register a new residence upon arrival, but nearly 13 percent failed to register a point of destination upon leaving a residence.[84] This situation is what made it relatively easy for people to lose or obscure their past. According to Yagoda, lack of citizen compliance with registration laws was a significant hindrance to police ability to hunt for criminals and escapees.[85] Police did not resolve this problem until after World II, in part as a result of a special police commission sent to occupied Berlin in summer 1945. The commission spent several weeks studying the German residence registration system that had been in use during the 1920s and 1930s. In his report, L. Chizhikov, the head of the commission, recommended that the Soviets follow the German system, in which all citizens were required to fill out departure forms in triplicate when moving from a residence. In the Soviet context, these forms would then be filed, respectively, in central oblast- or re-public-level passport bureaus, and in the central passport administration in Moscow. The report devoted a great deal of space—replete with photographs of card catalog boxes, identity stamps, even fasteners used to attach documents to papers—to a detailed description of filing and storing techniques used by the German police. Chizhikov also noted that the German system worked so well because police were required to verify their registration catalogs every six months, and "to bring to responsibility" any citizen in violation of regulations.[86]

THE SECOND SERFDOM ARGUMENT

Historians often refer to the absence of passportization in rural areas as the most common example of the discriminatory character of the Soviet passport system. The vast majority of peasants were not issued passports and, so the argument goes, they were therefore tied to the land, denied the right to travel freely, in a kind of second serfdom.[87] The Bolsheviks may well have been antipeasant, but the second serfdom argument represents a misreading of how the passport and residence registration system worked. In fact, the passport system reflected an increasingly complicated hierarchy of privileges and restrictions, of exclusions, partial exclusions, and graduated constraints on movement that affected the entire Soviet population. In Stalin's corporate kind of state socialism, rural inhabitants were at or near the bottom of this hierarchy of privileges and access, but peasants were not the only category of the population to be tied down to their residence and workplace. All those in state militarized occupations found themselves under similar restrictions. Such restrictions applied, of course, to all soldiers and NKVD internal forces, but they also applied to all police, including firefighters, certain medical professionals, defense industry workers, and all employees on key rail lines. Commanders or employers confiscated employee passports, and issued workers *spravki*. These employees needed special permission to travel or leave their place of employment. A number of enterprise heads in nonmilitarized sectors also engaged in the practice, albeit illegal, of confiscating passports, in order to try to hold labor turnover to a minimum.[88]

Most rural inhabitants were not issued passports during the 1930s, but it is an important point to note that they had the right to possess passports if they had legitimate reason to travel to, and work and reside in, areas that were passportized. This is an important distinction to make in order to understand how officials thought about the lack of rural passportization. In fact, many millions of peasants received passports who worked on Soviet state farms or on collective and state farms within certain distances of urban, strategic, or border areas. More important, the lack of passportization in most rural areas no more tied peasants to the land than the possession of passports allowed other citizens to move freely. Peasants living on collective farms, of course, needed written permission—the infamous *spravki*—to leave for work in other places. *Kolkhozniki* were not free simply to move to a city to live and to look for work. They did so only under certain regulations—secure employment or relatives already registered in the place of destination. This was a severe restriction on individual freedom, but it was a restriction imposed by employment and hiring laws, not by the absence of passportization. Even peasants holding passports needed permission to leave their farms. Like any citizen from nonpassportized areas, a *kolkhoznik* who was transferred to industrial employment through collective labor contracts received a temporary passport for one year, which was then renewed for three years. This passport rolled over to a "permanent" five- and then ten-year passport if the *kolkhoz-nik*-turned-factory-worker remained industrially employed.

Legally, most industrial workers were allowed the freedom to leave an enterprise and to seek employment in other towns or parts of the country, and this was a labor right that distinguished them from rural farm workers.[89] Yet residence laws placed constraints on the employment mobility of all citizens, regardless of hiring laws. Citizens holding passports, as well as non–passport holders, needed secure employment or support of relatives to remain for more than a short period of time in regime areas away from their registered domicile. As the list of regime areas and cities expanded during the 1930s, this restriction discriminated against large segments of the population, industrial as well as rural workers, denying them access to the best resources and most desirable places to live and work. It was not so much the lack of passports that tied rural inhabitants to their place of residence, but labor and residence laws, which affected all citizens, whether urban or rural.

In the late 1930s, the regime broadened the range of restrictions on free labor movement. By that time, it was clear that passport laws were working relatively well to prevent social contamination, but employment and residence laws were not working as they should to control industrial labor movement. High rates of turnover continued in factories, as workers, like "disruptive" peasants, attempted to improve their living conditions by moving. As the country began preparing for war, Stalinist officials enacted draconian labor laws in 1940, with further restrictions throughout the 1940s and early 1950s. These laws acted as the urban equivalent of the harsh laws put in place several years earlier to restrict rural work migration. Between 1940 and 1956, several million workers were convicted of violating work residence laws that tied them to their factories and enterprises, unless they received special permission to leave for other employment. If peasants suffered under a second serfdom, so, eventually, did all workers in the Stalinist state.[90]

The reasons for not passportizing rural areas in the 1930s were complex, but very likely had to do with logistical problems and with the original purpose of passportization. According to the initial decree, this was to "count and cleanse" the population, and both of those goals had supposedly been accomplished in rural areas even before passportization.[91] Dekulakization and collectivization had supposedly purged the countryside of socially hostile elements. Rural passportization was therefore not needed for purposes of social cleansing. According to an early draft of passport procedures, rural passportization was also not necessary for the purpose of counting. A census of the rural population already existed, according to the author of the draft, in the form of village soviet resident lists, which were supposedly kept under strict control of local police.[92] Thus, if passportization was not needed as a means to purge rural areas, neither was it needed, at least in the view of leaders, in order to keep peasants tied to their places of work. The priority, then, for passportization was to "fix" the urban population—to purge and register urban residents and to protect the cities. Originally, passportization functioned as the urban equivalent of dekulakization, and the original passport instructions made this goal clear, although officials quickly adapted passport repression to much broader policing purposes.[93] By early 1936, in fact, Yagoda lamented that the regime could not police the countryside using passport laws in the same ways it had "cleansed" the cities.[94] This statement testified simultaneously to the effectiveness of passport and resident laws as policing mechanisms and to the continuing problems, despite collectivization, of controlling the countryside.

Overhaul of the passport system in both 1940 and again in 1952 called for passportization of the entire Soviet population. The 1952 passportization proposals from police foresaw complete coverage by 1956.[95] The Politburo under Khrushchev tabled these proposals for later consideration, and they were then rejected outright by the Brezhnev regime in the late 1960s. The reasons why the regime rejected rural passportization after World War II remain unclear, but the argument is more plausible for this period than for the 1930s that leaders were motivated specifically by worries about rural labor drain. As residence restrictions on other groups were lifted gradually during the 1950s, passportization came, in fact, to function mainly as a discriminatory practice against rural inhabitants. Rural inhabitants received passports as a matter of course only in the 1970s.

SOVIET PASSPORTS IN COMPARATIVE PERSPECTIVE: LEVELING AND TRANSPARENCY

The system of internal passport identification was not peculiar to the Stalinist period or to the Soviet Union. The tsarist regime introduced a system of internal passports, which the Bolsheviks abolished as one of their first revolutionary acts against the oppressive system of tsarist rule. In fact, Bolshevik actions paralleled those of the French revolutionaries a century earlier—ironically so, since the Bolsheviks, like the French revolutionaries, reintroduced a system of identification as a necessary measure against social disorder and counterrevolutionary threat.[96] By the late nineteenth century, identity systems were well developed in all European states. As governments further centralized and bureaucratized their civic policies, they imposed increasingly standardized forms of identity on their citizens. Whether to achieve greater civic inclusion—as Max Weber and more recently Charles Tilly have argued—or to achieve greater social control, as Foucault argued, states began to apply categories of identity that tended to blur social and regional distinctions and to create a uniform state administrative system and a homogenous citizenry.[97]

In their work on identity, Jane Caplan and John Torpey invoke Tocqueville, Tilly, and Weber to assert that the emergence of a central authority governing an increasingly homogenous population is a hallmark of the modern state.[98] This tendency, according to Charles Steinwedel, characterized tsarist Russia as well as other European states. Writing about parish registers and internal passports, Steinwedel notes that, in order to achieve greater civic inclusion, tsarist ministers, particularly Petr Stolypin and Sergei Witte before him, began to blur the legal distinctions among religious confessions and estate status groups. This in turn led to the kind of "leveling of the governed" characteristic of other states. In Russia, this process made estate status (*soslovie*) and religious confession, the two primary identity markers, less useful as a means of structuring the empire's civic order. After 1905, when identity documentation became most widespread, categories of estate and religion decreased in usage. The state's more frequent identification of subjects by nationality and ethnicity was one sign of this change.[99]

In some ways, the Soviet passport system, as it evolved, reflected similar trends, but it also differed significantly from these trends. In most European states, identity regimes tended to impose civic (if not social) homogeneity on populations, the "leveling" of which Caplan and Torpey write. Categories of inclusion and exclusion corresponded to the physical borders of the nation and the property boundaries of places of incarceration. In other words, as states homogenized civic forms of identity so too they homogenized civic space. In contrast, and as the foregoing discussion shows, the Stalinist civic order did not reflect the "Newtonian" universe of civic administration supposedly characteristic of late nineteenth-century Europe. Social groups in the Soviet Union did not interact with the state and each other according to universally administered laws. Bodies in the Stalinist cosmos interacted in ways analogous to medieval notions of Aristotelian space, in which objects in different spaces, or spheres (earthly or celestial) obeyed different laws of motion.[100] In the Soviet Union, different categories of the population occupied different geographic spaces and interacted with the state and each other according to laws peculiar to each group and the space that that group inhabited. This system evolved in increasingly complex ways as police continued to differentiate the regulations governing mobility and civic rights. As a result, the accretion of regulations became difficult to enforce, let alone to understand. By the end of the decade, few officials in the Soviet Union understood all the different kinds of passport restrictions and regulations— to whom they applied and under what conditions. The system readily lent itself to abuse both by citizens hoping to avoid restrictions, and by officials easily bribed to issue illegal passports and residence permits, or unwitting enough to enforce regulations unfairly.[101]

The development of hierarchically differentiated identity regimes in the Soviet Union seems to run counter to the processes of administrative uniformity and civic leveling supposedly characteristic of other European states. Yet discussions of identity policies in European states usually focus only on the metropolitan areas of those states and do not include identity regimes set up in colonial areas. If we consider the latter, then the Soviet passport system does not look so exceptional. During the 1930s, Soviet colonization policies and policies of discrimination tended to cut along social lines of demarcation rather than along lines of ethnic difference. Still the different identity regimes that characterized the Soviet state corresponded, in large part, to a colonial model of geography, replete with the colonial language of settlers, penal colonies, core lands, and distant territories. Despite the change in semantics from "colonization" to "mastery," Soviet deportation policies, and the hierarchy of identity regimes associated with those policies, reflected, in the extreme, the administrative construction of geography and identity used by other European powers.

CONCLUSIONS

Soviet leaders originally designed the passport system to protect cities and control mass migration during the chaotic years of the early

1930s.[102] The passport and residency system evolved throughout the 1930s to encompass much broader and significantly different functions. In the early 1930s, when the state first issued internal passports, citizens were required to state their national identity as well as their social class status, yet class still counted as the primary defining criterion of inclusion and exclusion. The mass repressions associated with collectivization and dekulakization were based on class and, initially, residence and rationing privileges associated with the new passport system were also based on social criteria of class and occupation. Within a short period of time, however, police officials abandoned class and occupation as useful categories for monitoring the population, keeping cities safe from undesirable populations, and organizing social policies of privilege and exclusion. By the mid-1930s, Yagoda was pressing to have permanent notations placed in passports based, not on vague distinctions of social status or background, but on specific criteria of criminality and social marginality. Yagoda did not get his way entirely, but by the mid-1930s, residence privileges and restrictions were based increasingly on such specific notations, regardless of class or occupational status. Over the course of the 1930s, alienness or nearness became increasingly associated with social deviance and marginality. Criminality and marginality became, in effect, the new class boundaries.

Police utilized passport and residency laws to fight crime and maintain social order. At the same time, passport and residency laws also provided the regime with a powerful tool to enforce redistribution of the country's population through operations of mass repression and deportation. In this way, passport laws became part of the Soviet state's apparatus, increasingly dominated by police organs, to colonize and integrate peripheral areas of the former empire. Forms of repression based on passport and residence laws also provided a mechanism for authorities to clear suspect ethnic populations from border and other strategically sensitive regions of the country. Thus, various criteria—class purity, public order, internal colonization, and territorial security—merged in the state's forced migration and internal passport policies during the 1930s.

Determined people could, with relative ease, bypass passport and residency laws if they chose or needed to do so. Many people created and re-created their identities—through illegal migration, falsifying passport information, multiple moves, rehabilitative work, or other means.

They did so for any number of reasons: to hide, engage in criminal activities, claim certain rights, become good Soviet citizens, or most often to obscure stigmatizing backgrounds. Individual identities changed and evolved constantly, but always within the framework of identities created by the regime and implemented through the passport and residency registration system. That system reinforced a categorical imperative in Soviet policing and social policies and an already strong tendency to fix atavistic characteristics upon segments of the population. Police and other Soviet officials rejected the biological basis of determining social deviance, which had so fascinated other European and American observers. Yet Soviet officials believed in a social and ethnic atavism that produced recidivist criminals, incorrigibly harmful social elements, and enemy nations even within Soviet borders. Passport and residency laws provided police, or so they believed, with the means to identify, separate, and, if necessary, exterminate those groups.

9 "Once and for All Time"

Background to the Great Purges

Consider that, in the Narym and Kuzbass areas, there are 208,400 exiled
kulaks; another 5,350 live under administrative exile and include White
officers, active bandits, and convicts, and former [tsarist] police officials.
This is the broad base . . . on which to build an insurgent rebellion.
—Sergei Mironov, Chief of the Western Siberian NKVD, June 1937

IN 1936, YAGODA BELIEVED that the problem of social order had
been solved. His report to Sovnarkom in the early months of that year
declared as much. Within a year, however, he had been ousted as head
of the NKVD and replaced by Nikolai Yezhov, and leaders were wor-
rying about the supposedly large numbers of socially dangerous populations loose in the country. They were so worried that, in the summer
of 1937, they ordered the political and civil police to launch mass
roundups and executions of supposedly anti-Soviet elements. These
mass operations (*massovye operatsii*), as they were called, were part of
what became known as the Great Terror, which lasted from late July of
1937 through November of 1938. During that period close to 800,000
people were arrested, and some 367,000 were shot under NKVD Operational Order 00447. Hundreds of thousands were deported or in-
terned in camps and penal settlements. In the order that launched the
mass operations, Yezhov declared it his intention to eradicate dangerous populations "once and for all time."[1]

A great deal of mystery surrounds the events that are described as the
Great Terror. This and the next chapter sort through what is known
and not known, and add detail from archives in order to fill out a picture of what happened in 1937 and 1938. The primary focus here, as
in other chapters, is on the mass social repressions, rather than on the

purges as a whole. The mass social repressions were often referred to as the mass operations, and I will follow this nomenclature. These mass operations were related to but distinct from other operational aspects of purges during these years, and these chapters will discuss the differences and similarities as well as analyze the purges as a whole from the perspective of the mass operations.

Two distinctions should be made at the outset. The first is semantic: it is a misnomer to call the mass purges that swept the Soviet Union in the late 1930s the Great Terror. Certainly, the purges were a terror for those many who suffered, and to insist on proper nomenclature is not an attempt to relativize or apologize for the heinousness of that tragedy. Nor is it merely a splitting of definitional hairs to insist on calling the events of 1937 and 1938 purges rather than terror. The distinction is important for historical reasons of understanding motives and origins: how leaders and ordinary people understood what was happening and what they were doing or experiencing. Leaders and police officials understood the mass operations as a cleansing, a literal purge of the body politic. They did not regard what they were doing as terror, which was the term Lenin and the Bolsheviks used, unapologetically, during the revolutionary wars of 1918–24. Thus, "mass purge" or "mass purges" is an accurate historical description of what occurred in the late 1930s. That term distinguishes these events from processes of mass repression that came before and after, as well as linking them with each other. "Once and for all time" was the phrase Yezhov used to characterize the goal of that cleansing, not in the sense of an extermination policy, but in terms of engineering Soviet society and making it safe for socialism.

A second distinction also needs to be made — not a semantic one, but an operational one between the selective purges of state and Party organs and institutions and the mass operations against whole social categories of the population. The former, as many histories and memoirs have shown, struck hardest at elites within the Soviet and Party bureaucracies. The purge campaign relied heavily on a ritualized process of denunciation, arrest, and interrogation. The Party purge, especially, involved a laborious process of document review and appeal. Individual arrests could generate thick case files, and interrogations could last for weeks and months. In contrast, the operations mounted under authority of Order 00447 encompassed a much broader spectrum of criminal and socially marginal groups. Denunciations played a part in some aspects of the mass operations, but many who fell victim to this process were targeted not because of any specific criminal or political act which they supposedly had committed, but because they belonged to a suspect social category. Or they were simply arrested at random. In other words, the purge process focused on individuals, the mass operations on population categories. Often, those arrested under authority of Order 00447 never saw an interrogator, and were rarely held in isolation in individual cells. More often than not, victims of the mass operations were arrested, processed, and executed or imprisoned in mass numbers. There were no thick case files, only a few sentences on an arrest order, if that. Though related, the purges of Party and state institutions were distinct from the mass operations. They derived from different policing policies, different political concerns, and different operational trajectories within the NKVD.

ON THE EVE

As previous chapters have shown, changes in policing practice from the early to the mid-1930s reflected a shift in Stalinist policies. By ending mass repression in rural areas, police authorities remonopolized control over violence in society, even as the regime moved away from a revolutionary program of social restructuring to one of protecting state interests and establishing public order. Campaigns of mass repression continued after the end of dekulakization, but under more professionalized police control, and not through mass mobilization of revolutionary violence. Authorities channeled mass repression through operational directives associated primarily with newly enacted passport and residency laws, and laws against socially "dangerous" populations. As such, mass or categorical forms of repression became more a mechanism to police deviance and marginality than a weapon to remake class relations. Authorities continued to apply measures of social discrimination and repression against traditional enemies of the regime — former landowners, tsarist officials, clerics, those identified as kulaks — but repressions associated with measures of social defense during the mid-1930s targeted petty criminals, former convicts, social marginals, and deviants as a new kind of enemy. These groups posed a threat to the state since, in mass numbers, they siphoned off state resources and were nonproductive members of Stalin's new society. By the mid-1930s, class war had turned into repression of traditional categories of social deviants and marginal populations.

Policing marginality and deviance became the new class war, as laid out by Stalin in January 1933, and both the civil and political police joined this "war" with vigor and with all the resources of a powerful state. By early 1936, Yagoda could report notable success in the fight to secure public order, protect state property, and contain dangerous populations. Significant problems still plagued the state's policing efforts. The NKVD was still a long way away from the organization that Yagoda envisioned. Numbers were still woefully inadequate, as were qualifications of both civil and political police officials. Prophylactic policing was still only an ideal. Police surveillance and agent systems remained underdeveloped. Effective policing was carried out often through campaign-style forms of repression associated with passport and residence laws and campaign-style operations of social defense. The passport system could be counted as a significant advance toward the goal of universal social surveillance, but police enforced passport and residence laws more often in the breach than in practice. Illegal migration, trade, and speculation continued to siphon off state resources and to threaten state economic plans. Youth crime remained a large problem, despite the draconian measures that police had inaugurated, and petty crimes, especially theft of both private and state property, seemed resistant to increasingly harsh punitive measures. Still, policing measures set in motion in 1932 and 1933 were, by 1936, beginning to have an effect, at least in Yagoda's perception. Social marginals were being pushed out of major urban areas. Crime rates were dropping, especially in key cities, due largely to police sweeps and social defense laws. NKVD operations had cleared border areas of suspect and potentially disloyal populations. Most important, through the multilayered system of police registration, the regime now had a system, albeit unwieldy, to identify and isolate dangerous individuals and populations. Despite weak enforcement of passport and residency laws, many of those regarded as socially harmful were, by mid-decade, contained in camps, colonies, or special settlements. A certain normalcy was returning to Soviet society, and Yagoda, at least, was disposed to believe that this was due in no small measure to his social policing policies.[2]

Yagoda's new policing system worked changes in both the civil and the political police. Professionalization, reorganization, and integration of the *militsiia* into the OGPU changed that organization most of all. By 1935 and 1936, Yagoda had none of the doubts about civil police that he had had in 1931 and 1932. Yagoda complained, still, about distractions, about police corruption, and about lack of professional qualification, but by the mid-1930s, the *militsiia* was no longer the hodge-podge local constable system that it had been in the 1920s. By the end of the social defense campaigns, the civil police was fully militarized and fully subordinated to the political police. Civil police answered to the higher authorities of the state, and ultimately to the political police, rather than to the representatives of local soviets. The *militsiia* was fully integrated, at least on paper, into the state's system of social surveillance. Centralization brought professionalization, and Yagoda attempted to professionalize the civil police into an effective if still evolving part of his Soviet gendarmerie.

Stalin's new class war changed the political police as well as the *militsiia,* and was reflected in the transformation of the OGPU into the NKVD SSSR. That transformation culminated a successful strategy of expansion and adaptation by the OGPU's leaders, in particular Yagoda, to the change in political culture and state priorities after 1932. This adaptation mirrored the transformation of the Cheka in the 1920s, but also differed significantly from that previous reincarnation. During the 1920s, the security apparatus had suffered a significant decrease in numbers and budget, even as its leaders refashioned it from an extraordinary organ of revolutionary terror into a constitutive organ of the new state in defense of public order. The OGPU gradually expanded its authority after the threat of dissolution in 1922 and the crisis of 1924, but it did so within a relatively weak central state system, and in constant conflict with rival agencies, especially with the republic NKVD system and with the republic justice commissariats. Expanded, again, as an organ of revolutionary mass repression during collectivization, the OGPU emerged in 1932 facing something of the same crisis that it faced in 1922.

Yagoda steered the OGPU through the transition of the early 1930s. As in 1922, so in 1932, the OGPU transformed itself from a weapon of revolutionary class war into an organ of public order, this time not in conflict with the civil police, but by incorporating civil police and carceral institutions into a new policing empire. The new NKVD was not merely a chief administration under Sovnarkom, as had been the old OGPU. Yagoda and other leaders of the OGPU ruled over an all-union commissariat with all the resources of the federal state at their command. Rapid expansion of power and jurisdictional authority made the NKVD into one of the most important commissariats under Stalin, but enhanced status and power were not the only consequence of changes in the political police. The methods of mass repression used by the OGPU during collectivization and dekulakization produced a lasting effect on the institutional culture of the OGPU. Despite Stalin's call for new tactics, ingrained habits of mass repression and administrative justice were hard to change, the more so since they proved relatively effective in the new kind of social war of the 1930s. In the context of a weak civil state and an underdeveloped policing system, campaign-style operations and mass, categorical kinds of repression continued as primary methods to secure social order and to protect state interests.

Stalin, of course, was key to the transformation of the police. Without him, the political police could easily have found itself in the same position as it did in 1924. It was Stalin who created the powerful centralized state of the 1930s. It was Stalin's redefinition of class war that gave the OGPU a new lease on its institutional life, as it was the Great Leader's penchant to solve state personnel problems by "sending some Chekists." Yet the transformation of the OGPU was not all Stalin's doing. Certainly, Stalin gave direction to the state's policies of repression and the role of the political police, but Yagoda proved a deft bureaucratic in-fighter, and it was he who positioned the political police to take on new roles. Stalin gave direction and sanction, but it was Yagoda who engineered the successful transformation of the civil police and OGPU. Yagoda simultaneously militarized the former, and he "domesticated" the latter by turning the OGPU into an organ of social as well as political policing. It was Yagoda who incorporated the state's system of custodial institutions under the political police and built that system into a massive empire of punitive labor and economic colonization. It was Yagoda who pushed the police into numerous areas of social policy. More than any other single individual, it was Yagoda who was the architect of Stalin's political and social policing system.

By the mid-1930s, then, the NKVD was more than just a weapon to protect the state against its political enemies. Through mass forms of repression, first in rural and then in urban areas, and through its vast system of camps, colonies, and settlements, the NKVD had become deeply involved in the social, economic, and territorial construction of the Soviet state. The large masses of people that the police raked in each year comprised a system of cheap, even slave, prison labor. Through the administration of its custodial populations, especially its exile and special settlements, police encroached on and essentially took over the state's colonization and settlement program of new lands. The system of colonies, special settlements, and exile regimes constituted a complex hierarchy of categories of what police and regime officials regarded as more or less dangerous populations and more or less socialist territories. Where these populations were put, and the gradations of privileges and restrictions placed on them, constituted a nomenclature or ordering of both the population and the territory of the country. This ordering of society and territory affected more than the socially dangerous and marginal. Through administration of the passport and residency system, police ordered the whole population of the country into a hierarchy of privilege and restriction. Administration of the passport system turned the NKVD from an organization to fight political enemies and criminals into an organization of mass social engineering.

TURNABOUT

Yagoda created the Stalinist policing system. He organized that policing system to accomplish the tasks that Stalin set forth for defense of the state. In the early and mid-1930s, following the dekulakization and collectivization campaigns, Yagoda accepted Stalin's assessment that criminality and social disorder posed the greatest danger to the state. Dealing with these dangers was not only a social priority, but a political one, the equivalent of political struggle against counterrevolution. Stalin and other leaders supported this policy line at first, but after the murder of Sergei Kirov, the Leningrad Party chief in December 1934, Stalin's priorities began to shift, and he began to lose confidence in his police chief. By autumn 1936, Stalin was ready to oust Yagoda for continuing this line in the operational policies of the NKVD.

In Sepember 1936, Stalin engineered Yagoda's removal as head of the NKVD. In a telegram from his vacation home in Sochi, Stalin, along with A. A. Zhdanov, another secretary of the Party's Central Committee, recommended to the Politburo that it remove Yagoda and appoint Nikolai Yezhov to the position of commissar of the NKVD. Yagoda, the telegram went on, had failed to destroy the Trostkyist-Zinovievist bloc inside the Soviet Union. This reference was, of course, to two of Stalin's old rivals for political power in the Party — Leon Trotsky and G. Ia. Zinoviev. The threat of these two former Party leaders had long ago been neutralized by Stalin, but he feared, or rather fantasized, that they had joined forces and stood behind an organized network of agents, saboteurs, and foreign governments, using every means, including murder of high officials, to unseat himself and the Communist Party from power. In Stalin's view, Kirov's murder was part of this plot. Much speculation has surrounded Kirov's death, and many have believed that Stalin, in fact, engineered it in order to start a purge to secure his power and position. Several historians have cast doubt on this version. They have argued that, very likely, Kirov was murdered for the reasons to which the murderer confessed — jealousy over an affair between Kirov and the murderer's wife. Still, the murder of the Leningrad Party secretary, one of the highest-ranking Party members and a close confidant of Stalin, shocked the leader. In his paranoia, Stalin easily believed that the killing was the work of his personal political enemies.[3]

After Kirov's murder, Stalin's concern about the threat of organized political subversion mounted, and he set in motion a series of reviews and purges. His first priority was a purge of the Leningrad security organs, and then a wider purge of the Party, as well as a review and purge of the NKVD. It was to this process of hunting down political oppositionists that Stalin referred when he described Yagoda as inadequate to the tasks of the political security of the state. It was in the context of assessing the Kirov murder that Yezhov, as Party secretary, had written Stalin in early 1935 about the woeful state of the NKVD's intelligence and agent system in fighting active counterrevolutionary elements in the country.[4] Indeed, Stalin's mistrust of Yagoda now went so deep that he bypassed his police chief to involve Yezhov directly, as a Party secretary, to conduct a secret review of the NKVD. By late summer of 1936, Yezhov had gathered enough information to write a damning report about Yagoda, accusing him of having been deeply involved with Stalin's political enemies in the so-called Right Opposition. This report sealed Yagoda's fate, as well as Yezhov's promotion. Stalin, however, did not imediately broadcast his suspicions about Yagoda. Accusations of outright counterrevolution would come out only later, when Yagoda was finally arrested in March 1937. In the September 1936 telegram to the Politburo from Sochi, Stalin and Zhdanov confined themselves to the more neutral but still ominous assessment that Yagoda was "far from capable" of carrying out the primary task of protecting the Party and state from the organized political conspiracy that had gathered around leaders of the "Right" Opposition. Yagoda, Stalin insisted, was to be removed and replaced with Yezhov.[5]

Once in his new post, Yezhov began a high-level purge of those who had been close to Yagoda. These purges touched a number of ranking oblast and *krai* NKVD leaders, and key figures in the central NKVD administration. In November, Yezhov removed M. I. Gai as head of the *Osobyi Otdel* — the department in charge of political security in the military — and replaced him with I. M. Leplevskii, who had been NKVD chief in Belorussia. Gai was reappointed to head the Eastern Siberian NKVD until his arrest in April 1937. At the same time, and most important, Yezhov removed G. A. Molchanov, a longtime associate of Yagoda, from his post as head of the Secret Political Department. This was a key position, since that department handled agent and informant networks. V. M. Kurskii, formerly head of the Western Siberian NKVD, replaced Molchanov, who was demoted to head the Belorussian NKVD post made vacant by Leplevskii's promotion. Molchanov remained in his new position for several months only, and was arrested in February 1937, just prior to Yagoda's arrest. The purge continued and, in April 1937, Yezhov appointed M. P. Frinovskii, former head of the NKVD border and internal forces, as overall head of the GUGB, and as assistant commissar of the NKVD. Frinovskii replaced Ia. S. Agranov, who thereafter served briefly as head of the Secret Political Department and, as a measure of demotion, as head of the Saratov oblast NKVD. Agranov was arrested in July 1937.

By early 1937, Stalin was ready to launch an open assault on Yagoda, not only for his sins of omission, but for his sins of commission. Yezhov's criticisms at the February–March Party plenum in 1937 reiterated the failures of the previous NKVD chief to protect the state against its political enemies, but Yezhov went further. For the first time, Yezhov linked this failure to Yagoda's emphasis on social policing policies throughout the previous years. Yezhov harshly criticized Yagoda for focusing the energies of the political police too much on issues of social order, and for failing to reorient the methods of police work in general from mass forms of social policing to counterintelligence and agent-operational work. What had been official policy was now described as a dangerous distraction from the real threat of underground political organizations and foreign intelligence services.[6]

Yezhov's criticisms at the plenum signaled a turnabout in political policing priorities. Yezhov's reforms of the GUGB and NKVD, which he had already begun, reflected his attempt to untangle and separate the social order functions of the police from the functions of state security, which were supposed to belong to the GUGB. Administratively and operationally, Yezhov sought to reorient the GUGB toward the fight against political opposition, understood not as social disorder but as direct, organized political subversion and spying. Thus, Yezhov jettisoned the economic crimes section of the GUGB, which had drained so much operational time and energy. He placed responsibility for the fight against organized crime in the hands of a newly organized and strengthened police department, the OBKhSS (*Otdel bor'by s khishcheniem sotsialisticheskoi sobstvennosti*). In a major reorganization, and as a direct result of the February–March plenum, Yezhov also created a new railroad police department within the structure of the GURKM. He clearly distinguished its functions from those of the newly reformed Transport Department of the GUGB. In a draft directive for the Central Committee, Yezhov outlined the functions of the new railroad police department of the GUGB. "The Transport Department of the GUGB," wrote Yezhov, "will be freed from functions of securing social order on railroad lines, maintaining public order in train stations, fighting against theft of socialist property, hooliganism, and child homelessness. These functions are to be transferred to the newly formed railroad police, which will be subordinated to the GURKM NKVD." According to Yezhov, officers of the Transport Department of the GUGB were to engage themselves exclusively in the fight against counterrevolutionary sabotage of the country's vital rail systems. What this meant in practice is not entirely clear, but whatever Yezhov intended, it is clear that he wanted to get the GUGB — the organ of state security — out of the business of guarding mail cars, rounding up hooligans from train yards, chasing itinerant kids, robbers, and hobos riding on trains, patrolling train stations, and checking for ticket violations.[7]

Whatever other reorganizations Yezhov carried out are a matter of speculation. It is not known whether he streamlined and reoriented the work of the NKVD's agent informant networks, which he claimed needed to be done. Neither is it clear to what extent he purged the

NKVD apparatus and fundamentally reorganized it. Despite his initial reforms, Yezhov never entirely separated the *militsiia* from the GUGB. The government separated the two organs only in 1940, after Yezhov's brief but bloody tenure, and after the leadership of the NKVD passed to Lavrentii Beria. Yet the separation of internal policing functions from the functions of state security began under Yezhov, immediately following the February–March 1937 plenary meeting of the Central Committee.

TURNABOUT, AGAIN

Yezhov's criticism of Yagoda and NKVD policies was sharp and unequivocal. No one could have misunderstood his intent to change the previous policies of the NKVD. Yet just five months after the February–March plenum, in late July 1937, Yezhov issued the now infamous Operational Order 00447. That order began the mass social operations of 1937 and 1938, and it was followed quickly by other orders for mass repression of different national minorities and other groups.[8] According to Order 00447, and by decree of the Politburo, the NKVD was charged to begin mass shooting or imprisonment of several categories of socially harmful elements. Leaders regarded former kulaks, bandits, and recidivist criminals among the most dangerous of these groups, alongside members of anti-Soviet parties, White Guardists, returned émigrés, churchmen and sectarians, and gendarmes and former officials of the tsarist government.[9] By the end of November 1938, when leaders stopped the operations, nearly 768,000 individuals had been caught up in the police and GUGB sweeps. Nearly 387,000 of those individuals had been arrested as category I enemies. Those who fell into this category were scheduled to be shot, while the remaining arrestees, in category II, were to receive labor camp or high-security prison sentences from eight to ten years.[10]

How are we to understand these operations and the order that initiated them? The mass operations of 1937–38 seem to have been a direct contradiction of Yezhov's new turn in the NKVD. Except for the scale and the level of violence, these mass operations were similar in many details to the kinds of campaigns that Yagoda had conducted against marginal populations and criminal elements. They involved the same kind of operational procedures — procedures that Yezhov had condemned —

and were directed against similar kinds of social groups — groups that Yezhov had declared were not the affair of the organs of state security. Once again, GUGB officers and units, in addition to the police, found themselves in the business of large-scale social purging. In campaign style, they rounded up criminals, itinerants, beggars, gypsies, so-called kulaks, and a host of other categories of suspect people.

The return to mass social repression not only contradicted Yezhov's turn in NKVD policies; Order 00447 also seemed to belie the success of Yagoda's policies. In his March 1936 report on crime, Yagoda informed Sovnarkom that, with a few exceptions, the problem of social disorder had been resolved. Rates for nearly every major crime had declined, and although he recommended extension of campaigns against socially harmful elements, Yagoda looked forward to an increasingly stable social situation. Nor did there seem to be deep concern about the economy that would explain a return to mass forms of repression. Industrial production continued to be a concern, as various commissariats failed to meet plans. The harvest of 1936 had proved difficult, as usual, and high officials were aware that famine conditions had reappeared in some areas, especially in rural Western Siberia. Yet these problems did not seem to alarm officials too much, and there was no talk of kulak sabotage, or the necessity to take any kind of extraordinary measures.[11] Finally, there seems to have been little warning or open discussion and debate within the ranks of the Party elites about the need for mass purging, nor were there any mass propaganda campaigns to prepare the population. In the great collectivization and dekulakization drives of the early 1930s, there were open discussions in higher Party organs about a crisis in the countryside, and there had been much heated debate about what was to be done. When Party leaders finally did embark on collectivization, they prepared the ground with widespread propaganda campaigns, and attempts to mobilize segments of the population. This was not so in 1937. At first glance, the mass operations of 1937 and 1938 seemed to arise abruptly, with little or no warning, and constituted a sharp break with previous policies.[12]

ORIGINS

That there was little open discussion or debate among Party leaders, as there had been about dekulakization, is not surprising. By the mid-

and late 1930s, Stalin's style of dictatorship had changed. He relied less and less on the traditional mechanisms of discussion and regular meetings of the Politburo and Central Committee. These bodies met less frequently than in the early 1930s, and their function seemed to have become more and more a means to legitimate decisions already discussed and taken by Stalin and his close associates. Substantive decisions were made increasingly by Stalin and the small number of his closest aides. These included Molotov and Kaganovich, and often Georgii Malenkov, who headed Party affairs. Yezhov served to execute policies, and he was certainly privy to decisions that affected policies of repression, but he was not a trusted member of Stalin's intimate entourage. Policies were discussed informally and personally either in Stalin's private office or in his dacha near Moscow, with little recorded evidence, and with little discussion by the larger bodies of Party and state power. Stalin wielded power through the Politburo and the Central Committee. By the late 1930s, however, these organs no longer functioned with the same independent power that they had in earlier years of the dictatorship. By 1937, they had become the classic rubber stamp for Stalin's personal assumption of authority.[13]

Although no recorded evidence exists of discussions about mass repression, there are many indirect clues about leaders' thinking during this period. In fact, there was a logic to the purges. Several historians have noted, for example, a connection between the mass purges with promulgation in 1936 of the much heralded "Stalinist" constitution. The new constitution guaranteed civil rights to former kulaks and other socially marginal populations, including voting privileges and right of property protection. The constitution, in effect, declared an end to class war within the country and extended an inclusive hand to populations that had been for years marginalized or openly repressed by the regime. The progressive and ameliorative tone of the new constitution in turn emboldened former kulaks, religious sects, and other groups, which had been long repressed, to reassert rights and claims as full citizens of the new Soviet society. Such demands overwhelmed local authorities and set off a wave of concern among Party and state authorities about the resurgence of anti-Soviet elements. Concern turned to near panic when, according to the new constitution, union-wide elections were scheduled for late 1937 for representative seats to the Supreme Soviet. Worried about a backlash against Soviet power by millions of antiregime voters, leaders undertook a typically Stalinist solution to the problem. In the summer of 1937, Stalin launched a massive cleansing operation in advance of the elections. Summarizing these arguments, one scholar has asked, rhetorically, "[C]an the Yezhovshchina not be seen as an attempt to remove those from society who did not fit into the few formalized and ascribed class categories of a homogenized Soviet state?"[14]

There is no doubt that the upcoming elections and the consequences of the new constitution played a role in leaders' motivation to rid the country of dangerous populations. Indeed, discussions of the constitution and upcoming elections featured prominently in the remarks of Party leaders at the February–March plenary meetings of the Central Committee in 1937. This was the forum that Stalin used to stage-manage the case against enemies of the regime, and thereby to launch the mass repressions and the devastating purges of the Party and state apparatus. Mass social repression was a way, once and for all, in Yezhov's words, to take care of various domestic problems that had plagued the regime for a number of years. Marc Junge and Rolf Binner are correct in describing the mass repressions of the late 1930s as a form of social engineering on a grand and brutal scale.[15] Yet, domestic explanations for the mass repressions do not go far enough. Those arguments do not explain the social repressions in contextual relation to the simultaneous repressions against other sectors in Soviet society: against various national minorities, chief among them Germans, Poles, Asians, and Finns, as well as large numbers of military officers, and Party and state officials. The nationality repressions alone accounted for 335,513 sentences in 1937 and 1938, fully half as many as the 767,397 sentenced under Order 00447. The bloody purges of the Party, state, and military apparatus increased arrest numbers still further. In total, some 2.5 to 3.1 million people were arrested in these years as part of various purges.[16] The military purges, especially, decimated the senior officer core of the Soviet military, carrying away 84 percent of the General Staff. By the end of 1938, some two-thirds of all delegates to the 1934 Seventeenth Party Congress were under arrest, usually on trumped-up charges of being part of Trotskyist and Zinovievist plots. Every one of the oblast and *krai* Party heads was under arrest or had already been shot.[17]

Purging on such a scale was a complex as well as bloody business. Different groups were arrested under different operational orders and for different reasons. Purging of the Party elite, for example, arose out of a different set of political and operational dynamics than did the mass repressions of social and ethnic groups. The mechanics of purging also differed from group to group. Many were arrested individually, undergoing lengthy interrogations and torture. Many others were arrested in mass numbers and sentenced without the formalities of interrogation, confession, or police hearing or trial. Still, there existed an overall strategic conceptualization in Stalin's mind that linked all these different kinds of purges, and the concern here is to understand the mass social purges of the late 1930s within that larger strategy. Constitutional changes and elections played a role in leaders' decision to launch the purges, but other considerations need also to be examined in order to explain the mass repressions and simultaneous purges in the Party, state, and military bureaucracies.

WAR AND REBELLION:
THE INTERNATIONAL DIMENSION

One of the clues to understanding the mass social purges can be found in the changing language of NKVD circulars and reports. One of the key documents in this chain was a report dated 17 June 1937 to Robert Eikhe, Party head in Western Siberia, by Sergei Mironov, head of the Western Siberian UNKVD. In the report, Mironov described operations to root out "Kadet-monarchist and SR organizations" in Western Siberia. These underground organizations, according to Mironov, had united under orders from the Japanese intelligence service into an overall organizational front called the "Russian General Military Union (ROVS)." The organizations in this union were preparing a "revolt and a seizure of power" in Siberia to coincide with an invasion by the Japanese army. Mironov described the various branches of this union, which the NKVD had uncovered through its agent and operational work, as well as the locations of these organizations. He also named various officials involved in them under cover of their positions as local state functionaries, and he estimated the numbers involved in the various conspiracies.

However dubious were the substantive conclusions of Mironov's report, his writing reflected, in part, Yezhov's new policy emphasis on the struggle against underground political organizations. His report fell fully in line with the new policy directives, as laid out by Yezhov, in operational meetings and in the February–March Party plenum. At the same time, Mironov made a connection that had not been made previously, between the work of these underground groups and the problem of marginal and other suspect populations. "Consider," wrote Mironov, "that in the Narym and Kuzbass areas there are 208,400 exiled kulaks; another 5,350 live under administrative exile and include White officers, active bandits and convicts, and former [tsarist] police officials. . . . This is the social base for their organizing work — kulaks and *spetspereselentsy* scattered across the Narym and in the cities of the Kuzbass. . . . It is clear then the kind of broad base that exists on which to build an insurgent rebellion."[18]

This language of conspiracy (*zagovor*) and social rebellion differed from the language used in the course of the mass operations to clear cities of harmful elements during the mid-1930s. NKVD and Party authorities had long seen a link between criminal and other marginal populations on the one hand, and anti-Soviet, even counterrevolutionary elements, on the other hand. The unrestricted movement of large numbers of socially marginal people threatened social contamination and economic disruption. Throughout the 1930s, however, operational policies directed against socially marginal populations had been separate from operational activities directed against political opponents of the regime and against opposition political organizations. The two operational lines involved different goals and different methods, the one line distinguished by methods of mass social policing, and the other by agent-operational work. In 1937, NKVD and Party leaders connected these two threats and merged operational trends that had previously been distinct. Leaders had come to believe that political enemies were manipulating the criminal and marginal population of the country to unite and not only engage in the kind of secret sabotage of which Stalin had first spoken in 1933, but to rise up in organized rebellion. Mironov's warning, therefore, was not just about the threat of social contamination or economic disruption caused by socially harmful populations, and it was not just a repetition of the same rhetoric about quiet sabotage. Mironov warned about the formation of organized, conspiratorial, and insurgent opposition to the regime. His was a language that tied socially suspect populations to active political organization and to military uprisings.

The threat of armed insurgency was new. This was a threat far more dangerous than the threat of social disorder or economic disruption. But what precipitated this sudden escalation of rhetoric? The historian Oleg Khlevniuk has argued that the sudden and frantic fear of armed uprising originated in foreign policy concerns, specifically in Stalin's reading in late 1936 of uprisings in the rear against the Republican regime in Spain during that country's civil war. As Khlevniuk points out, Stalin followed NKVD agent reports from Spain carefully, and was deeply impressed by the role of so-called fifth-column underground organizations. The term "fifth column" originated in the Spanish civil war, as a reference to diversionary and partisan activities by anti-Republican forces during the siege of Madrid. Having surrounded the city with four columns of regular troops, Franco's forces relied on the aid of a "fifth" column of diversionary forces inside the capital to bring about an uprising and the downfall of the Republican regime. According to Khlevniuk, Stalin feared this type of insurgency movement in the Soviet Union in the increasingly likely event of war. He feared that enemy states and internal political enemies would attempt to organize the same kind of fifth-column uprisings in the Soviet Union should war break out and hostile powers such as Germany and Japan invade.[19]

In his report, Mironov raised the specter not just of armed uprising, but of armed uprising during war. This reference to war was also new. The context of impending war was missing from previous campaigns against social marginals and policies of ethnic deportation, and it was the decisive context for the origins of the mass purges of 1937 and 1938. Certainly, Stalin and other leaders had warned for years about the threat of capitalist encirclement, but the talk among leaders in late 1936 and early 1937 was of the real prospect of invasion and war, not a vague threat.[20] In 1937, in other words, Soviet leaders began to perceive the outlines of what they believed were organizing efforts for insurgent activities in a coming war with Japan and Germany.

Explanation of the mass purges of 1937 and 1938 in the context of war and insurgency is convincing. It is the only explanation that puts the mass social operations within a larger political strategy of purging that included national minorities, ranking military officers, and large numbers of state and Party officials.[21] This argument also makes sense of the sudden change in language by Stalin and those around him in late 1936 and early 1937. Indeed, Stalin's talk at the February–March plenum in 1937 was peppered with the specific threat of war, the work of enemy agents, and sabotage by internal enemies. Mironov's report in the summer of 1937 was also full of talk of "rebellious moods" and organizing activities by oppositionist and foreign-directed agents and underground organizations. In their memoirs, both Molotov and Kaganovich explained and attempted to justify the mass repressions of the late 1930s in these terms. Both talked of fifth-column diversionary activities and made reference to the heightened perception among leaders in the late 1930s that war was inevitable. The Party and state purges of those years, and the mass social cleansing that became known as the Great Terror, were fully justified in their view in order to protect the rear of Soviet forces.[22]

Mironov's assessment of the danger to the country from harmful populations applied to rural as well as to urban areas. This rural aspect also distinguished the discussion about harmful elements in 1937 from previous assessments. The discussion about anti-Soviet elements in the summer of 1937 was not just about making cities safe for socialism, as it had been during the mid-1930s social defense campaigns. In 1937, police and leaders were talking about the organized military threat that marginal populations posed throughout the entire country, and especially in rural areas. In fact, Yezhov began Order 00447 with a reference, not to protecting cities, but to the threat from the countryside. He noted that "a significant number of former kulaks, those previously repressed, those hiding from repression, and escapees from camps, exile, and labor colonies have settled in rural areas." He wrote further that significant numbers of anti-Soviet elements — including sectarians, members of previous anti-Soviet parties, bandits, repatriated White officers, and others — "have remained in rural areas, nearly untouched." These, along with a "significant cadre of criminals" — including rustlers, recidivist thieves, armed robbers, escapees, and others — posed a significant danger to the country as the source of "all sorts" of anti-Soviet and diversionary crimes.[23] Despite Yagoda's optimistic pronouncements in early 1936 about having contained this danger, now, a year later, with Yagoda discredited, the country's leaders suddenly saw the country full of dangerous populations. Under Yagoda's leadership, the NKVD had secured major cities, or so Yagoda had claimed, while police had lacked the resources and, as Yagoda noted in March 1936, the authority, to extend that control to rural areas of the country. In contrast, Yezhov's operational assessment in July 1937 was much more dire. Anti-Soviet elements had begun to filter back into regime cities, industrial sites, the transport and trade system, collective and state farms, and other rural areas and "unprotected" towns and cities. This was not due to a limitation on police authority, according to Yezhov, but resulted from a lack of political vigilance and insufficient policing and surveillance measures.

THE ENEMY WITHIN: KULAKS, EXILES, SECTARIANS

The fear of war and its domestic consequences makes sense not only of the shift in language, but also of a shift in attitude and policies toward a number of groups within Soviet society. High Party officials focused special attention at the February–March plenum meetings on the numbers of dangerous populations abroad in the country. Each group posed its own threat and, together, a cause for considerable concern among leaders. First and foremost among these populations were, of course, kulaks and former kulaks. Robert Eikhe had been in the forefront of Party secretaries who, in 1935 and 1936, had encouraged Party leaders to reconcile with former kulak exiles, arguing that they should be restored rights and integrated into Soviet society.[24] At the plenum, however, Eikhe, as well as other regional Party heads suddenly changed their line. Eikhe described the presence of former kulaks, and exiles in general in Western Siberia, as a serious threat to the regime, as these were groups which would continue to fight against Soviet power. Similarly, I. D. Kabakov, the head of the Sverdlovsk oblast Party organization, worried about the "large influx" of "alien elements" into the area's factories and workplaces. The head of the Turkmenistan Party organization, Ia. A. Popok, noted that large numbers of kulaks had passed through camps and colonies and were now working in the guise of "honest" laborers. Many others had returned to their homes and were brazenly demanding restoration of their land and property, basing their demands on articles of the new "Stalinist" constitution that had been promulgated in 1936.[25]

Such assessment of the situation in the country reflected the paranoia of the day, but leaders had reasons for concern. Yezhov's description of the social dynamics of Soviet repressive policies during the 1930s was, for the most part, accurate. Dekulakization had sent over two million peasants into exile. The campaigns of social defense that followed had cleared the cities of suspect and marginal populations. Through pass-portization and clearing operations in the mid-1930s, groups which the regime deemed anti-Soviet had been sent into exile or had been driven out of regime cities and border areas and had taken refuge in nonregime towns and in the countryside. There they had stayed, while many others had fled exile and camps, or had been released. The latter contingent was a sizeable one, and included a significant proportion of those who had been dekulakized in the early 1930s and had served their five-year exile terms or had been released under the amnesty campaigns of 1934 and 1935. Indeed, the end of kulak and other exile terms in the mid-1930s had precipitated a mass flight from controlled police areas and special settlements. Before Yagoda was able to plug this breach with a law to prohibit resettlement, close to 80 percent of those given rights — about 23,500 out of 31,300, according to Berman, the head of the Gulag system — left their labor settlements. The gold industry in Sverdlovsk oblast lost over 50 percent of its labor force in the first week after the initial restoration of rights. In many areas, reported Berman, whole settlements were nearly abandoned.[26] Former kulaks continued to leave the regions of their exile, even after the 1935 law prohibiting this. They did so either by illegal flight or by persistent appeals to be permitted to return to areas where they had family. Bolstered by restoration of their rights, former and soon-to-be-released deportees were not shy about petitioning local police, both civil and political, as well as local civil administrations. They did so, according to reports, in large numbers, and local government and police officials found themselves caught between two conflicting demands. On the one hand, clear bureaucratic instructions demanded that local officials not grant rights of return settlement or property restitution to former kulaks and criminals. On the other hand, citizens presented petitions with specific references to constitutional statutes of restitution and amnesty. Caught in the middle, local officials found themselves at a loss, and continued to seek clarification from higher authorities about what line to take toward these petitions.[27]

Those having served out exile terms or camp terms began to flow back to their homes, also in large numbers, and this heightened police fears of recontamination. In April 1937, Vyshinskii replied, in a circular distributed to all procurators, to a typical request from a local procurator, this one from the Orenburg executive committee, which sought clarification about return of exiles. Like other local officials, the

Orenburg authorities had been inundated with demands from those having finished exile sentences to be allowed to return to their homes, despite routine NKVD refusals to allow this. Vyshinskii explained, again, the various distinctions set forth in passport laws and in the extraordinary directives from the NKVD. Certain ex-convict categories and those exiled and released under social danger laws were allowed the right of return, while other ex-convict categories were not allowed this privilege. Former kulaks were not permitted to return to their previous homes.[28]

While Vyshinskii tried to split legal hairs, police sought a simpler way to deal with the problem of returning exiles. As the Orenburg letter showed, local NKVD passport offices simply denied the right of return to all former exiles and camp inmates. This was common police practice, despite laws to the contrary. On more than one occasion, Yagoda sent internal NKVD orders to deny right of movement and return to any and all ex-convicts and freed exiles, despite differentiations within the law. In the spring of 1937, once again, Molchanov, Yagoda's deputy, had had the temerity to submit a proposal to ban all ex-convicts and exiles from return to any regime location. The proposal caused an outburst of heated exchanges within Sovnarkom, just several months after the drawn-out fight over passport notations, and the proposal was quickly quashed. Still, Molchanov's proposal served as a reminder of the categorical way in which police sought to deal with dangerous populations. Coming just several months before the launch of mass purges, it also provided a barometer of police thinking about the threat that marginal populations posed.[29]

Demands by former kulaks and exiles for return of property was a serious problem by 1937, the more so since many of these demands were driven by the new constitution. The new constitution granted a wide range of rights to citizens, even and especially to those who had been exiled, been denied voting rights, and had served prison sentences. The ameliorative aspects of the new constitution precipitated a wave of legal demands on the state, especially against property seizures during dekulakization in the early 1930s. In many areas, local authorities were overwhelmed by such demands, and did not know how to respond. At an October 1935 Supreme Court special session devoted ostensibly to the fight against banditry, a Ukrainian court official, Yevm[iniuk], took his turn, not to discuss banditry, but to draw attention to what he believed was a far more pressing problem — the "crushing" number of civil cases involving property return. Nearly three times as many such cases clogged local courts in Ukraine, he declared, as all criminal cases combined.[30] In Western Siberia, a special envoy of KSK, Rozit, wrote in February 1937 that the problem of property complaints by those whose rights had been restored was, legally, an "open" issue, and potentially explosive. Local Party organizations could not possibly return such property, much of which was being used for other purposes, but neither could they refuse action on the basis that "it was all a long time ago." Rozit anticipated that such complaints would mount with promulgation of the new constitution, and would become a major point of social conflict in regions.[31]

Those who abandoned hopes for property return settled where they could. Those who could not return to their former homes or live in regime areas — ex-convicts, freed exiles, deportees, and "alien" elements of all sorts — found work where they could, often in low-level positions: in rural, village, or small town administrations, as teachers, accountants, clerical workers, as minor civil servants, and in trade and cooperative organizations.[32] Hundreds of thousands, if not millions, of people found themselves in these situations. Marginalized by the regime, they eked out a life at the edges of the country's hinterlands. In Yezhov's 1937 view of the world, however, these populations were once again suspect, their very situation proof that they had "infiltrated" back into the institutions of Soviet life. In the view of Stalinist leaders, such people were waiting for the signal, for the right moment of invasion and war, to rise up and sabotage socialist construction and the defenses of the country. In his vivid paranoia, Stalin described to the February–March plenum delegates how easy it would be for such saboteurs to blow up bridges and dams, and to spirit strategic plans to enemy headquarters.[33] It was Stalin's unrealistically wild fantasy that the country's exiled and socially marginal populations were organized in one large conspiracy and were waiting for a signal to rise up against the regime. Stalin may have been paranoid, but the Great Leader was certainly accurate in his calculations of social arithmetic. Hundreds of thousands, if not millions, of disaffected and disenfranchised individuals and families peopled the towns, villages, and cities of the country.

The problem in rural areas involved more than just former kulaks and exiles. Dissatisfaction with the *kolkhoz* system combined with serious economic difficulties in 1936 and early 1937 to cause mass flight from collective farms. Throughout 1936, the number of peasants joining *kolkhozy* still exceeded the number who left or were excluded by a rate of about three to two. These numbers were reason enough for alarm, but by late 1936 and early 1937, the rate of those leaving was nearing the rate of those being enrolled. By spring of 1937, in several key areas, such as Western Siberia and in the Urals, collective farms were losing more members, overall, than they were gaining. The flight of working-age men was especially widespread and hit a number of regions especially hard. An early 1937 NKVD report from Voronezh oblast reported that in some villages literally all the working-age men had fled.[34] According to a Central Committee report, *kolkhozniki* left farms in increasing numbers because of harsh management policies and impoverished living conditions, at times bordering on starvation. At the same time, the number of peasant households establishing themselves as *edinolichniki,* separate from collective farms, was growing in alarming numbers. Peasants withdrew from collectives in order to establish themselves and their families as individual farm families, or they left in order to try to find work in industrial centers.[35] Officials attempted to stem this labor migration tide by refusing to issue *kolkhozniki* passports, which the latter needed to leave their regions of residence. Denial of passports in turn resulted in further petitions by farmers to local prosecutors for violation of rights. And all of this came to the attention of central authorities in Moscow. In April, Vyshinskii protested to TsIK that the denial of passports to *kolkhozniki* was occurring on such a widespread scale that such denials amounted to a form of mass repression and, therefore, was illegal according to the 8 May 1933 Central Committee resolution that proscribed mass repression in rural areas.[36] Central GUGB officials became concerned enough about peasant unrest that, in December 1936, the central GUGB issued an order to all oblast and *krai* heads. They were to start compiling special reports about peasant withdrawals from collectives, as well as about other "anti-Soviet" activities, especially of kulak settlers in conjunction with promulgation of the new constitution.[37]

Angered by renewed hunger and continuing impoverishment, and trapped on their farms by the regime, peasants showed an often openly hostile face to authorities. The increased tension in rural areas showed in local reports by political and police authorities. In January 1937, for example, the assistant chief prosecutor for Western Siberia, Pozdniakov, visited several collective farms in the Belovo region as a plenipotentiary of the district's Party committee. His task, a yearly one for all officials in the Siberian Party, was to ensure compliance by farms in meeting their grain procurement quotas and to ensure that local officials were mobilized in the all-out effort. In his report, Pozdniakov described strong resistance in numerous farms he visited, supposedly organized by unspecified counterrevolutionary elements. When, for example, he entered the club hall to address a general meeting of *kolkhozniki* at the Voroshilov collective farm, Pozdniakov was greeted with shouts of "We are starving!" and "We are naked and have no shoes. All our grain has been taken!" Pozdniakov reported several other incidents that he regarded as blatant counterrevolutionary provocations, and he also described the open fear expressed by the regional Party head, Guseev. Following the general meeting at the Voroshilov farm, Guseev warned Pozdniakov privately "not to press the issue of grain fulfillments. Otherwise," he said, "they might kill you (*inache, eshche mogut ubit'*)." By not specifying the third-person pronoun, the local Party chief left open the question of who "they" were. Presumably, "they" were kulak elements, except that all those at the meeting were *kolkhozniki*, and *kolkhozniki*, by definition, were not a counterrevolutionary social stratum. Pozdniakov concluded in his report that local Party officials were cowed by these unspecified "counterrevolutionary elements," that local authorities had not taken a hard enough line against them, and that these authorities did not have control over their regions. Pozdniakov nonetheless realized that Soviet authority was weak in the region and, to impose its will, still needed to rely on outside plenipotentiaries and other forms of assistance from central Party and Soviet organs.[38]

Such a state of affairs was not peculiar to the Belovo region. Regular reports by local NKVD officers and Party heads on "political-moral conditions" in their regions expressed the same sense of isolation and embattlement as did the Belovo Party boss. Local political and NKVD officials worried about the small number of Communist actives in their regions, a growing number of peasant households withdrawing from *kolkhozy*, and hostile moods of *kolkhozniki*. These simmered just below the social boiling point, and just as often could boil over into beatings of farm officials, mass refusals to work, and even murder of plenipotentiaries. In some parts of the country, local Communists expressed fear of traveling about in their own regions alone.[39] As rumors about a new constitution gathered force, local leaders also worried about the rise in religious sectarian activity. As one MTS political officer reported, rumors were widespread that the new constitution would not only legalize but sanction the revival of religion. He noted already a rise in the number of proselytizing groups of self-ordained priests in his region.[40] Another Party head wrote that several lay priests were stirring up converts in *kolkhoz* villages. They used the argument that, according to the new constitution, if mothers did not have their babies baptized, they would be expelled from the *kolkhoz*.[41] Still another rumor had it that the new constitution allotted three priests to every village.[42]

Such musings were not confined to local authorities. Special reports by UNKVD officials echoed the rising levels of dissatisfaction, frustration, and outright rage by peasants.[43] By the time of the February–March plenum, leaders were reading the preliminary material collected for the 1937 population census. What they read only added to their mounting concern about hostile populations. Beatings of census takers by villagers were already well known, as were at least some murders, and harassment of election officials. At the plenum meetings, Robert Eikhe underscored what he called the "most backward, the most dangerous moods" that existed within the population. Eikhe in fact seemed taken aback both by the extent of the bleak impoverishment in the country and by the hostile attitude of the population. He equated the two in his remarks to the February–March plenum delegates, declaring "This was made clear to us during the census. . . . In every region [we] found dilapidated and abandoned villages, and whole districts in cities in the same condition. We had to bypass all of these." S. V. Kosior, secretary of the Ukrainian Party, made similar comments, noting that "We found sluggishness and conservatism even in cities, and I am not talking just about small towns. . . . We found the most terrible primitiveness . . . as well as anti-Soviet sentiments."[44] Shocked by the impoverishment and primitiveness that surrounded them, Soviet leaders feared that this would lead to a popular backlash against the regime's vision of a shining socialist society.

As local reports confirmed, one of the most troubling findings from the census involved the level of religious activity in the country. In his speech to the February–March plenum, Andrei Zhdanov declared that anti-Soviet elements, in particular priests and "sectarians of all kinds," were organizing in preparation for upcoming elections of local representatives to the Supreme Soviet. Emboldened by the legal rights guaranteed under the new constitution, these groups were now revealing themselves and were organizing anti-Soviet political parties. E. M. Iaroslavskii, head of the Union of the Fighting Godless (*Soiuz voinstvuiushchikh bezbozhnikov*), told his audience that close to 40,000 religious organizations were legally registered in the country, making up about one million religious activists, and that surely many more underground religious sects and organizations were also at work to organize anti-Soviet elections. In the same vein, Kosior noted that the census revealed "exceptionally fanatical" religious beliefs among the populace, which, in turn, nourished "undisguised hatred" toward socialist society.[45] Both Eikhe and L. I. Mirzoian, secretary of the Kazakh republic Party organization, warned about large numbers of religious activists in their areas who were working against Soviet power. Mirzoian and Ia. A. Popok, the Turkmenistan Party head, warned in particular about the strength of Islamic groups, which were highly organized and purportedly actively anti-Soviet.[46]

Despite years of repression, the census showed that a full 57 percent of the adult population—those over the age of sixteen—listed themselves as "believers." A surprising 44 percent of those between the ages of twenty and twenty-nine, a purely Soviet generation, also claimed religious beliefs. Iaroslavskii declared that in more than a few "backward" regions, the proportion of believers of one kind or another reached close to 80 percent of the adult population. Worse yet, according to Iaroslavskii, even a large number of collective farm administrators had belonged to churches at one time or another.[47] To what extent religious belief was tied to active anti-Soviet sentiments is difficult to assess, but certainly leaders believed that there existed a demonstrable connection. Like other speakers, E. G. Yevdokimov, Party head of the Azov–Black Sea oblast, connected religious beliefs specifically to anti-Soviet activities, and particularly to the threat against the regime's agrarian politics. The goal of anti-Soviet believers, declared Yevdokimov, was to register as many believers as possible and to return the churches to their place as centers of power. Summarizing what he believed was the eventual goal of sectarians, Yevdokimov described a situation in which "Everything will go back to the way it was, and there will be no *kolkhoz*."[48] Yevdokimov's comments were fairly typical of those offered by regional

Party heads. Judging from such comments, these leaders feared a serious backlash against Soviet power that would follow from the country's new constitution.

CRIMINALS AND EX-CONVICTS

Criminals and ex-convicts constituted another category of potential recruits for an insurgency, according to Yezhov's Order 00447. This perception was also clear in leaders' discussions, although it is difficult to determine (as with other populations) to what extent such fears were justified. What is more interesting is that leaders believed that this group was ripe for insurgency not simply because it was a criminal or marginal class, but because of the particularly harsh campaigns that the regime had waged against even petty criminals and rule breakers. Also of interest is that regime leaders believed that criminality and criminals still posed a significant threat in 1937, even after several years of mass campaigns against them. In an effort to gauge the dimensions of this threat and to contain it, Yezhov wrote to Stalin in April 1937 that, monthly, the NKVD released over 60,000 convicts from camps, prisons, and lockups at the end of their terms of confinement. According to Yezhov, only several thousand of these would find socially useful work and be rehabilitated, and the NKVD was prepared to assist these individuals. According to Yezhov, however, the great majority of released convicts returned to a life of crime. This "sad fact" was not due to any failure on the part of camps to fulfill their rehabilitative function. In Yezhov's assessment, the criminal class, especially recidivists, was simply incorrigible and refused rehabilitative efforts.[49]

Supposedly, this group could be contained and tracked through residence restrictions and registration of passport and conviction information. Yezhov could not guarantee Stalin, however, that the NKVD was capable of isolating the population of criminals in the country. Widespread corruption within the passport system, lax enforcement of registration practices, and loopholes in residence laws allowed many thousands to slip out of sight of the NKVD and to "infiltrate" back into cities and other areas of the country out of police control. Passport officials in camps and in regions where prisons and colonies were located were easily bribed to issue "clean" passports. These allowed the bearer to travel anywhere in the country, containing no restrictive stamps or other compromising information. Names could be changed or expunged from card catalogs. Blank passports could easily be bought, indeed, in the dozens and hundreds. In 1936, alone, police failed to account for several tens of thousands of stolen passport blanks. If they could not obtain a false passport, ex-convicts could use the tried and true method and move and move again, counting on lax police enforcement of registration laws, to lose any trace of their criminal past.

Yezhov's estimate of 60,000 convicts released monthly from detention seems high at first reading. Certainly, Yezhov may have exaggerated the figure some, but it may not be so surprising, if we remember that many thousands of people were held in local jails for terms of up to a year. These were not counted in camp, colony, or settlement populations, and consisted of large numbers of minor rule breakers, rustlers, pickpockets, and other petty criminals. The number of this population is impossible to determine, but it must have been sizeable, considering anecdotal evidence of police and other officials. Indeed, although the problem of crime and public order in 1937 was undoubtedly not as widespread as in the very early 1930s, that problem seems not to have been ameliorated to any significant degree, despite concerted police campaigns, harsh sentences, and Yagoda's assessments in early 1936. The police chief Mikhail Shreider wrote in his memoirs about jails in Ivanovo "overflowing" with "bandits and recidivists," when he was head of the RKM in the oblast in late 1936 and early 1937.[50] Western Siberian officials often reported on mass theft of livestock from farms, products from warehouses, and especially coal and other fuels from depots, not to mention the constant hiding and pilfering of grain. Eikhe noted in late 1935 that workers in certain areas not well policed, especially in the Taiga, could not leave animals out overnight. Chickens, cows, pigs, dogs were all brought in to huts and living quarters. Horses had to be kept under guard. "Mass theft of livestock is a fact of everyday life," he remarked to a meeting of the district's Party executive committee.[51] In May 1937, the Chair of the Kalinin oblast executive committee reported, in despair, that a significant number of ex-convicts were settling in the oblast after their release from camps and prisons — nearly 5,000 in 1935 and 4,523 in 1936, who could be identified and counted as ex-convicts. This number did not count the many more who settled illegally by hiding their backgrounds. City and oblast officials were at a loss to employ this population, and many were turning again to crime after unsuccessfully trying to find work.[52] A Leningrad NKVD report from early 1937 provided an astonishing estimate that 2.3 percent of the city's population consisted of escaped convicts and criminals, while that same contingent made up as much as 5.4 percent of the general population of the oblast.[53]

In order to seal this breach in the country's defenses, Yezhov suggested to Stalin the novel idea to allow camp troikas and courts to extend the sentences of criminal convicts. This could apply to anyone in custody, he wrote, who infringed labor discipline regulations, engaged in "hooliganism," or refused to engage in rehabilitative work. Sentences could be extended for up to three years at a time.[54] Unable to enforce passport laws, and having failed to return to a policy of universal residence ban, Yezhov suggested to Stalin yet another solution to the criminal contamination problem — simply to keep criminal convicts in custody. Both Krylenko and Vyshinskii objected to such a practice. Both argued that convicts could only be resentenced for breaking specific statutory laws, not for something as vague as labor discipline infractions or refusal to engage in rehabilitation programs. And in any case, they argued, such matters should not be handled by ad hoc NKVD troikas, but by the legally constituted special courts that held jurisdiction over camps and prisons.[55] A special commission convened by Sovnarkom sympathized with Yezhov's desire to keep hardened criminals out of cities and industrial areas, but commission members objected to Yezhov's proposals. Yet again, they cited current laws, which allowed ex-convicts, except for those convicted of especially serious crimes, to settle in cities and industrial sites, and some even in regime areas.[56]

Vyshinskii, Krylenko, and Sovnarkom members responded to Yezhov's proposals within the context of the law, and of solving the problems of employing and reintegrating the country's criminal class. High government officials exchanged a copious number of memoranda over this issue, which involved a number of major commissariats. Even the trade union leadership weighed in on the matter, if only to note that it had no authority to force member unions to employ or support ex-convicts. Vyshinskii even produced letters from former criminals in an effort to bolster the case for rehabilitation programs. Yet none of the sides involved in these exchanges could know Stalin's intent or the direction he was moving, with the exception of Yezhov, the NKVD chief, and Molotov, Stalin's confidant and the head of Sovnarkom. Stalin was not interested in rehabilitating criminals. Yezhov's response to Stalin was primarily about finding a way to identify and isolate the country's criminal class as a potential enemy population — and of finding a way, eventually, to destroy that population.

THE ORGANIZERS: EX-COMMUNISTS AND "FOREIGNERS"

Kulaks and former kulaks, criminals, ex-convicts, exiles of all kinds, *lishentsy* and former *lishentsy*, and other socially marginal groups: these were supposedly the disaffected populations from whose ranks would emerge the recruits for rebellion. As noted above, however, these recruits needed organization and leaders. Soviet leaders' concerns focused not just on mass social disaffection, but on the combination of mass disaffection and active organizational efforts by disaffected elements within the state and Party. In other words, Stalin was worried about a "cadre revolt," as well as mass uprisings among the population.[57] Stalin's fear of oppositional groupings in the military, and the bloody purges that resulted, have been well documented, as have the purges within the NKVD. Other clues, as well, point to the connection between Stalin's fear of a coming war and his attempt to suppress any fifth-column organizational activities inside the Soviet Union. As early as December 1936, for example, Stalin, through Yezhov, directed heads of key commissariats to compile lists of suspect personnel at the oblast and *krai* level. Accordingly, in a secret memorandum from 20 December, Vyshinskii ordered republic-, *krai-*, and oblast-level procuracy heads to compile lists of officials who had had ties with opposition parties in the past, and a separate list of "any officials who at any time showed vacillation during the period of struggle with various oppositions." Vyshinskii required procuracy heads to draw up such lists secretly, by themselves.[58] Analogously, in February 1937, Malenkov, the head of Party affairs in the Central Committee, prepared for Stalin a similar list of potentially disgruntled Party and former Party members. Malenkov drew up this document in specific preparation for the February–March plenum meetings in 1937. Malenkov drew Stalin's attention to the fact that over 1.5 million former Party members, excluded from the Party since the early 1920s, were at large and worked in all sorts of institutions — factories, enterprises, state offices, and rural and urban administrations. Some 315,528 individuals had been excluded within the previous two years, in the course of Party card reviews. This number amounted to a little more than 13 percent of the overall number of Party members in 1935. In some factories, the number of expelled Party members exceeded the number of Communist actives. This was a disturbing fact, warned Malenkov. These people had at least some organizational experience, based on their Party work, and posed a threat as potential organizers of anti-Soviet activities. Interestingly, the largest single group among them — 86,888 or 27.5 percent of the total — were excluded because they were "socially alien and harmful elements." Stalin underscored this figure and this category in bold pencil, as he did the number of those excluded as "Trotskyist-Zinovievists."[59] In his reading, the two categories were closely linked. Speaking to the February–March plenum delegates, Stalin referred to Malenkov's report. Using the language of diversionaries and fifth-columnists, Stalin raised the prospect that such numbers provided a "reserve" organizing force for the regime's enemies.[60] In his remarks to the February–March plenum, Robert Eikhe echoed Stalin's warnings, referring to the large numbers of former Party members in Western Siberia. According to Eikhe, in fact, the number of those excluded from the Party since the mid-1920s in Western Siberia outnumbered active Communists: there were some 93,000 expelled Party members, compared to 44,000 still active Party members as of January 1937. Many of the former, he declared, were openly hostile to the regime. Eikhe, too, underscored the Party political experience of these "enemies" and their potential to act as organizing agents for anti-Soviet groups.[61]

Disgruntled communists constituted a major threat as organizing agents, but so did the large numbers of foreigners in the country. In Stalin's view of the world, not just some, but all foreigners constituted a threat as potential spies. The memoirs of foreign diplomats in Moscow during the late 1930s are filled with comments about the strange atmosphere that prevailed in the country. Nearly all Soviet officials understood that contact with any foreigner was dangerous, even contact in the course of professional and necessary diplomatic and trade business. Yet "foreigner" was a word that encompassed more than diplomats and other government representatives. That word included political refugees, guest workers, and those granted Soviet citizenship from other countries, as well as gypsy populations that had crossed from central European countries into the Soviet Union during the 1930s. Thus, for example, the large numbers of workers from other countries who had settled in the Soviet Union in the 1930s were now suspect as spies, saboteurs, and underground organizers. By 1937, this number ran into the tens of thousands.[62] This group was hit particularly hard by the mass repressions of 1937 and 1938, as were the ranks of foreign opposition parties that had taken refuge in the Soviet Union.

Stalin suspected all of these populations as potential spies. As a result, and as with other groups, he set the NKVD to making lists. In the first weeks of 1937, the NKVD drew up registers of all foreign citizens residing in the country. Central police officials ordered local offices to verify addresses and activities. On the basis of this review, the criminal investigative branch of the police, the *ugolovnyi rozysk,* distributed a register of all foreign citizens who could not be found. The list, from February, consisted of 766 names arranged in alphabetical order. Following each name was information on nationality, passport and visa numbers, and last registered address. The investigative police issued an urgent order to all local branches to search for these individuals as "most wanted."[63]

In a similar vein, an NKVD decree from March ordered the police Visa and Registration Department to submit lists of all foreigners granted citizenship since 1 January 1936.[64] And in yet another — and remarkable — document, the country's civil police chief, Bel'skii, issued a circular in the spring of 1937 declaring simply and boldly that it was an "already well-documented fact" that the "overwhelming majority" of foreigners in the country were the "organizing agents" of hostile foreign powers. Bel'skii noted that local police were not to take direct action against foreigners in their areas. The main weapon to be used against these spies was agent-operational work, but Bel'skii let local police officials know that they, too, could do their part against these enemies. Bel'skii instructed local police to keep special track of foreigners in their areas, and to take various measures to restrict their movements, "so as to hinder their ability to engage in spying and diversionary actions." Measures included delays in processing travel requests, restrictions of physical movement and contact, and lengthy review of documents.[65]

The fear of foreigners that so characterized the regime in the late 1930s stretched to cover ethnic minorities living in the Soviet Union. Any national group was suspect that had community or ethnic ties to populations living in other states. Those of German, Polish, and Finnish extraction were most suspect, of course, as were Korean and Chinese minorities living in Siberia. Soviet leaders had for some years feared the potential danger posed by these populations. Border cleansing campaigns had focused on ethnic minorities, especially along the country's western boundaries, from as early as 1933. One of the first systematic efforts to identify such populations came to light in 1934, in a circular from the Central Committee to the Moscow oblast Party committee. The circular required that NKVD bureaus in Moscow factories begin to register activities and members of certain ethnic populations who were regarded as hostile to the Soviet Union. The first priority was given to Germans, Koreans, Finns, Letts, Lithuanians, and Poles. Individuals of these ethnic extractions were to be progressively excluded from the enterprises of the city, especially from high-level positions important for the work of an enterprise. It was necessary, as well, to pay special attention to the activity of the members of a second group of "nations": Jews, Armenians, Crimean Tatars, Chechens, Ingushetians, and Ossetians. According to the circular, the NKVD organs of the enterprises, as well as the central Party organs, were to be immediately informed of any expression of discontent over work conditions, Soviet power, or other aspects of Soviet life, from these categories of workers.[66]

Leaders were not content simply to monitor these populations. Large-scale deportation of ethnic populations started in 1935 and 1936 and coincided with the campaigns to clear cities of anti-Soviet and socially harmful elements. Deportations of national minorities continued under special orders throughout the late 1930s, but these operations also merged with mass repressions in 1937 and 1938 under Order 00447. Indeed, separate orders were issued for nationality operations against Germans and Poles almost simultaneously with the order against kulaks and social marginals. By 1937, as Terry Martin and others have shown,[67] leaders came to regard these ethnic populations as "enemy nations," potentially, and even inherently, hostile to Soviet power. These groups suffered heavily during the mass purges of 1937 and 1938.

One of the groups targeted as "foreign" was, in fact, not made up of foreign citizens or even of ethnic minorities, but of ethnic Russians who had worked on the Harbin rail line during the 1920s and 1930s. This was the rail line owned and run by the Soviet Union, which connected the Trans-Siberian *magistral* to the Manchurian city of Harbin. In the mid-1930s, when Japanese forces entered Manchuria, Soviet authorities sold the rail line to them, and many thousands of rail workers returned to the Soviet Union. These *kharbintsy* came to have a categorical identity all their own in NKVD files, and they became suspect in 1937. Indeed, Yezhov issued a separate operational order against the *kharbintsy* in September, and it reflected the shrill and categorical attitude of the regime toward "foreign" populations. The "overwhelming majority" of these workers, Yezhov wrote, had been recruited by the Japanese secret service to infiltrate the Soviet Union, especially the transport industry, to act as organizers, spies, and saboteurs in the coming war. The NKVD, having discovered this plot, now ordered that the *kharbintsy* workers be rounded up and executed as traitors, spies, and diversionaries.[68]

CONCLUSIONS

Here, then, were the elements that gave the Great Purge its particular characteristics and virulence. The dekulakization campaigns of the early part of the decade formed one background for the mass repressions of the late 1930s. Dekulakized peasants made up the largest single category of those who fell under suspicion and were arrested in 1937 and 1938 under Order 00447. The social defense campaigns of the mid-1930s formed a second and equally important background. The conflation of social disorder with counterrevolution, especially, influenced state and NKVD policies and methods. The mechanisms employed during the repressions of 1937 and 1938 were similar to those used earlier to gather up undesirable populations and, in 1937 and 1938, the NKVD targeted many of the same social groups. Similarly, campaigns to contain suspect ethnic minorities also formed part of the background to the mass purges of the late 1930s. Yet it was not the threat of social disorder alone that generated the mass repressions of the late 1930s. The fear of opposition political organizations — Trotskyists, Zinovievists, et al. — haunted leaders after the murder of Sergei Kirov. Gearing up the state security machinery to battle suspected opposition groups became an increasing priority for leaders, even as they continued operational policies to control marginal and other undesirable "elements" within the population.

Each of these concerns — over class opposition, social disorder, underground political subversion, and national contamination — had generated separate political responses and operational policies throughout the 1930s. These concerns and policy lines coalesced in 1937. By 1937, leaders were convinced that oppositionists, working with foreign agents, were actively organizing socially disaffected populations into a fifth-column force. Leaders worried that invasion, which seemed increasingly likely in the late 1930s, would be the signal for armed uprisings by these groups, as well as by purportedly disaffected ethnic minorities. Indeed, the threat of war was key. That threat, made real, introduced an especially virulent element into Soviet policies of repression and gave to those policies a sense of political urgency.

The various fears of Soviet leaders combined in a deadly way within the context of imminent war and invasion, but the policy lines that merged in the purging process were not new. They were familiar to all political and civil police officials. If anything was surprising to policing officials, it was the seemingly sudden turnabout from Yezhov's policy line laid down in late February and early March 1937. The scale and deadliness of the purge process were also new. Stalin, through Yezhov, launched the massive purge of Soviet society in 1937 and 1938 in order to destroy what leaders believed was the social base for armed overthrow of the Soviet government. The following chapter explores the dynamics of that purge process.

10   The Mechanics of
Mass Purging

Isn't it time Stalin wrote another "Dizzy with Success" article?
—*Chief of the Penza NKVD, September 1937*

THE FEBRUARY–MARCH plenary sessions of the Central Committee confirmed Stalin's assessment of the dangers facing the country. Resolutions of the Central Committee recognized the imminent threat from a coalition of increasingly hostile powers. The same resolutions affirmed the growing danger inside the country. A massive number of anti-Soviet organizations were quietly but steadily spreading their tentacles and coordinating their efforts, positioning themselves for subversive activities and outright rebellion in the event of war. Agents of gloom were fanning dissatisfaction among the populace, and rebellious "moods" affected large segments of Soviet society. The Party's Central Committee concurred that the Party and police must act quickly and decisively to deal with these threats.

Stalin and his new political police head had already started a wide-scale purge, even before the plenary meetings, of old Bolshevik leaders and Party members, as well as of large numbers of specialists in the economy, sciences, education, and in the press. Between October 1936 and February 1937, Yezhov oversaw the arrest of some 2,116 individuals who supposedly had been working actively in anti-Soviet blocks or for hostile governments. These arrests included the sensational arrest of longtime Bolshevik leaders such as Aleksei Rykov and Nikolai Bukharin, as well as numerous other highly placed and well-known

Party members. The plenum wholeheartedly approved of these arrests and the general line laid out by Stalin, Molotov, and Yezhov at the meetings.[1] This approval provided Stalin with a major victory by connecting, for the first time, the former Party majority leadership with counterrevolutionary plots. At the same time, the plenary sessions also gave Stalin, and more specifically, the NKVD, a nearly unchecked mandate to initiate repression on a broad scale. The mass purges launched in late July 1937 fulfilled that mandate with a particularly Stalinist kind of viciousness.[2]

This chapter recounts the sequence of events leading up to the mass operations under Order 00447, and details the progress of the purges once they started. While clues are sparse about the timing of the mass operations, evidence is abundant for the operational aspects of the purges, and this chapter focuses particularly on the interrelationship between central and local dynamics. Although covered under the same operational orders, the purging process played out differently in urban, rural, and border regions. These local peculiarities help explain the different patterns of the purges in different areas of the country, as do the personalities of the executioners that Stalin assigned to different regions at different times. Following the trail of Stalin's favored killers provides a significant insight into the leader's perceptions about the social and political dynamics in the country. Local peculiarities account for much about the purges, but a detailed account of the purges reveals Stalin's controlling hand at the key junctures and turning points of the whole process. This chapter emphasizes the significant role played by the civil police, and it details the steps by which purging became "industrialized" into a bureaucratic process of mass-production killing. The process of bureaucratization became an important and necessary mechanism of the purges, a response to relentless pressure for more arrests, and a mechanism that transformed the scale and intensity of Stalin's killing machine.

The purpose of the purges was to rid the country of its criminal and anti-Soviet classes, and yet, judging by post-purge assessments, this chapter concludes that the purges failed to achieve their purported goal. Crime levels in the country seemed hardly to have been affected by the waves of mass arrests of supposed criminal and antisocial classes. Circulars about crimes and levels of social disorder read much the same in the late 1930s as in the middle and early years of the decade. The mass purges supposedly cleansed Soviet society, but of what is not at all clear. What is clear is that the Great Purges of 1937 and 1938 devastated the Soviet Union. Stalin's brutal assault on Soviet society destroyed the lives of hundreds of thousands of people and affected millions. The Great Purges rank as one of the greatest acts of state violence in the twentieth century.

THE FOUR-MONTH GAP

Arrests and purges of state and Party bureaucracies continued after the February–March plenary meetings, most spectacularly in a sweeping purge of top military officials, but also of high officials in the agricultural commissariats.[3] Still, Stalin and Yezhov delayed the start of mass social and ethnic repressions until midsummer. Official sanction for these purges came only on 2 July. On that day, and with apparently little prior discussion, the Politburo issued the infamous decree on anti-Soviet elements, which started the purge process in motion.[4] Following the 2 July decree, preparations for mass operations came in a rush of orders and activities. The following day, Yezhov telegrammed a directive to all regional administrative heads of the NKVD to compile lists of "all kulaks and criminals who have been released or escaped from camps and exile." NKVD heads were to make two lists. The first comprised the "most dangerous elements" who were to be shot. The second list was to include the less active, but still dangerous, elements, who were to be exiled. The task of compiling lists by itself required an enormous amount of work, since lists in any particular region grew to thousands of persons. Yet Yezhov demanded these lists by 8 July, and making lists was but one of a number of preparations that had to be carried out quickly.[5] As regional police administrations rushed to make lists, Yezhov called an operational meeting for 16 July in Moscow of all UNKVD heads, that is, the heads of district- and oblast-level NKVD administrations. In turn, police officials had to brief and prepare their subordinates for operational activities. Operational units had to be assembled, and personnel of the judging troikas had to be approved. Any one of these activities could have taken weeks, and some local officials did, in fact, request deadline extensions. Yezhov, however, was relentless, and pushed the police apparatus to be prepared for operations by the beginning of August.

Thus, a matter of only a few weeks separated the first Politburo resolution about anti-Soviet elements in early July from the onslaught of operations in late July and August. But this sudden hectic rush came after a nearly four-month hiatus from the end of the Central Committee plenary sessions in early March. The timing and sequence of these events is curious and raises a number of questions about the motivations behind the purges. The issue of delay seems to be a particularly vexing problem. Resolutions of the plenary sessions approved Stalin's assessment of the need for large-scale purges. So, why was there a four-month gap between the February–March plenum meetings and the onset of the mass purges? This question may seem to be an example of academic hair-splitting, but it is an important one. Differing interpretations of that gap speak to the issue of motivations, and how power relations worked in the Stalinist regime. Some have argued that, in initiating mass purges, Stalin was being driven by policies and pressures that he did not initiate. In this scenario, Stalin acceded to a mass purge of society only in response to pressure by regional Party heads, which erupted at the February–March meetings and continued throughout the spring and summer. Regional leaders, according to this interpretation, feared a social backlash against their power from a populace emboldened by rights granted under the 1936 constitution, that would be expressed in elections to the Supreme Soviet scheduled for December 1937. Supposedly, Stalin agreed to a mass purge in exchange for local leaders' cooperation in implementing constitutional changes and elections.[6] Other scholars have argued that Stalin was already intent on a campaign of mass repression as early as February and March, and that he hesitated for different reasons. Despite approval of his policies of widespread political purging, Stalin was not yet certain of full approval for mass social repression from within the Central Committee, and even from within the Politburo. In this interpretation, Stalin maneuvered for another several months after the close of the plenum in order to prepare the way for a mass purge of society.[7]

Little direct evidence exists to support one or the other argument, but what evidence there is suggests that Stalin intended to engage in mass purging, and that mobilizing preparations were underway already in the spring and early summer of 1937. That evidence also suggests that, while local Party leaders favored a major campaign of social repression, resistance to purge operations arose, in all places, from within the NKVD.

LISTS AND A MEETING

Throughout the spring and early summer of 1937, NKVD central authorities geared up for a major purge of Soviet society and its governing institutions. One of the most important aspects of those preparations, and one for which some second-hand evidence exists, involved a meeting of UNKVD heads and plenipotentiaries in mid-July, 1937. Yezhov called that meeting, which took place in Moscow, just weeks before the scheduled start of operations. At the meeting, Yezhov told his audience that the previous NKVD commissar, Yagoda, a confessed diversionary spy, had done little to safeguard the country and its leaders and, in fact, had allowed the security services and the country to become inundated with enemies. Yezhov warned his listeners that a sweeping purge of social enemies was in the making, and that operational heads should prepare their staffs for large-scale operations. Yezhov then reeled off "approximate" numbers of people to be arrested in different republics, oblasts, and districts. According to one of the officers in attendance, V. A. Styrne, from Ivanovo, there was "deathly silence" in the hall as Yezhov read off the figures. Styrne and his colleagues were "struck dumb" by such large numbers of people supposedly to be arrested as enemies. When Yezhov had finished reading, the Omsk oblast NKVD chief E. P. Salyn' protested, saying that it was impossible that such large numbers of enemies could be at large in his oblast. In any case, he supposedly declared, it was "unacceptable" to estimate how many people were to be arrested and shot even before a preliminary investigation had been conducted. According to Styrne, Yezhov reacted to Salyn''s protest with a shrill outburst, with much waving of hands. Yezhov accused Salyn' of being the first enemy from Omsk to be unmasked, and ordered the sergeant at arms to arrest the Omsk chief.

This apocryphal story was recounted by Styrne to Mikhail Shreider, the civil police chief of Ivanovo oblast, who recorded it in his memoirs.[8] As with other details in his memoirs, Shreider confused his facts. Shreider wrote that the meeting took place sometime in April, when in fact it was held on 16 July. Shreider's account of Salyn''s arrest was also not quite accurate. In reality, Salyn' remained at his post as head of the Omsk NKVD until his arrest in August 1937.[9] Either Styrne or Shreider overdramatized the Salyn' incident, and Shreider misremembered his chronology by several months. Despite these confusions, the tone Shreider ascribes to the July NKVD gathering rings true, as does the expression of surprise and reluctance by at least some regional NKVD chiefs. At least four other police officials questioned the need for a mass purge, arguing that, with such hasty preparations, many innocent people would be unjustifiably accused. Like the Omsk chief, these others also came under Yezhov's criticism, and eventually were arrested. According to several eyewitness accounts, Yezhov resorted to outright threats and intimidation of those subordinates who seemed to be "operationally inert," and who did not show the requisite aggressiveness in ferreting out enemies.[10]

That police officers were surprised by Yezhov's pronouncements is understandable. His call for a mass social purge contradicted the tone and policy line laid down by Stalin and Yezhov just a few months earlier at the Party plenum. The GUGB was no longer supposed to be in the business of mass social policing. Those had been the policies of the discredited Yagoda. Yet here was Yezhov telling his subordinates to prepare for exactly those kinds of operations, and on an unprecedented scale. So too, it was patently absurd, and an insult to the professionalism of those sitting in the audience, to imagine that such large numbers of enemies could be loose and wreaking havoc and sabotage in the country. UNKVD heads knew, of course, even before the 16 July meeting, that a purge of anti-Soviet elements was in the offing. The Politburo resolution of 2 July had noted that, and local police heads were already putting together lists when they were summoned to Moscow. Yezhov used the numbers in those lists to put together the figures he read off at the operational meeting. Still, it seems that at least some of the officers present did not conceive of a purge on the scale Yezhov outlined. Indeed, Yezhov cautioned his subordinates that the numbers he read out did not constitute the final tally. The categories to be purged, he warned, would be broadened beyond kulaks and criminals to include *kharbintsy*, Poles, Germans, and members of what Yezhov described as "kulak–White Guardist groupings" in the Party and the Soviet administrative apparatus. He warned regional police heads to prepare for more purging.[11]

The reluctance shown toward Yezhov at the July meeting was not, apparently, the only resistance by subordinates. Even before the operational meeting, at least seven UNKVD heads responded to Yezhov's 2 July instructions with requests for extensions of the five-day deadline to compile lists of enemies. The head of the Tatar republic NKVD asked for a whole month's extension. Others noted that their lists were very provisional.[12] Such foot dragging in the face of a direct and urgent order was not the usual practice in the NKVD, and it could have been an indication of reluctance to comply with Yezhov's demands. How much resistance there was to the push for a mass social purge is unclear, and many police heads no doubt responded enthusiastically to the call. Still, initial resistance was strong enough, apparently, that, on 10 July, Yezhov submitted a list to the Central Committee of thirteen regional police heads to be removed immediately from their positions. There is no explanatory text attached to the recommendation, but the timing of the recommendation is telling. Yezhov made the recommendation two days after the deadline had passed for compiling lists, and less than a week before the operational meeting in Moscow. Given this timing, and the flurry of concentrated activity surrounding preparations for the purge, it seems likely that Yezhov's recommendation for disciplinary action was related to his instructions of 3 July, and to the reluctance or inability of subordinates to comply with those instructions.[13]

Either by removal or by intimidation, Yezhov brought reluctant subordinates into line. In the meantime, the business of making lists moved ahead, and Stalin and Yezhov monitored the process closely. Stalin, working through Yezhov, adjusted the lists submitted from regions. In some cases, the numbers submitted to be shot were adjusted upward and in other cases downward. Stalin and Yezhov raised the limits in seventeen regions and lowered the limits in nineteen regions, approving the numbers from four regions. The two leaders also adjusted numbers for the second category of detainees, those to be imprisoned or exiled. In this category, they raised limits for eighteen regions and lowered numbers for twenty-two. The overall number of people to be repressed, according to an 11 July Politburo decree, amounted to 187,000, some 20,000 less than initial limits submitted from forty regions of the country.[14] What strategic considerations went into these adjustments is unclear, although it would seem that Yezhov and the central apparatus of the NKVD had some kind of orienting figures already at hand, despite the charge to local police officials to take the initiative in making lists and setting limits. This is not surprising, given the centralized organization of registration catalogs in Moscow. Central authorities could have been working on their own lists as a check on local efforts. Stalin, no doubt, also had his own ideas about the distribution of populations in the country that he believed posed the greatest danger to the regime.[15] In any case, Stalin and Yezhov kept a close watch on numbers submitted by local police heads.

EARLY SIGNS

Apart from compiling lists, purging on a mass social scale required significant organizational preparation, and there were signs that organizational changes to gear up for the purges were underway already in the spring. Some of those changes involved reorganization of operational units. Although ubiquitous, regional branches of the NKVD were not adequately staffed to take on the tasks that would be demanded of them. In Western Siberia, for example, the political police could count 600 to 700 operational officers to cover 124 regions.[16] Cities such as Novosibirsk and Tomsk had a higher concentration of officers than did outlying regions, but the number of operational staff per region remained as it had been throughout the mid-1930s—about three to four officers per region. These numbers were hardly adequate to fulfill normal duties, let alone extraordinary demands. At the same time, administering dozens if not hundreds of regional offices from the oblast-level UNKVD administration was slow and cumbersome. In order to beef up staff at the local levels, and to facilitate administration of the purges, Yezhov ordered that each oblast, and even cities, be divided into a number of operational sectors, each sector overlapping and including several regions. Yezhov's order placed an officer-grade commander, usually a major or a captain, or at least a lieutenant, in charge of each sector, and assigned a number of operational officers to each sector. In many oblasts and urban areas, department heads of the civil police, particularly the *ugolovnyi rozysk,* were assigned duty as heads of operational sectors.[17]

Many of these operational sectors were formed in the hectic rush of preparations during July 1937. In peripheral areas of the country, however, the NKVD formed operational sectors already by late April or early May. On 11 May, central procuracy officials discussed how to respond to these changes so that local procuracy officials could oversee the newly formed sectors. Those discussions revealed that the operational sectors were to be headquartered in larger towns. Procuracy leaders decided that jurisdiction for the sector would fall to the procuracy administration in the towns where headquarters were located. These organizational reforms were widespread enough that procuracy officials decided not to respond to individual inquiries, but to send a general circular letter to advise all oblast procuracy administrations of the corresponding changes.[18]

Interregional operational sectors existed during the early 1930s, also for outlying or large regions. These sectors, however, were eliminated by 1935 as administrative reforms subdivided large territories into smaller regions. As a result of these reforms, and in order to avoid duplication, the NKVD folded its operational sectors into the newly formed regional administrative departments.[19] Reformation of these sectors in late April or early May 1937 does not seem related to other reforms, and does not appear to have been a permanent structural reorganization. These changes were very likely part of Yezhov's preparation for a mass action, for the specific purpose of carrying out mass purges. Operational units for each sector were made up of rank-and-file officers already assigned to regions in each sector, and officers who worked in the oblast administration. New recruits, drawn from recent graduates of NKVD, Party, and Komsomol schools, were assigned to supplement operational units. Students in NKVD academies and schools were also rushed through to graduation and assigned to operational units.[20]

Other signs in the spring and early summer indicated movement toward some kind of mass action. In April, the Politburo approved formation of an emergency crisis council, comprised of Stalin, Molotov, Kaganovich, Voroshilov, and Yezhov. This crisis council was empowered to take emergency action on issues of a secret nature. According to the historian Viktor Danilov, this council provided Stalin and his inner circle the institutional means to deepen the purges by bypassing the formal process of Politburo approval.[21] In a related move, and also in April, the Politburo broadened the authority of the NKVD's *Osoboe soveshchanie* by subsuming under it the functions of the special civil police sentencing boards, the *militseiskie troiki*. Created in May 1935,

the police troikas adjudicated the expulsion, deportation, and imprisonment of socially dangerous "elements." Although police boards continued to operate in 1937, the decree in April of that year now placed
the struggle against socially dangerous elements directly under control
of the political police, along with expanded jurisdiction over repression
of suspected spies, wreckers, and diversionary elements. The decree still
limited administrative sentencing of these groups to five to eight years
exile or imprisonment, but it was an ominous sign that policing of social marginals was explicitly linked to struggle against groups considered a direct threat to the security of the state—interesting, too, that
individuals deported under this order had only to be suspected of subversive activities. The sentencing board did not need to prove violation
of law, although it was required to submit written reasons for suspicion. This was one more in a series of prophylactic measures that would
escalate in the coming weeks and months into a massive purging operation.[22]

The NKVD acted quickly on this new authority, launching campaigns
against different groups. In late May, the Politburo approved an operation drafted by Yezhov to deport from Moscow, Leningrad, and Kiev
former oppositionists and people who had been expelled from the Party,
as well as relatives of these individuals. In Moscow alone, the list that
Yezhov compiled numbered over 6,000 people, 1,160 of whom had no
"visible means of employment." Yezhov's operational draft foreshadowed later formulations linking marginal populations with the threat of
insurgency. Yezhov wrote that such a population provided a considerable "base" of support for the "harmful forces" working against Soviet
power. By June, when the operations began, the list of cities to be
cleared expanded to include the Party resort of Sochi, and the industrial centers of Taganrog and Rostov on Don.[23] In late May and June,
police launched still other operations to clear "declassed elements" from
rail lines. When informed of this at a 19 June meeting of procuracy
heads, Vyshinskii ordered a letter be sent to Yezhov declaring his support for renewing the campaigns against "these 35-ers" (tridtsatipiat-
niki). This was an odd epithet, and very likely a reference to the original operational order against socially dangerous elements, number
00192, from May 1935.[24]

A curious incident in June also indicated preparations for some kind
of emergency police action. Without warning to Vyshinskii, or any dis-

cussion, the Moscow civil police head issued instructions to his department and section heads exempting them from normal arrest procedures. The exemption included the necessity to obtain procuracy sanction for arrests. Vyshinskii reacted by instructing the Moscow procurator to protest and block the new arrest procedures. It is difficult to imagine that the police chief issued these instructions on his own authority; more likely he was following orders from higher officials. Neither is it clear whether Moscow was the only city affected, but it seems equally clear that such instructions would not have been issued had the police not been planning a large operation. In any case, the instructions mimicked those that would be issued more broadly in a little over a month's time in preparation for the mass purges. The Moscow incident was an odd occurrence just on the eve of the purges.[25]

Yezhov issued instructions on 3 July to UNKVD heads to start compiling lists for purge operations. Instructions arrived from Moscow, according to the deposition of P. A. Yegorov, an assistant chief of the NKVD in Western Siberia, "that . . . ordered us to compile lists of all counterrevolutionary elements among social aliens and [lists] of all criminal recidivists."[26] Thus, the NKVD Operational Department prepared surveys, based on work records, passport information, police records, and other registries of "alien and anti-Soviet elements" working and living in the district. These populations were said to have "infiltrated" or alternately "saturated" such crucial infrastructural systems as the Tomsk railroad lines, as well as other rail, river, and road transportation networks, grain storage centers, and rural and local village governing councils. Yezhov's orders arrived in early July, but already in June, regional-level NKVD offices were filing reports to the district NKVD leaders on numbers of enemies and their activities in their regions. These reports carried the same tone and wording as the major summary report submitted by the district NKVD head, Mironov, to Eikhe in mid-June. Enemies were everywhere, as were conspiracies to bring about rebellion. The district was infiltrated by anti-Soviet elements.[27]

There are hints, then, that by mid-June, NKVD officials in Western Siberia were already gearing up for a coming purge and were already making lists. Yet Eikhe, the Western Siberian Party chief, also needed to warn local Party activists that a mass purge was in the works. Many local officials would already have known about a purge, if only by rumor, but Eikhe needed to make clear that the purge would encompass peasants, specifically *kolkhozniki,* as well as criminals, exiles, and other marginal populations. Doing this was a tricky business since, by definition, *kolkhozniki* were loyal Soviet citizens, and starting a mass purge of peasants would run directly counter to several years of regime policy. Indeed, with the end of dekulakization, much of the repression in the countryside had been directed against low-level officials rather than against peasants. During the mid-1930s, collective farm chairs, rural council officials, and other local officials took the brunt of blame for agrarian problems and the dysfunctional workings of the collective farm system. Repression among these groups had taken a heavy toll of some one million arrests between 1934 and 1937, while the regime had tried to lure peasants onto the farms with ameliorative policies of stabilization. A mass purge of peasants would reverse this policy, and Eikhe needed to find a way to finesse this turnabout. *Kolkhozniki* had to be demoted, in a sense, to mere peasants again (*kres'tianin*) so that they could be reclassified as kulaks and then repressed.

Eikhe accomplished this turnabout, not by sending a circular letter, but by sending out special plenipotentiaries to the various regions. As in earlier campaigns, Eikhe sent one of his favorite Party bulldogs, the assistant district prosecutor, Pozdniakov. Pozdniakov had been out and about already in January 1937, assessing the situation in rural areas and warning local rural leaders about the need for vigilance. As in January, so in June, Pozdniakov chastised local officials in several regions for adhering to the "attitude" that the class enemy had been defeated. As in January, so in June, Pozdniakov exhorted local officials to remain ever-vigilant against a ubiquitous enemy. In one respect, however, the language he used in June of 1937 differed markedly from the language he had used in January. In January, he had talked in elliptical terms about anti-Soviet elements. In June, however, he got right to the point. He spoke in specific rather than vague terms about the threat to the socialist countryside. "It is anti-Soviet," he said bluntly, "to believe that peasants cannot be wreckers." This was the signal that repression against officials had ended, and large-scale repression of peasants would begin again. In reporting the results of his tour to Eikhe, Pozdniakov recounted the numerous examples of "peasant-kulaks" he had encountered who engaged in anti-Soviet agitation or outright sabotage. To Pozdniakov and other high Party leaders in Western Siberia, peasants were no longer protected by their socialist identities as collective or state farm workers. The countryside was suddenly full of peasant kulaks and needed to be cleansed.[28]

JUNE PLENARY MEETINGS

Plenipotentiary reports such as the one submitted by Pozdniakov re-inforced the warnings contained in reports that were arriving from local NKVD offices, and these reiterated the warnings in Mironov's summary report to Eikhe in June about the potential for rebellion. In fact, Mironov's report may have played a key role in the process that led to Order 00447. On the basis of that report, Eikhe telegrammed the Cen-tral Committee about the presence in Western Siberia of rebellious kulak populations and other anti-Soviet elements. He reiterated the same threat at the June plenum of the Party's Central Committee. No stenographic record was made of the first several days of that plenum, which lasted from the twenty-third to the twenty-ninth of the month. Fragmentary evidence, however, suggests that Eikhe made a strong case for mass repression, based on the situation in Western Siberia.[29] Ye-zhov's thesis for the plenum also referred to the situation in Western Siberia in the same language as Mironov's report. The district was in a pre-rebellion state, where a "major [diversionary] organization" had united a "partisan-rebellious cadre of *spetspereselentsy*," into a poten-tially counterrevolutiionary force. The subversive organization that Yezhov named was none other than the ubiquitous anti-Soviet military union, the ROVS, about which Mironov had warned. Interestingly, Yezhov's thesis included twelve points about counterrevolutionary ac-tivities. Ten of these concerned conspiratorial groups in state, Party, or military organizations. Only two of the twelve mentioned mass-rebel-lious situations—the one in Western Siberia, and an analogous situation in Orenburg oblast. There, mass numbers of Cossack populations were supposedly organizing for an uprsing.[30]

The ordering of Yezhov's thesis points casts doubt on the argument that Stalin was being pressured by local leaders to engage in mass social repression.[31] Rather, Eikhe's presentation and Yezhov's theses speak more to Stalin's careful and typical scripting of the plenum in order to achieve his goals. The Orenburg and Western Siberian situations pro-vided Stalin with the pretext he wanted in order to justify the purges and to begin a campaign of mass social repression. On 28 June, based on

Eikhe's telegram and report to the plenum, the Politburo formally ac-knowledged the threat in Western Siberia of a "counterrevolutionary rebellious organization," made up of exiles and kulaks. The resolution approved the application of shooting sentences to all "activists" of such an organization. In order to expedite the review of cases outside of nor-mal judicial processes, the Politburo also approved formation of an ad-ministrative board—a *troika*—made of Eikhe, Barkov (the district pros-ecutor), and Mironov.[32] This was the first of the purge troikas and the model for the rest. Several days later, on 2 July, the Politburo approved the circulation of a letter to all republic, oblast, and district Party heads, which addressed the issue of "anti-Soviet elements." That letter called for the establishment of troikas similar to the one set up in Western Siberia throughout all autonomous republics, oblasts, and every *krai* in the country. The organization of the troikas followed the same basic pattern and consisted of the oblast or district Party head, the chief procurator, and the NKVD chief.[33]

Using Western Siberia as a pretext and as a model was consistent with Stalin's previous practice. In 1928, he used peasant resistance in West-ern Siberia as the pretext to implement forced measures of grain pro-curement, a policy that led quickly enough to the bloody drive for col-lectivization and dekulakization. In 1930, Stalin appointed Robert Eikhe as district Party chief, and Eikhe proved himself a trusted mem-ber of Stalin's elite. Eikhe was ruthless, and Stalin counted on him sev-eral times to help script and carry out harsh repressive policies.[34] In the autumn of 1934, in response to continuing peasant resistance in the dis-trict, Eikhe requested permission from the Politburo to set up special troikas to shoot a number of offenders, and to publicize this process as an example to the population.[35] The scenario that played out in June 1937 resembled the scenario from October 1934. The difference be-tween 1934 and 1937 was that in 1934, Stalin limited the use of troikas and extrajudicial executions to a short period of time, to fewer numbers of people, and to just several areas of the country—Western Siberia and the Far Eastern district. In 1934, Stalin needed to make examples in order to break spontaneous and sporadic resistance to the regime's poli-cies. In 1937, however, Stalin believed or convinced himself and the Party that the country was facing a potential uprising. This latter situ-ation justified and demanded the wider use of violent repression.

The Politburo instruction of 2 July gave local authorities little time to make their lists—just five days—and this deadline precluded any pretense of drawn out investigative activity. Central authorities most certainly expected local officials to compile lists simply by categories and names of people taken directly from NKVD registries.[36] There is also a distinct possibility that central NKVD officials already had figures, taken from their own centralized catalogs, and supplemented those numbers with figures arriving from localities. In any case, the process was, by necessity and in typical NKVD fashion, hasty and crude, with little attention given to accuracy of information. It was the epitome of mass repression by category, by list.

In Western Siberia, as in other parts of the country, Yezhov's 3 July order set in motion a flurry of activity. Time was short, even if district authorities already possessed information from regions. In Novosibirsk, NKVD authorities commandeered a building in the city's center as a clearing house to cull registry lists. Officers brought registry catalogs to the site and received permission from the district Party committee to "mobilize" NKVD academy students and Komsomol activists. These were set to the task of poring through the *kartoteki* and registry information to pull together lists of exiles, known criminals, and ex-convicts, as well as other groups who fit the category of socially dangerous. By July 8, Mironov had already submitted to Eikhe a detailed list of "enemies" who allegedly had infiltrated grain procurement and processing centers in the district.[37] Mironov attended the 16 and 17 July meetings in Moscow, and was back in Novosibirsk for a 25 July meeting with his own subordinate NKVD heads. At that meeting, Mironov read a draft of what would become Order 00447. Mironov told his officers that the order was in the final stages of approval at the "directive level," meaning the Politburo. He also informed officers of the quotas that had been established for the two categories of those to be repressed, and he gave instructions on how to write the cases and sentences of those to be arrested in simplified form. Mironov said that an operational directive would follow soon, and that all units should be prepared for immediate operations.[38]

OPERATIONAL ORDER 00447

On 31 July 1937, the Politburo approved and Yezhov issued Order 00447. The order placed Yezhov's deputy, M. P. Frinovskii, in charge

of its execution. The order called for operations to begin between 5 and
15 August and to continue for a period of four months. The order gave
an overall quota figure of 259,450 individuals to be arrested; of these,
72,950 were to be shot as category I enemies. The remainder were to be
sentenced to internment in camps or high-security prisons from eight
to ten years. As noted above, Order 00447 listed troika members for
each autonomous republic, district, and oblast and it gave troikas extraordinary powers to pass sentences of execution. The Politburo had
approved the occasional and limited use of troikas during the 1930s,
but this was the first time since the dekulakization campaigns in the
early 1930s that administrative boards were given such sweeping authority and on such a countrywide scale.[39] Troikas were instructed to
process cases quickly, with only the minimum of accusatory information
based on shortened arrest and indictment forms. In this hasty process,
operational officers were told not to bother with the procedural requirements of face-to-face interviews with witnesses or even with the
accused.[40] Yezhov underlined the importance of the operation by requiring NKVD heads to submit telegraphed, classified reports every five
days on the progress of the operation. Political police units were to take
special care to maintain secrecy in order to prevent flight of the contingents to be arrested, or the formation of resistance bands.

Secrecy was important, in operational particulars, and in general.
Yezhov, for example, stressed the need for strict secrecy in carrying out
shooting sentences, especially the time and place of executions.[41] In the
25 July operational meeting in Novosibirsk, Mironov also stressed secrecy in this aspect of the operations. He elaborated, instructing that
operational commanders were responsible for finding appropriately discreet places for executions. Places of execution and burial were to be
kept strictly secret. After executions were carried out, burial grounds
were to be hidden, as much as possible, "so as not to become places of
religious fanaticism for believers or contras" (*kontriki,* slang for counterrevolutionaries). Mironov directed, more generally, that the numbers
involved in the repressions be kept strictly secret. He familiarized officers with arrest quotas for the district, in order, as he said, to impress
them with the scale and importance of the operations, but he warned his
officers that, once noted, they were to forget these figures. "The numbers that you hear should die in your head; those of you who can,
should wipe these figures from your head; those of you who are not

able to forget them should try to do so, anyway, since the slightest mention (*razglashenie*) of general figures will land the perpetrator in front of a military tribunal." Mironov warned his officers that "under no circumstances" were they to divulge, even to procuracy officials, how many arrests were being made in each of the two categories. At the end of his talk, Mironov reiterated that officers maintain secrecy in carrying out all aspects of the operations, lest the NKVD itself be the outlet for public knowledge of the mass repressions.[42]

This kind of secrecy went beyond the normal conspiratorial practices of the political police. Once informed about the operations, even Vyshinskii bound his subordinates to silence. In a secret memorandum from August, the chief prosecutor warned those involved in troikas not to divulge aspects of the operation even to colleagues and subordinates within the procuracy apparatus.[43] This was an unusual measure, one of the only times—perhaps the only time—that Vyshinskii demanded such discretion from his subordinates. Monitoring NKVD conduct was one of the primary tasks of the procuracy system, and one that was discussed openly. Issues of NKVD conduct, and especially arrest procedures and numbers, provided constant fare for procuracy operational meetings. Yet beginning in the autumn and then into January 1938, Vyshinskii allowed less and less discussion of the NKVD in operational gatherings. In an operational meeting in January 1938, for example, the chief procurator from the Uzbek city of Kakanda tried to raise the issue of relations with the NKVD. Vyshinskii cut him short in mid-sentence. "That question," Vyshinskii said curtly, would be "handled secretly." After this short exchange, the chair of the session quickly closed discussion and returned the floor to Vyshinskii for his closing remarks.[44]

Regime officials were not in the habit of making public arrest figures from mass operations, but neither were they shy about public knowledge of repression. Public reporting of show trials of supposed counterrevolutionaries, ranging from the sensational trials of Bolshevik leaders in Moscow to public trials in nearly every oblast and district in the country, was an important part of the purge process in 1937 and 1938. These show trials served a legitimizing and didactic purpose, and Central Committee officials gave precise instructions to local leaders on how many such trials they were to hold and what kind of charges were to be brought. Instructions always included reminders to publicize the trials widely through press reports and in meetings. The mass repressions were a different matter. The regime's leaders attempted to keep the scale of these purges secret, and to keep overall information about them limited, as much as possible, to commanding personnel and participants.

Why this was so is unclear, except for the obvious reason that officials worried about negative public reaction should knowledge of mass repression become widely broadcast. Trials of well-known figures, and even reports of counterrevolutionary plots and underground organization were one thing. Such organizations could be described publicly as dangerous and vaguely ubiquitous, but public knowledge that police were engaged in mass shootings of citizens was another matter altogether. That knowledge had to be kept secret. The very nature of mass repression, of course, made it difficult to keep the operations secret, but the attempt to limit knowledge stemmed apparently from purely political rather than moral considerations. Leaders such as Molotov and Kaganovich justified the purges even into their old age, as did officers and rank-and-file political policemen, at least those who survived the purging process. Depositions of officers arrested after the purges reveal no remorse, only regret, at most, that "some" procedural rules were not followed. One officer in attendance at Mironov's Novosibirsk operational briefing in July 1937 later recorded that he and his colleagues received their commander's report with "boisterous approval" (*shumnym odobreniem*). To these men, the danger was real and the enemy everywhere.[45]

In addition to secrecy, one other aspect distinguished the mass purges from previous practices of social repression. As Mironov described to his NKVD officers, normal legal procedures were to be suspended for operations carried out under Order 00447. No procuracy sanctions were needed for arrests. Mironov instructed operational commanders to provide the district procuracy office only with a list of names and only after arrests were made. Lists were to include the minimal amount of information. In addition to names, lists should indicate whether those arrested were kulaks or criminals, under what statute they were arrested, and the date of arrest. "That is all that you should put into the list that goes to the procuracy," said Mironov.[46] Reemphasizing the need for secrecy and control of information, Mironov told his subordinates that they were to prepare only four copies of arrest lists. A list of those to be arrested would be sent to the heads of regional and city NKVD offices in each operational sector of the district. Heads of operational sectors would keep one copy of arrest lists for their own records. A third copy would go to the district-level operational commander for review by the troikas, and one list would go to the district-level procuracy office. In this way, complete lists of arrests for the entire district would exist only at the central district level—in the NKVD headquarters, the records of the troikas, and in the chief procurator's office. Heads of operational sectors would have lists only for their sectors, and regional commanders would know of arrests only in their respective regions.

These procedures violated the constitution as well as long-established procedural codes, and they made it virtually impossible for procurators to review cases or protest arrest decisions. The problem lay not only in the sheer number of arrests; there were no case materials for procurators to review, only lists of arrest protocols. Moreover, local procurators were excluded entirely from the process, since they did not even receive arrest lists. These went only to the district chief procurator, who was a member of the area's troika sentencing board. Thus, the NKVD set up the operations not only to expedite the process of repression, but to make the purge full proof against procuracy interference. Indeed, Yezhov and UNKVD commanders made it clear that no punishments would follow from mass arrests, and that central authorities would overlook simplified procedures.[47]

Such methods were justified on the grounds of state security and as emergency measures, and Vyshinskii fell dutifully into line in accepting these procedures. And that line was surely set down by Stalin and no one else. As head of the Western Siberian NKVD, Mironov was a powerful man, but he did not have the authority alone to suspend constitutional and legal norms. Neither did Yezhov, for that matter, though not for want of trying. Throughout the 1930s, political police carried out arrests while ignoring procuratorial sanction, and Yezhov, and Yagoda before him, did little to stop the practice. On the other side, procuracy officials complained often, and were not afraid to use their authority to nullify such arrests. As late as March 1937, Vyshinskii issued a stern warning to local prosecutors reminding them to monitor and prevent violations of arrest procedures, particularly attempts to carry out arrests without prior sanction.[48] In June, as noted above, Vyshinskii again reacted strongly, this time to an order from the chief of the Moscow police to exempt the city from the normal arrest procedures. Vyshinskii instructed his deputy Bomash to protest the order and to draft a letter to the Moscow police chief, requiring him to rescind the order as unconstitutional, and as a violation of procedures established as far back as the 8 May 1933 instructions on arrests and mass repressions.[49]

The Moscow police order may very well have been issued in conjunction with preparations for the mass purges. If so, Vyshinskii had not yet been informed of the special circumstances under which the operations were to proceed. He was soon brought into the picture. By August, Vyshinskii instructed deputies who sat on troikas not to interfere in NKVD arrests. "Observance of procedural norms and prior arrest sanctions are not required," he wrote. Troika decisions were final and not to be protested, except under extraordinary circumstances, and then only to Vyshinskii directly.[50] Vyshinskii was not afraid to take on Yagoda or Yezhov over issues of NKVD violations, so his sudden turnabout must have been the result of a direct communication from either Stalin or, more likely, Molotov. Judging by correspondence and stenographic records, it was Molotov who dealt with Vyshinskii throughout much of 1937 and 1938 over questions of procuracy activities and jurisdiction. In any case, Vyshinskii offered no objections in principle to the suspension of legal procedures, indeed justifying the emergency measures with the infamous line about history, itself, setting outdated laws aside.[51]

FIRST PHASE: JULY 1937–JANUARY 1938

As in the early 1930s, the peasant "kulak" bore the brunt of the police's repressive campaigns, at least in Western Siberia. By October 1937, 14,886 kulaks and 5,009 individuals with criminal records had been arrested and sentenced by special NKVD troikas in the *krai*. As of the above date, authorities had sentenced 9,843 of this number to be shot and 5,568 to terms of eight to ten years in labor camps.[52] An additional 3,480 individuals had also been swept up in the hunt for criminals and kulaks that summer. Police listed these individuals, fitting into neither category, simply as "other counterrevolutionary elements." In related operations, police (including the *militsiia* and GUGB units) netted an additional 3,702 individuals with unsavory backgrounds. The latter included several former Russian princes, counts, and landowners —74 in all—646 former White army officers, 400 former "bandits" and tsarist police officials, 236 former commercial trade agents, 450 priests or believers, and 149 former members of the Socialist Revolutionary Party. In all, police sweeps in the summer and autumn of 1937 led to the arrest of 25,413 kulaks, criminals or former criminals, and other socially dangerous elements in Western Siberia. By 5 October, NKVD special troikas had passed sentences on 19,421 of all those arrested; 12,876 had been sentenced to execution and 6,093 had received sentences of eight to ten years in labor camps. Only 452 individuals received the lightest sentence recorded—five years in a camp. One hundred thirty-four of those arrested had been released, and the cases of only 31 individuals had been transferred to the regular court system. By early October, authorities had carried out sentences on 9,525 individuals.

The figures reported above were included in two separate reports, or *svodki,* prepared by the operational secretariat of the Western Siberian NKVD for the district Party's central committee. One of the *svodki,* a summary report of all mass operations to date, broke down the arrest and sentencing figures by region, fifteen in all, and included the original target figures for arrest in each region.[53] Target figures were given for each of the social groups of kulaks and criminals to be arrested, and these target figures were further divided into category I or II for each social group. Category I arrestees were considered especially dangerous types to be executed or given maximum sentences in confinement. Category II included those to be sentenced to varying periods in labor camps. Target limits for kulaks and criminals were listed in the first columns of the table. Actual arrest figures, broken down in the same manner, were listed in the second set of columns. The columns that followed included the numbers in each social grouping sentenced to shooting, or to labor camps for ten, eight, or five years. The final page of the table provided a summary for the whole of the *krai.*

From this table, it is clear that the NKVD in Western Siberia concentrated their first series of mass operations in the summer of 1937 in the traditionally unruly areas of the south and west: Biisk *raion,* the cities of Barnaul and Tomsk, Stalinsk *raion,* the mining district of Kemerovo, and the Marinsk, Kamensk, and Cherepanov *raiony.* These had been centers of strong peasant resistance to collectivization in the early 1930s, and areas to which many exiles and former kulaks had returned during the course of the decade.[54] In addition, these regions had all experienced large-scale immigration during the decade of the 1930s of workers seeking employment in the new industrial towns, and of large numbers of marginal populations pushed east by the imposition of passport and rationing restrictions in western cities of the Soviet Union. From similar reports in early autumn, it is clear that police also targeted the mostly non-Russian Altai and Narym areas, and the industrial cities of the Kuzbass. The latter, too, had seen strong resistance to Stalinist policies, both agrarian and industrial, and had undergone a large influx of new populations during the industrialization period of the early 1930s. As a result, police regarded the populations in the Western Siberian areas as especially dangerous.

One of the major police operations in Western Siberia in the summer of 1937 targeted the system of grain procurement centers throughout the district. Already by 8 July of that year, Mironov had submitted a report to the Party's secretariat, based on information gathered by *raion*-level police, that detailed the "extreme contamination" of the procurement system by "class-harmful and criminal elements."[55] Based on a review of the thirty largest centers, Mironov estimated that 400 to 500 such individuals were working in responsible positions, and these did not include another 259 that had already been removed and arrested. In addition to the dreaded and ubiquitous kulaks, Mironov listed other dangerous groups: White officers, former *lishentsy,* former small-time traders and commercial agents, and former convicts. Interestingly, Mironov also named groups of political refugees working in procurement centers as suspect populations. The latter included people who had fled from Germany, Poland, the Baltic states, Romania, and finally, from the Far East—the *dal'nevostochniki.*[56]

At the end of his report, Mironov included a list of 218 names. Each name was followed by a brief designation of the individual's job and what made that person suspect as a member of a harmful social category. At the Barnaul procurement center, for example, the driver Kamenets was suspect as a refugee from Romania. The assistant manager of the same center, Kurzhamov, was related to a kulak family and was, himself, an "unstable element." The typist Tamara Koroleva was the wife of a former White officer; L. V. Livshits, who worked as a clerk at the Zyriansk center, was serving a five-year sentence of administrative exile from Leningrad; and Mikhail Polkovnikov, a mechanic at the Biisk center, was suspect because he had been stripped of his voting rights in 1929. The report gave no information why Polkovnikov had lost his rights or whether, according to the new constitution, he had, in fact, regained them. Many of those included on the list were *lishentsy* or former *lishentsy*. Many were on the list because of a past criminal conviction or because of kulak connections. Thus, Vasilii Kliushkov, an agronomist, was on the list because his father had been a kulak exiled to the Narym region. Others were either married to a kulak or in some other way related to a kulak family.

As Mironov's lists showed, the peasant "kulak" and other exiles were the main targets of mass repression in 1937 and 1938, at least in Western Siberia, although the widespread campaign of repression of those years was more than another dekulakization campaign. In the country, in general, the first mass waves of arrests and executions appear to have been made up largely of criminals already in custody, the unemployed, those with previous convictions and police arraignments, and individuals in other marginal populations who could easily be identified and rounded up. By mid-August 1937, just two weeks after Order 00447 was issued, nearly 200,000 individuals had already been arrested in just 57 oblasts of the country, and 14,305 had already been sentenced.[57] As Iunge and Binner have pointed out, review of the arrest protocols of these individuals shows that many were already in police custody and awaiting trial, or were individuals under suspicion, whose cases could not be sent to court for lack of evidence, or whose cases had been quashed. "There were many such cases in the files of the *ugolovnyi rozysk*," write Iunge and Binner, and this is confirmed by the police chief Mikhail Shreider. In his memoirs, Shreider noted that, in summer of 1937, his jails were bursting with criminal arrestees. He recalled the strong pressure from the beginning of the mass operations to hand over the many criminals in his custody to the GUGB as political terrorists and diversionaries. The cases of these individuals were easily transferred to the newly formed troikas, which were already in session and reviewing cases by the end of the first week of August.[58]

Shreider claimed that he resisted the pressure to give "his" criminals to the purge troikas, but this appears to have been exactly what happened in at least two other oblasts. In the Western oblast, near the border with Poland, NKVD operational units had already arrested by 1 August twice as many individuals under category I as the number prescribed in Order 00447 (2,000 instead of 1,000). Similarly, in Omsk, Order 00447 provided for a limit of 1,000 arrests under category I, but within days after the issuing of the order, the Omsk UNKVD listed over 3,000 people under category I arrest. By mid-August, the Omsk UNKVD held 5,444 people under category I.[59] At the same time, the Omsk troika did not carry out its first review of cases until the fifth or sixth of the month. Very likely, in both the Western and Omsk oblasts, many of the UNKVD "arrests" under Order 00447 were no more than a bureaucratic transfer of case files from judicial to troika jurisdiction, and a reclassification of criminal offenders into dangerous political insurgents.

Mass convictions of criminals and marginals under Order 00447 served an important purpose—not just to get quick results, but also, and importantly, to clear already crowded jails for the many who were to follow. In 1933, the OGPU and police faced a similar problem at the start of the social defense campaigns, when Yagoda, Stalin, and the Politburo were considering mass arrests of socially marginal populations in the wake of dekulakization. Jails were overcrowded then, as well, with large numbers of criminals, dispossessed people, petty lawbreakers, and the human flotsam and jetsam of Stalin's agrarian and industrial policies. In the earlier preparation for mass repression, the OGPU solved the problem of overcrowded jails in part by mass transfer of existing prisoners to newly opened special settlements. Most however, were simply released—nearly 400,000 people. These measures freed up nearly half a million prison spaces in 1933, which were quickly filled again with those arrested under passport and other social defense laws. In 1937, political leaders did not consider release as an option; nor for that matter did NKVD officers worry about the procedural codes prescribing limits on numbers of prisoners. The main concern in 1937 was the physical amount of space available to put the expected influx of arrestees. In the summer of 1937, the NKVD solved the problem of overcrowded jails and space by a simple and brutally expedient redefinition of prisoners under Order 00447—by incarcerating most in camps as politically dangerous, and by executing the rest as active counterrevolutionaries. The difference in the way the regime handled petty criminals during the social repressions of the early 1930s and the purges of the late 1930s is striking, an indication of how attitudes had changed toward the country's marginal and criminal populations. The change in policy was also indicative of the changed perception of threat by the regime's leaders, and the fear of war and its consequences.

By the end of September and beginning of October 1937, a number of oblasts and districts were already reaching their initial arrest limits. Such was the case in Omsk and the Western oblast, of course, but also in Western Siberia, in Orenburg oblast, and in other areas of the country. As they reached initial arrest quotas, regional police and Party officials appealed to central authorities to raise limits. Requests flowed along one of several lines. In some cases, oblast, *krai,* and republic Party committees appealed to the Central Committee, which meant of course, a letter to Stalin or to Stalin and Molotov. In other cases, the head of the regional UNKVD appealed to Yezhov, as head of the NKVD, but also in his capacity as a Central Committee secretary. In most cases, requests to raise limits were signed jointly by the head of the Party committee and the UNKVD chief, and were addressed to the Central Committee, specifically to Stalin and Yezhov. By the end of the year, Party or police leaders, or both, had requested increases in arrest limits in nineteen republic, oblast, and *krai* territories. These nineteen represented about one-third of all administrative territories in the country.[60] Stalin or the Politburo approved these requests—at times recommending even higher limits than those requested—which raised the official arrest limit under Order 00447 by as many as 40,000 individuals by year's end. As arrest tables show, however, the overall number of people repressed during the mass purge exceeded the official limit, even with the increases. This was so since, in a number of cases, Stalin approved requests without official Politburo consideration. In a number of cases, Yezhov also approved increases without consulting Stalin. Overall, some 300,000 people were arrested over and above original limits without Politburo approval.[61] In some oblasts, limits were raised two and three times, as was the case in Orenburg, Western Siberia, and in the Western oblast. In the ultimate absurdity, officials in Novosibirsk considered exchanging quotas from the Altai of different categories of arrestees, since the latter territory had not yet reached its limit.[62]

Pressure to increase quotas came from above as well as from below. In many cases, in fact, requests for upward revisions came in the wake of pressure from the center. For example, a wave of requests and approvals followed Yezhov's circular telegram in early November to intensify repressive campaigns against anti-Soviet "elements" and national minorities. Similar increases followed the first and second extensions of Order 00447 in December 1937 and late January 1938. Many increases resulted from competition among "careerist-oriented" officers, and this was a competition that Yezhov encouraged. One of Yezhov's assistants, Lulov, testified that "UNKVD heads knew that those who reached their given limit . . . were given a new limit from the Narkom, and they were seen as the better officers, better and faster than others in fulfilling and overfulfilling Yezhov's directive to rout the counterrevolution." Lulov recalled an incident in which the head of the Ivanovo UNKVD, A. P. Radzivilovskii, stopped into his office, just after a meeting with Yezhov. Radzivilovskii was bursting with pride that Yezhov had commended his work and had given him a new, higher arrest quota. Lulov later mentioned the incident to Yezhov, who commented, in turn, "Good for Radzivilovskii. He came to see me and I gave him a new quota." Lulov reported similar incidents involving other officers as typical behavior in the atmosphere fostered by Yezhov.[63]

STALIN'S KILLERS

Radzivilovskii's career exemplified how the patronage or clan system worked in the NKVD, and how that system contributed to the spiraling increase in arrest numbers during the mass purges. Radzivilovskii was a Komsomol recruit from the Caucasus who climbed quickly through the ranks to a position in the mid-1930s in Moscow under the infamous S. F. Redens, the head of the Moscow oblast UNKVD. Under Redens' patronage, Radzivilovskii worked as head of the Secret Political Department and then as assistant head of the Moscow oblast UNKVD. These were powerful positions, and they enabled Radzivilovskii to create his own "family" of appointees, mainly of regional-level UNKVD heads and their assistants. According to a later deposition by one of Radzivilovskii's deputies, the chief kept the loyalty of his appointees in a fashion typical of the culture of the political police—by dispensing favors such as apartment assignments, and by keeping a current file of compromising material on all his staff.[64] Using both the carrot of material benefits and the stick of threatened exposure, Radzivilovskii, like other ranking officers, built networks of loyal subordinates and protected himself from incrimination.

As head of the UNKVD, Radzivilovskii also came into contact with Lazar Kaganovich, one of Stalin's closest aides, and then head of the Moscow Party organization. It was with the active support and encouragement of Kaganovich and Redens that Radzivilovskii helped put Moscow into "first place" in the fight against counterrevolution and the enemies of the people.[65] Published records and archeological excavations, especially in the Kuntsevo region, south of the city, testify to the brutal intensity of the mass purges in and around Moscow, which was largely the work of Redens and his deputy, and of the local UNKVD heads who answered to their patrons.[66] Radzivilovskii pleased his superiors well enough, receiving an Order of Lenin medal from Kaganovich, so that Yezhov entrusted him to head the UNKVD in Ivanovo, and to carry out purges there in the same manner and with the same support as he had in Moscow. Shreider, who had known Radzivilovskii since the mid-1920s, encountered him again in Ivanovo, when the former was assigned as head of the *militsiia* in that oblast. Radzivilovskii was a changed man, according to Shreider—schooled first in the "cynical careerism" of Yagoda's NKVD, and then transformed completely by just a year working under Yezhov. Yezhov's "school of falsification . . . completed [Radzivilovskii's] transformation into a consummate careerist, not in the least squeamish to use any methods in order to ingratiate himself with those higher up, and in that way to move himself up closer to the heights of power." With the arrival of Radzivilovskii and his "company" in Ivanovo, the numbers of arrests and executions rose sharply in the oblast, according to Shreider. Radzivilovskii boasted of his "work" in Moscow, and of his special relations with Party and NKVD leaders. His personal association with Redens, Yezhov, and Kaganovich emboldened Radzivilovskii to carry out his assignment in Ivanovo with the ruthless confidence that he was accomplishing the "special" tasks of the Party and the government.[67]

Shreider came into conflict with Radzivilovskii on numerous occasions over the use of the civil police in purge arrests, interrogations, and executions. Tensions became so strained that Shreider became convinced he would be arrested if he stayed longer in his post in Ivanovo. He was familiar with the NKVD officers' practice to concoct "provocational" information about rivals or those who stood in the way in order to have them arrested. This was the other side of the coin of the clan system, and contributed to mass bloodbaths among rival groups. Shreider understood this well, having suffered demotion for his involvement in an anti-Yagoda group during the early 1930s. He also knew that reassignment was a good way to avoid the fate of arrest.[68] In

December 1937, Shreider used his own still high connections in the NKVD police hierarchy to obtain a reassignment. This was easy enough to do, since arrests within the NKVD organs had left a number of positions vacant. One of those vacant posts was in Western Siberia. In January 1938, Shreider arrived in Novosibirsk to take up his new post as head of the RKM in the newly formed Novosibirsk oblast.[69] Unfortunately for Shreider, his new posting amounted to a jump from the proverbial frying pan to the fire, for the head of the UNKVD in Western Siberia was Grigorii Fedorovich Gorbach, one of Stalin's most energetic killers.

Gorbach's career, like that of Radzivilovskii, accounted for some of the worst excesses of the purges. His career also exemplified the way in which Stalin and Yezhov used the rotating assignment of particular officers to manipulate the purge process. Arriving in a new posting with their own "clans," officers such as Gorbach could renew and intensify the purge cycle by using the excuse that the previous leaders had been slow or inefficient, or had themselves been counterrevolutionaries. Just a week prior to the start of the mass operations, for example, Gorbach was assigned, on the personal recommendation of Stalin, to head the UNKVD of Omsk oblast. That oblast, in the southwest of Siberia, had been a major center for deportation of peasants and socially dangerous types throughout the 1930s. Stalin was supposedly not pleased with the low arrest quotas that had been sent in by the previous UNKVD chief, and he sent Gorbach to replace that predecessor.[70] Arriving in Omsk in late July, Gorbach immediately requested an increase in category I arrests from the modest number of 479 to 1,000. As noted above, arrests tripled even that number by the start of the operations, and increased yet again one and a half times by mid-August to 5,444 individuals. Still not satisfied, Gorbach requested a final limit of 8,000. Stalin personally approved Gorbach's request and raised it to 9,000 arrests.[71]

Having accomplished his task in Omsk, Gorbach received a new assignment in mid-August 1937 to Novosibirsk, the center of the Western Siberian territory. Shreider met Gorbach there in early January 1938. By that time, Gorbach had done in Western Siberia what he had done in Omsk, nearly tripling the number of those arrested under category I from the original quotas (from 5,000 to nearly 14,000).[72] Shreider was "shocked and overwhelmed" by the level of repression in the oblast, especially the mass arrest of some 25,000 military veterans who had fought in the Russian imperial army during the war with Germany from 1914 to 1918. These veterans were supposedly part of the military-monarchist conspiracy in the territory to overthrow the Soviet regime. Shreider quickly understood that the "bloody" progress of the purge in Novosibirsk far outstripped even what he had seen in Ivanovo under Radzivilovskii.[73] Within a month of his arrival in Novosibirsk, Shreider again pressed for reassignment, and received a new posting to Kazakhstan in February 1938. Gorbach remained in Western Siberia until the spring. In late May 1938, he was assigned to the Far East territory where, stationed in Khabarovsk, he requested and received permission to increase overall arrest quotas from 10,000 to 20,000. Gorbach's killing spree ended with his own arrest in November 1938, one of the first of Yezhov's underlings to be purged when Stalin began to wind down the purges, and to execute, in turn, the executioners.[74]

Some of the worst excesses of the purges occurred in the oblasts that came under Gorbach's control. His personal sadism meshed well with Stalin's paranoia, and with Stalin's strategy. Stalin used his loyal executioner to clean out areas of the country—the southern Urals, Western Siberia, and the Far East—that had been the most inundated with exiles and socially marginal populations. Similarly, Stalin had Yezhov assign another uniquely qualified sadist, V. A. Karutskii, to head the UNKVD in the Western oblast. This area, too, was particularly vulnerable, "saturated" with marginal populations who had been deported from or denied residence in the major capitals of Moscow, Kiev, and Leningrad. In addition, explained Karutskii in early August 1937, the recently arrested Party leaders in the oblast had not pursued dekulakization in the early 1930s with appropriate vigor and, as a result, only 5,000 of 22,000 supposed kulaks had been exiled from the area. Thus, according to Karutskii and the newly appointed Party secretary, D. S. Korotchenkov, kulak and anti-Soviet elements in the oblast constituted a major potential threat in case of war, especially given the proximity of the oblast to the western frontier. Karutskii, who had been removed from his post in Western Siberia for excessive drinking, was assigned to the Western oblast as a second chance to redeem himself. He did so by overfulfilling his arrest quotas even as Order 00447 was put into effect. Already by the end of July, he had arrested 2,000 former kulaks, twice as many as the original quota, and in early August, Karutskii informed Yezhov of an additional 11,000 "counterrevolutionary" and "criminal elements." Under Karutskii, as noted above, the Western oblast UNKVD came to rival the Omsk police under Gorbach, in rates of arrest of the local population. Both served well the purpose of the purges to rid the country of populations that the regime regarded as dangerous.[75]

PHASE II: OCTOBER 1937 – FEBRUARY 1938

Arrests of former kulaks and social marginals were not the only mass repressions in the late summer and autumn of 1937. In addition to arrests under Order 00447, UNKVD units also began rounding up large numbers of people belonging to certain ethnic minorities. These so-called nationality operations were carried out under their own separate orders. Yezhov issued the first of these orders on 25 July 1937 just days before the antikulak and anticriminal operations—Order 00439, to arrest all German refugees in the country as well as German nationals working in enterprises as guest workers. Deportation and arrest operations would follow in the coming years against the large population of citizens of German descent in the central Volga and Western Siberian regions. Arrests of large numbers of Polish immigrants and refugees began with Order 00485, issued on 11 August 1937. Similarly, NKVD Order 00593, issued in late September, called for the arrest of all those who had worked on the Harbin railroad line, who were made up of people of different nationalities, including many Russians, but were all regarded by the regime's leaders as "alien" elements. The *kharbintsy*, in leaders' evaluation, were contaminated by foreign influence, and were therefore potential spies for the Japanese. By mid-September, nearly 31,000 *kharbintsy* had been arrested. Likewise, in late 1937, 170,000 citizens of Korean descent were exiled from border regions in Siberia. The Koreans were not regarded as political enemies, but they were nonetheless forced to leave their homes and to move *en masse* to new settlements in Kazakhstan and Uzbekistan. In 1937 and 1938, political police mounted mass arrest operations also against Latvian immigrants and citizens of Latvian background, as well as those of Finnish origin. In all, by mid-September, nearly 228,000 people had been arrested under the so-called nationality operations. This figure did not include the Korean deportees, but did include substantial numbers of refugees and citizens of Greek, Romanian, and Iranian descent, as well as other ethnic groups.[76]

These nationality purges decimated the foreign refugee and ethnic communities that they affected. The "Polish operations" alone resulted in the repression in some form of nearly 20 percent of that community —some 131,000 out of a population registered at 656,000 in 1937. The "German operations" led to the arrest of about 5 percent of that community.[77] In order to process such numbers, special troikas (*osobye troiki*) were set up, which in fact consisted of the same functionaries as those who sat on the 00447 troikas—the Party secretaries, chief procurators, and NKVD heads of republics, oblasts, and autonomous regions. Review of so many files was such a burdensome task that the regime quickly authorized the formation of two-man boards (*dvoiki*), consisting of UNKVD and procuracy heads, and often just NKVD heads. These officials reviewed files in the most expeditious manner possible— by simply signing what the NKVD gave them.

The nationality operations began in late summer and autumn of 1937, and ran unabated throughout 1938. The operations against kulaks and criminals, by contrast, intensified and peaked in the late autumn of 1937 and the early winter of 1937/1938. By the end of December 1937, the NKVD had arrested some 600,000 people under Order 00447. This number represented nearly 78 percent of the total number of 770,000 arrested by the time the operations were brought officially to a close in November 1938. The intensity of mass arrests that autumn and winter had much to do with the original deadline for the operations, which was mid-December 1937. As that deadline approached, Yezhov began issuing circulars to maintain the pace of arrests. This pressure created a problem for local UNKVD units. The first wave of mass arrests in August and September exhausted the numbers most easily accessible for repression—those listed in various *kartoteki* and active police investigative files, and those already in detention. The pressure for more arrests forced operational units and local UNKVD administrators to come up with new contingents when few were easily available. P. A. Yegorov, then an UNKVD chief in Tomsk, recalled the increasing flow of telegrams from Gorbach, in Novosibirsk, beginning in late September and early October: first 1,500, then another 2,000, then 3,000 more, and so on. And these were not maximum limits as were the quotas listed in the original order. The new limits were minimum quotas, Yegorov recalled. In other words, units were not allowed to arrest fewer than the number specified, while no upper limit was given.[78]

This was a new kind of pressure, and it marked a turning point in the mass repressions. Up until October, arrests had been based on lists of names, which officers had compiled from political and civil police records. The control figures from the original order were based on those lists and corresponded to the names of real people. Thus, regardless of the moral and legal issues of guilt or innocence, there existed at least a professional logic to the arrests in the first phase of the purges. Political policemen believed in this professional logic; they believed in the veracity of their catalogs. The logic of this process led many *Chekists*, at least according to Yegorov, to justify the early phase of the purges, and to distinguish that phase from the later phases. Figures after October, by contrast, were not based on any kind of "investigative" or even catalog work. The new figures were abstract ones, and did not correspond to any lists or names in registry catalogs or police files. Whatever qualms officials such as Yegorov may have had about the first waves of arrests, they understood clearly that these new control figures were fictional, the more so since these figures were minimal limits. As September moved into October, and the control figures kept coming, Yegorov recalled that "many of us no longer understood the sense of continuing the operations."[79] Officers complained to oblast officials that their arrests were no longer based on any kind of investigative or agent work. (At least, officers might justify perusal of lists drawn from *kartoteki* as "investigative" or "agent" work.) The head of the Penza NKVD mused to his assistant that perhaps it was time for Stalin to write another "dizzy with success" article to stop the cycle of repression that was spinning out of control.[80] In turn, higher police officials made no pretense about the fictional character of the new limits. I. A. Mal'tsev, assistant head of the Novosibirsk oblast UNKVD, reported to an operational meeting in December that he did not really care who was arrested, so long as the oblast met its quota.[81]

The pressure to meet ever-increasing arrest quotas turned the anti-Soviet operations into a "frantic" and "terrible" (*strashen*) kind of competition, in Yegorov's description. The turn in policy after October, created, in his words, a "force that swept up innocent people who never had anything to do with anti-Soviet organizations, and for whom there existed no compromising material whatsoever."[82] This is an interesting turn of phrase, showing that Yegorov, like many other officers, believed that the initial wave of mass repression was legitimate, and that the individuals arrested posed, in fact, a threat to the state. Yegorov, like others, justified the first arrests, but believed that something had gone terribly wrong after October. Still, and despite his misgivings, neither Yegorov nor others could stop the spiraling upward curve of insanity. Those officers who refused to continue arrests were themselves arrested. Most were afraid to speak up or to protest. Others opted out by taking their own life. Rates of suicide increased among *Chekists*.[83] Only the Central Committee of the Party, and Stalin, could stop the arrests, Yegorov wrote. And, of course, what Yegorov did not write was that there were many who were quite willing and ready to continue the arrests. Thus, apart from the overall question of moral sensibilities, many political police officers felt a sense of professional outrage at the turn in repressive policies after October. Indeed, for most, and certainly for Yegorov, moral and professional sensibilities were combined. He was not being disingenuous when he looked back on the first phase of the mass repressions as justified, but then condemned the policies that followed. Beginning in October, the mass purges entered a phase that few, except the most blind or the most cynical, could mistake for anything other than a horrific fiction.

MASS-PRODUCTION KILLING: THE BUREAUCRATIC DYNAMICS OF REPRESSION

Willingly or unwillingly, UNKVD officers found ingenious ways to meet or exceed their control figures. In the frantic hunt for people to arrest, some officers turned to names in "dead" files—the files of cases closed or of people long ago acquitted.[84] Yet officers ran through these files quickly. Other officers were not even that selective, nor did they have time to be so. In order to maximize the use of personnel and time, for example, operational units began to conduct group rather than individual arrests. Units would single out several adjacent villages and arrest individuals living close together, or several relatives within a single household.[85] In urban areas, police arrested numbers of people in the same office or factory department, or in the same apartment building. In other instances, officers simply picked up people randomly off the streets who looked suspicious, for whatever reason. The task of mass arrests was easiest in the case of the nationality operations. In the Kuntsevo region south of Moscow, large numbers of German and Latvian refugees worked and lived in close communities and in the same enterprises. These were easy targets for the intensified arrest quotas pressed on local UNKVD officials. In some cases, whole workshops and enterprises were paralyzed by the arrest of the overwhelming majority of workers. In cases of mass arrests in institutions, families, or neighborhoods, officers would create a fictive conspiracy among the arrestees in order to justify the detention of so many people living and working in such close proximity to each other.[86]

As numbers of arrests increased, so did numbers of people in holding cells and jails. Forty to sixty people in a cell for four people was not unusual. The task of handling the masses of people in detention was overwhelming. Operational units were so busy arresting, they rarely had time to interrogate prisoners or to write and type the confession and sentencing protocols that were necessary for case reviews by troikas. At the same time, the crush of prisoners in detention had to be processed. To help clear this bottleneck, commanders relied, at least in some areas, on the tried and true system from the early 1930s of allowing certain prisoners to manage other prisoners. Self-management during the purges, however, was very unlike the relatively benign corruption involved in self management by prisoners during the early part of the decade. Yegorov described the use of prisoner "aides" who organized new arrivals into likely groups of "conspirators." Most of the time, these conspirators had never met until they were arrested. The prisoner aide softened up the arrestees, telling them that they should sign group protocols, convincing them that this was in their interest and that they would get off lightly. Clerical staff could simply type up the signed protocols, which were passed on to jailers by the prisoner aides. Interrogating officers often never saw the people who supposedly confessed to crimes. In this way, operational units could focus on the number one task of arrests.[87]

These methods proved effective, even necessary, as arrest limits began to climb. Arresting and processing by groups was much more bureaucratically efficient than arresting and interrogating individuals. Still, arresting people in increasingly large numbers created a bottleneck in clerical work. All of the confessions and arrest protocols had to be typed and organized into case files to be sent to the troikas. Witnesses had to be found to "testify" to knowing or hearing what the "conspirators" were planning. Witness depositions also had to be typed and signed. In this swirl of activity, operational commanders deputized not only civil police, but staff from all departments of the NKVD bureaucracy, and even from outside the NKVD. Officers needed help with a wide range of tasks, from clerical work to participation in arrest units. In a number of areas, nearly all of the NKVD personnel were pressed into service, even typists, firemen, and civil service employees. Yegorov remembered that he was forced to deputize local tax clerks, Party functionaries, and Komsomol members to participate in raids and arrests. Typewriters became a priority and typists much sought after. Dispatchers and secretaries were especially valuable in this regard, as were any office staff. Local teachers were conscripted, if they had not already been arrested, and even those who had been arrested were sometimes employed, as were staff members of the civil registry offices.[88]

Falsification of charges, confessions, and witness accounts took on a mass-production character. The process of repression was broken down into its component parts, reproduced in mass numbers, and then assembled for final output to the sentencing boards. In January 1938, a special prosecutor on the Kirov railroad line described in a report how this "conveyor" system worked. In the context of this report, "conveyor" referred not to the oft-cited practice of continuous interrogations, but to the bureaucratic assembly-line character of the purge machine. The procurator, a certain Vorob'ev, submitted his report in the form of a rare complaint to his superiors about investigative methods used by local political police officials and operational groups. This report is worth replicating in some detail, since it provides an extraordinary view into the world of the mass operations.

Vorob'ev wrote that in early January, a special NKVD plenipotentiary arrived in the Kirov railroad region to conduct investigations of political sabotage. The plenipotentiary, M. V. Pukhov, was attached to the Petrozavodsk branch of the GUGB Transportation Department. As it turned out, the local NKVD was short on office space, so Pukhov appealed to Vorob'ev to lend him both space and personnel. In making his appeal, Pukhov said that he had "much work to do, serious work, and a very short deadline." Vorob'ev noted that, since he had a light case load at the time (only one case, he wrote!), he could spare himself and five of his staff to assist Pukhov.

Having secured office space and staff, Pukhov got down to work. First, he gathered eyewitnesses—eight that Vorob'ev named, and "others." These witnesses consisted of railroad technicians, as well as the chair of the local railroad trade union committee, and an administrator, a certain Lakmanov, from the local hospital clinic. Next, Pukhov briefed each witness. He told each that he needed "eyewitness accounts against so-and-so, and so-and-so . . . he had a whole list already made up." Pukhov told witnesses not to be afraid to sign depositions. The perpetrators, he said, "have already been shot; you will not be called into court; your deposition is needed only to formalize the case. We will write the protocol, then you stop by and sign it." As Pukhov's statement implied, the political police were having trouble keeping up with paperwork, shooting detainees before officers could write up the witness depositions. Still, bureaucratic formalities had to be attended to, and Pukhov's statement gave meaning to the urgency of his deadline.

After assembling his witnesses, Pukhov set Vorob'ev and his staff to work. Their task was to write up the witness depositions. Pukhov provided them examples of the kinds of charges to write, and the kinds of evidence that was needed. He cautioned his charges not to be too repetitive, but to vary the wording of accusations slightly.

> He gave me, for example, three to four witness names and where they worked. That way, I could fill out the first informational part of the deposition form. I took a blank form, filled out the top part [the name, address, and place of work], and then wrote that 'I [the witness] understand that I give a truthful deposition, in accordance with statute 95 of the criminal code.' Then, I began my [fictional] interview with the absent witness. I asked him or her the relevant questions, then provided the relevant answers myself.

Vorob'ev found that he had "no lack of imagination," and that his depositions came out "smooth and flowing."

In the evening, Pukhov and Vorob'ev called in their witnesses to sign depositions. Some witnesses signed without even reading, noted Vorob'ev. Others balked upon reading their accounts. "Their eyes got real big, and they refused, steadfastly, to sign what I had written." Pukhov "calmed" the reluctant ones, reassuring them, again, that the individuals in question had already been shot, and that they, the witnesses, would not have to appear in court and swear to what they were asked to sign. Through a mixture of cajoling and outright threats, Pukhov got nearly all the witnesses to sign. In a couple of cases, he gave reluctant citizens "financial encouragement" to do their duty and to quell their fears. In one case, Pukhov took it upon himself to sign the name of a witness who could not even be bribed. At the end of their several days of work, Pukhov handed Vorob'ev two hundred rubles "to cover staff costs."

In reporting this incident, Vorob'ev tried to walk a fine line. In the atmosphere of the purges, he certainly understood that he had no choice but to do as Pukhov requested. At the same time, Vorob'ev knew, and admitted, that what he and Pukhov had done was illegal and criminally liable. "In plain Russian, what we did was a fraud (*podlog*)." In a parody of understatement, Vorob'ev wrote that "with such investigative methods and actions, personal freedom in our country cannot be guaranteed." Vorob'ev wrote that he was "fed up" with his stint as a "fiction writer." He noted that other NKVD operational units were working in the same way in the region, and he finished rhetorically, by asking "Was Pukhov acting correctly? Do we allow such investigative methods?" Vorob'ev responded to his own questions in the same rhetorical vein by expressing doubt, but he nonetheless asked his superior to "clarify" the issue for him. In a laconic reply, the head of the USSR procuracy Transport Department, G. Roginskii, noted that he would "send an investigative team" to sort out the matter. No further record exists of the incident.[89]

Mass falsification of charges was commonplace during the purges, driven by the pressure on operational commanders to keep up with arrest demands. At the same time, these methods did not resolve the pressure on prison space; instead, they created a bottleneck at the next stage of the purge process. Soon, a huge backlog of cases built up to be reviewed by the troikas. This backlog led to a typical bureaucratic response. In November, Yezhov issued a circular that criticized the overcrowding in jails. Yezhov reminded his subordinates that such overcrowding constituted a violation of procedural codes and, with legalistic fastidiousness, he instructed subordinates to move people out of confinement by shortening the period of time from arrest to sentencing.[90] Officers were already hard pressed to keep up with arrests, let alone the paperwork of writing arrest protocols and evidence reports to be submitted to troikas. In turn, troika members were also inundated with massive numbers of case files to review and to sentence. In anticipation of large numbers of arrests, Yezhov had secured permission for arrest units and troikas to simplify procedures of evidence and review. These procedures were written into Order 00447. Operational officers and troikas had been using these procedures since the beginning of the mass operations. After October, these simplified procedures underwent still further simplification.

Indeed, the increasing insanity of the mass repressions can be seen in the changing physical appearance of the paper it generated. Arrest protocols during the first weeks and month of the mass operations reflected an effort to justify sentences. These protocols included a paragraph and sometimes a whole page of investigative description of supposed crimes, contacts, and subversive activities. As the year progressed, protocols became shorter and shorter. By December and early January, protocols often contained only a single sentence or two, with a one-word sentencing recommendation. Officers were either so pressed for time, or so cynical, that they made no pretense of investigative summary.[91] Troika members, in turn, began to review whole lists or "albums," instead of individual case files. They passed sentences on hundreds of people in a single session, sometimes on thousands during an afternoon or an evening. The Central Committee commission that investigated the mass purges noted in its 1956 report that, in general, troikas simply rubberstamped the accusations presented in the highly abbreviated arrest protocols. At the commissariat and national procuracy level, Yezhov, Vyshinskii, and their deputies were also pressed for time. Molotov and Vyshinskii, for example, reviewed the sentences of over one thousand people in one night, sent from several Leningrad oblasts. Yezhov finally pushed the review of sentences on to department heads. These officials, in turn, made "no effort" to confirm the validity of the lists. They had neither the time nor the interest, regarding the review task as an interruption of their normal duties.[92] In many oblasts, case review and sentencing were carried out solely by the UNKVD chief since, by December 1937, many chief prosecutors, judges, and oblast-level secretaries had been arrested and their posts remained vacant or filled by temporary appointees.[93]

The frenetic speedup of arrests created a macabre mass-production chain of events. As NKVD units attempted to keep up with quotas, they arrested indiscriminately and in mass numbers, rather than individually. As the number of arrests jumped, so did the number of people in jails, which in turn led to the bureaucratic necessity of mass review and sentencing, often of hundreds and thousands in a single day or night. Finally, the speedup in arrests and sentencing led to a consequent speedup in the carrying out of sentences. Those sentenced to shooting were executed within weeks and even days of their arrest.

The component parts of this mass production process did not always occur sequentially. In the first weeks of the purges, lists created from police files and address registers generated arrest protocols. These led to arrests, which then led to charges. Next came review and sentencing by troikas, and finally execution of sentences. Beginning in October, with the change to minimum quotas, this chain of events was at times reversed. Police arrested massive numbers of people and then generated lists of enemies and conspiracies from the names of those arrested. In many cases, arrestees were shot or sent to camps before evidentiary protocols were written. These latter were written in mass numbers to correspond to the sentences already carried out. The component parts of this process—arrest, charges, troika review and sentencing, and execution—were connected only by the necessity of bureaucratic form and consistency. Political police officials worried little about guilt or innocence, or about the fate of individuals. Uppermost in their minds was the necessity to ensure that their paperwork was in order—and to increase arrest numbers, of course. Always to increase the numbers.

There was no mechanism that could stop or slow this process. Yegorov was not simply trying to duck responsibility when he wrote that only Stalin could have stopped the purges. Yegorov was correct. The impetus for mass repression came from the initial political decisions by Stalin and those close to him. Yet it is in the bureaucratic minutiae that we find the perpetuating mechanism of the purges. The pressure to arrest was relentless, and the bureaucratic machinery of repression fed on itself. There was no time for appeal, let alone investigation of facts or interrogation. The normal prosecutorial oversight process had also ceased to function, in fact had been suspended. Vorob'ev's letter of complaint seems to have been an exception. Most prosecutors did not interfere or speak out about abuses. In many oblasts and regions, there were no procurators to speak out. Many procurators had been arrested and not replaced. Those who remained heeded Vyshinskii's prudent advice not to interfere. With no internal or external brake, the purges ground on through November and December 1937, into January 1938, and then beyond.

EXECUTIONS

Executions of those in category I followed in mass numbers from mass arrests and mass sentencing. In fact, as the numbers of detainees increased, so did the percentage of those executed. As one scholar has pointed out, the large majority of those executed were executed in the last months of 1937 and first two months of 1938. Part of the explanation for this jump in the proportion of executions lies, no doubt, in the rush by operational units to meet deadlines for ending operations, to tidy up loose ends, as it were.[94] There was, however, another bureaucratic logic at work, which followed from the mass character of the purges. As the pressure to arrest large numbers of people increased, so did the pressure to process people in mass numbers. As noted above, processing large numbers of arrestees was most effectively done through their organization into networks of conspiracies. In this way, whole groups of people—dozens, perhaps hundreds—could be reviewed, en masse, in one "case." Those who confessed to "organized" conspiracies were, of course, found guilty en masse, and therefore sentenced and shot en masse. Thus, as the purges took on a collective bureaucratic character, the proportion of those sentenced to shooting rose and also took on a collective bureaucratic character. In other words, the dynamics of processing prisoners in mass numbers created a bureaucratic imperative to shoot people in mass numbers. Collective processing of arrestees also had the advantage of clearing much needed space for new arrivals.

Executions were supposed to be carried out by the heads of operational units—political police officers and carefully chosen deputies. As Barry McLoughlin points out, this practice distinguished Stalinist mass execution policies from those of German death squads during World War II. In the latter case, officers gave the orders, but enlisted soldiers carried out the executions. In the Soviet mass purges, officers did the shooting. The Leningrad UNKVD chief, for example, participated in the executions of over a thousand arrestees in the autumn of 1937.[95] As noted above, executions were to be carried out in out-of-the-way places, usually in wooded areas and often on the grounds of UNKVD zones.[96] In at least one instance, Yezhov reprimanded a UNKVD chief for carrying out executions in the courtyard of a local prison. This was not a good idea, wrote Yezhov. The gunshots could be heard by the local populace, and the proximity of executions to holding cells could, Yezhov chided, "lead to rumors among the prisoners." Yezhov instructed the UNKVD commander to move the site of executions to a more remote location.[97]

Operational commanders were instructed to include only political police personnel in executions, but the pace of arrests and sentencing led many to draw in regular police in order to keep up with numbers. In his memoir, Shreider adamantly declared that he resisted participation in executions. At least, he did not admit to participating in the gruesome task of these squads. In a number of oblasts and regions, however, local police heads, as well as heads of the criminal investigative branches, the *ugolovnyi rozysk*, were pressed into duty. Shreider did recall that, when he arrived in Novosibirsk, the assistant who met his train informed him almost immediately that Gorbach was using civil police in execution squads. Prisoners were led to a bathhouse where, under the pretense of a bath, they were crowded into a small space. Political and civil police then surrounded the bathhouse, firing into the group. Yegorov, among others, also told of the widespread use of regular police for executions.[98]

In Novosibirsk, Shreider fought a losing battle with Gorbach over the use of civil police in mass operations. Shreider was a ranking UNKVD officer, and he could cite operational jurisdictions and authority to some degree in order to protect his officers and keep them from being drawn into the mass operations. On occasion, Shreider appealed directly to V. V. Chernyshev, the head of the GURKM, in Moscow. Chernyshev would intervene directly with Yezhov, who would restrain Gorbach. In this way, Shreider was at least successful, so he claimed, in forcing Gorbach to release *militsiia* officers from duty on execution squads. Still, Shreider was Gorbach's subordinate, and the mass operations took precedence over other UNKVD functions. As Shreider recounted, Gorbach commandeered office personnel and equipment—typewriters were especially valued—and police cars and vans. On more than one occasion, Shreider found that when he called from his office, he had no car or driver, both having been commandeered for an operation associated with mass arrests.[99]

Shreider's account is somewhat disingenuous. He depicts a situation in which there was a clear-cut distinction between normal and legal policing duties and mass repression of political enemies. In fact, Order 00447 named criminals, ex-convicts, and social marginals as a major category of the population targeted for mass arrest. The order also and explicitly directed civil police to participate in this aspect of the operations. While Shreider attempted to deny *militsiia* involvement in mass repression, he also referred to the large numbers of criminals that were filling up jails, and were being brought into custody by civil police. In

Novosibirsk, between the spring and the end of autumn, at least seven thousand individuals were caught up in mass operations carried out by civil police.[100] It is difficult to know overall how many of these individuals there were, and how officials decided whether to send their cases for review through the UNKVD troikas or through the regular police troikas, which were still operating in 1937. The so-called *militseiskie troiki* had been revived in April 1937 and, at the height of the mass repressions, they constituted one of the three types of administrative sentencing boards at work. These included the NKVD special troikas for handling arrests under Order 00447, the *dvoiki* for processing cases under the various nationality operations, and the police troikas for reviewing cases of social harmfuls and criminals. The jurisdiction between the police and NKVD troikas was blurred, since criminals and social harmfuls also fell within the arrest jurisdiction of Order 00447. In some cases, oblast officials traded off contingents of prisoners from one to the other in order to stay within or to fulfill arrest quotas. This was the case in the Western oblast in July 1937. There, political police transferred to the civil police boards the cases of thousands of people arrested under Order 00447 so as not to exceed quotas under the mass operations.[101] (Such a distinction would not have come into play, of course, after October, if some limits were minimum rather than maximum numbers.) Yet it is still unclear how any one individual may have fallen under the jurisdiction of a civil police troika, instead of under the purview of a special NKVD troika. The decision to arrest an individual under one or the other jurisdiction may have been arbitrary, but individuals who came under the police troikas could count themselves fortunate, since the authority of these troikas was limited to sentences of up to five years in camps or settlements and they could not impose death sentences. Shreider noted that these police boards were as busy as the mass operations troikas and, in fact, he lamented that many hard-core criminals who came under his police jurisdiction got off rather lightly, in his view, with just five years.[102]

URBAN OPERATIONS

Political police officers often referred to the mass operations by the shorthand name of antikulak operations. This was so since most of those arrested under Order 00447 were former kulaks and exiles, and most of the operations to round up these people took place in rural and industrial areas of the country. Most of the kulak operations were carried out by political police. Hence, in their experience, the mass operations were primarily antikulak operations. However, the mass operations were more than a second dekulakization. In urban areas, the mass operations targeted primarily social marginals, passport violators, ex-convicts, known or suspected "hooligans," the unemployed and homeless, and those suspected of criminal activities. In absolute figures, more people were arrested under the rubric of kulak than from the criminal or socially marginal world of cities, but the proportions of the latter categories were nonetheless significant. In Novosibirsk, the mass purges carried away some seven thousand individuals, but this amounted to approximately 6–8 percent of the adult male population of the city.[103] As well, it was civil police, not political police, who were primarily responsible for rounding up these categories of people. In general, civil police were spared participation in the more gruesome aspects of the repressions, although, as noted above, they were at times pressed into service for execution squads. The major exception involved the heads of criminal investigative units, who were routinely assigned these duties. Police, especially officers of the *ugolovnyi rozysk*, were routinely included in arrest squads. In addition, it seems from arrest photographs that the NKVD used the *ugolovnyi rozysk* offices for initial documentation of prisoners. In Leningrad, at least, *ugolovnyi rosyzk* commanders also headed up major operational units during the mass operations.[104] Shreider's efforts to draw distinctions and to exonerate the civil police are understandable. The civil police, however, were deeply involved in the mass repressions.

Civil police officials participated in the mass repression campaign more or less willingly. Shreider, for example, walked a fine and dangerous line. He tried to fulfill his duty, as he understood it, while protecting himself and his staff from involvement in the worst aspects of the repressive machinery. Shreider was, in fact, threatened on several occasions with arrest for his resistance to political police superiors, until in 1938, he was actually arrested and, of course, charged with counterrevolutionary conspiracy. Fortunately for him, his arrest came late in the purge process, and he was exonerated of the worst political charges following Yezhov's removal from power. Shreider was convicted on various minor charges of professional misconduct. Eventually, he was released and lived out his natural life.

Shreider had no qualms about conducting a hard campaign against criminals under statutes of the criminal code, even as he opposed the politicized process of mass repressions. Some police administrations simply refused to engage in mass arrests of any kind, although whether this was for moral reasons or simply out of bureaucratic inertia is not clear. In September 1937, for example, in a reprimand circulated to all NKVD offices, Yezhov criticized the Tatar republic police for laxness in fulfilling its duties under Order 00447. As proof, Yezhov noted that, in August, Tatar police detained only 695 social harmfuls in the whole of the republic. Most of these were, according to Yezhov, petty speculators, beggars, and small-time hooligans. Social harmfuls and criminals were sentenced through "regular" police troikas and received only light sentences. Many were simply fined, and were assessed small fines, at that. The average fine amounted to "no more" than 34 rubles. Police conducted no organized campaigns against hooligan gangs, which literally controlled certain sections of cities and towns. The passport departments of the police were in "complete" disarray. Chaos in passport work not only created a major public inconvenience—as many as nine hundred citizens waiting in line for passport renewal—but seriously hindered police in the fight to identify and track political enemies and social harmfuls.[105]

The consequences of this laxness in duty were serious. This was, after all, 1937, and Yezhov was inclined to punish all but the most zealous officials. In all, eleven ranking officials—including the head of the republic's civil police, Aitov—were placed under arrest and charged with unspecified crimes of professional and political misconduct. The assistant chief was removed from his post and barred from work again in the NKVD. The heads of the *ugolovnyi rozysk* and the Passport Department were sanctioned for misconduct and corruption.[106] Several similar surveys in the late summer and early autumn of 1937 served as warnings to police administrations to take Order 00447 seriously. Interestingly, these surveys were of peripheral police administrations or border force commands—in the Azov–Black Sea territory, and in the republics of Kazakhstan, Georgia, Armenia, and Turkmenistan.[107] Yezhov found reason, however, to be dissatisfied with civil police commitment even in the capital city. In August, Yezhov ordered that the central address registration bureau in Moscow, which was administered by the GURKM, be placed under direct control of the Second Department of the GUGB, the Operational Department.[108] Yezhov gave no specific reason for this transfer of authority, but it very likely arose as the result of bureaucratic incompetence rather than of lack of zeal or active resistance by civil police officials. Yezhov wanted to make certain that political police had direct and unfettered access to the city's address registries. This was important as the purges moved into the phase of unlimited quotas.

By most accounts, police officials in Moscow and in other major urban centers showed no hesitation in carrying out arrests under Order 00447. Indeed, many welcomed the new campaign as an opportunity, once and for all, to rid their streets of undesirable social types. "We are cleaning out Moscow," said a police precinct captain to a mother who protested her son's arrest in November 1937. The young man, Kiril Korenev, had been picked up under Order 00447 because of his record of two previous convictions on petty theft. Police also claimed that Korenev was unemployed and therefore a social harmful. "We are finally getting rid of your kind," said a policeman to Korenev.[109]

Korenev received an eight-year camp sentence, pronounced by the Moscow oblast *troika,* but at least he was not sentenced to shooting. Many were shot, of course, including M. A. Kozlovskii, a railroad dispatcher from Saratov oblast. Police arrested Kozlovskii in September 1937 under Order 00447. He was sentenced to shooting for drunkenness and consorting with criminals. In a later deposition, one of the arresting officers, a certain Rudin, head of the Saratov oblast *ugolovnyi rozysk,* claimed that police officials had no hesitation about rounding up social marginals and former criminals. Rudin added, however, that he and his officers had no idea what kind of harsh sentences awaited those whom they arrested. "That was a matter handled entirely by the troikas," reported Rudin. There was no place on arrest protocols for officers to recommend sentences, according to Rudin, and civil police officers were not consulted about sentencing.[110]

Rudin made out well. He was promoted to major and transferred from Saratov. At the time of his deposition, in 1939, he was working in the Moscow oblast criminal investigative department. His claims of ignorance must certainly be suspect, in part because Rudin made these remarks in response to a procuracy investigation of illegal arrest and sentencing procedures. In order to protect himself, Rudin may have exaggerated the extent of his isolation from responsibility during the mass purges. If he was head of the criminal investigation department of a major oblast in 1937, Rudin would likely have been involved in all aspects of the mass operations, even and especially as a participant in mass execution squads. He very likely knew all too well what awaited those arrested under mass operation orders. Still, there is a grain of truth in his deposition. The mass repressions in urban areas had a different dynamic than those carried out in rural areas and smaller towns. Mass operations in rural areas and towns required major logistical and propaganda preparations. The state's turn against peasants in 1937 was a complete turnabout from the previous policy of persecuting local officials. Reorganization of operational units, the influx of new personnel, and the change in propaganda about enemies surely made clear even to low-level NKVD officials that something big was happening, and something different from the usual kind of repression campaigns.

The situation was different in urban areas. To many urban civil police officials, operations under Order 00447—to round up social marginals and criminals—must have had a familiar feel, at least in the first phases of the repression. After all, police had been mobilized for any number of social cleansing and social defense campaigns in the preceding years. Order 00447 may have looked like yet one more "once and for all time" campaign, yet again directed against the same "anti-Soviet" categories of the population. As in 1933 and 1934, and then in 1935 and 1936, police were told once again in 1937 to rout out and round up the "usual suspects"—social marginals, passport violators, suspected criminals, etc.

The sense of business as usual would have been reinforced by the mechanics of the purge process. Rudin reported that neither he nor any of his subordinate officers saw or read Order 00447. "Everything was done by memo or by oral instructions that came from [GUGB] Major Stromin [head of the Saratov oblast UNKVD]." In giving orders to begin rounding up people, Stromin simply made reference to Order 00447. According to Rudin, *militsiia* officers were told simply to make lists of all those who had convictions or who had been detained (*privod*) by police. The lists were put together by the precinct heads in each region or *raion*, each with an order for arrest. Officers were told that it did not matter whether the individuals had committed a specific crime. Police officers were told to include anyone with a criminal or detention record. At first, the lists were compiled by the oblast-level *ugolovnyi rozysk*. Rudin and the head of the Oblast *militsiia* were to countersign the lists before they were passed on to the GUGB for action. After a while, however, Stromin by-passed this intermediary step. He sent political police plenipotentiaries directly to the regional precincts to collect the lists. "[Stromin] claimed that sending the lists through us slowed the process too much, and that we often wrote the charges incorrectly, which meant that the lists had to be sent back for further investigation." Further investigation meant, of course, writing the criminal charges in the acceptable bureaucratic form. As noted above in the case of Vorob'ev, the Kirov railroad line prosecutor, writing criminal charges for the purge troikas required a certain practice, and local police officials were apparently not well versed in the particulars of this kind of bureaucratic paper work. In fact, Rudin noted without irony, and with a certain professional pique, that proper evidentiary work had always been a weak spot with the oblast police. Local police officers were notoriously undereducated and the oblast-level civil police administration was constantly having to send criminal investigations back to the regions because they had been incorrectly or incompletely done. During the purges, and under the pressure of arrest quotas, political police officials did not tolerate the bureaucratic semiliteracy of local police. GUGB officers streamlined the process of writing evidentiary charges. They collected the lists directly from the regions and then wrote the charges themselves. Or, as in the case of Vorob'ev, they conscripted literate professionals to help with the task.[111]

Based on the lists put together by local police, arrest squads began their work of rounding up individuals. Local police were often the ones who made the arrests, but their role ended once they transferred prisoners to the jurisdiction of the GUGB and the troikas. As Rudin noted, civil police were not involved in determining the sentences of those they arrested. Nor, it seems from several sources, were police even involved in the process of writing evidentiary charges. Thus, local police would not even have known if arrestees were to be sent through the regular police sentencing boards or through the mass purge troikas. It is difficult to believe that someone in Rudin's position remained ignorant of the fate of those he arrested or of the scale of the mass purges. It is possible, however, that local police officials did not entirely understand what was unfolding around them, even though they were a part of it. They would have understood that the scale of the mass operations in 1937 and early 1938 was more extensive than that of the social defense campaigns of the mid-1930s. As noted above, many police officials in fact welcomed the renewed campaign against marginal and criminal populations in their cities. The bureaucratic processing of arrestees was also somewhat different in the mass purges than in previous campaigns. At the same time, the social groups targeted in the urban aspects of the mass operations were the same as in the social defense operations of earlier years. The operational aspects of mass roundups were also much the same as in previous campaigns. Civil police officials may or may not have understood what was happening overall, but they could at least shield themselves from the implication of criminal responsibility. So far as is known, no action was taken against Rudin for his part in the mass operations.[112]

DENOUEMENT

The Politburo twice extended the purge operations under Order 00447, once in mid-December 1937, and again in late January 1938. Operations did not officially come to a close until November 1938, when the Politburo ordered a final cessation. The order to end operations and to disband the troikas was issued over the signatures of Stalin and Molotov on 17 November, and it created a final spasm of intense activity to finish up cases and send them for sentencing. Most operations under Order 00447, however, were winding down already by February and March 1938. By the end of January, as noted above, more than 600,000 of the 748,000 arrested under 00447 had already been sentenced. An additional 148,000 individuals became victims of the mass purges in 1938, but these arrests occurred mainly in border areas where the regime's leaders feared that most sabotage would be carried out during an invasion. After January, the Politburo and NKVD leaders seemed to lose interest in the operations. No more memorandums arrived in oblast headquarters pushing local officials to arrest more people. In fact, just the opposite. In January, when officials in the Tatar republic requested an increase in arrest quotas, the Politburo, for the first time, denied the request. This effectively ended the mass operations in that republic. In February and March, the Politburo refused requests for continuation in other oblasts, and operations in these parts of the country wound down in like manner.[113]

This was a remarkable turnaround in just a matter of weeks, but curtailment of arrests under order 000447 did not signal an end to mass purges, only a refocusing of effort. Under pressure from the Politburo, the NKVD was turning its attention increasingly to operations against ethnic minorities and foreigners. The latter operations had started more slowly than operations under Order 00447, and they peaked later. Arrests of criminals and kulaks spiked in late 1937, tapering off after January 1938. By February, the bulk of arrests under the various nationality orders were yet to come. During 1938, from January through November, political police arrested over 300,000 people under the various nationality orders.

The Politburo ordered cessation of all mass operations in its 17 November decree. That memorandum signaled a major turn in policy, finally, against mass repression, and marked the end of Yezhov's violent leadership of the state's security organs. According to the Politburo order, the special sentencing boards were to be disbanded, and any arrests were to be carried out only with the sanction of the procuracy. The country was to return to the phase of legality that had existed prior to the start of the mass purges. Within days of this order, Yezhov was relieved of his position and replaced by Lavrentii Beria, the former head of the NKVD in Georgia. In a replay of the events of late 1936 and early 1937, Yezhov was charged, as was Yagoda before him, with crimes of counterrevolutionary sabotage. Yezhov, so it was alleged, had allowed the infiltration of the NKVD by anti-Soviet elements. He had deceived the Party and the government and encouraged a mass repression of innocent citizens through the simplified and hasty mechanism of the purge process. Stalin and Molotov took no responsibility for the excesses of the purges, of course, and all blame fell on Yezhov and his clan within the NKVD. Yezhov was sentenced to death and executed in February 1940.[114]

Yezhov's fall from grace and power began the final chapter in the mass purges. On 26 November 1938, a week after the 17 November Politburo resolution, Beria issued his own internal NKVD order nullifying Order 00447 and the other mass repression orders. Beria's order listed eighteen orders or additions that were no longer in force. All pending cases under these orders were to be sent to the corresponding procuracy level for review in judicial courts.[115] In the wake of these events, Beria launched a purge of the NKVD, specifically of those who had been close to Yezhov, and who had been most active in the purge process. The cycle of purge and recrimination repeated itself. As Beria purged the NKVD, the procuracy began an investigative review of the illegalities committed by the NKVD during 1937 and 1938. The commissions involved in the investigation were inundated with tens of thousands of petitions. Many of those fortunate enough to be still alive petitioned their convictions and sentences from their places of exile and imprisonment. Others petitioned on behalf of dead or missing relatives. The procuracy reviewed several thousand cases in the course of 1939 and 1940, and many convictions were overturned. This process did nothing to bring back the dead; for the living, however, rehabilitation of a family member meant the restoration of rights and at least some dignity, and it often involved the restitution of or compensation for lost property. On the other hand, many hundreds of thousands of convictions remained in force. These victims of repression, whether living or dead, remained officially enemies of the state.

CONCLUSIONS

The consequences of the purges were devastating. Apart from the appalling loss of life, the disruption caused by the purges re-created the conditions of social chaos that mass social cleansing was supposed to remedy. The purges were supposed to have rid society and its institutions of dangerous elements and strengthened the country in preparation for a coming war. On the contrary, the legal, judicial, and social-order institutions of Soviet society were in nearly complete disarray as a result of the purging of their personnel. Many parts of the country were without judges, bailiffs, or procuracy officials, and the ranks of police, both civil and political, were stretched thin by arrests and transfers. By 1940, many officers in service had only one to two years' experience, if even that.[116] The country's infrastructure was in a shambles. The losses to the military high command are well documented and often cited, but the same was true in other key state sectors. Numbers of train collisions increased dramatically in 1939 and 1940 as a result of inexperienced drivers, dispatchers, and switch operators trying to cope with the demands placed on them. Accidents in mines, and in industry in general, jumped due to the loss of experienced workers and managers. Similar problems arose in nearly every area of public and state service.

The forced migration of the population and the disruption of millions of lives nullified any stabilizing effects and social control that were supposed to have resulted from social purging and enforcement of passport and residence laws. Hundreds of thousands of escapees roamed the country. They and many more were obliged to falsify their identities, often obtaining fake documents and being forced into criminal activity. Family members ignored travel bans and made their way to the east, to the camp areas where they knew or believed their loved ones had been sent. Train stations and small towns in exile and penal areas were inundated with people, often sleeping in and around the stations, with no documents, and looking "ragged."[117] Social institutions could not cope with the sharp rise in numbers of orphan and unsupervised children. This was a resurgent problem on a scale almost as widespread as after the great collectivization and dekulakization campaigns in the early 1930s. Forced migration and illegal buying and selling caused a "sharp rise" in speculation in 1939, as millions of people fell outside of the official market and trade mechanisms of the state. Crime rates rose, and police were at a loss to cope, their ranks so drained by the purges. Soviet society had changed much in the two years of the mass purges. Hundreds of thousands of people had been murdered by the state. The lives of millions of people had been violently disrupted. All this was justified in the name of domestic order and state security. And yet, to read reports from the government, police, judicial, and procuracy organs, it seemed like very little had changed. Descriptions of crime, illegal migration, speculation, hooliganism, street children, and graft and corruption differed little from the same kinds of complaints, admonishments, and descriptions of the early and mid-1930s.[118]

So ended the Great Purges—in a morass of death and chaos, with little intended effect. The purges were an unmitigated social catastrophe, horrific in their cruelty and monstrous in their arbitrary bureaucratic banality. The purges were eclipsed in their devastating effects on Soviet society only by the war. Much had happened in the two years of the purges, and it was only the beginning of much worse to come.

11 Outside the Margins
The Case of Kiril Korenev

We will send you to a place where even cows don't graze.
—*Police inspector Gogolev to Kiril Korenev, November 1937*

THE DEVASTATING EFFECTS of the great purge can be measured statistically by the hundreds of thousands of people arrested and then executed or imprisoned. The effects of the purge can be measured by the demographic dislocation, economic costs, and loss to the professional infrastructure that it caused. This scale provides a valuable perspective, which is useful for historical generalization and comparison. The devastation wrought by the purges may also be seen from the perspective offered by individual biography, a powerfully emotive and personalizing view that is also valuable as a form of social history. Viewing the purge through the story of one who was its victim can tell us much about how individuals coped with the arbitrary and repressive forces of the police and the state, but biography can also tell us much about the details of how the policing system worked—or how it failed to work the way it was supposed to work.

The case of Kiril Kirilovich Korenev offers a view of the mass purges from the perspective of one of its victims. Korenev's story is not the typical story that has been published in numerous variations. He was not arrested for political crimes under the usual charges of spying, sabotage, or anti-Soviet agitation or opposition. He was not anti-Soviet, he was not a secret Trotskyist, or in any way particularly political. Rather, he was arrested as a socially dangerous "element" under authority of Operational

Order 00447. He was arrested by the civil police in Moscow in November 1937, and he was sentenced to a labor camp for his past convictions of hooliganism and for being unemployed. His story, then, is not a story about political repression, nor is it a story about life in Soviet prisons and hard labor camps. Korenev did not spend time in a political prison. He did not endure days and weeks of psychological and physical torture and isolation, nor the interrogations that were so much a part of being a political prisoner. What is interesting about Korenev is not his life in prisons or camps. We know much already about the harsh conditions and strategies of survival in the Soviet forced labor system. What is interesting about Korenev is his life outside the camps, on the run. His arrest in 1937 began an odyssey of imprisonment, escape, and life outside the law, which lasted for nearly four years. We can reconstruct this period in his life from his extensive dossier, which runs to 255 pages. His file provides a detailed account of his travails as a prisoner and an escapee in Eastern Siberia. Through the file, we can reconstruct how he fashioned and refashioned false identities, how he forged passports, registration, and other identity papers, and how he moved from place to place and in and out of cities, farms, and industrial sites. The dossier contains depositions, reports from police and procuracy officials, and letters from Korenev to his mother, Sofiia, written under assumed names. The file also preserves the numerous letters and petitions from Korenev's mother to reverse his sentence and to win her son's release. His letters, along with other materials from his case file, belong to the USSR procuracy archive and are housed in the Russian state archives in Moscow.[1] Korenev's file would sound incredible as a movie script; it is all the more remarkable for being true.

Korenev's story is unusual as biography, but it also tells us much about the system of social control that the Stalinist regime attempted to put into place during the 1930s. As described in chapter 8, the passport and residence registration system, introduced in 1933, provided police with the primary mechanism to accomplish this goal—to track and control the country's population. By enforcing its complex provisions, police and policymakers hoped to check the unhindered exodus of people from the countryside to the cities; they hoped to channel population flows between urban and rural areas, between regions of the country, and between major industrial sites. Police, especially, employed the passport and registration regime in an attempt to cleanse cities and strategic areas of itinerants, criminals, and other undesirable populations.

The passport system was supposed to restrict the free movement of social marginals, keep them confined in the areas set aside for them by the regime—whether in colonies, camps, or particular regions of the country—and prohibit them from gaining access to the residence and commodity privileges that belonged to "normal" Soviet citizens. In short, officials saw in the passport system a means to fix populations socially and geographically in ways that reinforced the hierarchies of privilege and punishment built into the Stalinist social order.

And yet, we know that people of all social levels moved by the hundreds of thousands, by the millions, during the 1930s. They moved about the great stretches of the empire in legal and illegal ways. Despite the ban on them, itinerants, beggars, criminals, and other social outcasts made their way along roads, rail lines, and water ways; gypsies moved across the countryside, much as they always had done; tens of thousands of orphaned children swarmed onto trains, into train depots, through city back streets and marketplaces. Thieves, con men, and prostitutes plied their trades in cities and construction towns, and political exiles moved and moved again to find work and to settle in places where they should have been prohibited. How did all these people move about, obtain work, settle down, or stay in one place for a time, then pick up and move on? How were large segments of the population able to sidestep the strict provisions of the passport and residence registration system? This is an especially perplexing problem for the 1930s, the period of rapid police expansion and harsh repression. How did large numbers of people move about in a highly policed state where all were supposed to have a place and to stay in that place?

There is much in Korenev's story that can help to answer these questions. The materials in his file tell us how, in practice, the system of passport control and residency registration worked (or did not work), how police operated, and, despite a pervasive system of police surveillance, how difficult it was for authorities to trace individual people as they slipped from one identity to another and from one place to another. Combined with police and passport control records, Korenev's story offers a valuable microanalysis of social movement and surveillance under the Stalinist dictatorship.

The case file of Korenev is unique as archive material, but the documents in this file reflect experiences of many people in the Soviet Union during the 1930s. I refer here not to the specific criminal activities of Korenev, but to his marginal status within Soviet society, to his constant movement, and, consequently, to the numerous aliases that he acquired and then discarded. The 1930s, especially, was a decade when traumatic social upheaval and the whims of official policies forced millions of people to uproot themselves and their families, to refashion their social identities, and, in fact, to lead multiple lives. Official policies marginalized and criminalized many activities and social categories in a seemingly arbitrary manner, and often after the fact. Korenev, for example, was deemed socially harmful in 1937 for a minor criminal conviction in the early 1930s, for which he had served a sentence and been released and rehabilitated. People could also be criminalized simply by association. Nearly everyone had something to hide—a conviction, a previous job dismissal, a socially "alien" family connection. Many carried with them their own "alien" past or previous association with now-suspect political groups or associations. Soviet criminal law and other state policies forced people to construct their lives in ways that obscured these connections. Thus, the detail of the story recounted here—a life led in and out and on the margins of the law—magnifies on a personal scale the arbitrary ways by which people could be made legitimate or not, depending on the whims of official politics, circumstance, and local authority. The experiences recounted in Korenev's file reveal the brutalizing and often tragic absurdities in which people found themselves during the 1930s.

SOTSVREDELEMENT

Korenev's story began in 1915, when he was born the son of Sofiia Brodskaia and Kiril Aleksandrovich Korenev. Korenev's parents were active and longtime Socialist Revolutionaries in tsarist Russia. In an ironic foreshadowing of their son's fate, both Sofiia and Kiril Aleksandrovich were arrested, sentenced to exile in Siberia, and escaped several times over before they met and married in either 1914 or 1915. Theirs was a hard but not untypical life in the circumstances of war and illegal political activity. Sofiia bore five children of her own, of which three survived childhood (one infant died under the difficult circumstances of exile), and she took in two more children of a friend and comrade, a fellow woman revolutionary, who had also died in exile. After the October revolution, the family settled in Moscow where, according to Sofiia, her husband served as one of the first agricultural commissars under Lenin. Korenev, the father, left the SRs in 1922 and died in 1927, when his son, Kiril, was twelve. By the time the younger Korenev reached his teens, then, his mother was already widowed and struggling to make ends meet as a middle-aged and ailing pensioner. According to accounts by both Korenev and his mother, the two did not get along and quarreled often. Sofiia made certain her son attended a good school, but Korenev nonetheless "became tied to the streets" early on in life. In fact, Korenev spent much of his childhood growing up unsupervised on the streets of Moscow.[2] This is how he first came into contact with criminal life and with the police.

As a teenager, Korenev was one of the tens of thousands of *beznadzorniki* of the 1930s—unsupervised children who inundated urban areas, especially Moscow, during the chaotic years of Stalin's "socialist offensive." During the early 1930s, the numbers of orphan and unsupervised children in the USSR reached unprecedented proportions, the consequence of social dislocation caused by Stalin's harsh policies of agrarian collectivization and rapid industrialization. The resulting problems of juvenile gangs and juvenile crime that arose during this period overwhelmed the various social agencies in charge of children's homes and orphanages. Korenev was not an orphan, but the lure of life on the streets and the influence of street gangs was powerful. Soon, Korenev "slid onto the path of crime."[3] By the time he was eighteen, in 1933, Korenev had been held in police detention no less than six times for hooliganism and petty theft. By this time, also, the regime had launched its campaigns against socially harmful elements, and troublemaking juveniles such as Kiril were often one of the targets of police sweeps of cities to clean them of socially dangerous "elements." Sure enough, Korenev fell victim to the police campaigns of social defense. In November 1933, Korenev was picked up for robbery and came into contact for the first time with the political police. On 13 November, he was sentenced by the Moscow oblast OGPU *troika* to three years in a camp as a social harmful.

Korenev did not serve out his term. He was given early release in October 1934, as part of a general amnesty. Under recognizance of his mother, he was allowed to return home to Moscow. Within days of his return, however, Korenev was again arrested, this time for armed robbery. Korenev, along with some other youths, taunted and robbed a woman who, it turned out, was the wife of a dispossessed kulak. As mitigating circumstances, Korenev's mother pointed out that the woman was not only a kulak, but a church elder who concealed her identity, as well as her robes and crosses. The robbery, apparently, exposed this identity. Moreover, the weapon involved in the robbery turned out to be a child's toy pistol that was loaded with rubber bullets. Nonetheless, as Sofiia wrote, "a fact is a fact." Her son had engaged in armed robbery and had to face the consequences. The consequence for Kiril was a five-year sentence to a corrective labor camp. In this instance, however, the sentence, which Sofiia regarded as mercifully mild, was handed down not by the OGPU, but by a regular court. By October 1934, the OGPU had reorganized into the NKVD. As part of that reform, most of the OGPU troikas were disbanded and their cases sent to regular courts. As a result, Korenev's case fell under statutes 162 and 165 of the criminal code and came before the Moscow oblast criminal court. It was this court that sentenced Korenev to his second term as a convict.[4]

Korenev served part of his second sentence under jurisdiction of the infamous White Sea NKVD camp administration. Fortunately, he was not sent to work on the canal of the same name, but was assigned to the Tulomstroi construction site as a forced labor prisoner. Korenev worked there as a dispatcher's assistant and, at least for a time, worked, apparently, in the central White Sea administration at Medvezh'egorsk, near Lake Onega. Korenev made the most of his circumstances and put his education to use by taking part in the political-social life of the camp and helping to edit a newspaper. Notes in his camp file describe him as a good and honest worker.[5] Sofiia even managed to visit him while he worked in the camp administration. Korenev eventually wrote an article about his experience for *Komsomol'skaia Pravda,* the newspaper of the Communist Youth League. In a "Letter to a Friend," Korenev described his social "redemption" through work. He praised the Soviet system of justice and the Stalinist constitution, and begged his fictional friend, an upstanding Komsomol member, to forgive him and to accept him back into the companionship of socialist society. After "careful screening," the newspaper published Korenev's "Letter" on 4 January 1937. Three days later, by order of the TsIK, the NKVD gave Korenev early release. The TsIK order granted Korenev full citizenship rights, which was important, since this allowed him to receive an unrestricted passport. Under normal circumstances, an ex-convict who bore a criminal record for armed robbery would not have been allowed to live in a so-called regime area. He or she would have been issued a passport by the camp authorities with a special notation that would have permitted residence and work only in non-regime cities or areas. Although many found ways around this law, it officially barred hundreds of thousands of citizens from living in a number of desirable locations, such as major cities and industrial sites. This part of the passport law condemned socially marginal groups to life in the more impoverished areas of the country.

Korenev was fortunate. Because of his exemplary behavior and "honest" work as a prisoner, and also because he had immediate family who lived in Moscow, the NKVD permitted him to be issued a passport to live in the capital city. With the publication of his article, Korenev also became a corresponding staff writer for *Komsomol'skaia Pravda*. Thus, Korenev also had socially useful employment, another legal condition for residence in a regime locality. As a result of his employment, he enjoyed the protection and patronage—*shefstvo*—of the prestigious newspaper, and this was more than just symbolic. As a staff writer for *Komsomol'skaia Pravda* he also became a member of the Soviet Writer's Union. On several crucial occasions in the next few years, the newspaper and the Union acted as an intermediary between Korenev and Soviet authorities.

Accounts vary about Korenev's deportment during the next few months of his life. According to police reports, he could not reintegrate into normal Soviet life, despite his good fortune. He drank heavily, quarreled often with his mother, did not work, and was known by local police as a troublemaker and a street brawler.[6] According to accounts by his mother and, later, the USSR procurator's office, on the other hand, Korenev lived an exemplary life. Although he had difficulties at home, these did not spill over into his work life. At work, supposedly at the newspaper, Korenev conducted himself in the best possible way. He was a "disciplined and good-natured" worker.[7] In the short run, of course, it was the police version that counted. Police in Korenev's precinct arrested Korenev again in November 1937 and charged him under statute 7-35-b of the Soviet criminal code. The precinct supervisor, Solov'ev, informed Korenev that he was being arrested as a socially dangerous element; that is, he had no definite place of employment or residence, and he also had a criminal record of two convictions for armed robbery. According to his later deposition, Korenev protested the charge. He insisted that he was employed and had a permanent residence. Further, citing the constitution, he declared that arresting him for having previous convictions was illegal. He had committed no specific crime, and his past could not be held now against him. According to Korenev's mother's account, Solov'ev responded to her son: "The constitution does not apply to tricksters. You were convicted under statutes 162 and 165, and that means you are a thief and a robber and are subject to isolation and exile. . . . there is no protection for tricksters, no matter that [you expiated your crimes] long ago."[8] Solov'ev's deputy, Chief Inspector Gogolev, added a further threat. "We are going to send you away for good," he told Korenev, "and without a court." When Korenev protested, again, that he had committed no crime, Gogolev replied that that did not matter. "We'll solder together whatever statutes we need." Using a common expression of the day—*kuda Makar teliat ne gonial*—Gogolev promised Korenev that they would send him to a place of exile so far away no one would ever find him, literally, a place where cows don't even graze. Gogolev played with the colloquial name in that expression, several times referring to "Makar places (*v makarkinskikh mestakh*)." Korenev replied that such "Makar places" hadn't existed in the country for at least twenty years, and under the new constitution, could not exist. Gogolev promised Korenev that, in fact, such places existed. "We're going to send you to hell at the end of the earth, and you'll get to know the joys of such places."[9]

Two days after Korenev's arrest, Sofiia met with Solov'ev to protest her son's detention. By this time, Korenev had been sent to a central prison somewhere in Moscow and Solov'ev either did not know or did not wish to tell Korenev's mother where her son had been sent.[10] Neither would he tell her under what statute Korenev had been arrested. Instead, he gave her a similar answer to the one that he had given Korenev. All that he volunteered was: "Your son is an enemy of the people —a thief and a robber," he said; "we are cleaning out Moscow (*My ochishchaem Moskvu*)." Sofiia appealed immediately to the regional procurator, who had oversight authority over the police, and who, by law, was required to sanction any police arrest. The procurator, Krasnopevtsev, informed her that he was unaware that her son was employed and had a permanent place of residence. The police, it seems, had informed him otherwise. In any case, all that did not matter, he told her. Sofiia asked, then, on what grounds her son had been arrested. The procurator replied, simply, "His past."[11]

Receiving no help from Krasnopevtsev, Sofiia took her protest to the Moscow city procurator, Maslov. Sofiia confronted Maslov in December, nearly two months after her son's arrest. Maslov agreed that the police had no case, basing their arrest only on Korenev's past record of convictions. He issued instructions for Korenev's release, but apparently too late. According to Sofiia's account, her son's "nonexistent" case had already been transferred from civil police and criminal court jurisdiction to that of the state security organs and the NKVD special troikas. Maslov informed Sofiia that her son had already been sentenced by the NKVD to a closed regime labor camp as a socially dangerous element. Maslov refused to take further action. "In these matters," he told Sofiia, "we [the procuracy] do not argue with the NKVD."[12]

In fact, Korenev had fallen victim to the nationwide campaign of mass repression that began in the summer of 1937 under Order 00447. NKVD depositions later confirmed that police arrested Korenev under authority of that order, and that they arrested him not for a specific crime, but because he had a record of past convictions. That was why police regarded him as a socially dangerous element. And as Chief Inspector Gogolev grimly promised, Korenev was not sentenced by a court. As in the early 1930s, Korenev was once again sentenced, in extrajudicial procedure, by an NKVD *troika*.

Police supposedly charged Korenev under statute 7-35-b for having no gainful employment or place of residence. In later depositions, however, Korenev's mother noted that this was changed to a charge under one of the paragraphs of the infamous statute 58, the broad statute covering punishment for counterrevolutionary activities. Possibly, having learned that Korenev was employed and a legal resident of Moscow, police realized that the case they had made against Korenev was absurd. They did not wish to let him go, and so changed the charge. Their decision to do this may also have been influenced by Korenev's behavior after his arrest. He did not go quietly. Korenev began writing letters of protest immediately. He demanded to see procuracy officials, threatened suicide and self-starvation and, along with other prisoners, staged a riot in the Moscow jail to which he had been sent. According to the head of the Moscow city police, Panov, Korenev's actions cost him dearly, as did his "impudence" at his "hearing" before the Moscow city *troika*. Korenev, it seems, had the temerity to demand proof of a crime. He "forgot his position" as a twice-convicted felon and openly challenged the authority and competence of the head of the *troika*. The latter, Stanislav Redens, was the head of the entire Moscow oblast NKVD apparatus. This was a high position and Redens was, indeed, one of the most powerful Chekists of the 1930s.[13] The Moscow NKVD *troika* sentenced Korenev on 17 November 1937 to eight years in a closed regime labor camp. Panov told Sofiia that her son was lucky to get off with that.[14]

A. V. TUMANOV

The NKVD, indeed, shipped Korenev to a faraway place. Korenev fell under the administration of the Buriat NKVD railroad camp system, the Burzheldoroglag. After more than a month in transit, he, along with 2,455 other prisoners, ended up in what Korenev described later as "a small, out-of-the-way railroad station" not far from the city of Birobidzhan, in Eastern Siberia. NKVD records make clear that this was the NKVD-run rail station at Izvestkovaia. The actual work site, a logging camp to which he was transferred, lay deeper in the taiga, some distance away from the rail line. The logging camp was run under the administration of the Burzheldoroglag.[15] Korenev described the next months of his life in a letter to his mother. He did not wish to reveal his identity, or his convict past, to anyone who might read the letter other than his mother, so he wrote under a pseudonym, and in thinly disguised wording.[16] According to Korenev, he arrived at his new "workplace" in late December 1937 or early January 1938. Upon arriving, he and his fellow "workers" discovered quickly that the "local leaders" (i.e., the camp administrators) were "simply a pile of criminals." The working conditions and living accommodations "prepared" for the new arrivals "exceeded anything I had ever seen for their meanness and illegality." Korenev soon had serious run-ins with the "bosses." He also feared that the conditions were so bad that his health would be seriously threatened. (Korenev had suffered several serious lung and kidney infections over the years, and his legs were also weak from serious bouts of frostbite.) "It was too much for me," he wrote, "and I realized that my only option was to leave the place."

According to his case file, Korenev, along with several other inmates, fled the logging camp in early February 1938. Their plan was to head for Birobidzhan. In his letter home, Korenev explained, in cryptic language, that, "due to complicated reasons," he had no money and no transport and, as a result, was forced to spend a number of days in the woods, along the rail line. Very likely, Korenev had no documents as well, and could not risk being picked up along roads or in towns. Wandering with no food and with little clothing to protect him from the cold, he fell ill from hunger and exposure, and "landed" in "a clinic in some small town, in the middle of nowhere." There, he "hovered for a number of days between life and death," but slowly began to recover. From later records, it is clear that Korenev traveled at the time under a false name. Still, he did not explain how, as a stranger with no documents in a sensitive area of the country, he was able to recuperate in a clinic in a small town without drawing police attention. He certainly arrived at the clinic under suspicious circumstances. According to his own account, a policeman found him lying unconscious and took him for nearly dead. He was taken immediately to the clinic. This part of Korenev's story testifies either to the sympathetic cooperation of the local population or to the laxness of local police, or to both.

In any case, Korenenv was not detained, and his brush with death was the first of several. In his letter, he wrote that after recuperating, he made his way to Vladivostok. He did not mention to his mother that, before arriving in Vladivostok, he took a detour, as planned earlier, to Birobidzhan. There, however, with no identity papers and no money, he could get no work. He turned to robbery, and survived in this way for a number of weeks, from his escape in February until his recapture in early April 1938. His rearrest resulted from a robbery attempt turned bad. Unfortunately, having broken into an apartment with another escaped convict, he was discovered by the owner's mother. Neither police nor procuracy records make clear what happened, but the confrontation ended, tragically, in the woman's murder. Korenev and his accomplice were armed with a "cold" weapon, most likely a knife. Korenev was apprehended, and he gave his name as A. V. Tumanov. Interestingly, police were forced to accept the alias, as is shown by the fact that Korenev's case file for the robbery was identified under the name Tumanov. Police may have attempted to trace Korenev under his alias, and if so, they very likely realized that Tumanov was not his real name. Without any other documentation to trace, however, they were forced to take Korenev's word about his identity. Police might have suspected that he was an escapee from a camp. Yet, given the large number of escapes from camps, trying to trace his identity by inquiring about recent escapees was probably impossible to do. Thus, Korenev acquired a new identity. He now had two case files, one under the name Korenev in the NKVD camp administration in Izvestkovaia, and one under the name Tumanov in Birobidzhan.[17] These were the first two of several identities he was to acquire.

After their initial investigations, police transferred Korenev to the central NKVD prison in Khabarovsk, the center of the Eastern Siberian *krai*. Police held him in Khabarovsk while his case was further processed. According to a later police deposition, Korenev mentioned that he noticed, during one of his interviews, that his case file lay separately from other files on a desk. He concluded correctly from this that his case would not be heard in a regular court, but was to be transferred to the jurisdiction of the extrajudicial NKVD *troika* board of the Eastern Siberian *krai*. The case officer who compiled the later deposition wrote: "Korenev, being a sufficiently astute person, quickly evaluated his situation—a criminal past, and now awaiting punishment for a particularly egregious crime." In his later deposition, Korenev explained that, aware of the seriousness of his situation, he convinced his cellmate, a certain Ivan Rozhnov, to cooperate in a ruse to "switch cases," that is, to switch identities. Here is how it was supposed to work. Rozhnov had been sentenced to three years in a work camp for hooliganism, and he was already scheduled to be shipped out of the Khabarovsk prison soon. "When the transport came to gather their shipment," according to Korenev, "I took Ivan Rozhnov's place, while Ivan Rozhnov stayed behind as me." The plan was that Ivan would confess the switch after nine or ten days, allowing "Tumanov" enough time to try again to escape.[18]

Unfortunately for Ivan Rozhnov, the switch worked too well. Korenev, posing as Rozhnov, was shipped out of Khabarovsk. Rozhnov, however, either failed to confess the switch or failed to convince prison and police officials that he was not, in fact, "Tumanov." Later case records reconstructed what happened next. "Tumanov's" case did, in fact, come before the NKVD *troika* in Khabarovsk on 29 April, and he was sentenced to death by shooting. According to NKVD files, the sentence was carried out on the same day.[19] Several years later, during an investigation of his various identities, police showed Korenev the file of "Tumanov," which had been sent from Khabarovsk. Korenev acknowledged that the identifying photograph accompanying the file was not his, but that of Ivan Rozhnov. From this statement, it is clear that the NKVD in Khabarovsk had believed the ruse, and had even attached the wrong photograph to "Tumanov's" case file. With the execution carried out, the NKVD closed the case file, and it remained in the NKVD offices in Khabarovsk. Two files now existed within the Siberian NKVD system on Korenev, but they were separate and unconnected. One file under the name Korenev showed him as missing from the Burzheldoroglag camp system, and one, in Khabarovsk under the name Tumanov, listed him as executed.

In fact, Korenev was alive, having cheated death a second time, and was on his way to Vladivostok under the alias Ivan Rozhnov. Once again, we reconstruct events from later depositions. As Rozhnov, Korenev traveled under NKVD guard in a prisoner transport train. The train arrived at a transshipment junction near Vladivostok on 19 April 1938. From there, Korenev, like the other prisoners, was to be shipped to points farther along in the camp and prison system. At the junction, guards disembarked their prisoner-wards to sort and reload onto different trains. Several transports were already at the junction and several hundred or even several thousand prisoners ended up mixed together in a disorderly fashion. Here, Korenev found his chance. Taking advantage of the confusion, Korenev managed to separate himself from the other prisoners and guards and to slip away from the transport.[20]

EMEL'IAN MAKARKIN

Korenev made his way to the city of Vladivostok proper, but he was, again, without documents, and Vladivostok was a regime city. This meant that police would probably be more rigorous in the enforcement of passport and registration laws. Korenev knew this and decided on what he hoped would be an appropriate strategy to create a believable identity. He explained in a later deposition: "Since I had no documents, I knew I needed some kind of verifiable information, some kind of biographical information, no matter how brief, about someone local. If I was apprehended without documents, I could give that name and some biographical details." Korenev hoped that the information would be convincing enough that the police would at least release him on his own or his "family's" recognizance, while they checked the information. The plan, of course, was that, once released, Korenev would again flee.

Korenev made his way to the Vladivostok dock area. There, he struck up an acquaintance with a dock worker, supposedly, by the name of Emel'ian Makarkin, and none too soon. On the evening of 25 April, just a week after his flight from the NKVD transport, Korenev was found drunk and asleep in a ship's coal bunker. Police found in his possession ("next to him") what appeared to be stolen items.[21] He was apprehended as an undocumented person and then arrested on the suspicion of robbery. In keeping with his strategy, he gave police the name of Emel'ian Makarkin as his own, but the strategy failed him. Police did not release him, as he had hoped. Since they charged him with robbery, rather than just lack of documentation, they held him in jail under investigative detention.

Here, the various accounts create a mystery. An NKVD *troika* sentenced Korenev, again, on 14 May 1938, nearly three weeks after police arrested him, to three years in a labor camp, under the name of Emel'ian Makarkin. One NKVD report notes that he was sentenced as a socially dangerous element, but another declares that he was sentenced for robbery.[22] One account notes that the sentence was for only three years because "Emel'ian Makarkin" had no previous convictions. Normally, such a case would have been heard in a regular court, but "Emel'ian Makarkin's" case was heard by an NKVD *troika*—very likely, because "Emel'ian Makarkin" had no documents to prove his identity. Yet, the sentencing of Korenev under the name Emel'ian Makarkin does not make sense. Supposedly, Emel'ian Makarkin was a real person. He lived and worked in Vladivostok. This means he had a passport and was registered in the city. Why were police and NKVD investigators unable to discover the real identity of Emel'ian Makarkin, and realize that the individual they were holding was an imposter? The passport and registration system was often ineffective and officers were lax in keeping records current, but it is difficult to believe that the system was so corrupted that police could find no trace of a registered individual living in a regime city in which the search was initiated. Perhaps Korenev gave the name of Emel'ian Makarkin but provided fictitious information about residence in another, nonregime city. Still, police would have had three weeks, at least, to inquire and discover that no such person was registered.

There is an alternate explanation to this mystery. The evidence that Emel'ian Makarkin was a real person came from Korenev, as part of a deposition given in October 1940. The officer who took the deposition reported it as fact, but Korenev may have lied in the deposition. In fact, this is a likely scenario, and the clue to this version lies in the last name. Korenev gave Vladivostok police Emel'ian's family name as Makarkin, which was ironically similar to the name Makar, the name bandied about by the Moscow police officer, Gogolev, who arrested Korenev in 1937. Korenev may have recalled the use of that name and its association with a place "in hell at the end of the earth." It stretches the bounds of credibility to believe that Korenev coincidentally met someone with such a last name. Most likely, and with a certain amount of bitter humor, Korenev deliberately chose that name to give Vladivostok police in April 1937. Indeed, this was the conclusion that Korenev's mother also drew, after reading a letter from her son sent from the Lisii Island camp, near Vladivostok. Korenev wrote this letter in September 1938 under the pseudonym of Makarkin. Through her own inquiries, Sofiia already knew about the conversation between Gogolev and Korenev during his original arrest. Putting the two names together, she made the connection between Makar and Makarkin. She explained the connection in one of her many protest letters to the procuracy to have her son's case reviewed. Using such a name was characteristic of her son's sardonic and bitter sense of injustice.[23] If this latter version is true, and Emel'ian Makarkin was not a real person, then that would explain why Vladivostok police apparently could find no such person. Having no other way to document Korenev's real identity, police had no choice but to accept this identity and to sentence Korenev under the name Emel'ian Makarkin.

Whatever the explanation for this mystery, the NKVD accepted Korenev's claim to be Emel'ian Makarkin. He was sentenced as that person and was once again transported to a penal logging camp, this time to the island of Lisii. It was from this island that Korenev wrote to his mother in late September 1938, posing as Emel'ian Makarkin, a close friend of the family.[24] By this time, Korenev had been in the logging camp for four months, his longest single stretch of time in one place since his transport from Moscow. In addition to a recitation of his adventures, Korenev described some of the life of the camp, and his various administrative jobs. He wrote that he had already sent his mother three letters, but had no idea if they had arrived. Korenev requested that his mother send clothing, shoes, money, and other goods to the camp, but he added a proviso that she not delay, since he might be leaving soon (!). Korenev did not spell out the implication, but clearly he was planning another escape, and he needed clothing other than that issued by camp authorities. Korenev had gotten smarter, realizing that during previous escapes he had had to steal in order to survive and to establish an identity, and this was what had gotten him caught. This scenario Korenev hoped to avoid in any future escape, and he let his mother know this in his cryptic sentences. Thus, he wrote, "I have nothing to wear . . . and I do not want to do anything illegal." In order to underscore his request and the reason behind it, Korenev reminded his mother how "strange" he had appeared during their "visit together at Lake Onega and Medgor." The latter was a coded reference to Sofiia's visit to her son during his first camp stint from 1934 to 1937. In describing this "happy" memory, however, Korenev left absent any mention that he was, in fact, a prisoner at the time. Finally, Korenev requested of his mother that, if she in fact received the letter and replied, to do so "in the same style and form" as he had written. This was a warning, of course, that she should address her letter to Emel'ian Makarkin.[25]

Korenev filled his letter with coded references, creating a fictitious past that only his mother could decipher. He acknowledged that he was serving time at Lisii, having been convicted as a *sotsvredelement,* but he presented himself as Emel'ian Makarkin, convicted by mistake as a social harmful. This was due, he claimed, to the fact that his documents had been stolen and he was not registered. Korenev, as Makarkin, reflected on this "inhuman" fate and its injustice. In fact, Korenev was writing about the twists and turns of his own fate. "What an inhuman, terrible, and difficult . . . situation I find myself in," he wrote, "and how deeply and without hope I have fallen. . . . I fail to understand how all this suddenly got dumped on me (*valit'sia vdrug mne na golovu*). Is this all a bad accident or a conscious blow? What for?" Expressing his innocence, again in coded language, Korenev also expressed remorse for his criminal activities since his arrest and escapes, and he pleaded for understanding. "I cannot consider myself guilty of anything," he continued, "neither before my departure [his arrest and exile from Moscow], nor later, when I had to act as necessity demanded, and anyone who thinks to reprimand or judge this or that among my actions should step into my skin and see how he behaves." After so much had happened to him, Korenev concluded, he had lost faith and could hope for nothing normal ever again. "Behind is a string of strange, inexplicable events; ahead is a joyless, unclear future, without promise, without a goal. What remains to me is only to try to make the time go quickly in the hope that some kind of extraordinary event will occur to bring me back to where I was." Korenev was writing about his own life, but his words also reflected the fate of his generation.[26]

Korenev made good his expressed intention to escape, but not from Lisii. He remained on the island for several more months until late April 1939, when he fell ill with a recurring kidney ailment. According to his letters home, he was ill a lot during these months, and this last bout brought him close to death. The illness was serious enough that camp authorities transferred Korenev to a hospital on the mainland where doctors gave little hope for his recovery. However, he cheated death yet a third time, and recovered sufficiently by late May or June to be transferred to an NKVD mining colony in Artem, north of Vladivostok. After a hiatus of several months, from May to September, Korenev reestablished contact with Sofiia. After an exchange of several letters, she proposed in September to come visit. Korenev wrote that she should not make the journey, for several reasons, but for the main reason that, "at any minute, they can herd me (*ugnat'*) to another place, somewhere even more remote." Whether this was another veiled warning is not clear, but on 11 November, according to later investigation, Korenev escaped from the Artem colony.

MIKHAIL ROMANENKO

Having escaped, Korenev somehow got to Vladivostok, where his immediate problem was to get hold of identity papers. He was in a regime city and therefore ran the high risk of being caught without proper identification papers, *dokumenty*. Yet he was unable to leave the city by any kind of public transportation without showing a passport. Korenev committed a burglary in order to obtain documentation, and obtained a passport in the name of Mikhail Romanenko.[27] He then fled the city of Vladivostok and made his way back to Khabarovsk. Why he chose to return to Khabarovsk is unclear, but once there, he went to the local offices of *Komsomol'skaia Pravda*, located in the city's Central Hotel. There he told newspaper officials that he was a former corresponding member and editor in the Moscow offices of the newspaper, that he had been in a labor camp and had been released, but that his release papers had been stolen. Remarkably, Korenev used his real name, probably realizing that the newspaper would try to verify his identity.[28] Newspaper officials did, in fact, verify by telegraph that he was a correspondent, and the paper's editor believed his story that he had been released and that his documents had been stolen. On the basis of this story, the Khabarovsk office of the newspaper advanced Korenev sixty rubles, and he left. He then committed another robbery, this time of the apartment of an NKVD official. He took some money, but most important, he stole the official's uniform, though not his passport. He still traveled under the alias and stolen documents of Mikhail Romanenko.[29]

Korenev managed to evade police for only a short time, for they apprehended him again on 24 November, still in Khabarovsk, under unknown circumstances.[30] Korenev attempted to pass himself off as Romanenko, but police quickly caught him out, using fingerprint and other information contained in passport files, and he acknowledged his identity as Emel'ian Makarkin. Under this name, of course, police could trace him as a runaway from the Vladivostok camps administration, Vladivostoklag, and they may or may not have made the link between the identities of Makarkin and Korenev. NKVD officials maintained that at the time of his arrest as Romanenko in November 1939, they knew him only as Makarkin, and had no information linking him to the identity of Korenev. Disputing this, Korenev's mother claimed that the NKVD was aware of the link as early as October 1938, when Korenev was still on Lisii, since she informed NKVD officials that they were holding her son, Kiril Korenev, under the name of Makarkin.[31] It is very likely that both claims were true. Central NKVD officials knew of the connection between Korenev and Makarkin, but local officials in Khabarovsk may not have known of the connection, even if they had sent an inquiry to Vladivostok. Such inquiries were often lost or routed to offices that had incomplete or wrong information. Whatever the case, and even if Khabarovsk police connected Romanenko-Makarkin to Korenev, the NKVD officials who arrested Romanenko-Makarkin in November 1939 did not make the crucial and damning link between Romanenko-Makarkin-Korenev and Korenev-Tumanov. Police made no connection to Korenev's identity as Tumanov, and to the robbery turned to murder in 1938, or to Korenev's identity as Ivan Rozhnov, the unfortunate individual executed in his place in April 1938.

This failure to connect Korenev to Tumanov or Ivan Rozhnov is interesting. Korenev, posing as Romanenko-Makarkin, sat in the same prison, in Khabarovsk, where the cases of Tumanov and Ivan Rozhnov had been adjudicated, and Korenev might have worried that someone would recognize his face, or make a connection between his various identities. This did not happen for one or more of several reasons. The case file for Tumanov had been handled as part of the mass operations under the special troikas, not the regular police, so the file would not have been easily accessible to criminal police in late 1939, even if they were looking for a connection. Moreover, the case file for Tumanov was not yet connected to the name Korenev, at least not in Khabarovsk police registries, and there would have been no reason for police officials to look for a connection. Finally, Korenev's second arrest in Khabarovsk took place in late November 1939. The years of the mass repressions were already over. Thousands of individuals had passed through the Khabarovsk police and NKVD system within those two years, and it was not likely anyone would have recognized Korenev. Also likely is that the police and NKVD officers who had handled Korenev's case in 1938 had themselves been swept away in the purges and counterpurges of the period. Ironically, the very confusion and mass character of the mass operations guaranteed Korenev a certain amount of anonymity and protection.

KORENEV-MAKARKIN-ROMANENKO

Police in Khabarovsk returned Korenev, still under the alias Emel'ian Makarkin, to the Vladivostok NKVD camp administration in Artem, from which he had escaped. By February, 1940, camp officials had prepared charges against Korenev for his November 1939 escape and robberies. This time, however, and for the first time, Korenev's case was adjudicated through the regular court system, rather than through an NKVD *troika*. The end of the mass purges in November 1938 finally put a stop to the activities of the special sentencing boards, and Korenev's fate was now to be decided according to the regular procedures of the criminal and judicial system. In April, in accordance with judicial procedures, the Primorsk district procurator for camps, Kondrashev, confirmed the NKVD indictment and sent it for a hearing by the district judicial court.[32] Korenev was indicted by both Kondrashev and camp officials under the aliases of Makarkin and Romanenko. Interestingly, Kondrashev included the name Tumanov as one of Korenev's aliases. This was one of the first police or procuracy documents to make the connection, but this connection did not seem to affect the indictment. Kondrashev made this connection from a summary of information about Korenev sent by the central passport office in Moscow. Among other items, that summary listed Korenev as having been arrested as Tumanov, in Birobidzhan, although it mistakenly dated the arrest to December 1938 instead of to April 1938. (By December 1938, Korenev was already a prisoner on the island of Lisii, as Makarkin.) There was no substantive information about Korenev's arrest as Tumanov, and Kondrashev, preparing his indictment in April 1940, most likely passed over the brief reference to Tumanov.[33] Kondrashev indicted Korenev as Korenev-Makarkin-Romanenko for the November 1939 escape from Artem and subsequent robberies. Korenev remained in Artem, but on 4 May 1940, he escaped yet again.[34] Once again he was apprehended, and once again he gave a false name, this time of Nikolai Orlov. It is unclear how long Korenev eluded police, or how, once recaptured, police officials identified him as Makarkin-Romanenko, but they did so, and easily. On 31 May, the Primorsk judicial court sentenced Korenev, alias Makarkin-Romanenko to an additional one and a half years for his escape from Artem, and for robberies committed under statutes 82 and 162 of the criminal code.[35]

The story of Korenev's various escapes and identities is remarkable. Yet the tale told so far is only half the story. Korenev did not realize that during the years of his various camp confinements and escapes, high procuracy and NKVD officials in Moscow were attempting to trace him. These attempts are a story in and of themselves that cannot be fully explored here, but part of it is pertinent to the themes explored in this chapter. The search from Moscow helps explain how Korenev's various identities finally caught up with him.

SOFIIA

As noted above, Korenev's mother, Sofiia, actively pursued a review of her son's case after his arrest. For nearly a year, she received contradictory answers about the charges lodged against her son, about his sentence, about whether the courts or the NKVD had sentenced him, and where he had been sent. Interestingly, much of this contradictoriness arose, not because of conscious attempts on the part of police and NKVD officials to obfuscate; in fact, it appears that various officials were insultingly frank about the information they thought they knew. Rather, different bureaucracies—the police, the NKVD, and the procuracy—possessed conflicting information about Korenev's case. Little effort was made to coordinate and check this information, and Sofiia received the impression that she was talking about different versions of her son's life, depending on which official sat in front of her.[36] The rapid turnover of officials due to purge and counterpurge complicated Sofiia's inquiries. In two years, from late 1937 through late 1939, she confronted no fewer than five officials, one succeeding the other, in the position of assistant chief prosecutor for oversight over the NKVD prison system. Sofiia had to educate each one in the details of her son's case. In the weeks and month after her son's arrest, she wrote scores of petitions, and sought interviews with dozens of police and higher NKVD officials. She got nowhere with the police and NKVD. The arresting police officers, Solov'ev and Gogolev, ridiculed her and her son, treating Sofiia like "some kind of half-crazed old woman," saying her son got what he deserved, that she was "wasting her tears." Aside from the many insults, the justification for her son's arrest ultimately boiled down to the frightening combination of routine police bullying and the arbitrary and nearly unlimited power given to the police during the mass operations. "The police can do what it wants, without any kind of court," said Solov'ev.[37]

At least the police talked with Sofiia. Repeated requests to see NKVD administrative officials were denied. Her petitions to Yezhov were returned with the same one-word notation: refused. Patient and numerous appeals to various Moscow city procuracy officials also availed Sofiia little. Either they agreed with the sentence, not having reviewed the case file, or, frightened, they refused to help. But, Sofiia persisted—and not quietly. She appealed to her deputy representative in the Supreme Soviet. She appealed to *Komsomol'skaia Pravda,* and the editors of the paper formally and officially supported her petitions and offered crucial copying and typing services. Sofia was not the meek mother she was told to be by police officials. She had been a revolutionary activist, had suffered exile, and had herself escaped several times. She knew hardship, she knew the law and her rights under the "Stalinist" constitution, and she was not intimidated by threats. Sofia's petitions over the years showed a keen ability to summarize and present facts. She kept meticulous records of meetings and of what was said and by whom. She did not shrink from calling the behavior of high officials what it was—criminal—either by conscious, hypocritical design or by negligent incompetence. Sofiia's straightforward recounting of events amounted to a withering and damning indictment of a brutal system, and of the "cruel" people who were part of that system, who "consistently violate the constitution . . . who deceive the populace, who [sow] disbelief in the law."[38] Sophia persisted, and she finally gained the attention and help of Andrei Vyshinskii, and then of Beria, Yezhov's successor, as well as of Mikhail Pankrat'ev and V. M. Bochkov, Vyshinskii's successors as chief procurator.

Sofiia first wrote to Vyshinskii directly in January 1938, fully two months after her son's arrest, and after two months of inaction by procuracy and police officials. As the previous chapter showed, those months—November and December—were some of the most intense in the campaigns of mass arrests and killings under Order 00447. Police were under enormous pressure to maintain the pace of arrests, and procuracy officials were under direct orders not to interfere. No wonder that police dismissed the complaints of an aged pensioner mother. No wonder procuracy officials refused to help. At first, Sofiia's letter to Vyshinskii seemed to fare no better than her previous appeals. She received no answer to that or to a second letter.[39] Finally, in July 1938, Sofiia wrote directly to Stalin. What effect this letter may have had is unclear, although Sofiia believed that it was this letter that finally evoked a response, since she was summoned several weeks later to the central procuracy office for oversight over the NKVD. In fact, the letter to Stalin may have played little or no role. Although Sofiia received no acknowledgment from Vyshinskii, the procuracy office began an inquiry into the case even within several days of receiving the first letter in January. By late May 1938, Vyshinskii had prepared a protest against Korenev's conviction, which was submitted to the NKVD's *Osoboe soveshchanie* in early June. Vyshinskii appealed Korenev's case as an example of illegal arrest. The procuracy contested the police version that Korenev had had open association with criminal elements, was unemployed, and had no official residence in Moscow. The latter was patently false, since Korenev lived with his mother. Vyshinskii cited the police evidence of criminal connections as too vague to be given credence. On the contrary, the procuracy complaint produced testimony from officials at *Komsomol'skaia Pravda* that Korenev had been not only employed but had been an exemplary worker.[40] Vyshinskii's complaint was successful. In July of 1938, the *Osoboe soveshchanie* heard the case and acquitted Korenev of the original charges.

As it turned out, winning Korenev's acquittal was the easy part. After the acquittal, the NKVD and the USSR procuracy's office of oversight over the NKVD attempted to trace Korenev, but they failed, and they failed repeatedly. They could trace Korenev to his first camp, the NKVD railroad camp at Izvestkovaia, but from the Burzheldoroglag they received contradictory information. In response to Moscow's requests, a physical search revealed that he was not in the camp to which he had been assigned, or in any of the several camps or colonies under the Burzheldoroglag administration. Yet, neither did the camp administration have any record that Korenev had escaped. Thus, officially, Korenev was listed as a prisoner of the Burzheldoroglag, but he was not there. Further, according to the Burzheldoroglag administrators, they could not even verify in their records that Korenev had, in fact, physically arrived at the camp to which he had been assigned. Thus, if he had escaped, they were not certain whether he had escaped after or before his arrival at the camp with the two thousand other prisoners in his transport.[41]

There the trail went dead. Even the highest officials of the NKVD and the procuracy could not trace Korenev's various identities and escapes. The trail stayed dead until October 1938, when Sofiia received the letter from her son, then in the island labor camp under the alias Emel'ian Makarkin. She turned this over to the procuracy and the NKVD, and both agencies contacted the administration of the Vladivostoklag. Officials of Vladivostoklag confirmed that they held a prisoner named Emel'ian Makarkin, but they refused to release him. Their refusal stemmed from two problems, both associated with the issue of identity. The first problem was one of simple proof. Camp officials refused to release Korenev unless and until they could obtain proof that the prisoner Emel'ian Makarkin was, in reality, the person identified as Korenev. Later records show that proof of identity required either fingerprint or photographic evidence that the two persons were the same individual. The gathering of this evidence was a time-consuming process and involved the physical locating of files in various places—at least in Moscow, in Izvestkovaia, and in Khabarovsk—and their transfer to Vladivostok. Still, this was a rather straightforward bureaucratic process, assuming that files had not been misplaced.

The second problem delaying Korenev's release was more complicated. The individual Korenev might have been illegally arrested and be subject to release, but camp officials held an individual named Emel'ian Makarkin who had been convicted on specific charges of false identity, robbery, and being a socially dangerous element. Camp officials, and now the NKVD leadership of the Primorsk district, were reluctant to release that individual. In one telegram, Vladivostoklag officials wrote laconically: "We have instructions to release Korenev, we will not release Makarkin." A procuracy official summed up the problem of bureaucracy and identity succinctly when he told Sofiia: "As Korenev, your son should be freed, but as Makarkin, he will sit in prison."[42]

Other problems delayed action on Korenev's case. Unfortunately for Sofiia and her son, officials tracked Korenev's location and false identity in November and December 1938, and this turned out to be bad timing. The purges that decimated the procuracy system also affected the ranks of the NKVD. It was in these months that Stalin brought the mass repressions to a halt and turned on Yezhov and the NKVD system that had carried out the mass repressions. Beria replaced the now disgraced Yezhov and a large number of NKVD officials were either arrested or otherwise replaced. Understandably, these changes affected the central leadership of the NKVD and created chaos. As a result, ongoing work of these bureaucracies either came to a halt or slowed considerably. Within the course of several months, all the individuals who had been working on Korenev's case were changed and changed again. Sofiia had to start all over again with a new set of NKVD officials.[43]

Matters dragged on for several months during the winter and spring of 1939. Sophia and procuracy officials continued to press for information about and release of Korenev. Their requests were met with either silence from camp officials, or baffling delays while files and identities were being checked. The chief procurator in charge of camp oversight, a man named D'iakonov, apologized profusely for the delays, and said that the problems lay with the slowness of local officials. D'iakonov promised Sofiia that answers would be forthcoming, and that her son would soon be freed.[44] In the meantime, Sofiia maintained contact with Korenev, who began to take an active part in the Lisii camp life. As he had done while in camp in the mid-1930s, he took up writing articles and advocating for fellow prisoners. Sofiia sent him money each month, as well as other packages with newspapers and books. Korenev began to use his own name, signing articles and his own petitions, one of which he sent to Beria in the spring of 1939. *Komsomol'skaia Pravda* also submitted a supporting petition to Beria for Korenev's immediate release.[45]

Inexplicably, none of this activity produced the expected results. In May 1939 came the word from a camp doctor that Korenev had been taken seriously ill with a recurring kidney problem, and had been transferred to a hospital in Vladivostok. Sofiia then lost contact with her son until August when an NKVD official in Vladivostok informed her that Korenev had been transferred to the mining camp at Artem. Sofiia took this news to a procurator with whom she had been working, a man named Dimakov. Through Dimakov, Sofiia wired her son money and letters. The news from him revealed, however, that his situation at Artem was worse than on Lisii, not better, and that he placed less and less hope in the prospect of release. Mother and son exchanged several more letters and, in that exchange, Korenev informed his mother that he had not received the money or other items she had sent to him. In September, Sofiia resolved to go to Artem to try to push matters. As noted above, Korenev pleaded with her not to make the trip.

Abiding by her son's wishes, Sofiia continued to press NKVD officials in Moscow, and by October, she believed that the case was, again, moving to resolution and release of her son. The camp procurator at Artem had interviewed Makarkin and was finally satisfied that Makarkin and Korenev were the same person. All the other information—from camp records, police files, and passport catalogs—coincided. So did accounts in the various petitions from Sofiia and her son. NKVD officials told Sofiia that everything was in order. All that was needed was the final approval for release by Dimakov. When Sofiia arrived in Dimakov's office, however, both of them received a shock. The file that the NKVD had sent to Dimakov was not that of Korenev-Makarkin, but of Korenev-Tumanov.

The exchange of files and identities is inexplicable, at least on the basis of the documents included in Korenev's case file. The NKVD had a file on Korenev as Makarkin, and a case file for Tumanov, but it is unclear how police connected Tumanov's identity with that of Korenev. Nor is it clear how central NKVD officials could have mistakenly sent the case file of Korenev-Tumanov to Dimakov in place of the file for Korenev-Makarkin. Korenev had been careful to keep the two identities separate. In all his correspondence, he omitted any reference to events in Birobidzhan and Khabarovsk from April 1938. Sofiia believed, as did procuracy and central NKVD officials, that Korenev had gone straight to Vladivostok after his escape from the logging camp. All the central NKVD documents, as well as those from the Vladivostok NKVD administration, repeat this version. In these documents, Korenev was known only by the alias Makarkin. Neither NKVD nor procuracy officials, nor Sofiia, made the connection between Korenev and Tumanov. In fact, when Sofiia and Dimakov saw the Korenev-Tumanov file for the first time, both believed that there had been a mix-up, that the person named Korenev-Tumanov was not Sofiia's son. It is understandable that they thought this since, as later documents revealed, the photograph and information in the file were those of the unfortunate Ivan Rozhnov, mistakenly identified as Tumanov. Still, it is unclear who made the connection between Tumanov and Korenev. Just as puzzling is that central NKVD officials did not notice anything amiss when they reviewed the file of Korenev-Tumanov, even though they were the ones who sent the file to Dimakov, and who reassured Sofiia that everything was in order for the release of her son. Very likely, those same officials did not bother to look at the file before sending it to Dimakov; otherwise they would have realized their "mistake," or launched a further inquiry.

That central NKVD authorities possessed the Korenev-Tumanov file provides insight into how the NKVD worked. In their months of investigations, officials very likely culled any information available from likely oblast and district offices about anyone with the name of Korenev or his known aliases. Receiving a directive for information, Khabarovsk police officials would have found the file for Korenev-Tumanov and sent the file physically to Moscow. Sending the file would have taken a number of days, and most likely weeks. Korenev's case was, of course, not the only case under investigation, and the movement of hundreds if not thousands of case files around the country at any one time helps explain why such investigations took so long. As noted above, Korenev's arrest as Tumanov was also noted in a brief entry in his passport card in the central NKVD passport catalogs in Moscow. When reviewing the actual case files, however, Moscow authorities must have concluded that the passport entry for Korenev, K. K. was wrong. Clearly the file of Korenev-Tumanov was of a different person than that of Korenev-Makarkin.

It remains a mystery how Korenev's name became associated with the file for Tumanov. Possibly, Korenev may have given his real name to Birobidzhan and Khabarovsk officials in April 1938 if they discovered his Tumanov alias to be false. This might explain the police's Passport Department notation, cited above, of Korenev's arrest as Tumanov in Birobidzhan. Police were required routinely to make duplicate copies of any biographical information about arrestees, and to file that information in local passport catalogs and send copies to regional and central passport departments. It is remarkable that during the mass purges, when local police processed hundreds of people daily, the routine procedures of every-day bureaucracy ground on. Then again, perhaps it is not so remarkable, since the mass operations were, themselves, the ultimate example of a horrific bureaucratic machine. Whatever the case, police believed in their files, and in the information contained in those files. And the files of Korenev-Tumanov and Korenev-Makarkin showed two separate individuals. In the course of their investigations, NKVD officials must have concluded that the Korenev-Tumanov executed in April 1938 could not be the same person as the Korenev-Makarkin who was alive and on the island of Lisii. Lacking eyewitness accounts, this would have been the only conclusion possible, given the photographs and biographical information contained in the two files. In October and November 1939, only Kiril Korenev knew the truth about what had happened in Khabarovsk.

And Kiril Korenev was nowhere to be found. On 11 November 1939, Korenev made good his escape from Artem, and his escape and recapture precipitated the next chain of events in this strange story. As recounted above, Korenev committed robbery in Vladivostok to obtain documents in the name of Mikhail Romanenko, he made his way back to Khabarovsk, and identified himself to the local editors of *Komsomol'skaia Pravda*. When editors of the paper's central office in Moscow received the inquiry to confirm Korenev's identity, they contacted Sofiia with the news that her son was, apparently, free. Korenev, as well, telegraphed his mother with the same news. This news she shared with

Dimakov, and both were overjoyed and surprised. Both believed that Korenev had been officially released, but Sofiia wondered how, after two years, events could have moved so quickly. Dimakov reassured her, although he, too, was surprised by the apparent speed of events. NKVD officials had told Sofiia in October that all was in order. Then, the mix-up with the files had occurred, but that confusion apparently did not affect the process of release. In fact, explained Dimakov, the mix-up might have hastened Korenev's release. Central NKVD authorities, as well as local officials, might have been embarrassed by the mistake, and have moved all the more rapidly to correct the situation. Dimakov had, in fact, wired the local procurator, Kondrashev, to authorize the release. Once the decision was taken by the NKVD and confirmed by the procuracy, her son would have been released immediately. So explained a jubilant Dimakov, who congratulated Sofiia and insisted that, when Korenev arrived in Moscow, he wanted to meet such an extraordinary young man.[46]

Sofiia and Dimakov had it all wrong, of course, and it did not take Sofiia long to realize that something was not right. By mid-December, with no other word from her son, Sofiia began to worry. She broached the "dreaded" question with Dimakov that perhaps her son had not been released, but had escaped. Interestingly, central NKVD officials also did not know what had happened. Over the next weeks, from late December 1939 through early January 1940, both Dimakov and D'iakonov repeatedly telegraphed their subordinates and counterparts in Vladivostok and Artem to ascertain Korenev's fate. They contacted Artem camp officials, the head of the Vladivostoklag camp system, and Kondrashev, the Vladivostoklag procurator. Their repeated telegrams went unanswered for weeks. Finally, on 15 January 1940, D'iakonov received a terse telegram from an official of the Vladivostoklag administration that Korenev was "missing," and that "measures" were "being taken." This was followed the next day by a fuller cablegram from a Chief Lieutenant, Mishustin, assistant head of the Vladivostoklag administration. Korenev had fled the Artem camp on 17 November.[47]

This series of exchanges is revealing. Surprisingly, it took nearly a month for NKVD officials either to act on D'iakonov's request, or to ascertain that a prisoner was missing. Also surprisingly, these same NKVD officials not only got the date wrong (Korenev fled on 11 not on 17 November), they also did not know that Korenev had been recaptured, that he was under arrest in Khabarovsk, and had been for three weeks already. This lapse is surprising, since Khabarovsk police quickly ascertained Korenev's alias and had contacted officials of the Artem camp that they were holding a runaway. Somehow, that information did not make it into the right file or into the right hands. When Vladivostok officials inquired about Korenev's whereabouts from Artem camp officials, they were told that the prisoner had escaped, but they were not told that Korenev had been recaptured. Thus, Vladivostok authorities instigated a search for a prisoner who was already under detention. Indeed, Korenev may already have been on his way back to Artem by the time he was listed as missing. According to information from Khabarovsk police, Korenev was returned to the Artem camp sometime in the second or third week of January 1940.

Korenev's escape from Artem proved a bitter irony. NKVD officials had consented finally to Korenev's release, almost literally on the eve of his escape. His original sentence had not only been overturned, but so had the three-year sentence issued by the Vladivostok *troika* against him as Makarkin in May 1938. Had he not bolted, Korenev would have been freed. Instead, by February 1940, he was back in camp, and officials were preparing a new set of indictments against him. In February, Lieutenant of State Security Bashko of the Vladivostok camp administration submitted formal charges of flight and robbery against Korenev, alias Makarkin and Romanenko. In April, Kondrashev, as the corresponding procurator, confirmed the charges and submitted his indictment to the Primorsk district court. In early May, Korenev attempted one last escape, and was rearrested under the name Orlov. On the last day in May, the court sentenced Korenev, now with the aliases Makarkin, Romanenko, and Orlov, to sixteen months' imprisonment. Korenev was back where he began.

ABSURDITIES

Sofiia began anew. She pushed Dimakov and D'iakonov to protest the May 31 sentence. The slow machinery of bureaucracy began, again, to clank into movement. This time, however, Sofiia did not have the full support of the procuracy. D'iakonov, it seems, was reluctant to take up the matter again. In his view, and in the view of his office of prison oversight, Korenev had showed himself "unrehabilitated" by his escapes

from Artem. In a summary prepared by his assistant, Makushin, D'iakonov refused to support Sofiia's request for a review of the sentence.[48] In
the meantime, Dimakov, overall head of the procuracy's office of
NKVD oversight, had moved on and was replaced by chief procurator
V. M. Bochkov. Sofiia traveled to Vladivostok to be near her son.
Records are unclear, but Sofiia either convinced Bochkov to pursue the
review, or she convinced Kondrashev, in person in Vladivostok, to do
so. In either case, by late summer, Kondrashev was ready to submit a
formal protest of Korenev's sentence, that is, of the very indictment he
had written in April. Sofiia pressed her case by telegraphing Bochkov
from Vladivostok to "give instructions to D'iakonov to conclude the
release of [her] son."[49] When D'iakonov got word of this, he telegraphed Kondrashev on 29 August, and demanded to know on what
grounds Kondrashev was planning to protest Korenev's sentence.
Within several days, on 4 September, D'iakonov telegraphed Kondrashev again. This time, he told Kondrashev bluntly that he would not
support a protest, and that Kondrashev should "acquaint" himself with
new material that was being sent to the head of the Primorsk UNKVD
office.[50]

The "new material" proved Korenev's undoing. Someone had put the
pieces together, or at least had raised the suspicion that Korenev-
Makarkin and Korenev-Tumanov were the same person. By mid-Octo-
ber 1940, Artem camp authorities had reviewed the files sent to them
and were interrogating Korenev about Tumanov and the events of
spring 1938. The interrogations occurred on 16 and 18 October. Kondrashev's report to D'iakonov from 31 October summarized the results
of the investigation and the interrogations. Police officials showed Korenev the photograph attached to the file identified as Korenev-Tumanov. They asked if he recognized the individual. At first, Korenev said
that he had never seen the man. When officers informed Korenev that
the man had been executed, Korenev broke down and confessed the
man's identity as Ivan Rozhnov. He confessed the switch that had taken
place, and he confessed his part in the robbery and accidental murder
that had led to his arrest as Tumanov.[51]

Korenev's admission confirmed to police that Ivan Rozhnov had been
executed in Korenev's place. No doubt, this discovery was an unpleasant surprise to Korenev as well. Having no information to the contrary,
Korenev assumed that, according to their plan, Rozhnov had informed

officials of the switch without serious consequences. Learning the truth two years later, Korenev spilled out the whole story: his escapes, his identities, his life on the run, his life on the margins of Soviet society. Korenev's various identities were now fully revealed, as were the various files that contained the scattered pieces of his life: Korenev-Tumanov-Rozhnov-Makarkin-Romanenko-Orlov.

On the basis of this new investigation, officials charged Korenev anew, this time for the crimes committed as Tumanov. Interestingly, Korenev was not charged with murder, but under the banditry law, statute 59-3. It is not clear why they chose this statute, since it was usually applied in circumstances of collective and sustained activities. It could have applied to the apartment robbery turned murder, since Korenev was with an accomplice, and Korenev's robberies certainly continued over a period of several years. Also, this statute carried a stronger penalty than simple robbery, and could possibly lead to a capital sentence. Again, Kondrashev wrote the indictment, which he submitted to the Primorsk court in late December 1940.[52]

In December 1940, the NKVD transferred Korenev from a labor camp to the central UNKVD prison in Vladivostok. There he awaited a new trial by the Primorsk district judicial court.[53] Nothing was simple in this case and, here again, the problem of identity and bureaucratic jurisdiction arose. In late January, the case came up for a hearing, but the court refused to accept the indictment as it was. As Kondrashev reported to D'iakonov, the court demanded further proof of Korenev's various identities. More to the point, the court noted that a capital sentence had been passed by the former NKVD *troika* in April 1938, but that sentence had neither been carried out nor vacated. The court returned the case to the procuracy to clarify whether the execution order remained in force, or whether it was null and void. That issue had to be resolved before the court could hear the new charges of banditry.[54]

Kondrashev was also confused. He, in turn, requested clarification from the central procuracy office in Moscow whether the case belonged to the NKVD or to the judicial courts. In bland bureaucratic language, he "requested" that the question "be placed before the NKVD to carry out the sentence of the UNKVD *troika* or to vacate said sentence and submit the case for a new [judicial] review."[55] In other words, was Korenev to be shot or to be given a new trial? Once again, Korenev's life hung in the balance, and once again, his fate hung on the decision of the

NKVD. As it turned out, this was an issue that required a new hearing before the NKVD's *Osoboe soveshchanie.*

D'iakonov was not well disposed toward Korenev, but he put forward a strong deposition in Korenev's favor, citing the various mitigating circumstances. The murder was accidental, and Korenev had been sentenced illegally in the first place. Yet presentation of mitigating circumstances was not the decisive argument. The short summary of the procuracy's argument is curious. Procuracy officials acknowledged that it was "necessary" to carry out the death penalty on Korenev, but then they noted, without further explanation, that the decision of the former NKVD *troika* from April 1938 "cannot be carried out." On that basis, they requested that the case remain under the jurisdiction of the judicial courts.[56] Records provide no clarification why the *troika* decision "could not" be carried out, but the *Osoboe soveshchanie* agreed. On 12 May 1941 the death sentence was commuted, and Korenev's case returned to the jurisdiction of the Primorsk district judicial court. Korenev had escaped death a fourth time.[57]

The decision to commute Korenev's death sentence and the return of his case to the judicial courts is the last document in the case file. Korenev's fate remains unknown, although it seems, at least, that he avoided the sentence of death by shooting. Whether he was sentenced by the Vladivostok court to further prison or camp time is unclear. Nor is it clear if the procuracy requested a death penalty. Most likely not, since such a demand is not contained in any of the indictment documents. Once again, Sofiia traveled to Vladivostok, this time for a new trial. She continued to argue that her son should be freed, based on the decision overturning his original 1937 conviction. She argued that any confinement to which Korenev might be sentenced for crimes committed while as a prisoner had already been fulfilled by his illegal imprisonment.

In a final irony, the decision to have Korenev's case heard by the judicial courts came in mid-May, just one month before the German invasion of the Soviet Union in June 1941. No doubt in May Korenev hoped that the court might free him finally. Yet, Korenev's chance of survival over the next several years might have been better if he stayed in the camps, rather than being freed and, very likely, conscripted into the army. We do not know his fate, however. Korenev's file ends with the decision to try his case in May 1941. It is unclear whether he was convicted or acquitted, what his sentence was, or where he ended up. Attempts to trace him or his family have proved fruitless. As with many of Stalin's victims, Korenev's fate remains a mystery.

CONCLUSIONS

Korenev's tale reveals, dramatically, the gaps and appalling ineffi-ciencies that existed in the system of social surveillance and police con-trol of the 1930s. That system was designed to deal with categories rather than persons. Police could identify, extract, and deport whole populations in a single operation. The regime's leaders could engineer the whole of society, but the massive policing machinery they built to do this had difficulty keeping track of a single individual. Korenev ac-quired and discarded identities numerous times. He moved with relative ease from place to place using falsified or stolen documents. His claims about who he was went largely unchallenged, even when local author-ities should have routinely checked his impersonations. Police ques-tioned their assertions only and not until Korenev came under suspi-cion for a crime. In the case of arrest, police might uncover a false identity rather quickly, but the layers of bureaucracy were extremely cumbersome and slow to trace a person's true identity, or to connect one identity to another. Normally, officials sent out chits, usually in the form of telegrams, asking other departments in other cities and regions if they possessed information about a particular individual. This method yielded little reliable information and was extremely time-consuming.[58] Police in a regional center sent and received hundreds of requests each month, and these had to be individually researched in files. Even tele-graphed and repeated orders from central to local authorities got lost or otherwise went unanswered for weeks. Cross-checking names against aliases was nearly impossible, unless an alias was known. Tracing indi-viduals to various identities became easier once fingerprinting became standardized and widely used, but this method was still in its infancy during the 1930s. In the case of Korenev, police used fingerprint analy-sis only to confirm the information Korenev had already given his in-terrogators. Ultimately, police had to accept an individual's word about his or her identity, unless extraordinary circumstances brought infor-mation to light, or unless an individual volunteered information about his or her background.

The passport and registration system, designed to make Soviet society transparent to the regime, also produced the opposite effect; it encouraged large numbers of people to obfuscate—to falsify parts of their biography or to create wholly fictitious ones. And Soviet citizens did just that by the hundreds of thousands and millions.[59] It is difficult to know the overall dimensions of this kind of falsification. Most citizens probably falsified their identities in small ways—on application documents, for example, omitting the name of a suspect relative, or their own previous membership in a politically unacceptable group or party. Fewer, but probably still a considerable number of people, picked up and moved and then moved again and in the process created whole new identities—bureaucratically and legally—for themselves and their families. This category included professional criminals, but it also encompassed large segments of the population dispossessed of their land, or otherwise persecuted, and forced into a marginal existence of exile and migration. This category included individuals such as Korenev. These people were criminalized simply, and tragically, by the regime's ever-widening definition of social groups and activities deemed harmful and anti-Soviet. Korenev's hapless fate personified Yezhov's casual remark on the eve of the mass purges, that the destruction of a few thousand innocent people should not overly concern police officials. Korenev was one of those people, and he was a lucky one. He narrowly escaped death on several occasions. Still, his life was destroyed, as were the lives of many close to him, or with whom he came into contact. Korenev's story was one of many such stories. His story was repeated not in the thousands, but in the millions.

12 The War and
Postwar Trends

THE NATURE OF POLICING and repression changed during and after the war. Categorical and mass forms of repression continued, even intensified, but these campaigns targeted different populations than before the war. Mass deportations, for example, hit ethnic communities hard inside the 1939 borders of the country, as they did in the new territories annexed in 1939 and reoccupied after 1945. Mass administrative repression of "socially dangerous elements" also continued in the new territories. In the occupied Baltic republics and in the western border regions of Ukraine and Belorussia, political and civil police carried out the same kinds of mass social and political repression that had been characteristic of the 1930s. Within the country's pre-1939 borders, however, the nature of social policing changed after the war, from administrative repression based on categories of identity to judicial convictions for breach of law. This change did not mean that levels of repression decreased. On the contrary, levels of penal incarceration and deportation reached all-time highs in the years from 1945 to 1953. Millions of people found themselves under arrest and then convicted for infractions of labor discipline, and of antitheft and other harsh laws associated with Stalin's extractive policies of economic reconstruction. But these people were convicted by judicial courts rather than by police administrative boards. They were convicted for specific violations of laws rather than for potential disloyalty based on a suspect social or ethnic background. In the realm of social politics, people were repressed for what they did rather than who they were.[1]

Soviet leaders continued to employ political police methods—the kind of secret, extrajudicial policing that dominated the 1930s—primarily in the country's new territories, as well as in some regions of the Caucasus. In these areas, the security of the state was at risk, as local authorities faced serious insurgency movements against Soviet rule all along the country's new borders.[2] Inside the pre-1939 territories, in contrast, leaders depoliticized social-order policing and the fight against criminality, even as they increased the role of civil police and courts in the continuing widespread repression of the population. This shift was reflected in reforms to separate civil from political policing. During the war and postwar years, a series of bureaucratic reorganizations hived off the *militsiia* from the state security organs, and placed it under the former NKVD, now known (in consequence of the renaming of all people's commissariats as ministries) as the Ministry of Internal Affairs, the *Ministerstvo vnutrennikh del,* or MVD. Meanwhile, the political police became a separate Ministry of State Security, the *Ministerstvo Gosudarstvennoi Bezopasnosti,* or MGB. To those sentenced to prisons, camps, colonies, or penal settlements, the difference maybe mattered little whether they were arrested by political or civil police, but there was a difference, and a significant one. Social-order kinds of policing during the postwar years was not nearly as deadly as police repression in the 1930s, and this change reflected a general demilitarization of the social sphere, if not a reduction in levels of repression. In the country's pre-1939 territories, then, the goal, and therefore the methods, of repression changed from the 1930s to the postwar years. No longer was repression aimed at isolating or eliminating enemies of the state. In the postwar era, leaders employed widespread forms of repression to discipline a society in service to state economic reconstruction.[3] The changes in the goal and methods of repression also reflected changes in notions of citizenship and the relation of citizens to the state. All of these changes—in policing practice, bureaucratic organization, and ideas of citizenship—gained momentum in the last years of Stalin's life and resulted in large-scale amnesties after the dictator's death, but many of the changes discussed in this chapter began even in the last years of the

1930s. This was especially true of the structure and nature of social policing.

CIVIL POLICE

The purges of the late 1930s took a heavy toll on police numbers and qualifications. This toll can be seen in the changing demographics of the police forces. By 1940, nearly 24 percent of all civil police had worked in the *militsiia* less than one year. Such a low level of experience resulted partly from expansion in the size of the force. With redivision of a number of oblasts, the demand for more police led Sovnarkom in 1938 to grant a request for 20,000 additional staff. Incorporation of railroad police into the RKM also increased its size. In early 1939, the RKM employed 182,000 people.[4] By mid-July 1940, that number had increased by 31,000, for a total of about 213,000 officers and staff, excluding police academy students. Thus, in a period of one and a half years, the *militsiia* expanded by 17 percent over its 1939 level, but the increase in numbers of positions accounted for only 14.5 percent of those hired within the same period of eighteen months. By mid-1940, as noted above, nearly one-quarter, 24 percent, of police had worked in the RKM for less than one year. Thus, some 3,000 individuals—9 to 10 percent of police staff hired in 1939 and the first months of 1940—were hired as replacements, not to fill new positions.[5] There could have been a number of reasons for replacing staff, including retirements, dismissals, and resignations, but certainly some of that turnover, perhaps most of it, was the result of purges.

The effect of the purges was even more pronounced in statistics of the commanding officer ranks. Command staff positions increased at about the same rate as rank-and-file ones, by about 17 percent between January 1939 and July 1940. As of July 1940, however, 31 percent of the 98,545 command staff had worked in the NKVD for less than one year.[6] Thus, since January 1939, 14 percent—about 13,800 officers—had been hired or promoted to fill vacated rather than new positions. As with rank-and-file staff, many of these replacements were hired very likely due to high rates of voluntary turnover, but many positions were likely vacated due to arrest. Most officers came to the RKM from previous experience in the regular military forces or the NKVD military forces. This was true for 71 percent of rank-and-file police and 83 percent of command officers. Less than 2 percent were recruited from the ranks of the GUGB or OGPU. This pattern of recruitment fit more the practice of European police forces than Yagoda's original vision of an integrated and interchangeable civil police and state security force.[7]

By 1940, police forces were beginning to recover from the effects of the purges, but were still about 8 percent below strength.[8] The war took another heavy toll. In the first months of the war, the RKM lost nearly one-quarter of its strength due to conscription. These numbers were replaced, if replaced, by many who were underqualified or exempt from military service due to physical handicap, pensioner status, or who were described as "criminals and others avoiding military service."[9] By 1947, police numbers were still low—only 201,000, down from a force of 213,000 in 1940.[10] Under strength, underequipped, and underqualified, police had difficulty coping with the massive dislocation and social disorder created by the chaos of the war and the regime's policies in its aftermath. The problems police authorities faced were analogous, if not entirely similar, to those they had faced in the early 1930s. Social displacement and mass migration, criminality, unemployment, even starvation, were exacerbated by the destruction of the cities and their infrastructure, and by the collapse of the trade and distribution systems. Masses of people moved across the landscape through cities and villages singly and in large groups. People ignored passport and residency laws. In 1946 alone, police registered over 1.26 million passport violations, and these were only the number of violations that actually came to their attention. In Leningrad in 1947, police registered 49,144 passport violations, and 173,000 in Moscow for the same year.[11] In 1946, police expelled a quarter of a million people from regime cities who were "looking for food," but had no registration papers. That number reached over half a million in 1947. In just the four years between 1948 and 1952, police charged some 5.5 million people with passport violations. The majority of these people received fines, but 127,000 were charged with criminal violations and sentenced to some sort of prison or camp punishment.[12]

To police authorities, the increase in numbers of passport violators was a sign that the police were beginning to enforce residency laws more effectively. This was no doubt true, but the figures also testified to the scale of social chaos that gripped the country, and authorities admitted that the number of those convicted of residence violations was nonetheless low compared to the number of people actually moving through the cities. In Vilnius alone, over 30,000 people a day arrived in the city's train stations during the first months of 1947. According to police, these people were looking for food, as well as shelter. Few if any of them possessed passports or other officially recognized identity documents.[13] Authorities in the Krasnoiarsk district pleaded to have the city of Norilsk placed under special residence restrictions to stop the inundation of the town by itinerants, former convicts, and outright criminals.[14] Between 1940 and 1946, the population of Sverdlovsk more than doubled, in large part as a result of the arrival of evacuees from more western cities, but also with a significant "contingent" of ex-convicts from nearby NKVD camps. The latter accounted for some four thousand in-migrants in 1946, according to local police.[15] In border areas, especially in the still unfenced border reaches of Central Asia and the Caucasus, contraband activities went nearly unchecked. Goods and people moved with little interference across the borders with Turkey, Iran, and Afghanistan. In Sukhumi, the Black Sea resort town, the city soviet estimated that in 1946, over one thousand foreign nationals and individuals with no clear citizenship status lived in the city without proper residence papers.[16] Similarly, in the Georgian border port of Batumi, crime rates rose dramatically, according to local officials, due to the unchecked influx of undocumented itinerants and foreign smugglers. The proximity of the Turkish border, the mild climate, and the presence of military and naval stores and import and export facilities made the city a prime target for large-scale in-migration.[17]

CHANGES IN CRIMINALITY AND POLICING

If the war brought mass dislocation and migration, it also brought a change in the nature of criminality. Before the war, according to police assessments, the most common form of theft was that of money in the form of embezzlement, and of industrial goods and finished products from enterprises. With the breakdown of the trade and distribution system during and after the war, the most common kind of theft became that of agricultural and prepared food products, and especially of the ration cards and coupons needed for purchase of scarce goods. Relatedly, crimes of speculation also focused on the sale of services and access to food. This stood in contrast to the main focus of speculation during the middle and latter years of the 1930s on resale of industrial goods, raw materials, and manufactured commodities. The shift in criminal activity toward services, and toward food and access to it, repeated a similar pattern during the early 1930s. During the harsh period of collectivization, famine, and rapid industrialization, outright theft of grain and other food products had ranked high in the registry of serious crimes against the state. After the relative stabilization of the mid-1930s, crimes of theft against the state focused on goods and materials. In the immediate postwar period, as in the early 1930s, theft of food commodities and crimes of bribery, graft, and other forms of bureaucratic corruption were not just crimes of greed and venality; these were crimes of necessity for survival in a system of scarce commodities and services. In these circumstances, it is not surprising that, in the mid- and late 1940s, theft of state property and crimes of bureaucratic corruption soared to a level not seen since the first years of state collectivization.[18]

Police forces were ill equipped to deal with these problems, in part as a result of decreases in numbers and qualifications, and also as a consequence of territorial expansion. The size of the country had grown considerably since the prewar years. In a February 1946 request for an increase in police, the Interior Minister, S. N. Kruglov, noted that, since 1939, twenty-two new oblasts had been added, including Kaliningrad and new areas in Transcarpathia and in southern Sakhalin. There were more than 160 new regions, 24 new major cities, and over 100 new workers' settlements. To date, authorities had been forced to staff new areas with police from existing territories. Increases in railroad and water transport police had further drained manpower from the ranks of the territorial police. Some 33,000 officers had been transferred since 1937 from territorial to branch divisions, even as the subdivision of administrative territories inside the pre-1939 borders had created an even greater demand for command staff and rank-and-file police officers. Police ranks were stretched dangerously thin, more so than at any time since the early 1930s. Kruglov presented a litany of local Soviet organs urgently requesting an increase in police to deal with problems of social disorder. Requests poured in from every part of the Soviet Union. The country was underpoliced as well as undergoverned. The situation of disorder, warned Kruglov, was moving out of control of the Ministry of the Interior.[19]

The MVD received additional police staff, but the increase in numbers was not in itself sufficient to deal with the problems of social disorder. Changes in the dynamics of criminal activity and the effects of the war necessitated fundamental changes in the way the country was policed. If the dynamics of major crime shifted from goods to services, so did the locus of criminal activity—from the streets and marketplaces to enterprises and offices. At least, this was leaders' perception of where the greatest danger lay to the state. During the 1930s, authorities were obsessed with the fear of disaffected and marginal social groups, the so-called socially dangerous elements, and the key role these groups allegedly played in criminal activity and potential political opposition. Professional crimes and institutional corruption were rampant in the 1930s, as police often complained, but the priority for state policing was the identification and isolation of dangerous social populations. Yagoda declaimed on numerous occasions about the significant danger to the state posed by petty speculators and criminals. Policing this danger was accomplished largely through social defense campaigns using passport and residency laws—mass sweep operations of city sectors, market districts, transportation nodes and arteries, and other public gathering places. Mass sweeps may have had some effect during the mid-1930s, or so police officials claimed, but such tactics were ineffective in the immediate aftermath of the war. The street-focused policing of the 1930s could not get at the rising level of enterprise-centered criminal activity that so concerned officials after the war. Policies of repression that targeted marginal populations proved ineffective against white-collar criminal activities committed by the millions of employees in state enterprises and cooperatives. Nor were such tactics effective against the gargantuan losses arising from the activities of large-scale, organized criminal rings that operated out of enterprises and state bureaucracies.[20] The priorities and tactics of policing had to shift from defense against ostracized or "alien" elements to the disciplining of Soviet citizens.

There was another reason why policies of mass repression were ineffective. Mass surveillance and policing methods of the 1930s were based largely on an increasingly complex system of passport and residency laws enacted in the early part of the decade. That system had almost completely broken down during and after the war. An MVD report from 1949 summarized the problem in the typically stilted phrasing of Soviet bureaucratic culture:

> During the course of the war, significant numbers of passport blanks and secret passport instructions fell into the hands of the enemy, and into hands of the criminal element. Reregistration of passports and other measures carried out by the MVD could not, therefore, guarantee against the inappropriate use of Soviet passports for purposes harmful to our state goals.[21]

The laconic statement underscored what every policeman knew. Policing based on documented identities was ineffective in the immediate aftermath of the war. Authorities could not be certain that passports presented to them were genuine; nor, in many, cases could officials verify the identities of passport holders through other means. Civil registries had been destroyed in many cities and rural areas, making background or passport checks difficult, if not impossible. In addition, hundreds of thousands of passports had been reported lost or stolen during and after the war. Citizens often had few or no documents that could verify their identity in order to receive a new passport.[22] At the same time, and according to the same report, prewar passport documents were too easily forged or illegally modified, and, thus, too easily open to "abuse by the criminal element."[23] Mass evacuations and migrations added to the problem of "fixing" the population using techniques of the 1930s passport and residency laws. In other words, passports had lost their effectiveness as a means of mass social surveillance in the chaotic postwar conditions of the Soviet Union.

By 1949, MVD officials were preparing proposals for a revamped passport system, but one not tied to mass forms of overt police repression. Use of passport laws for purposes of mass social repression was politically untenable after the war, as well as practically ineffective. Soviet leaders had understood the practical and political problems associated with mass policing even before the social purges of 1937 and 1938. Yezhov criticized the social policing policies that had characterized the 1930s, and that had drawn the state security organs into the business of social control. In the early months of 1937, he began to restructure the NKVD, moving functions of railroad and other transportation policing, which had come under the political police, into reorganized branches of the civil police. In 1938, Yezhov initiated a special branch for fighting banditry under the GURKM, and a new elite criminal investigation branch, the Department for Combating Theft of State Property—the *Otdel bor'by s khishcheniem sotsialisticheskoi sobstvennosti*—an awkward name with an equally awkward acronym, OBKhSS. Yezhov's reforms, though significant, were interrupted, with catastrophic consequences, by the onset of the very kind of mass purges in 1937 and 1938 that he claimed to deplore. Lavrentii Beria, who succeeded Yezhov as head of the NKVD, continued the process of depoliticizing and restructuring the state's police forces. In 1941, Sovnarkom formally separated the civil and political police. The new Commissariat of State Security (*Narodnyi Komissariat Gosudarstvennoi Bezopasnosti,* NKGB) incorporated the old OGPU-GUGB structure. The Commissariat of Internal Affairs, the NKVD, encompassed the remaining administrations under the old NKVD, including the civil police (the GURKM), and the GULAG and firefighting administrations. The political and civil police structures merged and separated again several times during the war and after, but within the 1939 borders of the country, the principle and practice of separating the two organs and their functions was well established even before the end of the war.[24]

As the locus of criminality shifted, so did police strategy. The dramatic increase in institutional forms of theft and corruption forced police to turn away from the ineffective methods of mass repression against social marginals, and to turn instead to the use of agents, informants, and undercover police work to ferret out crime and corruption in institutional settings. This shift amounted to a turnaround in policies from the 1930s, a decade in which both Yagoda and Yezhov downplayed and even mistrusted policing policies based on informant networks. During the 1930s, operational officers disdained informant work, and possessed neither the resources nor, often, the desire, let alone the competence, to engage effectively in this kind of work. The turn back toward this strategy during the 1940s reflected both the changed nature of criminality, or at least police perception of that change, and the prestigious status of the recently formed OBKhSS. In 1940, even before the start of the war, the NKVD began a serious effort to bring order to its agent and informant work, inaugurating a purge of idle or "socially alien" elements from informant and agent rolls. The commissariat opened training schools for agents and began to recruit and build a new system of networks.[25] The chaotic conditions of the war gave this strategy added urgency. A 1944 report noted that "Mass theft and speculation have become such problems that they require mass agent work. No longer is it sufficient to place just one agent in an enterprise." As a result of new priorities, recruitment of agents and informants within OBKhSS increased yearly, from 1,424 agents and 40,723 informants in 1942 to 6,076 agents and 126,693 informants by mid-1944. Officials reported an overall increase in recruitment since before the war of 315 percent, and this during a time when police ranks were being drained by military conscription. Some of this increase came from staffing of territories taken back from German occupation, but most resulted from the strengthening of work at *krai* and oblast levels of police administration.[26]

After the war, yearly expansion of informant networks was rapid: nearly 23,000 were added in 1946, and over 30,000 in 1947. By 1947, OBKhSS alone boasted an agent and informant base numbering 308,579 people. As of January 1948, the number had grown to 338,858, of whom 14,555 were residents, that is, police officers or specially trusted informants who controlled agents or other informants. Case officers controlled nearly 18,500 agents, and residents managed over 305,000 informers. OBKhSS employed nearly 10 percent of its officer cadre, 32,258 people, in the maintenance of these networks.[27] In keeping with new policing priorities, over one-third of agents and informers, 123,524, worked in enterprises of the agricultural ministry, which included state and collective farms, as well as in financial and accounting offices of the ministry's bureaucracies. The next largest group—45,237, or 13 percent —were deployed in the struggle against speculation. Other bureaucracies of special concern included the food, meat, and dairy ministry, and the trade ministry. Police operated 29,548 informants in offices of the former and 21,000 in enterprises of the latter.[28]

The shift in policing strategy toward informant and agent work resonated in the way cases arose and were brought to court. During the 1930s, Andrei Vyshinskii, the state's chief procurator, frequently chastised his own agency's investigators, noting that the vast majority of cases involving enterprises arose as the result of surveys by social control organs, such as the Soviet Control Commission. This was true, as well, of cases that came to the attention of police. Less than 5 percent of such cases in the mid-1930s arose out of information generated by informants or agents.[29] By the late 1940s, however, the situation had changed. Fully 29 percent of OBKhSS cases in 1946 were generated by undercover and agent-operational work, while in a number of oblasts, that number reached as high as 38 to 52 percent.[30]

Many of the same problems plagued agent and informant work in the 1940s as in the 1930s. Reports complained about the low or inappropriate qualifications of police agents, the sporadic character of informant reporting, and the inability of police to filter, coordinate, and operationalize informant information. Much of the information that police received led only to petty lawbreakers, not to big crime rings, despite aggressive campaigns to infiltrate agents into organized gangs.[31] The potential for corruption within the police still concerned higher authorities, though such criticism was not as strong in the 1940s as in the prewar decade. It is difficult to assess if, in fact, informant and undercover policing was effective, or more effective than it had been during the prewar years, but probably it was so, if only because police gave such priority to this type of investigative work. In any case, the new emphasis placed on informant and agent work amounted to a strategy of public cooptation into social policing. In the prewar decade, Party leaders mistrusted that strategy, given their suspicions of anti-Soviet "elements" hiding in the population. As well, grandiose plans in the early 1930s to set up systematic informant networks had come to little, resulting in a bloated and ineffective system that officials believed to be a major source of criminal corruption and political infiltration. Scientific social surveillance centered on the increasingly complex system of information gathering in card indexes, which was tied closely and increasingly to the passport and residence registration system introduced in the early 1930s. Throughout that decade, social policing through enforcement of passport and residence laws remained the most effective means of social control and fighting criminality. Both of these practices —registration of information and enforcement of passport laws—were carried out as professionalized police activities. They did not rely on active public participation, in fact were designed to operate as secret bureaucratized processes out of the public view. Mass public participation in social policing became tenable only during and after the war, both out of necessity, given the changing nature of criminality, and because of ideology, given leaders' new sense of legitimacy and the demilitarization of the social sphere.

MASS FORMS OF REPRESSION

Administrative forms of mass repression continued during the 1940s, but the focus of that repression shifted from peasants, petty criminals, and marginal social groupings to ethnic populations. Deportation of such populations had begun already during the mid-1930s, with the targeting of Germans, Finns, and Poles, but these deportations involved only partial extraction of groups deemed potentially harmful. Criteria for deportation or arrest included ethnic background, but were based primarily on the main threat of suspected political or class leanings. Thus, the "Greeks" to be deported from Black Sea regions in the mid-1930s were suspected of foreign ties, but were selected mainly on the suspicion that they had resisted collectivization during the early 1930s.[32] It was during the mass purges of 1937 and 1938 that the regime's leaders began to perceive whole ethnic populations as potential enemies. Wholesale deportation of Koreans, Poles, and other groups is well documented from that period. These repressions continued through the war, with the resettlement of the Chechen and Ingush peoples, as well as others. Large-scale deportations also continued of nearly all ethnic populations that were close to or in occupied areas, including Germans, Poles, Finns, Iranians, Afghanis, Armenians, Georgians, Kalmyks, and Crimean Tatars, as well as other groups. By 1952, a little over 1.8 million out of the total of 2.75 million *spetspereselentsy* (1,810,140 of the 2,753,000) were listed under the nationality category; they had been exiled because of their nationality rather than specifically for their class or other social status.[33]

Social deportation campaigns continued after the war and into the late 1940s, but brought in fewer people than ethnic campaigns—about 678,000 new settlers to the country's special settlements between 1945 and 1952.[34] Most important, however, was that both social and ethnic contingents of *spetspereselentsy* came primarily from new territories, and to a much lesser extent from areas inside the pre-1939 borders of the country. In the seven years after the war, the regime exiled close to 50,000 peasants as kulaks who resisted collectivization in oblasts and republics along the country's new western borders, especially from west-

ern Ukraine, Belorussia, and the Baltic areas. Peasants or rural inhabitants who resisted Sovietization policies were also included in contingents listed as nationalist sympathizers, as well as in contingents simply
listed as deportees from particular areas. Many thousands of the former
came from Ukrainian areas and were categorized under the label *Ou-
novtsy*, from OUN, the initials of the *Organizatsiia Ukrainskikh Na-
tsionalistov*, or Organization of Ukrainian Nationalists. Other contingents, also numbering in the tens of thousands, came from Soviet
Moldavia, the Baltics, and the western oblasts of Ukraine.[35] Contingents from newly occupied territories also included large numbers of
people under the catch-all category of "socially dangerous elements"
and disloyal (*neblagonadezhnye*) populations. Police used this category
to rid new areas of petty criminals and socially marginal groups who
might have been susceptible to recruitment into nationalist movements.

Inside the pre-1939 borders of the Soviet Union, large-scale social repression also continued after the war, but in changed form. Inside the
country's 1939 borders, the regime ceased the practice of nonjudicial repression through administrative sentencing boards. The infamous police
troikas of the 1930s, constituted in various incarnations, were disbanded once and for all under the 17 November 1938 Politburo decree
"On Arrests, Procuracy Oversight, and the Conduct of Investigations,"
which brought the mass purges to a close and regulated, once again,
civil and political police activity. The *Osoboe soveshchanie* of the
NKVD continued to hear political cases in administrative sessions, until
it was finally dissolved in 1953, but the regime did not revive the use of
troikas after 1938.[36] Instead, the regime's leaders turned back to the
courts and the legal codes, and they did so with a vengeance. During just
the war years, courts convicted over 9 million people for violation of the
basic labor discipline law, published in June 1940. Between 1940 and
1953, courts sentenced close to 4 million people specifically to labor
camps for violation of labor and work discipline laws. Courts convicted
another 5.5 million people for theft of socialist property, theft of private
property, robbery, hooliganism, and speculation.[37] Leaders amnestied
those convicted under labor laws during the war by a decree from July
1945, but police began immediately to arrest workers again in large
numbers. In just the last six months of 1945, according to the country's
assistant chief prosecutor, G. N. Safonov, courts convicted 540,000
workers under labor discipline laws. In some factories, the numbers sent

to courts or convicted reached anywhere from 15 to 20 percent of the work force. Workers were arrested and convicted in such large numbers that arrest lost its "preventive" and "social-educational" purpose, becoming instead a "routine fact of daily life."[38]

Large-scale social repression also included the hundreds of thousands yearly whom police fined, deported from regime areas, or arrested for violating passport and residence laws. In the postwar years, nearly 4 million people suffered restrictions on where they could live, which barred them legally from work and residence in some 340 designated regime cities of the country, as well as from large territories near border areas and resort locations. Restrictions applied not only directly to the millions of individuals under restriction, but also to their immediate families. In the impoverished conditions of the country during the postwar era, such restrictions effectively condemned millions of citizens and their families to lives of deprivation, even long after paying the debt for their crimes through "corrective" labor and supposed rehabilitation. Such a pervasive form of discrimination forced its victims to break the law, settling in cities and areas where they were not allowed to live. Between 1943 and 1953, over 5 million people were charged with passport violations. Most of these were fined, as much as 100 to 200 rubles, a considerable sum when a worker's salary amounted to an average of 900 rubles monthly. During the same period, courts convicted 127,000 people under criminal statutes of the passport laws and sentenced them to camps or prison terms.[39]

Social repression enforced through passport laws both created and testified to the huge number of marginal people in the country. War invalids were prominent in this population. Unable to find work in major cities or on farms, they were condemned to lives of begging and indigence. Wanderers, adventurers, criminals, the unemployed, youth gangs, and religious sectarians made up large numbers of the Soviet Union's marginal classes, as did a host of other groups, such as demobilized soldiers, ex-convicts, and members of displaced ethnic groups who had fled exile or been released.[40] During the 1930s, regime officials had treated socially marginal populations and statutory criminals as serious political threats to the state. These populations were placed, for the most part, under the purview of the political police and the NKVD's nonjudicial sentencing boards. After 1938, regime officials still regarded statutory crimes as socially and economically serious, but these types of crimes, as well as criminals and other social deviants, were handled through the civil police and the regular court system. Like other forms of criminality, leaders depoliticized these kinds of social disorders, coding them, as in the 1920s, as a part of the social rather than the political sphere.

This shift in the mechanics of repression had at least two major consequences. The most important consequence was that social repression became less deadly, if still pervasive. The regime criminalized or marginalized millions of people through its harsh laws, condemning them to lives of misery and impoverishment, but it did not kill them. Mass social repression, enforced through passport and residence laws, continued to be a fundamental way by which the regime related to its citizens, but in the postwar years, this kind of repression was designed to function more as a form of social "disciplining," not, as in the 1930s, as a mechanism of state security. The change in function altered the responsibility of enforcement, the other major consequence, placing an added burden on an already overstrained judicial and police system. Like other sectors of civil government, the court, prosecutorial system, and police suffered serious depletion of personnel during the war. Courts were as understaffed with underqualified officials as they had been in the 1930s. Yet much of the social repression during the prewar decade had been carried out by political police and special sentencing boards. Stalin, at least, as well as Yagoda and other police officials, did not trust the judiciary with matters of policing state security, which, during much of the 1930s, they equated with social order. As a result, courts were inundated with civil and criminal cases, but did not have the extra burden of adjudicating mass numbers of cases of politicized social repression.

After the war, the burden of large-scale social repression, at least inside the 1939 territorial borders, fell on civil court officials who were forced to apply the draconian laws passed by Soviet leaders. During the 1930s, court officials might requalify a crime to a lesser charge—charging someone with hooliganism, for example, rather than with anti-Soviet agitation—in order to avoid passing a harsh sentence. Some of this practice no doubt continued in the postwar period, as well. Yet sentences for minor infractions were often harsh, and courts had little choice but to pass maximum sentences. Minor theft violations, for example, were subject to a mandatory sentence of eight to ten years' hard labor. In this way, the judiciary was incorporated into the state's repressive machinery in the postwar era in a way that had not occurred during the 1930s. During the prewar decade, political police went around the courts and the procuracy, often using administrative sentencing procedures. Procuracy and court officials reacted strongly against these practices, and not only because of perceived violations of law. Conflicts between the NKVD and other agencies turned not just on points of legality but also on jurisdiction. Procuracy and court officials always claimed that social repression was the business of civil police and courts, not political police and administrative sentencing boards. Many of the complaints about NKVD practices were not only about violating citizens' rights, but about violating legal procedure that vested the responsibility for social order in the civil rather than the political sphere of government. In the postwar period, Stalin and other leaders used political police for many tasks, but no longer for social-order policing. Courts, as a result, became the primary means by which leaders attempted to impose discipline on Soviet society through the implementation of widespread forms of judicial repression.[41]

DEMILITARIZATION AND CHANGES IN SOCIAL REPRESENTATION

The shift from nonjudicial to judicial forms of repression reflected a shift in leaders' perception of danger to the state. This shift amounted to a form of demilitarization, not just from the war, but from the sense of state emergency that had existed throughout much of the 1930s. In the postwar period, political authorities still regarded statutory criminals and marginal populations as a threat to social order, but no longer as a threat to the political stability of the regime. This change can be seen in the tone of reports from the MVD to Stalin and Molotov on crime and problems of social dislocation. These reports lacked the shrill and politicized hysteria of pronouncements from the 1930s. Stalin had set this hysterical tone in his January 1933 speech to the Party plenum by identifying crime as the new form of class war, and criminals as a major enemy population. Following suit, Yagoda, as well as other officials, branded all social marginals as a counterrevolutionary threat to the state. According to this view, petty criminals, passport violators, and former exiles provided the recruitment fodder for anti-Soviet rebellions. By the late 1940s, this kind of social representation had disappeared from official discourse. Police and interior ministry officials reported crime figures in a straightforward manner. Reports referred to a beggar as a beggar, a thief as a thief. Police and political authorities described speculation as an economic threat associated with anti-Soviet behavior, but speculation and speculators were no longer regarded as political enemies.[42]

Police and courts expressed the requisite concern about criminality, vagrants and itinerants, anti-Soviet types, mass migration, and all the social ills associated with the chaotic postwar era. Indeed, as noted above, the breakdown in social order associated with the war and its aftermath was likely as serious as any the regime had faced since the early 1930s—arguably more serious, given the collapse of the country's infrastructure. Yet, social disorder no longer carried the same political valence as in the early 1930s. And it was not just the tone of reports that changed, but also the representation of disorder. After the war, MVD reports to Stalin and Molotov categorized crimes, as in the 1920s and earlier, in a simple hierarchical arrangement according to the descending number of incidents in each category. This contrasted with the way the NKVD organized reporting during the 1930s, according to the perceived danger of each category to the regime and its policies.[43] By the late 1940s, the MVD had reverted to nominal and simple numerical categories of representation that were consistent with the practice of professionalized police forces throughout Europe during the nineteenth and early twentieth centuries. This change was one more indication that Soviet political leaders perceived crime in a different way than they had during the prewar decade.

It is difficult to pinpoint exactly the reasons for these changes in perception, but very likely, the shift had to do with the perceived cause of social disorder. Throughout the 1930s, leaders understood criminality as a consequence of class resistance to the state's socialist offensive in industry and agriculture. Criminality and marginality were defined in terms of class war and opposition to the building of socialism. Thus, policing had a political as well as a social and economic goal and came under the authority of the political police. In the view of Soviet leaders, hostile foreign governments and oppositionist agents sought to exploit criminal and antisocial behavior. As the threat of war loomed larger in the late 1930s, leaders tied representations of criminality and social dis-

order increasingly to the threat of invasion and organized uprising. That
threat formed the background to the mass purges of the latter part of
the decade. In contrast, leaders could view the social disorder that characterized the Soviet Union after World War II as the nonpoliticized consequence of an externally caused crisis—invasion, war, and occupation.
The social consequences of criminality and disorder remained serious
after the war, but the defeat of the Axis powers resolved and removed
one fundamental threat to the state. Dekulakization and the mass purges
of the 1930s had, supposedly, removed the other fundamental threat of
domestic class opposition. Patriotic mobilization of the population during the war assured its loyalty to the regime. Thus, after the defeat of the
country's internal and external enemies, social disorder was no longer
seen as a form of class war. Crime was no longer a mortal political
threat to the survival of the state, to be crushed by counterinsurgency
methods of repression. Instead, problems of social disorder, though serious, became a matter of social discipline, to be handled by judicial
punishment. The catharsis of military victory brought a new sense of legitimacy to the regime, and wrought a change in policy tone as well as
policy substance.[44]

These changing perceptions and priorities can be charted in judicial
statistics, as well as in the tone and forms of representation found in
official reports. The records of judicial repression cited above show
clearly that the regime's leaders perceived problems of work and economic discipline as the most serious threat to the state, and to the ability of authorities to carry out the government's policies.[45] Work tru-
ancy and labor desertion laws passed in the early 1940s remained in
effect well after the war and into the early 1950s. Courts convicted millions of people under these laws, many times more than under laws
against personal injury and against assault and theft of private property. MVD authorities underscored the primary importance of economic
discipline. Decrees by the Politburo, Sovmin (the *Sovet ministrov,* or renamed Sovnarkom), and the Central Committee repeatedly focused on
different aspects of economic crimes and state protection against theft
and economic loss. In the course of two years, Sovmin passed no fewer
than seven decrees to strengthen campaigns against agricultural loss
through outright theft and embezzlement. Between 1943 and 1947, the
MVD or Sovmin passed thirteen decrees or orders to strengthen undercover and agent work against theft or embezzlement, and bribery re-

lated to theft and embezzlement, in various branches of the state and economy.[46] Authorities regarded theft of socialist property as such a serious threat that they passed a new law to supersede the August 1932 law. The 4 June 1947 law was broadened to include embezzlement and various forms of white-collar crime. The numbers convicted under that law also soared into the hundreds of thousands.[47]

All these decrees and orders reflected a near-obsessive fixation by Party and state officials on problems of social and economic order, but those problems were read as being strictly social and economic in nature, not as involving political opposition. Gone from these documents was the rhetoric of the 1930s. Police, Party, and government correspondence made no mention of intentional sabotage by hostile "elements." There were no warnings about internal class enemies and spies working through criminal elements to undermine the Soviet state and the building of socialism. No policeman viewed itinerants and beggars as counterrevolutionary threats to the state. In a major speech about passportization from 1947, an MVD official described in glowing terms the success of residence and passport laws during the 1930s and 1940s in catching criminals. He made no mention of these laws as an instrument of state security, as had both Yagoda and Yezhov—as a "weapon" to identify and contain dangerous populations and to track and capture spies and dangerous class enemies. Postwar official discourse about crime and social order was cast in the language of social discipline and not the rhetoric of the danger of political insurgency.

One telling incident highlights the change in perception of social danger. In February 1948, the Leningrad city executive committee passed a resolution allowing enterprises to hire labor "from among the unorganized population." While this resolution only recognized what was already a widespread practice, it provoked objection from the head of police, Kruglov. In fact, this same resolution, passed by Leningrad authorities in 1935, had precipitated a sharp, shrill, and lengthy response from Yagoda, then the head of the NKVD. In the earlier version of this conflict, the city came out on the short end in its collision with the police. In 1935, Yagoda and the NKVD convinced Sovnarkom that hiring workers outside of formal state contracts posed a serious threat to security. According to Yagoda, such a practice allowed the infiltration of cities and factories by subversive and dangerous social "elements."[48] In 1948, as in 1935, the matter reached the highest level of the government. In the 1948 round of the conflict, Kruglov objected, as had his predecessor, though not overtly for reasons of state security, but simply because the practice, so he claimed, violated passport regulations which had been put in place as a result of the 1935 Sovnarkom resolution.

In 1948, the outcome of this conflict was the opposite of the outcome in 1935, and the reasons for the difference were significant. Kruglov did not have the status that Yagoda had in 1935, nor did Stalin take the kind of active role in the daily minutiae of domestic economic issues in 1948 as in the prewar decade. Most important, in the 1948 instance, Sovmin did not perceive the security of the state at risk if enterprises hired workers outside of officially sanctioned contracts. The perception of social danger that had characterized the 1930s no longer dominated leaders' attitudes toward issues of social order. Beria and his deputy Ivanov supported the Leningrad city resolution, as did the procurator general, Safonov, the justice minister, K. P. Gorshenin, and Rodionov, the head of the Russian republic's Council of Ministers. All agreed that enterprises could hire whomever they wished, so long as employees did not violate other laws, and enterprises could provide living space for workers.[49]

One other nuance of postwar official discourse on crime and social disorder stands out. Internal MVD correspondence from the postwar years does not reveal the same level of concern about weapons in the general population as was apparent during the 1930s. In the prewar decade, mass deportation and urban sweep operations nearly always carried statistics about the number of weapons seized, whether guns or knives, and NKVD authorities initiated several campaigns specifically to confiscate "hot" and "cold" weapons from various segments of the population. After the war, concern about weapons does not seem to have been a high priority among police and Party officials, except in the newly acquired territories where special police and military units fought large-scale organized insurgency movements. Inside the pre-1939 borders of the country, police authorities expressed little concern about these issues. It is reasonable to assume that large numbers of weapons and ammunition would have been available among the populace in the wake of a major war, much more so than in the prewar decade. Yet authorities expressed more fear of knives and hunting rifles in the 1930s, as weapons to be used in potential uprisings, than they did about weapons of war in the late 1940s.

THE NEW TERRITORIES

Policies of repression in the new territories contrasted sharply with policies inside the pre-1939 borders, as did the representation of problems of social order. By the 1940s, for example, the regime's officials were no longer deporting inhabitants as kulaks from areas inside the country's pre-1939 boundaries. By the time of the war, rural areas purportedly had been pacified and cleared of hostile populations. Officials regarded inhabitants as loyal citizens. Even many hundreds of thousands of those who had been dekulakized were granted their rights as full citizens and rehabilitated. The numbers of those released were significant. In the ten years from 1941 to 1951, the regime freed close to 883,000 "former" kulaks from special settlements. More than 400,000 such deportees were freed between 1946 and 1952, and about half of those, some 200,000, were freed in the three years between 1948 and 1952.[50] Large-scale social repression continued after the war. In the pre-1939 territories, however, rural malcontents were more often than not convicted by judicial courts for various kinds of work infractions or for theft or economic crimes rather than branded as anti-Soviet kulaks. Ten years earlier, such infractions had warranted deportation as a kulak, but not in the late 1940s.

Policies of dekulakization reached their zenith in newly occupied territories even as officials released hundreds of thousands of previous deportees from older territories. In the postwar years, hundreds of thousands of kulak contingents arrived in special settlements from the newly occupied regions of Western Ukraine, Belorussia, Moldavia, and the Baltic. These deportees were rural inhabitants who had resisted collectivization and other Sovietization policies. Similarly, criminal and socially marginal populations in the new territories fell into the same categories of "socially dangerous elements" that had characterized such groups during the 1930s. In the new territories, police rounded up and deported urban malcontents and social marginals in the same manner and under similar orders that police had used against marginals during the social defense campaigns of the mid-1930s. Beria's order from May

1941, for example, applied specifically to the three newly acquired Baltic republics. The six-page order called for "cleansing" these areas of "anti-Soviet, criminal, and socially dangerous elements." The wording was similar to the various social repression orders of the Yagoda years, as was the identification of marginals as both anti-Soviet and potentially counterrevolutionary. In the postwar period, up to the early 1950s, approximately 400,000 people were deported under the above categories from the newly acquired territories along the country's western borders.[51]

Authorities carried out "sovietization" in the new territories with a vengeance. In the western areas of Ukraine, where nationalist resistance was strong, half a million people suffered some kind of repression in the years from the end of the war to 1952. Over 153,000 were killed in clashes with Soviet forces and police, while some 134,000 found themselves under arrest. The majority of those repressed were deported, either as socially dangerous or as family members of those arrested or killed. In Lithuania, nearly 10 percent of the population (270,000) suffered some form of repression at hands of Soviet authorities.[52] In the new territories, police and security organs lumped statutory criminals and "bandits" in the same categories as insurgents, as in the 1930s, and these dangerous "elements" came under the operational jurisdiction of the state security organs. This was true, as well, for activities described as banditry, as well as other criminal activities, in the border regions of the Caucasus and Central Asia. Operations against these kinds of crimes and groups were carried out by special units of the security organs, border guard troops, the elite units of the administration for fighting banditry, and special gangs or "extermination units" (*istrebitel'nye otriady*) put together to hunt down and kill political bandits.[53] The antibanditry administration (*Glavnoe upravlenie bor'by s banditizm,* or GUBB) had been formed in 1938, as part of reforms to separate political from civil policing. Originally, the GUBB was placed under the civil police administration, an indication that the regime no longer regarded banditry as political, but as part of the criminal sphere. This reorganization was consistent with the attempt to demilitarize the social sphere after the great purges. After the war, however, and largely due to bandit and insurgency activities in the new territories, the GUBB was reincorporated into the MGB, but its jurisdiction was limited primarily to the new territories and the southern border regions of the country.[54]

In the volatile border regions and new territories, then, leaders pursued the same policies as in the rest of the country in the 1930s, conflating social order with state security. In these areas, such perceptions were probably justified. In the postwar years, the Soviets found themselves faced with serious nationalist resistance and insurgency movements in these regions. The dislocation, shortages, and hardships caused by the war were further compounded by the revolutionary and repressive policies of the new Soviet regime of harsh collectivization and property confiscations. The resulting social chaos bred both widespread criminality and resistance movements, and made it difficult to separate criminal activity from politically motivated insurgency. The two shaded easily into each other, and police and security organizations saw both as a threat to the state.

PASSPORTIZATION

Passportization policy in the new territories also differed from that in the older territories. Originally, police planned passport practices in new territories to follow those in the pre-1939 borders. Rural inhabitants were not to receive passport documents, which were distributed in urban, military, and industrial areas, and along border zones. As of early 1946, some 680,000 citizens of Latvia had been issued Soviet passports, while about 1 million still carried older documents or affidavits from local authorities. In all, fifty-nine cities and towns had been passportized, as well as border zones. In February 1946, however, the Latvian Party secretary, Ia. Kalnberzin, and the head of Latvia's Sovmin, V. Latsis, issued a joint request to Sovmin SSSR to passportize all citizens of the republic, rural as well as urban. In the original request, Latsis and Kalnberzin wrote laconically, and obliquely, that the widespread use of old pre-Soviet identity documents, combined with the lack of Soviet passports, "might give rural citizens the incorrect impression about their legal rights as Soviet citizens." In discussions at Sovmin in Moscow, Kruglov, the MVD head, opposed the request, arguing that passport practice in Latvia should not differ from that in other republics. The secretary of the powerful Politburo member Georgii Malenkov weighed in with the same objection in Malenkov's name. Kruglov reminded members that passportization had not been carried out in rural areas of the country since it was not necessary. Rural inhabitants were already counted in registries or local village soviets. These citizens, he noted, were issued passports when they traveled out of their areas of registration. The same system should be adopted in Latvia, he argued.[55]

The Latvian officials dropped the matter for the time being, but Latsis broached the issue again with Kruglov and Molotov personally on a visit to Moscow later in 1946. Subsequently, in 1947 and 1948, officials carried out passportization of the entire population, and not only of Latvia, but of all three Baltic republics. The reasons, as elaborated in MVD reports, clarified the motives behind Latsis's originally oblique wording. Exchanges about passportization in the new republics also highlighted the original reasons why officials had passportized urban but not rural populations during the 1930s. These exchanges show that the way passportization was carried out was not designed particularly to discriminate against peasants or to control labor migration; the reasons had to do with state security and the most effective way of counting and controlling the whole population. In the new republics, as MVD documents made clear, passport and residence registration worked fairly effectively in urban areas to isolate criminals, social marginals, political activists, and other "anti-Soviet elements." In contrast, there existed no effective system of documenting and registering the rural population, as there was within the pre-1939 borders. The "large majority" of the population in new territories still carried passports issued by the former bourgeois government of Latvia, and even various types of affidavits and passes issued by German occupation authorities, most of which still bore the swastika stamp. Given the chaotic situation of documenting identity, and in the context of an insurgent civil war, rural areas had become a haven for criminals and insurgents. The latter could hide and change identities easily outside of towns, and local authorities had little idea of who came and went, who belonged and who did not in their regions. Passportization was therefore necessary, in order to document and register legitimate residents and to enable police and security organs to ferret out bandits and oppositionists.[56]

Social control tied to state security was the primary justification for passportizing the whole of the Baltic populations, but officials noted a second and equally important reason to issue passports to all citizens, at least in Latvia. As officials explained, the populace of the new republics had become accustomed to internal passport documents, since such documents had been issued to all adult citizens by previous governments.

The absence of a Soviet passport disconcerted many, making them question their rights, and even the authority of Soviet power, and provided an opening for nationalist movements to make inroads in rural areas. The same officials claimed that rural citizens and those in small towns had raised the issue numerous times with local authorities, believing that the new Soviet government should issue them passports, as had previous governments. Apart from issues of security, Latvian leaders believed that passportization of the entire populace would strengthen the ties of these relatively new citizens to the Soviet state. Here was the meaning of Latsis's original and obscure justification. A passport was a tangible sign of citizenship, which officials believed would strengthen the legitimacy of Soviet power in the new territories, especially in areas where authority was not yet fully established and where nationalist movements competed for citizens' loyalty.[57]

Inside the 1939 borders, changes in passport laws after the war reflected a mixture of conflicting demands and trends. Many in the police, Party, and government understood that the current passport system was unwieldy and practically impossible to enforce. The two- and three-tiered system of regime cities and forbidden zones covered hundreds of cities, towns, and strips of territory. Few understood the bewildering tangle of residence restrictions, to whom they applied, for how long, and under what circumstances. The hundreds of thousands of "residents" who peopled the system of penal colonies, special settlements, and exile zones was also a cumbersome administrative problem, not to mention a political one, let alone the millions who filled the country's Gulag system. The destruction of the war, combined with the postwar chaos, made the passport system almost unworkable. Local authorities complained on the one hand about an ineffective passport system that allowed unchecked migration, and on the other hand about residence restrictions that hindered the hiring of needed labor. Deportees inundated officials, singly and in mass numbers, with petitions for restoration of rights, and police officials began to question both the legality and practicality of the cumbersome and restrictive passport and exile system.

Some deportees took matters into their own hands and simply walked away from their places of exile. Such deportees were categorized officially as "runaways," and their departure was classified as "flight" or "escape" (*pobeg*). For those living in special settlements or in exile, "escape" was not as difficult as might be expected. Settlements were not labor camps and had no barbed wire. Many exiles were settled in with local populations. Their exile was enforced by a monthly visit to the local police station to register. Most did not possess passports, only affidavits, or *spravki*. If they had passports, their passports were stamped with restrictive wording limiting them to the area of their exile. These conditions did not hinder those who wished to flee, the more so since interior ministry police were remarkably lax in their administration of exiles. When ordered in 1948 to compile lists of exiles and runaways under their administration, local authorities could not do so. Lists were misplaced, registries did not exist, and in many cases, local police simply did not bother with monthly registration. And this was true even in supposedly special regime settlements.[58] Thus, deportees melted away from their settlements in large numbers. Many settled near their former places of exile, but many others walked or otherwise made their way to their former homes. The number of runaway deportees did not reach the level of the early and middle 1930s, when tens of thousands fled camps or settlements yearly, but the postwar numbers were also significant. Officials registered runaways in the thousands yearly.[59] The country's leaders regarded the problem of runaways as a crisis, and pressed local police and other authorities to be more vigilant in finding and detaining runaways. In November 1948, in an effort to stem the flow, the government drastically increased the penalties for flight, from an already draconian eight years' imprisonment to twenty years of forced labor.[60] Local authorities reacted to this pressure mainly in the breach. During the immediate postwar years, the country was full of migrants wandering singly and in large numbers as refugees, demobilized soldiers, released convicts, adventurers, or as those seeking work or a new life. Groups of deportees, thus, probably looked no more unusual than any other group of wandering people, and would have attracted little attention. Given the breakdown in the passport system, there would be little to distinguish them from anyone else with little or no documentation. Reaching their former homes, deportees often attempted to reoccupy their old houses and plots of land, if these had not been put to other use. Some rented land from collective farms, if they had the resources, and took up lives as *edinolichniki*—independent household farmers. Others settled in nearby villages or towns to pick up their lives in trades or as employees in local enterprises. According to police reports, most deportees did not bother to try to hide themselves from authorities, and local authorities did little to stop deportees from reoccupying their old homes, once they reached their destinations.[61]

PERMANENT EXILE

The response of Stalin and other political leaders to this situation was to freeze and enforce the current system. During the course of 1948 and 1949, Sovmin and the Presidium of the Supreme Soviet passed a series of decrees to tighten control over exiles, increase punishment for flight, and stem the legal release of deportees and prisoners. Besides increasing the penalty for escape attempts, leaders decreed that exiles were to be regrouped into harsher, nearly inaccessible areas—in eastern and northern Siberia, especially in the Kolyma region, farther away from rail and transport lines in Western Siberia, and farther away from settled areas in Kazakhstan. Administration of those groups deemed especially dangerous was to be transferred from the interior ministry to the MGB, which was charged to intensify agent work among and surveillance of deportee communities. In yet another move, the Presidium of the Supreme Soviet decreed in November 1948 that deportation orders for all groups exiled during the war years were to remain in effect indefinitely. This decree affected ethnic groups for the most part, but was applied as well against criminal and socially dangerous exiles. A similar decree in February 1948 affected camp inmates who had been sentenced for "especially dangerous" anti-Soviet crimes. In practice, this meant that those nearing the end of their terms of exile or imprisonment—usually five to eight years—were to be rearrested on the same charges, and resentenced to exile in penal settlements. The joint MVD/MGB order that put this decree into effect further instructed police to rearrest those who had already been released. Many of those affected had, after release, resettled with their families and found work, and were rebuilding their lives outside of the Gulag system. Close to 22,000 people suddenly found themselves thrust back into the world of camps, prisons, colonies, and special settlements.[62]

The 1948 decrees expressed the kind of atavism that had come to characterize leaders' attitudes before and during the war. The decrees were a throwback to the essentialist categorization of the population during the middle and late 1930s. Social and ethnic backgrounds were immutable, and some backgrounds were good and some were suspect. Ethnic groups that had been deported during the war as potentially dis-loyal were permanently branded with that suspicion. So, too, were those who were serving exile sentences for reasons of class background or criminal history. The decrees allowed for no kind of rehabilitation or reintegration of those condemned as socially harmful or potentially dis-loyal. According to the 1948 decrees, these populations would remain permanently marginalized and second class.

DISMANTLING MASS REPRESSION

Police authorities enforced passport and residence laws as best they could. In 1948 and 1949, MVD officials increased monetary fines for passport infractions, and lengthened prison sentences for statutory vi-olations.[63] They duly noted in yearly reports the increased numbers of passport violators being picked up and deported from cities. They touted a jump in the number of runaways returned to exile or camps, and a reduction in the numbers of those engaging in flight. At the same time, government authorities, police, and officials in the interior min-istry understood that harsher enforcement of the existing system would not resolve problems of social order and the growing crisis of adminis-tering the country's custodial populations. Neither could police enforce the unwieldy passport and residence system that had grown up over the years. In short, the attempt to tighten social controls and repress in-creasing numbers of people was unworkable. Letters and reports from authorities in charge of exiles and camps made this clear. Special set-tlements and colonies were in collapse and on the verge of starvation. Money for food and basic supplies was negligible, yet these expenses still consumed larger and larger portions of the government's budget. By the early 1950s, uprisings in a number of camps had already taken lives and provoked major concern among political leaders.[64] It is no wonder that, within weeks of Stalin's death, on 5 March 1953, his successors announced a general amnesty and began a major overhaul of passport and residence laws. That leaders acted so quickly in this matter testified to its seriousness. Given the nature of the proposals, it is clear that some officials had been rethinking the whole system.[65]

One of those officials was, ironically, Lavrentii Beria, successor to Yezhov as head of the NKVD, and the individual most responsible, after

Stalin, for the mass deportations of the war years. After the war, Beria continued to play an important role in policing matters as head of the MVD and as a vice chair of Sovmin. On Stalin's death, he was reinstated as the head of the newly combined MVD and MGB. This appointment was brief, as Beria became the first major victim of the power struggle following Stalin's death. Fearful of Beria's power, his fellow colleagues in the Party's Presidium had him arrested in July 1953. Beria was held until December. He was tortured, tried, and condemned in secret, and finally executed.

Before his arrest, however, and in his position as head of the MVD, Beria moved quickly to begin dismantling the country's large custodial system and the arcane system of passport and residence laws. The reasons for such a turnabout are not clear. Beria made his arguments on the basis of citizens' rights and especially economic necessities, as well as the impracticalities of enforcement, but he may also have been motivated by his power struggle with other top leaders, such as Georgii Malenkov, in the rush to distance themselves from Stalin's policies. Whatever the mix of motives, Beria pushed successfully to have all exiles returned to the administrative authority of the civil police, the MVD. He further instructed his deputies to review a number of laws on exiles with the goal of rescinding the postwar decrees condemning deportees and former convicts to permanent exile.[66] Under Beria's authority, MVD officials also began to make recommendations for lifting exile orders on a number of ethnic and social groups exiled during the war and after, and on those whose terms of exile had expired.[67]

In May 1953, Beria made his most sweeping proposal, to eliminate almost entirely the system of residence restrictions associated with passport laws. In his letter of recommendation to the TsK Presidium, Beria condemned the system that banned millions of citizens from over 340 cities and forbidden zones. "Thus, if you glance at a map of the USSR," he wrote, "it is possible to see that the whole country is mottled (*pestrit*) with regime cities and forbidden zones where citizens are banned who have previous convictions and are ex-convicts." He emphasized the hardships suffered by citizens and their families who were barred from the "industrial and cultural centers" of the country. He stressed the tremendous loss to the economy that resulted from such restrictions, and the necessity for those restricted to violate bans in order to find work and provide for their families. Beria encouraged the Presidium to abolish the two-tiered system of category I and II regime cities. He recommended that all restrictions be lifted as "unnecessary," except for several major cities, including Moscow, Leningrad, Vladivostok, Sevastopol, and Kronstadt. In these key places, he suggested, restrictions should be placed only on those convicted of the "most serious" crimes. In order to bolster his argument, Beria noted that residence restrictions such as those in force in the Soviet Union existed "in no other country." He pointed out that in a number of countries, "the USA, England, Canada, Finland, and Sweden," the population carried no internal passports at all.[68]

Beria's recommendations were the result of multiple revisions within the MVD, whose officials had been reviewing passport laws even before Stalin's death. Initial recommendations for a revamping of the passport system were put forward in March 1953, and were made still within the Stalinist framework. This set of recommendations retained the two-tiered system of regime cities and residence restrictions, as well as restrictions on a number of groups exiled during the war. Responding to the flood of requests from local authorities, the head of the MGB, S. D. Ignat'ev, supported yet a further expansion of the list of regime areas beyond that which already existed. In his comments, Ignat'ev proposed adding eight more cities to the regime I status list, as well as twenty regions near existing regime cities. He further proposed to establish a seventy-five-kilometer regime zone around Baku and the port city of Sukhumi in Georgia, and to add the city of Tupase in the Krasnodar territory to the list of regime II cities. As part of this recommendation, Ignat'ev also proposed adding a proportionate number of new police to help enforce passport laws.[69]

Stalin's demise and Beria's appointment as the new head of the combined MVD and MGB precipitated a dramatic turnaround. By April, and under pressure no doubt from Beria, the head of the police, Stakhanov, put forward a set of recommendations that lifted exile orders for all groups that had been banished originally for only a five-year period. In his recommendations, Stakhanov justified the removal of exile status by noting that extended exile orders had been illegal, since they were promulgated by operational order of the NKVD or MGB without the government's consent, meaning without a decree from either Sovnarkom or Sovmin. The April recommendations, however, retained the two-tiered system of regime-status restrictions.[70] By late May, yet a third set of recommendations had gone so far as to suggest lifting bans on most exiled populations, or keeping them only temporarily. These recommendations also argued for lifting exile orders on all children of exiles. The May proposals also eliminated the two-tiered list of cities where residence bans applied.[71]

The May 1953 recommendations accorded with Beria's recommendations to the TsK Presidium, but no sooner had these been issued than some officials began to suggest reinstatement of restrictions. "What regulating levers will be left in the hands of the police if we eliminate residence restrictions," asked one anonymous official in response to the April proposals circulated among top officers.[72] An official named Fedotov, identified only as an official of the MVD administration, also objected to the removal of so many cities from the list of regime areas. He urged that a number of cities be put back on the restricted list.[73] The head of the police Operational Department, Gorokhov, pleaded that if so many people were to be released and the number of regime cities reduced, then at least stamps be placed in the passports of those still forbidden to live in regime areas. This proposal was rejected, since Sovmin ordered that all stamps be removed from passports so as not to prejudice their holders.[74]

By September, final proposals reflected some retrenchment from Beria's recommendations in May. MVD officials supported the reinstatement of regime status for all republic capitals, as well as another seventeen cities, in addition to the major centers proposed in May. Special status was extended once again to border zones and to a number of regions bordering sensitive border zones, according to the pre-1953 passport regulations. The list of crimes for which residence restrictions applied was reduced considerably from earlier laws, but expanded from the shortened list of May 1953. These crimes included counterrevolutionary activity and agitation, banditry, hooliganism (if more than two convictions), premeditated murder, and theft of personal property, if perpetrated by a gang member or as a repeat offense.[75]

MVD officials worried about the double effect of releasing millions of prisoners and exiles and simultaneously lifting residence restrictions. For police and local officials, this was their worst nightmare. Under the new regulations and amnesties, cities would be exposed to invasion by outcast and criminal classes, and local authorities would have few means to protect themselves. Many officials openly feared the chaotic consequences of such a radical reform. Their fears were not unfounded. During the period 1953–57, the regime released some several million people. They were given passports that allowed them access to most of the country. Millions of people thus made their way back to their former homes or to new places to start life again. Among these millions were ethnic populations bent on retrieving their former territories. Many returned to former homes or plots of land to find them occupied, and at times had to fight to win back what had been taken from them. Among the many released were also the drifters, the displaced, the maladjusted, and the true hooligans—young men unemployed, uneducated, and used to violence as a way of life in camps and prisons. Also released were the legions of drunkards, beggars, criminals, and hundreds of thousands of workers and farmers, separated from families and brutalized into inhumanity by prisons, camps, and colonies. These populations were the marginalized victims of harsh laws and social repression, but they nonetheless posed a major problem of readjustment and criminality in the communities to which they returned. Local authorities had cause to fear this invasion, as did the Soviet "middle" classes who feared for their safety and demanded protection. The historian V. A. Kozlov has documented the mass social disorders and the social-political "crisis" of the 1950s and 1960s that swept the Soviet Union. Waves of mass unrest in the form of strikes, food riots, ethnic conflicts, gang wars, and other mass disorders (even at sporting events) often escalated into violence, involving armed conflict among participants and between participants and police. Disorders were sparked by local conditions and occurrences. Yet Kozlov is no doubt correct to suggest that the increase in levels of violence in Soviet society during these years had its origins in the Stalinist system of mass social repression, and in the explosion of anger, anarchy, and lawlessness that resulted when the regime dismantled that system and the policing mechanisms that enforced mass repression.[76] The agony of prolonged social violence was one of many legacies of the Stalinist state.

Conclusions

Repression, Citizenship, and Stalin's Socialism

THE SOVIET POLICE AND security organs acquired unprecedented power during the 1930s. This is not surprising, given the ideology and predilections of Stalinist leaders, the constant atmosphere of crisis, and the militarized character of the state during that decade. Neither is it surprising, and for the same reasons, that the regime's leaders related to the Soviet people largely through the police. The contexts of class war, domestic disorder, and imminent invasion shaped how regime officials and police categorized and dealt with the Soviet population. As a result, social and ethnic identities, as represented by passport and residency laws, became associated primarily and directly with mechanisms of police repression and perceptions of threat. Police and security organs used their power not only to repress real and perceived political opponents of the regime. Given nearly unlimited license, political and civil police shaped the Soviet body politic in blunt and brutal ways, and in accordance with the ideology of the regime's political leaders and their changing perceptions of danger and state security. In other words, citizens' relationships to the state were militarized in a constant tension of crisis. Officials categorized the population according to the level of threat they perceived from any particular group. Police officials routinely and administratively suspended civil rights of appeal for those groups deemed a threat to state security.

Not only did police gain increasing authority to deal with dangerous categories of the population. Through administration of the passport system, police usurped the traditional right of local governments to identify who was and who was not an enemy or an alien element. And with the victory of socialism, declared in 1933, the criterion of enemy shifted from traditionally defined class enemies—smallhold peasants and small-scale traders—to new groups—increasingly to those who fell into the social margins of Soviet society. Petty criminals, vagrants, "former people," the dispossessed and disenfranchised became, for Stalin and Soviet leaders, the new class enemy, as did a range of ethnic minorities. Socially dangerous elements and enemy nations became the focus of much of the Soviet police repression of the 1930s, up to and including the mass repressions of 1937 and 1938.

As the previous chapters have shown, class had declined as a social marker, at least for policing purposes, already in the mid-1930s. During much of that decade, policies of repression focused on deviancy and marginality, in addition to political opposition, regardless of class status or background. During and after the war, nationality came to replace class as a key criterion defining a citizen's identity and status. If in the early 1930s, class was everything and police officials still argued about whether nationality mattered, by the mid- and latter part of the decade this issue was settled. Nationality mattered as much as if not more than class. Nationality became a primary determiner of people's status, especially of those belonging to a suspect ethnic minority. As other historians have noted, the attitudes of leaders about ethnicity hardened into definitions of primordial beginnings and inherent traits.[1] Analogously, attitudes toward social groups hardened around the intractable and anti-Soviet traits of criminality, recidivism, and marginality, but not around markers of class.

The victory in the war changed this dynamic. The war gave to leaders a new sense of authority and legitimacy and complicated an already changing role for police. In a new era of state legitimacy, social and ethnic identity and the criteria of privilege and repression became dissociated from the litmus test of state security, at least inside the country's 1939 borders. The relationship of individuals and groups to the state became associated with more traditional understandings of citizenship— civil rights, violations of law, nationality, and service to the state. The last two criteria became especially important, even as the criterion of class declined in importance as a marker of identity, privilege, and repression. After the war, and inside the 1939 borders, policing and state repression continued on a large scale, but focused on traditional categories of statutory lawbreakers and the unproductive. Moreover, while there were millions of people who were arrested for violations of labor laws, theft of state property, and other violations of social discipline, these groups fell within the purview of courts and civil police, not the political police. Political police, and militarized units of the civil police, continued to engage in campaigns of suppression against national resistance movements and organized bandit activities, largely in the border republics and regions of the country.

Markers of nationality and social deviancy were important, but the war brought into being yet another identity regime, which superseded social and national categories as a criterion of privilege and exclusion. After the war, service to the state supplanted class and even nationality as the key criterion that defined a citizen's relation to the state. The importance of service is striking when examining the many debates about amnesties and passport reforms in the late 1940s and early 1950s. Discussions internal to the MVD about passport reforms in 1949 and 1950, in particular, raised issues of continuing exile restrictions that had been placed on various social and national groups during the 1930s and the war. These discussions generated much argument, but all who were party to them agreed that one criterion, in particular—extraordinary service to the state—could, in individual and even in collective cases, mitigate a person's or group's undesirable social or national background. Even by the middle years of the 1930s, service to the state, especially extraordinary acts, began to replace labor as a primary criterion for social rehabilitation. For a time, in fact, until the war with Finland and then the Second World War, rehabilitative labor and state service were largely identical, but it was service more than labor that was important, as exemplified by the rehabilitation of former kulaks and criminals for award-winning work on the state's penal farms. Simple rehabilitative labor was not enough. Conscientious fulfillment of labor tasks was insufficient to secure return to full citizenship status. The latter was achieved only by exemplary labor service, a form of extraordinary service to the state. After 1940, military service, and especially war veteran status, became the major criterion of reinstatement and privilege, which overrode both class status and national origins. Military and other forms of extraordinary service became the primary criterion by which individuals (in the case of the Koreans, even a whole category of the population) gained social rehabilitation and reintegration.[2] In discussing the categories of the population forbidden to live in regime areas, the draft passport regulations from 1949 specifically exempted from the bans "families of convicts, or those released from exile or prison who have been awarded Orders of the Union of SSR, or who are veterans of war, or others who have performed special service to the Motherland." Similarly, proposals for amnesties of different groups also appealed to wartime service as a justification for lifting restrictions.[3]

The most important criterion that the regime's officials employed to consider rehabilitation of repressed groups after the war turned not on nationality or class, but on service to the state, and primarily military service and sacrifice. Sacrifice and service overrode everything, regardless of a citizen's or group's ethnicity or social background. The criterion of service became applied more broadly, and was more suited, to the era of state economic reconstruction that characterized post-war Stalinism. Stalin may have remained tied to older notions of state security and martial law socialism, but by the late 1940s, the Great Leader was being left behind by the history and the state that he had done so much to create. In his 1953 criticisms of the carceral and restrictive passport systems, Beria articulated a new set of standards on which to build the Soviet state and Soviet socialism. His arguments against the Gulag and the restrictive passport system were made not on the basis of state security, but mainly on the basis of cost to the state's economy and the loss of productive labor. Stalin's martial law socialism was giving way quickly to a new kind of socialism and a new kind of state, an authoritarian service state more than a class state, and more than a nationality state or a simple police state.[4] This transition did not occur whole cloth or quickly. Many aspects of Stalinism remained to shape social and state development. Still, Stalin's death in March 1953 hastened the evolution to a new era in the Soviet Union and to a new phase of Soviet socialism.

Notes

INTRODUCTION

1. For a classic description of different types of arrest, see Alexander Solzhenitsyn, *The Gulag Archipelago, 1918–1956: An Experiment in Literary Investigation,* trans. Thomas P. Whitney (New York, 1973), 5–12.

2. For three recent and articulate statements of modernity as social improvement and state interventionism, see Zygmunt Bauman, *Modernity and the Holocaust* (Ithaca, 1991); Anthony Giddens, *The Consequences of Modernity* (Stanford, 1990); and James C. Scott, *Seeing Like a State: How Certain Schemes to Improve the Human Condition Have Failed* (New Haven, 1998). Giddens takes a broader and more detached view of modernity than that found in the cautionary tales told by Bauman and Scott. For a definition of modernity as state interventionism in the Soviet context see, especially, David Hoffmann, "European Modernity and Soviet Socialism," in *Russian Modernity: Politics, Knowledge, Practices,* ed. David Hoffmann and Yanni Kotsonis (New York, 2000), 245–61; Stephan Kotkin, "Modern Times: The Soviet Union and the Interwar Conjuncture," *Kritika: Explorations in Russian and Eurasian History* 2 (2001): 111–64. For counterarguments, see Terry Martin, "Modernization or Neo-Traditionalism? Ascribed Nationality and Soviet Primordialism," in *Stalinism: New Directions,* ed. Sheila Fitzpatrick (London, 2000), 348–67; Jörg Baberowski, ed., *Moderne Zeiten? Krieg, Revolution und Gewalt im 20. Jahrhundert* (Bonn, 2006); idem, "Zivilisation der Gewalt: Die kulturellen Ursprünge des Stalinismus," *Historische Zeitschrift* 281 (2005): 59–102. For a neutral reading, see my "Modernity and Backwardness on the Soviet Frontier: Western Siberia during the 1930s," in *Provincial Landscapes: Local Dimensions of Soviet Power, 1917–1953,* ed. Donald Raleigh (Pittsburgh, 2001), 194–216.

3. Hoffmann emphasizes the systematic, rational origins of modern kinds of social engineering.

4. In addition to the works cited above, see also Anthony Giddens, *The Nation-*

State and Violence (Cambridge, 1985); Bernd Weisbrod, "Military Violence and Male Fundamentalism: Ernst Juenger's Contribution to the Conservative Revolution," trans. Pamela E. Selwyn, *History Workshop Journal* 49 (Spring 2000): 69–94; Elisabeth Domansky, "Militarization and Reproduction in World War I Germany," in *Society, Culture, and the State in Germany, 1870–1930,* ed. Geoff Ely (Ann Arbor, 1996), 427–63; Michael Geyer, "The Militarization of Europe, 1914–1945," in *The Militarization of the Western World,* ed. John Gillis (Rutgers University Press, 1989), 68–85; Jane Caplan and John Torpey, eds., *Documenting Individual Identity: The Development of State Practices in the Modern World,* (Princeton, 2001); and the essays collected in Amir Weiner, ed., *Landscaping the Human Garden: Twentieth-Century Population Management in a Comparative Perspective* (Stanford, 2003). In the last work, see in particular, Amir Weiner, "Landscaping the Human Garden" (1–17), Peter Holquist, "State Violence as Technique: The Logic of Violence in Soviet Totalitarianism" (19–45), and Elisabeth Domansky, "The Transformation of State and Society in World War I Germany" (46–63). For a nuanced discussion of the positive and negative aspects of "modernity" in shaping society, see Clifford Rosenberg, *Policing Paris: The Origins of Modern Immigration Control between the Wars* (Ithaca, 2006), esp. 209–12.

5. Sheila Fitzpatrick was one of the first scholars to analyze early Soviet efforts to ascribe class identities to the Soviet population in order to differentiate between enemies and allies and to implement class-discriminatory policies on that basis. Others, especially Golfo Alexopoulos, Juliette Cadiot, Francine Hirsch, and Terry Martin, have done much to show how the regime attempted to refashion social, ethnic, and national identities, and Elena Osokina has written about the ways in which the regime divided the population according to access to scarce supplies of food, commodities, and living space. Sheila Fitzpatrick, "Ascribing Class: The Construction of Social Identity in Soviet Russia," *Journal of Modern History* 65 (December 1993): 745–70; Golfo Alexopoulos, *Stalin's Outcasts: Aliens, Citizens, and the Soviet State, 1926–1936* (Ithaca, 2003); Juliette Cadiot, "Qu'est-ce que la nationalité?" in *L'invention des populations: Biologie, idéologie, et politique,* ed. Hervé le Bras (Paris, 2000), and "How Diversity was Ordered: Lists and Classifications of Nationalities in the Russian Empire and the Soviet Union, 1897–1939," *Ab Imperio* 4 (December 2002): 181–210; Francine Hirsch, *Empire of Nations: Ethnographic Knowledge and the Making of the Soviet Union* (Ithaca, 2005); Terry Martin, *An Affirmative Action Empire: Nations and Nationalism in the Soviet Union, 1923–1939* (Ithaca, 2001); Elena Osokina, *Za fasadom stalinskogo izobiliia: Raspredelenie i rynok v snabzhenii naseleniia v gody industrializatsii, 1927–1941* (Moscow, 1998). On taxation policies and census techniques as ways to categorize and sort the Soviet population, see David Kertzer and Dominique Arel, eds., *Census and Identity: The Politics of Race, Ethnicity, and Language in National Censuses* (Cambridge, 2002); Alain Blum and Martine Mespoulet, *L'Anarchie bureaucratique: Statistique et pouvoir sous Staline* (Paris, 2003).

6. Historians have only recently turned their attention to the study of social marginals (*sotsial'nye marginaly*) as a distinct social stratum in Soviet history, with its own changing sociological definitions and dynamics. Writing about the Stalinist era, Sergei Krasil'nikov identifies "marginals" as one of five distinct "estates," or *soslovie:*

the *nomenklatura,* or the new service "nobility"; workers; specialists and white-collar workers (*spetsy i sluzhashchie*); peasants (later *kolkhozniki,* or collective farm workers); and marginals (*marginaly*). Krasil'nikov defines marginals as remnants of the prerevolutionary privileged classes, exiles (*spetspereselentsy*), the disenfranchised (*lishentsy*), and "others." S. A. Krasil'nikov, *Na izlomakh sotsial'noi struktury: Marginaly v poslerevoliutsionnom obshchestve (1917–konets 1930-kh gg)* (Novosibirsk, 1998). See also S. A. Krasil'nikov, ed., *Marginaly v Sovetskom obshchestve 1920–1930-kh godov: Istoriografiia, istochniki: Sbornik nauchnykh trudov* (Novosibirsk, 2001).

7. Histories of repression and political police under Stalin usually overlook the social-order policing campaigns of the 1930s, perhaps because these campaigns were not overtly political. Robert Conquest, for example, leaves out social-order policing in his two studies of Stalinist repression. Robert Conquest, *The Harvest of Sorrow: Soviet Collectivization and the Terror-Famine* (New York, 1986), and *The Great Terror: A Reassessment* (New York, 1990). More recent studies by J. Arch Getty and Oleg Naumov also pass over social-order kinds of repression. J. Arch Getty and Oleg Naumov, *The Road to Terror: Stalin and the Self-Destruction of the Bolsheviks, 1932–1939* (New Haven, 1999); and J. Arch Getty, " 'Excesses Are Not Permitted': Mass Terror and Stalinist Governance in the Late 1930s," *Russian Review* 61 (January 2002): 113–38. For exceptions, see the brief discussions of repression of social marginals in V. N. Zemskov, *Spetsposelentsy v SSSR, 1930–1960* (Moscow, 2003), 45–46; and N. Vert and S. V. Mironenko, eds., *Istoriia stalinskogo Gulaga: Konets 1920-kh–pervaia polovina 1950-kh godov. Sobranie dokumentov v 7-mi tomakh,* vol. 1: *Massovye repressii v SSSR* (Moscow, 2004), 68–69. For more extensive coverage, see Paul Hagenloh, "Police, Crime, and Public Order in Stalin's Russia, 1930–1941" (Ph.D. diss., University of Texas, 1999); idem, " 'Socially Harmful Elements' and the Great Terror," in *Stalinism: New Directions,* ed. Sheila Fitzpatrick (London, 2000), 286–308; idem, " 'Chekist in Essence, Chekist in Spirit': Regular and Political Police in the 1930s," *Cahiers du monde russe* 42/2–4 (April–December 2001): 447–76; Gabor Rittersporn, "Vrednye elementy, 'opasnye men'shinstva' i bol'shevistskie trevogi, in *V sem'e edinoi: Natsional'naia politika partii bol'shevikov i ee osushchestvlenie na Severo-Zapade Rossii v 1920–1950-e gody. Sbornik statei,* ed. Timo Vihavainen and Irina Takala (Petrozavodsk, 1998), 101–19; David R. Shearer, "Social Disorder, Mass Repression, and the NKVD during the 1930s," *Cahiers du monde russe* 42/2–4 (April–December 2001): 505–34; idem, "Crime and Social Disorder in Stalin's Russia: A Reassessment of the Great Retreat and the Origins of Mass Repression," ibid., 39/1–2 (1998): 119–48.

8. For the most comprehensive history of the Soviet political police, see V. M. Chebrikov, *Istoriia Sovetskikh organov gosudarstvennoi bezopasnosti: Uchebnik* (Moscow, 1977). On civil police and policing, see A. V. Borisov, A. N. Dugin, and A. Ia. Malygin, *Politsiia i militsiia: Stranitsy istorii* (Moscow, 1995); V. M. Pervushin, *Istoriia organov vnutrennikh del Rossii: Sbornik nauchnykh trudov* (Moscow, 1999); Louise Shelley, *Policing Soviet Society: The Evolution of State Control* (New York, 1996); George Lin, "Fighting in Vain: The NKVD RSFSR in the 1920s" (Ph.D. diss., Stanford University, 1997); and Hagenloh, "Police, Crime,

and Public Order." On political police, law, and state formation see O. I. Cher-dakov, *Formirovanie pravookhranitel'noi sistemy Sovetskogo gosudarstva v 1917–1936 gg: Istoriko-pravovoe issledovanie* (Saratov, 2001); L. P. Rasskazov, *Karatel'nye organy v protsesse formirovaniia administrativno-komandnoi sistemy v Sovetskom gosudarstve, 1917–1941 gg* (Ufa, 1994). On repression, law, and state formation more broadly, see V. M. Kuritsyn, *Istoriia gosudarstva i prava Rossii, 1929–1940* (Moscow, 1998); V. Kudriavtsev and A. Trusov, *Politicheskaia iustitsiia v SSSR* (Moscow, 2000); A. G. Zviagintsev and Iu. G. Orlov, *Prigovorennye vremenem: Rossiiskie i Sovetskie prokurory XX vek, 1937–1953* (Moscow, 2001); Peter H. Solomon Jr., *Soviet Criminal Justice under Stalin* (Cambridge, 1996).

9. On the role of ideology and the change in views of deviance from the 1920s to the 1930s, see, especially, David L. Hoffmann, *Stalinist Values: The Cultural Norms of Stalinist Modernity, 1917–1941* (Ithaca, 2003), 177–78. For an overview of Stalin's socialist offensive, see, especially, R. W. Davies, *The Socialist Offensive: The Collectivisation of Soviet Agriculture, 1929–1930* (Cambridge, 1980), and idem, *Soviet Economic Development from Lenin to Khrushchev* (Cambridge, 1998).

10. A number of scholars have noted the subordination of the civil to the political police, but they make little of it. Many, of an earlier generation of scholars, note the merging as part of the inevitable logic of Stalinist totalitarianism. Others, who write specifically about political repression, tend to overlook police reorganization and its implications for social-order kinds of repression. For the former, see for example, Robert Conquest, *The Soviet Police System* (New York, 1968); Boris Levytsky, *The Uses of Terror: Soviet Secret Police 1917–1970* (New York, 1967), esp. 75. For the latter, see Getty and Naumov, *Road to Terror,* and Getty, "'Excesses Are Not Permitted'." For two exceptions, see Shelley, *Policing Soviet Society,* and Lin, "Fighting in Vain." Shelley's overview does not explore in depth the implications of the merging, and Lin stops with the subordination of civil to political police in 1930. For more thorough coverage, see Hagenloh, "Police, Crime, and Public Order"; idem, "'Chekist in Essence'"; and Shearer, "Social Disorder, Mass Repression, and the NKVD."

11. OGPU stood for *Ob'edinennoe gosudarstvennoe politicheskoe upravlenie* (Combined State Political Administration). This was the name of the political police before its incorporation into the newly created Commissariat of Internal Affairs, the NKVD SSSR, in late 1934. Once incorporated, the OGPU was renamed the GUGB, *Glavnoe upravlenie gosudarstvennoi bezopasnosti* (Chief Administration for State Security).

12. Hagenloh emphasizes increasing involvement of political police in public policing policies as an incremental and unintended consequence of social crisis in the early 1930s, and of failed attempts by civil police to quell rising criminality. Hagenloh, "Police, Crime, and Public Order," 114; idem, "'Socially Harmful Elements,'" 299; idem, "'Chekist in Essence,'" 449. In this book, I also emphasize the breakdown in public order and the inadequacy of civil policing as a source of crisis in the early 1930s. At the same time, I argue that involvement of political police in social-order kinds of policing resulted from Stalin's direct intervention, and from an ideological and policy shift from the 1920s, based on a new understanding of state security and class war. See also Shearer, "Crime and Social Disorder," and especially "Social Dis-

order, Mass Repression, and the NKVD," 516–18. For the most recent expression of Hagenloh's arguments, see Paul Hagenloh, *Stalin's Police: Public Order and Mass Repression in the USSR, 1926–1941* (Washington, D.C., forthcoming 2009).

13. Through employer records, reports of local Party activists, and even citizen denunciations, as Alexopoulos explains in *Stalin's Outcasts*.

14. On militarization of police forces in general in European states after World War I, see Gerald Blaney Jr., ed., *Policing Interwar Europe: Continuity, Change, and Crisis, 1918–1940* (Basingstoke, 2007), 3–7.

15. Neither the civil nor the political police under Stalin were subordinated to the military, as were most gendarme forces during the nineteenth century, and the civil police, at least, did not live in barracks. Many units of the Soviet political police, and especially the units of the internal forces, did live in barracks, and were organized by military rank. Both the civil and political police under Stalin were subordinated to military law and discipline. On Western European gendarme forces, see Clive Emsley, *Gendarmes and the State in Nineteenth-Century Europe* (Oxford, 1999); Herbert Reinke, "'Armed As If for War': The State, the Military, and the Professionalization of the Prussian Police in Imperial Germany," in *Policing Western Europe: Politics, Professionalism, and Public Order, 1850–1940*, ed. Clive Emsley and Barbara Weinberger (New York, 1991), 55–73; David H. Bayley, *Patterns of Policing: A Comparative International Analysis* (New Brunswick, 1985); Howard C. Payne, *The Police State of Napoleon Bonaparte, 1851–1860* (Seattle, 1966). On the Russian gendarmerie, see V. S. Izmozik, *Zhandarmy Rossii* (St. Petersburg, 2002); Z. I. Peregudova, *Politicheskii sysk Rossii, 1880–1917* (Moscow, 2000); Ye. I. Shcherbakova, *Politicheskaia politsiia i politicheskii terrorizm v Rossii (vtoraia polovina XIX–nachalo XX vv)* (Moscow, 2001); M. I. Siznikov, A. V. Borisov, and A. E. Skripilev, *Istoriia politsii Rossii (1718–1917)* (Moscow, 1992); E. P. Sichinskii, ed., *Istoriia pravookhranitel'nykh organov Rossii: Sbornik nauchnykh trudov* (Cheliabinsk, 2000).

16. For exceptions, see Cynthia Hooper, "Terror from Within: Participation and Coercion in Soviet Power, 1924–1964" (Ph.D. diss., Princeton University, 2003), 151–57, on informant networks and card registries in the 1930s. See also David R. Shearer, "Elements Near and Alien: Passportization, Policing, and Identity in the Stalinist State, *Journal of Modern History* 76 (December 2004): 835–81. On civil police use of informants and card registries, see Hagenloh, "Police, Crime, and Public Order," 55–59, 67–76, 95–102.

17. Reasons for this lapse are not entirely clear, but may have to do, in part, with previous lack of access to archives. As well, as noted above, most histories have focused on overtly political forms of opposition and repression and ignored forms of social repression.

18. For the most comprehensive studies in English, see Lynne Viola, *Peasant Rebels under Stalin: Collectivization and the Culture of Resistance* (New York, 1996), and idem., *The Unknown Gulag: The Lost World of Stalin's Special Settlements* (New York, 2007). In Russian, see the monumental document collection V. Danilov, R. Manning, and L. Viola, eds., *Tragediia sovetskoi derevni: Kollektivizatsiia i razkulachivanie. Dokumenty i materialy v 5 tomakh, 1927–1939* (Moscow, 1999–2004).

19. For the role of the OGPU during collectivization, see also Lynne Viola, "The Role of the OGPU in Dekulakization, Mass Deportations, and Special Settlements in 1930," *The Carl Beck Papers in Russian and East European Studies*, no. 1406 (Pittsburgh, 2000).

20. Narodnyi komissariat vnutrennikh del.

21. Solomon, *Soviet Criminal Justice*, 166, 172–173; Getty and Naumov, *Road to Terror*, 122–23, 172.

22. GANO, f. 3, op. 2, d. 813, l. 24.

23. GANO, f. 3, op. 9, d. 977, ll. 94–100.

24. In some ways, this shift reflected the conservative shift in legal culture about which Solomon writes, and it also reflected some of the shift about which Timasheff wrote in his famous argument of the Great Retreat. At the same time, I do not go so far as Timasheff. The regime continued to be a revolutionary regime in that it did not retreat from state control over the economy, collectivization, or Communist Party monopoly over political power. Solomon, *Soviet Criminal Justice*, and Nicholas Timasheff, *The Great Retreat: The Growth and Decline of Communism in Russia* (New York, 1946).

25. For the former viewpoint, see especially Getty, "'Excesses Are Not Permitted.'"; and Getty and Naumov, *Road to Terror*, esp. 136–37. See also Baberowski, "Zivilisation der Gewalt," 95. For the latter argument, see especially Gabor Rittersporn, *Stalinist Simplifications and Soviet Complications: Social Tensions and Political Conflicts in the USSR, 1933–1953* (Reading, 1991). For a critique of the argument of Stalinist repression as irrational, see Holquist, "State Violence as Technique."

26. For an early description of the mass purges as social prophylaxis, see F. Beck and W. Godin, *Russian Purge and the Extraction of Confession* (New York, 1951), 228–36. See also Alexander Solzhenitsyn's classic study, *The Gulag Archipelago*, 1:77. For one of the best recent treatments of the origins of the great purges, see Oleg Khlevniuk, "The Objectives of the Great Terror," in *Soviet History, 1917–1953: Essays in Honor of R. W. Davies*, ed. Julian Cooper, Maureen Perrie, and E. A. Rees, (Basingstoke, 1995), 158–76. For a view of the mass purges as a constitutive aspect of Bolshevik ideology or culture, see Jörg Baberowski, *Die Rote Terror: Die Geschichte des Stalinismus* (Munich, 2004); idem, "Zivilisation der Gewalt," and Holquist, "State Violence as Technique."

27. Of the many such arguments, see especially Walter Laqueur, *The Fate of the Revolution: Interpretations of Soviet History from 1917 to the Present* (New York, 1987); Martin Malia, *The Soviet Tragedy: A History of Socialism in Russia, 1917–1991* (New York, 1994); Richard Pipes, *Communism, the Vanished Specter* (Oxford University Press, 1994). For an older but still serviceable survey of such arguments, see Giuseppe Boffa, *The Stalin Phenomenon*, trans. Nicholas Fersen (Ithaca, 1992).

28. For an English-language formulation of this position, see Jörg Baberowski's review of Getty and Naumov, *The Road to Terror*, and Lewis Siegelbaum and Andrei Sokolov, eds., *Stalinism as a Way of Life*, in *Kritika: Explorations in Russian and Eurasian History* 4/3 (Summer 2003): 756. See also Baberowski's "Zivilisation der Gewalt," esp. 97–101. Baberowski attributes Stalin's personal penchant for

violence to his Georgian cultural roots, but he also underscores a more fundamental Bolshevik culture of violence that nurtured a Stalin and allowed him to become the tyrant he was. The penchant to use violence was an essential if not an inherent trait of Stalinist Bolshevism. Ibid., 62.

29. Hannah Arendt, *The Origins of Totalitarianism* (New York, 1973); Norman Naimark, *Fires of Hatred: Ethnic Cleansing in Twentieth-Century Europe* (Cambridge, Mass., 2001).

30. Holquist, "State Violence as Technique," 44. See also Baberowski, "Zivilisation der Gewalt" and Amir Weiner, "Nature, Nurture, and Memory in a Socialist Utopia: Delineating the Soviet Socio-Ethnic Body in the Age of Socialism," *American Historical Review* 104/4 (October 1999): 1114–55.

31. Lenin employed mass repression during the struggle for power, but he drew back from the use of mass terror during the phase of "peaceful construction," making the famous argument, in Bukharin's encapsulation, that there should be no third revolution. Among the many works on Lenin, see especially Moshe Lewin, *Lenin's Last Struggle* (New York, 1968), 106–16. See also the astute reading by Lars T. Lih, "Political Testament of Lenin and Bukharin and the Meaning of NEP," *Slavic Review* 50/2 (Summer 1991): 241–52.

32. See especially Moshe Lewin, *The Making of the Soviet System: Essays in the Social History of Interwar Russia* (New York, 1985), 202–8 on different Leninisms; 281–85 on the legal and extralegal state; and 304–10 on different ideologies. On different visions of state construction within Soviet socialism, see also James W. Heinzen, *Inventing a Soviet Countryside: State Power and the Transformation of Rural Russia, 1917–1929* (Pittsburgh, 2004), esp. chaps. 4 and 5, and Markus Wehner, *Bauernpolitik im proletarischen Staat: Die Bauernfrage als zentrales Problem der sowjetischen Innenpolitik, 1921–1928* (Cologne, 1998). On different visions of industrial state building, see my *Industry, State, and Society in Stalin's Russia, 1926–1934* (Ithaca, 1996).

33. Peter Solomon's study, *Soviet Criminal Justice*, emphasizes a similar tension between judicial and extrajudicial practices.

34. F. Chuev, *Sto sorok besed s Molotovym* (Moscow, 1991), 390–93.

CHAPTER 1. A NEW KIND OF CLASS WAR

1. RGASPI, f. 17, op. 2, d. 514, ll.14–17.

2. Collective and Soviet, or state, farms. *Kolkhozy* were legally constituted as cooperatives, while *sovkhozy* were state enterprises whose farmers were paid employee wages.

3. RGASPI, f. 17, op. 2, d. 514, l. 16.

4. RGASPI, f. 17, op. 2, d. 514, l. 17.

5. GARF, f. 9474, op. 16, d. 79, l. 470b.

6. Comments reported in procuracy report on crime, GARF, f. 8131, op. 37, d. 48, l. 67.

7. GARF, f. 8131, op. 37, d. 48, l. 67.

8. GARF, f. 9401, op. 12, d. 135/doc. 119. I am grateful to Paul Hagenloh for help in reconstructing Yagoda's speech. For a more complete description of this

speech, see Paul Hagenloh, " 'Socially Harmful Elements' and the Great Terror," in *Stalinism: New Directions,* ed. Sheila Fitzpatrick (New York, 2000), 286–308.

9. RGASPI, f. 17, op. 2, d. 598, ll. 12, 41–43, respectively. These remarks were made at the February–March 1937 Central Committee plenum. Given the highly politicized and scripted nature of that session, we should approach these comments with caution. Still, in substance, they seem to be an apt description of political police policy during the mid-1930s. See also Yagoda's directive to operational departments of the GUGB, as well as the police, in March 1936, to free themselves from unnecessary tasks and to "focus on priorities of aggravated robbery, murder, and theft of socialist property." GARF f, 9401, op. 12, d. 135, doc. 31/4.

10. GARF, f. 9415, op. 5, d. 475, ll. 6–7.

11. A. Shliapochnikov, "Prestup'nost' i repressiia v SSSR." *Problemy ugolovnoi politiki,* vol. 1 (Moscow, 1935), 75–100, here 99.

12. Ibid., 75. For similar comments, see, for example, N. Krylenko's comments in N. Krylenko, "Proekt ugolovnogo kodeksa Soiuza SSR" in *Problemy ugolovnoi politiki,* 1:21, 23; G. Volkov, "Nakazanie v Sovetskom ugolovnom prave," ibid., 74; A. Vyshinskii, "K reforme ugolovno-protsessual'nogo kodeksa," ibid., 35. See also Lazar Kaganovich's August 1932 speech to a Moscow police conference in RGASPI, f. 81, op. 3, d. 151, l. 12.

13. GARF, f. 393, op. 84, d. 4, l. 21. See also the 1927 report to Sovnarkom on incidents of banditry as a "local" criminal activity. GARF, f. 5446, op. 55, d. 1532, l. 1.

14. On professionalization of police, see Clive Emsley and Barbara Weinberger, eds., *Policing Western Europe: Politics, Professionalism, and Public Order, 1850–1940* (New York, 1991), ix–x; Raymond B. Fosdick, *European Police Systems* (1915; Montclair, 1969. Reprint of 1915 edition), 10–11; David H. Bayley, "The Police and Political Development in Europe," in *The Formation of National States in Western Europe,* ed. Charles Tilly (Princeton, 1975), 347; Richard J. Evans, *Rereading German History: From Unification to Reunification, 1800–1996* (London, 1997) esp. chap. 6, "Police and Society from Absolutism to Dictatorship," 65–86.

15. For more on the OGPU takeover of the police, see chapter 3.

16. GARF, f. 9415, op. 5, d. 475, l. 38.

17. GARF, f. 8131, op. 37, d. 48.

18. GARF, f. 8131, op. 37, d. 48, l. 227.

19. GARF, f. 8131, op. 37, d. 48, l. 228.

20. GARF, f. 3316, op. 64, d. 1523, l. 103.

21. A. Gertsenzon, "Problema edinogo ucheta prestuplenii i nakazanii," in *Problemy ugolovnoi politiki,* vol. 3 (Moscow, 1937), 95–120, here 98.

22. GARF, f. 9474, op. 16, d. 79, l. 48.

23. In the first quarter of 1934, for example, the number of reported thefts of all kinds in the city of Moscow numbered 35,775, but courts convicted only 5,875 offenders for theft during the same period. GARF 8131, op. 37, d. 48, l. 233.

24. GARF, 8131, op. 37, d. 48, l. 174.

25. GARF f. 393, op. 84, d. 4, l. 22.

26. GARF, f. 7511, op. 1, d. 147, l. 90.

27. Shliapochnikov, "Prestupnost' i repressiia v SSSR," 36.

28. GARF, f. 8131, op. 3, d. 48, ll. 175–76, 225–26. See also Shliapochnikov,

"Prestupnost' i repressiia v SSSR," 92, for a similar argument that rates of conviction for hooliganism had dropped because many such cases were being handled more and more by administrative means.

29. All comments from GARF, f. 9474, op. 16, d. 79, ll. 47–48.

30. GANO, f. 20, op. 1, d. 220, ll. 10–120b.

31. GARF, f. 8131, op. 37, d. 48, ll. 68–69.

32. GARF, f. 9492, op. 2, d. 42, ll. 133, 136.

33. GARF, f. 8131, op. 37, d. 48, ll. 68–69.

34. GARF, f. 5446, op. 14a, d. 755, l. 2.

35. GARF, f. 7511, op. 1, d. 147, l. 90.

36. Wages in light industry averaged 150 rubles per month.

37. GARF, f. 9415, op. 5, d. 484, l. 61a.

38. See the Soviet Control Commission report in GARF 7511, op. 1, d. 147, ll. 90–91.

39. GARF, f. 9415, op. 5, d. 484, l. 61a.

40. GARF, f. 9415, op. 5, d. 484, l. 60.

41. GARF, f. 9415, op. 5, d. 477, l. 76.

42. GARF, f. 9415, op. 5, d. 477, l. 76.

43. GARF, f. 9415, op. 5, d. 477, ll. 8–9.

44. GARF, f. 9415, op. 5, d. 499, l. 13.

45. GARF, f. 9415, op. 5, d. 499, ll. 4–5.

46. GARF, f. 9415, op. 5, d. 477, l. 33.

47. GARF, f. 5446, op. 15a, d. 1073, l. 186.

48. For example, workers by occupation, but who did not carry proper residence permits. GARF, f. 5446, op. 15a, d. 1071, l. 25.

49. GARF, f. 5446, op. 15a, d. 404, l. 188.

50. GARF, f. 5446, op. 16a, d. 404, l. 11.

51. GARF, f. 5446, op. 16a, d. 404, l. 13.

52. GARF, f. 5446, op. 16a, d. 404, l. 13.

53. GARF, f. 5446, op. 16a, d. 404, l. 13.

54. GARF, f. 5446, op. 16a, d. 404, l. 14.

55. GARF, f. 5446, op. 16a, d. 402, ll. 4–5.

56. GARF, f. 5446, op. 15a, d. 1071, l. 25.

57. GARF, f. 8131, op. 37, d. 48, esp. ll. 35–42, on difference in grain and bread prices as a reason for speculation, incorrect convictions for speculation, and the problem of defining speculation.

58. GARF, f. 5446, op. 16a, d. 402, ll. 3–15.

59. GARF, f. 5446, op. 16a, d. 402, l. 14.

60. GARF, f. 5446, op. 16a, d. 402, ll. 4–6.

61. GARF, f. 5446, op. 16a, d. 402, l. 10.

62. Rimmel, "A Microcosm of Terror, or Class Warfare in Leningrad: The March 1935 Exile of 'Alien Elements,'" *Jahrbücher für Geschichte Osteuropas* 48/4 (2000): 528–51.

63. GARF, f. 5446, op. 16a, d. 402, ll. 11–12.

64. GARF, f. 5446, op. 16a, d. 402, l. 12.

65. GARF, f. 5446, op. 16a, d. 404, l. 16.

66. See G. F. Grinko's letter to Sovnarkom 23 January 1934 and Yagoda's vigorous defense of police activities from 26 February 1934. GARF, f. 5446, op. 15a, d. 1073, ll. 186 and 187 respectively.

67. GARF, f. 5446, op. 16a, d. 404, l. 17.

68. GARF, f. 5446, op. 16a, d. 404, l. 17.

69. GARF, f. 9415, op. 5, d. 492, l. 35.

70. GARF, f. 9415, op. 5, d. 492, l. 35.

71. For the 1931 comment, see GARF, f. 8131, op. 37, d. 20, l. 42. Official assessments of the overtly political character of banditry remained consistent throughout the 1930s. See below, notes 77 and 78.

72. GARF, f. 9415, op. 5, d. 492, l. 36.

73. This account is taken from a letter summarizing the events from G. Musabekov, chairman of the TsIK, Azerbaijan SSR to Sergo Ordzhonikidze. RGASPI, f. 85, op. 1s, d. 127, ll. 1–10.

74. RGASPI, f. 85, op. 1s, d. 127/ l. 6.

75. Eric Hobsbawm, *Primitive Rebels: Studies in Archaic Forms of Social Movement in the 19th and 20th Centuries* (New York, 1965). Originally published as *Social Bandits and Primitive Rebels* (New York, 1959). See also Lynne Viola, *Peasant Rebels under Stalin: Collectivization and the Culture of Resistance* (New York, 1996), 175, 179.

76. The report on the Nakhichevan rising twice noted that the center of the revolt and of bandit activities in the area coincided with the areas of strongest resistance to Bolshevik power in 1919–21. For the most explicit argument that collectivization was a continuation of the peasant war of 1919–20 see Andrea Graziosi, *The Great Soviet Peasant War: Bolsheviks and Peasants, 1917–1933* (Cambridge, Mass., 1996).

77. For the 1934 report, see GARF, f. 8131, op. 37, d. 48, ll. 49–51.

78. GARF, f. 9474, op. 1, d. 91, l. 133.

79. GARF, f. 9474, op. 1, d. 91, l. 134. The report did not detail how the commission arrived at its conclusions.

80. In his memoir, Mikhail Shreider, head of the police in Novosibirsk and then Kazakhstan in 1937 and 1938, discusses banditry as one of the continuing and major problems. Mikhail Shreider, *NKVD iznutri: Zapiski chekista* (Moscow, 1995), 86.

81. GARF, f. 5446, op. 26, d. 18, l. 195.

82. GARF, f. 5446, op. 26, d. 18, l. 195.

83. GARF, f. 5446, op. 26, d. 50, l. 5.

84. GARF, f. 5446, op. 26, d. 18, l. 202.

85. GARF, f. 5446, op. 26, d. 50, l. 5.

86. GARF, f. 5446, op. 26, d. 18, l. 201.

87. GARF, f. 5446, op. 26, d. 50, ll. 4–5.

88. GARF, f. 5446, op. 26, d. 18, l. 201.

89. GARF, f. 5446, op. 26, d. 50, l. 2. See the remarkable memoir by Nicholas Voinov, *The Waif* (New York, 1955) for an autobiographical account of the life of a *besprizornik*-hooligan during the 1930s.

90. GARF, f. 5446, op. 26, d. 50, l. 3; GARF, f. 5446, op. 18a, d. 847, l. 201.

Voinov's autobiographical account squares with Sovnarkom's official assessment of the organized use of many homes for criminal activities. Voinov describes an even more widespread system of orphan criminal organization, which included protection racketeering, police bribery, and revenge murders of public (especially NKVD) officials.

91. See pp. 226–29.

92. F. Nakhimson, "K voprosu o bor'be s prestupnost'iu nesovershennoletnikh," in *Problemy ugolovnoi politiki,* 3:84.

93. Ibid., 86.

94. GARF, f. 3316, op. 64, d. 1619, l. 39.

95. Nakhimson, "K voprosu," 86–91.

96. Ibid., 91.

97. GARF, f. 3316, op. 12, d. 29, l. 4. *Privod* was not a formal arrest, but was a form of police intimidation in which police would take a person to the local station and register his or her name in a catalog of troublemakers. Lists of those with *privody* were used later during the deadly mass purges of the late 1930s.

98. GARF, f. 3316, op. 64, d. 1523, l. 19.

99. GARF, f. 8131, op. 38, d. 6, l. 61. On socially harmful elements, see Paul Hagenloh, "'Socially Harmful Elements'"; Gabor Rittersporn, "The Impossible Change: Soviet Legal Practice and Extra-Legal Jurisdiction in the Pre-War Years," Paper given at the University of Toronto, Munk Centre for International Studies workshop, March 1995; David R. Shearer, "Social Disorder, Mass Repression, and the NKVD during the 1930s," *Cahiers du monde russe* 42/2–4 (April–December 2001): 505–534; and "Crime and Social Disorder in Stalin's Russia: A Reassessment of the Great Retreat and the Origins of Mass Repression," Ibid., 39/1–2 (1998): 119–48.

100. For Yagoda's comments, see GARF, f. 9401. op.12, d. 135, doc. 31. See also GARF, f. 8131, op. 37, d. 58, ll. 138–39 on arresting individuals as social harmfuls who had not committed a statutory crime. The National Socialist regime in Germany also treated vagrants and vagabonds not only as criminals, but also as a political threat to the state. Officials and laws under the Weimar Republic did not regard marginal groups as a political danger, but public officials did use the language of "antisocial elements" (*asoziale Elemente*), and passed custodial laws allowing police to round up vagrants and undocumented people and place them in detention work camps. Wolfgang Ayass, "Vagrants and Beggars in Hitler's Reich," in *The German Underworld: Deviants and Outcasts in German History,* ed. Richard J. Evans (London, 1988), 210–37, esp. 222–24 and 235 n. 49. For discussion of the word "element" as used in both the Russian and Soviet contexts, see Peter Holquist, "To Count, to Extract. to Eliminate: Population Politics in Late Imperial and Soviet Russia," in *A State of Nations: Empire and Nation Making in the Age of Lenin and Stalin,* ed. Ronald Suny and Terry Martin (Oxford, 2001), 111–44. After the 1848 revolutionary upheavals in the German states, police also conflated public disorder with political threat. Gendarmerie were particularly active in rounding up criminal and other marginal groups as part of antirevolutionary policing. Evans, *Rereading German History,* 68.

101. GARF, f. 1235, op. 141, d. 1650, ll. 1–3.

102. GARF, f. 9415, op. 3, d. 6, l. 1.

103. Stuart Finkel, "An Intensification of Vigilance: Recent Perspectives on the Institutional History of the Soviet Security Apparatus in the 1920s," *Kritika: Explorations in Russian and Eurasian History* 5/2 (Spring 2004): 306.

104. Golfo Alexopoulos, *Stalin's Outcasts: Aliens, Citizens, and the Soviet State, 1926–1936* (Ithaca, 2003).

105. GARF, f. 9415, op. 3, d. 1, ll. 278–79.

Chapter 2. Police and Social Disorder

1. GARF, f. 393, op. 84, d. 24, l. 10. A. V. Borisov, A. N. Dugin, A. Ia. Malygin, et al., *Politsiia i militsiia Rossii: Stranitsy istorii* (Moscow, 1995); O. I. Cherdakov, *Formirovanie pravookhranitel'noi sistemy Sovetskogo gosudarstva v 1917–1936 gg: Istoriko-pravovoe issledovanie* (Saratov, 2001), 124; V. M. Kuritsyn, *Istoriia gosudarstva i prava Rossii, 1929–1940* (Moscow, 1998); L. P. Rasskazov, *Karatel'nye organy v protsesse formirovaniia i funktsionirovaniia administrativno-komandnoi sistemy v sovetskom gosudarstve, 1917–1941* (Ufa, 1994).

2. GARF, f. 5446, op. 13a, d. 1320, ll. 1–3.

3. GARF, f. 393, op. 84, d. 24, l. 13.

4. GARF, f. 1235, op. 72, d. 340, l. 21; GARF, f. 393, op. 84, d. 24, l. 13.

5. GARF, f. 1235, op. 72, d. 340, l. 21.

6. GARF, f. 1235, op. 72, d. 340, l. 1400b. This report put the number of uniformed state *militsiia* at 37,673; *vedmilitisiia* at 58,341; and *ugolovnyi rozysk* officers at 5,014.

7. GARF, f. 5446, op. 13a, d. 1316, l. 110b.

8. GARF, f. 9515, op. 3, d. 31, l. 5.

9. GARF, f. 9515, op. 3, d. 31, l. 7.

10. GARF, f. 9415, op. 3, d. 31, l. 7.

11. GARF, f. 9415, op. 3, d. 1, l. 159.

12. GARF, f. 393, op. 84, d. 24, ll. 10–11, GANO, f. 47, op. 5, d. 160, l. 31, GARF, f. 1235, op. 141, d. 910, l. 29. In 1928 in the Trotsk region of Leningrad oblast, the precinct chief received 94 rubles a month in salary. The five policemen under him received 44 rubles per month. GARF 393, op. 78, d. 21, l. 3.

13. GARF, f. 1235, op. 141, d. 910, l. 33.

14. GARF, f. 1235, op. 141, d. 910, l. 33.

15. GARF, f. 1235, op. 141, d. 910, l. 24, 9415, op. 3, d. 3, l. 59.

16. GARF, f. 393, op. 78, d. 21, l. 2.

17. GARF, f. 9415, op. 3, d. 1, l. 76.

18. GANO, f. 47, op. 5, d. 160, l. 24.

19. GANO, f. 47, op. 5, d. 160, l. 24. Poor service and living conditions and corruption described above for police in Western Siberia reflected a national pattern. For similar descriptions for the whole of the RSFSR and the Ukrainian SSR, see GARF, f. 393, op. 1, d. 24, ll. 12–15, f. 1235, op. 141, d. 910, ll. 24–40, f. 5446, op. 15a, d. 1130, ll. 8–9. See also Yagoda's 1934 critical review of poor performance and corruption in the Western Siberian police administration in GARF, f. 9401, op. 12, d. 135, doc.13.

20. GARF, f. 1235, op. 72, d. 340, l. 3.

21. GANO, f. 47, op. 5, d. 160, l. 28.

22. GANO, f. 47, op. 5, d. 160, l. 32.

23. GARF, f. 393, op. 84, d. 24, l. 14.

24. GARF, f. 393, op. 84, d. 24, l. 14.

25. See description of police activities and problems in the Trotsk rural region of Leningrad oblast, 1928–29, in GARF, f. 393, op. 78, d. 21.

26. GARF, f. 1235, op. 141, d. 910, ll. 38–39.

27. GARF, f. 393, op. 84, d. 24, l. 11.

28. GARF, f. 8131, op. 37, d. 19, ll. 43–102.

29. GARF, f. 393, op. 78, d. 75, ll. 132–34. The tendency toward corruption in this kind of police work is not surprising, nor is the procuracy's assessment of recommendation for greater procuracy oversight over the *ugolovnyi rozysk*. These kinds of undercover activities conducted by agents had led inevitably to the *ugolovnyi rozysk* losing contact with the "healthy" influence of the "working masses."

30. GANO, f. 47, op. 5, d. 160, ll. 26, 29, 32, 36–37.

31. GARF, f. 9401, op. 12, d. 135, doc. 13.

32. GARF, f. 9401, op. 12, d. 135, doc. 13.

33. GARF, f. 9401, op. 12, d. 66, ll. 176–176ob. In 1934, in contrast, Yagoda relieved of command several police officials in Uzbekistan for misuse of confiscated funds, and their distribution as favors to people outside the police or OGPU. GARF 9401, op. 12, d. 166, ll. 126–126ob.

34. GARF, f. 9415, op. 5, d. 474, ll. 1–1a.

35. GARF, f. 9401, op. 12, d. 135, doc. 22. A report from November of 1934 reported 124,068 total state police. GARF, f. 5446, op. 16a, d. 1270, l. 28. Such numbers, of course, do not necessary indicate an increase in police crime rates from the 7 percent of 1930, but most likely better supervision by central authorities over local units.

36. Moscow oblast population taken from V. B. Zhiromskaia, *Demograficheskaia istoriia Rossii v 1930-e gody: Vzgliad v neizvestnoe* (Moscow, 2001), 38–39. On numbers of police, see GARF, f. 1235, op. 72, d. 340, l. 21. On the 1933 population, see GARF, f. 1235, op. 141, d. 1650, l. 29.

37. David Englander, "Police and Public Order in Britain 1914–1918," in *Policing Western Europe: Politics, Professionalism, and Public Order, 1850–1940*, ed. Clive Emsley and Barbara Weinberger (London, 1991), 90–138; Anja Johansen, *Soldiers as Police: The French and Prussian Armies and the Policing of Popular Protest, 1889–1914* (Burlington, 2005), 25. In 1905, the city of Essen counted a population of 230,000 and 270 uniformed police officers, a ration of 1:836. This did not count militarized police and soldiers garrisoned in the city. Elaine Glovka Spencer, *Police and the Social Order in German Cities: The Düsseldorf District, 1848–1914* (DeKalb, 1992), 90.

38. GARF, f. 9401, op. 12, d. 135, doc. 26.

39. GARF, f. 9401, op. 12, d. 135, doc. 26.

40. On public order in Moscow during the 1930s, see David Hoffmann, *Peasant Metropolis: Social Identities in Moscow, 1929–1941* (Ithaca, 1994).

41. GARF, f. 9415, op. 5, d. 478, l. 49, f. 5446, op. 26, d. 18, l. 201, f. 9415, op. 5, d. 479, l. 13.

42. GARF, f. 5446, op. 15a, d. 1130, l. 4.

43. Yagoda reported a total police force in 1932 of 98,292, which included cadets as well as street officers and command staff. GARF, f. 5446, op. 13a, d. 1320, l. 5. See also TsIK (RSFSR) report on police in GARF, f. 1235, op. 141, d. 910, ll. 24–40.

44. GARF, f. 5446, op. 13a, d. 1320, l. 6.

45. GANO, f. 3, op. 1, d. 550, l. 18.

46. Records of the Soviet labor colonies administration, the GULAG, showed that in the country as a whole, between 1932 and 1935—the first half of the decade—133,435 *spetspereselentsy* fled their colonies, while only 44,343 of those escapees were returned. GARF, f. 9479, op. 1s, d. 89, l. 217. The head of the Western Siberian GULAG reported in 1934 that, yearly, only about 15 percent of escapees in the district were recaptured. V. P. Danilov and S. A. Krasil'nikov, eds., *Spetspereselentsy v zapadnoi Sibiri, 1933–1938* (Novosibirsk, 1994), 197. Escapes from colonies and camps continued on a "massive and threatening" scale throughout the first half of the 1930s. GANO, f. 47, op. 5, d. 160, l. 3.

47. From a letter by Party plenipotentiary T. R. Ryskulov to Party leaders, 9 March 1933, reproduced in A. V. Kvashonkin et al., eds., *Sovetskoe Rukovodstvo: Perepiska, 1928–1941* (Moscow, 1999), 204–25, 205. For a recent discussion of the flight of Kazakhs during collectivization, see Niccolo Pianciola, "Famine in the Steppe: The Collectivization of Agriculture and the Kazak Herdsmen, 1928–1934," *Cahiers du Monde russe,* 45/1–2 (January–June 2004): 137–92, here 153–55.

48. These figures are included in the police report from January 1932. GANO, f. 47, op. 5, d. 160, ll. 6–7.

49. GANO, f. 47, op. 5, d. 160, l. 44.

50. GARF, f. 5446, op. 14a, d. 762, l. 7.

51. GANO, f. 3, op. 1, d. 550, ll. 177–78.

52. GANO, f. 47, op. 5, d. 166, ll. 140–41.

53. GANO, f. 47, op. 5, d. 175, ll. 2, 4.

54. GANO, f. 47, op. 5, d. 175, l. 2.

55. GANO, f. 47, op. 5, d. 175, l. 7.

56. At the time, only Moscow, Leningrad, Kiev, and Kharkov had regime status. Novosibirsk did not receive this coveted status until the mid-1930s.

57. GANO, f. 47, op. 5, d. 175, l. 2.

58. Lars T. Lih et al., eds., *Stalin's Letters to Molotov, 1925–1936* (New York, 1995), 228.

59. GANO, f. 47, op. 5, d. 192, l. 1.

60. GANO, f. 47, op. 5, d. 192, l. 64.

61. GANO, f. 47, op. 5, d. 192, l. 64.

62. GANO, f. 47, op. 5, d. 192, l. 66.

63. GANO, f. 3, op. 1, d. 550, l. 181.

64. GANO, f. 47, op. 5, d. 160, l. 33.

65. GANO, f. 3, op. 1, d. 550, ll. 182–83.

66. Nicholas Voinov, *The Waif* (New York, 1955).

67. GANO, f. 3, op. 1, d. 550, ll. 178, 181. See also the December 1933 letter

to the head of the Western Siberian Soviet, M. Domarev, the chief of the Western Siberian RKM, acknowledging the existence of widespread corruption and ties to criminal gangs in the district's *militsiia*. GANO, f. 47, op. 5, d. 175, l. 159.

68. GARF, f. 9401, op. 8, d. 41, l. 1.

69. V. M. Kuritsyn, *Istoriia gosudarstva i prava Rossii, 1929–1940* (Moscow, 1998), 99.

70. N. V. Petrov and K. V. Skorkin, *Kto rukovodil NKVD, 1934–1941: Spravochnik* (Moscow, 1999), 35–36.

71. GARF, f. 9401, op. 8, d. 41, l. 2.

72. GARF, f. 9401, op. 12, d. 70, ll. 205–7.

73. GARF, f. 9415, op. 5, d. 475, l. 7.

74. Kvashonkin et al., *Sovetskoe Rukovodsto*, 165–66. More to the point, Andreev complained that local OGPU officials were too closely tied to local railroad administrators and connived with them to cover up problems on their roads.

75. GARF, f. 5446, op. 13a, d. 1030, l. 9. Sovnarkom took subsequent action in the autumn to increase OGPU presence on rail lines, in some cases taking over direct administration.

76. GARF, f. 5446, op. 14a, d. 762, ll. 7–8.

77. RGASPI, f. 81, op. 3, d. 94, ll. 146–48.

78. RGASPI, f. 81, op. 3, d. 94, l. 142. Yagoda reported 2,900 OGPU staff transferred to political departments in 1933. GARF 9401, op. 8, d. 41, l. 2.

79. RGASPI, f. 81, op. 3, d. 94, ll. 76–86.

80. GARF, f. 1235, op. 72, d. 340, l. 14.

81. GARF, f. 1235, op. 141, d. 910, l. 40. GANO, f. 47, op. 5, d. 160, l. 18.

82. GARF, f. 1235, op. 72, d. 340, l. 14.

83. GARF, f. 9415, op. 3, d. 3, l. 52, f. 9401, op. 12, d. 126, l. 222.

84. In 1928, a police report listed 405 village bailiffs in the Trotsk region near Leningrad, a considerable number, and many more than the number of police. GARF, f. 393, op. 78, d. 21, l. 7.

85. GARF, f. 9415, op. 3, d. 3, l. 49.

86. GANO, f. 47, op. 5, d. 160, l. 16.

87. GARF, f. 9401, op. 12, d. 135, doc. 21. On reorganization, see GARF, f. 5446, op. 13a, d. 1314, ll. 8–10.

88. GARF, f. 393, op. 84, d. 24, l. 17.

89. GARF, f. 5446, op. 13a, d. 1314, l. 8.

90. GANO, f. 47, op. 5, d. 160, l. 16.

91. GARF, f. 393, op. 84, d. 24, l. 17.

92. GARF, f. 393, op. 84, d. 24, l. 17.

93. GANO, f. 47, op. 5, d. 160, l. 18.

94. GANO, f. 47, op. 5, d. 160, l. 18.

Chapter 3. A Soviet Gendarmerie

1. V. Vinogradov, *Genrikh Yagoda: Narkom vnutrennikh del SSSR, general'nyi komissar gosudarstvennoi bezopasnosti. Sbornik dokumentov* (Kazan', 1997), 89–93.

2. N. V. Petrov and K. V. Skorkin, *Kto rukovodil NKVD, 1934–1941: Spravochnik* (Moscow, 1999), 9.

3. On centralizing tendencies in police administration, see Paul Hagenloh, "Police, Crime, and Public Order in Stalin's Russia, 1930–1941" (Ph.D. diss., University of Texas, 1999), esp. chap. 1, "'Chekist in Essence, Chekist in Spirit': The OGPU Takeover and the New Stalinist Police"; idem, "'Chekist in Essence, Chekist in Spirit': Regular and Political Police in the 1930s," *Cahiers du Monde russe* 42/2–4 (April–December 2001): 447–76; David R. Shearer, "Social Disorder, Mass Repression, and the NKVD during the 1930s," *Cahiers du Monde russe* 42/2–3-4 (April–December 2001): 505–34.

4. On these conflicts, see especially Stuart Finkel, "An Intensification of Vigilance: Recent Perspectives on the Institutional History of the Soviet Security Apparatus in the 1920s," *Kritika: Explorations in Russian and Eurasian History* 5/2 (Spring 2004): 309; George Lin, "Fighting in Vain: The NKVD RSFSR in the 1920s" (Ph.D. diss., Stanford University, 1997); Nicholas Werth, "L'OGPU en 1924: Radiographie d'une institution à son niveau d'étiage," *Cahiers du Monde russe* 42/2–4 (April–December 2001): 397–422; Vladimir N. Haustov, "Razvitie sovetskikh organov gosudarstvennoi bezopasnosti: 1917–1953 gg," ibid., 357–74; A. M. Plekhanov, *VChK-OGPU v gody novoi ekonomicheskoi politiki, 1921–1928* (Moscow, 2006), esp. 99–115; Paul Hagenloh, "Police, Crime, and Public Order," 21–32, and "'Chekist in Essence,'" 451–53; S. A. Krasil'nikov, "Vysylka i ssylka intelligentsii kak element Sovetskoi karatel'noi politiki 20-kh–nachala 30-kh gg.," in *Diskriminizatsiia intelligentsii v poslerevoliutsionnoi Sibiri (1920–1930-e gg): Sbornik nauchnykh trudov*, ed. S. A. Krasil'nikov and L. I. Pystina, *Minuvshee*, no. 21 (1997): 179–239. Hagenloh, Werth, and Lin stress the intensity of these conflicts, while other authors downplay the seriousness of the threat to the OGPU. See also A. Ia Malygin, "Organy vnutrennikh del v period provedeniia novoi ekonomicheskoi politiki (1921–1929)," in A. V. Borisov, A. N. Dugin, A. Ia. Malygin, et al., *Politsiia i militsiia Rossii: Stranitsy istorii* (Moscow, 1995), 114–39, and L. P. Rasskazov, *Karatel'nye organy v protsesse formirovaniia i funktsionirovaniia administrativno-komandnoi sistemy v sovetskom gosudarstve, 1917–1941* (Ufa, 1994), 162–230.

5. *Gosudarstvennoe politicheskoe upravlenie* and *Ob'edinennoe gosudarstvennoe politicheskoe upravlenie*. A. I. Kokurin and N. V. Petrov, *Lubianka: Organy VChK-OGPU-NKVD-NKGB-MGB-MVD-KGB, 1917–1991* (Moscow, 2003), 5–6.

6. On the function of information gathering, see, especially, Peter Holquist, "'Information is the Alpha and Omega of Our Work': Bolshevik Surveillance in Its Pan-European Context," *Journal of Modern History* 69 (September 1997): 415–50; V. S. Izmozik, *Glaza i ushi rezhima: Gosudarstvennyi politicheskii kontrol' za naseleniem Rossii v 1918–1928 godakh* (St. Petersburg, 1995). In contrast to Holquist and Izmozik, Werth, especially, stresses the importance of the OGPU's continuing role as an organ fighting counterinsurgency, more so than as an information gathering agency. See Werth, "L'OGPU en 1924."

7. Finkel, "An Intensification of Vigilance," 306, and Plekhanov, *VChK-OGPU v gody novoi ekonomicheskoi politiki*, 135–37.

8. In his history of the OGPU during the 1920s, Plekhanov describes a process

of jurisdictional expansion based on the politicizing of ordinary criminality by OGPU officials, a process that Stalin broadened still further during the 1930s. Plekhanov, *VChK-OGPU v gody novoi ekonomicheskoi politiki*, 137.

9. GARF, f. 393, op. 43, d. 83, l. 8 on change in the penal code. See also Lin, "Fighting in Vain," 77–122.

10. Between four and six thousand yearly in 1925–28, jumping to 8,761 in 1929 and then nearly 180,000 in 1930, the first year of collectivization. GARF, f. 9401, op. 1, d. 4157, ll. 202–03. On troikas, see V. Danilov, R. Manning, and L. Viola., eds., *Tragediia Sovetskoi derevni: Kollektivizatsiia i raskulachivanie. Dokumenty i materialy v 5 tomakh*, vol. 5: *1937–1939*, book 1: *1937* (Moscow, 2004), 601 n. 57. On jurisdictional expansion of OGPU troikas, see Plekhanov, *VChK-OGPU v gody novoi ekonomicheskoi politiki*, 136–37.

11. Finkel, "An Intensification of Vigilance," 309. Lin and Krasil'nikov also stress the importance of these events in shaping the role of the political police in Soviet society and state organization.

12. See pp. 65–67.

13. On the tsarist policing system, see M. I. Siznikov, A. V. Borisov, and A. E. Skripilev, *Istoriia politsii Rossii (1718–1917)* (Moscow, 1992); A. V. Borisov, A. N. Dugin, A. Ia. and Malygin, *Politsiia i militsiia: Stranitsy istorii* (Moscow, 1995), 45–67; Z. I. Peregudova, *Politicheskii sysk Rossii, 1880–1917* (Moscow, 2000), 27–100; N. P. Eroshkin, *Istoriia gosudarstvennykh uchrezhdenii dorevoliutsionnoi Rossii* (Moscow, 1968), 213–15.

14. On the history of the NKVD in the early 1920s, see Borisov, *Politsiia i Militsiia*, 114–26. See especially Rasskazov, *Karatel'nye organy*, 212–14.

15. Dzerzhinskii recommended already in 1924 that the civil police and the *ugolovnyi rozysk* be subordinated to the political police. Plekhanov, *VChK-OGPU v gody novoi ekonomicheskoi politiki*, 135.

16. GARF, f. 1235, op. 72, d. 340, l. 14.

17. GARF, f. 393, op. 84, d. 24, l. 140b.

18. O. I. Cherdakov, *Formirovanie pravookhranitel'noi sistemy Sovetskogo gosudarstva v 1917–1936 gg: Istoriko-pravovoe issledovanie* (Saratov, 2001), 114.

19. Lin, "Fighting in Vain," 129–30.

20. Ibid., 137.

21. On *Rabkrin*, see E. A. Rees, *State Control in Soviet Russia: The Rise and Fall of the Workers' and Peasants' Inspectorate, 1920–1934* (New York, 1987).

22. Lin, "Fighting in Vain," 155.

23. L. Kosheleva et al., *Pis'ma I. V. Stalina V. M. Molotovu, 1925–1936* (Moscow, 1995), 215.

24. O. V. Khlevniuk, *Politbiuro: Mekhanizmy politicheskoi vlasti v 1930-e gody* (Moscow, 1996), 30. See the letter in Kosheleva et al., *Pis'ma*, 214.

25. Khlevniuk, *Politbiuro*, 28–29.

26. Lin, "Fighting in Vain," 160. RGASPI, f. 17, op. 3, d. 806, ll. 16–17.

27. GARF, f. 5446, op. 12a, d. 1141, ll. 61–62. Now published in A. I. Kokurkin and N. V. Petrov, eds., *Lubianka: Organy VChK-OGPU-NKVD-NKGB-MGB-MVD-KGB, 1917–1991. Spravochnik* (Moscow, 2003), 526–27.

28. Lin, "Fighting in Vain," 160.

29. Ibid.

30. The historian A. Ia. Malygin makes a similar argument, that Stalin and OGPU officials expanded control piecemeal over police organs as part of an overall plan to deprive national republics and autonomous regions of power over internal affairs that had been guaranteed under the 1924 constitution. Each measure, writes Malygin, "came closer to the planned goal, and was taken only after [leaders] became convinced that there would be no undesired reaction." Malygin, "Organy vnutrennikh del," in Borisov et al., *Politsiia i militsiia*,142.

31. GARF, f. 1235, op. 141, d. 910, l. 43, f. 9415, op. 5, d. 475, ll. 3–4, 7.

32. GARF, f. 9415, op. 5, d. 475, ll. 5, 7.

33. GARF, f. 9415, op. 5, d. 475, l. 5.

34. GARF, f. 9415, op. 5, d. 475, l. 9.

35. GARF, f. 9415, op. 5, d. 475, l. 9.

36. GARF, f. 9415, op. 5, d. 475, l. 8.

37. GARF, f. 9415, op. 5, d. 475, l. 34.

38. GARF, f. 9401, op. 12, d. 1, l. 59.

39. GARF, f. 9415, op. 5, d. 475, l. 5. Usov specifically acknowledged the resistance "in a number of regions" by justice officials to police subordination.

40. GARF, f. 5446, op. 12a, d. 1141, ll. 3–4. Officials of the Supreme Court also objected to the expanded arrest and investigative functions of the civil police. See GARF, f. 3316, op. 64, d. 1292, ll. 5–50b.

41. GARF, f. 374, op. 27, d. 1923, l. 40.

42. For further discussion of this letter, see Hagenloh, "Police, Crime, and Public Order," 31–32, and "'Chekist in Essence,'" 453.

43. See, for example, a 1933 report by the Siberian *militsiia*, which included a section on public participation. GANO, f. 47, op. 5, d. 160, l. 15.

44. Kokurkin and Petrov, *Lubianka: Organy,* 49. Even Yagoda's reference to the "civilian" population reflected his understanding of the police as a militarized force.

45. GARF, f. 5446, op. 12a, d. 1141, l. 45 defined military crimes as those committed by operative and administrative economic personnel against the established service procedures.

46. GARF, f. 5446, op. 13a, d. 1320, l. 6.

47. GARF, f. 5446, op. 12a, d. 1141, l. 45.

48. Kokurkin and Petrov, *Lubianka: Organy,* 531. Even leaders referred to police work as beneath the Cheka. After Kirov's murder in 1935, Nikolai Yezhov, under Stalin's orders, purged the Leningrad political police organization. He noted that of 280 purged, 180 were sent to camps, and another 100, whom he found not qualified for OGPU work, could possibly be used in police or ZAGS (the civil registration bureau run by the NKVD) but not in Cheka work. RGASPI, f. 671, op. 1, d. 118, l. 37.

49. For police involvement in the 1933 Western Siberian harvest campaign, see GANO, f. 47, op. 5, d. 160, ll. 119–28. See also Borisov et al., *Politsiia i militsiia,* 150.

50. GARF, f. 374, op. 27, d. 1992, ll. 1–5.

51. See the Western Siberian report in GANO, f. 47, op. 5, d. 160, ll. 1–33,119–

28. For the contrary view that higher police and OGPU authorities resisted the participation of local *militsiia* in collectivization and dekulakization duties, see Hagenloh, "Police, Crime, and Public Order," 82–83, and "'Chekist in Essence,'" 461.

52. GANO, f. 47, op. 5, d. 160, ll. 8, 10, 27.

53. Given the low numbers of police in Western Siberia, it is not clear where these one thousand police came from, or whether they were really police officials.

54. GANO, f. 47, op. 5, d. 160, l. 10.

55. GARF, f. 9415, op. 3, d. 3, ll. 48–49.

56. For the designation *pri OGPU*, see Kokurkin and Petrov, *Lubianka: Organy*, 56.

57. As of 10 April 1933, 833,938. GARF, f. 5446, op. 15a, d. 1073, l. 31.

58. GANO, f. 47, op. 5, d. 160, l. 44.

59. V. N. Khaustov, V. P. Naumov, and N. S. Plotnikova, eds., *Lubianka: Stalin i VChK-GPU-OGPU-NKVD, ianvar' 1922–dekabr' 1936* (Moscow, 2003), 399–406.

60. RGASPI, f. 17, op. 162, d. 14, l. 96.

61. Khaustov et al., *Lubianka: Stalin*, 811 n. 116.

62. Ibid., 811 n. 115.

63. Ibid., 435.

64. Ibid., 436; I. Zelenin et al., *Tragediia Sovetskoi derevni: Kollektivizatsiia i raskulachivanie. Dokumenty i materialy v 5 tomakh*, vol. 3: *Konets 1930–1933* (Moscow, 2001), 746–49.

65. Khaustov et al., *Lubianka: Stalin*, 436–40.

66. GARF, f. 5446, op. 14a, d. 757.

67. Khaustov et al., *Lubianka: Stalin*, 448.

68. See also RGASPI, f. 17, op. 162, d. 15, ll. 2, 14.

69. RGASPI, f. 17, op. 162, d. 15, ll. 161, 164.

70. This represented something of a return to favor for Bel'skii, who had been removed from active OGPU duty after siding with the losing faction in a struggle against Yagoda in 1931 and 1932. Leonid Naumov, *Bor'ba v rukovodstve NKVD v 1936–1938 gg* (Moscow, 2003), 19.

71. RGASPI, f. 17, op. 3, d. 937, l. 28.

72. See Peter H. Solomon Jr. on a similar contradiction in applications of the 25 June 1932 decree on revolutionary legality and the 7 August 1932 law on theft, in *Soviet Criminal Justice under Stalin* (Cambridge, 1996), 160–61.

73. GARF, f. 5446, op. 15a, d. 1073, l. 34.

74. GARF, f. 5446, op. 15a, d. 1130, ll. 1–10, here 1.

75. GARF, f. 5446, op. 15a, d. 1130, l. 10.

76. GARF, f. 9401, op. 12, d. 137, ll. 23–24.

77. GARF, f. 9401, op. 12, d. 137, ll. 24–27.

78. GARF, f. 9401, op. 12, d. 137, ll. 24–27.

79. Khaustov et al., *Lubianka: Stalin*, 12.

80. Ibid., 448, 487, 508.

81. On formation of the *spetskollegii*, see GARF, f. 5446, op. 16a, d. 126.

82. Solomon, *Soviet Criminal Justice*, 153–69.

83. RGASPI, f. 17, op. 3, d. 965, l. 75.

84. See also Solomon, *Soviet Criminal Justice,* 158.

85. GARF, f. 9415, op. 3, d. 1, l. 128.

86. GARF, f. 5446, op. 13a, d. 1320, l. 5.

87. GARF, f. 5446, op. 16a, d. 1270, l. 28.

88. GARF, f. 5446, op. 22a, d. 130, l. 22, and f. 9401, op. 8, d. 58, l. 1, respectively. Note here an apparent improvement of discipline, as well.

CHAPTER 4. INFORMANTS, SURVEILLANCE, AND PROPHYLACTIC POLICING

1. On prophylactic policing, see V. M. Pervushin, *Istoriia organov vnutrennikh del Rossii,* no. 2: *Sbornik nauchnykh trudov* (Moscow, 1999), 38–39.

2. See, for example, Iurii I. Shapoval, "The Mechanisms of the informational activity of the GPU-NKVD: The Surveillance File of Mykhailo Hrushevsky," *Cahiers du Monde russe* 42/2–4 (April–December 2001): 207–30; Volodymyr Semystiaha, "The Role and Place of Secret Collaborators in the Informational Activity of the GPU-NKVD in the 1920s and 1930s," ibid., 231–44.

3. On the tension that arose in general between leaders' need for popular participation and their mistrust of the population, see Cynthia Hooper, "Terror from Within: Participation and Coercion in Soviet Power, 1924–1964" (Ph.D. diss., Princeton University, 2003), esp. chap. 2.

4. Police utilized popular denunciations during such campaigns as the purging of Leningrad in 1935, and in certain aspects of the purges of 1937 and 1938. Leslie Rimmel, "A Microcosm of Terror, or Class Warfare in Leningrad: The March 1935 Exile of 'Alien Elements,'" *Jahrbücher für Geschichte Osteuropas* 48/4 (2000): 528–51. Scholars are divided over the extent to which police authorities utilized denunciations in Germany during the Third Reich. Robert Gellately has argued that Gestapo practices of repression were often driven by denunciations, while Eric Johnson has argued that the Gestapo was much more wary of such forms of public participation in policing and repression. Robert Gellately, *Backing Hitler: Consent and Coercion in Nazi Germany* (New York, 2001), 190–204; Eric Johnson, *Nazi Terror: The Gestapo, Jews, and Ordinary Germans* (New York, 2000).

5. On the 1920s, see Stuart Finkel, "An Intensification of Vigilance: Recent Perspectives on the Institutional History of the Soviet Security Apparatus in the 1920s," *Kritika: Explorations in Russian and Eurasian History* 5/2 (Spring 2004): 314 n. 65; Hooper, "Terror from Within," 123–25, 142–44.

6. Finkel, "An Intensification of Vigilance," 315. Finkel summmarizes a difference of emphasis between those who stress the surveillance gathering functions of the OGPU in 1920s and those who argue that, despite efforts to gather information, this function was not as important as semimilitary activities, such as combatting banditry and insurgent movements, and conducting espionage. Here, I develop the argument that in the 1930s, social surveillance became increasingly important, but technologies and practices of information registration were more important than human agent and informant surveillance. For a similar argument, see the internally produced history of the political police, V. M. Chebrikov et al., *Istoriia Sovetskikh organov gosudarstvennoi bezopasnosti* (Moscow, 1977). In their respective chapters, I. M. Nikitan and I. S. Rozanov emphasize the weakness of agent-informant

work during the 1930s. They stress that the main emphasis in political policing during the decade centered on mass arrests, and that the practice of identifying anti-Soviet elements on the basis of agent information begun seriously only in 1939. Ibid., 271–83, 309–10.

7. RGASPI, f. 671, op. 1, d. 118, l. 34. See also the "Instruktsiia o postanovke informatsionno-osvedomitel'noi raboty okruzhnykh otdelov GPU USSR, Khar'kov 1930," in Dzheffri Burds, *Sovetskaia agentura: Ocherki istorii SSSR v poslevoennye gody (1944–1948)* (Moscow, 2006), 169–206; Hooper, "Terror from Within," 156–57.

8. RGASPI, f. 671, op. 1, d. 118, ll. 525–26. That many were paid, and paid well, or received special and lucrative favors, see Semystiaha, "The Role and Place," 243–44.

9. Nicolas Werth, "L'OGPU en 1924: Radiographie d'une institution à son niveau d'étiage," *Cahiers du Monde russe* 42/2–4 (April–December 2001): 411.

10. A. I. Kokurin and N. V. Petrov, *Lubianka: Organy VChK-OGPU-NKVD-MGB-MVD-KGB, 1917–1991. Spravochnik* (Moscow, 2003), 574.

11. Werth, "L'OGPU en 1924," 399, 410.

12. N. V. Petrov and K. V. Skorkin, *Kto Rukovodil NKVD, 1934–1941: Spravochnik* (Moscow, 1999), 34.

13. GARF, f. 9401, op. 8, d. 41, ll. 11, 12. Nikita Petrov notes an increase between 1933 and 1935 from 20,898 to 23,188. "Le Personnel des organes de sécurité soviétiques, 1922–1953," *Cahiers du Monde russe* 42/2–4 (April–December 2001): 376.

14. V. Vinogradov, *Genrikh Yagoda: Narkom vnutrennikh del SSSR, general'nyi komissar gosudarstvennoi bezopasnosti: Sbornik dokumentov* (Kazan', 1997), 421.

15. See Yagoda's comment to this effect, especially on the ineffective use of MTS political police officers, in August 1934, ibid. 421–22.

16. GARF, f. 9401, op. 8, d. 41, l. 12. UNKVD staff increased in Belorussia from 460 to 803 (74.5 percent); in Western Siberia from 669 to 1,097 (64 percent); in the Far East from 406 to 1,185 (187 percent), and in Kazakhstan from 403 to 889 (120 percent). Moscow, of course, received a large influx of officers as well, with an increase from 699 to 1,020 (46 percent).

17. GARF, f. 9401, op. 8, d. 41, l. 12.

18. GARF, f. 9401, op. 8, d. 41, l. 12.

19. Peter Holquist, "'Information is the Alpha and Omega of Our Work': Bolshevik Surveillance in its Pan-European Context," *Journal of Modern History* 69 (September 1997): 415–50.

20. GARF, f. 9415, op. 5, d. 575, l. 56.

21. GARF, f. 9415, op. 5, d. 475, ll. 55–56.

22. See the report, critical of "secretive" police methods, in GARF, f. 393, op. 78, d. 75, ll. 133–34.

23. GARF, f. 9415, op. 5, d. 475, l. 55.

24. See Yagoda's statements to this effect in GARF, f. 9401, op. 12, d. 138, l. 2, and f. 9401, op. 12, d. 66, doc. 122.

25. Yagoda openly encouraged political police operational heads to utilize civil police sources, especially in peripheral areas. In 1934, he chastised GUGB officers,

saying that he had told them "repeatedly" that civil police, whether in factories or in rural areas, were important sources in setting up agent work. "We should use this mass of people, select the best, in order to strengthen our tentacles (*shchupal'tsa*)." Vinogradov, *Genrikh Yagoda*, 421.

26. GARF, f. 9415, op. 5, d. 475, ll. 56–58.

27. GARF, f. 9415, op. 5, d. 475, ll. 56–57, 111–13, f. 9415, op. 3, d. 1, ll. 48–49, 55–57, 70–72, 111–20. On the general organizational structure of the civil police, see, especially, Paul Hagenloh, "Police, Crime, and Public Order in Stalin's Russia, 1930–1941" (Ph.D. diss., University of Texas, 1999), 48–52. On police attempts to establish informant networks, see also ibid., esp. 67–68, 100–106.

28. Such comments seemed to run counter to Yagoda's 1934 exhortation that political police utilize civil police in their operational work. See above, note 25. On the other hand, such contradictory comments were common as the lines blurred in the 1930s between what was regarded as civil and what political criminality.

29. GARF, f. 9415, op. 5, d. 475, ll. 39–40.

30. GARF, f. 9415, op. 5, d. 475, l. 72.

31. GARF, f. 9415, op. 5, d. 488, l. 21.

32. GANO, f. 3, op. 9, d. 973, l. 12.

33. GARF, f. 9415, op. 5, d. 488, l. 23. In her autobiography, Mary Leder notes, however, that she usually met directly with a plainclothes officer of the NKVD. Mary M. Leder, *My Life in Stalinist Russia: An American Woman Looks Back* (Bloomington, Ind., 2001), 154–55, 171–72.

34. GARF, f. 9415, op. 5, d. 488, ll. 23, 27, 49.

35. GARF, f. 9415, op. 3, d. 1, l. 44.

36. GARF, f. 9415, op. 5, d. 488, ll. 13–17.

37. GARF, f. 9415, op. 5, d. 491, ll. 1, 280b.

38. GARF, f. 9415, op. 5, d. 491, ll. 5, 26.

39. GARF, f. 9415, op. 5, d. 491, ll. 5, 26.

40. GARF, f. 9415, op. 15, d. 488, ll. 30, 81.

41. GARF, f. 9415, op. 5, d. 488, ll. 46–48 provides a list of enterprises, places of work or locations, numbers of informants in place, and the number still needed.

42. GARF, f. 9415, op. 5, d. 488, l. 81.

43. See GANO, f. 47, op. 5, d. 166, ll. 143, 149.

44. GARF, f. 9415, op. 5, d. 488, l. 82.

45. GARF, f. 9415, op. 5, d. 488, l. 84.

46. GARF, f. 9415, op. 5, d. 488, l. 83.

47. GARF, f. 9401, op. 12, d. 66, doc. 122, ll. 2–3.

48. GARF, f. 9401, op. 12, d. 66, doc. 122, l. 2.

49. See complaints in GARF, f. 9415, op. 5, d. 488, ll. 57–99, f. 9401, op. 12, d. 66, doc. 122, ll. 3, 6.

50. GARF, f. 9401, op. 12, d. 66, doc. 122, ll. l, 2.

51. GARF, f. 9415, op. 5, d. 491, ll. 12–120b.

52. GARF, f. 9401, op. 12, d. 66, doc. 122.

53. GARF, f. 9415, op. 5, d. 497, l. 2.

54. How Yagoda came to this conclusion is unclear; neither did he provide ex-

amples to substantiate this claim. GARF, f. 9401, op. 12, d. 66, doc. 122, ll. l. 2; GARF, f. 9401, op. 12, op. 138, d. 2.

55. GARF, f. 9401, op. 12, d. 138, ll. 2–20b.

56. GARF, f. 9415, op. 5, d. 498, ll. 19, 26, 50, f. 9415, op. 5, d. 499, ll. 1–5, 13–17.

57. GARF, f. 9415, op. 5, d. 498, l. 1.

58. GARF, f. 9401, op. 12, d. 138, l. 3. See also Hagenloh, "Police, Crime, and Public Order," 115.

59. RGASPI, f. 671, op. 1, d. 118, ll. 4,6.

60. RGASPI, f. 671, op. 1, d. 118, ll. 4, 40; GARF, f. 9401 (Prikazy NKVD za 1937), ll. 1–3.

61. RGASPI, f. 671, op. 1, d. 118, ll. 6–7.

62. RGASPI, f. 671, op. 1, d. 118, ll. 8–9, 25.

63. RGASPI, f. 671, op. 1, d. 118, ll. 8, 27.

64. RGASPI, f. 671, op. 1, d. 118, ll. 8, 29–30.

65. RGASPI, f. 671, op. 1, d. 118, l. 27. Yezhov did not discuss the dilemma that it was exactly these and only these types of informants who could effectively infiltrate deep into the criminal world or the opposition political world.

66. RGASPI, f. 671, op. 1, d. 118, ll. 26–27.

67. RGASPI, f. 671, op. 1, d. 118, l. 33.

68. RGASPI, f. 671, op. 1, d. 118, l. 32.

69. RGASPI, f. 17, op. 2, d. 597, l. 11. Yezhov was, in fact, criticizing the campaign-style management policies of Yagoda, cutting and then recruiting in mass numbers in a short period of time.

70. A. G. Tepliakov, "Personal i povsevdnevost' Novosibirskogo UNKVD v 1936–1946," *Minuvshee: Istoricheskii al'manakh* 21 (1997): 242. I am grateful to Gabor Rittersporn for this reference.

71. RGASPI, f. 671, op. 1, d. 118, ll. 29–30.

CHAPTER 5. CATALOGING THE POPULATION

1. One set of figures from the *ugolovnyi rozysk*, for example, reported two thousand cases investigated in 1930. Another set from the *militsiia* showed four thousand cases investigated by the *ugolovnyi rozysk* for the same year. GARF, f. 9415, op. 5, d. 475, ll. 55, 61–62.

2. See, for example, GARF, f. 9415, op. 5, d. 486, which gives both a statistical and narrative account of police activities in the Moscow oblast for 1932. GARF, f. 9415, op. 5, d. 494 consists of statistical and narrative reports for the first quarter of 1933 for the Caucasus and Central Asian police administrations. GARF, f. 9415, op. 5, d. 486 gives a similar account of crime and police activities in Leningrad for 1932.

3. See the forms and descriptions, taken from 1931, in GARF, f. 9415, op. 3, d. 1, ll. 12–36, and f. 9415, op. 5, d. 475, ll. 60–63, 72–73.

4. GARF, f. 9415, op. 5, d. 475, ll. 55–58.

5. GARF, f. 9415, op. 5, d. 475, l. 73.

6. V. N. Khaustov, "Razvitie sovetskikh organov gosudarstvennoi bezopas-

nosti, 1917–1953 gg," *Cahiers du Monde russe,* 42/2–4 (April–December 2001): 370.

7. GARF, f. 9401, op. 12, d. 138, l. 7.

8. GARF, f. 9401, op. 12, d. 137, doc. 15.

9. See Yagoda's instructions to police in GARF, f. 5446, op. 15a, d. 1130, l. 2. See also the joint RKM and GUGB instruction from November 1935 on searching for wanted individuals, both political and criminal, in GARF, f. 9401, op. 12, d. 138, doc. 52. Also GARF, f. 9410, op. 12, d. 106 on coordination of searches for escapees.

10. GARF, f. 9415, op. 5, d. 475, l. 76.

11. GARF, f. 9415, op. 5, d. 475, ll. 67, 76, 82.

12. GARF, f. 9515, op. 5, d. 575, l. 68.

13. GARF, f. 9415, op. 5, d. 475, ll. 73–74.

14. GARF, f. 9415, op. 5, d. 457, ll. 74–75.

15. GARF, f. 9415, op. 5, d. 475, ll. 74–75.

16. On debates about how to define nationality in internal passports, see especially Francine Hirsch, *Empire of Nations: Ethnographic Knowledge and the Making of the Soviet Union* (Ithaca, 2005), 293–97.

17. GARF, f. 9415, op. 5, d. 475, ll. 76–77.

18. GARF, f. 9415, op. 5, d. 475, l. 71.

19. GARF, f. 9401, op. 12, d. 138, l. 20b.

20. GARF, f. 9415, op. 5, d. 475, ll. 78–79.

21. GARF, f. 9415, op. 5, d. 475, l. 77.

22. See, for example, an instructional booklet for precinct heads from 1936, GARF, f. 9401, op. 12, d. 135, doc. 133. See also GARF, f. 9401, op. 12, d. 138, l. 18 for a 1935 statement that current passport information was "the foundation" of any police search activity.

23. GARF, f. 9415, op. 5, d. 475, ll. 81–83.

24. GARF, f. 9401, op. 12, d. 138, l. 20b.

25. GARF, f. 9401, op. 12, d. 138, ll. 4–5.

26. GARF, f. 9415, op. 3, d. 8, l. 56. Also GARF, f. 9401, op. 12, d. 138, ll. 2–3 for the complaint that precinct inspectors were not paying attention to information on illegal residents.

27. GARF, f. 9401, op. 12, d. 138, l. 18.

28. GARF, f. 5446, op. 71, d. 176, l. 122.

29. GARF, f. 5446, op. 71, d. 176, l. 120.

30. GARF, f. 9401, op. 12, d. 106, l. 11.

31. Settlement inhabitants, for example, reported to local police only once a week, and it was up to the settler to go see the police.

32. GARF, f. 9401, op. 12, d. 138, ll. 18–19.

33. V. Vinogradov, *Genrikh Yagoda: Narkom vnutrennikh del SSSR, general'nyi komissar gosudarstvennoi bezopasnosti. Sbornik dokumentov* (Kazan', 1997), 421–22.

34. GARF, f. 9479, op. 1, d. 89, l. 217.

35. GARF, f. 9479, op. 1, d. 89, ll. 217–18.

36. GARF, f. 9415, op. 5, d. 475, l. 47.

37. See GARF, f. 9401, op. 12, d. 106, l. 11 for reference to a 21 April 1935 special NKVD order to take extraordinary measures to stop runaways and recapture escapees.

38. GARF, f. 9401, op. 12, d. 106, ll. 25–27, f. 9415, op. 3, d. 9, ll. 35–36.

39. GARF, f. 9401, op. 12, d. 138, ll. 6–6a.

40. GARF, f. 9415, op. 5, d. 494, l. 172.

41. GARF, f. 9401, op. 12, d. 138, ll. 7–12. For reasons of manpower, this could not have been possible in the case of the lowest civil police level, the precinct.

42. GARF, f. 9401, op. 12, d. 138, ll. 18–22.

43. GARF, f. 9415, op. 3, d. 1, ll. 26–27.

44. GARF, f. 9401, op. 12, d. 138, l. 19.

45. GARF, f. 9415, op. 12, d. 138, l. 3.

46. Terry Martin, "*Uchet* and *Nastroenie:* Information Report and the OGPU Surveillance System" (unpublished paper, 2000).

47. Even after reforms, police rarely updated residence and registration information in a timely manner, and NKVD search capabilities still worked ineffectively. GARF, f. 9401, op. 12, d. 138, l. 18. See the series of critical memoranda by Frinovskii and Yezhov from August 1937 in GARF, f. 9401, op. 12, d. 66, l. 161.

48. GARF, f. 9415, op. 5, d. 475, l. 47.

CHAPTER 6. THE CAMPAIGNS AGAINST MARGINALS

1. For other discussions about policing policies, see Paul Hagenloh, "Police, Crime, and Public Order in Stalin's Russia, 1930–1941" (Ph.D. diss., University of Texas, 1999), esp. chap. 3, "Criminality, Policing, and 'Socially Harmful Elements' in the Mid-1930s"; idem, "'Socially Harmful Elements' and the Great Terror," in *Stalinism: New Directions,* ed. Sheila Fitzpatrick (London, 2000), 286–308; idem, "'Chekist in Essence, Chekist in Spirit': Regular and Political Police in the 1930s," *Cahiers du Monde russe* 42/2–4 (April–December 2001): 447–76; David R. Shearer, "Crime and Social Disorder in Stalin's Russia: A Reassessment of the Great Retreat and the Origins of Mass Repression," ibid., 39/1–2 (1998): 119–48; idem, "Social Disorder, Mass Repression, and the NKVD during the 1930s," *Cahiers du Monde russe* 42/2–4 (April–December 2001): 505–34. Hagenloh stresses the evolution of policies against social harmfuls as driven by the internal dynamics of policing tactics against criminals. I argue for a more top-down interpretation, in which the ideology of class war, considerations of state security, and the intervention of leaders, Stalin in particular, drove much of the policing strategy during the 1930s.

2. On militarization of railroad "defense" and the role of political police, see GARF, f. 5446, op. 13a, d. 1030, ll. 1–3.

3. O. V. Khlevniuk, R. U. Devis (R. W. Davies), et al., *Stalin i Kaganovich: Perepiska, 1931–1936 gg* (Moscow, 2001), 260.

4. V. N. Khaustov, V. P. Naumov, and N. S. Plotnikova, *Lubianka: Stalin i VChK-GPU-OGPU-NKVD, ianvar' 1922–dekabr' 1936* (Moscow, 2003), 316–19.

5. Ibid., 319.

6. GARF, f. 5446, op. 13a, d. 1030, l. 2. See also GARF, f. 9415, op. 3, d. 2, ll. 217–217ob.

7. A peculiarity of the Soviet system, in which an individual could be indicted, tried, and sentenced in a court without having been formally arrested.

8. Khaustov et al., *Lubianka: Stalin,* 343–44.

9. GARF, f. 3316, op. 64, d. 1356, ll. 1–2.

10. RGASPI, f. 17, op. 162, d. 14, l. 103. No information is given in the document on how many were taken or where they were sent.

11. Gijs Kessler, "The Peasant and the Town: Rural-Urban Migration in the Soviet Union, 1929–1940" (Ph.D. diss., European University Institute, Florence, 2001), 57, 59. For other descriptions, see Andrea Graziosi, *The Great Soviet Peasant War: Bolsheviks and Peasants, 1917–1933* (Cambridge, Mass., 1996); Eugene Kulischer, *Europe on the Move: War and Population Changes, 1917–1947* (New York, 1948), esp. 88–98; N. A. Ivnitskii, *Kollektivizatsiia i raskulachivanie (nachalo 1930-kh godov)* (Moscow, 1994); I. Zelenin et al., *Tragediia Sovetskoi derevni: Kollektivizatsiia i raskulachivanie. Dokumenty i materialy v 5 tomakh,* vol. 3: *Konets 1930–1933* (Moscow, 2001), 32–33, 634; Sheila Fitzpatrick, "The Great Departure: Rural-Urban Migration in the Soviet Union, 1929–1933," in *Social Dimensions of Soviet Industrialization,* ed. William G. Rosenberg and Lewis H. Siegelbaum (Bloomington, Ind., 1993), 15–40.

12. Kessler, "The Peasant and the Town," table A-3, summary of statistical data from 1936.

13. Ibid., 59.

14. Ibid., 133–134; Jeffrey J. Rossman, "The Teikovo Cotton Workers' Strike of April 1932: Class, Gender, and Identity Politics in Stalin's Russia," *Russian Review* 56/1 (1997): 44–69.

15. Kessler, "The Peasant and the Town," 135.

16. Ibid.

17. GARF, f. A-374, op. 23, d. 198, l. 24. See also a note to the same effect by B. A. Balitskii to the Central Committee from 23 November 1932. "'Izmeneniia pasportnoi sistemy nosiat printspial'nyi kharakter': Kak sozdavalas' i razvivalas' pasportnaiia sistema v strane," *Vestnik arkhivov* 6 (1997): 104.

18. "Izmeneniia pasportnoi sistemy," 104; Khaustov et al., *Lubianka: Stalin,* 339–40.

19. Khaustov et al., *Lubianka: Stalin,* 391–94; Zelenin et al., *Tragediia,* 3:634–38.

20. Khaustov et al., *Lubianka: Stalin,* 393.

21. Ibid., 393.

22. Khaustov et al., *Lubianka: Stalin,* 392–93.

23. Graziosi, *Lettere da Kharkov: La Carestia in Ucraina e nel Caucaso del Nord nei rapporti dei diplomatici italiani* (Turin, 1991), 109–10, cited in Kessler, "The Peasant and the Town," 136.

24. Leaving 3,596 unaccounted for. O. B. Mozokhin, *Pravo na repressii: Vnesudebnye polnomochiia organov gosudarstvennoi bezopasnosti s 1918 po 1953 gg.* (Moscow, 2006), 129–31.

25. Khaustov et al., *Lubianka: Stalin,* 810 n. 110.

26. GARF, f. 5446, op. 15a, d. 1096, doc. 15.

27. RGASPI, f. 17, op. 3, d. 909, l. 107.

28. GARF, f. 5446, op.14a, d. 740, ll. 1–10.

29. GARF, f. 9401, op. 12, d. 137, doc. 15.

30. GARF, f. 9401, op. 12, d. 137, doc. 15.

31. GARF, f. 9415, op. 3, d. 9, l. 33.

32. GARF, f. 9401, op. 12, d. 137, doc. 1.

33. GARF, f. 5446, op. 14a, d. 740, l. 71.

34. GARF, f. 5446, op. 14a, d. 740, ll. 72–73.

35. GARF, f. 1235, op. 141, d. 1650, l. 27.

36. GARF, f. 9401, op. 12, d. 137, doc. 46.

37. GARF, f. 9401, op. 12, d. 137, doc. 48, ll. 202–4.

38. See discussion of this law in a July 1934 review of the criminal code in GARF, f. 3316, op. 64, d. 1523, ll. 19–20.

39. GARF, f. 1235, op. 141, d. 1650, l. 31.

40. GARF, f. 1235, op. 141, d. 1650, l. 30.

41. GARF, f. 1235, op. 141, d. 1650, l. 30, f. 3316, op. 64, d. 1227, l. 90.

42. GARF, f. 1235, op. 141, d. 1650, l. 29.

43. RGAE, f. 1562, op. 329, d. 131, l. 3. Contrast, however, the figure of 50,000 for the whole year with the figure of 98,000 for the period January to April, which shows that, in fact, the population recovered and began to grow again quickly.

44. GARF, f. 1235, op. 141, d. 1650, l. 28.

45. See, for example, Politburo approval in February 1933 of an OGPU operation to sweep Magnitogorsk of criminal elements, and approval in January 1934 of an OGPU operation, to last three months, to sweep Kharkov of déclassé elements. RGASPI, f. 17, op. 3, d. 914, l. 3, and f. 17, op. 162, d. 15, l. 164.

46. GARF, f. 9479, op. 1, d. 19, ll. 7, 9.

47. Khaustov et al., Lubianka: Stalin, 316.

48. Ibid., 425; GARF, f. 5446, op. 15a, d. 1071, l. 25, f. 5446, op. 15a, d. 1073, l. 186.

49. GARF, f. 5446, op. 15a, d. 1073, l. 25.

50. Khaustov et al., Lubianka: Stalin, 427, for example.

51. RGASPI, f. 17, op. 3, d. 946, l. 65.

52. A. I. Kokurin and N. V. Petrov, GULAG (Glavnoe upravlenie lagerei), 1918–1960 (Moscow, 2002), 432.

53. GARF, f. 8131, op. 37, d. 48, l. 1.

54. Khaustov et al., Lubianka: Stalin, 558.

55. RGASPI, f. 588, op. 2, d. 155, ll. 66–67.

56. V. Vinogradov, Genrikh Yagoda: Narkom vnutrennikh del SSSR, General'nyi komissar gosudarstvennoi bezopasnosti. Sbornik dokumentov (Kazan', 1997), 423–24.

57. On the difficulties of keeping Moscow cleaned of professional beggars, Yagoda wrote "We expel them and they come back again." N. Vert and S. V. Mironenko, eds., Istoriia stalinskogo Gulaga, Konets 1920-kh—pervaia polovina 1950-kh godov: Sobranie dokumentov v 7-mi tomakh, vol. 1: Massovye repressii v SSSR (Moscow, 2004), 257.

58. RGASPI, f. 588, op. 2, d. 155, l. 67.

59. On Vyshinskii's duplicitous positions, see especially, Peter H. Solomon

Jr., *Soviet Criminal Justice under Stalin* (Cambridge, 1996), 157–58; and A. G. Zviagintsev and Iu. G. Orlov, *Prigovorennye vremenem: Rossiiskie i Sovetskie prokurory XX vek, 1937–1953* (Moscow, 2001), 7–94.

60. On socially dangerous elements, GARF, f. 8131, op. 38, d. 11, ll. 39–40. On strengthening legal procedures, "Ob usilenii nadzora za revoliutsionnoi zakonnost'iu," 11 May 1935, in Zviaginstev and Orlov, *Prigovorennye vremenem*, 439–42.

61. GARF, f. 8131, op. 38, d. 11, l. 18.

62. RGASPI, f. 588, op. 2, d. 155, l. 66. Now published in "Izmeneniia pasportnoi sistemy," 109–11.

63. GARF, f. 8131, op. 38, d. 6, l. 61; GANO, f. 20, op. 1, d. 220, ll. 32–33.

64. GARF, f. 9401, op. 12, d. 135, doc. 148. On campaigns against social harmfuls, see, especially, Hagenloh, "Police, Crime, and Public Order," 114–46; idem, "'Socially Harmful Elements'"; Gabor Rittersporn, "Vrednye elementy, 'opasnye men'shinstva' i bol'shevistskie trevogi," in *V sem'e edinoi: Natsional'naia politika partii bol'shevikov i ee osushchestvlenie na Severo-Zapade Rossii v 1920–1950-e gody: Sbornik statei,* ed. Timo Vihavainen and Irina Takala (Petrozavodsk, 1998), 101–19; Shearer, "Social Disorder, Mass Repression, and the NKVD," and "Crime and Social Disorder," 134–37.

65. Note, again, that the higher number of those indicted than arrested was a peculiarity of the Soviet justice system, in which a person could be indicted and tried without having been arrested.

66. GARF, f. 8131, op. 37, d. 70, l. 138.

67. GARF, f. 9401, op. 1, d. 4157, l. 203.

68. GARF, f. 9414, op. 1, d. 1155, l. 5.

69. GANO, f. 20, op. 1, d. 220, l. 34, f. 47, op. 5, d. 227, ll. 81–82.

70. GANO, f. 20, op. 1, d. 220, l. 32.

71. GANO, f. 20, op. 1, d. 220, ll. 1–10b.

72. GANO, f. 20, op. 1, d. 220, l. 32.

73. GARF, f. 5446, op. 18a, d. 904, l. 3.

74. GARF, f. 5446, op. 18a, d. 904, l. 16.

75. RGASPI, f. 17, op. 163, d. 1059, l. 119. In a note from Vyshinskii to Stalin and Molotov, 8 April 1935, the chief procurator wrote that he had received a telegram from the procurator of the East Siberian district, Fridberg, requesting that he be allowed to extend the 16 March 1935 directive on aggravated theft to the new construction areas in Ulan-Ude, Cheremkhovo, and Usol'e. Fridberg wrote that the civil and police administration of these sites supported his request. Vyshinskii recommended granting the request. Politburo members agreed.

76. GARF, f. 9401, op. 12, d. 135, doc. 31.

77. GARF, f. 5446, op. 15a, dd. 1071 and 1073, esp. l. 186, and f. 8131, op. 37, d. 71, l. 220.

78. GARF, f. 9401, op. 12, d. 142, ll. 1–20b, f. 5446, op. 16a, d. 404, ll. 11–17.

79. An NKVD circular letter from September 1935 from the head of the EKO GUGB, Mironov, both criticized and sympathized with the task of EKO operational and agent groups, but the letter nonetheless noted the failure of agent investigative work to curtail the deficit problems created by illegal selling and speculation. GARF, f. 9401, op. 12, d. 142, ll. 16–17.

80. GARF, f. 5446, op. 57 (*postanovleniia Sovnarkoma za 1936*), No. 1285, l. 124. GARF, f. 5446, op. 16a, d. 404, ll. 4–9 for the October 1935 directive.

81. GARF, f. 9401, op. 12, d. 142, ll. 1–20b.

82. GARF, f. 8131, op. 37, d. 73, l. 19 and f. 9401, op. 12, d. 142, l. 1. By way of comparison, in all of 1935, according to Yagoda, 104,645 individuals had been apprehended on charges or suspicion of speculation. GARF, f. 5446, op. 18a, d. 904, l. 4.

83. Terry Martin, "The Origins of Soviet Ethnic Cleansing," *Journal of Modern History* 70 (December 1998): 813–61; *An Affirmative Action Empire: Nations and Nationalism in the Soviet Union, 1923–1939* (Ithaca, 2001), 345–43.

84. See Khaustov et al., *Lubianka: Stalin,* 582–84 for S. Kosior's memorandum about strengthening Ukrainian border areas, and targeting especially villages with Polish and German settlers.

85. Alain Blum, "Administrative Forms, Demographic Forms and the Limit of Ascribing Identity" (paper presented to the American Association for the Advancement of Slavic Studies, Washington D. C., 1991).

86. Martin, "Origins," esp. 847–50; Pavel Polian, *Ne po svoei vole: Istoriia i geografiia prinuditel'nykh migratsii v SSSR* (Moscow, 2001). See also I. L. Shcherbakova, *nakazannyi narod: Repressii protiv rossiiskikh Nemtsev* (Moscow, 1999); and A. E. Gur'ianov, *Repressii protiv poliakov i pol'skikh grazhdan* (Moscow, 1997).

87. Polian, *Ne po svoei vole,* 87–90, and GARF, f. 5446, op. 18a, d. 209.

88. GARF, f. 8131, op. 37, d. 59, l. 183–98.

89. GARF, f. 8131, op. 37, d. 59, l. 1870b. See also D. M. Smirnov, *Zapiski chekista* (Minsk, 1965), 46 on the practice of interviewing local activists.

90. Indeed, early surveys by Getty, Rittersporn, and Zemskov do not include nationality deportations in counting repression, neither do they count the many who were expelled from cities or sent back to home villages during times of famine or urban purges. See J. Arch Getty, Gabor Rittersporn, and Viktor Zemskov, "Victims of the Soviet Penal System in the Pre-War Years: A First Approach on the Basis of Archival Evidence," *American Historical Review* 98/4 (October 1993): 1017–49. As discussed in the previous chapter, there is almost no way to estimate the latter numbers.

91. L. A. Rimmel, "A Microcosm of Terror, or Class Warfare in Leningrad: The March 1935 Exile of 'alien elements,'" *Jahrbücher für Geschichte Osteuropas* 48/4 (2000): 528–51.

92. See Khaustov et al., *Lubianka: Stalin,* 613–16 for Zakovskii's request to Yagoda for a purge. See Yagoda's letter to Stalin supporting Zakovskii's recommendation, ibid., 617 and 820 n. 157. The operational order for this purge is in GARF, f. 9479, op. 1, d. 28, ll. 3–5. See Zakovskii's report to Yagoda on the operation in Khaustov et al., *Lubianka: Stalin,* 654–57, which gives a figure of 11,700 expelled. On the Leningrad and Karelian operations, see GARF, f. 9479, op. 1s, d. 30, ll. 13–14b. I am grateful to Lynne Viola for this and other references to f. 9479. On the Kalinin operations, see GARF, f. 8131, op. 37, d. 71, l. 225. For a discussion of Stalin's sensitivity to borderlands, especially when the "center" was weak or threatened, see Alfred J. Rieber, "Struggle over the Borderlands," in *The Legacy*

of History in Russia and the New States of Eurasia, ed. S. Frederick Starr (Armonk, 1994), 61–90; and "Stalin, Man of the Borderlands," *American Historical Review* 106/5 (December 2001): 1651–91.

CHAPTER 7. POLICING JUVENILES, POLICING DEBATES

1. GARF, f. 393, op. 84, d. 24, l. 170b.
2. GARF, f. 9415, op. 3, d. 1, l. 177.
3. GARF, f. 9415, op. 3, d. 1, l. 2780b.
4. GARF, f. 9415, op. 3, d. 1, l. 1770b.
5. GARF, f. 9415, op. 5, d. 478, ll. 45, 40 respectively.
6. GARF, f. 9415, op. 5, d. 479, l. 14. Overall, statistics of the GURKM received from eighteen *kraia* in the second half of 1931 showed that police apprehended (*bylo zaderzhano*) 26,230 underage individuals. In the first quarter of 1932, data from fifteen *kraia* showed 11,202 underage offenders apprehended. GARF, f. 9415, op. 5, d. 479, l. 13.
7. GARF, f. 9415, op. 5, d. 489, l. 18.
8. GARF, f. 9415, op. 5, d. 479, l. 22.
9. GARF, f. 5446, op. 14a, d. 515, ll. 1–3. See also Paul Hagenloh, "Police, Crime, and Public Order in Stalin's Russia, 1930–1941" (Ph.D. diss., University of Texas, 1999), 165.
10. GARF, f. 5446, op. 26, d. 18, ll. 259–69 for the July draft and ll. 32–41 for the September draft. Also GARF, f. 5446, op. 71, d. 176, ll. 16–29 for the July draft.
11. In fact, Chubar' penned this recommendation in June in handwritten notes of talking points for a report he was to give to the Central Committee. He based his recommendation on the police-dominated subcommission on child crime. GARF, f. 5446, op. 26, d. 18, l. 228.
12. See GARF, f. 5446, op. 26, d. 18, ll. 259–69 for the July draft and 32–41 for the September draft. Also GARF, f. 5446, op. 71, d. 176, ll. 16–29 for the July draft. In an early draft from June (GARF, f. 5446, op. 26, d. 18, l. 67), the placement commission was called a troika, a word struck from the later draft. No doubt, this word carried connotations of the political troikas that commission members wished to avoid, and also because these commissions were to include four people rather than the traditional three.
13. GARF, f. 5446, op. 26, d. 50, l. 42.
14. GARF, f. 5446, op. 26, d. 50, l. 43.
15. GARF, f. 5446, op. 26, d. 50, l. 44.
16. GARF, f. 5446, op. 26, d. 50, ll. 77–87.
17. Presumably, Narkompros retained control over the country's still large system of orphanages.
18. GARF, f. 3316, op. 64, d. 1612, l. 93–102 for the final April draft.
19. GARF, f. 3316, op. 64, d. 12, ll. 22–26. In making these arguments, Krupskaia avoided public mention of the most glaring cause of child homelessness, the brutal policies of the regime during the early 1930s.
20. RGASPI, f. 17, op. 163, d. 1059, ll. 22–26, Protokol 24 from 26 April 1935.

See the published decree in *Sobranie zakonov i rasporiazhenii* 32 (20 June 1935), 473–76. The sections on police operations were not included in the published law. On the work of the Chubar' commission, see also Hagenloh, "Police, Crime, and Public Order," 179–80.

21. Summarized in GARF, f. 5446, op. 16a, d. 1270, l. 5.

22. GARF, f. 5446, op. 16a, d. 1270, l. 7.

23. *Sobranie zakonov* 19 (May 1935), 262.

24. Addendum reproduced in O. V. Khlevniuk, A. V. Kvashonkin, et al., *Stalinskoe Politbiuro v 30-e gody* (Moscow, 1995), 144–45.

25. RGASPI, f. 17, op. 163, d. 1059, ll. 23–24. Peter Solomon stresses Stalin's personal role in formulation of the 1935 juvenile delinquent law. Peter H. Solomon Jr., *Soviet Criminal Justice under Stalin* (Cambridge, 1996), 197–203, esp. 201. See also Hagenloh, "Police, Crime, and Public Order," 140–41; David R. Shearer, "Crime and Social Disorder in Stalin's Russia: A Reassessment of the Great Retreat and the Origins of Mass Repression," *Cahiers du Monde russe* 39/1–2 (1998): 129–130; Gabor Rittersporn, "Between Revolution and Daily Routine: Youth and Violence in the Soviet Union in the Interwar Period," in *Sowjetjugend 1917–1941: Generation zwischen Revolution und Resignation,* ed. Corinna Kuhr-Korolev, Stefan Plaggenborg, and Monica Wellmann (Essen, 2001), 66.

26. Voroshilov's letter was precipitated by an account of a sixteen-year-old convicted murderer who was sentenced to only five years' incarceration. Khlevniuk, Kvashonkin, et al., *Stalinskoe Politbiuro,* 144.

27. Ibid., 144. GARF, f. 3316, op. 64, d. 1612, l. 100.

28. GARF, f. 3316, op. 64, d. 1612, ll. 99–100.

29. GARF, f. 3316, op. 64, d. 1612, l. 67.

30. GARF, f. 3316, op. 64, d. 1619, l. 39.

31. GARF, f. 9474, op. 10, d. 49, ll. 4–5.

32. GARF, f. 5446, op. 18a, d. 904, l. 6. On antijuvenile campaigns, see also Hagenloh, "Police, Crime, and Public Order," 141–42, 186–90. On judicial reaction, see Solomon, *Soviet Criminal Justice,* 204–8. In contrast to the aggressive police reaction, Solomon argues that judges often refrained from using their full sentencing power.

33. GARF, f. 1235, op. 2, d. 2032, ll. 26–27.

34. GARF, f. 5446, op. 16a, d. 591, l. 21.

35. GARF, f. 1235, op. 2, d. 2032, l. 26.

36. Sarah Davies, "The Crime of 'Anti-Soviet Agitation' in the Soviet Union in the 1930s," *Cahiers du Monde russe* 39/1–2 (January–June 1998): 142–67,

37. For Vyshinskii's letter, see GARF, f. 8131, op. 37, d. 70, ll. 103–6. For Yagoda's reply, see GARF, f. 8131, op. 37, d. 70, ll. 138–42.

38. According to Vyshinskii, the *militsiia* initiated 2,401,412 criminal cases. Investigation of these cases resulted in the detention of 2,430,585 people. Police arrested 539,519 of those detained. In the end, however, police quashed 431,276 cases and the procuracy vacated about the same number. GARF, f. 8131, op. 37, d. 70, l. 1340b.

39. GARF, f. 8131, op. 37, d. 70, ll. 103, 105. Vyshinskii did not elaborate restrictions, other than those already in place to send political cases through courts.

40. From a speech to operational heads of the newly formed NKVD, 1934. V. Vinogradov, *Genrikh Yagoda: Narkom vnutrennikh del SSSR, general'nyi komissar gosudarstvennoi bezopasnosti. Sbornik dokumentov* (Kazan', 1997), 410.

41. Ibid., 417–18. This was also Yezhov's assessment in a 1935 report to Stalin. "Officers don't know laws and are proud of it. In general, they have low educational levels and do not read." RGASPI, f. 671, op. 1, d. 118, l. 34.

42. The historian N. S. Plotnikova confirms that even Yagoda did not understand the relation that was supposed to obtain between the political police and the procuracy. N. S. Plotnikova, "O deiatel'nosti osobogo soveshchaniia pri NKVD SSSR," *Istoricheskie chteniia na Lubianke, 1999 god* (www.fsb.ru/history), 2.

43. GARF, f. 5446, op. 18a, d. 849, ll. 1–4.

44. A. Vyshinskii, "K reforme ugolovno-protsessual'nogo kodeksa," *Problemy ugolovnoi politiki,* vol. 1 (Moscow, 1935), 26–39.

45. Ibid., 34.

46. GARF, f. 8131, op. 38, d. 11, l. 44, f. 3316, op. 64, d. 1619, l. 380b.

47. Vyshinskii, "K reforme," 35.

48. Thus, Vyshinskii's participation in the show trials of the mid- and late 1930s was not a contradiction of his support for due process and rights, but a consistent extension of his views of the public character of repression.

49. GARF, f. 8131, op. 37, d. 68, ll. 48–150.

50. GARF, f. 8131, op. 37, d. 70, l. 103.

51. GARF, f. 8131, op. 37, d. 68, ll. 69, 90–92, 106.

52. For Sol'ts's comments, see GARF, f. 8131, op. 37, d. 68, ll. 42–43.

53. GARF, f. 8131, op. 37, d. 68, l. 251.

54. GARF, f. 8131, op. 37, d. 68, l. 82.

55. The report was, in fact, compiled by the head of the RKM, Bel'skii. GARF, f. 5446, op. 15a, d. 1130, ll. 2–, f. 8131, op. 37, d. 71, ll. 220–26.

56. GARF, f. 5446, op. 18a, d. 904, ll. 2–14.

57. GARF, f. 9401, op. 12, d. 135, doc. 31, ll. 1–5.

58. Yagoda's assessment. GARF, f. 5446, op. 18a, d. 904, l. 2.

59. GARF, f. 9401, op. 12, d. 137, l. 24, and doc. 14, ll. 1–2.

60. GARF, f. 5446, op. 18a, d. 904, l. 3.

CHAPTER 8. PASSPORTS, IDENTITY, AND MASS POLICING

1. For recent work on the passport system, see Gijs Kessler, "The Passport System and State Control over Population Flows in the Soviet Union, 1932–1940," *Cahiers du Monde russe* 42/2–4 (April–December 2001): 478–479; eadem, "The Peasant and the Town: Rural-Urban Migration in the Soviet Union, 1929–40" (Ph.D. diss., European University, Florence, 2000); Nathalie Moine, "Passeportisation, statistique des migrations et contrôle de l'identité sociale," ibid., 38/4 (1997): 587–600; eadem, and "Le Système des passeports à l'époque stalinienne: De la purge des grandes villes au morcellement du territoire, 1932–1953," *Revue d'Histoire moderne et contemporaine* 50/1 (January–March, 2003): 145–69. In Russian, see E. N. Chernolutskaia on the Soviet Far East, "Pasportizatsiia dal'nevostochnogo naseleniia," *Revue des Etudes slaves* 71 (1999): 17–33; and V. P. Popov, "Pas-

portnaia sistema v SSSR (1932–1976)," *Sotsiologicheskie issledovaniia* 8 (1995): 3–14 and 9 (1995): 3–13. In the same vein, see Paul Hagenloh, "Police, Crime, and Public Order in Stalin's Russia, 1930–1941" (Ph.D. diss., University of Texas, 1999), esp. chap. 5, "The Passport System, Social Quarantine, and the Mass Operations of 1937–1938"; idem, " 'Socially Harmful Elements' and the Great Terror," in *Stalinism: New Directions,* ed. Sheila Fitzpatrick (London, 2000), 295–300. See also David R. Shearer, "Elements Near and Alien: Passportization, Policing, and Identity in the Stalinist State," *Journal of Modern History* 76 (December 2004): 835–81. While Popov stresses the use of the passport system to discriminate against the peasantry, Moine's groundbreaking studies first examined the passport system as a means of controlling migration and protecting cities. Kessler focuses on passportization as a means to regulate migration between rural and urban areas, and Hagenloh emphasizes the use of passportization as a means of criminal control. This chapter coincides with and extends the work of these scholars to include a comparative dimension, further discussion of the geographic-social aspects of Soviet passportization, and an examination of the evolution of passport laws within the context of bureaucratic conflicts and conflicting state visions. The chapter also emphasizes the function of the passport system as a tool of mass public surveillance and social engineering.

2. For the most thorough discussion, see Francine Hirsch, *Empire of Nations: Ethnographic Knowledge and the Making of the Soviet Union* (Ithaca, 2005). See also Alain Blum, "Λ l'origine des purges de 1937," *Cahiers du Monde russe,* 39/1–2 (January–June 1998): 169–96; Kessler, "The Passport System," esp. 495–501; Moine, "Passeportisation."

3. Golfo Alexopoulos, *Stalin's Outcasts: Aliens, Citizens, and the Soviet State, 1926–1936* (Ithaca, 2003).

4. See above, p. 116.

5. Alain Blum, "Administrative Forms, Demographic Forms and the Limit of Ascribing Identity" (paper presented to the American Association for the Advancement of Slavic Studies, Washington, D.C., November 2001), 1; Moine, "Passeportisation," 590–91.

6. RGASPI, f. 671, op. 1, d. 118, l. 4.

7. GARF, f. 1235, op. 141, d. 1650, l. 31.

8. " 'Izmeneniia pasportnoi sistemy nosiat printsipial'no vazhnyi kharakter': Kak sozdavalas' i razvivalas' pasportnaia sistema v strane," *Vestnik arkhivov* 6 (1997): 111.

9. V. N. Khaustov, "Razvitie sovetskikh organov gosudarstvennoi bezopasnosti: 1917–1953 gg," *Cahiers du Monde russe* 42/2–4 (April–December 2001): 370 for reference to 1.2 million under surveillance.

10. Michel Foucault, *Discipline and Punish: The Birth of the Prison,* trans. Alan Sheridan (New York, 1977), 171.

11. In addition to previous chapters, see David R. Shearer, "Social Disorder, Mass Repression, and the NKVD during the 1930s," *Cahiers du Monde russe* 42/2–4 (April–December 2001): 519–29; idem, and "Elements Near and Alien"; Paul Hagenloh, " 'Chekist in Essence, Chekist in Spirit': Regular and Political Police in the 1930s," ibid., 469; idem, " 'Socially Harmful Elements,' " 296–300.

12. GARF, f. 9415, op. 5, d. 494, ll. 172–73.

13. The precision which officials ascribed to social nomenclature based on passport identities bordered on the absurd. In a March 1934 memorandum, the Western Siberian police chief, Domarev, reported that, based on passportization to date, exactly 4.5 percent of the district's population was of the "socially alien element." In a further piece of absurdity, Domarev, apparently having miscalculated, struck out the typed figure of 4.5 percent and handwrote "2.5 percent." GANO, f. 47, op. 5, d. 160, l. 155.

14. GARF, f. 5446, op. 15a, d. 1096, ll. 1–23.

15. GARF, f. 9415, op. 3, d. 6, l. 1.

16. GARF, f. 9415, op. 3, d. 3, ll. 55–56.

17. GARF, f. 8131, op. 38, d. 6, l. 61.

18. GARF, f. 8131, op. 37, d. 68, l. 7.

19. GANO, f. 47, op. 5, d. 160, ll. 155-56. A common complaint from ordinary people was how unfair it was that former kulaks and convicts should receive passports that gave them as much right to social privileges as workers and other "upstanding" Soviet citizens. GANO, f. 47, op. 5, d. 160, 157-58.

20. GANO, f. 47, op. 5, d. 160, ll. 158-59.

21. For the best descriptions in English of ethnic and national operations, see Terry Martin, *An Affirmative Action Empire: Nations and Nationalism in the Soviet Union, 1923–1939* (Ithaca, 2001), esp. chap. 8, "Ethnic Cleansing and Enemy Nations"; and Amir Weiner, *Making Sense of War: The Second World War and the Fate of the Bolshevik Revolution* (Princeton, 2001), chap. 3, "Excising Evil." See also Terry Martin, "The Origins of Soviet Ethnic Cleansing," *Journal of Modern History* 70 (December 1998): 813–61.

22. Lynne Viola, *The Unknown Gulag: The Lost World of Stalin's Special Settlements* (New York, 2007), 24.

23. GARF, f. 5446, op. 16a, d. 1252, l. 26.

24. Nicholas Werth, "L'OGPU en 1924: Radiographie d'une institution à son niveau d'étiage," *Cahiers du Monde russe* 42/2–4 (April–December 2001): 413. On Western Siberia as an extreme duty area, see GARF, f. 9401, op. 12, d. 273, l. 86.

25. Comments made at the June 1937 conference of regional Communist Party heads of the Western Siberian District. GANO, f. 3, op. 2, d. 828, l. 11.

26. See Hiroaki Kuromiya, *Freedom and Terror in the Donbas: A Ukrainian-Russian Borderland, 1870s–1990s* (New York, 1998); David R. Shearer, "Modernity and Backwardness on the Soviet Frontier: Western Siberia during the 1930s," in *Provincial Landscapes: Local Dimensions of Soviet Power, 1917–1953,* ed. Donald Raleigh (Pittsburgh, 2001), 194–216.

27. One should admit here a certain contradiction in calling Western Siberia, for example, a frontier and describing it in colonial terms as well. Western Siberia fit more into the scheme of a frontier, such as the American West of the nineteenth century, a place contiguous to the core state and as yet not fully assimilated, but a place to be tamed and eventually assimilated. As Peter Blitstein has pointed out, however, there is a difference between policies of assimilation and discrimination, which were characteristic of nation-states, and colonial policies of empire, which were de-

signed to maintain separation and exclusion between metropole and colony. In some senses, Western Siberia, as well as other Soviet "distant" places, fit into both categories incompletely, and into neither category completely. Peter Blitstein, "Why the Soviet Union Was Not an Empire, and Why It Matters" (unpublished paper).

28. The designation of penal colonists as "special settlers" distinguished them from voluntary settlers, whom the government also encouraged to settle in the non-European areas of the Soviet Union. In the mid- and late 1920s, government documents and officials referred to the process of settling underdeveloped areas as colonization (*kolonizatsiia*), although in keeping with their "special" status, penal colonists were engaged in what was described as *spetskolonizatsiia*. The language of colonization was quickly dropped in favor of the more neutral term of "mastering," but, in the late 1920s, officials still used the language of colonization unabashedly. See, for example, the VTsIK decree from 18 August 1930 "O meropriatiiakh po provedeniiu spetskolonizatsii v Severnom i Sibirskom kraiakh i Ural'skoi oblasti," reprinted in S. N. Golotik and V. V. Minaev, *Naselenie i vlast': Ocherki demograficheskoi istorii SSSR 1930-kh godov* (Moscow, 2004), 117. Also, see GARF, f. 3260, op. 9, dd. 6, 27, 28, 34, all of which, from 1928 and 1929, refer to colonization and resettlement plans. See, however, an exception in the 1936 report by I. I. Pliner, assistant head of GULAG, on plans to "colonize" territory associated with construction of the Baikal-Amur rail line. GARF, f. 9479, op. 1, d. 36, ll. 28–29, reprinted in T. V. Tsarevskaia-Diakina, ed., *Istoriia stalinskogo gulaga, Konets 1920-kh—pervaia polovina 1950-kh godov: Sobranie dokumentov v 7-mi tomakh*, vol. 5: *Spetspereselentsy v SSSR* (Moscow, 2004), doc. 49, 226–27. On colonization, see Edward Hallett Carr, *Socialism in One Country, 1924–1926* vol. 1 (New York, 1958), 519–30. More recently, see Niccolo Pianciola, "Famine in the Steppe: The Collectivization of Agriculture and the Kazakh Herdsmen, 1928–1934," *Cahiers du Monde russe*, 45/1–2 (January–June 2004): 153–59.

29. Thus, Soviet deportation policies were not unique, but reflected, in the extreme, colonizing policies carried out by other European empires. On Australia, see Robert Hughes, *The Fatal Shore: The Epic of Australia's Founding* (New York, 1987); L. L. Robson, *The Convict Settlers of Australia* (Melbourne, 1965); George Rudé, *Protest and Punishment: The Story of the Social and Political Prisoners Transported to Australia, 1788–1868* (London, 1978); A. G. L. Shaw, *Convicts and Colonies: A Study of Penal Transportation from Great Britain and Ireland to Australia and Other Parts of the British Empire* (Melbourne, 1966). In France, penal legislation to allow mass colonial deportation of vagrants, beggars, recidivist criminals, and other social marginals was enacted in stages between 1883 and 1885. See Robert Nye, *Crime, Madness, and Politics in Modern France: The Medical Concept of National Decline* (Princeton, 1984), 59–95. Richard Evans discusses various German states' attempts in the nineteenth century to export recidivist criminals, political revolutionaries, and other undesirables, an effort hampered by the lack of overseas colonies. State ministries were forced to contract with South American governments and even with Russia to ship these populations away. After unification, the issue of penal colonies arose again, following the models of Britain and France, within the larger national drive to acquire overseas possessions. The penal project was eventually abandoned, as Evans explains, for several reasons, not the

least of which was that the British experience, at least, had not worked well and their deportation policies were being scaled back. Richard J. Evans, *Tales from the German Underworld: Crime and Punishment in the Nineteenth Century* (New Haven, 1998), 40–81.

30. GARF, f. 9401, op. 12, d. 130, doc. 75.

31. RGAE, f. 1562, op. 329, d. 131, l. 3.

32. GARF, f. 9401, op. 12, d. 137, ll. 125–27. By 1940, 175 cities and 460 other regions carried this distinction, which prompted leaders to distinguish further between regime categories I and II. Moine, "Le Système des passeports," 156.

33. See the comment by the head of the *militsiia*, L. N. Bel'skii: "The best indicators of reduced crime come from cities with populations over 50,000, a significant number of which are regime [cities]. These cities (120 in number) are under special control by the Chief Administration of the Police." GARF, f. 8131, op. 37, d. 71, l. 220. See also Yagoda's similar assessment in GARF, f. 9401, op. 12, d. 135, doc. 31, l. 3. In addition, see the report on crime in regime cities in GARF, f. 9401, op. 12, d. 135, l. 146.

34. GARF, f. 8131, op. 37, d. 71, l. 226.

35. GARF, f. 5446, op. 14a, d. 740, l. 157.

36. GANO, f. 3, op. 1, d. 550, l. 18.

37. From a letter by Party plenipotentiary T. R. Ryskulov to Party leaders, 9 March 1933, reproduced in A. V. Kvashonkin et al., eds., *Sovetskoe Rukovodstvo: Perepiska, 1928–1941* (Moscow, 1999), 204–25, here 205. Pianciola, "Famine in the Steppe," 171.

38. GANO, f. 4, op. 34, d. 26, l. 2.

39. Mikhail Shreider, *NKVD iznutri: Zapiski chekista* (Moscow, 1995), 86–87, 98–99.

40. GARF, f. 5446, op. 18a, d. 845, ll. 31–32.

41. See examples of these requests in GARF, f. 5446, op. 14a, d. 740.

42. Shreider, *NKVD iznutri,* 99–100.

43. GARF, f. 9401, op. 12, d. 137, doc. 67. Reprinted in Vert and Mironenko, *Spetspereselentsy v SSSR,* doc. 35, 209. GARF, f. 9401, op. 12, d. 130, doc. 75.

44. GARF, f. 9401, op. 12, d. 137, docs. 7, 21, 36.

45. GARF, f. 5446, op. 22a, d. 69, l. 47.

46. Sheila Fitzpatrick emphasizes the corporate character, or *soslovnost'*, of Stalinist society in her article "Ascribing Class: The Construction of Social Identity in Soviet Russia," *Journal of Modern History* 65 (December 1993): 765–68.

47. GARF, f. 5446, op. 20a, d. 931, l. 2, f. 8131, op. 37, d. 83, ll. 43–44.

48. This amounted to the social equivalent of what Martin refers to as the emergence of "primordial" views of nationality, which also crystallized in the early and mid-1930s. Terry Martin, "Modernization or Neo-Traditionalism? Ascribed Nationality and Soviet Primordialism," in Fitzpatrick, *Stalinism: New Directions,* 348–67.

49. GARF, f. 9479, op. 1s, d. 29, l. 12. Reprinted in Vert and Mironenko, *Spetspereselentsy v SSSR,* 207–9.

50. GARF, f. 9479, op. 1, d. 29, l. 11.

51. GARF, f. 9479, op. 1, d. 30, ll. 1–5.

52. GARF, f. 8131, op. 37, d. 59, ll. 17–19.

53. GARF, f. 9479, op. 1, d. 30, ll. 14–15.

54. GARF, f. 5446, op. 22a, d. 69, l. 31.

55. M. N. Gernet, "Predislovie k rabote *Prestupnyi mir Moskvy* (1924)" in M. N. Gernet, *Izbrannye Proizvedeniia* (Moscow, 1974), 435. For other European views, see Robert Nye, *Crime, Madness, and Politics;* Daniel Pick, *Faces of Degeneration: A European Disorder, c. 1848–c. 1918* (Cambridge, 1989). Lombroso's most synthetic work in English was *Crime: Its Causes and Remedies* (London, 1911).

56. G. I. Volkov, *Klassovaia priroda prestuplenii i sovietskoe ugolovnoe pravo* (Moscow, 1935), esp. chap. 4, "Kritika burzhuaznykh teorii prestupleniia."

57. GARF, f. 9401, op. 12, d. 135, doc. 31.3.

58. Berman, the head of GULAG, expressed the view already in 1933 that recidivists could not be rehabilitated. N. Werth and G. Moullec, *Rapports secrets soviétiques: La société russe dans les documents confidentiels, 1921–1991* (Paris, 1994), 44.

59. GARF, f. 9401, op. 12, d. 137, doc. 69. This order led to so many questions from local police that an April 25 circular further elucidated it. The original order was not rescinded, but the new circular recommended that such individuals not be expelled unless there existed "compromising" information about the social danger they posed. GARF, f. 9401, op. 12, d. 130, doc. 70.

60. GARF, f. 9401, op. 12, d. 135, doc. 31, ll. 3–4.

61. GARF, f. 5446, op. 22a, d. 69, ll. 2–13.

62. GARF, f. 5446, op. 22a, d. 69, l. 46.

63. "Obiazatel'no, ia ubegu." The criminal had in mind the relative ease with which people could escape camps, if they so chose. GARF, f. 5446, op. 22a, d. 69, l. 45.

64. GARF, f. 5446, op. 22a, d. 69, l. 31.

65. See the summary tables in Pavel Polian, *Ne po svoei vole: Istoriia i geografiia prinuditel'nykh migratsii v SSSR* (Moscow, 2001), 245–49. See also Iu. A. Poliakov et al., *Naselenie Rossii v XX veke: Istoricheskie ocherki*, vol. 1: *1900–1939* (Moscow, 2000), esp. chaps. 13–15.

66. GARF, f. 9479, op. 1, d. 19, l. 9. See the request to Stalin by Robert Eikhe, Party head in Western Siberia, in summer 1933, to remove recidivist criminals from agricultural colonies. According to Eikhe, criminals too easily escaped, formed bandit gangs, and terrorized the colonies. RGASPI, f. 558, op. 11, d. 64, l. 36.

67. GARF, f. 8131, op. 37, d. 70, l. 166, f. 9401, op. 12, d. 137, doc. 149.

68. GARF, f. 5446, op. 15a, d. 1175, l. 12.

69. GARF, f. 5446, op. 15a, d. 1175, l. 12.

70. GARF, f. 5446, op. 15a, d. 1175, ll. 8–9; emphasis in original.

71. GARF, f. 5446, op. 15a, d. 1175, l. 6.

72. GARF, f. 5446, op. 16a, d. 1332, l. 2.

73. GARF, f. 5446, op. 16a, d. 1332, l. 2.

74. GARF, f. 5446, op. 18a, d. 845, ll. 31–32.

75. The previous year, in December 1934, Yagoda had made the same recommendation. No record exists of the discussion surrounding this earlier recommendation, but it was apparently quashed. See GARF, f. 5446, op. 16a, d. 1270, l. 30.

76. GARF, f. 5446, op. 18a, d. 845, l. 32.

77. GARF, f. 5446, op. 18a, d. 845, l. 34.

78. GARF, f. 5446, op. 18a, d. 845, ll. 28–30, f. 8131, op. 71, dd. 118–20.

79. These same arguments were made in 1953, when the then Council of Ministers abolished the system of regime cities and residence restrictions. By that time, somewhere between 2 and 10 million people (2 million alone between 1945 and 1953) had lived under such restrictions since they were put in place in the early 1930s. See the 1956 decree in Andrei Artizov, ed., *Reabilitatsiia: Kak eto bylo: Dokumenty prezidiuma TsK KPSS i drugie materialy, mart 1953–fevral' 1956* (Moscow, 2000), 45–48.

80. GARF, f. 5446, op. 18a, d. 845, l. 28.

81. GARF, f. 5446, op. 18a, d. 845, l. 23.

82. GARF, f. 5446, op. 18a, d. 845, ll. 15–17.

83. For the handwritten editorial changes, see GARF, f. 5446, op. 18a, d. 845, l. 12. For the published draft, see ll. 1–2.

84. RGAE, f. 1562, op. 20, d. 52, l. 18.

85. GARF, f. 9401, op. 12, d. 137, doc. 25; RGAE, f. 1562, op. 329, d. 131, ll. 10–11.

86. GARF, f. 9415, op. 5, d. 463, ll. 36–37, 48, 65.

87. In Russian, see the otherwise excellent article by Popov, "Pasportnaia sistema v SSSR." In English, see especially Marc Garcelon, "Colonizing the Subject: The Genealogy and Legacy of the Soviet Internal Passport," in *Documenting Individual Identity: The Development of State Practices in the Modern World,* ed. Jane Caplan and John Torpey (Princeton, 2001), 83–100; John Torpey, "Revolutions and Freedom of Movement: An Analysis of Passport Controls in the French, Russian, and Chinese Revolutions," *Theory and Society* 26/4 (1997): 837–68. Both Garcelon and Torpey, as well as Popov, describe the passport system more or less as involving a simple dichotomy between rural and urban populations. Both Garcelon and Torpey provide a succinct and valuable description of early Soviet identity regimes during the 1920s—from revolutionary repudiation of tsarist practices to the gradual reimposition of passports under rapid industrialization, collectivization, and the social chaos of the early 1930s. I disagree, however, with Garcelon's description of passportization as "an array of disciplinary practices [that] linked rewards and punishments to degrees of public conformity to standardized ideological discourses" (Garcelon, "Colonizing the Subject," 88). Passportization acted as a mechanism for behavioral disciplining only in part, in the case of restrictions placed on former criminal convicts, for example. The great majority of citizens were given passport privileges or restrictions based not on ideologically prescribed behavior but on ascribed social or ethnic status.

88. Of course, there were significant differences in living and work conditions between collective farm workers and those in militarized occupations. The latter lived at the top of the supply system, with the exception of rank-and-file soldiers, but passport restrictions were nearly identical to those placed on farm workers. In contrast, however, employees in militarized sectors also came under the harsh strictures of military tribunals, rather than the jurisdiction of regular courts. For the illegal practice of passport confiscation, see GARF, f. 9415, op. 3, d. 38, l. 3. For

passport restrictions applied to railroad employees on various lines, see RGASPI, f. 17, op. 163, d. 1061, l. 76; GARF, f. 9401, op. 12, d. 137, doc. 63; GARF, f. 5446, op. 14a, d. 719, ll. 1–2.

89. For urban workers' complaints that the passport system tied them to their place of work and residence as a result of confiscation of their passports by employers, see GANO, f. 47, op. 5, d. 160, ll. 155–59.

90. These laws called for harsh sentences in labor camps for various infractions of labor discipline, including leaving a place of employment without permission. Donald Filtzer, "Labour Discipline and Criminal Law in Soviet Industry, 1945–1953" (paper delivered at the Sixth World Slavic Congress, Tampere, Finland, 2000), 1; Yoram Gorlizki, "Rules, Incentives, and Soviet Campaign Justice after World War II," *Europe-Asia Studies* 51 (1999): 1245–65.

91. See the Politburo protocol from 15 November 1932 in "Izmeneniia pasportnoi sistemy," 104.

92. GARF, f. 5446, op. 14a, d. 740, l. 6.

93. GARF, f. 9401, op. 12, d. 137, l. 78. The first general section of instructions defines the function of police in setting up the passport system. The first and primary function was to set up passport distribution and residence registration. Then, "to conduct a purge (*ochistki*) of regime places of kulak, criminal and other antisocial elements, as well as of persons not connected to production and work." The next point required police "to register (*uchet*), on the basis of passportization, the infiltration of nonregime areas and enterprises of kulaks, criminal and other antisocial elements, and to conduct operational measures in accordance with that *uchet.*"

94. GARF, f. 5446, op. 18a, d. 904, l. 3.

95. GARF, f. 5446, op. 86a, d. 7932, l. 70.

96. On France, see Torpey, "Revolutions and Freedom of Movement."

97. Max Weber, *Economy and Society,* trans. G. Roth and C. Wittich, 2 vols. (Berkeley, 1978) 1:223–25; Foucault, *Discipline and Punish.*

98. Caplan and Torpey, *Documenting Individual Identity,* 5; Charles Steinwedel, "Making Social Groups, One Person at a Time: The Identification of Individuals by Estate, Religious Confession, and Ethnicity in Late Imperial Russia," ibid., 68.

99. Steinwedel, "Making Social Groups," 77–81.

100. Which is why cannonballs traveled in an arc and fell to earth while, in the accepted wisdom, celestial bodies traversed perfect eternal circles. J. L. E. Dryer, *A History of Astronomy from Thales to Kepler* (New York, 1953), 414–15.

101. On the increasing complexity of the passport system, see especially Moine, "Le Système des passeports."

102. Kessler, "The Passport System," 479–81; Moine, "Le Système des passeports," 144.

CHAPTER 9. "ONCE AND FOR ALL TIME"

1. First published in abbreviated form in *Izvestiia TsK KPSS,* 1989, no. 10, 81–82; *Trud,* 4 June 1992, 4. For the full text of the order, see Iu. M. Zolotov, ed., *Kniga pamiati zhertv politicheskikh repressii* (Ulianovsk, 1996), 766–80. For a

more recent and partial publication, see N. Vert and S. V. Mironenko, eds., *Istoriia stalinskogo gulaga, Konets 1920-kh–pervaia polovina 1950-kh godov: Sobranie dokumentov v 7-mi tomakh,* vol. 1: *Massovye repressii v SSSR* (Moscow, 2004), 267–75.

2. It is difficult to ascertain to what extent urban stabilization was also the result of deliberate policies, begun with the second Five Year Plan, to increase investment in trade and consumer goods, and to allow trade mechanisms to operate again. Yagoda, at least, believed that much of the social stability was due to police activities.

3. O. V. Khlevniuk, *Politbiuro: Mekhanizmy politicheskoi vlasti v 1930-e gody* (Moscow, 1996), 141.

4. See pp. 153–56.

5. For full text and comments, see O. V. Khlevniuk et al., *Stalin i Kaganovich: Perepiska, 1931–1936* (Moscow, 2001), 682–83. See also A. I. Kokurin and N. V. Petrov, *Lubianka: Organy VChK-OGPU-NKVD-MGB-MVD-KGB, 1917–1991. Spravochnik* (Moscow, 2003), 824 n. 176.

6. RGASPI, f. 17, op. 2, d. 597, ll. 8–10, 12–14.

7. GARF, f. 5446, op. 20a, d. 479, l. 36.

8. Orders against German citizens (25 July 1937); against Poles (11 August 1937); against former workers on the Manchurian railroad (20 September 1937); against Latvians (30 November). Vert and Mironenko, *Istoriia stalinskogo gulaga,* 1:267–85.

9. Ibid., 269.

10. See the tables of those arrested in Mark Iunge and Rol'f Binner, *Kak terror stal "bol'shim": Sekretnyi prikaz No. 00447 i tekhnologiia ego ispolneniia* (Moscow, 2003), 122–36.

11. R. W. Davies, "The Soviet Economy and the Launching of the Great Terror," in *Stalin's Terror Revisited,* ed. Melanie Ilic (New York, 2006), 11–37.

12. For the clearest and most recent statement of this view, see J. Arch Getty, "'Excesses Are Not Permitted': Mass Terror and Stalinist Governance in the Late 1930s," *Russian Review* 61 (January 2002): 115.

13. O. V. Khlevniuk, A. V. Kvashonkin, et al., *Stalinskoe politbiuro v 30-e gody: Sbornik dokumentov* (Moscow, 1995), 16.

14. Barry McLoughlin, "Mass Operations of the NKVD, 1937–8: A Survey," in *Stalin's Terror: High Politics and Mass Repression in the Soviet Union,* ed. Barry McLoughlin and Kevin McDermott (London, 2003), 142. J. Arch Getty and Iu. N. Zhukov, especially, stress the context of Supreme Soviet elections and constitutional changes. Getty, "'Excesses Are Not Permitted'," and J. A. Getty and O. V. Naumov, *The Road to Terror: Stalin and the Self-Destruction of the Bolsheviks, 1932–1939* (New Haven, 1999); Iu. N. Zhukov, "Repressii i konstitutsiia SSSR 1936 g," *Voprosy istorii* 1 (2002): 3–26. For the most comprehensive overview of domestic policy considerations, see McLoughlin, "Mass Operations: A Survey," and Iunge and Binner, *Kak terror stal "bol'shim,"* esp. sec. 5, "Bol'shoi terror s tochki zreniia prikaza No. 00447," 205–59. Although both Getty and Iunge and Binner stress the domestic context, Getty stresses the irrationality of the great purges, while Iunge and Binner stress the "social engineering" rationality of the great purges. Getty,

"'Excesses Are Not Permitted'," 116, 135–36; Iunge and Binner, *Kak terror stal "bol'shim,"* 242–43.

15. Iunge and Binner, *Kak terror stal "bol'shim,"* 242–43. Iunge and Binner distinguish their broad contextual argument about social engineering from the interpretation put forward by Getty and Zhukov about the specific importance of the Soviet elections. As Iunge and Binner point out, fear of voting results, alone or even predominantly, cannot explain the mass purges. Elections in December 1937 did not change or threaten any existing power relations, and yet the purges continued and intensified throughout 1938. Iunge and Binner, *Kak terror stal "bol'shim,"* 212–13; Getty, "'Excesses Are Not Permitted'," 125–26; Zhukov, "Repressii," 113.

16. On the nationality purges, see Terry Martin, *An Affirmative Action Empire: Nations and Nationalism in the Soviet Union, 1923–1939* (Ithaca, 2001), 338. For the overall figure of 2.5 million, see Getty and Naumov, *The Road to Terror,* 590. V. N. Zemskov gives one of the highest authoritative numbers of overall arrests during the 1937–1938 purges, 3,141,444. In *Naselenie Rossii v XX veke: Istoricheskie ocherki.* vol. 1: *1900–1939,* ed. V. B. Zhiromskaia (Moscow, 2000), 318.

17. E. A. Rees, "The Great Purges and the XVIII Party Congress of 1939," in *Centre-Local Relations in the Stalinist State, 1928–1941,* ed. E. A. Rees (London, 2002), 191–94.

18. GANO, f. 4, op. 34, d. 26, l. 2. V. Danilov, R. Manning, and L. Viola, eds., *Tragediia sovetskoi derevni: Kollektivizatsiia i raskulachivanie. Dokumenty i materialy v 5 tomakh, 1927–1939,* vol.5: *1937–1939,* book 1: *1937* (Moscow, 2004), 256–58.

19. Oleg Khlevniuk, "Prichiny 'Bol'shogo Terrora': Vneshnepoliticheskii aspekt" (unpublished manuscript) and "The Reasons for the 'Great Terror': The Foreign-Political Aspect" in *Russia in the Age of Wars, 1914–1945,* ed. S. Pons and A. Romano (Milan, 2000), 159–69. For detailed discussion of the nationality purges in the context of the foreign affairs argument, see Terry Martin, "Modernization or Neo-Traditionalism: Ascribed Nationality and Soviet Primordialism," in *Stalinism: New Directions,* ed. Sheila Fitzpatrick (London, 2000), 348–67; and "The Origins of Soviet Ethnic Cleansing," *Journal of Modern History* 70 (1998): 813–61. For other statements of the foreign policy context, see Hiroaki Kuromiya, "Accounting for the 'Great Terror,'" in *Jahrbücher für Geschichte Osteuropas* 53/1 (January 2005): 86–101; David R. Shearer, "Social Disorder, Mass Repression, and the NKVD during the 1930s." *Cahiers du Monde russe* 42/2–4 (April–December 2001): 505–34; and Marc Jansen and Nikita Petrov, *Stalin's Loyal Executioner: People's Commissar Nikolai Yezhov, 1895–1940* (Stanford, 2002), 79.

20. That Stalin and Soviet leaders considered the threat of war real and imminent is evidenced by reports from the foreign branch of the GUGB in February 1937 about discussions between American, British, and French leaders. These discussions focused on the implications of the Spanish civil war broadening into a general European conflagration, which would pit Germany, Italy, and Japan against the Soviet Union. V. N. Khaustov et al., eds., *Lubianka: Stalin i glavnoe upravlenie gosbezopasnosti NKVD, 1937–1938* (Moscow, 2004), 79–82.

21. Iunge and Binner acknowledge that foreign policy considerations may have

played a part in Stalin's decision to engage in mass purging, but they insist that the mass social purge of the late 1930s must be explained in terms of Stalin's grand domestic design of social engineering. McLoughlin makes a similar argument. Iunge and Binner, *Kak terror stal "bol'shim,"* 243–44; and McLoughlin, "Mass Operations: A Survey," 143. While Getty disputes the social engineering argument, he too emphasizes domestic considerations. Getty, "'Excesses Are Not Permitted'," esp. 135–36. Certainly, Stalin may have viewed the mass operations as social engineering on a grand scale, but the domestic origins arguments do not explain why Stalin launched the purges specifically in summer 1937, and not a year or two or three earlier. Such arguments also do not explain, as noted further on in this chapter, why the mass operations differed so in scale and violence from previous policies designed to deal with the same socially marginal groups. Arguments that focus on domestic considerations alone may be persuasive in explaining the origins of the mass purges, but are not as persuasive when considering the mass operations within the whole context of the purges.

22. F. Chuev, *Sto sorok besed s Molotovym* (Moscow, 1991), 390–91, 416; L. M. Kaganovich, *Pamatnye zapiski* (Moscow, 1996), 13–14.

23. Zolotov, *Kniga pamiati*, 766.

24. See one of Eikhe's proposals in GARF, f. 8131, op. 37, d. 58, ll. 170–78. For further discussion, see David R. Shearer, "Modernity and Backwardness on the Soviet Frontier: Western Siberia during the 1930s," in *Provincial Landscapes: Local Dimensions of Soviet Power, 1917–1953,* ed. Donald Raleigh (Pittsburgh, 2001), 194–216.

25. L. P. Kosheleva, O. V. Naumov, and L. A. Rogovaia, eds., "Materialy fevral'sko-martovskogo plenuma TsKVKP(b) 1937 goda," *Voprosy istorii* 6 (1993): 25, 27. Cited also in Khlevniuk, "Prichiny 'Bol'shogo Terrora,'" 80.

26. GARF, f. 9479, op. 1, d. 29, l. 12.

27. See the "special communication" from the UNKVD of the Tatar republic from January 1937 in Danilov et al., *Tragediia,* 5/1:83. On the special place of peasants and kulaks in purge considerations, see ibid., esp. 7–50; Sheila Fitzpatrick, *Stalin's Peasants: Resistance and Survival in the Russian Village after Collectivization* (Oxford, 1994), 238–54; Gabor Rittersporn, "'Vrednye elementy,' 'opasnye men'shinstva' i bol'shevistskie trevogi: Massovye operatsii 1937–1938 gg. i etnicheskii vopros v SSSR." in *V sem'e edinoi: Natsional'naia politika partii bol'shevikov i ee osushchestvlenie na Severo-Zapade Rossii v 1920–1950-e gody: Sbornik statei,* ed. T. Vikhovainen and I. Takala (Petrozavodsk, 1992), 99–122.

28. GARF, f. 5446, op. 20a, d. 931, l. 2.

29. GARF, f. 8131, op. 37, d. 83, ll. 67–70.

30. GARF, f. 9474, op. 1, d. 87, l. 38.

31. GANO, f. 923, op. 1, d. 1347, ll. 1–2. See also Danilov et al., *Tragediia,* 5/1:16.

32. The poet Nadezhda Mandel'shtam was but one famous example, exiled to a semirural area of Kazakhstan, where she lived out the 1930s after the arrest of her husband.

33. Kosheleva et al., "Materialy," *Voprosy istorii* 3 (1995): 13–14.

34. Danilov et al., *Tragediia,* 5/1:18.

35. 1936 materials show that from *kolkhozy* throughout the USSR 196,728 households were excluded, and 463,446 households left voluntarily. At the same time, 1,019,433 households joined *kolkhozy*. As of July 1937, 226,398 households joined *kolkhozy*; 129,236 left voluntarily and 39,369 were excluded. RGASPI, f. 17, op. 120, d. 334, l. 21.

36. GARF, f. 3316, op. 64, d. 1885, ll. 1–10b; Danilov et al., *Tragediia,* 5/1:230–31.

37. Danilov et al., *Tragediia,* 5/1:79.

38. GANO, f. 3, op. 2, d. 810, ll. 15–28, here 15 and 28 respectively.

39. GANO, f. 3, op. 2, d. 810, ll. 3–5 on fears by farm chairmen of their own farmers; GANO, f. 3, op. 1, d. 591, l. 148 on a rash of bandit shootings of local Soviet officials;

40. GANO, f. 3, op. 2, d. 726, l. 45.

41. GANO, f. 47, op. 1, d. 233, l. 150b.

42. GANO, f. 47, op. 1, d. 233, ll. 18, 139–40.

43. Danilov et al., *Tragediia,* 5/1:17–20.

44. Kosheleva et al., "Materialy," *Voprosy istorii* 6 (1993): 5, 8.

45. Kosheleva et al., "Materialy," *Voprosy istorii* 5 (1993): 4–5 (Zhdanov) and 14 (Iaroslavskii); Kosheleva et al., "Materialy," ibid., 6 (1993): 8 (Kosior).

46. Iunge and Binner, *Kak terror stal "bol'shim,"* 197 n. 95.

47. B. B. Zhiromskaia, *Demograficheskaia istoria Rossii, 1930-ie gody: Vzgliad v neizvestnoe* (Moscow, 2001), 193–94.

48. Stalin interrupted Yevdokimov to declare his agreement with this assessment. Kosheleva et al., "Materialy," *Voprosy istorii* 7 (1993): 10. Local officials, especially NKVD officials, reported often on rumors that Soviet power would soon fall, either through revolt or invasion, and the *kolkhoz* system would be abolished. Some rumors took the form that peasants needed to withdraw from farms before invasion, since collective farmers would be treated harshly under a new anti-Soviet government. See, for example, GANO, f. 3, op. 2, d. 643, l. 95. Iunge and Binner believe that the tension between religious believers and local authorities was exaggerated by both contemporaries and by later historians. *Kak terror stal "bol'shim,"* 170.

49. GARF, f. 5446, op. 22a, d. 69, l. 46. See also above, pp. 267–68. In fact, Yezhov's "assistance" amounted to a recommendation that trade unions take on the function and cost of finding work for willing ex-convicts. As noted in the previous chapter, trade union leaders balked at such a proposal. On Yezhov's letter and its implications, see also Jansen and Petrov, *Stalin's Loyal Executioner,* 81–82; Paul Hagenloh, "'Socially Harmful Elements' and the Great Terror," in Fitzpatrick, *Stalinism: New Directions,* 300; Gabor Rittersporn, "'Vrednye elementy,' 'opasnye men'shinstva,' i bol'shevistskie trevogi," 103. I am grateful to Paul Hagenloh for directing me to this document.

50. Mikhail Shreider, *NKVD iznutri: Zapiski chekista* (Moscow, 1995), 41, 46.

51. I. V. Pavlova, "Robert Eikhe," *Voprosy istorii* 1 (2001): 82.

52. GARF, f. 5446, op. 22a, d. 69, ll. 18–19.

53. V. A. Ivanov, "Operatsiia NKVD SSSR po prikazu No. 00447 protiv ugolovnikov v Leningradskoi oblasti," 8 (paper delivered at the conference "Stalin-

izm v Sovietskoi provintsii, 1937–1938: Massovaia operatsiia na osnove prikaza No. 00447," Moscow, 12–15 October 2006).

54. GARF, f. 5446, op. 22a, d. 69, l. 44.

55. GARF, f. 5446, op. 22a, d. 69, ll. 21–22.

56. GARF, f. 5446, op. 22a, d. 69, l. 31.

57. Khlevniuk, "Prichiny 'Bol'shogo Terrora,'" 70.

58. GARF, f. 8131, op. 38, d. 16, l. 13, f. 8131, op. 38, d. 19, l. 19.

59. RGASPI, f. 17, op. 2, d. 733, ll. 110, 115. Those excluded for corruption made up the second largest category, 65,030 individuals or 20.6 percent. The number of those excluded for being identified as supposed Trotskyists-Zinovievists amounted to 17,486 individuals or 5.5 percent. The number who were brought into the Party by bypassing Party procedures and who had been excluded for this reason was 20,985, or 6.7 percent.

60. Kosheleva et al., "Materialy," *Voprosy istorii* 6 (1993): 21–22. Also cited in Khlevniuk, "Prichiny 'Bol'shogo Terrora,'" 79.

61. Kosheleva et al., "Materialy," *Voprosy istorii* 6 (1993): 5–6.

62. Andrea Graziosi estimates that in the early 1930s, approximately 2–3 percent of the industrial work force were foreign workers. *A New Peculiar State: Explorations in Soviet History 1917–1937* (New York, 2000), 227.

63. GARF, f. 9401, op. 12, d. 138, doc. 18.

64. L. P. Rasskazov, *Karatel'nye organy v protsesse formirovaniia i funktsionirovaniia administrativno komandnoi sistemy v Sovetskom gosudarstve, 1917–1941 gg.* (Ufa, 1994), 316.

65. GARF, f. 9401, op. 12, d. 135, doc. 139.

66. Tsentral'nyi arkhiv obshchesvtennykh dvizhenii Moskvy, (TsAODM), f. 25, op. 1, d. 27, l. 3, "TsK VKP(b), TsK Plenumy goroda Moskvy," 24.9.1934 and TsAODM, f. 28, op. 3, d. 28, l. 3 from 12 December, 1935.

67. Martin, "Origins of Soviet Ethnic Cleansing"; idem, *An Affirmative Action Empire,* esp. 335–45.

68. Vert and Mironenko, *Istoriia stalinskogo gulaga,* 1:281–83; A. Ia. Razumov, ed., *Leningradskii martirolog,* vol. 3: *Noiabr' 1937 goda* (St. Petersburg, 1998), 583–85.

CHAPTER 10. THE MECHANICS OF MASS PURGING

1. For a detailed account of arrests, see Marc Jansen and Nikita Petrov, *Stalin's Loyal Executioner: People's Commissar Nikolai Yezhov, 1895–1940* (Stanford, 2002),

2. See especially discussion and resolutions in V. Danilov, R. Manning, and L. Viola, eds., *Tragediia sovetskoi derevni: Kollektivizatsiia i raskulachivanie. Dokumenty i materialy v 5 tomakh, 1927–1939,* vol. 5: *1937–1939,* book 1: *1937* (Moscow, 2004), 26, 162–68.

3. In late May, several high-ranking military officers were arrested, including Marshal Mikhail Tukhachevskii. He and several other officers were tried secretly and executed in June. In mid-April, A. I. Yakovlev, one of Stalin's close advisors and head of the Agricultural Department of the Central Committee, instructed the

NKVD to begin arrests of officials in the land and agricultural commissariats. Danilov et al., *Tragediia*, 5/1:29–30.

4. Ibid., 319.

5. Ibid.

6. J. Arch Getty, " 'Excesses Are Not Permitted': Mass Terror and Stalinist Governance in the Late 1930s," *Russian Review* 61 (January 2002): 126.

7. This is the argument put forward by V. P. Danilov in *Tragediia*, 5/1:28.

8. Mikhail Shreider, *NKVD iznutri: Zapiski chekista* (Moscow, 1995), 41–42.

9. N. V. Petrov and K V. Skorkin, *Kto rukovodil NKVD, 1934–1941: Spravochnik* (Moscow, 1999), 374.

10. Jansen and Petrov, *Stalin's Loyal Executioner*, 82–86; Danilov et al., *Tragediia*, 5/1:33, 602–3.

11. Ibid., 603.

12. Ibid., 33.

13. RGASPI, f. 17, op. 163, d. 1156, ll. 21–23. See the list of people removed in Danilov et al., *Tragediia*, 5/1:34.

14. Getty, " 'Excesses Are Not Permitted'," 127–28; Danilov et al., *Tragediia*, 5/1:35.

15. Getty argues that the reduction reflected Stalin's attempt to curb the push from local leaders for purging. " 'Excesses Are Not Permitted'," 128.

16. A. G. Tepliakov, "Personal i povsednevnost' Novosibirskogo UNKVD v 1936–1946." *Minuvshee: Istoricheskii al'manakh* 21 (1997): 241.

17. Thus, from the beginning, civil police were deeply implicated in the purges. V. A. Ivanov notes the active role of civil police in Leningrad in "Operatsiia NKVD SSSR po prikazu No. 00447 protiv ugolovnikov v Leningradskoi oblasti" (paper delivered to the conference "Stalinizm v sovetskoi provintsii, 1937–1938: Massovaia operatsiia na osnove prikaza No. 00447, Moscow, 12–15 October 2006).

18. GARF, f. 8131, op. 37, d. 83, ll. 43–44.

19. Petrov and Skorkin, *Kto rukovodil NKVD*, 37–38.

20. Tepliakov, "Personal i povsednevnost'," 248, 256. See also Yezhov's March 1937 speech to a group of Komsomol activists recently mobilized into the NKVD in A. I. Kokurin and N. V. Petrov, *Lubianka: Organy VChK-OGPU-NKVD-MGB-MVD-KGB, 1917–1991. Spravochnik* (Moscow, 2003), 569–82.

21. Danilov et al., *Tragediia*, 5/1:28.

22. RGANI, f. 89, op. 73, d. 10, ll. 35–36.

23. N. Vert and S. V. Mironenko, eds., *Istoriia stalinskogo gulaga, Konets 1920-kh–pervaia polovina 1950-kh godov: Sobranie dokumentov v 7-mi tomakh*, vol. 1: *Massovye repressii v SSSR* (Moscow, 2004), 311.

24. GARF, f. 8131, op. 37, d. 83, l. 70.

25. GARF, f. 8131, op. 37, d. 83, l. 71.

26. Yegorov gave his deposition in 1938, after his arrest during Beria's post-Yezhov purge of the NKVD. See letter in GARF, f. 8131, op. 32, d. 6329, ll. 12–16. Also published in Uimanov, *Repressii: Kak eto bylo. Zapadnaia Sibir' v kontse 20-kh-nachale 50-kh godov* (Tomsk, 1995), 95; Vert and Mironenko, *Istoriia stalinskogo gulaga*, 1:313–25.

27. GUGB reports about the Tomsk and other rail lines are contained in the se-

cret section (*sekretnaia chast'*) of the Western Siberian district Party Committee archive group, GANO, f. 4, op. 34, d. 8 and f. 4, op. 34, d. 12, from spring and summer 1937. For regional-level reports, see GANO, f. 4, op. 34, d. 22.

28. January comments, GANO, f. 3, op. 2, d. 810, ll. 15–27; June comments, GANO, f. 47, op. 1, d. 233, ll. 16–17.

29. See the reference to Eikhe's speech in Iu. N. Zhukov, "Repressii i konstitutsiia SSSR 1936 g," *Voprosy istorii* 1 (2002): 23–24.

30. Danilov et al., *Tragediia*, 5/1:306.

31. This is the main argument put forward by J. Arch Getty in "'Excesses Are Not Permitted'."

32. RGANI, f. 89, op. 73, d. 48, l. 31.

33. Politburo resolution reproduced in Mark Iunge and Rol'f Binner, *Kak terror stal "bol'shim": Sekretnyi prikaz No. 00447 i tekhnologiia ego ispolneniia* (Moscow, 2003), 78–79.

34. On Eikhe, see I. V. Pavlova, "Robert Eikhe," *Voprosy istorii* 1 (2001): 70–88.

35. RGASPI, f. 558, op. 11, d. 64, l. 88.

36. This is what NKVD officials did in Western Siberia, according to the head of the Secret Political Department, K. K. Pastanogov. A. G. Tepliakov, "Organy NKVD Zapadnoi Sibiri v 'kulatskoi operatsii' 1937–1938 gg" (paper delivered at the conference "Stalinizm v sovetskoi provintsii, 1937–1938: Massovaia operatsiia na osnove prikaza No. 00447," Moscow, 12–15 October 2006), p. 4.

37. GANO, f. 4, op. 34, d. 4, ll. 51–64.

38. Mironov's speech is published, in part, in Iunge and Binner, *Kak terror stal "bol'shim,"* 81–83. See also Uimanov, *Repressii,* 129.

39. Police passport troikas operated from 1935 on, but were allowed only to pass sentences of confinement up to five years.

40. See the instructions by Mironov to NKVD operatives from July 1937 in Iunge and Binner, *Kak terror stal "bol'shim,"* 82.

41. Vert and Mironenko, *Istoriia stalinskogo gulaga,* 1;274.

42. Iunge and Binner, *Kak terror stal "bol'shim,"* 81, 83.

43. Reprinted ibid., 98–99.

44. GARF, f. 8131, op. 15, d. 3, l. 107.

45. S. A. Papkov, *Staliniskii terror v Sibiri, 1928–1941* (Novosibirsk, 1997), 211. For regret about "procedural" mistakes, see the deposition of police captain Rudin in GARF, f. 8131, op. 37, d. 131, l. 38. For depositions of NKVD officers arrested in 1939, see GARF, f. 10035, op. 1, d. 55763.

46. Iunge and Binner, *Kak terror stal "bol'shim,"* 82.

47. Danilov et al., *Tragediia,* 5/1:603.

48. GARF, f. 8131, op. 38, d. 19, l. 16.

49. GARF, f. 8131, op. 37, d. 83, ll. 70–71.

50. Quoted in Iunge and Binner, *Kak terror stal "bol'shim,"* 98. What "extraordinary" meant in this context was not clarified, although at least one example will be discussed below.

51. Ibid., 26.

52. Calculated from charts, GANO, f. 4, op. 4, d. 26, ll. 4, 14.

53. GANO, f. 4, op. 34, d. 26, ll. 10–14. The target figures were most likely taken from estimates provided by local NKVD offices.

54. For a discussion of peasant resistance to collectivization in Siberia, see James Hughes, *Stalinism in a Russian Province: Collectivization and Dekulakization in Siberia* (Basingstoke, 1996).

55. GANO, f. 4, op. 34, d. 4, ll. 51–64.

56. GANO, f. 4, op. 34, d. 4, l. 51. *Dal'nevostochniki* may well have been Asian migrants.

57. Andrei Artizov, ed., *Reabilitatsiia: Kak eto bylo: Dokumenty prezidiuma TsK KPSS i drugie materialy, mart 1953–fevral' 1956* (Moscow, 2000), 320.

58. Iunge and Binner, *Kak terror stal "bol'shim,"* 38. Shreider, *NKVD iznutri,* 46. Shreider claimed that, at least at the beginning of his term in Ivanovo, he was able to resist this pressure.

59. Iunge and Binner, *Kak terror stal "bol'shim,"* 128, 130 n. 121. See also A. A. Petrushin, *"My ne znaem poshchady": Izvestnye, maloizvestnye i neizvestnye sobytiia iz istorii tiumenskogo kraia po materialam VChK-GPU-NKVD-KGB* (Tiumen', 1999), 137.

60. Iunge and Binner, *Kak terror stal "bol'shim,"* 42–43.

61. See the table ibid., 136.

62. On increases in limits, see ibid., 43–44, and O. Hlevnjuk, "Les mécanismes de la 'Grande Terreur' des années 1937–1938 au Turkménistan," *Cahiers du Monde russe,* 39/1–2 (1998): 204. On borrowing limits, see GANO, f. 4, op. 34, d. 26, l. 7.

63. Artizov, *Reabilitatsiia,* 319–20.

64. Vatlin, *Terror raionnogo masshtaba,* 17.

65. Shreider, *NKVD iznutri,* 54.

66. Vatlin, *Terror raionnogo masshtaba: Massovye operatsii NKVD v Kuntsevskom raione Moskovskoi oblasti 1937–1938 gg.* (Moscow, 2004), 19–25, 94–98.

67. Shreider, *NKVD iznutri,* 53, 55.

68. Ibid., 84–85. In Western Siberia, Ignatii Barkov became a victim of the kind of provocation that Shreider feared for himself. Barkov was arrested by the UNKVD in February 1938. In a memorandum, the head of the Novosibirsk UNKVD then wrote that a search of the procurator's office produced many files of "compromising, provocational" materials on NKVD officers. Clearly, the UNKVD understood that Barkov was collecting damning information and biding his time until circumstances permitted him to take action against the political police. Unfortunately for Barkov, the police got to him before he could get to them. Knowing full well what awaited him, Barkov committed suicide shortly after his arrest by throwing himself out a fifth-floor window of the NKVD building in Novosibirsk. He was being led from an interrogation room. GANO, f. 4, op. 34, d. 48, l. 26.

69. In November, the Western Siberian district was divided into several smaller administrative units. The core of the old territory became the Novosibirsk oblast.

70. Iunge and Binner, *Kak terror stal "bol'shim,"* 40.

71. Ibid., 40, 130.

72. Ibid., Chart, 126.

73. Shreider, *NKVD iznutri*, 91.

74. For more on Gorbach, see the table of arrest quotas in Iunge and Binner, *Kak terror stal "bol'shim,"* 122–36; and Barry McLoughlin, "Mass Operations of the NKVD: A Survey," in *Stalin's Terror: High Politics and Mass Repression in the Soviet Union,* ed. Barry McLoughlin and Kevin McDermott (London, 2003), 128–29.

75. Recounted in Iunge and Binner, *Kak terror stal "bol'shim,"* 41–42; and in Roberta Manning, "Politicheskii terror kak politicheskii teatr: Raionnye pokazatel'nye sudy, 1937," in Danilov et al., *Tragediia,* 5/1:70 n. 136.

76. According to the 1956 Shvernik commission, Artizov, *Reabilitatsiia,* 322. Interestingly, the Korean deportations were not considered part of the mass repression orders, since the Koreans, though forced to migrate, were not arrested or branded as openly anti-Soviet. Unlike criminal and anti-Soviet deportees, the Koreans were compensated, at least nominally, by the government for their move. Thus, while the regime's leaders regarded this group as potentially dangerous, they did not formally criminalize the Korean deportees. This group remained in a limbo status—much like the deported Japanese-Americans during World War II—until the mid-1950s.

77. Vert and Mironenko, *Istoriia stalinskogo gulaga,* 1:74. For the nationality orders, see ibid., 275–85. In addition to the nationality and anti-Soviet operations, Stalin also ordered the arrest of wives and children of citizens arrested under anti-treason laws. See ibid., 287. For detailed descriptions of the nationality operations, see I. L. Shcherbakova, ed., *Nakazannyi narod: Repressii protiv rossiiskikh nemtsev* (Moscow, 1999); L. S. Ermina, ed., *Repressii protiv poliakov i pol'skikh grazhdan* (Moscow, 1997); K. F. Liubimova, ed., *Butovskii poligon, 1937–1938: Kniga pamiati zhertv politicheskikh repressii,* 5 vols., (Moscow, 1999–2001).

78. Yegorov noted that this instruction came from the NKVD center in Novosibirsk, so it is unclear whether this represented a widespread phenomenon. Vert and Mironenko, *Istoriia stalinskogo gulaga,* 1:314–15.

79. Ibid., 314.

80. Tepliakov, "Personal i povsednevnost'," 258. The reference was to Stalin's article in 1930 that signaled a moderation in policies of forced collectivization. RGASPI, f. 558, op. 11, d. 57, l. 112. The officer, Filipov, and his assistant Berzon were arrested for this "counterrevolutionary" discussion.

81. Vert and Mironenko, *Istoriia stalinskogo gulaga,* 1:318–19.

82. Ibid., 315.

83. This according to Yegorov, ibid.

84. Tepliakov, "Personal i povsednevnost'," 258.

85. See descriptions in Vatlin, *Terror raionnogo masshtaba,* 29; and Liubimova, *Butovskii Poligon,* 3:27–28.

86. GARF, f. 8131, op. 37, d. 145, ll. 56–58.

87. Vert and Mironenko, *Istoriia stalinskogo gulaga,* 1:315.

88. On use of nonoperatives, even non-NKVD people in interrogations and mass operations, see Tepliakov, "Personal i povsednevnost'," 256; Vatlin, *Terror raionnogo masshtaba,* chap. 1; Yegorov, in Vert and Mironenko, *Istoriia stalinskogo gulaga,* 1:316.

89. GARF, f. 8131, op. 37, d. 69, ll. 8–10. For other examples of mass falsification, see for example Artizov, *Reabilitatsiia*, 344.

90. Iunge and Binner, *Kak terror stal "bol'shim,"* 39.

91. See examples of shortened arrest and sentencing documents in Liubimova, *Butovskii poligon*, 3:30.

92. Artizov, *Reabilitatsiia*, 344.

93. Yegorov, in Vert and Mironenko, *Istoriia stalinskogo gulaga*, 1:319; Peter H. Solomon Jr., *Soviet Criminal Justice under Stalin* (Cambridge, 1996), 244–47.

94. McLoughlin, "Mass Operations: A Survey," 131–32.

95. Ibid., 148 n. 75.

96. See the photographs and excavation reports on mass graves in the region of Kuntsevo, south of Moscow, in Liubimova, *Butovskii poligon*.

97. Reported in McLoughlin, "Mass Operations: A Survey," 132.

98. Shreider, *NKVD iznutri*, 86; Ivanov, "Operatsiia NKVD SSSR," 6; Tepliakov, "Personal i povsednevnost'," 254–55.

99. Shreider, *NKVD iznutri*, 86–88.

100. Tepliakov, "Personal i povsednevnost'," 255.

101. Iunge and Binner, *Kak terror stal "bol'shim,"* 42.

102. Shreider, *NKVD iznutri*, 87–88.

103. A. G. Tepliakov, "Organy NKVD," 6.

104. See the arrest photographs in Liubimova, *Butovskii poligon*, 4:7–8. On Leningrad, See Ivanov, "Operatsiia NKVD SSSR," 7.

105. GARF, f. 9401, op. 12, d. 66, ll. 286–88.

106. GARF, f. 9401, op. 12, d. 66, l. 289.

107. See GARF, f. 9401, op. 12, d. 66, ll. 211–67.

108. GARF, f. 9401, op. 12, d. 137, doc. 35.

109. GARF, f. 8131, op. 37, d. 132, l. 9.

110. GARF, f. 8131, op. 37, d. 131, l. 38.

111. GARF, f. 8131, op. 37, d. 131, ll. 36–37.

112. For other readings of the Kozlovskii case, see Cynthia Hooper, "Terror from Within: Participation and Coercion in Soviet Power, 1924–1964" (Ph.D. diss., Princeton University, 2003), 285–89; and Paul Hagenloh, " 'Socially Harmful Elements' and the Great Terror," in *Stalinism: New Directions*, ed. Sheila Fitzpatrick (London, 2000), 301–2.

113. In February and March, NKVD leaders and the Politburo declined several other requests to increase the number of arrests The requests came from the Tatar republic, Kalinin oblast, and Kursk oblast. Iunge and Binner, *Kak terror stal "bol'shim,"* 48.

114. Yezhov was removed as head of the NKVD 25 November 1938. He remained head of the water transport commissariat until April 1939 when he was arrested. Petrov and Skorkin, *Kto rukovodil NKVD*, 185.

115. GARF, f. 9401, op. 12, d. 249, ll. 456–61.

116. On time in service, see personnel charts in GARF, f. 9401, op. 8, d. 58, l. 6 and GARF, f. 9401, op. 8, d. 65, ll. 77–79. See above, pp. 407–8 for a more detailed description of the effects of the purges on police. On police inability to maintain social order and to protect citizenry from crime, see the 1939 report in GARF, f. 9401, op.

12, d. 231, tom 1, doc. 10. The purges not only affected police ranks, but devastated, as well, the informant and agent systems of both the civil and political police. Such was the assessment of K. K. Pastanogov, the head of the Secret Political Department of the West Siberian NKVD in 1939, who commented that the purges were conducted without any agent work, which resulted in the arrest and destruction of many valuable agents and networks. Tepliakov, "Organy NKVD," 4.

117. RGASPI, f. 558, op. 11, d. 65, l. 92.

118. See for example reports in 1939 of an "inpouring" of recidivist and other criminals into industrial centers. GARF, f. 9492, op. 2, d. 7, ll. 1–11. My thanks to Jim Heinzen for this reference. See also GARF, f. 9401, op. 12, d. 231, tom 1, doc. 10. See also descriptions of Leningrad in 1939 and 1940 in Ivanov, "Operatsiia NKVD SSSR," 8–9, and reports in late 1938 from Western Siberia of "sharp" increases in numbers of homeless children and juvenile crime, as well as in numbers of escapees. GANO, f. 4, op. 34, d. 68, ll. 1–8.

CHAPTER 11. OUTSIDE THE MARGINS

1. GARF, f. 8131, op. 37, d. 132. All other archive cites in this chapter are to this *fond, opis'*, and *delo*. I have tried to trace descendants of Korenev, but so far without success.

2. Ll. 6–7.

3. L. 7.

4. For Sofiia's description, l. 7. For the sentence, l. 155.

5. L. 8.

6. Ll. 8–9.

7. L. 37.

8. L. 8.

9. L. 98.

10. Solov'ev likely did not know where Korenev had been sent. According to later depositions, civil police often did not know the fate of those they arrested under Order 00447.

11. L. 9.

12. L. 730b.

13. Ll. 72–720b. See the biographical sketch of Redens in N. V. Petrov and K. V. Skorkin, *Kto rukovodil NKVD, 1934–1941: Spravochnik* (Moscow, 1999), 357–58. It seems unlikely that Korenev actually came face to face with the troika, since most of the 00447 cases were decided simply by list. Korenev's "hearing" may have consisted simply of a sentence being handed him by his jailers. Whatever comments he may have made about Redens were most likely made to a minor police official, and not in a direct confrontation during a troika hearing.

14. L. 72.

15. L. 141–42.

16. Ll. 67, 670b, 68.

17. It is highly likely, given the inventiveness with which Korenev concocted false identities, that he chose the name Tumanov for its association with fog (*tuman*) and, hence, with obscuring or obfuscating identity.

18. Ll. 212–13.

19. L. 232. A later procuracy summary listed the execution as having taken place on 1 June. See l. 213. The NKVD record is most likely the accurate account. During the mass operations, execution sentences were carried out almost immediately.

20. L. 213.

21. L. 143.

22. Ll. 155 and 143, respectively.

23. L. 98.

24. Korenev's letter is dated 20 September 1938. Sofiia received the letter about three weeks later, on 11 November. This she recorded on the copy she submitted to the procuracy office seeking her son's whereabouts.

25. Another coded reference may well have referred to identity documents that Korenev wanted his mother to send. In addition to the list of clothing, shoes, and money, Korenev also requested that his mother send "the things that Nikolai left behind during my last visit." L. 67ob.

26. Ll. 67–68. Korenev, of course, did not yet know of the execution of Ivan Rozhnov in his place.

27. Ll. 145, 147.

28. L. 128.

29. L. 145.

30. L. 146.

31. Ll. 78–79ob.

32. Ll. 147 and 145 respectively.

33. L. 136.

34. Ll. 213–14.

35. L. 155.

36. L. 71.

37. L. 73.

38. L. 72ob.

39. L. 73ob.

40. L. 37.

41. L. 141.

42. Ll. 100 and 99 respectively.

43. L. 74ob.

44. Ll. 74ob, 75.

45. L. 76.

46. Ll. 78–78ob.

47. Ll. 121–25. The date 17 November differs from that of 11 November found in other records. See ll. 145, 147. The earlier date is probably the more accurate. Between the date of his escape and his rearrest on 24 November, Korenev traveled to Vladivostok, engaged in two robberies, then took a train to Khabarovsk. Mishustin was either mistaken or did not wish to admit that a prisoner could be missing for so long unnoticed.

48. Ll. 155–155ob.

49. L. 154.

50. Ll. 148, 151.

51. See the report, ll. 161–62.

52. Ll. 211–14.

53. L. 214.

54. L. 231.

55. L. 231.

56. L. 2320b.

57. L. 244.

58. Searches for husbands to pay alimony showed the futility of these methods. Few men were ever found, even under their own names, and most men simply changed their names officially or took aliases to avoid detection.

59. See Sheila Fitzpatrick, *Tear Off the Masks! Identity and Imposture in Twentieth-Century Russia* (Princeton, 2005).

Chapter 12. The War and Postwar Trends

1. I do not consider here the increasing anti-Semitism of the postwar years. See Arno Lustiger et al., *Stalin and the Jews. The Red Book: The Tragedy of the Jewish Anti-Fascist Committee and the Soviet Jews* (New York, 2003); Joshua Rubenstein and Vladimir P. Naumov, eds., *Stalin's Secret Pogrom: The Postwar Inquisition of the Jewish Anti-Fascist Committee,* trans. Laura Esther Wolfson (New Haven, 2001); Robert Weinberg, *Stalin's Forgotten Zion: Birobidzhan and the Making of a Soviet Jewish Homeland: An Illustrated History, 1928–1996* (Berkeley, 1998); Yehoshua A. Gilboa, *The Black Years of Soviet Jewry, 1939–1953* (Boston, 1971); Amir Weiner, "When Memory Counts: War, Genocide, and Postwar Jewry" in *Landscaping the Human Garden: Twentieth-Century Population Management in a Comparative Framework,* ed. Amir Weiner (Stanford, 2003), 167–88. For a recent autobiographical account, see Mary Leder, *My Life in Stalinist Russia: An American Woman Looks Back* (Bloomington, 2001).

2. Jeffrey Burds, "Agentura: Soviet Informants' Networks & the Ukrainian Underground in Galicia, 1944–48," *East European Politics & Societies* 11/1 (1996): 89–130; idem, "The Early Cold War in Soviet West Ukraine, 1944–1948," *Karl Beck Papers in Russian and East European Studies* no. 1505 (Pittsburgh, 2001); Dzheffri Burds, *Sovetskaia Agentura: Ocherki istorii SSSR v poslevoennye gody, 1944–1948* (Moscow, 2006); Amir Weiner, *Making Sense of War: The Second World War and the Fate of the Bolshevik Revolution* (Princeton, 2001); E. Iu. Zubkova, *Pribaltika i Kreml', 1940–1953* (Moscow, 2008).

3. This kind of repression fit Vyshinskii's model of judicial repression for reasons of social discipline more than Yagoda's model of repression for reasons of state security.

4. GARF, f. 5446, op. 22a, d. 130, ll. 19–20.

5. Calculated from chart in GARF, f. 9401, op. 8, d. 58, l. 6.

6. GARF, f. 9401, op. 8, d. 58, ll. 6, 47.

7. GARF, f. 9401, op. 8, d. 58, ll. 6, 7, 50. On other recruitment patterns, see, for example, Elaine Glovka Spencer, *Police and the Social Order in German Cities:*

The Düsseldorf District, 1848–1914 (DeKalb, 1992). See also Raymond B. Fosdick, *European Police Systems* (1925; Montclair, 1969), 199–237.

8. GARF, f. 9401, op. 8, d. 58, l. 3.

9. A. V. Borisov, A. N. Dugin, and A. Ia. Malygin, *Politsiia i militsiia: Stranitsy istorii* (Moscow, 1995), 220.

10. GARF, f. 5446, op. 29a, d. 3246, l. 10.

11. GARF, f.9415, op. 3, d. 1424, ll. 4–5. Most of those violations, 45 percent, were for living without proper residence registration. Another 31 percent involved people with expired or otherwise invalid passports, while 16.4 percent had no passports at all.

12. GARF, f. 9415, op. 3, d. 1424, ll. 1–2. Ye. Iu. Zubkova, L. P. Kosheleva, et al., *Sovetskaia Zhizn', 1945–1953* (Moscow, 2003), 209. For the 1948–52 figures, see the report by Beria in V. Naumov and Iu. Sigachev, eds., *Lavrentii Beria, 1953: Stenogramma iul'skogo plenuma TsK KPSS i drugie dokumenty* (Moscow, 1999), 44.

13. GARF, f. 9415, op. 3, d. 1424, ll. 1–2.

14. GARF, f. 5446, op. 29a, d. 3246, ll. 49–50.

15. GARF, f. 5446, op. 48a, d. 2468, ll. 47–49.

16. GARF, f. 5446, op. 48a, d. 2469, l. 8.

17. GARF, f. 5446, op. 52, d. 3893, ll. 7–9.

18. This, according to an official police assessment. GARF, f. 9415, op. 5, d. 89, ll. 5–7. See also James Heinzen, "The Art of the Bribe: Corruption and Everyday Practice in the Late Stalinist USSR," *Slavic Review* 66/3 (Fall 2007): 389–412; Zubkova et al., *Sovetskaia zhizn',* 6. Interestingly, though, reviews by high state organs of increasing criminality do not mention bribery or corruption, focusing instead on such crimes as theft of state property and hooliganism. Zubkova et al., *Sovetskaia zhizn',* docs. 52–56; James Heinzen, "A Campaign Spasm: Graft and the Limits of the 'Campaign' against Bribery after the Great Patriotic War," in *Late Stalinist Russia: Society between Reconstruction and Development,* ed. Juliane Fürst (London, 2006), 123–41. Both James Heinzen and Cynthia Hooper note a conspiracy of silence on the part of leaders about corruption by officials, even as everyday bribery and corruption became a way of life and survival for Soviet citizens. James Heinzen, "A Campaign Spasm"; Cynthia Hooper, "A Darker 'Big Deal': Covering Up Party Crimes in the Post-WWII Era," in Fürst, *Late Stalinist Russia,* 142–63.

19. GARF, f. 5446, op. 29a, d. 3246, ll. 9–11.

20. See J. Heinzen, "Informers and the State under Late Stalinism: Informant Networks and Crimes against 'Socialist Property,' 1940–1953," *Kritika: Explorations in Russian History* 8/4 (Autumn 2007): 789–816.

21. GARF, f. 5446, op. 51a, d. 5020, l. 26.

22. Nearly 434,000 people reported lost passports in 1947, while another 145,232 reported passports stolen. GARF, f. 9415, op. 3, d. 1424, l. 11.

23. GARF, f. 5446, op. 51a, d. 5020, l. 26.

24. In 1941, Beria remained head of the NKVD, while V. N. Merkulov was appointed head of the new NKGB. At the same time, Beria was designated a vice chair of Sovnarkom, with supervisory control over both agencies. On the various orga-

nization changes, see A. I. Kokurin and N. V. Petrov, eds., *Lubianka: VchK-OGPU-NKVD-NKGB-MGB-MVD-KGB, 1917–1991. Spravochnik* (Moscow 1997).

25. GARF, f. 9415, op. 5, d. 89, l. 70b. See also Paul Hagenloh, "Policing Speculation after the Great Terror" (paper delivered to the Southern Conference of Slavic Studies, March 2004).

26. GARF, f. 9415, op. 5, d. 89, l. 9. See also Heinzen, "Informers and the State," 801–2.

27. GARF, f. 9415, op. 5, d. 98, l. 7.

28. GARF, f. 9415, op. 5, d. 98, ll. 7–8. This same report noted a related increase in numbers of conspiratorial apartments: by 391 in 1946 and by 660 in 1947, so that by 1948 OBKhSS operated 2,431 such apartments used for meetings with agents and residents.

29. See above, p. 150.

30. GARF, f. 9415, op. 5, d. 98, ll. 9, 13. Heinzen notes 34.2 percent in 1948. "Informers and the State," 804.

31. GARF, f. 9415, op. 5, d. 98, ll. 9–10. See also Heinzen, "Informers and the State," 803–4.

32. See above, p. 216.

33. V. N. Zemskov, "Spetsposelentsy (1930–1959)," in *Naselenie Rossii v 1920–1950-e gody: Chislennost', poteri, migratsii. Sbornik nauchnykh trudov,* ed. Iu. A. Poliakov (Moscow, 1994), 157–58, 165, 168.

34. Zemskov, "Spetsposelentsy," 162.

35. Ibid., 168. A significant number of deportee contingents were made up of repatriated soldiers, and especially Soviet soldiers and citizens who had fought in the Vlasov army against Soviet power. The latter included 148,078 deported en masse from NKVD holding camps in 1946 and 1947. Ibid., 161.

36. For a discussion of the decree, see above, pp. 367–68.

37. GARF, f. 9492, op. 6s, d. 14, ll. 14–15.

38. N. Vert and S. V. Mironenko, eds., *Istorii stalinskogo Gulaga: Konets 1920-kh—pervaia polovina 1950-kh godov. Sobranie dokumentov v 7-mi tomakh,* vol. 1: *Massovye repressii v SSSR* (Moscow, 2004), 546.

39. See Beria's description in a May 1933 report in V. Naumov and Iu. Sigachev, eds., *Lavrentii Beria, 1953: Stenogramma iul'skogo plenuma TsK KPSS i drugie dokumenty* (Moscow, 1999), 43.

40. See descriptions of postwar life, for example, in V. V. Denisov, A. V. Kvashonkin, et al., *TsK VKP(b) i regional'nye partiinye komitety 1945–1953* (Moscow, 2004), 330–33; and in Zubkova et al., *Sovetskaia Zhizn',* 168–72; 189–212, 268, 308–29, 344–53. See especially E. Iu. Zubkova, *Poslevoennoe sovetskoe obshchestvo: Politika i povsednevnost', 1945–1953* (Moscow, 2000), parts 1 and 2.

41. In rural areas, labor discipline laws were also adjudicated by local village and farm councils. According to the historian V. N. Zemskov, between 1948 and 1953, some 33,266 people were sentenced to exile for up to eight years in this manner. Zemskov, "Spetsposelentsy," 157.

42. See for example GARF, f. 9401, op. 2, d. 139.

43. See the categorization in GARF, f. 9401, op. 2, d. 199. For the 1930s, see above, pp. 27–29.

44. On the renewed sense of legitimacy, see Weiner, *Making Sense of War,* and Denisov, Kvashonkin, et al., *TsK VKP(b) i regional'nye partiinye komitety,* 8. According to several prominent scholars, that sense of legitimacy did not extend to the entire population, many of whom experienced a mixture of resignation and anger over the regime's harshly extractive priorities of reconstruction. See Donald Filtzer, *Soviet Workers and Late Stalinism: Labour and the Restoration of the Stalinist System after World War II* (Cambridge, 2002); Zubkova, *Poslevoennoe sovetskoe obshchestvo.*

45. Judicial statistics for the post-1938 years provide a more accurate index of official attitudes than statistics from the 1930s. Judicial conviction statistics from the 1930s did not reflect the various and significant forms of nonjudicial repression. These latter statistics reflected only the very tip of the iceberg, as it were.

46. See the lists in GARF, f. 9415, op. 5, d. 99, ll. 2–4.

47. *Ugolovnyi kodeks RSFSR* (Moscow, 1950), 142–43. In 1947, there were 800,000 convictions under the law; between 1947 and 1953, there were close to 2,400,000. Vert and Mironenko, *Istoriia stalinskogo gulaga,* 1:612–13.

48. See above, pp. 270–71.

49. GARF, f. 5446, op. 50a, d. 3896, ll. 1–8.

50. Zemskov, "Spetsposelentsy," 46, 152. These releases were specifically not applied to deportees of certain nationalities, such as Germans, Chechens, Kalmyks, and others.

51. On the 1941 order, see RGANI, f. 89, op. 18, d. 3, no. 89. On postwar deportations of kulaks and criminal, bandit, and dangerous elements, see Vert and Mironenko, *Istoriia stalinskogo gulaga,* 1:83–84.

52. Naumov and Sigachev, *Lavrentii Beria,* 46–49.

53. See descriptions of security and police operations against these groups in GARF, f. 9478, op. 1, dd. 865 and 764. See also Zubkova, *Pribaltika i Kreml',* esp. 191–257; Burds, "Agentura," "The Early Cold War," and *Sovetskaia Agentura;* Weiner, *Making Sense of War.*

54. On jurisdictions, see GARF, f. 9415, op. 3, d. 1424.

55. GARF, f. 5446, op. 48a, d. 2468, ll. 14–21. Originally, the request to passportize the whole population came from the Latvian MVD as a request to the republic Sovmin. GARF, f. 9415, op. 3, d. 1421, l. 1.

56. GARF, f. 5446, op. 48a, d. 2468, l. 19, f. 9415, op. 3, d. 1421, ll. 1–4, f. 9415, op. 3, d. 1425, ll. 2–4.

57. GARF, f. 5446, op. 48a, d. 2468, l. 20.

58. T. V. Tsarevskaia-Diakina, ed., *Istoriia stalinskogo gulaga, Konets 1920-kh —pervaia polovina 1950-kh godov: Sobranie dokumentov v 7-mi tomakh* vol. 5: *Spetspereselentsy v SSSR* (Moscow, 2004), 82, 568–600, 604–11.

59. As might be expected, the numbers of runaways were highest in the first chaotic postwar years—nearly 20,000 in 1947—and then dropped significantly each year after. See chart ibid., 707.

60. Vert and Mironenko, *Istoriia stalinskogo gulaga,* 1:585.

61. See Tsarevskaia-Diakina, *Istoriia stalinskogo gulaga,* 5:568, for example.

62. This decree for rearrest was issued in February 1948, and rearrest of those already released began on a large scale in the autumn. Vert and Mironenko, *Istoriia*

stalinskogo gulaga, 1:570–71. Also, Tsarevskaia-Diakina, *Istoriia stalinskogo gulaga,* 5:78–81, 625–28. For discussion of the November 1948 decree, see Zemskov, "Spetsposelentsy," 154.

63. GARF, f. 5446, op. 51a, d. 5020, ll. 10–12, 27. In addition, officials forbade immediate family members of those under residence restrictions from living in regime areas. This was to resolve the problem of ex-convicts converging on non-regime towns close to regime areas in which relatives lived. In these cases, those under restriction hoped to gain employment and eventual permission for residence with family members, or otherwise be able to stay in regime areas for long periods of time. Several town officials complained about the inundation of their areas by large numbers of undesirables. See GARF, f. 9415, op. 3, d. 1440, ll. 99–106.

64. For concerns about settlements, see V. V. Denisov, A. V. Kvashonkin, et al., *TsK VKP(b) i regional'nye partiinye komitety 1945–1953* (Moscow, 2004), 364–67. On camp uprisings, see Andrea Graziosi, "The Great Strikes of 1953 in Soviet Labor Camps in the Accounts of Their Participants: A Review," *Cahiers du Monde russe et soviétique* 33/4 (October–December 1992): 419–46.

65. For more detailed discussion of reforms from 1948 through 1953, see Nathalie Moine, "Le Système des passeports à l'époque stalinienne: De la purge des grandes villes au morcellement du territoire, 1932–1953," *Revue d'Histoire moderne et contemporaine* 50/1 (January–March 2003): 165–68; V. P. Popov, "Pasportnaia sistema v SSSR (1932–1976)," *Sotsiologicheskie issledovaniia* 9 (1995): 9–10.

66. See the report to Beria from May 1953, for example, in Vert and Mironenko, *Istoriia stalinskogo gulaga,* 1:595–97.

67. In early April 1953, the MVD recommended lifting restrictions on numbers of groups that were exiled during war, since, originally, their sentences were only for five years. GARF, f. 9415, op. 3, d. 1440, ll. 147–49.

68. Naumov and Sigachev, *Lavrentii Beria,* 43–46.

69. GARF, f. 9415, op. 3, d. 1440, l. 99.

70. GARF, f. 9415, op. 3, d. 1440, l. 133.

71. GARF, f. 9415, op. 3, d. 1440, ll. 228–36; Moine, "Le Système des passeports," 68.

72. GARF, f. 9415, op. 3, d. 1440, l. 145.

73. GARF, f. 9415, op. 3, d. 1440, l. 156.

74. GARF, f. 9415, op. 3, d. 1440, ll. 166–67.

75. GARF, f. 9415, op. 3, d. 1440, l. 229.

76. V. A. Kozlov, *Massovye besporiadki v SSSR pri Khrushcheve i Brezhneve, 1953–nachalo 1980-kh gg* (Novosibirsk, 1999), 13. See also Brian Lapierre, "Making Hooliganism on a Mass–Scale: The Campaign against Petty Hooliganism in the Soviet Union, 1956–1964," *Cahiers du Monde russe* 47/1–2 (January–June): 349–76; Sheila Fitzpatrick, "Soviet Parasites: How Tramps, Idle Youth and Busy Entrepreneurs Impeded the Soviet March to Communism," ibid., 377–408.

CONCLUSIONS

1. For the argument that this process took place earlier in the 1930s rather than later, see, especially, Yuri Slezkine, "The Soviet Union as a Communal Apartment,

or How a Socialist State Promoted Ethnic Particularism," in *Stalinism: New Directions,* ed. Sheila Fitzpatrick (New York, 2000), 333; and Terry Martin, "Modernization or Neo-Traditionalism? Ascribed Nationality and Soviet Primordialism," ibid., 348–67.

2. While military status was important for rehabilitation, this did not mean that war veterans as a whole received the benefits of privilege accorded them by their status. As a number of authors have shown, apart from certain symbolic gestures, war veterans, and especially invalids, were no more privileged than other segments of the population, and in the case of invalids, were often worse off. See the documents collected in E. Iu. Zubkova, L. P. Kosheleva, et al., eds., *Sovetskaia zhizn', 1945–1953* (Moscow, 2003), 308–31. See also E. Iu. Zubkova, *Poslevoennoe Sovetskoe obshchestvo: Politika i povsednevnost', 1945–1953* (Moscow, 2000), 28–36.

3. GARF, f. 5446, op. 51a, d. 5020, l. 10.

4. In this assessment, I agree with both Moshe Lewin and Robert Tucker, among others, who argue that the Soviet state evolved even under Stalin into a service state, with similarities to (though also differences with) the tsarist service state system. Moshe Lewin, *The Making of the Soviet System: Essays in the Social History of Interwar Russia* (New York, 1985), 307–8; Robert C. Tucker, "Stalinism as Revolution from Above," in *Stalinism: Essays in Historical Interpretation,* ed. Robert C. Tucker (New York, 1977), 99–100.

Index